SOCIAL SECURITY LAW IN CONTEXT

SOCIAL SECURITY LAW IN CONTEXT

NEVILLE HARRIS

with

Gillian Douglas, Tamara Hervey, Stephen Jones,
Simon Rahilly, Roy Sainsbury and Nick Wikeley

Foreword by John Mesher, Social Security Commissioner

OXFORD
UNIVERSITY PRESS

OXFORD

UNIVERSITY PRESS

Great Clarendon Street, Oxford OX2 6DP

Oxford University Press is a department of the University of Oxford.
It furthers the University's objective of excellence in research, scholarship,
and education by publishing worldwide in

Oxford New York

Athens Auckland Bangkok Bogotá Buenos Aires Calcutta
Cape Town Chennai Dar es Salaam Delhi Florence Hong Kong Istanbul
Karachi Kuala Lumpur Madrid Melbourne Mexico City Mumbai
Nairobi Paris São Paulo Singapore Taipei Tokyo Toronto Warsaw

and associated companies in Berlin Ibadan

Oxford is a registered trade mark of Oxford University Press
in the UK and in certain other countries

Published in the United States
by Oxford University Press Inc., New York

© Neville Harris 2000

The moral rights of the author have been asserted
Database right Oxford University Press (maker)

First published 2000

British Library Cataloguing in Publication Data
Data available

Library of Congress Cataloging in Publication Data

Harris, Neville.
Social security law in context / Neville Harris with Gillian Douglas ...[et al.].
p. cm.
Includes bibliographical references and index.
1. Social security--Law and legislation--Great Britain. 2. Great Britain--Social policy.
I. Title
KD3199 .H37 1999
344.41'02--dc21   99-050126

ISBN 0-19-876307-7 (Hbk)
ISBN 0-19-876308-5 (Pbk)

Typeset in Garamond by J&L Composition Ltd, Filey, North Yorkshire
Printed in Great Britain
on acid-free paper by
Biddles Ltd., Guildford and King's Lynn

Foreword

My usual walk to and from the Social Security Commissioners' office takes me past the Old Bailey. Carved above the main door of the Session House, opened in 1907, is the motto (taken from Psalm 72):

DEFEND THE CHILDREN OF THE POOR
AND PUNISH THE WRONGDOER

Would any criminal court built today advertise such an order of priorities, I wonder? Would it find a place among the platitudes and evasions in the mission statements of modern agencies and organisations?

There can be no doubt that the children of the poor still need their defenders. Yet many would point to the development of the welfare state as the major social achievement of Britain in the twentieth century. How then can it be explained that, after all those years of reforms and new schemes, with now a vast morass of legislation and a steadily growing proportion of public expenditure going on social security, health and education, there is still so much deprivation and despair to be seen all around us? Despite enormous advances in absolute material standards, the image of a gulf between the relatively comfortable two-thirds of the population and the insecure one-third, at best one step away from financial disaster, has echoes of the findings of the great Victorian social explorers into 'Darkest England'.

It is questions such as this which make the study of social security law so fascinating. At every level, from the most abstract theorizing about the welfare state down to the nuts and bolts of the conditions of entitlement to specific benefits, the subject is shot through with contradictions and compromises. There are constant tensions between the impulses towards the provision of security of income against the risks which a modern society creates and the desire not to undermine the disciplines of the labour market and the demands of family responsibilities. The shifting ways in which these tensions are resolved, and the conditions which we are prepared to impose on the most vulnerable groups, tell us a great deal about the nature of our society.

It is impossible to understand the present state of social security law without some knowledge of its historical development, as well as its present social and economic context. In this timely and welcome book Professor Neville Harris and his colleagues have supplied an accessible and authoritative survey of all those elements. Readers will often be struck by extraordinary continuities of underlying policy which can survive apparently fundamental changes in institutions and benefit structures. For instance, the Poor Law principle of 'less eligibility'—that existence on the Poor Law should always be less eligible than the life of an independent labourer of the lowest class—finds its counterpart in concerns about disincentives to work and in the complex rules for jobseeker's allowance and the New Deal. Readers will also be struck by how often recent history, or the sound reasons behind structures or practices, is forgotten, before those reasons have to be reinvented or rediscovered with surprise. One only needs to look at what a mess has been left by so many 'simplifications' or 'modernisations' of parts of the social security system to see the value of an appreciation of history.

This book is particularly timely as we approach the new century (and the unfairly derided section 173 of the Social Security Contributions and Benefits Act 1992 should be consulted for the precise date when that will begin). That not only prompts a reappraisal of the twentieth century's developments, but an evaluation of where things are going in the twenty-first century. The reappraisal may identify a significant gap between rhetoric and reality, for instance about actually defending the children of the poor or about the existence of a post-war consensus on social security in the light of what was actually done in implementation of the Beveridge Report. The evaluation of what is to come requires a similar exercise.

The amount of legislative activity on social security seems to be on a constantly increasing trend. The structure of benefits has become increasingly detailed, with many new benefits and new adjudicative structures being introduced. Added to that is the growth in the effect of European Community law, and soon the demands of the Human Rights Act 1998. In this state of constant change any attempt at an absolutely definitive statement of the law is out of date before it gets into print. What is needed is a treatment which deals with the law in a scholarly way, yet at the level of principle, enabling readers to make sense of the current state of affairs. Professor Harris and his fellow contributors constitute an able team of authors, with an impressive range of expertise and experience, and they deal with the most important areas of the subject in just that way. Their clear and objective analysis of controversial and difficult questions will ensure that this book is referred to for many years to come.

JOHN MESHER
Social Security and Child Support Commissioner
Professor Associate of Law, University of Sheffield

Preface

There is never an ideal time to write a book on social security law in Britain, because few legal areas change as rapidly. Nevertheless, the end of a long period of Conservative government in which the landscape of social security was significantly altered, and the election to office of a Labour Party committed to welfare reform and beginning to work through its legislative agenda, arguably makes this a better time than most. It provides an opportunity to reflect upon and evaluate the changes which have produced the social security system of today and to consider the possible future shape of social security provision in the welfare state of the twenty-first century.

The Labour Government elected to office in 1997 did not promise to sweep away the legislative and institutional structures underpinning the social security system, but it did announce a wide-ranging welfare reform agenda. Like the Conservatives in the 1980s, it has argued that the system needs a fundamental modernization and that Beveridge's true legacy was his vision and the values he espoused rather than the structures he set in place. The new Government's own vision was set out in a Green Paper (the first in a series presaging reforms) promising, in the words of its title, *New Ambitions for our Country: A New Contract for Welfare* (Cm. 3805) (1998). The Government proposed a reformed welfare system that would aim to promote 'opportunity instead of dependence', even 'empowerment not dependency' (ch.2), while alleviating poverty and ensuring the dignity of those unable to work because of severe disability, illness or old age. Achievement of these ambitions would take us (around the year 2020) into a Fourth Age of Welfare. Private and public provision would each play a part in this process.

The reforms have since begun in earnest. We have already seen: major changes to administration and adjudication and to substantive areas of benefit provision under the Social Security Act 1998; the introduction of the New Deal and the 'gateway to work'; and what could be the precursor to a more fundamental integration of tax and benefits system, the introduction of various new tax credit schemes, such as working families tax credit, and associated administrative changes. As we go to press, the Welfare Reform and Pensions Act 1999 has just completed its, latterly, rather turbulent passage through Parliament. It makes provision for 'stakeholder' pensions, new bereavement allowances and a host of other reforms, including changes to incapacity benefit. There might be an over-arching vision to welfare reform, but what the citizen can see is further proof of something the Green Paper itself has acknowledged: 'Reform is not a new challenge for social security. It is the norm' (Appx, para. 40).

The constant reform of social security law in Britain undoubtedly adds to the intrinsic fascination of the subject. In some ways, however, it also makes it inherently frustrating. Indeed, so intractable at times is the law that few would claim to be real legal 'experts' in the subject in the traditional sense. Generally the best that can be hoped for is an understanding of the key principles and structures, an ability to find one's way around the rules, and the capacity to make links between the different welfare benefits. Yet there are intellectual rewards for those who persevere with this infuriating subject. They go beyond the satisfaction gained from understanding how complex rules affect the entitlement of a particular person or a group of persons, a process spiced with a dangerous uncertainty as to whether one of the myriad new amendment regulations constantly appearing in this field might have come into force unnoticed and negated the conclusions drawn. In particular, by considering the law in its various contexts—theoretical, historical, social, political, and so on—one begins to understand the ways in which social security law impacts directly or indirectly on the whole social and economic fabric of the country. Social security entitlement at present costs the nation £100 billion each year and provides support to tens of millions of citizens. Entitlement is always conditional; and often the conditions that the law imposes aim to influence behaviour in various ways, for example by making claimants seek work or to live in accommodation that reflects their overall economic situation. Questions frequently arise as to whether the provision made meets particular social objectives—for example, alleviating poverty, assisting those who are disabled with the additional expense involved in living an independent life, or ensuring that pensioners can enjoy a degree of financial security. Questions also arise as to whether the system delivers what is broadly referred to today as 'social justice', which brings into play consideration of the framework of social citizenship rights, equality and other conceptual issues. The political dimension to welfare reform makes it also important to examine the ways in which, increasingly in recent years, ministers' rhetoric is reflected in policies aimed at attacking for political ends the entitlement of particular identifiable groups, such as lone parents, the young unemployed and asylum seekers.

While this book aims to provide an accurate, broad-ranging and up to date picture of social security law and policy in Britain, the legal content can obviously represent but a mere snapshot at the time of writing. However, the book also discusses future reforms which have been announced or for which provision has been made. It also aims to show (mostly in Part 2 (Chapters 3–5) but in the case of recent reforms, also in some of the later chapters) the historical context to social security, in order to bring out some of the continuities in the bases to the rules while also explaining the political, economic and other influences on reform of the law. Part 3 of the book (Chapters 6–8) examines the modern context, looking at: the characteristics of the modern benefits system and the legal framework both to national insurance (including pensions provision and reform) and the principal means-tested benefits; the administration and adjudication of benefits; and the European (specifically EC/EU) dimension to the subject (although discussion of EC law also occurs elsewhere). By mapping out the modern legal structure to social security here, this part aims to facilitate the subsequent (in Part 4) critical and focused review of the law as it applies to specific social issues (Chapters 9–15): gender and the family, welfare to work, education, disability, housing, money management/debt, and industrial injuries. The book begins (Part 1, Chapters 1 and 2) by placing the whole subject into a theoretical and broad social context, exploring themes such as poverty, social citizenship, and social control that recur at various points throughout the book. A thematic approach of the kind adopted in the book can give rise to problems of overlapping chapter content. A considerable effort has therefore been made to structure the book in a way that minimizes unnecessary duplication.

Given the contextual approach envisaged for this book, the vastness of the subject area, and the depth of analysis required, it would have been impracticable for one person to cover everything. I have been very fortunate in finding some first rate contributors, all highly expert in their respective fields of interest, to assist me in bringing this project to fruition. I am highly indebted to them and to John Mesher for his foreword. I also wish to thank Rhona Rowland, Lorraine Barton and Lynsey Thomas, who at various points provided research assistance. I am also very grateful to John Louth and Mick Belson at OUP for their support and assistance. Finally, but by no means least, I owe as ever the biggest debt of all to my wife and children.

The writing attempts to present the legal position as at the summer/early autumn of 1999 but references to the Immigration and Asylum Act 1999 and the Welfare Reform and Pensions Act 1999, both of which received the Royal Assent on 11 November 1999, have also been included. The House of Lords' ruling in *Nessa v Chief Adjudication Officer*, *The Times*, 27 October 1999 on the 'habitual residence' test, is the most recent case covered, squeezing in at proof stage.

Neville Harris
November 1999

Contents

Part 4 Specific Issues

Notes on Contributors

Gillian Douglas is Professor of Law at Cardiff University. Among other books, she has co-written *Bromley's Family Law* (9th edn.) with Nigel Lowe, and *Child Support: The Legislation* with Edward Jacobs. She is joint Case Editor of *Family Law* journal and an Assistant Editor of the *Journal of Law and Society*. She is a member of the Family Committee of the Judicial Studies Board and has served on the social security and child support appeal tribunals. As a member of the multi-disciplinary Cardiff Family Studies Research Centre, she has been involved in a number of major research projects exploring how both adults and children live through and cope with the immediate impact of separation and marital breakdown.

Neville Harris is Professor of Law in the School of Law and Applied Social Studies at Liverpool John Moores University. He is co-editor with Nick Wikeley of the *Journal of Social Security Law* and Senior Editor of *Education Law Reports*. His books include *Social Security for Young People* (1989), *Law and Education: Regulation, Consumerism and the Education System* (1993), and *Special Educational Needs and Access to Justice* (1997). He has also carried out research for the Law Society on welfare benefits work by solicitors' firms. He was a part-time member of the social security and child support appeal tribunals for a number of years and is now a part-time legal member of The Appeals Service.

Tamara K. Hervey is Reader in Law in the Department of Law at the University of Nottingham. She previously held lectureships in EC Law at the Universities of Manchester and Durham. She is author of *Justifications for Sex Equality in Employment* (1993) and *European Social Law and Policy* (1998) and she was the co-editor (with D. O'Keeffe) of *Sex Equality Law in the European Union* (1996).

Stephen Jones is a full-time legal member of The Appeals Service and he is Digest Editor of the *Journal of Social Security Law*. He was formerly a Senior Lecturer in Law in the School of Law and Applied Social Studies at Liverpool John Moores University, where his teaching areas included welfare law and mental health law.

Laura Lundy is a Senior Lecturer in Law in the School of Law at Queen's University, Belfast. She has a particular interest in social security law and has a number of publications in this field. She is a barrister, an Equal Opportunities Commissioner for Northern Ireland, and Vice-Chair of the Law Centre (Northern Ireland).

Simon Rahilly is a Senior Lecturer in Welfare Rights in the School of Law and Applied Social Studies at Liverpool John Moores University. He has researched and written on social security and housing for a number of years, including recent work, published in the *Journal of Social Welfare and Family Law*, on homelessness and immigration. As a past member of the Social Security Research Consortium he has also undertaken research on the social fund. He has been a board member of a housing association for ten years and has served as a member of the social security appeal tribunal.

Roy Sainsbury is a Senior Research Fellow in the Social Policy Research Unit at the University of York. He has researched and written about social security decision-making and appeals for a number of years. His extensive research projects have included work on housing benefit appeals, medical and disability appeal tribunals, and benefit fraud. He analysed the responses to the government Green Paper on social security decision making and appeals which preceded the Social Security Act 1998 (published by the Department of Social Security as *Consultation on Improving Decision Making and Appeals in Social Security: Analysis of Responses* (1997)).

Nick Wikeley is Professor of Law in the Faculty of Law at the University of Southampton. He is co-editor with Neville Harris of the *Journal of Social Security Law*. He is also General Editor of Ogus, Barendt, and Wikeley, *The Law of Social Security* (4th edn., 1995), author of *Compensation for Industrial Disease* (1993) and co-author (with Davis and Young) of *Child Support in Action* (1998). He has been a part-time chairman of the social security appeal tribunal and disability appeal tribunal, and he is now a part-time legal member of The Appeals Service.

Note on Decisions of the Social Security Commissioners

The book contains references to decisions of the Social Security Commissioners, either those by a single Commissioner or occasionally by a Tribunal of Commissioners (signifying a case considered to be particularly difficult on the law and/or legally important). The Commissioners hear appeals on a point of law from either party against decisions of an appeal tribunal (see further Chapter 8). There has been some discussion of late about the way that decisions of the Commissioners are reported. At present, selected decisions are reported (the selection being a matter for the Commissioners as a body). These are prefixed with the letter 'R'. Unreported decisions are prefixed with a 'C'. In either case the subsequent letters give an indication of the subject area of the appeal, such as 'IS' for income support. The numbers refer to the reference, registration or sequence number of the decision; the final numbers refer to the year of the decision (if it is unreported) or the year of reporting. Thus *R(IS)1/95* is the first reported income support decision in 1995 and *CDLA/58/1993* is an unreported disability living allowance case from 1993. Commissioners sometimes 'star' their decisions if they think that they are important and should be circulated to other Commissioners. Where '(T)' appears at the end of the decision reference this means it is a decision of a Tribunal of Commissioners.

Decisions of the Commissioners in England and Scotland are binding on the Secretary of State (or in a more practical sense on his/her officials) and on tribunals, whether reported or not, but the reported decisions are generally considered to carry greater authority and those of a Tribunal of Commissioners must be followed in preference to any conflicting decision by a single Commissioner. Decisions of the Northern Ireland Commissioners are considered to be of persuasive authority only in Great Britain, because they relate to different (although parallel and almost identical) legislation.

Table of Cases; Statutes; and Statutory Instruments

UK AND COMMONWEALTH CASES

COMMISSIONERS' DECISIONS

INTERNATIONAL TREATIES

EUROPEAN TREATIES

E.C. REGULATIONS

E.C. DIRECTIVES

UK STATUTORY INSTRUMENTS

SOCIAL FUND DIRECTIONS

Tables

List of Abbreviations

AA	Attendance allowance
AO	Adjudication Officer
Beveridge Report	Beveridge, *Social Insurance and Allied Services* Cmd 6404 (1942)
CAO	Chief Adjudication Officer
CPAG	Child Poverty Action Group
DAT	Disability appeal tribunal
DETR	Department of the Environment, Transport and the Regions
DfEE	Department for Education and Employment
DHSS	Department of Health and Social Security
DLA	Disability living allowance
DSS	Department of Social Security
DWA	Disability working allowance
DWA(G) Regs 1991	Disability Working Allowance (General) Regulations 1991 (S.I. 1991 No. 2887)
FC(G) Regs 1987	Family Credit (General) Regulations 1987 (S.I. 1987 No. 1973)
Green Paper (1985)	Secretary of State for Social Services, *Reform of Social Security*, Green Paper, Vols 1–3, Cmnds 9517–9519 (1985)
Green Paper (1998)	DSS, *New Ambitions for our Country: A New Contract for Welfare*, Green Paper, Cm 3805 (1998)
HB(G) Regs 1987	Housing Benefit (General) Regulations 1987 (S.I. 1987 No. 1871)
IB	Incapacity benefit
ICA	Invalid care allowance
IIAC	Industrial Injuries Advisory Council
IS(G) Regs 1987	Income Support (General) Regulations 1987 (S.I. 1987 No. 1967)
ITS	Independent Tribunal Service
JSA	Jobseeker's allowance
JS Act 1995	Jobseekers Act 1995
JSA Regs 1996	Jobseeker's Allowance Regulations 1996 (S.I. 1996 No. 207)

Ogus, Barendt, and Wikeley (1995)	A. I. Ogus, E. M. Barendt and N. Wikeley, *Law of Social Security* (4th edn) (1995)
SBC	Supplementary Benefits Commission
SERPS	State earnings-related pensions scheme
SSA	Social Security Act
SSAA 1992	Social Security Administration Act 1992
SSAC	Social Security Advisory Committee
SSCBA 1992	Social Security Contributions and Benefits Act 1992
White Paper (1985)	Secretary of State for Social Services, *The Reform of Social Security. A Programme for Action,* Cmnd 9691 (1985)
WFTC	Working families tax credit

Part 1

Theoretical and Social Contexts

1

The Welfare State, Social Security, and Social Citizenship Rights

NEVILLE HARRIS

1. INTRODUCTION

Analysis of social security law is often concerned with the detail of individual entitlement in specific circumstances and with the mechanisms for challenging decisions. Continuing legal analysis of this nature is indeed essential given the high level of complexity and, at times, obscurity, which characterises the present law, and which is in part the result of its frequent and often piecemeal amendment. There is, moreover, a need for a practical focus, as social security law impacts so directly on the lives of those in need of welfare benefits. However, when exploring an area of the law such as this where legislation is an instrument of government social policy, a degree of abstraction is necessary in order to understand the nature of the rules under consideration and to appreciate their overall effects. Thus throughout the chapters in this book there is an attempt to analyse the legislation and associated case law with reference to the wider social and policy contexts to the issues concerned. While at times engaged in detailed legal analysis and concerned with practical issues, the book therefore places a particular emphasis on a broader contextual approach to its subject.

As one pulls back further from the detail of the law and policy, one finds a conceptual framework which is traditionally the exclusive domain of social theorists but with which lawyers also ought to engage in order to understand the relationship between the substantive law and its social, economic and political role. The discussion below begins with the 'welfare state', an institution which, in the United Kingdom, is generally regarded as one whose creation and development represents perhaps the greatest social achievement of the twentieth century but which is also seen increasingly by some as merely a phase in the evolution of social policy in the West which is nearing a conclusion.

2. THE WELFARE STATE

A. Defining the Concept of a Welfare State

The social security system delivers a key element of the complex and highly regulated network of conditional support provided by the state to citizens who lack the financial or physical means to meet their basic needs. This overall network of support has traditionally formed the basic, primary, role of the welfare state. In fact, the 'welfare state' concept is sometimes used to describe part of the character of the particular state itself in addition to indicating the approach taken by a national state towards the delivery of welfare provision. Thus one may speak of a state as *being* a welfare state or as *having* a welfare state—the latter emphasising the conceptual distinction between 'welfare state' and 'statehood', which is more marked in states whose welfare systems tend towards the residual (operating a safety net of sorts but failing to offer comprehensive or universal provision as of right—see below), such as the USA or Japan.

Commentators have often observed that the concept of the welfare state defies precise definition,[1] but attempts have been made. Briggs[2] defined a welfare state as one in which:

organised power is deliberately used (through politics and administration) in an effort to modify the play of market forces in at least three directions—first, by guaranteeing individuals and families a minimum income irrespective of the market value of their work or property; second, by narrowing the extent of insecurity by enabling individuals and families to meet certain 'social contingencies' . . . and third, by ensuring that all citizens without distinction of status or class are offered the best standards available in relation to a certain agreed range of social services.

Looked at today, especially in the context of the UK, this construction might be regarded as representing more of a theoretical ideal than the outcome of an empirical observation. This is because the 'institutional' model of welfare that it represents (see below) has, in states whose welfare systems have traditionally conformed largely to it, come under increasing pressure either for economic reasons, as in the case of the Netherlands or Sweden,[3] or for a combination of economic and political/ideological reasons, as in the UK.[4] Between 1979–97 in particular, successive UK governments had an avowed commitment towards reducing the role of the state, a process which included a reduction in state welfare provision. A particular landmark was the 1985 Green Paper on *The Reform of Social Security*, in which part of the underlying philosophy

---

[1]   See, for example, D. Fraser, *The Evolution of the British Welfare State*, 2nd edn. (London: Macmillan, 1984), 238; N. Barr, *The Economics of Social Security*, 2nd edn. (London: Weidenfeld and Nicolson, 1993), 6.

[2]   A. Briggs, 'The welfare state in historical perspective' 2(2) (1961) *European Journal of Sociology* 221–258, 222.

[3]   A. Gould, 'The end of the middle way? The Swedish welfare state in crisis', in C. Jones (ed.), *New Perspectives on the Welfare State in Europe* (London: Routledge, 1993), 157–76; and see also G. Smedmark, 'The Swedish social insurance system: A model in transition' (1994) 47(2) *I.S.S.R.* 71–7.

[4]   J. Baldock notes that all industrial societies have been sharing the same economic difficulties resulting from the rising costs of social security as a result of higher levels of unemployment, an ageing population and worsening dependency ratios. He explains that in most European countries the debate about welfare has been conducted in fairly broad and consensual terms, whereas in Britain, 'the majority electoral system has excluded opposition parties from significant influence on policy, and . . . the Conservative Party [was] taken over by, what was for it, an unusually ideological leadership': J. Baldock, 'Patterns of change in the delivery of welfare in Europe', in P. Taylor-Gooby and R. Lawson, *Markets and Managers: New Issues in the Delivery of Welfare* (Milton Keynes: Open University Press, 1993), 24–37, at 26.

was that social security was no longer 'a function of the state alone', but 'a partnership between the individual and the state—a system built on twin pillars'.[5] Now, in its plans for welfare reform (see below), the Blair Government talks of maintaining a strong welfare state (albeit with a drive to reduce welfare dependency), but envisages that by 2020 private providers and mutual schemes 'will deliver a substantial share of welfare provision, particularly pensions'.[6] It argues that private provision does not mean residualisation of the welfare state but rather a means of modernisation, and enables the concentration of public resources for welfare on the most economically weak citizens. It is claimed that there will therefore be no diminution in the central concept of a welfare state, but a new emphasis on core values such as work.[7] The implications of this approach for the future of welfare in the UK are considered later.

An accurate and perhaps more all-embracing definition of a welfare state today than Briggs' is Mishra's simpler dual conceptualisation: the state accepts responsibility for welfare and (via legislation and other constitutional means) provides mechanisms—institutions and procedures—for the delivery of the services and other forms of provision required to meet basic needs.[8] In other words, the welfare state is defined partly by its functions and partly by the mechanisms which are developed to enable it to perform them. This dual definition can also be applied to social security specifically. Here there are highly complex mechanisms—represented by the administrative machinery, the legislative framework, and the wide range of often interrelated benefit schemes—for the provision of support. Most people's conception of social security is based on these tangible structures. Of course, these mechanisms will not only tend to differ from one state and political system to the next,[9] they will also change over time, in response to political, economic, and social change. For example, as noted above, an emphasis may be placed on private provision (as part of the 'welfare mix': see below). Thus the way that a welfare state is defined will itself need to change. For example, as Goriely observes: 'In 1945 [the welfare state] was an aspirational depiction of a new kind of state: by the 1960s it was a label applied to specific, central, public bureaucracies. Now it is often used to describe a minor and residual function of a state primarily concerned with other matters.'[10] The nature of the British welfare state today is discussed further below.

[5] Green Paper (1985), Vol. 1, para. 1.5.
[6] See Green Paper (1998), ch. 11, para. 7.
[7] Ibid., ch. 1. As Lundy explains in Chapter 10 below, this emphasis on work represents a continuity with both the Thatcher and Major Governments' social security policy.
[8] R. Mishra, *The Welfare State in Crisis* (Brighton: Wheatsheaf, 1984), p. xi and, more generally, ch. 1.
[9] For comparative studies, see L. Morris and T. Llewelyn, *Social Security Provision for the Unemployed. A Report for the Social Security Advisory Committee* (London: HMSO, 1991), ch. 7; P. Spicker, *Poverty and Social Security: Concepts and Principles* (London: Routledge, 1993), ch. 9; C. Jones (ed.), *New Perspectives on the Welfare State in Europe* (London: Routledge, 1993); A Cochrane and J. Clarke, *Comparing Welfare States: Britain in International Context* (London: Sage, 1993); J. Clasen, *Paying the Jobless* (Aldershot: Avebury, 1994); and H. Bolderson and D. Mabbett, 'Mongrels or thoroughbreds: A cross-national look at social security systems' *European Journal of Political Research* 28 (1995), 19–39.
[10] T. Goriely, 'Rushcliffe Fifty Years On: The Changing Role of Civil Legal Aid Within the Welfare State' (1994) 21 *J.L.S.* 545–66, 545.

B. Models of Welfare and Welfare Reform

The two chief models of welfare system are conceptualised as the residualist and institutional models.[11] Below there is discussion of where the present welfare state in Britain lies in relation to these models. The 'institutional' welfare state is premised on the notion that welfare provision is a normal and primary function of a modern industrial society.[12] The ideal on which the institutional model is based is that the welfare state should aim to maintain a reasonable standard of living for all, with a guarantee of more or less unconditional citizenship rights. The institutional model is associated with the redistributive function of welfare, in the sense that public welfare provision aims to redistribute resources in favour of those who derive the least advantage from the chief mechanism for wealth distribution—the market-based economic system.

Beveridge, whose 1942 grand plan[13] formed the basis for much of the immediate post Second World War development of social security, rejected the notion of redistribution across society as a whole. His notion of redistribution was simply that it should involve provision of income specifically to those whose earning power had been (temporarily) interrupted and during periods of heavy family responsibilities, rather than as part of a strategy to alleviate general poverty and inequality.[14] There was, however, a universalist thrust to many of Beveridge's key proposals—especially in the areas of social insurance and family allowances—which is why Beveridge's plan of welfare tends to be regarded as institutionalist. Universality in this context involves provision to all, entirely or almost entirely without regard for personal circumstances (although claimants need to fit into any broad categories of persons to whom entitlement to particular welfare benefits is restricted).

Following the so-called 'rediscovery' of poverty in the 1960s (see Chapter 2), the redistributive role of the welfare state came to greater prominence. As Lowe explains, in Britain 'poverty by the 1960s had been redefined as "relative deprivation", and so no significant reduction could be achieved without a major redistribution of resources between classes'.[15] Today, Townsend's definition of 'relative

---

[11] See Spicker, n. 9 above, 131. Spicker cites Titmuss's typology of welfare systems (R. M. Titmuss, *Social Policy: An Introduction* (London: Allen and Unwin, 1974)), which includes the residual and institutional models plus one other, the 'industrial achievement–performance' or 'handmaiden' model, under which welfare provision is structured more closely around economic aims and the needs of industry. The German system seems closest to this model, although it also has a residual character: here '[r]esidualism has been coupled with a strong economic commitment to the economic needs of society and a heavy dependence on the role of industry in providing occupational benefits. The focus falls on achievement in the market, and welfare provision is strongly linked to the occupational status and employment record of the recipient' (ibid., 127).
[12] L. Bryson, *Welfare and the State* (London: Macmillan, 1992), 56.
[13] Beveridge Report (1942). See Chapter 4 below.   [14] Ibid., para. 449.
[15] R. Lowe, 'A Prophet Dishonoured in his Own Country? The Rejection of Beveridge in Britain, 1945–1970', in J. Hills, J. Ditch and H. Glennester (eds), *Beveridge and Social Security: An International Retrospective* (Oxford: Oxford University Press, 1994), 131.

deprivation' as 'the lack of resources necessary to permit participation in the activities, customs and diets commonly approved by society'[16] is, according to Bryson, implied in any institutional model of welfare.[17] Such a definition is, of course, centred on the notion of inequality. An institutional model of welfare involves acceptance of a degree of redistribution to achieve greater equality, or 'relative equality'.[18] As noted above, the process aims to rectify the inequality that is a product of, and some would say is essential to, the operation of a market economy.[19] In this regard, it is also argued that the welfare state, through provision of services and benefits, aims to combat an injustice suffered by those who are worst off. In present-day political rhetoric, 'social justice' seems to involve the welfare state not only providing security for those who are incapable of earning income to support themselves through work (such as the elderly and severely disabled) but also guaranteeing disadvantaged individuals a measure of 'freedom' and 'opportunity' ('we must transform the welfare state from a safety net in times of trouble to a springboard for economic opportunity';[20] 'our ambition is nothing less than to: restructure the institutions of welfare in order to promote people's opportunity and independence').[21]

Reference has also been made, in this context, to the need for 'distributive justice'[22] in the face of this market inequality. Rawls argues that any theory of distributive justice must assert that basic rights and duties should be assigned equally to all and that social and economic inequalities should be tolerated only if they result in 'compensating benefits for everyone, and in particular for the least advantaged members of society'.[23] Economic liberals would reject the assertion that there is injustice here, because they do not regard the allocation of benefits by the market as being the result of a deliberate action or the result of applying particular moral principles.[24] The counter argument is that injustice is caused if a rectifiable inequality and the resultant disadvantage are ignored. As Plant has argued, '[f]ailure to attend to the welfare of those individuals who, through no fault of their own and largely owing to bad luck . . . find that they are unable to lead the kind of life which the culture of society defines as the norm of human fulfilment is deeply unjust'.[25] The record of the British welfare state in achieving any significant redistribution in practice has in fact been questioned;[26] and although some see the issue as

[16] P. Townsend, *Poverty in the United Kingdom* (Harmondsworth: Penguin, 1979), 47. See further Chapter 2 below.
[17] L. Bryson, *Welfare and the State* (London: Macmillan, 1992), 58–9.
[18] V. George and P. Wilding, *Ideology and Social Welfare* (London: Routledge, 1985), 98.
[19] See T. Novak, *Poverty and State Support* (Buckingham: Open University Press, 1988).
[20] Commission on Social Justice, *Social Justice: Strategies for National Renewal* (London: Vintage, 1994), 1.
[21] Green Paper (1998), ch. 11, para. 1.   [22] P. Townsend (1979), n. 16 above, 62.
[23] J. Rawls, *A Theory of Justice* (Oxford: Oxford University Press, 1972), 14–15.
[24] See, for example, F. A. Hayek, *Law, Legislation and Liberty Vol. 2.* (London: Routledge and Kegan Paul, 1976), 64 *et seq.*
[25] R. Plant, 'The very idea of a welfare state', in P. Bean, J. Ferris, and D. Whynes, *In Defence of Welfare* (London: Tavistock, 1985), 15–16.
[26] P. Taylor-Gooby, 'Two cheers for the Welfare State: Public Opinion and Private Welfare', (1982) 2(4) *Journal of Public Policy* 319–46 at 345.

contentious,[27] all the evidence points to increased rather than reduced income inequality.[28]

Under the 'residualist' model of the welfare state, primacy is given to family, voluntary, and market-based services—the supposedly ' "natural" sources of welfare'.[29] State provision should only come into play when there is a breakdown in these mechanisms.[30] As Bryson explains: 'Need rather than right is the basis of public provisions and these are kept to a minimum . . . eligibility is targeted only to the most disadvantaged and . . . No merit is seen in provisions that maintain people at more than subsistence level.'[31] Under residualism, the welfare state is not regarded as having any real redistributive function and there is a strong emphasis on private solutions to poverty, as noted above, including private insurance against contingencies such as unemployment or sickness. In part, therefore, the importance of the degree of intervention inherent in the institutional model of welfare relates to the inequalities produced by a market-orientated approach to the problem of poverty. Inequalities flow from the inadequacies of market-orientated provision to ensure that all individuals have equal access to welfare. For example, some individuals lack the knowledge, understanding, or prudence to make the necessary private arrangements; and some are 'bad risks' and may not be able to protect themselves.[32] Carney and Hanks explain that advocates of the market-orientated approach believe that 'high rates of economic growth will have a trickle-down effect on the standard of living of all sections of the community' by reducing unemployment, enhancing wages, and creating greater scope for occupational welfare (such as retirement superannuation).[33] Much lower priority is given by such advocates to public welfare provision, largely on the ground that it reduces incentives.

As noted above, with reference to Beveridge, the notion of 'universality' in social security provision tends to be associated with the institutional model of welfare. A social security system whose provision is characterised by 'selectivity'—where benefit support is targeted on those whose particular circumstances, including their income resources, meet specified (and often legally-defined) criteria of need—will often be associated with the residual model. This conceptual link is not automatic, however. For example, in the development of its social security system in the twentieth century, Australia placed a strong emphasis on means-testing, eschewing the universality of the essentially contribution-based western European social security systems. Nevertheless, it has been suggested that when subjected to international comparison the provision in Australia is 'on a par with the OECD norm and offers minimum

---

[27] See M. O'Higgins, 'Welfare, redistribution and inequality', in P. Bean, J. Ferris and D. Whynes, *In Defence of Welfare* (London: Tavistock, 1985), 162–79.
[28] A. Walker and C. Walker, *Britain Divided* (London: CPAG, 1997). See further Chapter 2 below.
[29] V. George and P. Wilding, *Ideology and Social Welfare* (London: Routledge, 1985), 40.
[30] L. Bryson, *Welfare and the State* (London: Macmillan, 1992), 56.
[31] Ibid.   [32] Ogus, Barendt, and Wikeley (1995), 8–9.
[33] T. Carney and P. Hanks, *Social Security in Australia* (Melbourne: Oxford University Press, 1994), 5–6.

benefits which in absolute terms are better than in most other OECD nations', so that 'the description of the Australian Welfare State as "residual" is misconceived'.[34] This demonstrates that the level of provision is a key factor in any characterisation of the welfare state. In the British social security system both selective and universal elements are present, despite a distinct shift towards the former since the early 1970s.[35] Thus in Britain, child benefit is available as a universal benefit for families with children, and a majority of full-time workers are covered by insurance benefits such as those concerned with sickness or unemployment, whilst benefits such as income support and council tax benefit are means-tested and subject to stringent conditions of entitlement.

The categorisation of a welfare state reflects, above all, what is often referred to as the 'welfare mix', a term used by commentators to acknowledge that, in all states, welfare provision emanates from a variety of sources—public, private, family/community, and so on.[36] The mix will vary between states and over time. If the UK has broadly adopted an institutional model post Beveridge, the welfare mix has certainly not remained static but has progressively assumed residualist characteristics, as noted above. For social security, the most significant period was the 1980s, when the insurance principle was seriously weakened and many areas of provision were cut (see Chapter 5). 'New Right' policies came to the fore, influenced by the ideology of economic liberalism and individualism.[37] An increasingly minimal role for the state was envisaged and private provision was encouraged; at the same time personal economic incentives and initiative, individual liberty, family unity, greater personal responsibility and reduced dependence on the decisions of others, and similar values, were promoted.[38] As regards future prospects for welfare, Blair's Labour Government claims to have rejected both a 'privatised future with the welfare state becoming a residual safety net' and the present institutional model enhanced by 'more generous and costly benefits'; it proclaims a 'third way [which] will take us into a third stage of welfare', involving a system which works actively to move people from welfare dependence and poverty, through education, training, and support.[39] Private provision will, however, be part of the new welfare mix which seems to be envisaged, as noted above.

New Labour's vision of a welfare state which puts an onus on work and self support, on private and public partnership in provision, and on preventing abuse of the

---

[34] F. G. Castles, 'The institutional design of the Australian Welfare State' *I.S.S.R.* (1997) 50/2, 25–41 at 40. Cf. Dean, who, referring to the work of Esping-Andersen, places Australia in the same category as the USA and Canada—liberal economic/welfare regimes with 'minimalist' welfare states: H. Dean, *Welfare, Law and Citizenship* (Prentice Hall/Harvester Wheatsheaf, 1996), 57.

[35] P. Spicker, *Poverty and Social Security: Concepts and Principles* (London: Routledge, 1993), 119. See further Chapters 4 and 5 below.

[36] P. Alcock, *Social Policy in Britain: Themes and Issues* (London: Macmillan, 1996), 16.

[37] The work of F. A. Hayek, *The Road to Serfdom* (London: Routledge and Kegan Paul, 1944) and *Individualism and the Economic Order* (London: Routledge and Kegan Paul, 1949), being particularly influential in so-called 'New Right' approaches to public policy from the late 1970s.

[38] See generally M. Friedman and R. Friedman, *Free to Choose* (London: Penguin, 1980).

[39] Green Paper (1998), ch. 2, paras 5 and 6.

system, carries an important social message about the morality of welfare entitlement: an 'enhanced sense of responsibility that lies at the heart of the new welfare
contract, with people not only taking more personal responsibility for their own and
their families' wellbeing, but also more collective responsibility for policing the new
system and preventing fraud'.[40] But there is also a wider economic dimension, in the
sense that welfare provision, particularly social security provision, on the scale of the
past twenty years is regarded as a hindrance to economic growth and prosperity by
increasing public expenditure, encouraging welfare dependency, and dampening personal effort.[41] The economic and political environment has been one in which there
is a constant struggle to cope with the problem of how to meet the spiralling cost of
state welfare provision without weakening still further a market-based economy by,
for example, increasing the burden of taxation. Mishra sees this economic dimension
as pre-eminent and argues that the increased emphasis among western states' 'dominant elites' on consumerism, free enterprise, and economic growth makes it 'unlikely
that universality as a principle of social provision can survive for long'.[42] Cox similarly observes the welfare state's disengagement with the notion of universality and
associated social rights (see below); he argues that two decades of reform have transformed the welfare state and he is critical of scholars who fail to recognise the cumulative effect of changes to welfare involving reductions in state provision.[43] Similarly,
Lister sees a fundamental undermining of the British welfare state under the influence of New Right politics and the Conservatives' economic agenda during the
1980s, as a result of departures in certain key areas from the fundamental 'cradle to
grave' commitment traditionally associated with it.[44] Indeed, some regard the political and economic pressure brought to bear on the welfare state as having put it into
'crisis'.[45] According to Mishra, we are seeing the end of the welfare state ideal of
eliminating poverty and securing the well-being of all: 'the post-World War II "welfare state" as a social formation has . . . passed into history'.[46]

Others are more sanguine, regarding the British welfare state as having weathered
the storm of both New Right politics and economic domination. Hills, and more

[40] Green Paper (1998), ch. 11, para. 6.
[41] But note the trenchant comment by C. Euzéby, 'Social security for the twenty-first century' 51(2)
I.S.S.R. 3–16 at 4: 'Worldwide . . . it is not the countries where social security is most advanced that are
showing the worst economic performance.'
[42] R. Mishra, 'Social policy in the postmodern world', in C. Jones (ed.) *New Perspectives on the Welfare State
in Europe* (London: Routledge, 1993), 18–40 at 35 and 36.
[43] R. H. Cox, 'The Consequences of Welfare Reform: How Conceptions of Social Rights are Changing'
(1998) 27(1) *J. of Social Policy* 1–16. See also J. Clarke, 'The problem of the state after the welfare state'
(1996) *Social Policy Rev.*, 8, 13–39, at 15–16. On the welfare cutbacks in the United States, particularly under
Reagan in the 1980s, see J. O'Connor, 'US Social Welfare Policy: The Reagan Record and Legacy' (1998)
27(1) *J. of Social Policy* 37–61.
[44] See R. Lister, 'Social Security in the 1980s', (1991) 25(2) *Social Policy and Administration* 91–107.
[45] L. Bryson, above n. 30, 56; J. Tweedy and A. Hunt, 'The Future of the Welfare State and Social
Rights: Reflections on Habermas' (1994) 21(3) *J. of Law and Society* 288–316, at 289.
[46] N. 42 above, 35. An extreme example is Chile, which privatised its entire social security system under
Pinochet: see J. Midgeley, 'Has social security become irrelevant?' (1999) 52(2) *I.S.S.R.* 91–9.

recently, Powell and Hewitt, for example, see reports of the demise of the welfare state as 'greatly exaggerated'.[47] In the area of social security specifically, the essential principles and core values underlying the welfare state are seen as broadly intact. Bradshaw, for example, reflecting on Conservative reforms, has observed that 'social security has remained fairly impervious to the most radical government in Britain since the war ... It has proved itself an extraordinarily robust institution, firmly embedded in the social and cultural life of the country'.[48] Moreover, Clarke and Langan observe that under the Major administrations from 1990 there was a 'softer approach' towards welfare, so that there was only a minor shift towards a more residual welfare state, in a 'new mixed economy of welfare' (involving greater involvement of the private and voluntary sectors, and a market/consumer approach to provision).[49]

In a sense, both sets of viewpoints are sustainable. It is true that the welfare state continues to play a central role in areas such as social security and health and that it retains many of the characteristics of twenty to thirty years ago. Nevertheless, Mishra and others are correct in identifying a fundamental shift of emphasis: the welfare state has proved to be far from immune from the force of political and economic change; there have been significant inroads into the principle of universality; the British welfare state has been weakened and the threat of further residualism looms large.

The Blair Government sees the welfare state as capable of guaranteeing universal protection, but considers that account must be taken of the economic reality which demands curtailment of the growth in welfare spending and, as noted above, seeks a far greater emphasis on individual involvement. Thus, as Frank Field has argued, in the future in the field of pensions, 'the bill ... can only be met by transferring a greater proportion of today's income to meet that cost. I do not believe that people will accept the transfer of income that is necessary unless the rules of the game are fundamentally changed. Hence the stakeholder principle, whereby each individual gains ownership over any new assets which are built up in the scheme'.[50] Field's proposals for 'stakeholder' welfare seek to harness self-interest, but in a way that is conducive to the public good and stresses a kind of new social morality about welfare.[51]

---

[47] J. Hills, 'Introduction', in J. Hills (ed.), *The State of Welfare: The Welfare State in Britain since 1984* (Oxford: Clarendon Press, 1991), 1; M. Powell and M. Hewitt, 'The End of the Welfare State', *Social Policy and Administration* (1998) 32(1), 1–13, at 11.

[48] J. Bradshaw, 'Developments in Social Security Policy', in C. Jones (ed.), *New Perspectives on the Welfare State in Europe* (London: Routledge, 1993), 45. See also, referring to 'the resilience of social security' despite benefit cutbacks in the early to mid 1980s: J. Bradshaw, 'A defence of social security', in P. Bean, J. Ferris, and D. Whynes (eds), *In Defence of Welfare* (London: Tavistock, 1985), 227–56 at 231–3.

[49] J. Clark and M. Langan, 'Restructuring Welfare: The British Welfare Regime in the 1980s', in A. Cochrane and J. Clarke (eds), *Comparing Welfare States: Britain in International Context* (London: Sage, 1993), 69–74.

[50] F. Field, *Stakeholder Welfare* (London: IEA, 1996), 21.

[51] See Field's earlier work *Making Welfare Pay* (London: IEA, 1995) and A. Deacon and K. Mann, 'Moralism and Modernity: The Paradox of New Labour Thinking on Welfare' (1997) *Benefits* September/October, 2–6.

There is not the space in this book for a detailed theoretical analysis of Field's, or indeed New Labour's, vision of the welfare state of the future.[52] Moreover, it is not clear precisely how far reform of the social security system will go, particularly following the resignation of Field from the office of Minister of State for Welfare Reform in July 1998. What seems likely overall is that Social Security reform will be based on an increasingly conditional or restrictive approach, as reflected already in the tightening up of incapacity benefit eligibility via the Welfare Reform and Pensions Act 1999, and there will be increased private sector involvement (for example, in relation to pensions). Such reform would represent a further residualisation of the traditional welfare state in Britain, at least in relation to social security, which, it has recently been argued, 'is set to become a semi-detached part of the welfare state'.[53] However, another way of approaching this involves reconceptualising the welfare state. One recent definition of the term 'welfare state' refers to 'government commitment and effort in Western industrialised countries to maintain a decent minimum standard of living through a high level of employment, general social programmes and anti-poverty measures'.[54] This is a broader definition and one which can accommodate the 'contractual' basis of welfare, including an element of private provision, which the Labour Government embraces.[55]

C. From National to European Welfare State?

Part of the rationale for developing private provision of welfare, as presented by New Labour, is the decline in national state power. Field has argued that the internationalisation of business, communications, and markets has reduced the ability of individual nation states to manage areas like jobs and welfare. Moreover, it is claimed that individual citizens no longer expect the state to deliver on these issues and, as Field has argued, 'look elsewhere for the services which were once the province of welfare states'.[56] In some spheres the state acts increasingly as little more than a facilitator and as an umpire, 'setting rules and ensuring fair play operates'.[57] As noted above, the new welfare state of the twenty-first century which Labour envisages would appear to be one premised on a reduction in state provision, beyond regulation.

[52] See P. Alcock, 'Making Welfare Work—Frank Field and New Labour's Social Policy Agenda' (1997) *Benefits* September/October, 34–8; R. Page, 'New Labour's New "Welfarism": Time to Re-write the Script' (1998) *Benefits* April/May, 10–11; A. Deacon and K. Mann, 'Moralism and Modernity: The Paradox of New Labour Thinking on Welfare' (1997) *Benefits* September/October, 2–6.
[53] R. Page, op. cit. n. 52 above, at 10.
[54] R. Mishra, 'Social policy in the postmodern world', in C. Jones (ed.) *New Perspectives on the Welfare State in Europe* (London: Routledge, 1993), 18–40 at 36
[55] See, for example, the proposals for funded pensions in DSS, *A New Contract for Welfare: Partnership in Pensions*, Cm 4179 (London: The Stationery Office, 1998).
[56] *Stakeholder Welfare* (London: IEA, 1996), 28.   [57] Ibid.

The emergence and development of international legal systems makes it particularly important to look beyond the realm of the national state when examining the institutional framework for policy development and the delivery of welfare. Outside the EU context, although current international treaties have not had a major impact on national social welfare policies in the United Kingdom, the incorporation of the European Convention on Human Rights following the enactment of the Human Rights Act 1988 is bound to increase the Convention's influence.[58] Turning to the United Kingdom's membership of the EC and, more recently, EU, this has only had a relatively limited impact on its social security system.[59] None the less, despite the UK's initial refusal to sign up to the Social Protocol and Agreement at Maastricht, Labour's desire to embrace 'social Europe'[60] (reflected in the recent adoption of the terms of the Agreement on Social Policy via the Amsterdam Treaty) means that the EU dimension could become increasingly important. This issue is discussed in depth by Tamara Hervey in Chapter 8, but some general points may be made here.

To the 'Euro-sceptics' in this country there is the threat of a supranational European welfare state; but this ignores the fact that the Social Chapter of the Treaty of European Union cannot compel states to harmonise their social security and many other welfare arrangements.[61] The operation of the EC, and now the EU, has facilitated the development of supranational policies which provide an additional layer of social policy (and legislation), imposed some external constraints on national policy making, and established some important rights (for example, in the case of both women and migrant workers).[62] Nevertheless, for various reasons (partly concerned with the EU's legislative and institutional framework), not only is there no European 'super state', or at least not in the form which mirrors the traditional image of a national state, but there is also no real movement towards a European welfare state.[63] Moreover, a number of commentators see difficulties for EU social policy in view of the Union's apparent contemplation of reduced state welfare provision in furtherance of its economic goals.[64] Hargreaves none the less argues that

---

[58] The human rights dimension to social rights in the UK is discussed in Section 4B of this chapter, below.

[59] T. Hervey, *European Social Law and Policy* (Harlow: Longman, 1998) and J. Ditch and P. Spicker, 'The impact of European law on the development of social security policies in the United Kingdom' (1999) 52(2) *I.S.S.R.* 75–90. See further Chapter 8 below.

[60] See, for example, The Labour Party, *New Labour: Because Britain deserves better* (London: Labour Party, 1997) (the general election manifesto), 37.

[61] Hervey, op. cit., n. 59 above, explains (at 202) that the amendments made at Amsterdam could, however, provide a basis for minimum harmonisation; but she says that the Council is unlikely to sanction significant EU provision in this field.

[62] Directives 79/7/EEC and 76/207/EEC and Regulation 1408/71. See Chapter 8 below and T. Hervey, *European Social Law and Policy* (Harlow: Longman, 1998).

[63] W. Streeck, 'Neo-Voluntarism: A New European Social Policy Regime' (1995) 1(1) *European L.J.* 31–59 at 57–8.

[64] E.g., Streeck, op. cit.; H. Storey, 'United Kingdom Social Security Law: European and International Dimensions—Part 1', (1994) 1(3) *J.S.S.L.*, 110–32; B.-O. Kuper, 'The Green and White Papers of the European Union: The Apparent Goal of Reduced Social Benefits' (1994) *J. of European Social Policy* 4(2), 129–37.

while the EU's social policy 'would need to make enormous advances to create a "super-state" providing welfare for all its citizens' there have been some advances, notably with regard to Social Policy Agreement post Maastricht Treaty (which now aims at social and economic cohesion, social protection, and raised living standards), giving the social sphere some independence from the economic policy.[65] However, while improved levels of social protection across the EU as a whole remains firmly part of the EC Commission's social policy agenda, reflected in a number of initiatives,[66] factors such as the principle of subsidiarity, the increasing emphasis on economic goals (such as European monetary union or 'EMU') and the lack of a comprehensive legal framework in this area, all limit supranational development of welfare policy.[67] Hervey concludes that '[t]here is no "European welfare state", nor is there likely to be, within the current Treaty framework and given the division of competence between EU and Member State-level institutions'.[68] As she points out, people within the Member States continue to derive their welfare entitlement—or, in EU terms, social protection—from the social legislation of their own state rather than that of the Community. Nevertheless, although its impact has been fairly limited to date, as noted above, the influence of EC law on those entitlements has grown, as Hervey explains in Chapter 8 below.

3. SOCIAL SECURITY

A. Defining 'Social Security'

This book focuses on one specific area within the ambit of the welfare state: the social security system. How should the term 'social security' be defined in this context?

It has been suggested that when the term 'social security' was first used, at least in a legal context, in the US Federal Social Security Act passed by Congress in 1935, this indicated a broad view of the objective of state support: from one which was conditional on insurance, and thereby restricted to insured workers, to 'a system of social protection for all in poverty and need'.[69] In the European context, or more specifically the EU context, the term 'social protection' is in current use to define the areas of social security support (and, in some usages, employment and health and safety protection) provided from within Member States and the Union as a whole.

---

[65] S. Hargreaves, 'Social Europe after Maastricht: is the United Kingdom really opted out', (1997) 19(1) *J.S.W.F.L.* 1–15, 9.

[66] Commission of the European Communities, *Modernising and Improving Protection in the European Union*, COM(97)102 Final (Brussels: Office for Official Publications of the European Communities, 1997).

[67] See K. Duffy, 'Combating social exclusion and promoting social integration in the European Union', in C. Oppenheim (ed.), *An Inclusive Society: Strategies for Tackling Poverty* (London: IPPR, 1998), 227–51.

[68] T. Hervey (1998), op. cit., n. 59 above, at 4.

[69] P. Watson, *Social Security Law of the European Communities* (Oxford: Mansell, 1980), 1.

However, the EU does not have an all-embracing concept of social security in the UK sense as its social security rules are merely ancillary to its aims of free movement and protection of workers: thus, for example, Regulation 1408/71 on migrant workers extends only to 'the classic branches of social security' (mostly insurance-based)[70] plus relevant 'special non-contributory benefits' and excludes 'social assistance'; and the social security equal treatment directive (EEC/79/7) extends only to benefits concerned with access to employment (such as sickness and unemployment benefits) but not to those such as income support which are intended to provide income maintenance during unemployment.[71] There is also reference in the EU context to the 'solidarity' role of social security: this is based on the idea that social security reflects a common social and economic commitment towards its recipients, particularly the unemployed.[72] (In this respect social security provision is closely associated with the notion of social citizenship: below.)

Titmuss's view of social services also embraced a definition based on common aims, rather than the mechanisms designed to achieve them.[73] For Atkinson, however, the term 'social security' has a dual meaning: it can be used 'either to denote an objective of government policy or to describe a set of policies'.[74] Generally, references to 'social security' in Britain today are to the latter: provision in respect of financial support by the state to individuals (or couples) or persons on whom individuals are dependent (such as parents or carers). This divergence from Titmuss's approach may partly be a reflection of the lack of emphasis placed in government policy in recent years on the important social objectives which the social security system aims to achieve.

Changes in the welfare mix mean that what also needs to be considered is the extent to which the concept of social security now extends beyond state provision to include private provision, albeit regulated by the state. In a sense this has always been part of the British social security system, as both employer and employee have contributed to social insurance schemes. Now, as noted above, we are set to see a shift further towards private provision under the Government's proposals on pensions. Any integration of the tax and benefits systems is also relevant to this definitional question. The Government has introduced a 'working families tax credit' in place of the current family credit scheme. In effect, support for low wage families might result from a reduced PAYE tax liability, although claimants will have the choice of receiving payments instead. There is also a 'childcare tax credit' to meet childcare costs of working parents on low incomes. As they reflect the specific

---

[70] H. Storey, 'United Kingdom Social Security Law: European and International Dimensions—Part 1' (1994) 1 *J.S.S.L.* 110–32, at 114. See also 239 ff below.

[71] See *Meyers v Adjudication Officer* C-116/94 [1996] 1 CMLR 461 and *Jackson and Cresswell v Chief Adjudication Officer* [1993] 3 All ER 265; see further Chapter 8.

[72] P. Spicker, *Poverty and Social Security: Concepts and Principles* (London: Routledge, 1993), 108–9.

[73] R. M. Titmuss, 'The social division of welfare', in *Essays on the Welfare State*, 2nd edn. (London: George Allen and Unwin, 1955), cited in P. Spicker, n. 9 above, 103.

[74] A. B. Atkinson, *Poverty and Social Security* (Hemel Hempstead: Harvester Wheatsheaf, 1989), 99. I tried to convey both meanings of the phrase in the title of my book *Social Security for Young People* (Aldershot: Avebury, 1989).

purposes of the social security system as a whole, these are clearly areas of social security within Titmuss's definition, even if their administration is to be undertaken by employees of the Inland Revenue rather than the Benefits Agency.[75]

Atkinson seeks to describe the broad aims of social security within what he sees as its three constituent branches:

Social security in developed countries typically combines three different elements: income-tested social assistance designed to relieve poverty, social insurance concerned with the provision of security and the spreading of income over the lifecycle, and categorical transfers directed at redistribution between specific groups.[76]

The objectives of social security referred to by Atkinson make no specific reference (although there is implicit reference) to some of the 'social risks'[77] (such as family change or sickness)[78] against which the social security aims to provide protection. What Atkinson shows, however, is that the social security system aims to provide a degree of economic security, both through insurance—which is intended to prevent an individual from suffering a fall in their living standard that is unexpected and considered unacceptable under the terms of the social security system—and 'income smoothing', which enables individuals to 'reallocate consumption over their lifetime' (for example, through pensions contributions for old age).[79] This demonstrates that while relief of absolute poverty is the 'most obvious function of the social security system',[80] it is certainly not the only one. *Relative* poverty, on the other hand, is a linking theme, and one may assert that the social security system aims to reduce the inequality which is related to it. Such a function would form part of the redistributive function of the welfare state, referred to above. Nevertheless, the practical reality is often that social security increases inequality by holding down the incomes of those who are dependent on it: for example, between 1979–1993/4 the income of the poorest 10 per cent of the population fell by 13 per cent in real terms (with housing costs included in the calculation), compared with an increase in the average income for the population as a whole of 39 per cent over the same period.[81] Undoubtedly one of the key factors has been the ending (in 1980) of the index-linking of major benefits to rises in wages.[82] The social security system can also reinforce gender and racial inequality (see below).

---

[75] See J. McCrae and J. Taylor, 'The working families tax credit' (1998) *Poverty*, No. 100, 7–9, 9. The authors comment that the working families tax credit will operate as a more generous form of family credit and that the reform seems 'more of a "re-branding exercise"' than a substantial reform of the benefits system. See further, Chapter 9.

[76] A. B. Atkinson, *Poverty and Social Security* (Hemel Hempstead: Harvester Wheatsheaf, 1989), 100.

[77] P. Watson, n. 69 above, 2.

[78] For a list of such risks, see the International Labour Organisation Convention No. 102.

[79] N. Barr, *The Economics of the Welfare State*, 2nd edn. (London: Weidenfeld and Nicolson, 1993), 10.

[80] P. Spicker, *Poverty and Social Security* (London: Routledge, 1993), 104–9.

[81] *Households Below Average Income 1979–1993/94* (London: The Stationery Office, 1996), 114. See further Chapter 2 below.

[82] See generally C. Oppenheim, 'The growth of poverty and inequality', in A. Walker and C. Walker (eds), *Britain Divided* (London: CPAG, 1997), 17–31.

Whatever degree of social and economic inequality exists in reality, it clearly ought to be implicit in social security's role in guaranteeing economic security that the level of support is adequate. It is in this respect that the dual conceptions of 'social security', as a description of the provision made and as a broad aim, come together. There might also be a necessary minimum standard of provision for a social security system as a whole, in terms of the range of 'social risks' covered by it. This is clearly recognised by Article 12 of the (revised) European Social Charter, which binds signatories to 'maintain the social-security system at a satisfactory level at least equal to that required for ratification of the European Code of Social Security' and to 'endeavour to raise progressively the system of social security to a higher level'. However, the Committee of Independent Experts (the main supervisory body) has noted a fairly consistent regression in provision.[83] Article 13 requires signatories to ensure adequate social assistance (which would include benefits paid on the basis of individual need). The adequacy of current benefit levels is discussed in later chapters.[84]

A definition based on the provision of financial support is probably broad enough to cover grants in respect of education, whether provided by the state or by local authorities, particularly where there is an element in respect of living costs. Also, if one accepts that another of the broad social aims of the social security system is the development of individual potential (a view articulated in the 1998 Green Paper), one might in any event regard education benefits as an aspect of social security provision. Generally, however, education grants are not classed as social security support by either researchers or practitioners, partly because policy is made by the Secretary of State for Education and Employment (although also by local authorities, who are responsible for determining policy on discretionary awards)[85] and partly because the primary purpose of this provision is seen as supporting studentship. Although mandatory awards (which are being replaced by loans) have in part been intended to cover basic living costs, it is the fact that these costs arise out of being a student *per se* that is seen as taking such awards (or loans) out of the realm of social security, as discussed in Chapter 11. In contrast, housing benefit and council tax benefit are intended to alleviate hardship and clearly and properly fall within the generally accepted definition of social security in the UK. A complete list of current social security benefits in the UK is provided in Chapter 6.

Although not traditionally defined by them, social security clearly also has both economic and political objectives. These are discussed in later chapters on, for example, unemployment and gender/families. Additionally, there is the role which social security plays in the exertion of social control (below), to which some of these specific objectives are related.

---

[83] Cited, in relation to 1988–9, in Storey, n. 70 above, at 120; and more recent reports cited in K. D. Ewing, 'Social Rights and Constitutional Law' [1999] *P.L.* 104–23, at 104 n. 4. This regression was partly the result of changes introduced under the Fowler reforms of 1986–8: see Chapter 4 below.

[84] See, in particular, the discussion of poverty in Chapter 2; and see also Chapter 14.

[85] See Chapter 11.

B. Social Security and Social Control

In addition to its specific aims in relation to poverty and economic security, discussed above, social security operates as a vehicle for social control.[86] Social control in this context 'is taken to mean the encouragement or enforcement of particular patterns of behaviour',[87] as for example in one of the principles of the 1998 Green Paper: 'The new welfare state should help and encourage people of working age to work where they are capable of doing so.'[88] This function is distinguishable from social security's 'internal goal' of 'mobilizing resources to meet needs'.[89]

To appreciate the extent of the social control aspect of social security it is necessary first to reflect upon the continuities and traditions within the welfare system and its underlying values. The modern day welfare state in Britain has, despite its Poor Law origins, developed during, and is thus largely the product of, the twentieth century.[90] Discussion of the political and social forces which gave birth to it and which shaped its early development are well documented and lie mostly outside the scope of this book; but the underlying values and assumptions in many areas of social security provision will be considered at a number of points, because since their early emergence they have been highly influential and remain so. These continuities include the rules designed to provide work incentives and those embodying various dependency assumptions concerning support expected from family members. The most significant long-standing principles embedded in, and enforced by, social security arrangements include those of self-help, 'lesser eligibility' (the Poor Law concept which involves keeping provision below the income of the lowest paid worker, to discourage dependency and encourage self-sufficiency), willingness to work (for example, by penalising voluntary unemployment through benefit reduction or disqualification) and means-testing, so that the claimant must answer detailed questions and experience various forms of bureaucratic control. In recent years the need to defeat 'welfare dependency' and benefit fraud[91] has formed the basis of the moral justification under both the Conservatives and New Labour for intensifying the social control dimension to social security (as in the controversial Benefit Integrity Project under which some disabled claimants were visited and questioned in their homes: see Chapter 12). The notion of social control implies not only encouragement, discouragement, or enforcement of particular forms of behaviour, as noted above, but more particularly a deliberate and systematic attempt by government or the administration to achieve particular social goals. An obvious example in recent years has been the attempt to

---

[86] See H. Dean, *Social Security and Social Control* (London: Routledge, 1991), especially at ch. 3.
[87] P. Spicker, *Poverty and Social Security* (London: Routledge, 1993), 108.
[88] Green Paper (1998), 'Principle One' (at the start of ch. 3).
[89] R. Plant, 'The very idea of a welfare state', in P. Bean, J. Ferris, and D. Whynes, *In Defence of Welfare* (London: Tavistock, 1985) 3–30, 16.
[90] See Chapters 3–5.
[91] The 1998 Green Paper identifies fraud as one of the 'three fundamental problems' with the current social security system: ch. 1, para. 5. An entire chapter (ch. 9) is devoted to the question of fraud reduction. It estimates the total level of fraud annually as £4bn. See also, DSS, Cm 4012 (1998).

encourage more lone parents into work; policies on lone parents are discussed in detail in Chapters 2 and 9.

In the sense that it may involve regulation of particular forms of behaviour, the social control function of the welfare state imparts, *inter alia*, a sense of the power of state bureaucracies and their officials and the apparent vulnerability of claimants.[92] This power, and the relevant prescription, may arise from detailed legal rules, as, for example, in the case of the rules requiring the parent with care of the child to co-operate with the Child Support Agency or face loss of benefit (see Chapter 9). But social control may also arise from the exercise of administrative discretion and decision-making. A good example is provided by the operation of the cohabitation rule, which originated in the 1920s and under which unmarried heterosexual partners who are deemed to be 'living together as husband and wife' are in effect treated as a married couple for benefit assessment purposes.[93] The rule was not subjected to the general reduction in the scope for discretion and the increased emphasis on defined entitlement in the British social security system after 1980.[94] Nevertheless, both the principle enshrined in the cohabitation rule and the way investigations were con-ducted by the Department were said 'to convey, with considerable sanction, official messages about what kind of behaviour is accepted and tolerated'.[95] By giving offi-cers and investigators a degree of discretion and a relatively wide scope for the exer-cise of individual judgment in cohabitation cases, the social control function has been exerted just as forcefully as if a more prescriptive code on the meaning of cohabitation had been adopted. (The rules–discretion dichotomy is discussed further below.) The operation of the social fund, which also depends upon the exercise of discretion underpinned by legal rules and official policy, offers further examples of social control, as in the way loans may be denied where it is considered that support could and should, for example, be obtained from a family member or voluntary organisation rather than from the fund.

Of course, it must be accepted that there are different forms of social control which may be associated with the social security system. The examples given above illustrate the social and economic sanctions which operate. The sanctions represent the 'stick', while the social wage represents the 'carrot'.[96] It is argued that the social security system through the provision of a social wage has long had the aim of pre-venting any weakening of the social fabric by containing or defusing popular dis-content and disorder resulting from widespread deprivation[97] (a purpose also

[92] See generally, H. Dean, *Social Security and Social Control* (London: Routledge, 1991) and H. Dean, 'Social Security: The income maintenance business', in P. Taylor-Gooby and R. Lawson, *Markets and Managers: New Issues in the Delivery of Welfare* (Milton Keynes: Open University Press, 1993), 96.

[93] See N. Harris, 'Unmarried cohabiting couples and social security in Britain' (1996) 18(2) *J.S.W.F.L.*, 123–46.

[94] See Chapter 4.

[95] T. Novak, *Poverty and the State* (Milton Keynes: Open University Press, 1998), 169.

[96] H. Dean, *Social Security and Social Control* (London: Routledge, 1991), 18.

[97] See ibid., ch. 2.

associated with the introduction of social security appeal systems in the 1930s).[98] At the same time, the broad background of bureaucratic control has increased the apparent helplessness of many claimants, contributing (along with the increasing recognition of the extent and effects of poverty) to the widespread development of welfare pressure group activity in support of the poor in Britain in the late 1960s. This has involved well-documented and continuing (although evolving) local and national campaigns against state responses to poverty and the sanctions associated with bureaucratic control in the administration of welfare benefits, and via recourse to law (including a 'test case strategy').[99]

4. SOCIAL CITIZENSHIP

A. Ideals, Values, and Policies

The recent revival of interest in the citizenship paradigm (particularly the rights-based model formulated by T. H. Marshall) has been part of the critical response to the New Right liberalism of the late 1970s and the 1980s and its policy effects, and an element in the defence of the social rights underpinning welfare entitlement. Under the notion of 'social citizenship', rights to welfare are said to provide a basic opportunity for participation in society through the guarantee of a minimum level of entitlement for all citizens. Social citizenship is thus a useful concept for consideration of the ideological basis for state welfare provision and not least in evaluating the state's role in the field of social security.[100] The citizenship ideal is, in part, premised on the notion that the principal function of the welfare state is both to protect the poor from the effects of poverty (indeed, 'properly understood, a poor citizen is a contradiction in terms')[101] whilst at the same time seeking to combat the structural inequalities which can restrict social, political, and economic participation by all citizens.[102] Attention in recent years has been focused not only on the long-term unemployed but in particular on the inequalities and social exclusion affecting specific

---

[98] T. Lynes, 'Unemployment Assistance Tribunals in the 1930s', in M. Adler and A. Bradley (eds), *Justice, Discretion and Poverty* (Abingdon: Professional, 1976); T. Prosser, 'Poverty, Ideology and Legality: Supplementary Benefit Appeal Tribunals and their Predecessors', (1977) 4 *British J. of Law and Society*, 39–60.

[99] See, for example, T. Prosser, *Test Cases for the Poor* (London: CPAG, 1983); C. Harlow and R. Rawlings, *Pressure through Law* (London: Routledge, 1993). See also F. Piven and R. Cloward, *Regulating the Poor* (London: Tavistock, 1972).

[100] See T. Carney and P. Hanks, *Social Security in Australia* (Melbourne: Oxford University Press, 1994), ch. 5. Hervey also sees social citizenship as a suitable theoretical issue around which to discuss the EU's role in the field of welfare by exploring the relationship between the internal market and social citizenship rights: T. Hervey, 'Welfare Rights as Social Citizenship: Can the EU Deliver?' (1998), Paper at the Jean Monnet Conference on EU Citizenship and Human Rights, University of Liverpool, 4 July 1998.

[101] D. Vincent, *Poor Citizens* (London: Longman, 1991), 205.

[102] To Marshall, 'equality of status is more important than equality of income': T. H. Marshall, 'Citizenship and Social Class', in T. H. Marshall and T. Bottomore, *Citizenship and Social Class* (London: Pluto, 1992), 3–51, 33.

social groups, especially women,[103] young people,[104] particular ethnic minorities,[105] the elderly,[106] and disabled people.[107]

The citizenship ideal was an important element of the underlying philosophical basis to the structure of the welfare state as it emerged post the Beveridge Report (1942);[108] and it reflected the 'welfare consensus' on which the social security system, and the welfare state in general, was built in the 1940s. According to Hewitt,[109] the consensual ethic provided the 'rational foundation for the welfare state's role in the wider political consensus of the postwar years'. It was influenced by the results of scientific inquiry (from the Booth and Rowntree surveys of living conditions at the turn of the century, through to Beveridge's emphasis on scientific measurement of basic subsistence requirements)[110] and the widely held belief that social administration could progressively achieve certain practical goals and that the state was particularly suited to the task of providing welfare. The Beveridge Report formed much of the policy basis for the legislation which laid down the foundations of the modern welfare state (see Chapter 3 below). In ideological terms, Beveridge may be seen as 'one of the main international architects of ... the social citizenship model of welfare'.[111] Beveridge advocated collectivist notions of universal welfare provision, which lay at the heart of the social citizenship paradigm, although his emphasis on insurance and contributions revealed an element of economic liberalism and individualism in his ideology.[112] Many of Beveridge's assumptions, particularly those about the role and aspirations of women in society[113] and about the extent of unemployment,[114] have, of course, weakened the longer-term durability of his version of social citizenship.

---

[103] L. Dominelli, *Welfare Across Continents—Feminist Comparative Social Policy* (Hemel Hempstead: Harvester Wheatsheaf, 1991); R. Lister, 'Citizenship Engendered', (1991) 11(2) *Critical Social Policy*, 65–71.

[104] See in particular G. Jones and C. Wallace, *Youth, Family and Citizenship* (Milton Keynes: Open University Press, 1993); R. Macdonald (ed.), *Youth, the Underclass and Social Exclusion* (Routledge: London, 1997); and N. Pearce and J. Hillman, *Wasted Youth* (London: IPPR, 1998).

[105] D. Vincent, *Poor Citizens* (London: Longman, 1991), 207.

[106] C. Oppenheim and L. Harker, *Poverty: The Facts* (London: CPAG, 1996), 60–2 and more generally, K. Woodward, 'Feminist Critiques of Social Policy' in M. Lavalette and A. Pratt (eds), *Social Policy—A Conceptual and Theoretical Introduction* (London: Sage, 1997), 98–100.

[107] See T. Buck, 'The Disabled Citizen', in R. Blackburn (ed.), *Rights of Citizenship* (Oxford: Mansell, 1993).

[108] Beveridge Report (1942).

[109] M. Hewitt, *Welfare, Ideology and Need: Developing Perspectives on the Welfare State* (Hemel Hempstead: Harvester Wheatsheaf, 1992), 20.

[110] See the discussion of poverty in Chapter 2 below.

[111] P. Baldwin, 'Beveridge in the Longue Durée', in J. Hills, J. Ditch, and H. Glennester (eds), *Beveridge and Social Security An International Perspective* (Oxford: Clarendon Press, 1994), 37.

[112] Ibid., 45.

[113] See E. Wilson, *Women in the Welfare State* (London: Tavistock, 1977) and L. Dominelli, *Women Across Continents: Feminist Comparative Social Policy* (Hemel Hempstead: Harvester Wheatsheaf, 1991). See further Chapter 9 below.

[114] Beveridge's proposals for comprehensive social insurance as the principal area of social security support were based on an assumption of near full employment and generally short-term unemployment: see generally, Bill Jordan, 'Want', (1991) 25(1) *Social Policy and Administration*, 14–26.

The social citizenship ideal which was articulated by Marshall in his seminal essay in 1950, 'Citizenship and Social Class', was premised on the inclusiveness and universality of the Beveridge welfare state. Social citizenship was one of three elements making up the status of citizenship. Marshall explained that citizenship is based on civil rights (for example those which provide for equality before the law and access to legal remedies), political rights (for example those relating to enfranchisement and fair elections), and social rights (rights to welfare). He said that the civil and political rights which emerged by the late nineteenth century had not by then brought about any real reductions in social inequality. Civil rights 'gave legal powers whose use was drastically curtailed by class prejudice and lack of economic opportunity' and political rights 'gave potential power whose exercise demanded experience, organisation and a change of ideas as to the proper functions of government . . . [which] took time to develop'.[115] Marshall went on to explain that these rights had, however, 'helped to guide progress into the path that led directly to the egalitarian policies of the twentieth century'.[116] Social rights were at a minimum at this time and 'were not woven into the fabric of citizenship'.[117] However, as the twentieth century progressed and a more egalitarian society developed, social rights were incorporated into the status of citizenship, including 'a universal right to real income which is not proportionate to the market value of the claimant'.[118]

The basic rationale for citizenship as an ideal is said to lie in its capacity for the social integration of each individual. Marshall saw rights to welfare as part of the mechanism by which such integration could be achieved.[119] He believed that social citizenship rights should guarantee at least a minimum level of economic wealth and security to all. The idea was that the citizen would be able to achieve a degree of economic and social status and security which was not dependent on the operation of the market. However, Marshall appeared to accept that the citizenship ideal had to be tempered by a degree of economic reality. Whilst the aim should be to remove inequalities that could not be regarded as 'legitimate', the standard of legitimacy might vary with the degree of economic necessity.[120] Marshall was also alive to the tension between individual claims to welfare and collective interests. The state, he argued, owed a responsibility to society as a whole and it followed that individual rights had to be subordinated to national policies and needs.[121] But he remained wedded to the notion of universal welfare as a key element of the citizenship paradigm. The issue was taken up by Titmuss, who supported universalism but looked at ways of developing a more selective approach in favour of those in the greatest need: a

---

[115] T. H. Marshall, 'Citizenship and Social Class', in T. H. Marshall and T. Bottomore, *Citizenship and Social Class* (London: Pluto, 1992), 27.
[116] Ibid.   [117] Ibid.   [118] Ibid., 28.
[119] T. H. Marshall, 'The Right to Welfare', in N. Timms and D. Watson (eds), *Talking About Welfare* (London: Routledge, 1976), 60.
[120] T. H. Marshall, n. 115 above, 45.   [121] Ibid., 35.

universal base with a selective superstructure.[122] Supporters of state welfare increasingly regarded conferment of rights as promoting social integration by symbolising the community's social recognition of and respect for individual members whose exclusion was under threat.[123] This attachment to the principle of social rights led to a fierce defence of them in the 1960s and 1970s when they were seemingly undermined by the high level of discretion which had developed within the benefits system (see below).

In recent years those in Britain who support the basic principle of citizenship advocated by Marshall have paid particular regard to the issue of social integration, at a time when selective social and economic policies and government efforts to support the market system have reinforced and perhaps even precipitated growing social and economic inequalities.[124] It is recognised that, in particular, poverty and the problems associated with it present the biggest threat to social integration.[125] Poverty is clearly linked to various other forms of social disadvantage (for example in areas such as educational attainment and health). Any group particularly susceptible to poverty, including the unemployed in general,[126] young people, women (especially lone parents), the elderly, and particular ethnic minority groups, would be prone to social exclusion and thus citizenship denial.[127] Lister has argued that the state, via the social security system, should combat such exclusion by, *inter alia*, providing a 'participation standard' of support.[128] Similarly, Harris argues that 'the purpose of a right to welfare is to guarantee that needs are met . . . If these needs are not satisfied then the individual's effective membership of the community is threatened.'[129] As we shall see below, there are, however, divergent views on how far support (in the form of welfare provision) for an entitlement model of citizenship should extend as a means of tackling social exclusion.

The importance of rights to welfare in fact lies not only in the guarantee of a basic standard of living *per se*, but also, theorists would argue, in the fact that the fullest enjoyment of the civil rights of citizenship is dependent on welfare if these rights are to be more than formal and remote guarantees. Indeed, the social rights of

---

[122] R. Titmuss, *Commitment to Welfare* (London: Allen and Unwin, 1968).

[123] D. Harris, *Justifying State Welfare* (Oxford: Basil Blackwell, 1987), 156.

[124] See generally the discussion in P. Taylor-Gooby and R. Lawson, 'Where do we go from here?: the new order in welfare', in P. Taylor-Gooby and R. Lawson (eds), *Markets and Managers: New Issues in the Delivery of Welfare* (Milton Keynes: Open University Press, 1993), 132–49.

[125] A. Vincent and R. Plant, *Philosophy, Politics and Citizenship* (Oxford: Basil Blackwell, 1984); P. Golding (ed.), *Excluding the Poor* (London: CPAG, 1986); R. Lister, *The Exclusive Society. Citizenship and the Poor* (London: CPAG, 1990); C. Oppenheim (ed.), *An Inclusive Society: Strategies for Tackling Poverty* (London: IPPR, 1998).

[126] See, for example, M. Watson, 'Citizenship and Welfare', in M. Lavalette and A. Pratt (eds), *Social Policy—A Conceptual and Theoretical Introduction* (London: Sage, 1997), 182–95, 192.

[127] P. Alcock, 'Why citizenship and welfare rights offer new hope for new welfare in Britain', (1989) 9/2 *Critical Social Policy*, 32–43; C. Oppenheim, 'Poverty and Social Exclusion: An Overview', in C. Oppenheim (ed.) (1998) op. cit., n. 125 above, 11–28.

[128] R. Lister, 'Social Security', in M. McCarthy (ed.), *The New Politics of Welfare* (Basingstoke: Macmillan, 1989), 104–131, 128.

[129] D. Harris, *Justifying State Welfare* (Oxford: Basil Blackwell, 1987), 147.

citizenship also hold the key to active participation in democratic processes and the capacity to contribute to civil society. Thus, among those who may be regarded as deprived of citizenship are many young homeless adults who do not have their names on the electoral register, and so will be unable to vote, and who may lack entitlement to welfare benefits.[130] Bernard Donoghue, chair of the British Youth Council, has commented that 'young people can only engage in active citizenship . . . if they have the education, the employment, housing, financial support and freedom from discrimination to do so'.[131] Participation is also conditional on liberty; and, as J. K. Galbraith has said, 'nothing, let us forget, sets a stronger limit on the liberty of the citizen than a total absence of money'.[132] In recognising the importance of such civil and political participation, citizenship of entitlement might be regarded as having a potentially stabilising effect on society. The social exclusion which might otherwise result is seen as not only divisive but also a threat to the social order.[133] Thus, as Barry explains, part of the rationale presented for the rights-based model of citizenship is that 'the presence of economic rights that pertain to citizenship prevents class conflict (in the Marxian sense) getting out of hand'.[134]

Nevertheless, some regard the conceptual basis to citizenship itself, as articulated by Marshall and proponents of his ideas, as in some respects exclusive. For example, Lister refers to the 'mantle of invisibility (which) cloaks women in much of the contemporary discourse around citizenship'.[135] O'Donovan explains that in current debates about citizenship, a 'universal model' of the citizen is presupposed, one which 'abstracts from specific characteristics of race, gender, ethnicity and class', whereas 'Marshall's citizen is of the male gender' and present laws continue to reflect that perception.[136] As Phillips says, such abstraction 'encourages the notion of the "individual" and "citizen" as a character of indifferent sex', so that 'in societies that are thoroughly saturated by gender, such indifference to sex can only reinforce the position of women'.[137] O'Donovan rejects the traditional model of citizenship under which women may be 'incorporated into the body politic', in favour of one which acknowledges difference and takes account of group rights;[138] but she notes the difficulties of achieving this and does not seek an abandonment of the principle of uni-

---

[130] R. Macdonald, 'Youth, social exclusion and the millennium', in R. Macdonald, *Youth, the Underclass and Social Exclusion* (London: Routledge, 1997), 167–97 at 178.

[131] The Children's Society, *Children in Focus, Young People and Citizenship—A Public Debate, 29 January 1992* (London: The Children's Society 1992). Proposals for the inclusion of citizenship studies within the National Curriculum in secondary schools were announced on 13 May 1999.

[132] J. K. Galbraith, 'The Good Society Considered: The Economic Dimension', Address at St David's Hall, Cardiff, Wales, 26 January 1994 (published as a pamphlet insert in the *J. of Law and Society*, 1994).

[133] D. Oliver, 'Active Citizenship in the 1990s' (1991) 44(2) *J. of Parliamentary Affairs*, 157–71 at 162.

[134] N. Barry, *Welfare* (Milton Keynes: Open University Press, 1990), 96.

[135] R. Lister, *The Female Citizen* (Liverpool: Liverpool University Press, 1989), 15.

[136] K. O'Donovan, 'Gender Blindness or Justice Engendered', in R. Blackburn (ed.), *Rights of Citizenship* (Oxford: Mansell, 1993), 12–30 at 12. See also R. Lister, n. 128 above .

[137] A. Phillips, *Democracy and Difference* (London: Polity, 1993), 115.

[138] The work of Iris Young is cited: I. Young, 'Polity and group difference: a critique of the ideal of universal citizenship' (1989) *Ethics*, No. 99, 250–74.

versal, equal, citizenship,[139] a principle which forms part of the value base to rights to welfare on which the citizenship ideal rests. Social justice and society's moral obligation to its members are other key values,[140] although these are undoubtedly relativistic notions whose meaning varies in line with prevailing social norms and political ideals. Such egalitarian and wider moral principles or goals are of course dissociated from the market. In applying them, citizenship of entitlement thus aims to compensate for the market's moral neutrality and, of course, its inequalities. Barry argues that in practice, however, existing welfare state policies and institutions are not always aimed at addressing the failure of the market, for they are often no more than 'a response to political pressure, brought about by electoral competition' rather than ethical considerations.[141] One result is that frequently the unequal situation of particular groups is not addressed by the welfare system.[142]

As we shall see further in Chapter 2, one group excluded from social citizenship in recent decades has been young people, particularly the unemployed. The general difficulties experienced by many young people of both genders (although each gender's experience is in some respects different)[143] in making the normative transitions from school to work and from childhood into adulthood has been apparent in many Western states for over a decade and is largely the result of unemployment caused by economic recession and structural change.[144] Some states have framed youth policies which reflect the basic philosophy of widening social participation through citizenship rights. Chisolm and Bergeret found that in EC (now EU) Member States that had an explicit youth policy, citizenship was 'the anchoring concept' which informed its nature and purpose; youth policies were 'rooted in the idea of socialisation for participation and for citizenship'.[145] International examples of particular relevance to young people have included a proposed 'Charter of Youth Rights', based on 'citizenship rights', supported by the European Foundation for the Improvement of Living and Working Conditions,[146] and Fragnière's proposal for citizenship for young people based on rights to, *inter alia*, 'an income, guaranteed or earned'.[147] In the UK, citizenship of entitlement was featured in the recommendations of the Commission

---

[139] N. 136 above, at 25–7.

[140] See D. Harris, n. 123 above; W. A. Robson, *Welfare State and Welfare Society: Illusion and Reality* (London: Allen and Unwin, 1976).

[141] N. 134 above, at 85.

[142] D. Taylor, 'Citizenship and Social Power', (1989) 9/2 *Critical Social Policy*, 19–31, at 20.

[143] See e.g. F. Coffield, C. Borrill, and S. Marshall, *Growing Up at the Margins* (Milton Keynes: Open University Press, 1986).

[144] For a useful collection of evidence, see House of Lords Select Committee on the European Communities, Session 1990–91, 14th report, Y*oung People in the European Community*, with Evidence, HL Paper 63–II (London: HMSO, 1991).

[145] L. Chislom and J.-M. Bergeret, *Young People in the European Community* (Luxembourg: Commission of the European Communities, 1991), 62.

[146] *Growing Up and Leaving Home: Recommendations of a European Seminar* (Luxembourg: Commission of the European Communities, 1990).

[147] G. Fragnière, *Strategies for Solving the Malaise*, Paper for the Public Parliamentary Hearing on Youth Unemployment, The Hague, 3–4 September 1985 (The Hague, Council of Europe, 1985), 2–3.

on Citizenship chaired by the Speaker of the House of Commons; the Commission called for the greater social and economic integration of young people.[148] An initiative was launched by the incoming Labour Government in 1997—the establishment of a Social Exclusion Unit, whose first work programme (running to July 1998) focused on a number of issues related to young people, such as truancy, school exclusion, rough sleeping, and the drugs culture.[149]

The way that the social citizenship ideal has underlain various policies concerning young people in recent years demonstrates its political potential. Indeed, while the theoretical debate continues, 'citizenship' is becoming an increasing populist notion in Britain. It was promoted by the Commission on Social Justice as one of the 'four principles' of social justice: 'Everyone is entitled, as a right of citizenship, to be able to meet their basic needs'.[150] Thatcherism also promoted its own, contrasting, vision of citizenship, one which places less emphasis on the moral imperative of meeting need and greater emphasis on the responsibilities of citizenship, on 'active citizenship'.[151] John Major's preface to the Government's *Citizen's Charter* in 1991 commented that 'citizenship is about our responsibilities ... as well as our entitlements'.[152] Similarly, the centre Left, in the form of the present Labour Government, has expressed its vision of the future relationship between state welfare and individual entitlement in terms of a 'new welfare contract between the citizen and Government, based on responsibilities and rights'[153] (see below). Both approaches put an emphasis on personal responsibility which reflects traditional notions of reciprocity in the state welfare context. Under this principle, social rights depend to some extent upon the capacity of the beneficiary of public services to compensate for his or her inability to make private provision in respect of welfare needs and for a failure to contribute to the community as a whole through the personal taxation system.[154] We will see in later chapters a number of areas of social security in which this principle has been extended in recent years—most notably through the reforms accompanying the introduction of the jobseeker's allowance, where claimants not only have to show that they are actively seeking employment but must also sign an agreement with the Employment Office committing themselves to taking various steps, including training. Putting the receipt of benefits on a kind of pseudo-contractual basis in this way is seen as enabling public provision of welfare to mirror private welfare provision. The US 'Workfare' concept, which

---

[148] Commission on Citizenship, *Report of the Commission on Citizenship* (London: HMSO, 1990); for discussion, see J. L. Murdoch, 'Encouraging Citizenship: Report of the Commission on Citizenship' (1991) 54 *M.L.R.* 439–41.

[149] See, for example, Social Exclusion Unit, *Truancy and School Exclusion: Report by the Social Exclusion Unit*, Cm 3957 (London: The Stationery Office, 1998).

[150] Commission on Social Justice, *The Justice Gap* (London: IPPR, 1993), 16.

[151] See D. Heater, 'Citizenship: A Remarkable Case of Sudden Interest' (1991) 44(2) *J. of Parliamentary Affairs*, 140–56, at 166–7.

[152] HM Government, *The Citizen's Charter*, Cm 1599 (London: HMSO, 1991).

[153] Green Paper (1998), ch. 11, para. 5.

[154] See J. Parker, *Social Policy and Citizenship* (Oxford: Clarendon Press, 1975), 146–7.

engaged Conservative ministers and under which claimants have to perform work (often on community projects) as a condition of receiving benefits, is also built on the notion of reciprocity and has attracted a degree of intellectual as well as political support (but also criticism).[155] It was operated on a trial basis in a few areas under the Conservatives.[156] The New Deal programmes which the Labour Government has established and which offer specific groups (principally young people, lone parents, the long-term unemployed, and the disabled) the option of subsidised employment or benefit while studying or training (see Chapter 10), represent a continuity with previous policy initiatives emphasising the intense conditionality of citizenship of entitlement. An emphasis on personal responsibility is also reflected in Field's commitment to a revival of the insurance concept[157] and the Government's plans for stakeholder pensions based on private provision.[158] The insurance principle constitutes one of the traditional areas of reciprocity in the social security system but has in fact been considerably weakened over the past two decades;[159] its long-term status under Labour is less than clear.

It is also important to see active citizenship as part of a new relationship between citizen and welfare state. The citizen has changed from being 'the passive recipient of the public largesse of the post-war period to the active consumer, customer or client of the later twentieth-century state'.[160] Consumer-citizenship rights are therefore seen more in terms of individual involvement and the exercise of choice, with a corresponding increase in accountability on the part of the provider. The problem with this approach to citizenship is that it emphasises individualism, which may be seen as inimical to citizenship's more collectivist orientation. The 'consumer' may be seen to act in a more self-interested way than the 'citizen', who is expected to be motivated by more altruistic feelings and by public-spiritedness.[161] Consumer-citizenship, in placing more emphasis on the individual to act on his or her own behalf, also presupposes both a capacity to participate in the processes involved and an equality of choice or opportunity. The fact that the poor are often disadvantaged in these terms means that consumer-citizenship may serve to widen social divisions and increase the level of inequality, working against the core purpose of social citizenship rights.[162] The greater onus placed on individuals to

---

[155] See R. Plant, 'The fairness of workfare', *The Times*, 16 November 1988; D. Green, 'Welfare and Civil Society', in F. Field, *Stakeholder Welfare* (London: IEA, 1996) 75–91, 85–6.

[156] See N. Harris, 'Workfare schemes' (1994) 1 *J.S.S.L.*, 50–1.

[157] F. Field, *Making Welfare Work* (London: IEA, 1995).

[158] See the Welfare Reform and Pensions Act 1999, Part I; and see Green Paper (1998), ch. 4 and DSS, *A New Contract for Welfare: Partnership in Pensions*, Cm 4179 (London: The Stationery Office, 1998).

[159] See Chapter 6.

[160] D. Oliver, *Government in the United Kingdom: The Search for Accountability, Effectiveness and Citizenship* (Milton Keynes: Open University Press, 1991), 32.

[161] S. Ranson, 'From 1944 to 1988: Education, Citizenship and Democracy', in M. Flude and M. Hammer (eds), *The Education Act 1988: Its Origins and Implications* (London: Falmer, 1989) 1–20, 15.

[162] See P. Golding (ed.), *Excluding the Poor* (London: Child Poverty Action Group, 1986); R. Lister, *The Exclusive Society* (London: CPAG, 1990).

play a more active role in the system may disadvantage those most in need of assistance, since they are often the people least able to participate effectively in their own interest.[163] More generally, there is a perception that government exhortation to active citizenship is a threat to the social element of citizenship guaranteed by the welfare state as conceptualised by Marshall,[164] because it presupposes a weakening of the role of state as provider. Charitable provision or family support may need to fill part of the gap resulting from this reduction in state welfare. However, although individual charitable action may be a facet of active citizenship, it may connote, for those dependent on such philanthropy, 'an exclusive rather than an inclusive concept of citizenship'.[165] Moreover, as Lister explains, it is only activity in the public sphere which will be recognised for the purposes of active citizenship: 'By and large, governments prefer not to quantify what goes on in the privacy of the home; it does not count.'[166]

Both the Commission on Social Justice (1992–4) and, more recently, Frank Field, have sought ways of combining the advantages of consumer-citizenship, which are seen as including the promotion of greater personal initiative and self-reliance and reduced dependency, with the traditional aims of social citizenship in promoting social integration, reducing inequality, and providing individuals with a degree of economic security. The Commission on Social Justice[167] analysed existing policies and sought to develop a framework of principles on which practical policies could be developed, with the aim of providing economic security for individuals, maximised individual social and economic opportunities, and 'the creation of a fairer and more just society'.[168] In the field of social security, the idea of an unconditional basic 'citizen's income' in place of national insurance benefits, personal tax allowances, and certain means-tested benefits was considered by the Commission. Its moral basis was centred on the social citizenship ideal, but the idea was rejected (at least in that form) partly on the ground that it 'does not require any *act* of citizenship' and would be likely to be criticised for offering 'something for nothing'.[169] On the other hand, a strengthening of social insurance was favoured, because of its 'ethic of mutuality' and its 'balancing of rights and responsibilities'.[170] There was an emphasis on incentives and opportunities to work, on offering 'a hand-up rather than a handout' (a phrase since adopted by Tony Blair as Prime Minister), and on providing a benefits safety net that is seen as preventing rather than merely relieving poverty.[171]

What is clearly evident throughout the Commission's proposals for reform of the welfare state is the notion of reciprocity, referred to above. For example, one of the

[163] J. Le Grand, 'The State of Welfare', in J. Hills (ed.), *The State of Welfare: The Welfare State in Britain since 1984* (Oxford: Clarendon Press, 1991), 358–60.

[164] See D. Oliver, op. cit., n. 160 above, 35.

[165] R. Lister, *The Female Citizen* (Liverpool: University of Liverpool, 1989), 16. Lister explores this theme further in *The Exclusive Society*, n. 162 above.

[166] Ibid. See also R. Lister, 'Citizenship Engendered', (1991) 11(2) *Critical Social Policy*, 65–71.

[167] Commission on Social Justice, *Social Justice: Strategies for National Renewal* (London: Vintage, 1994).

[168] Ibid., 412.　　　[169] Ibid., 262.　　　[170] Ibid., 232.　　　[171] Ibid., 222–3.

reasons that the principle of social insurance is so highly favoured is that it represents 'a contract between individuals and society'.[172] Marshall himself accepted that the obligations of citizenship had to be considered, but he was unable to bring them squarely into his notion of social citizenship. Looking at one of the principal duties, the duty to seek employment, which is today clearly central to both New Right/liberal visions of citizenship and is also a dominant theme in the Commission on Social Justice's proposals and in the 1998 Green Paper, Marshall concluded that it was 'no easy matter to revive the sense of the personal obligation to work in a new form in which it is attached to the status of citizenship'.[173] To Marshall, the obligations of citizenship were basically moral in nature, involving an internal element: thus the essential duty was not merely to work, but to 'put one's heart into one's work and work hard'.[174] Self-motivation and a sense of wanting to contribute to the greater good were the key, but Marshall accepted that while 'a successful appeal to the duties of citizenship can be made in times of emergency . . . the Dunkirk spirit cannot be a permanent feature of any civilisation'.[175]

The most forceful advocate of the moral dimension to social citizenship in recent years has been Frank Field. Despite his resignation from the office of Minister for Welfare Reform in July 1998, Field's basic approach forms the basis for the Government's broad strategy as set out in the 1998 Green Paper, and his ideas have sparked an ongoing debate. The central, unifying, concept developed by Field is that of stakeholderism. It seeks to harness the self-interest of the individual, which Field sees as inherent in human nature,[176] in a way that benefits or at least is consistent with the public good. As Hutton, who has similar views on this subject, argues, 'there needs to be a sense . . . that individuals are contributing to their own well-being', but as part of a general 'morality of welfare'.[177] Field is critical of what he sees as the way that the welfare state is unable to accommodate or harness the basic expression of self-interest: 'Welfare is instead pitted against self-interest in a way in which the public good can only be the loser. Hard work is penalised by the loss of entitlement. Incentives reinforce welfare dependency. Honesty is punished by a loss of income.'[178] The chief culprit in this is the means-test: 'Its rules actively undermine the whole fabric of our character. In doing so it is a cancer within the public domain helping to erode the wider moral order of society.'[179] Field wants, therefore, to minimise the role of means-testing and to develop the insurance concept in a way that gives individuals a personal stake in welfare, hence the notion of 'stakeholder welfare', and destroys the perception that welfare is simply something to be handed down by the state.

---

[172] Ibid., 231.

[173] T. H. Marshall, 'Citizenship and Social Class', in T. H. Marshall and T. Bottomore, *Citizenship and Social Class* (London: Pluto, 1992), 46.

[174] Ibid.   [175] Ibid.

[176] See, in particular, *Stakeholder Welfare* (IEA: London, 1996), section III.

[177] W. Hutton, *The State We're In*, rev. edn. (London: Vintage, 1996), 309.

[178] *Stakeholder Welfare*, op. cit. g n. 176 above, 20.   [179] Ibid.

Field is particularly attracted to the values represented by the principle of mutuality and collective self-help. He sees it as conducive to social solidarity and personal responsibility and independence. Similarly, Hutton, another proponent of stakeholding, seeks 'a culture in which common humanity and the instinct to collaborate are allowed to flower', with a welfare state offering an inclusive concept of citizenship based on, *inter alia*, 'collective risk-sharing'.[180] For Field, social citizenship would be derived from welfare provision 'to which each of us earns our entitlement, and will become ever more so if the stakeholder concept is realised in the reform of welfare'.[181] Earned entitlement would be based on new, broadened insurance provision (not necessarily exclusively in the public sector), and on fulfilment of more rigorous conditions of entitlement to basic income support by being required to plan, with guidance, one's own career or life plan: 'claimants will have both an opportunity and duty to build their own life rafts from dependency'.[182] The initial manifestations of this last proposal are the New Deal programmes introduced by the Labour Government. Alcock[183] regards Field's attempts to remoralise welfare through the mutuality concept as 'dangerous', because in his view there is no guarantee of social inclusiveness: indeed, '[i]n a socially and culturally divided society such as modern Britain welfare based on mutual self-help could reinforce social exclusion based on ethnicity, age, disability, gender and other social divisions'. There would not, he argues, be the same imperative to bring some categories fully into the welfare net as would clearly be the case with an inclusive state model of welfare. Field does acknowledge that means-testing has left many claimants deprived of equal citizenship as conceptualised by Marshall and he therefore envisages stakeholding as 'the new badge of citizenship' and says that the concept of citizenship will need to be redefined to accommodate it.[184] Field aims to maximise social inclusion 'through extension of stakeholder status to those who by chance (not choice) are outside a labour market through which stakeholding is acquired'.[185]

As things stand, although the rules designed to ensure that claimants must be actively seeking work are reinforced by an unwritten moral code based on an abhorrence of 'scrounging' and dependency on both the state and on the taxpayers who fund the welfare provision that it makes, such moral underpinnings barely touch the perceptions of claimants. That is not to deny that the majority of claimants do feel a moral obligation to support their families through work. Nevertheless, for those requiring state support, the obligation to seek employment or undergo training for work is enforced through such stringent conditions that social control rather than personal moral responsibility seems to predominate. Indeed, in times of high unemployment, the sense of demoralisation and pointlessness which can often pervade the search for work, and especially the feeling of being let down by society as a whole, destroys any prospect of building up the obligations of citizenship other

---

[180] W. Hutton, *The State to Come* (London: Vintage, 1997), 65.
[181] *Stakeholder Welfare*, op. cit., 37.   [182] Ibid., 34.
[183] P. Alcock, 'Welfare and Self-Interest', in F. Field, *Stakeholder Welfare*, op. cit., 52–3.
[184] F. Field, 'A Rejoinder', in F. Field, *Stakeholder Welfare*, op. cit., 112.
[185] Ibid.

than on this basis. For that reason, Field is making an important point about the need to redefine social citizenship or at least the way of ensuring it. This is certainly the view of Deacon.[186] He urges us to differentiate between the views of Charles Murray,[187] whose portrayal of an urban 'underclass' leading a parasitic and at times criminal existence with little sense of social and moral responsibility provoked a fierce attack by the sociological community with regard to its central premises,[188] and those of Field, even though the language of Field's attacks on lone parents, means-testing, and fraud bear close resemblance to those of Murray. Deacon regards Field as having a completely different agenda to that of polemicists like Murray. Field nevertheless acknowledges the existence of an 'underclass' in presenting the case for new policies to deal with social exclusion.[189] Lister, however, warns us of the exclusionist, value-laden language of an 'underclass': the more the poor are described in this way 'the easier it becomes for the rest of us to write them off as beyond the bounds of common citizenship'.[190]

B. Social Citizenship and Human Rights

The introduction of ever more stringent conditions of eligibility to social security benefits combined with cutbacks in support in particular areas (discussed in later chapters and including support for lone parents and young people and for tenants in general) has, as noted earlier, been seen by some as undermining social citizenship by weakening social citizenship rights. Partly for this reason, and also because of anxiety about the increasing power of government in the UK, there has in recent years been concern that basic social and economic rights may need greater constitutional underpinning, either through incorporation of the European Convention on Human Rights 1950 or other international human rights instruments into domestic law or perhaps through a 'Social Charter for Britain'.[191] It is felt that the constitutionalisation of social rights would give them added potency.[192]

---

[186] A. Deacon, 'Welfare and Character', in F. Field, op. cit., 60–71.

[187] See C. Murray et al., *Charles Murray and the Underclass—The Developing Debate* (London: IEA, 1996), which includes 'The Emerging British Underclass' and 'Underclass; The Crisis Deepens', first published in 1989 and 1994 respectively. See also C. Murray, 'All locked up in the American dream', *The Sunday Times*, 7 February 1999.

[188] See the various commentaries in ibid.; E. Mingione, *Urban Poverty and the Underclass—A Reader* (Oxford: Blackwell, 1996); and M. Adler, 'The Underclass: Rhetoric or Reality?' in L. Lundy et al. (eds), *In Search of the 'Underclass': Working Papers from the SLSA One Day Conference in Queen's University Belfast* (Belfast: Queen's University Faculty of Law, 1997), 108–16.

[189] See F. Field, 'Britain's Underclass: Countering the Growth', in C. Murray et al., *Charles Murray and the Underclass—The Developing Debate* (London: IEA, 1996), 57–60.

[190] R. Lister, 'In search of the "underclass" ', in L. Lundy et al. (eds), *In Search of the 'Underclass'*, above n. 188 1–16.

[191] N. Lewis and M. Seneviratne, 'A Social Charter for Britain', in A. Coote (ed.), *The Welfare of Citizens* (London: IPPR/Rivers Oram Press, 1992), 31–54; and K. D. Ewing, 'Social Rights and Constitutional Law' [1999] *P.L.* 104–23.

[192] J. Tweedy and A. Hunt, 'The Future of the Welfare State and Social Rights: Reflections on Habermas', (1994) 21(3) *J. of Law and Society*, 288–316.

Now the European Convention on Human Rights 1950 is being brought into national law following the enactment of the Human Rights Act 1998. One of the legal effects of the 1998 Act (from October 2000) will be that adjudicative bodies will (under section 3) have to construe national legislation in a way that is consistent with the rights laid down in the Convention. Additionally, although those rights will not prevail over statutory provisions, the higher courts will be able to issue, in relation to primary or secondary legislation, declarations as to incompatibility.[193] Moreover, ministers must now make a statement prior to the second reading of a Bill in either House that the Bill's provisions are compatible with the Convention rights (a 'statement of compatibility') or that even though the Minister is not able to make such a statement the Government wishes the House to proceed with the Bill.[194] A statement of compatibility was, for example, made in respect of the Welfare Reform and Pensions Bill, published in February 1999. Secondary legislation, which is used extensively in the field of social security in Britain, will now be amenable to challenge as to illegality for inconsistency with the Convention. Although the Convention does not have any provisions specifically concerned with social security (cf. UN Convention on the Rights of the Child, Art. 26—child's 'right to benefit from social security') there is already discussion of the possibility of challenging, for example, the 'habitual residence' test in its impact on the social security rights of immigrants, cuts in lone parents' benefits, and aspects of the child support scheme's administration, under the provisions of the Convention of general application concerned, in the case of immigrants, with freedom from discrimination on the grounds of race or national origins (Article 14) and, in relation to the other examples, with respect for private and family life (Article 8). Moreover, the appropriateness of adjudication arrangements following recent reforms (see Chapter 7), will rightly be judged with reference to Article 6(1), which provides for entitlement to a 'fair and public hearing within a reasonable time by an independent and impartial tribunal established by law'.[195]

A limited number of attempts to apply some of these provisions have been made in the past.[196] For example, in Commissioner's Decision *CG/97/1997* the claimant argued breach of Article 8 in a cohabitation case on widow's benefit; but the Commissioner ruled that absent the enactment of the Human Rights Bill the Article could not govern his decision in precedence over national legislation. This was con-

---

[193] Section 4. See further The Lord Chancellor, *Rights Brought Home: The Human Rights Bill* (London: The Stationery Office, 1997).

[194] Section 19(1). This duty came into force on the Royal Assent, in November 1998.

[195] Art. 6(1) applies to civil cases and criminal charges. See further E. Eichenhofer, 'A European Perspective on the Bill', in M. Adler and R. Sainsbury (eds), *Adjudication Matters: Reforming Decision Making and Appeals in Social Security* (Edinburgh: Department of Social Policy, University of Edinburgh, 1998), 39–44. Note that Eichenhofer explains (at 42) that Article 6(1) rights based on social insurance are 'civil rights' for the purposes of the Article, but those based on social assistance are not.

[196] See further, H. Storey, 'United Kingdom Social Security Law: European and International Dimensions—Part 1' (1994) 1 *J.S.S.L.*, 110–32 at 123–5. On an unsuccessful attempt to apply the Geneva Convention to asylum seekers' claims to income support, see *CIS 564/1994* and *CIS 7520/1995*, cited in J. Mesher and P. Wood, *Income-Related Benefits: The Legislation* (London: Sweet and Maxwell, 1998), 273. The UN Convention on the Rights of the Child will remain persuasive only.

sistent with the approach taken in several child support cases where Convention rights were argued.[197] The potential for challenges under the Convention has obviously increased significantly with the Human Rights Act 1998. For example, the complaint, ruled admissible by the Commission, that the differential treatment of widows and widowers for the purposes of survivors' benefits is potentially in breach of Article 14, read with Protocol 1 Article 1 (to be rectified via the Welfare Reform and Pensions Act 1999 sections 54 and 55), would now be possible without having to take a case to Strasbourg.[198] In the recent case of *O'Connor v Chief Adjudication Officer and the Secretary of State for Social Security*[199] the Court of Appeal considered very carefully (although ultimately rejected) an argument that regulations appearing to deprive a student of the right to social security were incompatible with the prohibition on denial of the right to education and with freedom from discrimination, under Article 2 to Protocol 1 and Article 14, respectively.

While the practical utility of the Convention rights is yet to be fully tested within the UK, the incorporation of the Convention is, in any event, certainly of considerable symbolic significance. Like the Beveridge report, which was similarly born out of a drive towards building a better society for all after the conclusion of the Second World War, the Convention itself is based on the principle of universality, which is at the core of Marshall's vision of citizenship first articulated in the year the Convention came into being. Moreover, whatever their precise legal effect, the above provisions clearly import a rights-based view of citizenship similar to that articulated by Marshall but increasingly coloured in recent years by a political emphasis on individual civic responsibility (to which the Convention itself makes only passing reference).[200]

5. RIGHTS, RULES, AND DISCRETION

As we saw earlier, the language of rights pervades citizenship theory. There are conceptual difficulties, however, with the description of 'rights' in the context of welfare. Although there is not the space in this book to explore rights theories fully, even in the context of rights to welfare,[201] it is important to build on the previous discussion of the welfare state and citizenship by considering some key elements of the conceptual framework.

The term 'rights' used in this context may describe a given opportunity to receive

[197] See *R(CS)2/95* and *CCS/11729/1996*.
[198] See J. Wadham and H. Mountfield, *Blackstone's Guide to the Human Rights Act 1998* (London: Blackstone, 1999), 113.
[199] [1999] E.L.R. 209. See pp. 351–2 below
[200] In Article 4, the Convention outlaws 'compulsory labour' but excludes from this 'any work or service which forms part of normal civic obligations'.
[201] See H. Dean, *Welfare, Law and Citizenship* (London: Prentice Hall/Harvester Wheatsheaf, 1996), offering a thoughtful theoretical review of the subject, particularly the nature of social rights.

state welfare; the rights concerned arise out of the statutory duties resting on the state which form co-relatives to them.[202] Rights theories acknowledge that rights may be hierarchical, and Galligan, for example, argues that the status of rights to welfare may depend on the moral arguments used to justify attaching to certain interests, generally referred to in this context as 'needs', the special status of rights. He suggests that 'arguments from utility, or from theories of justice or other ethical principles, may provide the moral basis for rights to welfare'.[203] Formal entitlement to welfare, while not directly linked in practice to a collective moral duty, might be shaped by it in the values promoted by any particular society, such as a belief that communal wealth should be shared on an equitable basis. Marshall regarded it as important that a moral duty on the part of society and its agencies should underpin citizenship rights (see above). But moral ideals concerned with equality, security, and redistribution of wealth have, as noted above, to compete against wider political and economic objectives. Harris therefore argues that the political task for the future should ideally be 'to make the moral duty an operative element in the politics of large societies' in order to create a society 'which belongs to all of its members in place of one belonging to the well-off, the talented, the lucky and the well-born'.[204] The wider the social divisions, the more important the political and legal recognition of citizens' rights to welfare, underpinned by a moral commitment, becomes. As Dworkin puts it:

The institution of rights is ... crucial, because it represents the majority's promise to the minorities that their dignity and equality will be respected. When the divisions among the groups are most violent, then this gesture, if law is to work, must be most sincere.[205]

Today, the increasing political and legal emphasis being placed on the reciprocal obligations of those in receipt of state welfare has begun to change the complexion of welfare rights. While it would be incorrect to regard the increasing conditionality of rights to welfare as having changed the fundamental legal basis to them or the means of their enforceability, those rights are nevertheless increasingly represented as 'contractual' in nature—reflected in, for example, the terms 'jobseeker's agreement' and 'New Deal'. In one sense this might be seen to strengthen those rights by reinforcing their moral basis (see Conclusion below) and accommodating a degree of individual choice. On the other hand, the imposition of conditions seems merely to reinforce the dominance of the state in such arrangements. Furthermore, a right to welfare thus begins to be seen more in negative terms—a right not to be deprived of entitlement. Another important change is the way that, contemporaneous with the increasing assumption by some welfare rights of 'private' characteristics (albeit of a largely sym-

---

[202] See R. Plant, H. Lesser, and P. Taylor-Gooby, *Political Philosophy and Social Welfare* (London: Routledge and Kegan Paul, 1980).

[203] D. J. Galligan, *Discretionary Powers: A Legal Study of Official Discretion* (Oxford: Clarendon Press, 1986), 187.

[204] D. Harris, *Justifying State Welfare* (Oxford: Basil Blackwell, 1987), 61.

[205] R. Dworkin, *Taking Rights Seriously* (London: Duckworth, 1978), 205.

bolic nature) noted above, other such rights are being replaced or supplemented via a process of privatisation of welfare. This is a process which clearly undermines the traditional collective basis of welfare rights.

The status of rights to welfare also depends on whether provision is based on discretion as opposed to rules. There is a contrast between, on the one hand, entitlement under prescribed rules specifying necessary and/or sufficient conditions and, on the other, the possibility of receiving support either by virtue of meeting gateway criteria of need (being old, unemployed, sick, etc) or, more importantly, satisfying the relevant decision-maker that one is a 'deserving' case. The last of these bases of entitlement is particularly discretion-based (although some discretion also arises through the interpretation of rules and the exercise of judgment in individual rule-based cases: see below). Indeed, a classic problem when speaking of welfare 'rights' lies in determining the extent to which it is correct to speak of rights in respect of provision which is dependent on the exercise of discretion. As Asquith and Adler point out, there is an inverse relationship between individual rights and administrative discretion.[206] Thus, the more discretion that rests with officials the fewer and weaker the 'rights' of the claimant. Indeed, a point may be reached where 'the very coinage of rights is debased' by the discretionary element.[207]

In practice, however, key areas of discretion within the social security system today operate within a tight regulatory framework which sets parameters for support and constraints for officials. A good example of this is the legal framework governing the social fund, discussed in Chapter 14. Leaving aside a small number of entitlement-based areas under the fund, the allocation of grants and loans, which occurs broadly on the basis of need, is constrained by the statutory framework which enables needs to be ignored if, for example, local office budget allocations are depleted and priority cases redefined as a result, or where support is available from another source (such as a relative or charitable organisation). Even though the fact that officers are required to take account of the 'nature, extent and urgency of the need'[208] implies a significant degree of discretion, decision-making is also constrained by the need to apply relevant directions made by the Secretary of State and to have regard to statutory guidance, the effect of which is to rein in such discretion. Indeed, discretion in relation to state welfare provision is always constrained by, at the very least, 'administratively created parameters', whilst the application of legal rules governing entitlement 'must involve discretion in the interpretation of that rule and of the circumstances of its application'.[209] Thus, as Dalley and Berthoud

---

[206] 'Discretion and Power', in M. Adler and S. Asquith, *Discretion and Welfare* (London: Heinemann, 1981), 12.

[207] D. J. Galligan, n. 203 above, 192.

[208] SSCBA 1992, s.140(1). Following the SSA 1998, this no longer applies to budgeting loans. See further Chapter 14.

[209] H. Dean, *Social Security and Social Control* (London: Routledge, 1991), 141; see also D. Bull, 'The Anti-Discretion Movement in Britain: Fact or Phantom?' (1980) *J.S.W.L.*, 65–83, at 68, and J. Dewar, 'Reducing Discretion in Family Law', in J. Eekelaar and T. Nhlapo (eds), *The Changing Family: Family Forms and Family Law* (Oxford: Hart, 1998), 233–50, at 235.

comment, in practice 'the difference between discretion and entitlement may not always be clear-cut'.[210] Commentators noted that when, in late 1980, detailed rules intended to replace the wide discretion resting with the Supplementary Benefit Commission to make exceptional needs payments for clothing, furniture, and so on, were introduced, there was a residual discretion—not only when considering whether a payment (a 'single payment') might be made to a person, in order to avoid a 'serious risk' to their health and safety, but also in the exercise of judgment when applying various rules to individual cases.[211]

Thus some discretion must inevitably characterise welfare provision, even if discretion is of a residual nature. Indeed, it is regarded as providing a necessary element of flexibility to deal with circumstances which rules cannot adequately anticipate in advance. This was acknowledged by the DHSS's review team in its report which formed the basis for many of the 1980 changes to the supplementary benefit scheme.[212] Recognition of individual needs was regarded as an overriding consideration by Titmuss. He favoured creative and individualised justice within a discretion-based system in which individual needs, which varied, could be catered for adequately.[213] Whilst the application of a rule to a particular case could, in a particular set of circumstances, have a result which defeats the object of the rule and has an unfair effect, discretion may, as Schnieder says, 'allow the decision-maker to promote the rule's purpose' and let him or her 'do justice'.[214] But Donnison has pointed to the serious drawbacks to a discretion-based system, including the relatively high cost of administration, the potential for conflict between claimants and officials and, more significantly, the absence of clear entitlement (which can hinder officials as much as claimants).[215] Another criticism of discretion is that although rules are not in themselves value free,[216] discretion is particularly susceptible to the exercise of prejudice and perverse moral judgment by individuals.[217] Rule-based systems are said to ensure greater consistency in decision-making; and their more public character, in contrast to the private quality of discretion, means that people may understand better how they are expected to behave and may order their lives accordingly.[218]

---

[210] G. Dalley and R. Berthoud, *Challenging Discretion: The Social Fund Review Procedure* (London: Policy Studies Institute, 1992), 5.

[211] See R. Lister, 'The New Supplementary Benefit Regulations: Comment' (1980) *J.S.W.L.*, 341–3 and M. Partington, 'Supplementary Benefits: Interpretation and Judgment' (1980) *N.L.J.* 548.

[212] *Social Assistance: A Review of the Supplementary Benefit Scheme in Great Britain* (London: DHSS, 1978), para. 9.48. See also, D. Bull, 'The Anti-Discretion Movement in Britain: Fact or Phantom?' (1980) *J.S.W.L.*, 65–83. See further Chapter 4.

[213] R. Titmuss, 'Welfare "Rights", Law and Discretion' (1971) 42 *Political Quarterly*, 113.

[214] C. E. Schnieder, 'Discretion and Rules: A Lawyer's View', in K. Hawkins (ed.), *The Uses of Discretion* (Oxford: Oxford University Press, 1992), 47–88, 61.

[215] D. Donnison, 'Supplementary Benefits: Dilemmas and Priorities' (1976) 5 *Journal of Social Policy*, 337–59 and 'Against Discretion' (1977) 41/780 *New Society* 15 September.

[216] See J. Mashaw, *Bureaucratic Justice* (Boston: Yale University Press, 1983).

[217] See T. Novak, *Poverty and the State* (Milton Keynes: Open University Press, 1988), 187. On the scope for officer discretion within the supplementary benefit scheme, see further pp. 108–11 below.

[218] Schnieder, n. 214 above , 75–7.

According to Galligan, the crucial issue arising from the rules–discretion debate was in fact 'whether rights to welfare were protected more effectively by a rule-based system or one that left some discretion to officials'.[219] It is certainly true that so far as individual claims to entitlement are concerned, rules are important in providing the safeguard of enforceability. Non-adherence to rules is easier to question than the exercise of discretion, under which officials exercise legitimated choice.[220] Discretionary decisions tend to be far less amenable to independent and objective scrutiny, including legal challenge, than those based on rules.[221] At the same time, proper mechanisms of enforcement of rule-based rights are said to have elevated public welfare entitlement to the same status as private law rights in a way that was consonant with the idea, which emerged in the United States in the 1960s, that rights to welfare should be conceived of as 'new property' rights.[222] Nevertheless, it would be wrong to assume that claimants are always able to challenge rights-based decisions effectively.[223]

So far as collective interests are concerned, rules can introduce and sustain a measure of proportional justice (an equity argument which is central to the notions of social citizenship deriving from Marshall's thesis discussed earlier). But, at the same time, rules will also restrict the overall level of support provided by the welfare state, and thus the resources expended on it. Prosser has argued that while this is going on, the Government can maintain a 'superficially liberal appearance' by claiming that the rules 'represent an advance towards "open government" and welfare rights'.[224] But rules which provide a clearer basis of entitlement hardly protect rights to welfare when they also effect a rationalisation of provision. There are many examples in the chapters that follow of new legislation having this dual effect. It should be stressed, however, that the anticipated level of certainty and clarity being produced by any reform is frequently overstated. Furthermore, adjudication regularly produces an interpretation unanticipated by the legislator.

6. CONCLUSION

In this chapter we have seen that there is a well-developed conceptual framework within which to understand the nature and functions of state welfare and social

---

[219] D. J. Galligan, n. 203 above, 191.

[220] J. Bell, 'Discretionary Decision-making: A Jurisprudential View', in K. Hawkins (ed.), n. 214 above, 96–7.

[221] N. Lewis, 'Discretionary Justice and Supplementary Benefits', in M. Adler and A. Bradley (eds), *Justice, Discretion and Poverty* (Abingdon: Professional Books, 1976) 77–89, and D. J. Galligan, n. 203 above, 192. See also Dalley and Berthoud, n. 210 above, whose fairly positive conclusions about the contribution of social fund review procedures is tempered by the comment that 'no grievance procedure can rescue a scheme (i.e. the social fund) from its inherent weaknesses'.

[222] C. Reich, 'The New Property', (1964) 73(5) *Yale Law J.*, 733–87.

[223] See J. Baldwin, N. Wikeley, and R. Young, *Judging Social Security* (Oxford: Clarendon Press, 1992).

[224] T. Prosser, 'The Politics of Discretion: Aspects of Discretionary Power in the Supplementary Benefits Scheme', in M. Adler and S. Asquith, *Discretion and Welfare* (London: Heinemann, 1981), 148–70, 168.

security in particular. Inevitably, it is a constantly evolving framework as, for example, notions of a welfare state or social citizenship have to be viewed against a background of political and institutional change. As a new century dawns, there is a sense in which the welfare state has reached a crossroads; the Labour Government seems determined that it should not continue along the same route. Other Western governments face similar choices about the future of their state welfare systems which have struggled to cope with demographic change (such as an ageing population and increased family breakdown), shifting employment patterns and continuing unemployment against a background of technological change. In the UK, even the Labour Party, a party founded on socialist principles, now embraces the private sector as a provider of welfare and training. Across Western states 'the term welfare "State" may become a misnomer as social provision becomes the responsibility of a broader network of organisations'.[225] Some are even beginning to raise questions about whether social security, in the traditional sense of state welfare provision, has a long-term future, particularly in view of its enormous cost.[226] Either way, in the short or medium term we are likely to see further residualisation of state welfare in this field.

Another feature of the changing conceptual framework is the way in which it is becoming necessary to regard rights to welfare as 'contractual' rather than based on simple entitlement. In this regard, the need for the unemployed to sign a jobseeker's agreement in order to receive benefit or to sign up for the 'New Deal' in order to receive support, noted earlier, are particularly symbolic. The underlying basis for this approach seems to be that the moral foundation of welfare rights—centring on the duty of the democratic state to care for its citizens—has been weakened, undermined by welfare dependency or scrounging and by abuse in the form of fraud. A contractual, reciprocal notion of welfare, which pervades the 1998 Green Paper proposals, may reinforce a new moral basis for social security in particular. As we have seen, the concept of stakeholderism seeks to combine the notion of individualism inherent in the contractual or reciprocal basis of welfare with a collectivism based on mutuality which state welfare no longer represents. Regardless of how far, if at all, the stakeholder principle is adopted, social security law is likely to face an interesting but even more complex future as New Labour's ideals are progressively translated into policies and then (further) specific programmes.

[225] H. Lazar and P. Stoyko, 'The future of the Welfare State' (1998) 51(3) *I.S.S.R.,* 3–36, 33.
[226] J. Midgley, 'Has social security become irrelevant?' (1999) 52(2) *I.S.S.R.,* 91–9.

2

Social Security and Society

NEVILLE HARRIS

1. INTRODUCTION

A serious study of social security law needs to take close account of the social context to the welfare state because of the interaction between the kinds of provision made and level of support offered by the benefits system and key social phenomena such as poverty, unemployment, the shape and role of the family, housing tenure, demography, and migration of people. Indeed, while state welfare provision is often seen as having wide social and economic objectives such as preserving social stability or maintaining social control for the benefit of the capital economy,[1] as noted in Chapter 1, it is also a response to specific social problems. The fact that the social security system touches the lives of so many individuals in society at any one time, and has the potential to affect all citizens at one time or another, underlines the extent of its overall social impact.

One of the clearest examples of this interaction between social security and society lies in the determination of benefit levels, and particularly the unofficial 'poverty line' which is traditionally represented by the minimum level of entitlement provided by the basic means-tested social security benefit. This basic assistance is available, subject to conditions and certain exceptions, to those whose income and capital fall below a prescribed amount. According to Walker, basic social assistance rates in fact became an official poverty line, 'because they provided a benchmark against which the standards of living and expectations of poor people could be measured'.[2] As Spicker explains, the notion of an official poverty line represented an attempt to 'operationalise' the concept—to create a measurement of poverty around which future social security provision could be developed.[3] Recognition of an *official* poverty line was not part of an attempt to present a universal definition of poverty. Indeed, as Veit-Wilson says, describing social assistance benefit rates as the official poverty line 'confuses the political decisions on standards and benefits with the scientific evidence of income needs'.[4] In fact, since the mid-1980s the Government has avoided linking

---

[1] I. Gough, *The Political Economy of the Welfare State* (London: Macmillan, 1979).

[2] See C. Walker, *Managing Poverty* (London: Routledge, 1993), 3. According to one report, between 1979–93, the number of people in poverty in Britain rose from 7.7 million to 11.3 million: Commission on Social Justice, *Social Justice in a Changing World* (London: I.P. P. R., 1993), 6.

[3] P. Spicker, *Poverty and Social Security* (London: Routledge, 1993), ch. 3.

[4] J. Veit-Wilson, *Dignity not Poverty—A Minimum Income Standard for the UK* (London: Commission on Social Justice, 1994), 8.

basic assistance rates to a notional poverty line, arguing that rises in benefit rates relative to incomes would mean more people being officially classed as 'poor' even though their living standard would not have fallen.[5] The Government started instead to publish statistics showing 'households below average income'; these statistics show the broad distribution of income (such as the make-up, in terms of age, employment status, etc, of the bottom quintile of income distribution) but do not provide any hard facts about actual levels of income experienced by those concerned.[6] Despite the de-coupling of poverty from social security rates for official policy purposes, the relationship between poverty and the social security system remains of the utmost importance. Basic social assistance—such as income support—is widely accepted as the 'safety net' against destitution, even though its effectiveness in this regard is frequently questioned.

The interaction between poverty and social security is in fact complex. This is in part because both the circumstances in which poverty arises and the ways that it is related to the income and expenditure needs of the most financially disadvantaged are so diverse. There have, however, been attempts to measure poverty in different ways in relation to, for example, discrete social groups, such as the elderly, lone parents, or children.[7] A further element of complexity derives from the fact that the value systems which categorise needs as warranting or not warranting state support are reflected in a highly elaborate network of legal definitions and conditions governing entitlement. The nature of this interaction means that it is extremely unsatisfactory to attempt a *general* evaluation of the social security system and its legal rules. It is partly for this reason that this book has adopted a thematic, issue-based, approach. A further difficulty in the interaction between poverty and social security is that there is not a clear and consistent perception of the role of social security— whether it should be to relieve and mitigate the effects of poverty or to prevent it altogether.[8]

As poverty is a linking theme in this book it is now appropriate to discuss here some of the key approaches to its definition and measurement. The discussion is of necessity brief and introductory.[9]

---

[5] Green Paper (1985) Vol. 1, 12.

[6] N. 4 above, 36. See, for example, DSS, *Households Below Average Income—A Statistical Analysis 1979–1993/94* (London: The Stationery Office, 1996).

[7] See, for example, the discussion of the determination of a poverty line for the elderly, in P. Whiteford and S. Kennedy, *Income and Living Standards of Older People*, DSS Research Report No. 34 (London: HMSO, 1995), 18–21. Child poverty has been considered in a wide range of studies, many of which have focused on social security benefit rates: e.g. M. Wynn *Family Policy: A study of the economic costs of rearing children* (Harmondsworth: Penguin, 1972); D. Piachaud, *The Cost of a Child* (London: CPAG, 1979); and S. Middleton, K. Ashworth, and R. Walker, *Family Fortunes* (London: CPAG, 1994).

[8] P. Alcock, *Understanding Poverty*, 2nd edn. (London: Macmillan, 1997), 211.

[9] Particularly recommended for further reading are ibid.; J. Mack and S. Lansley, *Poor Britain* (London: Allen and Unwin, 1985); P. Townsend, *Poverty in the U.K.* (London: Penguin, 1979); A. B. Atkinson, *Poverty and Social Security* (Hemel Hempstead: Harvester Wheatsheaf, 1989).

2. POVERTY

Attempts to assess the adequacy of social security provision need to focus on the means of defining the basic social problem—poverty—whose relief is widely perceived to be the central aim of the social security system. With poverty itself being such a complex phenomenon, it is hardly surprising that differing approaches have been adopted to its definition and measurement. Indeed, sociologists and economists seem to agree that there is no unambiguous and universally applicable definition of poverty.[10] Moreover, as poverty is now increasingly viewed from a global perspective,[11] such a definition may become even more elusive.

A. Absolute Poverty

Defining poverty in *absolute* terms, in other words with reference to whether or not a person has sufficient means to meet bare subsistence needs and to preserve physical well-being, seems inappropriate for a modern industrialised society. Indeed, there have been claims that absolute poverty has ceased to exist in Britain, of which those by the Duke of Edinburgh have attracted the greatest public attention.[12] Yet research continues to suggest that income support levels may be insufficient to meet some basic needs.[13] However, it is important to remember that in the Beveridge Report of 1942, social assistance rates were determined with reference to such basic standards: 'The flat rate of benefit proposed is intended in itself to be sufficient without further resources to provide the minimum income needed in all normal cases. It gives room and a basis for additional voluntary provision, but does not assume that in any case.'[14] Today, most people in Britain would acknowledge that a socially unacceptable level of deprivation could be experienced by a single person or family without their necessarily being in a state of absolute poverty (see below).

The work of Rowntree (along with less scientific but important research by Booth) at the turn of the century, and subsequently, demonstrated that a broad measurement of bare subsistence could be determined with reference to the cost of a basic diet and other essentials needed for physical efficiency—which Rowntree defined as 'primary' poverty (or 'P1'). Rent, clothing, and fuel were also taken into account. Later a minimum level of income (calculated with reference to the Human Needs of Labour (or HNOL) scale) was calculated to show the amount that people

---

[10] See, e.g., N. Barr, *The Economics of the Welfare State* 2nd edn. (London: Weidenfeld and Nicolson, 1993), 139–40 and C. Walker op. cit. n. 2 above.

[11] See, e.g., P. Townsend, *A Poor Future* (London: Lemos and Crane, 1996).

[12] The Arnold Goodman Charity Lecture, London, June 1994, reported in *The Times,* 10 June 1994.

[13] See, for example, the research by the Food Commission, carried out for the National Children's Home and reported in *The Guardian,* 1 February 1994: 'Basic benefit "will not buy children a workhouse diet"'. See also, D. Piachaud, *The Cost of a Child* (London: CPAG, 1979), the subsequent CPAG study by N. Oldfield and A. Yu, *The Cost of a Child: Living Standards for the 1990s* (London: CPAG, 1993), and R. Cohen, J. Coxall and A. Sadiq-Sangster, *Hardship in Britain. Being Poor in the 1990s* (London: CPAG, 1992).

[14] Beveridge Report (1942), para. 307.

might require for basic subsistence.[15] Although Beveridge placed considerable reliance on the work of Rowntree, adding a small margin of two shillings per week for 'inefficiency of purchasing', he is said to have failed to include a social element in his calculations, promoting instead 'a social minimum assistance as adequate without supplementation for social security'.[16] Minimum subsistence was the ostensible basis of national insurance benefits until 1954 and of national assistance rates until 1959;[17] but despite increases designed to reflect the increasing national prosperity they 'remained adequate for only a non-participating level of living'.[18] Indeed, Lynes calculated that, for example, while the incomes of those in receipt of national assistance rose in real terms between 1948 and 1961, they increased at a lower rate than the incomes of the population as a whole.[19] Veit-Wilson argues that Beveridge condemned many to an existence in poverty which was not recognised as such.[20]

All the means of measuring an absolute, normative, standard of poverty—with reference to a required minimum income, to expenditure needs or to actual consumption—have in any event proved problematic.[21] Setting a minimum income threshold for poverty, for example, is difficult given the possibility, in some cases, that individuals may borrow or use savings or receive benefits (including services) in kind. With regard to expenditure, various assumptions about the availability of goods at particular prices have to be made; and one has to ignore market imperfections and other factors, including cultural diversity and personal social inadequacy, that can affect levels of expenditure. The third factor, consumption, would have to be looked at in relation to a range or 'bundle' of items—housing, food, clothing, transport, and so on—for which needs and availability vary widely. As a result of these definitional problems, poverty tends to be defined in a 'multi-dimensional' way, which means that it is inevitably complex.[22] A major factor in this is the way that all measurements, especially those relating to income, would need to take account of the nature of the particular income unit involved—the household, family, and individual, and so on. Income measurement runs into the additional problem of how to identify income transfers within households or families. Such transfers have been described as 'untraceable',[23] although research has begun to reveal broad patterns— for example, we know that unequal sharing is likely to prevail and that in male–female households females are likely to have less control over or access to financial resources than men.[24]

---

[15] B. S. Rowntree, *Poverty: A Study of Town Life* (London: Macmillan, 1901) and (1918) and (1937) editions.

[16] J. Veit-Wilson, 'Condemned to Deprivation: Beveridge's Responsibility for the Invisibility of Poverty', in J. Hills, J. Ditch and H. Glennester, *Beveridge and Social Security: An International Retrospective* (Oxford: Clarendon Press, 1994), 97–117, 113.

[17] Ibid., 111.   [18] Ibid., 111–12.

[19] T. Lynes, *National Assistance and National Prosperity* (Welwyn: The Codicote Press, 1962), 45.

[20] N. 16 above, 113–14.   [21] Atkinson, n. 9 above, 10.   [22] N. Barr, n. 10 above, 139.

[23] R. O'Kelly, 'The Principle of Aggregation', in R. Silburn (ed.), *The Future of Social Security. A Response to the Social Security Green Paper* (London: Fabian Society, 1985), 81.

[24] J. Pahl, *Money and Marriage* (Houndmills: Macmillan, 1989); P. Alcock, *Understanding Poverty*, 2nd edn. (Houndmills: Macmillan, 1997), 104–6.

The idea that poverty can be assessed in absolute terms and that there can be a simple, single 'poverty line' also ignores gradations of poverty. We do not tend to think of people above or below a single line as not being or being poor. As Spicker explains, there are degrees of poverty which present it in comparative or relative terms: 'very poor', 'fairly poor', and so on.[25] In order to assess the degree of poverty one must look at living standards within society as a whole. On this basis rests the notion of relative poverty (see below), which has helped to explain why, at a time when living standards have risen in the post-war period, poverty has remained.

Perceptions of poverty have not, and do not, remain static. The optimism that followed the Beveridge-based welfare reforms of 1945–8 included a 'general feeling that the welfare state, coupled with high employment and rising real incomes, had indeed abolished poverty'.[26] This was reinforced by Rowntree's follow-up survey (with Lavers) in York in 1950, which, applying the HNOL measurement (which was higher than the subsistence-based national assistance scale rates—see above), appeared to show a significant decline in poverty compared with an earlier Rowntree study, in 1936.[27] But by the 1960s social awareness of unexpected levels of poverty among the general affluence grew following the publication of a number of studies, of which arguably the most important was that by Abel-Smith and Townsend[28] (indeed, Atkinson reports that it had a 'dramatic impact',[29] being published just before Christmas in 1965 and showing that nearly 4 per cent of the population had incomes below the national assistance threshold levels). Poverty was 'rediscovered and redefined' and at around the same time a new anti-poverty campaigning organisation, the Child Poverty Action Group, was born.[30]

B. Relative Poverty or Deprivation and Inequality

The redefining of poverty in the 1960s was based on acceptance of the need to regard a state of poverty as reached when a member of society experiences a standard of living below that which is considered generally acceptable. This approach, which has become more universally adopted, means that the standard for measuring poverty will vary over time as general living standards rise or fall. Moreover, poverty will be socially defined. One way of taking account of this social dimension is to acknowledge that one measurement of poverty involves assessment of the extent to which an individual's total resources enable him or her to participate in various normal social activities. This is essentially the approach followed by Townsend and used in other studies, and it is reflected in the concept of social citizenship discussed in Chapter 1, under which enjoyment of citizenship is dependent

---

[25] P. Spicker, *Poverty and Social Security* (London: Routledge, 1993), 50.
[26] A. B. Atkinson, n. 9 above, at 44.
[27] B. S. Rowntree and G. R. Lavers, *Poverty and the Welfare State* (London: Longman, 1951).
[28] B. Abel-Smith and P. Townsend, *The Poor and the Poorest* (London: Bell, 1965).
[29] A. B. Atkinson, n. 9 above, 45.
[30] D. Vincent, *Poor Citizens* (London: Longman, 1991), 162.

on, *inter alia*, having a level of income or wealth sufficient to enable the individual to achieve a threshold level of social participation. Poverty is associated with social exclusion and may be defined with reference to the relative lack of social participation among those least well off in financial terms compared with others in society. Poverty is thus seen as a relative concept.

On Townsend's view, poverty may be expressed in terms of a threshold of 'relative deprivation' experienced by each member of society. In relating this to an individual's personal wealth, account is taken not only of income but also other sources such as fringe benefits for employees, other benefits in kind, savings and investments.[31] The index of deprivation can be constructed on an objective basis, but it is possible to include in such measurement of relative poverty the subjective views of individual members of the public. Thus Gordon et al. assessed poverty levels partly with reference to the views expressed in opinion polls by the general public as to the minimum items and services to which personal access was needed in order to achieve an 'acceptable' way of life.[32] When Mack and Lansley[33] carried out a survey in which they sought to identify an acceptable standard of living with reference to perceived expenditure needs, they found a level of subjective expectation that would place 7.5 million people in a state of poverty. What this proves is that it is possible to identify minimum living standards from general social expectations as well as from more objective criteria. The problem is how to relate that to actual income and expenditure needs: as Veit-Wilson says, 'What no amount of descriptions of poverty can do is tell us at what income levels people could avoid it.'[34]

Research by the Family Budget Unit has at least demonstrated the disparity between income support rates and an amount calculated with reference to the cost of items which most people themselves regard as necessaries. In this process any items which three-quarters of the population possessed were included.[35] This calculation produced a low cost budget level which for families with dependent children necessitated a net cash income significantly higher than the relevant income support rate (for example, a couple with two children would need an extra £34 per week). Subsequent research, published in 1998, into a 'low cost but acceptable' living standard, which included items possessed by 80 per cent or more of UK households, showed a similar level of disparity (up to £39 in the case of a two-parent family).[36]

---

[31]   P. Townsend, *Poverty in the United Kingdom* (London: Allen Lane, 1979).

[32]   D. Gordon et al., *Breadline Britain in the 1990s* (Bristol: University of Bristol, 1995).

[33]   J. Mack and S. Lansley, *Poor Britain* (Allen and Unwin, 1985).

[34]   J. Veit-Wilson, *Dignity not Poverty—A Minimum Income Standard for the UK* (London: Commission on Social Justice, 1994), 30.

[35]   J. Bradshaw, *Household Budgets and Living Standards* (York: Joseph Rowntree Foundation, 1993). See also J. Bradshaw (ed.), *Budget Standards for the UK* (Aldershot: Avebury, 1993) and P. Townsend and D. Gordon, 'What is Enough? New Evidence on Poverty Allowing the Definition of a Minimum Benefit', in M. Adler, C. Bell, J. Clasen, and A. Sinfield, *The Sociology of Social Security* (Edinburgh: Edinburgh University Press, 1991).

[36]   H. Parker (ed.), *Low Cost but Acceptable: A minimum income standard for the UK, families with young children, January 1998 prices* (London: Polity Press and Zachaeus 2000 Trust, 1998).

Other research has also demonstrated that child allowances in income support rates offer significantly less than would be needed to meet most parents' perceived minimum standards.[37]

The notion of relative deprivation contemplates a normative element in the definition of poverty which means that there is a standard of living against which the circumstances of the poorest members of society can be judged. Campaigns to improve levels of social security support which alleviate poverty often focus on the inadequacy of benefit rates to prevent serious deprivation, as judged by comparison with such a normative standard. In some cases such a standard is defined in fairly precise terms.[38] In others, the definition is more aspirational, as in Article 27 of the United Nations Convention on the Rights of the Child (1989), which asserts 'the right of the child to a standard of living adequate for the child's physical, mental, spiritual, moral and social development'. Such an approach seems to recognise that although poverty is a relative concept, there is an absolute element in terms of a lack of basic requirements such as shelter, adequate food, clothing and footwear, and so on. The absolute element within relative poverty has been recognised[39] although often seems to be taken for granted in the context of the modern role of social security in Britain.

Relative deprivation itself is obviously linked to the more general issue of inequality. Jordan reminds us that 'whereas it is extremely difficult to prove that poverty is an identifiable condition characterised by specific forms of exclusion, it is rather easier to demonstrate that inequality of incomes has grown'.[40] Empirical assessment requires attention to be paid to the gap, which has widened since 1980, between benefit levels and average earnings. There has been a tendency in recent years to focus on this growing divide, blamed in particular on reductions in social security provision throughout the 1980s (including the abolition of statutory earnings index-linking of national insurance benefits from 1980),[41] as being indicative of both an increase in poverty levels and the entrenchment of poverty for the poorest section of society.[42] If poverty is defined in terms of having an income which is below 50 per cent of the level of average earnings (which the DSS uses as its 'statistical measure of inequality' but which also forms the basis of the working definition of poverty in a number of other European countries),[43] we can see that the

---

[37] S. Middleton, K. Ashworth, and R. Walker, *Family Fortunes* (London: CPAG, 1994).

[38] See, for example, D. Piachaud, *The Cost of a Child* (London: CPAG, 1979) and N. Oldfield and A. Yu, *The Cost of a Child: Living Standards for the 1990s* (London: CPAG, 1993).

[39] A. Sen, 'Poor, Relatively Speaking', (1983) 35(1) *Oxford Economic Papers*, 153–69.

[40] B. Jordan, *A Theory of Poverty and Social Exclusion* (Cambridge: Polity, 1996), 98.

[41] See e.g. T. Atkinson and J. Micklewright, 'Turning the Screw: Benefits for the Unemployed 1979–88', in A. Dilnot and I. Walker (eds), *The Economics of Social Security* (Oxford: Oxford University Press, 1989), 17–51.

[42] Calculations by Jane Millar of the University of Bath, based on government statistics, suggest that the proportion living in poverty in the UK rose from 10 per cent in 1979 to 24 per cent by 1991: 'Quarter of Britons "are below the poverty line"', *The Independent*, 1 September 1993. For a detailed examination, see C. Oppenheim and L. Harker, *Poverty: The Facts*, 3rd edn. (London: CPAG, 1996), ch. 9.

[43] Veit-Wilson, *Dignity not Poverty*, n. 34 above, at 24. For useful international comparisons of social security and poverty based on this and similar definitions, see J. Bradshaw, 'Developments in social security policy', in C. Jones (ed.), *New Perspectives on the Welfare State in Europe* (London: Routledge, 1993), 53–60.

proportion of people in this category tripled between 1953 and 1991.[44] Although it remained more or less constant between 1991and 1994 and then began to fall, in 1996–7 there was a renewed rise.[45] The entrenchment of poverty is further illustrated by the fact that inclusive of housing costs the income of the poorest 20 per cent of the population rose by 2.5 per cent between 1979 and 1994 (that of the bottom 10 per cent actually fell, by 13 per cent), compared with the average rise in incomes of 39 per cent over this period (those in the top quintile seeing their income rise by over 50 per cent).[46] Moreover, if we look at the proportion of individuals living in households in receipt of income-related benefits (which certainly gives a broad indication of overall levels of poverty), we can see a significant increase since 1979: from 17 per cent in that year, to 25 per cent in 1992–3.[47] An increase in poverty among children between 1979 and 1996 is even more marked (from 10 per cent of children to 33 per cent).[48] Nearly three million children were living in households with below average incomes in 1996–7, and 25 per cent of children were in the bottom one-fifth of income distribution.[49] Lister questions whether Labour's goal of social inclusion (see Chapter 1) is achievable without some attempt to redress this level of inequality.[50] CPAG, while applauding an announcement by Tony Blair in March 1999 that Labour would end child poverty within twenty years, has commented that a radical policy change is needed if that specific pledge is to be honoured.[51]

Charles Murray might be correct in his assessment of the intellectual approach to poverty when it was 'rediscovered' in the 1960s—that 'the poor were to be homogenised . . . [as though they] were all alike'.[52] Today, close attention is paid to the differential extent and impact of poverty across various social groupings.[53] All the evidence points to a greater prevalence of poverty among, for example, the single elderly (reinforcing the fact that poverty may be linked to particular stages in the life-cycle, sometimes short term as in the case of students), women (particularly those caring for children or sick or elderly relatives on their own), and ethnic minori-

---

[44] D. Piachaud, 'Poverty', in *The Guardian* 'Society', Beveridge Report 50th Anniversary Special, 4 March 1992.

[45] DSS, *Households Below Average Income—A Statistical Analysis 1979–1993/94* (London: The Stationery Office, 1996); C. Howarth et al., *Monitoring Poverty and Social Exclusion: Labour's Inheritance* (York: Joseph Rowntree Foundation, 1998).

[46] DSS, n. 45 above, 114. See also Commission on Social Justice, *The Justice Gap* (London: I.P.P.R., 1995).

[47] DSS, *Households Below Average Income—A Statistical Analysis 1979–1992/93* (London: HMSO, 1995), para. 2.8.

[48] C. Oppenheim and L. Harker, *Poverty: The Facts* (London: CPAG, 1996), 37; and P. Gregg, S. Harkness, and S. Machin, 'Poor Kids: Trends in Child Poverty in Britain, 1968–96' (1999) 20(2) *Fiscal Studies* 163–87.

[49] See C. Howarth et al., op. cit. See also L. Elliott, 'Two in five children born poor', *The Guardian*, 29 March 1999.

[50] R. Lister, 'From equality to social inclusion: New Labour and the welfare state' (1998) 18(2) *Critical Social Policy*, 215–25.

[51] M. Barnes, 'Comment' (1999) *Poverty* No. 103, 1.

[52] C. Murray, 'The Emerging British Underclass', in C. Murray, *Charles Murray and the Underclass—The Developing Debate* (London: IEA, 1996), 23–53, at 24.

[53] See A. Goodman, P. Johnson, and S. Webb, *Inequality in the UK* (Oxford: OUP, 1997).

ties who experience disproportionately high levels of unemployment.[54] Moreover, we can see, for example, that the social composition of the poorest section of society may change. The bottom decile in the income distribution span now contains less than half as many pensioners as in 1979 (pensioners' incomes have risen relative to certain other groups) but twice as many unemployed people (as the unemployment level has until recently been around three times higher) and around one-third more lone parents (largely due to the increase in the proportion of lone-parent families relative to two-parent families).[55]

In the final analysis, definitions of poverty will tend to inform rather than condition levels of social security support to meet basic needs. More importantly, they will provide a basis on which to evaluate both the level of support provided by the benefits system to particular individuals and in particular circumstances, and the assumptions on which it may be based.

3. THE SOCIAL IMPACT OF SOCIAL SECURITY

Even if social security alleviates absolute poverty, it undoubtedly leaves many people with a very low standard of living. As previous discussion has shown, basic levels of income support are so low that it would be erroneous to define those dependent on this benefit as other than poor. And even if income support recipients actually have sufficient income on which to survive, their poverty may be compounded by poor housing and personal health: 'poverty should carry a government health warning'.[56]

Poverty is a social phenomenon, produced in part, or sustained, by the social security system, which is intrinsically difficult to eradicate. Even the idea of establishing a minimum income standard, based on objective empirical data, which would aim to provide a 'single standard of decency' to guide social policy, would merely result in the poverty line being redrawn. Eradication of poverty would require far-reaching government measures to effect major economic and social change giving rise to a significant redistribution of wealth. Instead, the social security system, it is often claimed, deliberately reinforces poverty by providing levels of support intended to create incentives for many unemployed claimants to improve their

---

[54] J. Millar and C. Glendinning, (eds), *Women and Poverty in Britain* (Hemel Hempstead: Harvester Wheatsheaf, 1992); P. Alcock, *Understanding Poverty,* 2nd edn. (London: Macmillan, 1997); J. Millar, 'Women', in A. Walker and C. Walker (eds), *Britain Divided* (London: CPAG, 1997), 99–110; C. Oppenheim and L. Harker, *Poverty: The Facts,* 3rd edn. (London: CPAG, 1996), ch. 6; A. Bloch, 'Ethnic inequality and social security policy', in A. Walker and C. Walker (eds), *Britain Divided* (London: CPAG, 1997), 111–22; C. Oppenheim, 'Poverty and Social Exclusion: An Overview', in C. Oppenheim (ed.), *An Inclusive Society: Strategies for Tackling Poverty* (London: I.P.P.R., 1998), 11–25 at 17–18.

[55] N. 47 above, Tables D1–D3.

[56] Commission on Social Justice, *Social Justice: Strategies for National Renewal* (London: Vintage, 1994), 44; P. Philimore, A. Beattie, and P. Townsend, 'Widening inequality of health in northern England' (1994) 308 *B.M.J.* 1125–8. For the impact of benefit levels on living standards, see also E. Kempson, *Life on a Low Income* (York: York Publishing Services Ltd, 1996).

standard of living through their own efforts—particularly by looking for and obtaining work—but leaving in poverty those who are unsuccessful. Those incentives are
reinforced by sanctions imposed on those who fail to play by the rules governing the
work test: disqualification from benefit can take their income below the income support rate (see Chapter 10).

Yet for some, a wage may not in any event guarantee a higher income compared
with a life on welfare benefits. This is because of the operation of the poverty and
unemployment traps.

A. The Poverty and Unemployment Traps

A particular problem which has a major bearing on the social impact of social security in relation to entry to employment, arises from the poverty and unemployment
traps. In the case of both, unemployed persons receiving social security benefits are
'trapped', in the economic sense of being no better off, or perhaps worse off, in (low-
paid) employment rather than being in receipt of benefits.[57] One of the key factors
is undoubtedly low wage levels. The abolition of Wages Council protection for
young people in 1986 and the subsequent abolition of most of the remaining Wages
Councils in 1993 helped to depress wage levels at a time of high unemployment. The
Government's commitment to a minimum wage, now underpinned by legal requirements on employers in respect of most employees (in force from 1 April 1999),[58]
may, despite the relatively low level at which the minimum has been set, in the long
term help to reduce the numbers who are in this position.[59]

The unemployment trap affects families in particular. If they are in receipt of
income-based jobseeker's allowance or income support, their personal allowances will
include extra amounts in respect of dependants' needs[60] and will provide a passport to
other benefits, including free school meals, which are not currently available to the
employed. Means-tested benefits increase with family size (in terms of numbers of
dependent children), whereas wages do not, so larger families may receive a higher
income through income support than if the main wage earner was in employment. To
ameliorate this effect, child benefit payments reduce income support entitlement £
for £.[61] According to Bradshaw and Lynes, since the severance of the link between

---

[57] See generally, A. Dilnot, J. Kay, and N. Morris, *The Reform of Social Security* (Oxford: Clarendon Press,
1984); P. Minford et al., *Unemployment: Cause and Cure* (Oxford: Basil Blackwell, 1985); and N. Barr, *The
Economics of the Welfare State*, 2nd edn. (London: Weidenfeld and Nicolson, 1993), ch. 10.

[58] National Minimum Wage Act 1998 and the National Minimum Wage Regulations 1999 (S.I. 1999
No. 584). The minimum wage is currently £3.60 per hour for workers aged 22 or over (or £3.20 for the
first six months where accredited training is provided) and £3.00 per hour for those aged 18–21. There is
no minimum for those aged under 18. Among those excluded from the minimum wage are the self-
employed and members of the armed forces. Homeworkers—who tend to be very poorly paid—are
entitled to the minimum wage, unless classed as self-employed.

[59] See generally J. Millar, S. Webb, and M. Kemp, *Combining Work and Welfare* (Layerthorpe: York,
1997).

[60] E.g. IS(G) Regs 1987, Sched. 2.

[61] See Chapter 9.

benefit uprating and annual increases in average earnings in 1980, a larger gap has been opened up between those in and those out of work. Consequently, the unemployment trap has become 'less of an issue', although it is also argued that higher rent levels and consequent increases in the amount of housing benefit paid to unemployed people have exacerbated its effect.[62]

The poverty trap concerns the impact of marginal taxation rates in combination with loss of income-related welfare benefits as income from employment increases. It could mean that for every additional £1 in wages above a basic level there is only a tiny gain (if any) in the family's overall income. This in fact creates a 'long poverty plateau'; wages may have to rise fairly substantially before any significant gain in family income occurs.[63] Dilnot and Stark estimated that as a result of the combined effect of social security and taxation, more than 500,000 people could face marginal tax rates exceeding 60 per cent.[64]

Hypothetical examples are often used to illustrate the bizarre effect of the poverty trap. Dilnot and Stark, for example, looked at the situation of a hypothetical (albeit increasingly atypical) family comprising a married man, his non-working wife, and two children of primary school age, who all lived in rented accommodation (rent £20 per week, local authority rates £6 per week). They calculated that, taking account of the availability of family income supplement,[65] the family would have an overall income of £117.42 at a wage of £70 per week, and an income of £117.26 where wages amounted to £130 per week. This, as they rightly commented, was 'absurd'.[66] Family credit replaced family income supplement as an income-related benefit addition to low wages in 1988, a reform which was in part intended to reduce some of the worst effects of the poverty trap by withdrawal of certain passported benefits (such as free school meals) and through assessment of entitlement on the basis of net rather than gross income (although the effect was partly offset by the increase from 50 to 70 per cent in the rate of withdrawal of benefit as earnings increased). Nevertheless, research on the poverty trap since then has produced similar results to the earlier studies.[67] McLaughlin, for example, calculated in 1994 that a two-parent family with two children, with gross earnings of £185 per week, would have an income of only £13 per week more than an equivalent family with earnings of £65 per week.[68]

Lone parents, most of whom are women, often face a particularly stark choice;

---

[62] J. Bradshaw and T. Lynes, *Benefit Uprating Policy and Living Standards* Social Policy Report 1 (York: Social Policy Research Unit, 1995), 45.

[63] E. McLaughlin, *Flexibility in Work and Benefits* (London: I.P.P.R., 1994), 35.

[64] A. Dilnot and G. Stark, 'The Poverty Trap, Tax Cuts and the Reform of Social Security', in A. Dilnot and I. Walker, *The Economics of Social Security* (Oxford: Oxford University Press, 1989), 171.

[65] Basically, family income supplement (FIS) was, and its replacement family credit (FC) was also (until it was replaced by the working families tax credit: see below), a means-tested benefit paid on top of wages to those in low-paid, full-time employment who had one or more dependent children for whose needs they were responsible. These benefits are further explained in Chapters 4, 5 and 9.

[66] N. 64 above, at 170.

[67] E.g. R. Walker, 'Springing the Poverty Trap', (1994) 1(3) *New Economy* 163–7.

[68] E. McLaughlin, *Flexibility in Work and Benefits* (London: I.P.P.R, 1994), 39.

indeed, the work disincentive effect of the poverty and unemployment traps has been most particularly acknowledged in the case of this group. Family credit changes since 1992 designed to encourage lone parents into work have included: a reduction in the number of hours which need to be worked (from 24 to 16); a childcare disregard of up to £60 per week (which was increased to £100 from June 1998 along with an increase in the upper age limit for the younger children from under eleven to the September following the child's twelfth birthday); and a maintenance disregard of £15 per week. At the same time, cuts to income support (the abolition of the lone-parent rate of family premium[69] with a knock-on effect on housing benefit and council tax benefit entitlement)[70] are also intended to reduce the benefits 'cushion' that stops lone parents from seeking work. But often the work available is very low paid and childcare remains a problem,[71] although under the Government's National Childcare Strategy £300 million is to be made available for out-of-school childcare. Also, as in the examples above, calculations show that increases in earnings can produce only very small increases in overall income: for example, if a lone parent has two young children and works sixteen or more hours per week, an increase in earnings from £80 to £120 yields only £3.50 extra in household income (based on 1998 rates).[72] Nevertheless, a recent survey has found that following the changes made to it, family credit had a significant impact on work incentives.[73] Moreover, for all claimants, the weakening of the poverty trap under family credit has been partly offset by the fact that unlike income support and income-based jobseeker's allowance, family credit has provided no help with mortgage interest, although the differential was reduced somewhat following the 1995 reductions in income support mortgage interest payments.[74]

Reform proposals understandably focus on the work disincentive effects which the poverty trap and unemployment trap produce.[75] But there are no easy solutions

---

[69] The Child Benefit, Child Support and Social Security (Miscellaneous Amendments) Regulations 1996 (S.I. 1996 No. 1803). On the original rationale from this, see DSS, *Restructuring Benefits for Lone Parents, Note to the SSAC* (London: DSS, 1996).

[70] The Government's own estimates were that in 1998–9 60,000 lone parents would lose up to £7.15 per week in housing benefit and that 45,000 others would lose up to £2.20 per week: quoted in T. Macdermott, A. Garnham, and S. Holterman, *Real Choices—for lone parents and their children* (London: CPAG, 1998), 20.

[71] Ibid., 25–31; see also C. Oppenheim and L. Harker, *Poverty: The Facts*, 3rd edn. (London: CPAG, 1996), 103–7.

[72] T. Macdermott *et al.*, n. 70 above, at 32. See generally A. Bryson, R. Ford, and M. White, *Making Work Pay: Lone Mothers, Employment and Well-being* (Layerthorpe: York, 1997).

[73] R. Ford, A. Marsh, and M. Range, *What Happens to Lone Parents*, DSS Research Report No. 77 (London: The Stationery Office, 1998).

[74] See N. Wikeley, 'Income support and mortgage interest: the new rules' (1995) 5 *J.S.S.L.*, 168–78; and see Chapter 13 below.

[75] See e.g. Commission for Social Justice, *Social Justice: Strategies for National Renewal* (London: Vintage, 1994), 245–55, F. Field, *Stakeholder Welfare* (London: IEA, 1996) and the Green Paper (1998), which identifies (at ch. 1, para. 2) barriers to paid work, 'including financial disincentives', as one of the three key problems with the current benefits system.

to the problems which are posed.[76] Evidence suggests that increased benefit support is more effective than changes to tax thresholds.[77] None the less, even though the effect of very high marginal tax rates was alleviated by the introduction of family credit, the impact of this more generous benefit was to spread the burden of still high rates over more people.[78] The Government is now planning both to reduce income tax rates for low-paid workers while at the same time offering (from October 1999) more generous support through the new working families tax credit (WFTC), which, it is claimed, 'will mean that every working family with a full-time worker has an income of at least £180 per week'.[79] WFTC is paid via wages in the form of reduced tax liability or via a discrete payment. The rate at which benefit is withdrawn as wages increase—the taper—is 55 pence in the pound instead of 70 pence under family credit; and the threshold at which benefit begins to be reduced has been increased, thereby bringing some higher wage earners, previously too well off to qualify for family credit, into the scheme. Tax credit schemes have traditionally been criticised for reproducing many of the problems associated with means-tested benefits, 'including the contradictory and perverse incentives of the poverty trap'.[80] While the Government wants to minimise these adverse effects, WFTC seems likely to reduce the poverty trap only slightly; moreover, 'by bringing more people onto benefits, the WFTC is likely to extend the poverty trap to higher earners'.[81] WFTC is discussed further by Gillian Douglas in Chapter 9.

B. Social Impact: Some Examples

The social impact of social security law is a central concern of this book and is discussed at some length in evaluating benefit rules in subsequent chapters. We shall see that social security rules and policy can have a major impact on, for example, family relations, access to housing or the social and economic status of particular social groups. Meanwhile, analysis of a selection of recent policies having a particularly marked impact will illustrate the effects of changes to social security law. The influence of social security on behaviour is also important and is assessed later.

One social group targeted and particularly affected by the reform of social security in the 1980s and 1990s has been young people, especially those aged between sixteen

[76] Field, for example, acknowledges that a radical reform of welfare, aimed at significantly reducing the role of means-testing, would be required. D. Green questions many of Field's assumptions: 'Welfare and Civil Society', in F. Field (n. 75 above), 75–96. Means-testing also produces a 'savings trap' by virtue of the fact that under benefit rules there are capital limits. Above a prescribed level of capital, benefit will be reduced or eligibility will cease: see Chapter 6 below.

[77] A. B. Atkinson, *Poverty and Social Security* (Hemel Hempstead: Harvester Wheatsheaf, 1989), 189.

[78] Dilnot and Stark, op. cit., n. 64 above, 178; see also P. Alcock, *Poverty and State Support* (London: Longman, 1987), 127.

[79] Green Paper (1998), ch. 3, para. 30. There will also be a separate childcare credit.

[80] P. Alcock, *Understanding Poverty*, 2nd edn. (Houndmills: Macmillan, 1997), 232.

[81] J. McCrae and J. Taylor, 'The working families tax credit' (1998) *Poverty* No. 100, 7–9, 8. See also, E. McLaughlin, 'Taxes, benefits and paid work', in C. Oppenheim (ed.), *An Inclusive Society. Strategies for Tackling Poverty* (London: I.P.P.R., 1998), 95–111, at 102.

and twenty-four. Numerous and often fundamental changes to aspects of their entitlement to social security are said to have interfered in various ways with the normative social transition from childhood to adult status.[82] They have had this effect because they produced a reduction in or loss of independent entitlement which forced young people into greater dependency on parents and other family members. The changes have included: the abolition of the non-householder's contribution in supplementary benefit (which had helped young people who lived in their parents' house to contribute to their keep); cutbacks in allowances for young boarders (especially those living away from their home area); an increase in the general minimum age of entitlement to income support from sixteen to eighteen; and the introduction of an age dividing-line in income support personal allowance rates (later built into both contributory and income-based jobseeker's allowance), which resulted in young people aged under twenty-five automatically receiving what was a 'non-householder' rate even where they lived independently (so that they received over 20 per cent less benefit per week than they would have received prior to the reform).

The overall effect of these changes, designed ostensibly to weaken the 'school-to-dole' dependency culture or, as some have argued, simply to execute cuts at the minimum political cost by targeting a politically weak group, has thus been to prolong the period of dependence by young unemployed people on their families and to reinforce the status ambiguity of young people (as neither dependent children nor independent adults).[83] Despite subsequent reforms designed to offer a degree of social protection to the particularly vulnerable (such as young people leaving care), the changes are also said to have increased poverty and homelessness levels among unemployed young people living away from their families.[84] An overall effect is said to have been social exclusion and disaffection among many young people.[85] In the past, various training programmes have failed to create long-term work opportunities for young people, partly as a result of the variable quality of the programmes (which have been seen by young people as undermining the value of training/work schemes), and partly because of economic conditions which, until the past couple of years, have discouraged labour recruitment. The Labour Government has now introduced a New Deal programme for young people (aged 18–24) at a projected cost of £2.6 billion. It goes further even than the stringent conditions of jobseeker's allowance (see Chapter 10) by requiring all young people seeking support to take up, following a 'gateway period' of guidance (which runs for up to four months), one of four options (subsidised work, education or training, work with the Environmental Taskforce, or work with a voluntary organisation).[86] As the Green Paper states, 'For

---

[82] See N. Harris, *Social Security for Young People* (Aldershot: Avebury, 1989); G. Jones and C. Wallace, *Youth, Family and Citizenship* (Milton Keynes: Open University Press, 1992).

[83] Ibid. See also H. Dean, 'Underclass or undermined? Young people and social citizenship', in R. Macdonald (ed.), *Youth, the 'Underclass' and Social Exclusion* (London: Routledge, 1997), 55–69.

[84] Ibid.

[85] See generally, N. Pearce and J. Hillman, *Wasted Youth* (London: I.P.P.R., 1998).

[86] See the Social Security Amendment (New Deal) Regulations 1997 (S.I. 1997 No. 2863).

those who do not wish to take up offers of help there will be no "fifth option" of simply remaining on benefit'.[87] The social impact of these latest reforms will depend upon what happens to the young people when their New Deal period comes to an end. Will the New Deal merely postpone their entry into the ranks of the dependent unemployed, or will their enhanced employability result in a return to the era when young people moved rapidly into adult status via work?

The impact of social security policy on women has been equally important. While it would not be appropriate to discuss this issue in depth here,[88] some of the key issues and critical themes need to be highlighted. For many women, part of the social and economic impact of social security is said to be its continuing reinforcement of notions of dependency on male breadwinners (which was linked in particular to the Beveridge plan for social insurance and its subsequent development) and assumptions about women's role in childrearing. The national insurance system has disadvantaged women because their contributions are based on lower wages than men and they are likely to be affected by interruptions in employment resulting from maternity and child-rearing. Furthermore, aggregation of partners' income and capital under means-testing provisions not only makes assumptions that household resources are appropriately distributed within families but also serves in many cases to deprive women of independent income. In this way, income-related benefits to support families have tended to replicate and intensify gender dependencies within household.[89] One facet of this enforced dependency is the way that the 'cohabitation rule' has assumed the provision of financial support by men to women with whom they are deemed to be living as an unmarried couple, without any requirement that such support is actually being provided.[90] A potential consequence for women of this dependency assumption would be the reinforcement of poverty if relationship breakdown occurs.[91]

Lone parents, nine-tenths of whom are women, have attracted particular attention in this context.[92] The legal framework has been changed to extend opportunities to take up employment. For example, as we have seen, the availability of family credit was extended by reducing the minimum number of qualifying hours of employment to sixteen per week and by introducing a childcare costs allowance. As Gillian Douglas explains in Chapter 9, a New Deal programme has specifically targeted lone

---

[87] Chapter 3, para. 9.   [88] See further, Chapter 9 by Gillian Douglas.

[89] On dependency assumptions, see H. Land, 'Social Policy and the Family', paper presented at conference on 'The goals of social policy: past and future', University of London, 17–18 December 1987. On control of benefits, see J. Goode, C. Callender, and R. Lister, *Purse or Wallet? Inequalities and Income Distribution within Families on Benefits* (London: Policy Studies Institute, 1998).

[90] See further N. Harris, 'Social Security and Unmarried Cohabiting Couples in Britain' (1996) 18(2) *J.S.W.F.L.* 123–46.

[91] See L. Dominelli, *Women Across Continents* (Hemel Hampstead: Harvester Wheatsheaf, 1991); R. Lister, *Women's Economic Dependency and Social Security* (Manchester: Equal Opportunities Commission, 1992); and C. Glendinning and J. Millar (eds), *Women and Poverty in Britain* (Brighton: Wheatsheaf, 1987).

[92] See above. See also Chapter 9.

parents: since October 1998 it has been available to all lone parents on income support with children of school age. Unlike the New Deal for young people, it operates at present on a voluntary basis, with personal advisers guiding the lone parents who agree to participate towards specific work, education, or training opportunities.[93] Although undoubtedly intended to reduce dependency on welfare, this extension might at least be seen as a further acknowledgement that lone parenthood has become an established part of the social structure of Britain, as throughout much of Western society. Indeed, suggestions made in recent years both in Britain[94] and in the United States[95] that perhaps some of the exemptions, currently enjoyed by lone parents, from the requirement to be available for and engaged in the search for work, should be removed, in fact serve to reinforce lone parenthood's increasingly normative social status. Ironically, campaigns for greater gender equality in the social security system, reinforced increasingly by the application of non-discrimination provisions in EU law (see Chapter 8), may in fact have helped to foster such discussions by contributing to a changed social and economic climate regarding women's place in the workforce at a time of new economic realism.

Nevertheless, any government recognition of the normative status of lone parenthood has been accompanied by continuing stigmatisation of this social group as part of the welfare dependent 'underclass'.[96] In particular, the policy debates surrounding the introduction of the child support scheme in 1993 demonstrated that lone parenthood, and especially lone parenthood on benefits,[97] was regarded by some of those in power as an unnatural state. The child support system (discussed further in Chapter 9) has therefore sought to (re)construct artificially the traditional two-parent family by forcing absent parents to maintain their offspring, even though the carer parent and child(ren) may be no better off financially as a result. The parent with care also faces the threat of reduced benefit entitlement if she fails to co-operate with the Child Support Agency in its efforts to identify and trace the absent parent.[98] This reminds us that the most significant feature of the various social security policies relating to lone parenthood has been the intrusiveness of the public welfare system into the private sphere of the family. Moreover, requiring absent parents to pay has, in many cases, had the effect of shifting the basis of support from a public one under the social security system (some 730,000 lone parents were receiving

---

[93] According to Government figures, one-third of the first 3,500 to take part in the programme found work: DSS Press Notice 98/044, 2 March 1998, although it is not clear how much of this work was permanent and/or full-time.

[94] Commission on Social Justice, *Social Justice: Strategies for National Renewal* (London: Vintage, 1994), 240.

[95] Reported in Anon, 'Dethroning the Welfare Queen: The Rhetoric of Reform', (1994) 107 *Harvard Law Rev.*, 2013–30, at 2024–5.

[96] See, in particular, Charles Murray's 'The Emerging British Underclass' and 'Underclass: the Crisis Deepens', in C. Murray and R. Lister, *Charles Murray and the Underclass—The Developing Debate* (London: IEA, 1996), 23–53 and 99–135.

[97] Estimates suggest that approximately 70 per cent of lone parents receive income support: cited in Garnham and Knights, *Putting the Treasury First: The truth about child support* (London: CPAG, 1994), 10.

[98] See Chapter 9.

income support at the time of the enactment of the Child Support Act 1991; the number has since increased)[99] to a private one. Although a reduction in public expenditure is clearly sought, the reform also seems to be directed, unrealistically, at reducing the incidence of lone parenthood itself by limiting the apparent incentive of independent benefit entitlement. Indeed, the presence of increasing numbers of lone-parent families constitutes a social phenomenon which is linked by some on the right to the availability of social security support.[100] While it could be true that social security provision has an influence in a small number of cases (see below), over-emphasising such a link ignores the fact that lone parenthood is often simply a consequence of marital breakdown and divorce, which has been increasing over the past decade and a half throughout Western society.[101] (This issue is discussed further in section C below.)

Changes to social security law in the 1980s and 1990s have also altered dramatically the experience of the unemployed in general. Benefits provision became less generous and conditions of entitlement required ever-increasing efforts by the unemployed to justify the receipt of support under the social security system, for example through a more active and demonstrable search for employment and the acceptance of employment or training in appropriate cases.[102] Being unemployed and in receipt of benefits, moreover, became an increasingly 'negative experience'.[103] For example, the 'actively seeking work' condition for unemployment benefit and later jobseeker's allowance meant that claimants had to demonstrate to employment officers all the (failed) attempts to find work in the previous fortnight, with the result that the claimant had regularly to be confronted with his or her own sense of failure, adding to the psychological damage of unemployment.[104] Although the Government's welfare to work programme is primarily designed to weaken the dependency culture, its plans to introduce greater positivity, dignity (particularly in the case of the New Deal for the Disabled),[105] and more constructive help into the system—'For too long, governments have abandoned people to a life on benefits'[106]—are to be welcomed.

It is important to appreciate that while the impact of the social security system on society may have become more pronounced in recent decades, and is certainly more fully documented, it represents a continuity in the history of the welfare state, extending back through the household means-tests of the 1930s, the workhouse system and the Speenhamland system of the eighteenth and nineteenth centuries, and so on—developments which are discussed in Chapter 3. For example, the

---

[99] It reached just over 1 million in 1993 (Garnham and Knights, n. 97 above, 10) and stood at 1,009,000 in November 1997: DSS, *Social Security Statistics 1998* (Leeds: Corporate Document Services, 1998), Table A2.16.

[100] e.g. R. Harris, *Beyond the Welfare State* (London: IEA, 1988), 23.

[101] J. Bradshaw and J. Millar, *Lone Parent Families in the U.K.*, DSS Research Report No. 6 (London: HMSO, 1991). See part C of this section, below.

[102] See Chapter 10 by Laura Lundy.

[103] E. McLaughlin, J. Millar, and K. Cooke, *Work and Welfare Benefits* (Aldershot: Avebury, 1989), 93.

[104] See T. Buck, 'Actively seeking work' (1989) *I.L.J.* 258–65.

[105] See Chapter 10.   [106] Green Paper (1998), ch. 3, para. 6.

introduction of family allowances under the Family Allowances Act 1945 was as much an attempt to encourage childbirth following the period of low birth rates during the Second World War as a recognition of the needs of larger families.[107] Moreover, the history of the welfare state is replete with policies and rules designed to change social behaviour, as the discussion of social control in Chapter 1 sought to emphasise (and see below). A new development in the use of family allowances (now child benefit in Britain) to influence behaviour which is being discussed is the creation of disincentives to non-attendance at school through threat of withdrawal of benefit. This already occurs in the United States. The state of Wisconsin introduced a 'Learnfare' programme in 1988, under which parents' receipt of Aid for Families with Dependent Children (AFDC) is conditional upon their child's frequent attendance at school: absence for good cause is discounted. A failure to meet the attendance requirements in one month results in a loss of AFDC for the following month. Benefit will continue to be denied until the monthly attendance requirement is satisfied. Several other states, including Ohio, Maryland, and Florida, have since introduced their own Learnfare programmes.[108] Reid has argued that in Britain the withdrawal of some child benefit from parents of non-attending children, as happens in France, would be effective in reducing truancy levels here.[109]

It is, however, important to appreciate that part of the social impact of particular welfare policies may, in some circumstances, be unintended or at least relatively unimportant to the policy-makers or legislators (as, for example, in the general social marginalisation of the poor or sections of it). Indeed, even where policies are intended to deal directly with a particular social problem or set of problems, they may have broader effects on social stratification, as in the case of women and young people, referred to above.[110] Of course, any social or economic disadvantage caused to a particular social group will have political costs, which the Government has to weigh against the social or economic objectives which it is pursuing. It is obvious that, for example, tying child benefit to regular school attendance in the way suggested by Reid (above) might be politically divisive; and considerable controversy attended the Conservative Government's cutbacks to benefits for asylum seekers and Labour's plans in the Welfare Reform and Pensions Bill in 1999 to means-test incapacity benefit.[111] However, from a political perspective, curtailing entitlement in a specific set of circumstances may be seen as expedient or morally

---

[107] A further factor was the need to discourage unemployed persons with large families from reliance on insurance benefits (which then contained child dependants' allowances) rather than being in employment.

[108] B. D. De Noble, 'Reduction of Welfare Dependency Via Incentives To Recipients—Commendable Goal, But At What Cost?' (1993–4) 32(4) *U. of Louisville J. of Family Law* 885–900.

[109] K. Reid, 'The Education Welfare Service—some issues and suggestions', and 'Combating school absenteeism: main conclusions', both in K. Reid (ed.), *Combating School Absenteeism* (London: Hodder and Stoughton, 1988), 160–2 and 208–12.

[110] M. Adler et al., 'Towards a sociology of social security', in M. Adler, C. Bell, J. Clasen, and A. Sinfield, *The Sociology of Social Security* (Edinburgh: Edinburgh University Press, 1991), 9.

[111] See, on asylum seekers, Chapter 6 and M. Adler, 'The habitual residence test: a critical analysis' (1995) 2 *J.S.S.L.* 179–95, and, on incapacity benefit reform, Chapter 12 below.

defensible, despite its impoverishing effects for individuals, in order to achieve, for example, reductions in public expenditure and/or reinforcement of particular moral values such as family responsibility and the work ethic.[112]

C. To what Extent does Social Security Influence Social and Economic Behaviour among Individuals?

Whenever the case for reform of social security is put, assumptions are made about the ways that social security rules can influence behaviour, as discussed in relation to the poverty and unemployment traps above.

Means-testing of benefit clearly has considerable potential for influencing behaviour. For example, means-testing in relation to savings and other capital, with capital limits (for example, £8,000 in the case of income support), undoubtedly acts as a disincentive to save (sometimes referred to as the 'savings trap').[113] Indeed, there is a long association between means-testing and changes in behaviour—as in the departure of employed older sons and daughters from the household to avoid their income being included in the family's income for the purposes of the household means test in the 1930s.[114] Above all, means-testing is said to result in dishonesty[115] as claimants have an incentive to misrepresent their domestic situation (for example, on whether a single person is cohabiting) or their financial circumstances (for example, whether a lone parent is receiving maintenance or a claimant of jobseeker's allowance has undeclared earnings from part-time employment). Indeed, Field argues that 'Means tests are steadily recruiting a nation of cheats and liars'.[116] The extent of such dishonesty is said to be demonstrated by the scale of fraud,[117] but this often gives a distorted picture by ignoring the extent of honesty among the majority of claimants.

Measuring accurately the impact of social security on social and economic behaviour is difficult.[118] For one thing, the evidence is often inconclusive. This is even true of the standard assumption that over-generous provision is a cause of unemployment. Atkinson, for example, explains that while there is a large literature on the possible work disincentive effects of benefits (referred to by Creedy and Disney as the 'moral hazard question'),[119] the evidence is not wholly conclusive: for example, 'while

---

[112] This is the approach adopted by Frank Field in *Stakeholder Welfare* (London: IEA, 1996)—see Chapter 1 above.

[113] P. Alcock, *Understanding Poverty*, 2nd edn. (Houndmills: Macmillan, 1997), 229.

[114] See A. Deacon and J. Bradshaw, *Reserved for the Poor* (Oxford: Martin Roberton, 1983).

[115] F. Field, *Stakeholder Welfare* (London: IEA, 1996).   [116] Ibid., 11.

[117] See, for example, Green Paper (1998), ch. 9, which estimates the current cost of fraud as £4 billion but acknowledges that employers' and landlords' dishonesty also contributes to this total. See further Chapter 13, section 9 below, by Simon Rahilly.

[118] E. McLaughlin, 'Researching the Behavioural Effects of Welfare Systems', in J. Millar and J. Bradshaw (eds), *Social Welfare Systems: Towards a New Research Agenda* (Bath: University of Bath, 1996).

[119] J. Creedy and R. Disney, *Social Insurance in Transition. An Economic Analysis* (Oxford: Clarendon Press, 1989), 115.

there may be a significant link between benefits and unemployment duration, it does not stand out clearly from the data'.[120] Similar conclusions are drawn by Barr, following his review of the methodologies and results of domestic and international (including comparative) studies.[121] Moreover, the author's review of research findings on the impact of benefits provision on levels of youth unemployment led to the conclusion that 'at the very least there is considerable doubt about the precise significance of the "moral hazard" aspect of social security, where young people are concerned'.[122] On the other hand, Layard et al. are convinced that 'the unconditional payment of benefits for an indefinite period' is a 'major cause' of high unemployment levels in Europe.[123] They argue that the 'dramatic' fall in unemployment in Britain after 1986 was partially due to the more stringent application of the availability-for-work unemployment benefit rules and the Restart interviewing.[124] Entitlement to benefit is dependent on satisfaction of a very stringent work test which, as the discussion by Laura Lundy in Chapter 10 shows, has intensified with the introduction of jobseeker's allowance. Creedy and Disney argue that the strict enforcement of conditions of eligibility will tend 'to reduce the importance of moral hazard'.[125] Looking more generally at research evidence on behavioural responses to social security, Atkinson, however, concludes that it has failed to produce 'robust or widely-accepted answers to the basic question as to how income support affects economic behaviour'.[126]

One of the problems in assessing the impact of benefits on social and economic behaviour is the difference between the form and reality of social security, which researchers often ignore; Atkinson says that this difference is exemplified by the problem of incomplete take-up of welfare benefits[127] (discussed below). Theories about benefit-induced unemployment are based on the idea that it represents 'the classic response of "rational economic man" to unemployment benefit'.[128] The response is 'to prolong the duration of unemployment—whether for leisure or job search—and thereby reduce the time spent at work'.[129] But rationality cannot be assumed. For one thing, people are not always fully aware of all the facts or their implications when making their decisions, or may be influenced by feelings of uncertainty or anxiety, for example about the financial impact of taking low-paid employ-

---

[120] A. B. Atkinson, *Poverty and Social Security* (1989) (Hemel Hempstead: Harvester Wheatsheaf), 101.
[121] N. Barr, *The Economics of the Welfare State*, 2nd edn. (London: Weidenfeld and Nicolson, 1993), 202–4 and 260.
[122] N. Harris, *Social Security for Young People* (Aldershot: Avebury, 1989), 156.
[123] R. Layard, S. Nickell, and R. Jackman, *The Unemployment Crisis* (Oxford: Oxford University Press, 1994), 92.
[124] Ibid., 76. But see the comments by Laura Lundy at 324 below.
[125] J. Creedy and R. Disney, *Social Insurance in Transition. An Economic Analysis* (Oxford: Clarendon Press, 1985), 15.
[126] A. B. Atkinson, *Poverty and Social Security* (Hemel Hempstead: Harvester Wheatsheaf, 1989), 102.
[127] Ibid.
[128] M. Casson, *Youth Unemployment* (London: Macmillan, 1979), 39.   [129] Ibid.

ment. McLaughlin et al. found this last factor to be an important one in decisions concerning the take-up of work in some benefit-dependent families.[130]

Research continues to show that few people are attracted to unemployment by the level of benefits offered. This is hardly surprising because, as noted above, benefit levels have always been set at a sufficiently low level to deter unemployment among those able to work.[131] At the same time, the fact that unemployed people will tend to make judgments about the level of wages that would attract them to a job[132] means that comparisons between benefit levels and wages may well be made by claimants. The evidence shows that replacement income (benefits while unemployed) is on average significantly lower than normal income (when in work), especially where single people are concerned. For example, in 1986 the average replacement ratio (the ratio of replacement income to normal income, expressed in percentage terms) was 38 per cent for single persons without children, 48 per cent for a married couple with no children and 58 per cent for a married couple with children.[133] Although international comparisons are problematic because of the different conditions applicable to the award of benefit and variations in the duration of benefit, these ratios are lower than in most other Western democratic states.[134]

As noted earlier, benefits ceased to be uprated in line with earnings in 1980. For the most part price increases have been used instead. This method has clearly led to benefits being uprated at a lower rate than would have been the case had the link with earnings been preserved, and it has ensured that fewer persons experience high replacement ratios.[135] Nevertheless, it was estimated that in 1992 nearly 600,000 employees faced replacement ratios of over 70 per cent.[136] Even so, it has not been shown conclusively that the availability of benefit has a significant impact on levels of unemployment (or its duration),[137] and falling replacement ratios and tougher eligibility conditions in recent years would make such an assessment even more difficult to sustain.

There are other forms of behaviour and personal decisions which can potentially be affected by social security rules. But again the evidence is often inconclusive. For example, it would appear that the impact of reduced benefit entitlement on strike action is somewhat unpredictable; it clearly deters some individuals but merely hardens the resolve of others.[138] Another area of decision making concerns housing, including decisions about where to live and, in the case of young people, whether to

---

[130] E. McLaughlin, J. Millar, and K. Cooke, *Work and Welfare Benefits* (Aldershot: Avebury, 1989), 109.

[131] See ibid.

[132] L. Morris and T. Llewelyn, *Social Security Provision for the Unemployed*, SSAC Research Paper 3 (London: HMSO, 1991), 103–5.

[133] R. Layard, *How to Beat Unemployment* (Oxford: Oxford University Press, 1986), 47.

[134] Layard, Nickell, and Jackman, n. 123 above, at 74.

[135] J. Bradshaw and T. Lynes, *Benefit Uprating Policy and Living Standards*, Social Policy Report 1 (York: Social Policy Research Unit, 1995), 40 and 45.

[136] N. Barr, *The Economics of the Welfare State*, 2nd edn. (London: Weidenfeld and Nicolson, 1993), 202.

[137] E. McLaughlin, *Flexibility in Work and Benefits* (London: I.P.P.R., 1994), 15.

[138] See the evidence cited in L. Lundy, 'Income Support and Strikers' (1995) 2 *J.S.S.L.* 129–41.

leave home: research seems to support the view that reductions in social security for young people in the 1980s made it 'difficult for young men and women to leave home, whether to seek work, to escape domestic tension or simply to establish their independence'.[139] The extent to which the availability of social security influences family formation has also been considered. Some argue that the availability of particular forms of social security support for those with children encourages family formation. For example, Barr cites controversial evidence that a sharp increase in the number of female-headed households among blacks in the United States after 1960 was causally linked to benefit increases under Aid for Families with Dependent Children.[140] Hutton explains that in the UK there is a perception among politicians of the Right that 'Income support makes it attractive for teenage girls to have babies'.[141] However, George doubts whether the availability of a weekly child allowance in Britain influences a decision to have children, as a 'complex network of economic, cultural and demographic factors' will determine the matter.[142] Nevertheless, the availability of income support to lone parents was consistently argued, in the debates surrounding the introduction of the child support scheme in 1993, to have encouraged this form of family unit. But there is still no clear evidence in support of this assertion.[143] Indeed, so far as lone parenthood is concerned, it must be appreciated that apart from those in the under-twenty age group, more than half of lone parents have become lone parents because of the break-up of a relationship or the death of a partner.[144] On the other hand, the fact that a significantly higher proportion of unemployed than employed young people have children of their own suggests that a small minority of young people aged under eighteen, faced with a lack of benefit support unless a young mother or pregnant,[145] may attempt to improve their independent status and secure independent financial support by entering parenthood.[146] However, it could also reflect a lack of childcare facilities.

Many policy decisions about social security are inevitably made on the basis of their potential effect on behaviour. Account is often taken of past experience (for

[139] SSAC, *Sixth Report* (London: HMSO, 1988), para. 2.20. See also M. Murphy and O. Sullivan, 'Unemployment, Housing and Household Structure Among Young Adults' (1986) 15 *J of Social Policy* 205–22.

[140] See Barr, n. 136 above, 260.

[141] W. Hutton, *The State to Come* (London: Vintage, 1997), 7.

[142] V. George, *Social Security and Society* (London: Routledge and Kegan Paul, 1973), 126.

[143] A. Garnham and E. Knights, *Putting the Treasury First—The Truth about Child Support* (London: CPAG, 1994), 24.

[144] J. Payne and M. Range, *Lone Parents' Lives*, DSS Research Report No. 78 (London: The Stationery Office, 1998), 23. See also Garnham and Knights, *Putting the Treasury First*, n. 143 above, 4. See also n. 101 above.

[145] IS(G) Regs 1987 (S.I. 1987 No. 1961), reg. 13A and Sched. 1A para. 1.

[146] J. Coffield, C. Borrill, and S. Marshall, *Growing Up at the Margins* (Milton Keynes: Open University Press, 1986). There is some evidence to suggest that pregnancy can sometimes be viewed by some young women as a means of improving chances of obtaining a council house as well as improving their social status among their peer group: M. H. Banks and P. Ullah, *Youth Unemployment. Social and Psychological Perspectives*, Research Paper No. 61 (London: Department of Employment, 1987); C. Wallace, *For Richer, For Poorer. Growing Up In and Out of Work* (London: Tavistock, 1987). A homeless young single woman will have a 'priority need' for housing if she is pregnant: Housing Act 1996, s. 189.

example as to the effect of in-work benefits on decisions to take up employment). But the assumptions which form the basis for such decisions are often too simplistic, ignoring the complexity of the relationship between benefits and behaviour. This relationship is discussed further, in the context of specific areas of provision, in later chapters.

4. THE RESPONSIVENESS OF SOCIAL SECURITY TO SOCIAL AND ECONOMIC CHANGE

While it is generally accepted that there is a need for governments to plan strategically and exercise caution when changing the structure of the benefits system, not least because benefit reform will generally have a long-lasting social and economic impact, it is often argued that social security is insufficiently responsive to social and economic change. For example, it has been suggested that the benefits system has in general been slow to adapt to the increasing numbers of people, many of them women, in casual or part-time work.[147] Predicting future social and economic trends as well as benefit needs will be central to an effective reform of welfare provision.

Social change which is viewed as a potential threat to particular economic goals by increasing the potential burden of public expenditure, such as arising from an increasing demand for existing social security benefits, is likely to be responded to more swiftly or directly.[148] This is most graphically illustrated by the way the Government of the early 1930s responded to a huge rise in unemployment by instituting a substantial cut in unemployment benefit at a time of economic crisis,[149] and, in the 1980s, by the cutbacks to furniture grants within the supplementary benefit single payments system.[150] Equally, cases of spiralling expenditure *per se* resulting from demographic change may also be met by fundamental reform. The position of lone parents, for example, has not been immune from this kind of response in recent years (see above).

Ministers clearly seek to anticipate changes in the pattern of demand for social security when finalising their public expenditure plans. Indeed, a particularly long-term view is sometimes taken, as with the phasing out of the state earnings related pension scheme (SERPS), initially via the Social Security Act 1986, and moves towards increased private provision in the pensions field, which are intended to combat rising demand on the social security budget resulting from a projected massive increase in the proportion of the population who are above the age of sixty by 2020: the so-called 'pensions timebomb'.[151]

---

[147] E. McLaughlin, J. Millar, and K. Cooke, *Work and Welfare Benefits* (Aldershot: Avebury, 1989), 134; C. Walker, *Managing Poverty. The Limits of Social Assistance* (London: Routledge, 1993), 30; C. Hakim, 'Unemployment and Marginal Work in the Black Economy', in E. McLaughlin (ed.), *Understanding Unemployment* (London: Routledge, 1992), 154–9.

[148] See e.g. J. Bradshaw, 'Developments in social security policy', in C. Jones (ed.), *New Perspectives on the Welfare State in Europe* (London: Routledge, 1993), 44–63.

[149] See Chapter 3.   [150] See Chapter 4.

[151] See e.g. P. Johnson, *The Pensions Dilemma* (London: I.P.P.R., 1994). See further DSS, *A New Contract for Welfare: Partnership in Pensions*, Cm 4179 (London: The Stationery Office, 1998).

Social security reform may also be precipitated by social change which runs counter to, or challenges, a prevailing moralistic view underpinning government social policy, even though the true basis for change may be the economic or political case for Treasury-led cuts. There was certainly a heavily moralistic tone to the debates in the mid-1980s concerning the availability of board and lodging payments for young people under the supplementary benefit scheme; the introduction of severe restrictions was justified with reference to the need to prevent unemployed youth colonising seaside towns on the south coast of England, taking a prolonged holiday at the tax-payers' expense on the 'Costa del Dole'.[152] Indeed, young unemployed people in general were caught up in the moral panic over the emergence of an 'underclass' in society.[153] More recently, the 'habitual residence test' has been incorporated into the rules governing various income-related benefits as 'part of a process of narrowing access to benefit for people who the taxpayer should not be asked to support . . . [and] to deal with the well-documented abuse of these income-related benefits by some non-UK nationals, which has caused public anxiety'.[154] Similarly, the political (and media) reaction to an increase in the numbers receiving invalidity benefit—from 500,000 in 1975 to 1.5 million in 1992[155]—took the form of emotive claims that claimants were deceiving doctors into signing them as unfit for work (or that doctors themselves were 'going soft') and by moral indignation: 'people who work for a modest wage resent seeing neighbours, apparently as fit as themselves, living on invalidity benefit'.[156] The replacement of invalidity benefit with incapacity benefit (see Chapter 4) resulted in nearly 200,000 claimants losing entitlement to sickness-related benefit.

These reforms of the past few years sit easily with the more broad-ranging moral assault directed by both Conservative and Labour ministers at the welfare benefits 'dependency culture'. The extent of the dependency culture has not in fact been quantified; and, as noted above, there is in fact considerable empirical evidence substantiating claims that most unemployed people want to work. Indeed, Berthoud demonstrates that the increasing numbers receiving invalidity benefit were largely the product of changes in patterns of employment and in the labour market, particularly a tightening of the market making it more difficult for those who left work due to sickness to find another job: 'the increase [in invalidity benefit numbers] has not been caused by excessive ease of entry to the system, but by the difficulty of exit'.[157]

Idealism has always had some influence over the shape of social security reform since Beveridge. But while it was reflected in aspects of the Fowler reforms of the

---

[152]   See N. Harris, *Social Security for Young People* (Aldershot: Avebury, 1989), 76–86.

[153]   See R. Macdonald (ed.), *Youth, the 'Underclass' and Social Exclusion* (London: Routledge, 1997). See above.

[154]   DSS, *The Income-Related Benefits Schemes (Miscellaneous Amendments) (No. 2) Regulations 1994, Note for the Social Security Advisory Committee* (London: DSS, 1994).

[155]   DSS, *Social Security Statistics 1993* (London: HMSO, 1993), cited in R. Berthoud, 'The medical assessment of incapacity: a case study of research and policy' (1995) 2 *J.S.S.L.* 61–85, at 62.

[156]   Secretary of State for Social Security (24 January 1994), cited in R. Berthoud (ibid.), 64.

[157]   R. Berthoud, n. 155 above at 66.

1980s and underlies Labour's current and planned reforms, it is the political and economic agendas of government which have increasingly dominated the formulation of social security policy. The response to social and economic change has all too often been a hastily constructed one based on expediency rather than a carefully crafted one resting on particular ideals.[158]

5. TAKE-UP OF SOCIAL SECURITY

It is clear that not all people who are entitled to social security benefits actually claim them. Indeed, as Fry and Stark report, 'non-take-up of social security benefits is widely acknowledged to be one of the most serious problems facing the social security system'.[159] The reasons for non-take-up are in fact complex and diverse.[160] It is well known that ignorance and the complexity of both the benefits system and the claiming process are important factors[161] and that decisions about whether to claim are influenced by the amount of benefit that might be available (small weekly amounts are less likely to be claimed).[162] Certainly in the past, the social stigma in claiming means-tested benefits and being classified as a claimant has been a deterrent to the take-up of benefits such as supplementary benefit for some; and evidence suggests that it remains a problem in relation to current benefits.[163] Take-up of child benefit has always exceeded 90 per cent, largely because of its simplicity and lack of means-testing and stigma. We also know that take-up rates vary among the different claimant groups. Research has shown that pensioners are less likely to claim than others.[164] Take-up of income support and housing benefit is highest among lone parents and lowest among pensioners[165] (there are currently around one million pensioners who are not claiming income support to which they are entitled).[166] It seems that while a majority of people of retirement age regard the state pension as a right and something which is central to their money management, they tend to be resistant to claiming any additional income-related benefits, preferring to manage without them unless faced with a fairly dramatic change of circumstances.[167] Some ethnic

---

[158] See also the administrative and adjudication changes discussed by Roy Sainsbury in Chapter 7.

[159] V. Fry and G. Stark, 'The Take-Up of Supplementary Benefit: Gaps in the "Safety Net"?', in A. Dilnot and I. Walker, *The Economics of Social Security* (Oxford: Oxford University Press, 1989), 179–91, 179.

[160] See e.g. A. Corden: *Taking Up a Means Tested Benefit. The Process of Claiming F.I.S.* (London: HMSO, 1983).

[161] See A. Corden, *Changing Perspectives on Benefit Take-up* (London: HMSO, 1995).

[162] Ibid.

[163] C. Walker, *Managing Poverty. The Limits of Social Assistance* (London: Routledge, 1993), 151–6.

[164] Ibid. and V. Fry and G. Stark, n. 159 above.

[165] Government Statistical Service/DSS, *Income Related Benefits: Estimates of Take Up in 1992* (London: Government Statistical Service/DSS, 1995).

[166] Secretary of State for Social Security, *Annual Report by the Secretary of State for Social Security on the Social Fund 1997/98*, Cm 4003 (London: The Stationery Office, 1998), 5.

[167] H. Finch and G. Elam, *Managing Money in Later Life*, DSS Research Report No. 38 (London: HMSO, 1995). See further the discussion in Chapter 6, section 3A.

minorities are less likely to claim benefits, due to language or cultural barriers to claiming, a matter raised in Parliament in 1998.[168]

Take-up rates are, of necessity, always based on estimates, and the rates vary according to the benefit concerned. They are expressed both in terms of the proportion of possible recipients who actually claim a benefit ('caseload') and the proportion of total possible expenditure represented by actual expenditure in paying out the benefit ('expenditure'). Thus Government figures for income support take-up in 1995–6 show that there was an estimated 76–82 per cent take-up by caseload and 88–92 per cent take-up by expenditure.[169] These rates are higher than those for supplementary benefit in the 1970s.[170] The figures also confirm the continuing relatively low take-up rates for family credit: the take-up for the years 1991 and 1992 combined was 66 per cent in respect of caseload and 73 per cent by expenditure;[171] there was an increase, however, in 1995–6, to 69 per cent and 83 per cent respectively.[172] These figures contrast with an estimated take-up figure of 50 per cent (based on caseload) in respect of the benefit's predecessor, family income supplement, in 1984.[173] New benefits, particularly those which are complex and involve means-testing, are likely to suffer from initial take-up problems. The take-up of disability working allowance (which supplemented wages of disabled people on low incomes working at least sixteen hours per week, introduced in 1992: see Chapter 12) was well below 50 per cent by its second year;[174] by January 1998 just under 14,500 claimants were receiving it,[175] still some way short of the Government's estimate of 50,000 when the benefit was introduced. Take-up of disability living allowance (DLA) and attendance allowance is currently an estimated 50 per cent.[176]

Unfortunately, governments have not given sufficient emphasis to the need to improve take-up rates. Advertising campaigns by the DSS have tended to be very selective—in recent years focusing in particular on in-work benefits (arguably for the political reason that those who take up the benefit will cease to be entitled to unemployment benefits and will no longer be included in the unemployment statistics). Not surprisingly, since the 1970s welfare rights organisations have mounted local or occasionally national take-up campaigns,[177] particularly where a change in the law

---

[168] *Hansard*, H.L. Debs, Vol. 590, col. 184, 2 June 1998, *per* Lord Dholakia. See, generally, P. Alcock, *Understanding Poverty*, 2nd edn. (Houndmills: Macmillan, 1997), 161–2.
[169] DSS, *Social Security Statistics 1998* (Leeds: Corporate Document Services, 1998), Table H4.01. These rates show virtually no variation on the previous year: DSS, *Social Security Statistics 1997* (London: The Stationery Office, 1997), Table H4.01.
[170] C. Walker, n. 163 above, 151–2. [171] N. 165 above.
[172] DSS (1998), n. 169 above, Table H4.02.
[173] *Hansard*, H.C. Debs, Vol. 61, col. 460*w*, 12 June 1984.
[174] See K. Rowlingson and R. Berthoud, *Evaluating the Disability Working Allowance* (London: P.S.I., 1994). It was 21 per cent in 1996: see p. 392 below.
[175] DSS (1998), n. 169 above, Table E3.04. See further Chapter 12.
[176] *Hansard*, H.L. Debs, vol. 590, col. 182, 2 June 1998, *per* Baroness Hollis of Heigham (Under-Secretary of State for Social Security).
[177] See, generally, P. Alcock, *Understanding Poverty*, 2nd edn. (Houndmills: Macmillan, 1997), 244–7.

presents a benefit cut-off date. The 1998 Green Paper on welfare reform mentions take-up only in connection with the position of poor pensioners and DLA and attendance allowance. Moreover, although there is mention of new claim forms and better advice in benefit offices, increased take-up of benefits is not referred to in any of the 'success measures' which the Green Paper lists as performance indicators for evaluation of its proposed reforms. It is, however, referred to in the final chapter of the 1998 Green Paper on benefit fraud.[178] The appearance of a commitment to ensure that 'those eligible for claiming benefits are sought out and told of their entitlement' is perhaps a response to criticism of its absence from the earlier welfare reform proposals (above) as well as an attempt to inject a positive note into a document focused primarily on the negative. The Government has also established nine pilot schemes to investigate how best to identify pensioners who have an entitlement to income support and to encourage them to claim. The 1998 Green Paper on pensions promised (in rather vague terms) new measures to help ensure that the poorest pensioners receive the required help under the benefits system.[179] While these recent commitments are to be welcomed, overall much more could and should be done to improve take-up of benefits among all claimant categories.

6. CONCLUSION

A staggeringly large proportion of the population of Great Britain is dependent on social security provision. For example, in 1997, 9 million people—or approximately 15 per cent of the entire population—were the beneficiaries of income support or income-based JSA (either as one of 5 million recipients or 4 million dependants), while 4.6 million were in receipt of housing benefit.[180] Moreover, in 1997–8, 2.3 million people received payments of incapacity benefit.[181] It is axiomatic that any system of financial support on which there is such widespread reliance (despite incomplete take-up) and which is intended to cater for such a range of social needs will have a considerable impact on society as a whole. At the same time, the economic cost of maintaining the social security system—it currently takes up nearly 30 per cent of total public expenditure—makes social security particularly vulnerable to selective reform to meet economic goals. This economic pressure on social security expenditure is obviously particularly acute when social change—such as a relatively rapid growth in lone-parent families, long-term incapacity for work, or unemployment—increases the demand for social security.

By any definition, there are significant numbers within British society who regard

---

[178] DSS, *Beating Fraud is Everyone's Business*, Cm 4012, (London: The Stationery Office, 1998), ch. 9.

[179] DSS, *A New Contract for Welfare: Partnership in Pensions*, Cm. 4179 (London: The Stationery Office, 1998), ch. 11.

[180] DSS, *Social Security Statistics 1998* (Leeds: Corporate Document Services, 1998), Tables A2.01, A3.04 and C1.11.

[181] Ibid., Table D1.13.

themselves as poor and whose level of income places them within official definitions of poverty. But governments do not regard the solution to the problem of poverty in general as resting with the social security system. Instead, hopes are placed on economic growth and prosperity within the capitalist economy. Furthermore, although economic and social inequality have grown over the past twenty years, such inequality is apparently accepted as an inevitable feature of a capitalist society; thus it is not surprising that governments ensure that the social security system's role in wealth redistribution is limited. Social security is, however, increasingly perceived to have a role in encouraging many more individuals to take positive steps to lift themselves out of an avoidable state of poverty by working, or equipping themselves to find and undertake work, where capable of doing so.[182] For reasons of genuine conviction or mere expediency governments often embrace moralistic notions to underscore the arguments for such policies, combined with a belief that social security rules can and, at least sometimes, do influence social behaviour, even though the evidence for this is not wholly conclusive.

---

[182] Plant sees the Labour Government's welfare reforms as premised primarily on 'equality of opportunity' rather than 'equality of outcome': R. Plant, 'Supply Side Citizenship' (1999) 6. *J.S.S.L.* 124–136, 132.

Part 2

The Historical Context

3

Social Security Prior to Beveridge

NEVILLE HARRIS

1. INTRODUCTION

This is the first of three chapters tracing the historical development of the social security system. It is important for anyone attempting to make sense of the present social security system and its elaborate legislative and institutional framework to understand the evolution of the major areas of social security provision and be familiar with the key landmarks—primarily the major policy initiatives and pieces of legislation—along the way. In analysing these developments it is particularly necessary to take account of the political context in which they have taken place, particularly (as in Chapters 4 and 5) the Labour Party's social democratic welfare state programmes of the immediate post-war period and the emergence and domination of the 'New Right' Conservative ideology which embraced the rationalisation of welfare in the 1980s and much of the 1990s. It is also important to appreciate the economic context, such as the recession and high levels of unemployment between the wars (discussed in this chapter), to many of the developments in social security policy. This book does not, however, purport to offer a comprehensive history of social security; rather, the aim is to promote understanding of the present system in its historical context.

This chapter traces the history of social security from its Poor Law origins in England to the late 1930s. The main areas of social security are covered, although the size of the subject has necessitated some selectivity. Although the Beveridge Report of 1942[1] has had such enormous significance for the entire post-war evolution of the benefits system in the UK (and also had an influence elsewhere),[2] it is important to understand that many of the key features of post-war social security schemes—such as contribution-based insurance schemes and means-tested support, and principles such as registration and availability for work as a condition of entitlement to benefits for unemployment—have a much deeper history.

---

[1] Beveridge Report (1942).
[2] See J. Hills, J. Ditch, and H. Glennester (eds), *Beveridge and Social Security: An International Retrospective* (Oxford: Clarendon Press, 1994).

2. THE POOR LAW

The road to the present social security system can be traced back fairly easily to the Beveridge Report in 1942 and then further back to the National Insurance Act 1911. But no student of social security law can ignore the Poor Law, for, as Mesher has commented, 'while the precise forms and institutions of the Poor Law have been abolished, many of its underlying attitudes and policies remain firmly embedded in our current law and practice'.[3] Alcock refers to two surviving principles in particular which characterise modern-day means-tested benefits: that of less eligibility, namely that support for the poor should not improve their situation beyond that of the lowest paid worker, in order to discourage dependency; and the distinction between the 'deserving' and 'undeserving poor'—the former being seen as the hapless victims of uncontrollable circumstances (old age, sickness, and so on) and the latter being regarded as capable of supporting themselves if they made proper efforts to do so.[4]

The origins of the Poor Law lie in the fourteenth century. By the middle of that century the feudal system had collapsed and waged labour was being used. Mobility of labour developed and there was concern about resultant vagrancy among those who travelled in search for work. Legislation was enacted in 1388 in an attempt to counter it, but it was some time before assistance was offered to the vagrant poor. The government saw its role as the preservation of the peace and looked to the Church to help the poor. The local parish became the first agency with a role in poor relief. In 1536 parishes were authorised to collect money from parishioners to help the impotent poor and obviate the need for begging.[5]

One of the key features of the Poor Law which emerged was the concept of 'setting the poor on work'. The requirement to work applied to the able-bodied. The Poor Relief Act of 1576 required justices of the peace to provide the raw materials for the work to be carried out.[6] The Poor Law legislation was codified in 1598 and again in the Poor Law Act of 1601 (43 Elizabeth Chapter 2). In addition to the provision of work for the able-bodied, the Act of 1601 provided for the accommodation of the incapable poor in almshouses or 'poor-houses', whilst those who were able-bodied but idle would be punished in 'houses of correction'. Parishes were to administer poor relief through 'overseers' appointed to the parish by magistrates, who in turn were under the surveillance of the Privy Council.[7] The overseers could levy poor rates on property. However, only the poor who 'belonged' to a particular parish would be its responsibility. According to Fraser, legal disputes between

---

[3] J. Mesher, 'The Poor Law Strikes Back: 1909–1948–1984', in D. Hoath (ed.), *75 Years of Law at Sheffield, 1909–1984. The Edward Bramley Jubilee Lectures* (Sheffield: Faculty of Law, University of Sheffield, 1985). See also the examples given in R. Cranston, *Legal Foundations of the Welfare State* (London: Weidenfeld and Nicolson, 1985), 44.

[4] P. Alcock, *Poverty and State Support* (London: Longman, 1987), 85.

[5] D. Fraser, *The Evolution of the Welfare State*, 2nd edn. (London: Macmillan, 1984), 31.

[6] Ibid., 32.

[7] G. M. Trevelyan, *English Social History* (London: Reprint Society/Longmans, Green & Co: 1948), 172.

parishes were common; he comments: 'one suspects that often more time and money were spent on litigation than the sustenance of the pauper would have involved'.[8] Local parishes were concerned to minimise the costs arising from any increased burden on the poor rate. The Act of Settlement 1662 attempted to lay down rules governing connection with a parish. It did not fully resolve the problem however, and families were still cruelly removed from a parish which disowned them. Often family members who belonged to different settlements were separated. Finally, removal was restricted in 1795 and there was legislation to limit the break-up of families.[9]

A number of the provisions of the Elizabethan Poor Law affected the young. The 1601 Act in effect created a legal obligation for parents to exhaust their own resources for the support of a child before the local parish would be obliged to provide relief.[10] The pre-existing obligation on parents and children to support each other was extended to grandparents and grandchildren.[11] Furthermore, the requirement that the able-bodied poor should be set to work applied also to children whose parents could not support them. It should be noted that if a child was able to work the father had no support obligation under the Poor Law.[12] When children were considered old enough they would be compelled to take an apprenticeship and learn a craft.[13] In some cases, where children could not be supported by their families they could be separated from them without their families' consent, becoming, in effect, 'wards of the state'.[14] In the years that followed, child labour was much in demand and became for many poor families an important source of income.

Thomas Gilbert's Act (the Poor Relief Act) of 1782 enabled parishes to join together into unions. According to Fraser, most of the sixty-seven unions (formed out of 900 parishes) employed paid relieving officers. Poor relief often took the form of cash payments. Alternatively, the poor might be set to work for local parishioners (mostly farmers) on a rotation basis; this was known as the Roundsman system. At the end of the eighteenth century, allowances to supplement wages, which were insufficient to provide for basic needs at a time of inflated food prices resulting from bad harvests, were paid in some areas. As Trevelyan put it: 'As the loaf rose, the dole was to rise with it.'[15] Such an arrangement is often referred to as the Speenhamland

---

[8] Ibid., 34.

[9] See, generally, R. Cranston, *Legal Foundations of the Welfare State* (London: Weidenfeld and Nicolson, 1985), 22–5 and L. Charlesworth, 'The Poor Law: A modern legal analysis' (1999) *J.S.S.L.* 79–92.

[10] Poor Law Act 1601, s. 1.

[11] Ibid., s. 6; see Sir G. Nicholls, *A History of the English Poor law Vol. 1. A.D. 924–1714* (Westminster: P. S. King and Son, 1904), 190.

[12] R. H. Mnookin, *Child, Family and State. Problems and Materials on Children and the Law* (Boston: Little, Brown and Co, 1978), 168. On the position regarding illegitimate children, see Cranston, op. cit., 37.

[13] D. Oxley, *Poor Relief in England and Wales 1601–1834* (Newton Abbot: David and Charles, 1974), 73–4.

[14] P. Thane, 'Childhood in History', in M. King (ed.), *Childhood, Welfare, Justice* (London: B. T. Batsford, 1981), 17.

[15] N. 7 above, 473.

system, as its origin is said to lie in special arrangements agreed upon in that Berkshire village in 1795.[16]

The system of poor relief came under increasing intellectual attack for discouraging effort and endeavour on the part of its recipients and for depressing wage levels, which could have the effect of compelling 'a worker to become a pauper even when in work'.[17] There was growing concern in government about its rising cost.[18] Outdoor relief was considered to have been over-generous for some. Intellectual argument was also influenced by the free-market principles espoused in Adam Smith's *Wealth of Nations* in 1776, which helped to establish a climate of laissez-faire beliefs. It was considered that if the poor were given too much help they would not work. Ricardo referred to the need for an 'iron law of wages',[19] under which wages for manual labour ought not to rise much above subsistence levels.

A Commission was established to investigate poor relief and its Poor Law Report of 1834 recommended that the conditions of paupers should be made less eligible, in other words less attractive, than those of the lowest-paid independent workers. Able-bodied workers would be offered entry to the workhouse as a test of genuineness of need (the 'workhouse test') and outdoor relief would no longer be made available to them. A central body, the Poor Law Commission, would be established to supervise the unions responsible for poor relief (there had been reports of corruption among local Poor Law authorities). Under the Poor Law Amendment Act 1834, which effected these reforms, the Commission was also empowered to lay down general rules and directions, administered by assistant commissioners. The Commission was subsequently replaced by the Poor Law Board, in 1847, itself merged into the Local Government Board in 1871.

It is something of an understatement that 'the workhouse-test was used more harshly than intended'.[20] The workhouse proved to be one of the cruellest and inhumane of all institutions designed to 'help' or 'manage' the poor. At worst (conditions varied widely), there would exist a regime of near slavery, tied to completion of menial and soul-destroying tasks. Overall, the reforms failed to marry successfully what were the two principal objectives of the new Poor Law: to deter idleness and to provide humane relief. The stigmatisation of the poor that resulted from the application of the Poor Law 'became firmly rooted in popular culture',[21] and to some extent continues today. Moreover, many of the principles embedded in the Poor Law outlined above (such as the principle of lesser eligibility) and family responsibility seem to have also lasted into the twentieth century.[22] The fact that poor relief could

---

[16] See R. Cranston, n. 9 above, 40–1. [17] G. M. Trevelyan, n. 7 above, 474.
[18] The annual cost met by local ratepayers via the poor rate was £1 million at the end of Queen Anne's reign (1714) (ibid., 438), but in 1818 (the peak year for poor relief) £8 million was spent: D. Thomson, *England in the Nineteenth Century* (Harmondsworth: Penguin, 1975), 16.
[19] See Fraser, n. 5 above, 39. [20] Thomson, n. 18 above, 70. [21] Fraser, n. 5 above, 55.
[22] The principle of family responsibility was not only re-enacted in 1834 but was extended so that by 1930 it had encompassed stepfathers, married women with property and mothers of illegitimate children: A. Deacon and J. Bradshaw, *Reserved for the Poor—The Means Test in British Social Policy* (Oxford: Martin Roberton, 1983), 28 n. 1. Present-day means tests also reflect family responsibility.

take the form of a loan[23] offers an interesting comparison with the social fund budgeting loan and crisis loan schemes and the student loan scheme of today.

While the post-1834 (or 'New') Poor Law continued through the nineteenth century, a growing contribution to the relief of the poor was made by charities and through various philanthropic activities. For the better-off working poor, friendly societies, trade unions, and insurance companies increasingly offered schemes through which protection against the financial consequences of sickness or death could be arranged or the stigmatising effect of a pauper's funeral avoided.[24] But whilst Bismarck had offered German citizens state schemes of sickness and accident insurance by 1885,[25] it was not until well into the twentieth century before there was, in Britain, a state system of relief alternative to the Poor Law, despite the enormous social and ideological changes that characterised the late nineteenth century.

By the time that the Poor Law was subjected to the scrutiny of a Royal Commission from 1905–9 (see below), widespread changes in attitude towards poverty and its causes and effects had already helped to precipitate a more benevolent approach. There was growing awareness that poverty was not necessarily a matter of personal fault but that the major causes of poverty were economic. It was also realised that the free market was often unable to meet the need for basic provision (such as housing). There was also increasing evidence of the scale of poverty (especially following the publication of the Booth and Rowntree surveys around the turn of the century) and the effect of poverty on public health (Edwin Chadwick's *Report on the Sanitary Condition of the Labouring Population of Great Britain* (1842) having a prolonged influence). A changing political climate, growing democratisation and pockets of serious social unrest, including food riots in London, helped to precipitate change.[26]

Already, there had been state intervention in the form of a compulsory workmen's compensation scheme (under the Workmen's Compensation Act 1897), which guaranteed the right of the injured employee to compensation from the employer, subject to a maximum payment. Ogus comments that this scheme 'heralded the path' to social insurance in Britain.[27] Following a long campaign for old age pensions, and when it became politically expedient, non-contributory pensions were introduced, in January 1909, for those aged over seventy, under the Old Age Pensions Act 1908. Although the amount provided (five shillings per week) was meagre, 'pensions were paid through the Post Office and were quite separate from the Poor Law and immune from its moral stigma'.[28] Macnicol concludes that the 1908 Act was

---

[23] 1834 Act, s. 58.

[24] See A. I. Ogus, 'Great Britain', in P. A. Kohler, H. F. Zacker, and M. Partington, *The Evolution of Social Insurance 1881–1981* (London: Frances Pinter, 1982), 163–4.

[25] D. Zollner, 'Germany' in Kohler, Zacker, and Partington, op. cit., 25–6.

[26] See B. B. Gilbert, *The Origins of National Insurance in Great Britain* (London: Michael Joseph, 1966); J. Harris, *Unemployment and Politics* (Oxford: Clarendon Press, 1972); D. Vincent, *Poor Citizens* (London: Longman, 1991).

[27] N. 24 above, 176.

[28] D. Fraser, *The Evolution of the British Welfare State*, 2nd edn. (London: Macmillan, 1984), 153.

'probably the most radically redistributive piece of social policy ever introduced'; the Act benefited women (who made up the majority of the elderly and who in old age were worse off than men due to a lack of savings from employment combined with a greater longevity) and it targeted the poorest (those with an annual income of less than £31, with a sliding scale means-test for those with an annual income of £21 up to £31).[29] Those who were, or had been in the previous two years, in receipt of poor relief were not entitled to the pension. This restriction was lifted by the Old Age Pensions Act 1919.[30]

For the unemployed, the Poor Law remained the only form of public assistance. In London, however, distress committees (established under the Unemployed Workmen Act 1905) provided assistance to thousands of unemployed workers, at a time of growing unemployment.[31] The committees had to register, investigate, and classify unemployed persons applying to them for assistance, and then give whatever assistance they could, by providing temporary work, by aiding emigration, or in other ways, subject to the applicant satisfying certain conditions.[32]

The report of the Royal Commission on the Poor Law was published in 1909, but was not unanimous. The social reformers Beatrice and Sidney Webb signed a Minority Report. This, unlike the Majority Report which clung to some *laissez-faire* notions, was fully committed to a state system of welfare. But there were a number of areas of agreement between the Reports both in the need for reform of an anachronistic system of relief and in some of the measures which were required, such as the establishment of labour exchanges[33] and the development of a national scheme of unemployment insurance, building on the insurance principle reflected in existing trade union schemes.[34] The insurance principle was perhaps the most important of the recommendations to be acted upon (see below). A scheme of local public assistance was also proposed, in place of the local Poor Law administration under guardians. Public assistance authorities and committees managed by local authorities would administer assistance of various kinds (including social service type provision) (see below).

The Labour Exchanges Act 1909 empowered the Board of Trade to establish and maintain labour exchanges in places that needed them and to make regulations for their management. At first they extended only slowly, although there were 140,000 applications (21,500 of which were to the separate juvenile register) in the five weeks to 29 December 1911.[35] When unemployment insurance was introduced under the National Insurance Act 1911, registration at an exchange became a condition for

---

[29] J. Macnicol, 'Beveridge and Old Age', in J. Hills, J. Ditch, and H. Glennester, *Beveridge and Social Security: An International Retrospective* (Oxford: Oxford University Press, 1994), 74–5.

[30] See Ogus, Barendt, and Wikeley (1995), 215.

[31] W. H. Beveridge, *Unemployment. A Problem of Industry* (London: Longman, 1930), 119.

[32] Ibid., 23.   [33] Majority Report, Part VI; Minority Report, Part II.

[34] Majority Report, 632, para. 133.

[35] L. G. Chiozza Money, *Insurance Versus Poverty* (London: Methuen, 1912), 335 and 336.

receipt of benefit and led to a doubling of their use.[36] Beveridge argued that the Poor Law had aimed to offer relief 'without relieving unnecessarily' via 'the principle of deterrence—the making of relief so repellent that men might be presumed to have exhausted every other resource before they have accepted it'.[37] He viewed labour exchanges therefore as opening up 'a way of "dispauperisation" more humane, less costly and more effective than that of the "workhouse test"—the way of making the finding of work easy instead of making relief hard'.[38] But by the 1920s, when unemployment affected over one million people at any one time, the reality of experience among those queuing outside the labour exchanges was increasingly perceived to be one of humiliation.[39]

3. THE INTRODUCTION OF SOCIAL INSURANCE UNDER THE NATIONAL INSURANCE ACT 1911

The unemployment insurance scheme was brought into effect in March 1912 under the National Insurance Act 1911, which was steered through Parliament by Lloyd George. There were in fact two major strands of social insurance introduced under the Act: health insurance, providing medical treatment and sick pay for insured persons, and unemployment insurance. Both were funded by weekly contributions paid by employers, employees, and the state. There was also a maternity grant payable to the wife of an insured man or to an insured woman who qualified.

The scheme of social insurance placed an emphasis on individualism—the payment of contributions derived from earnings in employment in return for cover, which 'maintained, in a somewhat modified form, the exchange or reciprocal basis to social welfare',[40] giving rise in legal terms to something approximating to a contractual right and reflecting traditional values of thrift and self support. At the same time it incorporated collectivist principles, with workers' contributions being pooled into the insurance fund on a compulsory basis, this amounting to significant state interference. As Ogus explains, social insurance was a satisfactory compromise between these two extreme positions[41]—a compromise that operated on a political level to ensure widespread support for the scheme (although health insurance, influenced by the German scheme which Lloyd George had been impressed by when he had visited that country, did prove contentious; there was the opposition to it, or concern, from various vested interests—including friendly societies and the medical profession).[42]

The significance of unemployment insurance for the unemployed worker was that there was, for those whose trades were covered by the scheme (see below), an

---

[36] B. B. Gilbert, *The Origins of National Insurance in Great Britain* (London: Michael Joseph, 1966), 262.
[37] Beveridge (1930), n. 31 above, 215–16.
[38] Ibid., 216. The Poor Law workhouse test and the term 'pauper' were abolished in 1930.
[39] Vincent, op. cit., n. 26 above, 57.   [40] Ogus, op. cit., n. 24 above, 183.   [41] Ibid.
[42] Fraser, op. cit., n. 26 above, 163; Ogus op. cit., n. 24 above, 184–5.

effective alternative to the Poor Law or reliance on their own children for support. As Moroney says: '[A]s society becomes more industrialised it develops some form of social security system. Without such a system parents, however erroneously, viewed their children as their social insurance for old age and the greater the number of children, the greater the insurance. As collective social insurance mechanisms become available the perceived need ceases.'[43]

Unemployment insurance was to be based on two main principles. First, coverage would be narrow. There was concern that in trades where the risk of unemployment might be difficult to quantify the scheme might prove too expensive. It was therefore decided not to introduce a comprehensive scheme but rather one that was limited to particular trades where cyclical unemployment occurred: building, construction of works (railways and bridges, etc), shipbuilding, mechanical engineering, ironfounding, vehicle manufacture, and sawmilling;[44] during the First World War (1914–18) the scheme was extended to include munitions workers. Secondly, the scheme would have to be contributory (the employer, employee, and the state would each pay a contribution) 'if it were not to be ruinously expensive'.[45] Under the 1911 Act the employer's and employee's contributions were exactly the same (one penny for sixteen to eighteen year olds, one penny per day for those aged over eighteen who worked for two days or less per week, and two and a half pence per week for an over-eighteen year old who worked for more than two days). The state paid an amount equal to one-third of the total of the employer's and employee's contribution. Although the school leaving age was fourteen (with local authorities having the power to raise it to fifteen via local by-laws),[46] the age of entry into unemployment insurance was not reduced from sixteen to fourteen until the Unemployment Act 1934. To qualify for unemployment benefit an insured worker had to be at least seventeen years of age and to prove that he or she had been working in an insured trade for at least twenty-six separate weeks in the preceding five years.[47] Benefit was paid at a flat rate of seven shillings per week for those aged eighteen or over (or half that rate for seventeen year olds) for up to a maximum of fifteen weeks in any period of twelve months.

When the 1911 unemployment insurance scheme was reviewed in the early 1930s it was said to have been '"exiguous" and "narrowly cut" . . . it was, in fact, regarded as an assistance to men who needed nothing more than a "tiding over" of short tem-

---

[43] R. M. Moroney, *The Family and the State* (London: Longmans, 1976), 19.

[44] National Insurance Act 1911, Sixth Schedule.

[45] B. B. Gilbert, *The Origins of National Insurance in Great Britain* (London: Michael Joseph, 1966), 270.

[46] This power was not used: G. Rees and T. L. Rees, 'Juvenile Unemployment and the State between the Wars', in T. L. Rees and P. Atkinson, *Youth Unemployment and State Intervention* (London: Routledge, 1982), 18. Churchill had wanted to raise to school leaving age to 17: Gilbert, op. cit., 253. The Minority Report of the Poor Law Commission (at 342) recommended that 'in order to secure proper industrial training for the youth of the nation' employment below the age of 15 should be prohibited and there should be compulsory half-time employment and education up to the age of 18.

[47] National Insurance Act 1911, s. 86 and Seventh Schedule.

porary spells of unemployment'.[48] The scheme was only intended to meet immediate claims, and so the insurance fund profited from the fact that unemployment was generally very short-term at this time. Nearly half of the unemployed were back in work within a week and so were unable to draw benefit,[49] as it was not paid during the first week of unemployment. Levels of benefit were low, at around 22 per cent of average wages[50] and the scheme covered only a minority (around 2.5 million) of the labour force. Those who had lost their employment as a result of misconduct or who had left it voluntarily without 'just cause' were disqualified from benefit for six weeks.[51] Strikers were also barred from benefit. The scheme had been designed to be actuarially sound. In August 1914 the insurance fund showed a surplus of £3,185,000.

4. THE DEVELOPMENT OF SOCIAL INSURANCE BETWEEN THE WARS

The unemployment insurance scheme was extended after the First World War until the economic slump of the late 1920s and early 1930s placed such heavy demands on it that cutbacks were deemed necessary, leading to increased demand for alternative provision. Gilbert comments that 'the war and post-war depression destroyed [the] prudent, limited liability approach to unemployment insurance'.[52] The end of the First World War led to unemployment among returning service personnel and among the many young people who had obtained employment during the war in munitions factories, half of whom were unable to find alternative work.[53] Returning military lacked contributions records, and there were others who had undertaken work of value to the nation but who were engaged in trades not covered by the scheme. The Government was stung into almost immediate action by the political impossibility of forcing ex-military, just back from the fighting, and others who had supported the war effort, into dependence on the Poor Law.[54] It was the same political imperative which led to the establishment of council housing under Addison's Act (Housing and Town Planning Act) of 1919 ('homes for heroes'). Within the space of four weeks the Government developed the 'Out of Work Donation' for service personnel, and later civilians also, which in effect replaced unemployment insurance for those concerned until its phased discontinuation between 1919 and 1921. Unlike unemployment insurance, the Donation paid allowances for dependants. This

---

[48] Royal Commission on Unemployment Insurance *Final Report*, Cmd 4185 (London: HMSO, 1932), cited in B. Sadler, 'Unemployment and Unemployment Benefits in Twentieth Century Britain: A Lesson of the Thirties', in K. Cowling et al., *Out of Work. Perspectives of Mass Unemployment* (Coventry: University of Warwick, 1983), 19.

[49] Gilbert, n. 45 above, 285. [50] Sadler, op. cit., 19. [51] 1911 Act, s. 87(2).

[52] Gilbert, n. 45 above, 382.

[53] W. R. Garside, 'Juvenile Unemployment and Public Policy Between the Wars' (1977) 30 *Econ. History Rev.* 322–99 at 324.

[54] J. C. Brown, *Family Income Support—Part II: Children in Social Security* (London: Policy Studies Institute, 1984), 12–13.

happened because the 'Separation Allowance' which the Government paid to service personnel during the war, as an addition to the allotment from their pay in support of their dependants, contained dependency additions and it was considered necessary to continue these in the Out of Work Donation.

Dependency additions to unemployment insurance were, however, introduced in November 1921. By this time the scheme had been extended (by the National Insurance Act 1920) to nearly all employees outside agriculture and domestic service. Around 11 million workers were by now covered.[55] According to George, the payment of allowances for dependants marked a shift in emphasis in social security policy: 'The extension of social security benefits to cover the needs of the whole family ... reflected society's greater stress on the social service aspects of social security as distinct from its actuarial and narrowly defined economic aspects'.[56] But, in fact, the introduction of these additions owed more to government fear of unrest and other political factors; and the shift in policy was perhaps not all that dramatic, given the gradual move towards their introduction that had occurred via the Separation Allowances and Out of Work Donation (above).[57] These dependency additions to unemployment insurance were at first introduced into the scheme as a temporary expedient to meet 'winter hardships' following the reduction of unemployment benefit by 25 per cent in July 1921.[58] They provoked no controversy, although a Government attempt to impose an upper income limit was dropped, in the face of Parliamentary opposition.[59] The dependants' allowances were made a permanent feature of the unemployment insurance scheme by the Unemployment Insurance Act 1922.[60] Dependency additions were increased in 1923 (the child addition was doubled to two shillings per child; five shillings was paid in respect of a partner), and at the same time the fund out of which these additions had been paid (the Special Distress Fund) was amalgamated with the insurance fund. Dependency additions were to feature continuously in unemployment insurance and its successor schemes until abolition of the (by then much reduced) allowances in unemployment, sickness, and maternity benefits in 1984. By that time, the extension of means-tested and family allowances had reduced the need, and thus arguably the case, for these dependency additions. However, in the inter-war years the dependency additions proved impossible to withdraw, in view of the persistently high levels of unemployment.[61] It should be noted that there were no dependency additions to sickness benefits between the wars, which was a major anomaly and a cause of criticism.

The insurance scheme was extended in 1925 to bring contributory benefits cover-

[55] Ibid., 13.

[56] V. George, *Social Security and Society* (London: Routledge and Kegan Paul, 1973), 124.

[57] H. Land, 'The Introduction of Family Allowances', in Hall, Land, Parker, and Webb, *Change, Choice and Conflict in Social Policy* (London: Heinemann, 1975), 163; J. Macnicol, 'Family Allowances and Less Eligibility', in P. Thane (ed.), *The Origins of British Social Policy* (London: Croom Helm, 1978), 176 and 198 n. 16.

[58] Ogus, n. 24 above, 220.   [59] Macnicol, n. 57 above, 176 and 178.   [60] Section 1.

[61] J. C. Brown, n. 54 above, 14–15.

age to widows, who were entitled to the child dependency additions (above) in addition to a basic weekly benefit, and orphans; and a contributory pension was introduced for males and females aged sixty-five to seventy who were insured under the health insurance scheme.[62] The pension was 10 shillings per week (£1 for a married couple), compared with rates of 18 shillings for unemployment benefit and 15 shillings for sickness benefit. Later these inconsistent rates were to be rationalised by Beveridge.[63] The mechanics of contributory insurance funding 'effectively built a wall round the state pension scheme, insulating it from demands for "adequate" pensions and minimising its redistributive potential'.[64]

According to Sadler, social security policy in Britain in the 1920s was characterised by 'a clash between an ideological commitment to an actuarily sound insurance scheme and the social and political consequences of honest working men being forced into pauperism'.[65] Fear of the latter led to vacillations in government policy and a series of temporary expedients—'temporary because of the belief that the problem would disappear with the "return to normalcy", necessary because of the desire to avoid the consequences—social, political and financial—of using the Poor Law as a relieving body for the genuinely unemployed'.[66] One of these measures was 'extended benefit', which was designed to assist those who had exhausted their rights to insurance benefits. This benefit, described as 'uncovenanted benefit' at the time of its introduction in 1921 (under section 3 of the Unemployment Insurance Act 1921), provided a limited extension to entitlement. Benefit was paid at a uniform rate but subject to conditions and the exercise of ministerial discretion. Additions for dependants were available, and between 1921 and 1927 there were 1.3 million claims for them.[67] At first, extended benefit was paid for up to sixteen weeks during a period of eight months running from March to November 1921. At the end of this period a new period of twenty-two weeks began.[68] Further legislation was introduced to extend benefit for successive special periods. When the new (but short-lived) Labour government was elected to office in 1924 it made extended benefit of unlimited duration, replacing ministerial discretion with prescribed general conditions.[69]

The minister's discretion was soon restored, however.[70] Nevertheless, the Blanesburgh Committee, which had been appointed by the incoming Baldwin administration to review the insurance system, recommended abolition of the two separate schemes, to be replaced by a standard benefit which would be available as of right to those who met the basic contribution conditions. Those who could not

---

[62] Widows', Orphans' and Contributory Pensions Act 1925.
[63] See Ogus, n. 24 above, 219.
[64] J. Macnicol, 'Beveridge and Old Age', in J. Hills, J. Ditch, and H. Glennester, *Beveridge and Social Security: An International Retrospective* (Oxford: Oxford University Press, 1994), 80.
[65] Op. cit., n. 48 above, 19.   [66] Ibid.
[67] *Ministry of Labour Gazette*, May 1928, 161.
[68] See B. B. Gilbert, *British Social Policy 1914–1939* (London: B. T. Batsford, 1970), 82–3.
[69] Unemployment Insurance Act (No. 2) 1924, s. 1(1).
[70] Unemployment Insurance Act 1925, s. 1.

meet these and other conditions would be entitled to 'transitional benefit', which Fraser describes as 'yet another device to protect the unemployed from the Poor Law'.[71] Although, under the Unemployment Insurance Act 1927[72] which gave effect to these changes, entitlement became more generous in some respects, there were cutbacks in the rates of benefit paid to the young unemployed, although these were not as severe as the Blanesburgh Committee had proposed.[73] Transitional benefit involved an investigation of means and was subject to the minister's discretion, as had been uncovenanted benefit. The minister's discretionary power was, for example, used to exclude, unless hardship would be caused, 'single persons who are residing with parents or other relatives to whom, having regard to all the circumstances, they can reasonably look for support during unemployment'.[74] The exclusion of young people and married women with working husbands was one of a number of disincentives intended to prevent abuse and emphasise the 'temporary' nature of the benefit.[75]

It is important not to forget that despite the apparently growing generosity of the insurance scheme, there were strict conditions surrounding entitlement. There was, throughout, a concern to avoid abuse. When the unemployment insurance scheme was introduced in 1911 it had been assumed that, as Fraser explains, the proportionment of benefits to contributions would automatically prevent it: 'the malingerer, it was said, could only cheat himself since unnecessary claims would reduce entitlement to benefit when it was really needed'.[76] The abandonment of that principle in 1921 meant that other safeguards were considered necessary. The Unemployment Insurance Act 1921 and (No 2) Act 1924 introduced a condition that a claimant should be 'genuinely seeking work'. This led to disallowance of a significant number of claims, up to one in three in some areas, with over three million claims in all turned down on this ground from March 1921 to March 1930.[77] The 'genuinely seeking work' test was abolished in 1930, but was arguably reinstated in 1990 with the introduction via the Social Security Act 1989 of the 'actively seeking employment' requirement for both unemployment benefit and income support.[78] It was also built into the jobseeker's allowance scheme under the Jobseekers Act 1995.[79]

Another important move to prevent claims for benefit by introducing an element of compulsion to work was the programme of industrial transference which operated in a number of areas. It involved transferring registered unemployed workers from areas of labour surplus to those with a shortage of labour. In the first scheme, in 1927, unemployed miners were moved into industries in other areas; subsidies and

---

[71] D. Fraser, *The Evolution of the British Welfare State*, 2nd edn. (London: Macmillan, 1984), 187.

[72] 17 & 18 Geo.5 c.30.

[73] A. Deacon, *In Search of the Scrounger* (London: Bell, 1976), 43–53.

[74] W. H. Beveridge, *Unemployment. A Problem of Industry* (London: Longman, 1930), 276, n. 2.

[75] B. Sadler, 'Unemployment and Unemployment Benefits in Twentieth Century Britain: A Lesson of the Thirties', in K. Cowling et al., *Out of Work. Perspectives of Mass Unemployment* (Coventry: University of Warwick, 1983), 19.

[76] D. Fraser, op. cit. n. 71 above.

[77] Ibid., 188. [78] See Chapter 10 below. [79] Ibid.

allowances were payable to meet the costs of moving and other expenses. In that year, adult unemployment in the traditional mining communities of the Rhondda and Merthyr Tydfil stood at 21 per cent and 34.8 per cent respectively; juvenile unemployment in the latter was also high, at 25.6 per cent.[80] The transference of young people was also an important part of the programme as a whole. A separate juvenile transference scheme was introduced in 1928–9. Furthermore, whole families were moved under the household transference scheme.[81] Young unemployed people also faced the possibility of being required to attend a Juvenile Unemployment Centre (later retitled Juvenile Instruction Centres)[82] under pain of disqualification from entitlement to unemployment benefit.[83] Compulsion was deemed to be necessary so that the young could be 'saved from themselves': 'Reasonable allowance should be made for family circumstances, but suitable young men who are fit and able to take up a course of instruction, which offers good prospects of employment on completion, should not be permitted to stay at home in idleness.'[84]

The insurance scheme was generally improved in the period up to 1930. The Unemployment Insurance Acts of 1927 and 1930 led to all persons aged between sixteen and sixty-five employed under a contract of service in the United Kingdom being covered by the scheme. Benefit rates were increased under the 1930 Act, and the fixed period of disqualification for voluntary unemployment, set at six weeks, became a maximum. The Act was said, somewhat disparagingly, to mark 'the extreme limit of relaxation of [the] benefit rules'.[85] However, with transitional benefits unlimited in time and a charge upon the Treasury (the Labour Government shifted the burden away from the insurance fund in 1930), the rising tide of unemployment (it was by then above two million) as world economic recession and slump set in began to create immense budgetary pressure.[86] The numbers drawing transitional benefit more than doubled. Cuts in benefit were regarded as the only solution to a mounting budgetary deficit, but a majority of the Labour cabinet, although not the Prime Minister Ramsey MacDonald, preferred to resign rather than implement them. Following the general election that followed, the new National (coalition) Government cut insurance benefits and dependants' allowances by 10 per cent. The new benefit rates were to remain in force until July 1934. Standard benefit became payable for only twenty-six weeks. A 'thirty in two rule' (the claimant had to have paid thirty contributions

---

[80] Save the Children Fund, *Unemployment and the Child* (London: Longmans, 1933), 70.

[81] G. Rees and T. L. Rees, 'Juvenile Unemployment and the State between the Wars', in T. L. Rees and P. Atkinson, *Youth Unemployment and State Intervention* (London: Routledge, 1982), 23.

[82] These provided courses of instruction on a range of subjects. For further discussion, see N. Harris, *Social Security for Young People* (Aldershot: Avebury, 1989), 157–9.

[83] Unemployment Insurance Act 1920, s. 7(1)(v) and Unemployment Insurance Act 1930; see also University of Liverpool, *Report on Co-operation between The Unemployment Assistance Board, The Local Authority and Voluntary Associations in Liverpool* (Liverpool and London: University Press of Liverpool and Hodder and Stoughton, 1938), 13.

[84] The Commissioners for Special Areas in England and Wales, 1936, cited in R. C. Davison, *British Unemployment Policy. The Modern Phase since 1930* (London: Longmans, 1938), 110.

[85] Davison (ibid.), 8.   [86] Fraser, n. 71 above, 191–2.

in the previous two years), which had been recommended by the Blanesburgh Committee (above), was introduced. The 1931 changes led to one million people being cut off from insurance benefits.[87]

'Transitional payment' replaced transitional benefit[88] and acquired increasing significance for many people: there were 800,000 applicants for the benefit in 1931–2.[89] But to receive it claimants had to endure the notorious household means-test (see below) applied by the Public Assistance Committees of local authorities who administered the benefit. Benefit was paid at a rate that would not lead to a claimant drawing more than the normal insurance rate, including dependants' allowances.[90] Transitional payment was replaced by unemployment assistance following the Unemployment Act 1934 (see below). This Act followed the final report of the Royal Commission on Unemployment Insurance in 1932 which had recommended a number of improvements (including a lowering of the age of entry into the insurance scheme to fourteen and the establishment of a central non-political authority to administer transitional payments). Following the 1934 Act, insurance benefit could be claimed for up to fifty-two weeks, rates were raised and the employer, employee, and state paid equal contributions. The 1934 Act also introduced a right to an additional day's benefit, over and above the basic maximum, for those who had a record of five years' contributions (subject to satisfying the thirty in two rule (above) and certain other requirements).

By 1935 unemployment was falling rapidly, although at the end of that year there were still 1.6 million adults and juveniles out of work.[91] Following political pressure dependency additions to unemployment benefit were increased from two shillings to three shillings per child. Although the increase led to fears that insurance benefits might, in some cases, exceed the level of wages, the Government did not implement the Unemployment Insurance Statutory Committee's recommendation that the maximum payable overall should be four shillings per week.[92] There were no other significant developments with regard to insurance benefits until the Beveridge-inspired reforms immediately after the Second World War (see below). Unemployment continued to fall, although it rose slightly in 1938. The outbreak of war in 1939 created new demands for labour.

This period was important for rooting the insurance principle firmly in the social security system and is significant for establishing some of the conditions of entitlement which have continued to this day. The cuts of 1930–1 also demonstrated the vulnerability of social security to severe economic pressure on government. They

---

[87] Davison, n. 84 above, 15.
[88] Transitional payments were introduced via Order in Council under the National Economy Act 1931.
[89] A. Deacon and J. Bradshaw, *Reserved for the Poor—The Means Test in British Social Policy* (Oxford: Martin Roberton, 1983), 17.
[90] Ibid., 16.
[91] *Ministry of Labour Gazette*, December 1935, 480.
[92] J. C. Brown, *Family Income Support Part 2: Children in Social Security* (London: Policy Studies Institute, 1984), 15.

were most definitely a precedent for later rationalisations of benefits. The period also demonstrated that the insurance scheme could not meet the needs of all families, giving rise to a widespread need for means-tested assistance which even Beveridge was unable (later) to eradicate.

5. UNEMPLOYMENT ASSISTANCE

As noted above, 'transitional payments' were available from 1931 to those who had already been receiving insurance payments for twenty-six weeks and had therefore exhausted their entitlement, or those who had insufficient insurance contributions. 'Transitional payments' were paid at the labour exchanges, but were subject to a means-test administered by the local Public Assistance Committees (PACs). The administration of transitional payments by PACs was very unpopular. Although PACs received guidance from the Government on how to determine the amount of payment to make, the scales adopted by them varied considerably from one area to the next: 'Many take the line that there is no scale, and that each case is dealt with on its merits: others adopt the Unemployment Benefit scale and modify it slightly'.[93] But an even greater cause of dissatisfaction was the strict resources test and, more especially, the household means-test, applied by the PACs.

Transitional payments were aimed at those left in need by the insurance system. Thus the means-test which was applied was justified in terms of there being 'nothing unreasonable in asking them to demonstrate that need'.[94] However, the household means-test proved to be stigmatising and, for the many workers who had never previously had to seek this kind of assistance (under the Poor Law), there was the detailed and often humiliating process of in effect being forced into dependence on other members of the household, since it was assumed that each member's resources were available to meet the needs of a claimant member if their combined resources exceeded the scale rates applied by the PACs. Other household members could face detailed enquiries into their private affairs even if they themselves had not made a claim for benefit.[95] Young workers often left home in order to safeguard their parents' benefit. But the concept of 'collusive desertion' was developed: the young person's resources would be taken into account even if he or she was no longer present in the household. It was the doctrine of family responsibility being taken to an extreme. The household means-test, in forcing family members to contribute to each other's support, from often slender resources, did little to encourage family harmony; nor did it reward honesty:

---

[93] Save the Children Fund, *Unemployment and the Child* (London: Longmans, 1933), 37.

[94] A. Deacon and J. Bradshaw, *Reserved for the Poor—The Means Test in British Social Policy* (Oxford: Martin Roberton, 1983), 16.

[95] Ibid., 17.

[I]t provided occasion for family strife and even dishonesty . . . young men in particular, if they did not completely move from home in order to ensure their full rate of assistance, sometimes provided themselves with accommodation addresses. As one such young man commented to an enquirer, 'It's a terrible business when you've got to tell lies to get a miserable 15s a week'.[96]

Problems with local administration of transitional payments, especially the inconsistency in scales and the 'unpredictable discretion' of the PACs,[97] were tackled via the establishment of the unemployment assistance scheme under Part II of the Unemployment Act 1934. The scheme was administered by the new Unemployment Assistance Board (UAB). The UAB had six members who began work in July 1934 and submitted regulations laying down uniform rates of assistance, including age-related dependants' allowances. There was a uniform means-test, to be applied across the country. Poor Law administration (except that relating to poverty caused by sickness, old age, widowhood or incapacity) was progressively taken over from local PACs. The Poor Law was to survive as a 'gap-filling' provision until its final demise under the National Assistance Act 1948.

The unemployment assistance scheme covered all persons normally engaged in an occupation, and earning less than £5 per week, between the ages of sixteen and sixty-five, provided they had met the condition of registering at an employment exchange. The scale rates fixed by the UAB[98] contained dependants' allowances which were higher than those in the unemployment insurance scheme, so that some families (approximately 34 per cent) were better off on assistance.[99] On the other hand, when the UAB took over responsibility for those (about 800,000 in number) in the transitional payments class in January 1935 some were worse off than they had been under the local rate paid by the PAC. For some the cuts were 'monstrously large',[100] and there were storms of protest and even panic.[101] The Standstill Act 1935 ensured that all recipients of assistance received nothing less than the amount previously paid to them by the PACs. It defused the protests, but it was disliked by the UAB because of the anomalies it caused, which the UAB had been set up to eradicate.[102] It was suggested that the increased generosity of the unemployment assistance scheme in 1935 and 1936 was causing 'more malingering and more refusals of work than usual';[103] and there was concern that the guarantee of assistance from the Board operated against a necessary or desirable mobility of labour.[104] The UAB had to defend itself

[96] M. Bruce, *The Coming of the Welfare State*, 2nd edn. (London: B. T. Batsford, 1965), 240.
[97] B. Rogers, *The Battle Against Poverty. Vol. 2. Towards a Welfare State* (London: Routledge and Kegan Paul, 1969), 23.
[98] The fixing of the scale rates by the UAB is discussed in J. Macnicol, 'Family Allowances and Less Eligibility', in P. Thane (ed.), *The Origins of British Social Policy* (London: Croom Helm, 1978), 181–5.
[99] Deacon and Bradshaw, n. 94 above, 23.
[100] Ibid., 66.
[101] F. Miller, 'The British Unemployment Assistance Crisis of 1935' (1979) *J. of Contemporary History*, 329–51.
[102] Deacon and Bradshaw, n. 94 above, 24.
[103] R. C. Davison, *British Unemployment Policy. The Modern Phase since 1930* (London: Longmans, 1938), 71.
[104] Unemployment Assistance Board, *Report for 1938* (London: HMSO, 1939), 47.

against accusations that it was allowing young people to 'settle down on assistance and thereby become unemployable'.[105]

Standstill lasted for two years, but continuing concern about young males settling down to a life on assistance rather than working prompted an investigation of applicants aged under thirty by the UAB. The conclusion was that about 25–30 per cent of younger applicants had accepted and were resigned to unemployment and were unwilling to take active steps to improve their position—not simply because they preferred idleness, but because '[a]pathy and listlessness are bred . . . by a long period of unemployment'.[106] There was, however, strong evidence that the low wages paid to many younger workers were partly to blame for dependence on assistance.[107] In any event, this was the eve of the Second World War, which left few without work of one sort or another.

The means-test applied by the UAB was in many respects 'still the thoroughly objectionable Household Means Test',[108] although it operated rather more through rules than discretion. The effect of the household means-test was far-reaching. In October 1938 one-third of all unemployment assistance claimants were having their benefit reduced on the grounds of household income.[109] However, the fact that so many people were on the move or dislocated during the war years made the household means-test almost impossible to administer. It was virtually abolished by the Determination of Needs Act 1941, although often contributions by household members were still assumed (rather than being ascertained via an investigation of personal circumstances).[110] Nevertheless, means-testing has never disappeared. By the late 1960s it had a dominant role in the administration of social security benefits (see Chapter 4). The experience of the household means-test of the inter-war years reinforced a negative view of means-testing which began to be expressed at that time.

6. CONCLUSION

The social security system in operation in Britain by the outbreak of war in 1939 was based on two main and separate strands of provision: insurance benefits and means-tested assistance. While the former had been extended since its inception under the 1911 Act, it provided by no means the comprehensive protection against all major contingencies which Beveridge was soon to propose in his blueprint for the post-war

---

[105] Deacon and Bradshaw, n. 94 above, 25.

[106] Unemployment Assistance Board, op. cit., 48–9.

[107] R. C. Davison, n. 103 above, 73; A. J. Lush, *The Young Adult* (Cardiff: University of Wales Press Board, 1941), 28.

[108] B. Rogers, *The Battle Against Poverty. Vol. 2. Towards a Welfare State* (London: Routledge and Kegan Paul, 1969), 23.

[109] A. Deacon and J. Bradshaw, *Reserved for the Poor—The Means Test in British Social Policy* (Oxford: Martin Roberton, 1983), 29, n. 5.

[110] D. Fraser, *The Evolution of the British Welfare State*, 2nd edn. (London: Macmillan, 1984), 213.

welfare state. However, the insurance principle, first implemented in Germany, had become firmly established in Britain. A national scheme of means-tested provision, in the form of unemployment assistance, had also been developed in place of local schemes intended to support those whose needs could not be met by the insurance system. Thus we see the emergence of what are, despite the decline of insurance since the 1960s, the key features of the modern social security system in Britain. A work test and registration for employment as conditions of entitlement to unemployment benefit, and a means-test for basic assistance, are among the features of social security law which have continued to the present day.

Social security had also become established as a feature of everyday life. Millions of workers paid insurance contributions. Moreover, the economic difficulties of the 1920s and early 1930s had thrown hundreds of thousands of workers employed in labour intensive manufacturing and materials industries onto the 'dole'. Social security support had provided a lifeline for many. At the same time, the notion of the malingerer and scrounger developed, and rules and practices intended to apply the work test with rigour and to ensure genuineness of need were applied. While there was still a stigma attached to drawing the dole, and while the experience of the dole queue was humiliating for many, there was not the utter desperation and degradation of reliance on the Poor Law, the last vestiges of which were soon to be erased even if its underlying philosophy to some extent survived in the post-1945 social security system.

4

Beveridge and Beyond: the Shift from Insurance to Means-testing

NEVILLE HARRIS

1. INTRODUCTION

This chapter covers a crucial period in the evolution of the British social security system, starting with the Beveridge Report (1942), which formed a blueprint for the post-war welfare state and had an influence far beyond the United Kingdom. It examines the key elements of the Beveridge plan, which was based largely around a scheme of insurance-based benefits, and discusses the plan's implementation. It seeks to explain the influence of Beveridge's vision of a universal, insurance-based welfare system on the subsequent development of social security, and charts the gradual shift in the complexion of the social security system from being primarily insurance-based to placing an increasing emphasis on means-tested benefits to provide for basic subsistence needs.

2. THE BEVERIDGE REPORT

A. Introduction

Much has been written about the significance of the Beveridge Report[1] and the principles it espoused. As Glennester and Evans state, the report is today viewed as 'a unique statement of principle largely removed from its time and place'.[2] Beveridge's universalist vision was never fully translated into a practical reality,[3] but the report still provides a reference point for many analyses of the welfare state and social security in Britain, mainly because of the ideals which it embodied. Moreover, despite various benefit reforms over the years, and a progressive divergence from Beveridge's principle of comprehensive insurance protection, the British social security system continues to be based around the basic structures proposed in the report. As Alcock

---

[1] W. Beveridge, *Social Insurance and Allied Services*, Cmd 6404 (the Beveridge Report) (1942).
[2] H. Glennester and M. Evans, 'Beveridge and his Assumptive Worlds: The Incompatibilities of a Flawed Design', in J. Hills, J. Ditch, and H. Glennester (eds), *Beveridge and Social Security: An International Retrospective* (Oxford: Clarendon Press, 1994), 56–72, at 56.
[3] See R. Lowe, 'A Prophet Dishonoured in his Own Country? The Rejection of Beveridge in Britain, 1945–1970', in Hills, Ditch, and Glennester (eds), op. cit., 118–33.

comments, 'the broad labour-market insurance principle, supplemented by a means-tested safety net, are still the bases of entitlement to most social security benefits'.[4]

Although much of the Beveridge Report is concerned with matters of technical detail, especially as regards insurance benefits, it also refers to matters of principle—both the principles which guided Beveridge's general approach and those on which the detailed recommendations themselves were premised. Some were ideas that Beveridge had been developing over the previous thirty years, such as those relating to the role of insurance. Others were 'radical innovations that reflected the heightened consciousness of social change and social solidarity induced in Beveridge by the Second World War',[5] such as the principle of 'comprehensiveness' of coverage (with regard to both persons and needs).[6] Beveridge's conceptual and visionary approach was consistent with the mood of the times, expressing as well as contributing to 'the essential universalist spirit of war-time'.[7] The statements of principle that were put forward, such as 'freedom from want' ('Want' being one of the five 'giant' evils on the 'road to reconstruction', the others being Disease, Ignorance, Squalor and Idleness),[8] captured the public imagination and helped to make the report into a best-seller: more than half a million copies were sold, with 50,000 being sold in the United States within six months. At first, however, the report drew a cautious response from Churchill who did not want to bind his successor to reforms, when the economic conditions under which they would take place were as yet unpredictable. In 1944, however, Government plans were published (in white papers); implementation of the reforms (or at least a majority of them) occurred between 1945 and 1948 under Attlee's Labour Government.

Beveridge's plan proposed three complementary methods of security: (i) 'social insurance', which involved cash payments conditional upon a record of compulsory contributions; (ii) 'national assistance', also involving cash payments, but based on need at the date of claim; and (iii) voluntary insurance, which would enable the individual to exercise choice, would provide a higher standard of cover, and was to be encouraged by the state.[9] The Beveridge Report clearly incorporated both 'exchange' and 'unilateral' systems of welfare.[10] The former recognises that provision of welfare is part of a reciprocal or exchange relationship between the provider and recipient, under which they each have what represents a contractual obligation: one provides welfare while the other pays for it through his or her record of contributions. The latter, the unilateral system, involves a straight transference of resources to the individual from the state, although subject to conditions and restrictions (based on a test of need, but with the level of social protection being politically determined).

---

[4] P. Alcock, *Understanding Poverty,* 2nd edn. (Houndmills: Macmillan, 1997), 217.
[5] J. Harris, *William Beveridge: A Biography* (Oxford: Oxford University Press, 1977), 417.
[6] Beveridge Report (1942), para. 308.
[7] D. Fraser, *The Evolution of the British Welfare State,* 2nd edn. (Houndmills: Macmillan, 1984), 214.
[8] Beveridge Report (1942), para. 8.   [9] Ibid., para. 302.
[10] For a clear and well illustrated explanation of these concepts, see A. I. Ogus, 'Great Britain', in P. A. Kohler, F. Zacker and M. Partington (eds), *The Evolution of Social Insurance 1881–1981* (London: Frances Pinter, 1982), 232–6.

Beveridge's plans for insurance benefits, national assistance, and family allowances are discussed below. The Beveridge Report is also referred to in several later chapters when discussing various welfare benefits, hence the need for background here. Beveridge also covered industrial injuries benefits; his plans for them are more conveniently dealt with in Chapter 15, by Stephen Jones.

B. Insurance

Looking at the role played by the social security system today, and the prevalence of income-related and other non-contributory benefits, it is hard to appreciate the centrality of insurance to the Beveridge plan in 1942, which stated that the social insurance scheme was 'designed of itself when in full operation to guarantee the income needed for subsistence in all normal cases'.[11]

Under the Beveridge proposals, social insurance was to be based on six principles:[12]

(1) a flat rate of subsistence benefit (an exception to this principle would be made only where prolonged disability had resulted from industrial accident or disease);

(2) a flat rate of contribution (so that all insured persons 'whether rich or poor' would pay the same amount);

(3) unification of administrative responsibility;

(4) adequacy of benefit (this not only referred to a level of benefit which would meet subsistence needs but also included a proposal that benefit should be of unlimited duration without a means-test, which was not subsequently acted upon);

(5) comprehensiveness (in respect both of the person and the risks and needs to be covered);

(6) classification (to reflect 'the different circumstances of each of these classes and . . . many varieties of need and circumstance within each insurance class'[13]; Beveridge distinguished between full-time employment, self-employment and unpaid work as a 'housewife').

Social insurance benefits to be provided were to include unemployment benefit (of unlimited duration), disability benefit (for those physically incapable of work)[14], benefits in respect of industrial accident and disease (including industrial pension), training benefit (for people who needed to find 'a new means of livelihood'), funeral grant, maternity grant, maternity benefit, compulsory retirement pension, widow's benefit, and temporary separation benefit (for women whose marriage ended other than by widowhood).[15]

As noted above, Beveridge favoured a flat rate of contribution (although he set men's contributions higher than women's because men were expected also to meet

[11] Beveridge Report (1942), para. 23.   [12] Ibid., paras 303–9.   [13] Ibid., paras 303–9.
[14] There was no mention of mental incapacity here.
[15] This recommendation was not acted upon: see p. 262 below.

part of the benefit paid to housewives).[16] There would be no variation on account of income or, for the most part, the degree of risk affecting particular individuals or particular forms of employment. It is this lack of necessity for social insurance to relate contributions to risks that is often said (and was identified by Beveridge)[17] to be one of the key differences between this form of insurance and the private insurance schemes on which it is often said to be modelled.[18] Beveridge argued that public opinion favoured the idea that a compulsory insurance scheme should be based on the principle that individuals should 'stand in on the same terms; none should claim to pay less because he is healthier or has more regular employment'.[19] The flat rate principle accorded with liberal individualist philosophy, since there was no redistribution of wealth between the better off and less well off worker; and it also 'conveniently reflected the notion of social solidarity',[20] in the sense that rich and poor would be treated alike (as also in the rates of benefit each would receive). Beveridge also favoured unification of insurance (ending separate contributions for health (sickness) and unemployment insurance).

Beveridge identified six insurance classes. Employees (those under a contract of service or apprenticeship, irrespective of trade) were in Class I. Others gainfully occupied (essentially the self-employed) were in Class II. Class III comprised 'housewives' (married women of working age living with their husbands, who, if they worked, could contribute into Class I or II, as appropriate, or claim exemption from contributing, which meant that the only benefit they would be eligible for would be maternity benefit)[21]. Class IV comprised 'others of working age' (students aged over sixteen, unmarried women performing domestic duties without pay, persons of private means, and disabled people who did not qualify for benefit under the social insurance scheme). Young people who were below the age of sixteen comprised Class V. Those who worked beyond retirement age fell into Class VI. In some cases exemptions applied. For example, those in Classes II or IV who earned less than £75 per annum were to be exempt.[22] Those in Class I who were unemployed were to be 'excused' payment of contributions but were to be credited with them.[23]

The rates of contribution differed between many of the classes, where appropriate, in furtherance of Beveridge's belief that the system should reflect groups' different financial circumstances and their needs. In this regard he also proposed lower rates of contribution for eighteen to twenty and sixteen to seventeen-year-old contributors and recommended that the practicality of introducing regional variations in contribution and benefit rates should be explored.[24] In fact, although the National Insurance Act 1946[25] provided for men and women aged under eighteen to pay a lower contribution (with men always paying more than women) there was no departure from a single, national rate of employee's contribution in each class. Although

[16] Beveridge Report (1942), para. 357.   [17] Ibid., para 24.   [18] Ogus, n. 10 above, 222.
[19] Beveridge Report (1942), para. 26.   [20] Ogus, n. 10 above, 223.
[21] Beveridge Report (1942), para. 357.   [22] Ibid., para. 363.   [23] Ibid., para. 364.
[24] Ibid., para. 408.   [25] 1st Schedule, parts I–V.

Beveridge was attracted to a flat rate of benefit because of its simplicity and the fact that it would leave scope for voluntary additional provision,[26] he believed that the possibility of increasing the employer's contribution in cases where the employee's earnings were below a certain level should be explored. This suggestion was incorporated into the 1946 Act.[27]

The rationale for employers' contributions was based on the benefit to employers of the general improvement and discipline of their workers.[28] Beveridge argued that employers' contributions ought to be seen as 'an addition to wages', representing just a small extra element in the costs of production which was worthwhile in ensuring that the workforce was provided with security and maintenance during periods of unemployment or sickness and in giving the employer a real stake in the future of the social insurance scheme, which could be articulated through representations to the scheme's organisers.[29] Employers and employees paid the same rate of contribution until the National Insurance Act 1946 set employers' contributions at a lower rate.

Individual entitlement to insurance benefit, which Beveridge wanted to be of unlimited duration,[30] would depend on meeting the required contribution conditions. Beveridge concluded that, as with the unemployment insurance scheme before it, there should be an initial qualifying contributions test. For most benefits, twenty-six actual weekly contributions would have to have been paid, although no such test would apply to widow's or guardian's benefits.[31] To qualify for full benefit, the claimant would also need to have paid or been credited with forty-eight contributions in the preceding contribution year.[32] The intention behind the contribution conditions was both financial—to ensure that claimants had paid in a reasonable amount before drawing on the Insurance Fund, thereby helping to ensure that the Fund remained at adequate levels—and the more symbolic notion of 'contract' or reciprocity, bringing social insurance and private schemes into parallel. The contribution conditions for full benefit recommended by Beveridge were more strict than those which applied under the unemployment insurance scheme at the time (see Chapter 3 above), in part because benefit was going to be of unlimited duration. However, account would be taken of credited contributions, for which the pre-war schemes made no provision.

Despite the emphasis on universal, comprehensive benefits, Beveridge thought it undesirable to raise the level of benefits beyond the minimum, in case the incentive to work be undermined. He argued that flat rate contributions would open the door to flat rate benefits, although the individual would be able to make additional private

---

[26] Beveridge Report (1942), para. 307.   [27] 1st Schedule, parts I–V.
[28] Ogus, n. 10 above, 187.   [29] Beveridge Report (1942), para. 276.
[30] Ibid., para. 23. It was felt to be undesirable in principle to subject the genuinely unemployed and insured worker to a means-test after a certain period: para. 130. Accordingly, unemployment benefit was to be of unlimited duration, although some safeguards were necessary lest 'men . . . settle down to' life on benefits: ibid. The recommendations included attendance at a work or training centre for six months, in the case of adults (para. 131), a reform which was subsequently dismissed as impracticable.
[31] Ibid., para. 366.   [32] Ibid., para. 367.

provision if he or she could afford it. Work incentives would be encouraged not only by preserving the gap between subsistence benefits and wages (Beveridge in fact favoured a minimum wage which would reinforce this), but also by discouraging idleness through benefit disincentives (such as disqualification for voluntary unemployment, as under the existing unemployment insurance scheme) and a requirement (not in fact introduced until the late 1980s) to attend a course of training as a condition of receipt of benefit.[33] For young people, benefit was to be conditional on training right from the start.[34] Thus the emphasis Beveridge had many years earlier[35] placed on the need for both juvenile employment exchanges to co-ordinate training and work placement to avoid idleness and waste of abilities, reappears in this section of the Report.

Beveridge also gave serious consideration to retirement pensions,[36] for which separate contribution conditions were proposed.[37] It was clear that not everyone needed to draw a pension at the age of sixty or sixty-five,[38] and Beveridge considered that those still in employment should manage on their own resources (a decision primarily motivated by the need to keep the overall cost of the pension scheme within affordable limits).[39] To encourage people to carry on working beyond retirement age,[40] Beveridge proposed additional increments to the pension eventually paid to those who postponed their retirement, and an earnings rule designed to permit retired people to undertake a limited amount of paid employment without losing pension rights. These rules would apply during the first five years after retirement age. From the National Insurance Act 1946, which introduced most of Beveridge's pension proposals, until the late 1950s, flat rate contributory pensions formed the basis of benefit payments in retirement. The cost of supporting with a worthwhile pension an increasing number of people led to the introduction of earnings-related contributions in 1961. The development of pensions after Beveridge is discussed further below.

As noted above, benefits in respect of maternity were also part of the Beveridge plan for social insurance.[41] The plan envisaged the payment of a 'maternity grant' to all married women, whether gainfully employed or not, plus a separate 'maternity benefit', paid for thirteen weeks, for those who were gainfully employed but had

---

[33] See n. 30 above.   [34] Beveridge Report (1942), para. 131(ii).

[35] W. Beveridge, *Unemployment: A Problem of Industry* (London: Longmans, 1930), 211–16.

[36] For discussion, see generally, J. Creedy and R. Disney, *Social Insurance in Transition* (Oxford: Clarendon Press, 1985), chs 2 and 3.

[37] To qualify for the full pension, the claimant would have to have paid or been credited with an *average* of at least 48 contributions each year throughout his working life since the introduction of the scheme: Beveridge Report (1942), para. 367.

[38] Beveridge retained the discrepancy, which the Old Age and Widows' Pensions Act 1940 created, between the ages at which men and women qualified for a pension.

[39] Beveridge Report (1942), para. 236. The Labour Government of 1945–51 rejected Beveridge's plan for full pensions to be phased in over 20 years, preferring them to be provided immediately.

[40] See para. 245.

[41] Beveridge Report (1942), para. 341. A maternity grant had been paid under the National Insurance Act 1911, provided the wife or her husband were insured.

given up their employment during that period. The maternity *grant* was not intended to cover the whole cost of maternity (the Report explicitly stated that such cost 'has a reasonable and natural claim upon the husband's earnings'),[42] but was to be raised above the level of the grant in payment at the time. The maternity *benefit* was intended to provide an incentive for women to relinquish employment while expecting their child, and so it was to be paid at a higher rate than unemployment or disability benefit. The proposals were part of the package of incentives for marriage and motherhood put forward by Beveridge, who shared in a common concern about the effects of the declining birth-rate in the 1930s.[43]

Beveridge also made provision for widow's benefits, on the basis that widowhood was a contingency arising from 'one of the economic risks of marriage . . . the possibility that the marriage might end prematurely through the death of the husband'.[44] Prior to the Beveridge Report, widows had received a flat rate pension irrespective of age and whether or not they had dependent children, unless and until marriage or deemed cohabitation. Entitlement was based on the record of contributions of the widow's late husband.[45] At first widows only benefited if they were aged over sixty-five; this age threshold was later reduced to sixty and then fifty-five. Critics of the previous widow's pension could point to the fact that because it was paid to the widow irrespective of whether she had children, widows without dependent children might receive support that was unnecessary, in the sense that employment could be obtained. At the same time, the low rate of the flat rate pension disadvantaged widows with large families. According to Beveridge, the widow's pension was therefore 'inadequate in many cases and superfluous in other cases', and it took 'no account of real needs'.[46] Beveridge therefore proposed that widows should receive widow's benefit at a rate 50 per cent higher than unemployment and disability benefit for thirteen weeks, to facilitate adjustment to new circumstances; but thereafter, the widow would only receive subsistence level benefit (to be called 'guardian benefit') if there were dependent children, and the amount paid would be adjusted to take account of actual earnings.[47] Those aged sixty or over would qualify for retirement pension, if their late husband's contributions record was sufficient. All widows would be encouraged to train for employment through the provision of a training benefit paid while training was undertaken. After training, those without dependent children would become 'liable to work and contribute as a single woman', unless unable to take up work due to 'permanent disability'.[48]

The implementation of Beveridge's proposals on insurance benefits is discussed

---

[42] Para. 341.

[43] N. Timmins, *The Five Giants. A Biography of the Welfare State* (London: Harper Collins, 1995), 55. Timmins points out that, unknown to Beveridge, the birth-rate had by that time begun to rise.

[44] Cited in H. Glennester and M. Evans, 'Beveridge and his Assumptive Worlds: The Incompatibilities of a Flawed Design', in J. Hills, J. Ditch, and H. Glennester, *Beveridge and Social Security: An International Retrospective* (Oxford: Clarendon Press, 1994), 56–72, 68.

[45] Widows', Orphans' and Old Age Contributory Pensions Act 1925.

[46] Beveridge Report (1942), para. 153.   [47] Ibid. and para. 346.

[48] Ibid., para. 346 and Appendix A, para. 4.

further below. It will be seen that although several of Beveridge's principles were subsequently abandoned (flat rate contributions and benefits had all but disappeared by 1966) and insurance benefits were considerably eroded, the chief characteristics of the insurance scheme continued to be reflected in the benefits system.

C. National Assistance

As noted above, the Beveridge Report also contained recommendations on 'National Assistance', which was to be 'available to meet all needs which are not covered by insurance'.[49] Administration (within the new Ministry of Social Security) would replace the Poor Law and remaining local administered assistance.[50] National assistance was designed to maintain subsistence levels 'but it must be felt to be something less desirable than insurance benefit; otherwise the insured persons get nothing for their contributions'.[51] Accordingly, the Report proposed that assistance should always be subject to 'proof of needs and examination of means'.[52] Beveridge assumed that assistance would have only limited scope because the needs caused by unemployment would be met by an extension of unemployment insurance. Subsequently, in the Government's white paper in 1944,[53] it was acknowledged that it would not be possible to meet everyone's needs under a flat rate insurance benefit system and that the minority whose subsistence needs would not be met would require means-tested national assistance. When the national assistance scheme came into operation in 1948, under the National Assistance Act 1948, 675,000 insurance claimants sought this means-tested benefit to top up their benefit levels.[54]

D. Family Allowances

The third element of the social security scheme envisaged by Beveridge was family allowances, which involved a universal payment to those with child dependants (see below). Beveridge had become interested in the concept of family allowances in the 1920s. Although there was, at that time, resistance from many quarters to such payments, on the basis that they would undermine traditional notions of family responsibility,[55] the campaign for family allowances was gaining momentum. There was increasing recognition of the scale of family poverty and the fact that it was considerably worse in large families. The poverty surveys of Rowntree in York and the Pilgrim Trust in Liverpool, revealing the extent of poverty suffered by young children in particular, reinforced the convictions of the leading campaigner, Eleanor

---

[49] Beveridge Report (1942), para. 369.   [50] Ibid., paras 161–5.   [51] Ibid., para. 369.
[52] Ibid.
[53] Minister of Reconstruction, *Social Insurance, Part I*, Cmd 6550 (London: HMSO), para. 13.
[54] R. Lowe, 'A Prophet Dishonoured in his Own Country? The Rejection of Beveridge in Britain, 1945–1970', in J. Hills et al., n. 44 above, 118–33, 121.
[55] See V. George, *Social Security and Society* (London: Routledge and Kegan Paul, 1973), 125.

Rathbone, and her supporters.[56] Already there had been some recognition, in the form of state support, of the needs arising from responsibility for children—for example through the introduction of dependants' allowances in unemployment benefit (in 1921–2) (see Chapter 3) and the provision (from 1906) of free school meals. Land has commented, in relation to dependency additions, that 'the existence of a large group of men who received an income from the State which took account of their family size considerably strengthened the case for family allowances to be paid irrespective of the employment status of the parents'.[57]

Beveridge was impressed by Rathbone's *The Disinherited Family* (1924) and later claimed that it had 'converted' him to the cause of family allowances.[58] He became a member of the Family Endowment Society, as political and intellectual support for the movement grew. While Beveridge shared Rathbone's concern for family poverty, his motives in lending his support to the movement for family allowances were nevertheless wider than hers, being concerned also with the opportunity to arrest the decline in the birth-rate (as noted above) and to depress wage levels.[59] In 1924 Beveridge put forward proposals to the Family Endowment Council for a scheme of family allowances based on contributory insurance.[60] But there was disagreement about the most appropriate kind of scheme.[61] The 1930s are said to have been 'years of disappointment for the Family Endowment Society, in which the promise of the previous decade was not fulfilled'.[62] But by early 1943 the Government had committed itself to a national family allowances scheme.

The Beveridge Report presented three main arguments in support of a system of family allowances. First, they could guarantee a family a reasonable level of subsistence by taking account of the size of the family, unlike wages.[63] Secondly, by paying allowances regardless of whether the breadwinner was in or out of work, the differential between wages and benefits was not allowed to diminish to such an extent that work incentives would disappear.[64] Thirdly, the allowances could help to improve the birth rate 'both by making it possible for parents to bring [children] into the world without damaging the chances of those already born, and as a signal of the national interest in children, setting the tone of public opinion'.[65] Beveridge recommended a flat rate of eight shillings per child per week, but left the door open for future grading of allowances according to the child's age.[66] This figure was based on the cost of

---

[56] J. Macnicol, 'Family Allowances and Less Eligibility', in P. Thane (ed.), *The Origins of British Social Policy* (London: Croom Helm, 1978), 174.

[57] H. Land, 'The Introduction of Family Allowances', in Hall et al., *Change, Choice and Conflict in Social Policy* (London: Heinemann, 1975), 163–4.

[58] J. Harris, *William Beveridge: A Biography* (Oxford: Oxford University Press, 1977), 343.

[59] Ibid.   [60] Ibid., 344.   [61] Land, n. 57 above, 178.

[62] J. Macnicol, *The Movement for Family Allowances 1918–1945* (London: Heinemann, 1980), 36.

[63] Beveridge Report (1942), para. 411.

[64] Ibid., para. 412.

[65] Ibid., para. 413. As noted in Chapter 2, George doubts that the availability of a weekly child allowance can have this simple effect: V. George, *Social Security and Society* (London: Routledge and Kegan Paul, 1973), 126.

[66] Beveridge Report (1942), para. 421.

maintaining a child which, on post-1939 cost of living figures, amounted to nine shillings per week, but with downward adjustment by one shilling in respect of services provided by the state.[67]

The principle of parental responsibility was acknowledged by Beveridge in his recommendation that nothing should be paid for the first child of the family.[68] However, according to Land, it was the saving which Beveridge felt compelled to make (£100 million according to Beveridge's own estimate) which was the chief cause of this restriction: 'If Beveridge wanted his scheme to be accepted by the Government he had no alternative but to limit its scope by excluding from it the first child in every family.'[69] Thus Beveridge's talk of parental responsibilities was little more than a 'convenient rationalisation'.[70] There had been no prior suggestion that family allowances should be so limited (apart from Conservative proposals, on the grounds of economy, in the late 1930s). Moreover, no other social security allowances for dependants at this time excluded the first child. However, Beveridge did propose payment of an allowance for the first child where families were in receipt of a pension or other social security benefits.[71] Child tax allowances were to be retained. Family allowance was to be paid up to the age of sixteen or until the child left full-time education (if sooner).[72]

The rate of eight shillings per week which Beveridge proposed for family allowance was broadly comparable with the amounts available under unemployment assistance and unemployment insurance,[73] taking account of the fact that family allowance would not be payable for the first child. The Government, in response, proposed a figure of five shillings, referring to an anticipated expansion of services in kind, notably school meals and milk.[74] However, Macnicol notes a 'discrepancy between the private and public reasons' for cutting the allowance rate and claims that 'it is likely that the real reason was related to the general decision to abandon the Beveridge principle of providing subsistence benefits'.[75]

E. The Beveridge Report: Some General Conclusions

Much of the analysis of the Beveridge Report in recent years has been focused more on the principles and underlying assumptions reflected in its proposals than on the detail of his scheme. This is understandable, because the search for a way to re-formulate social security in Britain in the 1990s has concentrated on visionary and broad-ranging approaches. Glennester and Evans comment that Beveridge's 'sense of vision, his attempt to think on a large scale despite opposition . . . seems as necessary now as it was fifty years ago in a very different world'.[76]

---

[67] Ibid., para. 232.   [68] Ibid., para. 417.   [69] Land, n. 57 above, 201–2.   [70] Ibid., 202.
[71] Beveridge Report (1942), para. 419.
[72] Ibid., para. 423. The minimum school leaving age was not raised from 14 to 15 until 1947.
[73] Ibid., Table XXII.   [74] Macnicol, n. 62 above, 194.   [75] Ibid.
[76] H. Glennester and M. Evans, 'Beveridge and his Assumptive Worlds: The Incompatibilities of a Flawed Design', in J. Hills et al., *Beveridge and Social Security: An International Retrospective* (Oxford: Clarendon Press, 1994), 56–72, 71.

Beveridge's plan is evaluated at various points in this book, often when highlighting the ways in which his universalist vision of social insurance failed to be realised. In addition, reference is made to deficiencies in Beveridge's assumptions about the position of women in the family and the workforce (see in particular Chapter 9 by Gillian Douglas) and concerning the likelihood of full employment. Furthermore, Beveridge's expectation that an insurance-based scheme could cater for all the various circumstances of need was unrealistic. His insistence that a national housing element in respect of 'average' rather than actual rents should prevail as the only administratively practicable method of meeting housing costs,[77] and his reluctance to depart from the notion of a flat rate scheme, 'greatly weakened his claim that the rates of National Insurance benefits should be sufficient for "all normal" subsistence needs'.[78] Rather, as things turned out, the subsequent prevalence of unemployment, especially long-term unemployment, meant that assistance-based schemes, only briefly discussed by Beveridge (in the form of 'national assistance'), were to acquire perhaps greater social importance. Nevertheless, the role of insurance and of a possible way 'Back to Beveridge' has continued to assume a central position in debates about the future of social security.[79]

3. THE POST-SECOND WORLD WAR DEVELOPMENT OF SOCIAL SECURITY: THE DECLINE OF INSURANCE AND THE GROWTH OF MEANS-TESTING

A. Insurance Benefits (other than Old Age Pensions and Widow's Benefits)

Not all of Beveridge's recommendations were carried through into the National Insurance Act 1946. In particular, as noted above, the Labour Government did not accept his recommendation that payment of unemployment benefit should be of unlimited duration—a period of entitlement was therefore limited to six months—and appeared not to accept that social insurance should necessarily meet subsistence needs. Indeed, in setting benefit rates the Government made insufficient allowance for inflation, the rate of which had increased significantly on the pre-war level.[80] Moreover, although the Act gave effect to Beveridge's proposals for children's allowances to be paid for the only or eldest child where the parent was in receipt of unemployment or disability benefit or industrial pension or was a widow,[81] the allowance was set at seven shillings and sixpence rather than the eight shillings

---

[77] Beveridge Report (1942), paras 197–216.

[78] B. Jordan, 'Want', (1991) 25(1) *Social Policy and Administration* 14–26, at 19.

[79] See, for example, A. W. Dilnot, J. A. Kay, and C. N. Morris, *The Reform of Social Security* (Oxford: Clarendon Press/IFS, 1984); J. Creedy and R. Disney, *Social Insurance in Transition* (Oxford: Clarendon Press, 1985); Commission on Social Justice, *Social Justice: Strategies for National Renewal* (London: Vintage, 1994); F. Field, *Making Welfare Work* (London: IEA, 1995) and (idem.) *Stakeholder Welfare* (London: IEA, 1995).

[80] B. Jordan, n. 78 above.

[81] Beveridge Report (1942), Annex A, para. 6. See s. 23(1) of the 1946 Act.

recommended by Beveridge. In respect of other children of the family, the family allowance of five shillings per week (rather than the eight shillings recommended by Beveridge) was to be paid (see below).

The low rate of child allowances and the failure to guarantee subsistence level support overall, coupled with the fact that national insurance rent allowances were based quite unrealistically on a national figure rather than on local rents, meant that increasing numbers of claimants became dependent on supplementation of income via national assistance payments. The numbers rose from approximately 130,000 to 220,000 between July 1948 and December 1950 and the proportion of recipients of unemployment benefit requiring national assistance rose from 11 to 18 per cent over the same period.[82] Tomlinson comments that despite its commitment to the insurance principle, the post-war Government 'erected a welfare system which only delivered the long-proclaimed goal of a national minimum by underpinning the insurance system with a rapidly expanding National Assistance safety net'.[83]

Although the most obvious explanation for this increasing reliance on national assistance was that flat rate national insurance payments were incapable of meeting all claimants' needs, the Government diagnosed the problem as being due, to a large extent, to the lack of child dependency additions for second and subsequent children.[84] Child additions for second and subsequent children were introduced, although payable at a lower rate than for the first child, from 1951. The rates were equalised in 1952. The increased rates caused attention to be focused on the wage/benefit gap, to which the Government's response was to hold down the rate of child dependency additions. Under the Child Benefit Act 1975, child benefit was payable for the first and later children in place of family allowance. Entitlement to the child dependency additions to insurance benefits became harnessed to this benefit, a fact which was used to justify reductions in their value. Indeed, the practice adopted after 1979 of increasing the child dependency addition first and then deducting the increase in child benefit meant that 'the Government . . . cheated parents on "short-term" national insurance benefits out of 65p for each child'.[85] By November 1981 child benefit and child dependency additions combined were worth only 87 per cent of their 1979 value, and the SSAC noted that the principal effect of this drop in value was 'to weaken the role of the contributory benefits by increasing dependence on supplementary benefit'.[86] Child dependency additions were abolished in respect of most claimants in November 1984,[87] by which time their value had fallen to 15 pence per week. The objective was primarily to ensure that state child support for families in and out of work was provided on an 'even-handed' basis.

---

[82] National Assistance Board, *Annual Report 1951* (London: HMSO, 1951).

[83] J. Tomlinson, 'Why so Austere? The British Welfare State of the 1940s' (1998) 27(1) *J. of Social Policy*, 63–77, 75.

[84] See T. Lynes, *National Assistance and National Prosperity* (The Codicote Press: Welwyn, Herts, 1962).

[85] R. Lister, *Moving Back to the Means-test* (London: Child Poverty Action Group, 1980), 15.

[86] SSAC, *First Report* (London: HMSO, 1982), para. 3.30.

[87] Health and Social Security Act 1984, s. 13 and Sched. 5.

The contribution-based scheme of flat rate national insurance benefits continued under the National Insurance Act 1965. Many features were preserved, including the three waiting days before benefit would be payable, the conditions relating to unemployment benefit, such as availability for employment, and possible disqualification from benefit if dismissed from employment through misconduct.[88] But the Labour Party had committed itself to the reform of national insurance benefits. Although the promised raising of national insurance benefits (and abolition of national assistance) did not materialise, Wilson's Labour Government created an earnings-related supplement (ERS) to sickness and unemployment benefits, to be covered by additional graduated contributions. The ERS was introduced in October 1966.[89] It was, however, abolished in 1982 on the grounds of cost, at a time when unemployment had reached unprecedented levels.[90] Other changes after 1965 included amendment, in 1973 and 1975, of the rules relating to contributions; these were incorporated into the Social Security Act 1975.[91] There were further reforms to contributions (including a tightening up of conditions under the Social Security Act 1988)[92] before the scheme in the 1975 Act was consolidated in the Social Security Contributions and Benefits Act 1992.[93]

It was clear by the mid-1970s that a substantial number of people who became unemployed, considerably more than the residual category envisaged by Beveridge, were not being helped by the insurance scheme. The Supplementary Benefits Commission reported in 1977 that almost 'almost two-fifths . . . were entitled to no unemployment insurance benefit when they first became unemployed'.[94] The Commission also commented that: 'The national insurance scheme, at present levels of unemployment, has clearly failed in its original purpose of being the main source of help for people unable to find work.'[95] In 1980 the Treasury supplement to the insurance scheme was cut from 18 to 11 per cent, although financed in part by increases in contributions. A further weakening of the insurance principle occurred with the tightening up of the disqualification rules (the maximum period of disqualification was increased to thirteen weeks in 1983 and then to twenty-six weeks in 1986); and full-time students' entitlement was drastically curtailed.[96] The abolition of ERS in 1982 and child dependency additions (except for claimants of pensionable age or older) in 1984, and the tightening up of contribution conditions in the late 1980s, have already been mentioned.

Turning now to insurance in respect of incapacity for work as a result of sickness, the Beveridge reforms introduced under the National Insurance Act 1946 had

[88] See Chapter 10 below.   [89] National Insurance Act 1966.

[90] Ogus, Barendt, and Wikeley (1995), 76.

[91] These included new categories of contributions, such as the new Class 3 voluntary contributions (these only provided entitlement to widow's benefit or retirement pensions).

[92] See N. Wikeley, 'Training, Targeting and Tidying Up: The Social Security Act 1988' (1989) *J.S.W.L.* 277–92, 283.

[93] The current contributions system is mapped out in Chapter 6.

[94] Supplementary Benefits Commission, *Annual Report 1977* (London: HMSO, 1978), para. 7.10.

[95] Ibid., para. 7.9.   [96] See Chapter 11.

provided for a scheme of sickness benefits under which benefits in respect of such incapacity (at that time confined to physical capacity)[97] would be of potentially unlimited duration—or, at least, until the claimant was of pensionable age. Obviously, entitlement was dependent on meeting contribution conditions, which, under the National Insurance Act 1946, were more severe once the claimant had been in receipt of benefit for twelve months. Sickness benefit continued to be flat rate, in line with Beveridge's plan, until the introduction of an earnings-related supplement (paid for the first twenty-six weeks of incapacity for work) in 1966. As noted above, the supplement was abolished in 1982. The *long-term* sick were entitled, from 1971, to invalidity benefit—a flat rate 'pension' with an addition related to the age at the onset of incapacity. Invalidity benefit, which later became taxable, was paid, in place of sickness benefit, to those who had been in receipt of sickness benefit for six months. Under the Social Security and Housing Benefits Act 1982, statutory sick pay, a scheme intended to be administered by individual employers, replaced sickness benefit for a majority of workers; until the Statutory Sick Pay Act 1994 employers could claim reimbursement of a proportion of the cost from contributions liability. Meanwhile, for those who failed to meet the requisite contribution conditions but were incapable of work, the non-contributory invalidity pension (NCIP) was available, having been introduced by the Labour Government in 1975. The housewives' version of this benefit ((H)NCIP), however, discriminated against married and cohabiting women, for in order to qualify for it they had also to be unable to perform 'normal household duties'. The (H)NCIP was abolished in 1984 and in effect replaced by severe disablement allowance (SDA).[98]

As far as maternity benefits were concerned, these had been reformed in line with Beveridge's proposals under the National Insurance Act 1946. Maternity grant, which was flat rate, was intended to cover all confinement and post-confinement expenditure. By the 1970s it was still only £25.[99] Subsequent attempts to increase it were resisted.[100] As noted in Chapter 5 (below), it was abolished in 1987.[101] More

---

[97] Beveridge Report (1942), para. 330.

[98] For the background to the replacement of the NCIP (including the housewives' version) with the SDA, see L. Luckhaus, 'Severe Disablement Allowance: The Old Dressed up as New' [1986] *J.S.W.L.* 153–69 and Ogus, Barendt, and Wikeley (1995), 170–1. Given the fact that many (some 16,000) were expected to lose out as a result of the reform, transitional arrangements were introduced enabling those who had been entitled to NCIP to be eligible for SDA for so long as they were unable to work. But these arrangements did not eliminate the discrimination which had been present in the NCIP, and the arrangements were held to be in breach of the EC Equal Treatment Directive (79/7/EEC) (*Clarke v Chief Adjudication Officer* [1987] 3 CMLR 277). The European Court of Justice also held (*Drake v Chief Adjudication Officer* [1985] QB 166; [1986] 3 All ER 65) that the exclusion of married women from the invalid care allowance (ICA) was discrimination which breached the Directive. The ICA (see Chapter 12) had been introduced in 1976 to compensate (but on a flat rate basis) for lost income for those who had given up work to provide care for a disabled relative on a more or less whole-time basis. The discriminatory element was removed by the SSA 1986, s. 37.

[99] SSA 1975, s. 21.

[100] For example, the Black report on health inequalities in 1980 recommended raising it to £100, in order to put it at its 1948 value: N. Timmins, *The Five Giants. A Biography of the Welfare State* (London: Harper Collins, 1995), 379.   [101] SSA 1986, s. 38.

importantly, as far as insurance is concerned, the 1946 Act also provided for a maternity allowance, based on the woman's contributions alone, as a basic income replacement benefit. Under the Social Security Act 1975, the maternity allowance was paid for eighteen weeks, beginning with the eleventh week before the expected week of confinement. The Employment Protection Act 1975 introduced a right to statutory maternity pay (paid by employers for six weeks and calculated as nine-tenths of normal pay, minus the amount of the maternity allowance). However, following a review by the DHSS in 1980 and a further consideration via the 1985 social security white paper, maternity allowance was replaced, so far as the majority of cases were concerned, by statutory maternity pay (SMP), under the Social Security Act 1986 (see Chapter 5). The onus was shifted to employers to administer the scheme. Although employers could reclaim the full cost of SMP from their contributions liability, it was reduced to 92 per cent from 1994. Current provision is discussed by Gillian Douglas in Chapter 9.

In the light of these and other changes to national insurance (such as the abolition of statutory indexation of insurance benefit rates and the introduction of taxation on benefits), the central role of insurance benefits has increasingly been undermined.[102] Moreover, as the discussion in section E shows, there has been a substantial growth in other areas, notably in income-related benefits such as income support, housing benefit and family credit, which has weakened further the central position of the insurance scheme within the social security system. Although the broad divisions of the benefit system set out in the Beveridge plan (above) materialised, and indeed continued to provide the basis of the social security system for the next thirty years,[103] social insurance was never able to provide subsistence level support for the majority of people who needed it. There was a lack of government will to bear the political and economic costs of maintaining adequate support on any kind of actuarial basis as demand increased. Under the Conservatives post-1979 there was an ideological assault on the public sector and a drive to target provision as part of a rationalisation of welfare benefits, which led to an increase in means-testing and a serious erosion of the principles on which insurance was based. Overalll, social insurance has been shown to lack immunity from the changing policy goals of governments and administrators.[104] By 1984 the insurance principle was in serious decline—a decline which has not been arrested. Only a truly fundamental future reform of welfare can restore it to its central position envisaged by Beveridge. The importance and possible future of insurance are discussed further in Chapter 6.

---

[102] See T. Atkinson and J. Micklewright, 'Turning the Screw: Benefits for the Unemployed 1979–88', in A. Dilnot and I. Walker, *The Economics of Social Security* (Oxford: Oxford University Press, 1989), 125–57, and N. Wikeley, 'Unemployment Benefit, the State and the Labour Market' (1989) 16 *J. of Law and Society*, 291–309.

[103] See J. Clarke and M. Langan, 'The British Welfare State: Foundation and Modernisation', in A. Cochrane and J. Clarke, *Comparing Welfare States* (London: Sage, 1993), 19–48.

[104] J. Creedy and R. Disney, *Social Insurance in Transition* (Clarendon Press: Oxford, 1985), 211.

B. Pensions

Flat rate retirement pensions were part of the contributory national insurance scheme implemented by the National Insurance Act 1946. Amongst other things, the Act reflected the gender discrimination in the Beveridge Report's proposals:

Under the 1908 Act [women] had received an old age pension by virtue of citizenship and need; but Beveridge's proposals completed the trend begun in 1925, whereby the technicalities of insurance required that married women be seen as members of a household, eligible by virtue of their husband's contributions . . . .[T]he married woman's pension was rolled up within the joint pension, which, for the first time, was less than double the single rate.[105]

The rate at which retirement pension was paid under the 1946 Act (26 shillings for a single person and 42 shillings for a couple) represented a significant improvement on pre-war rates.[106] Nevertheless, it was not as high as the subsistence-related unemployment and sickness benefits, making it inevitable that pensioners would have to seek means-tested benefit to supplement their incomes. By 1954 over one-quarter of all pensioner households received payments from the National Assistance Board.[107] According to Macnicol, 'the extent of pensioner reliance on assistance supplementation was a major reason for the "rediscovery of poverty" in the 1960s'.[108]

The move away from flat rate pensions and towards pensions which were earnings related began with proposals, implemented in 1961,[109] for graduated pensions, funded by graduated contributions which were optional for employees until 1966.[110] By this time the increasing evidence of pensioner poverty and inequality and the undermining of income levels by the growing problem of economic inflation generated considerable interest in reform. Labour Government proposals in 1969 aimed to improve pension levels, relative to previous low earnings; the level of entitlement was to be based in part on lifetime earnings and adjusted to take account of rises in national wage levels.[111] The incoming Conservative Government in 1970 abandoned these proposals and instead proposed an earnings-related scheme, once again not implemented, despite the passage through Parliament of the necessary legislation.[112]

By the mid 1970s the proportion of the population over retirement age had risen by approximately 45 per cent since the time of the Beveridge Report.[113] Concern about the effects of this demographic change resulted in the financing of pensions

---

[105] J. Macnicol, 'Beveridge and Old Age', in J. Hills, J. Ditch, and H. Glennester, *Beveridge and Social Security: An International Retrospective* (Oxford: Oxford University Press, 1994), 73–96, at 94–5.
[106] The Government had abandoned Beveridge's idea for what tended to be referred to as the 'golden staircase', under which pensions would rise by biennial increments to 24 shillings and 40 shillings respectively.
[107] Macnicol (1994), n. 105 above, 93.   [108] Ibid., 95.
[109] Under the National Insurance Act 1959.   [110] National Insurance Act 1966.
[111] Labour's proposals were set out in *National Superannuation and Social Insurance: Proposals for Earnings-Related Social Security*, Cmnd 3883 (London: HMSO, 1969).
[112] The Conservatives' proposals were contained in a white paper entitled *Strategy for Pensions*, Cmnd 4755 (London: HMSO, 1971) and were enshrined in the SSA 1973.
[113] J. Creedy and R. Disney, *Social Insurance in Transition* (Oxford: Clarendon Press, 1985), 37.

becoming 'the major issue of social insurance policy'.[114] The Labour Government published a white paper in 1974.[115] Legislation followed, introducing, from 1978, the State Earnings-Related Pensions Scheme (SERPS), as well as permitting employees to contract out of the state scheme subject to prescribed conditions.[116] State pensions were thereafter made up of two components: there was a flat rate element (the 'basic component') and an earnings-related element (the 'additional component'). The additional component was calculated as one-quarter of the difference between the value of the insured's pensionable earnings and the basic flat rate pension, but it could be no higher than the upper limit for payment of national insurance contributions. In calculating earnings, the twenty best years of working life were taken into account, with the earnings adjusted to take account of increases in average earnings over the years in question.

It is clear that the introduction of SERPS was something of a leap in the dark. There was 'little experience, either in Britain or the rest of the world, on which to base any detailed analysis of the scheme's implications'.[117] The report on the financial effects of the Pensions Bill provided relatively short-scale projections.[118] Creedy and Disney argue that it was, nevertheless, quite clear from the beginning that there would be a need for substantially increased national insurance contributions.[119] By the early 1980s the overall cost implications of SERPS were giving concern to the Conservative Government. The scheme was discussed in the 1985 Green Paper, which recommended that it should be phased out (see Chapter 5).

C. Widow's Benefits

The National Insurance Act 1946 provided for a contribution-based widow's allowance to be paid for the first thirteen weeks after bereavement. Beveridge's proposed 'guardian benefit' (page 93 above) became widowed mother's allowance. His training benefit did not materialise. Those whose widowhood began after their fiftieth birthday or whose entitlement to widowed mother's allowance ended after they reached the age of forty (later fifty)[120] were eligible for a widow's pension. Provision was gradually extended in the ensuing years, such as via the introduction of child dependency additions in 1956 and, in 1966, the doubling of the entitlement period for widow's allowance (to twenty-six weeks) and the introduction of an earnings-related element.[121]

[114] Ibid.   [115] DHSS, *Better Pensions*, Cmnd 5713 (London: HMSO, 1974).
[116] Social Security Pensions Act 1975. The consent to a contracted-out scheme had to be obtained from the Occupational Pensions Board: SSA 1975, s. 30.
[117] Creedy and Disney, n. 113 above, 55.
[118] DHSS, *Social Security Bill 1975, Report by the Government Actuary on the Financial Provisions of the Bill*, Cmnd 5928 (London: HMSO, 1975).
[119] N. 113 above, 55.
[120] But note that a reduced rate in the allowance for those aged 40–49 came into operation in 1970.
[121] This was based on the late husband's recent earnings when in employment: Ogus, Barendt, and Wikeley (1995), 278.

Widow's benefits were brought within the remit of the Fowler reviews of 1984–5, when there was a drive to target those widows in the greatest need—those with children and older widows who, if not in employment, faced the greatest difficulty in making the transition to employed status—while cutting back provision made to others (see Chapter 5 below).

D. Family Allowances

The scheme of allowances introduced under the Family Allowances Act 1945 was less generous than Beveridge had proposed. As noted above, the Government set the rate at five shillings per week instead of eight shillings proposed by Beveridge. Land says that the lack of commitment to the standard proposed by Beveridge seriously weakened the overall benefits and long-term significance of the reform:

Family Allowances, described by the Chancellor of the Exchequer only three years before as 'the basic social service payment for children', had been reduced in scope to no more than 'ease the financial burden which at the present time oppresses parents with large families'. In the circumstances (and with the advantage of hindsight), it is difficult to believe that the Act was 'an Act of historic justice to the family' [as *The Times* had described it].[122]

The justification for Land's view lies in the fact that the Act was passed in isolation from the other social security reforms consequent on the Beveridge Report, that school meals and milk (which, as noted above, were to make up for the reduction in the allowance payable) were outside the control of the Minister of National Insurance, and, finally, that the family allowance scheme's future development had not been fully considered.[123] In the years that followed its introduction, the opportunity to build on the base of support provided by the initial scheme of family allowances, which was expected to be taken,[124] was ignored.[125] It was uprated only twice and the undertakings which had been given about benefits in kind were not completely honoured.[126] Despite the increases that occurred[127] the value of family

---

[122] H. Land, 'The Introduction of Family Allowances', in Hall et al., *Change, Choice and Conflict in Social Policy* (London: Heinemann, 1975), 223.

[123] Ibid.

[124] See J. Brown, *Family Income Support—Part II: Children in Social Security* (London: Policy Studies Institute, 1984), 46.

[125] The reason for this neglect of family allowances is not obvious. Ogus and Barendt suggested, in the third edition of *The Law of Social Security* (London: Butterworths, 1988) 389 (but not in the fourth edition, with Wikeley, 1995), that possible reasons might have included the timing of their introduction, the lack of support for the demographic arguments presented in favour of the allowances, and the relative lack of popularity of the benefit, compared with others, at the time.

[126] Ibid.

[127] The rate was increased in 1952 and an extra amount became payable for third and subsequent children in 1956: Family Allowances and National Insurance Act 1956. Also in 1956, the allowance became payable in respect of young people receiving full-time education, or in an apprenticeship, until the age of 18 rather than 16; from 1964 it became payable until the age of 19 (the present age-limit, although a new education allowance is proposed to replace it for those over 16) in such circumstances: Family Allowances and National Insurance Act 1964, s. 1.

allowances slipped in the 1950s and 1960s due to increases in the cost of living (with low-pay earners, who were gaining less from child tax allowances, suffering most).[128] This was symptomatic of the way that family allowances had become a 'notoriously neglected area of social policy'.[129] Moreover, the greater economic opportunities for women in the labour market reduced the relevance of family allowances to women's own, and indeed the family's, income.[130]

By the mid 1960s attention was becoming focused on family allowances as part of the debate about poverty prompted by its 'rediscovery' and in the light of increasing evidence of its effects on children and families.[131] The Labour Government considered abolishing child tax allowances and substantially raising family allowances, but in the event stalled on the former and only modestly increased the latter. Family allowances were increased twice in 1968, although these increases were 'a seemingly reluctant response to mounting evidence of the extent to which children were forced to live below the subsistence level approved by Parliament'.[132] To finance the increase and to achieve the avowed aim of making sure that non-taxpayers, as the poorest families, benefited most, child tax allowances were reduced by the so-called 'clawback' (which survived until 1975). This heralded an approach, involving joint consideration of family and tax allowances,[133] which precipitated the reforms of 1975 under which child tax allowances were progressively phased out[134] and family allowances were replaced by child benefit; unlike family allowances, child benefit was (and is) payable for the first child as well as subsequent children.

Child benefit, which included an additional payment in the case of lone parents (generally known as 'one parent benefit'), ran into some difficulties in the 1980s. It was frozen for three consecutive years, although this was partly offset by an increase in the payment for the first child. Although benefits for children and young persons were reviewed as part of the Fowler reviews, there was a separate review team and its findings were not published. Child benefit is analysed by Gillian Douglas in Chapter 9.

E. The Growth of Means-testing

Means-testing of benefits has traditionally many drawbacks. For example, it has tended to be resented by claimants because of its stigmatising effect and because it

---

[128] J. C. Brown, *Family Income Support—Part II: Children in Social Security* (London: Policy Studies Institute, 1984), 48.

[129] J. Macnicol, 'Family Allowances and Less Eligibility', in P. Thane (ed.), *The Origins of British Social Policy* (London: Croom Helm, 1978), 197.

[130] H. Land, 'The introduction of family allowances', in Hall, Land, Parker, and Webb, *Change, Choice and Conflict in Social Policy* (London: Heinemann, 1975), 225; see also Brown, n. 128 above, 50 and 51.

[131] Brown, n. 128 above, 51–2.

[132] J. Walley, 'Children's Allowances: an economic and social necessity', in D. Bull (ed.), *Family Poverty*, 2nd edn. (London: Duckworth, 1972), 113.

[133] Debate on the future of family allowances began to intensify with the publication of a series of recommendations on merger of tax and family allowances: ibid., 193–4.

[134] In respect of most child dependants, income tax allowances ceased to be paid from the tax year 1979–80: Finance Act 1979, s. 1(4).

gives rise to an invasion of privacy as authorities seek to ascertain private financial and living arrangements. It is clear that these factors also create a disincentive to take-up of the benefits concerned, noted in Chapter 2. Means-testing is also costly to administer as well as providing a potential source of friction between claimants and officials. As noted in Chapter 2, means-tests are also regarded as promoting dishonesty. Despite all of these problems, it is true to say that without the growth of means-tested benefits which has occurred under the post-Beveridge welfare state, the UK's model of welfare would have belonged more to the residualist end of the spectrum rather than being, if increasingly less securely, in the institutional zone.[135] In the post-war period means-tested benefits have become particularly important for what the EC has referred to as the 'new poor'—the growing numbers of long-term unemployed—and for families (especially the growing numbers of one-parent families, currently almost one million in number in the UK) and poor pensioners, many of whom are women.[136] This situation has been mirrored in other European states, notably Denmark, Germany and the Netherlands.[137] In Germany, for example, there were 750,000 claimants of Social Assistance in 1970, 1.4 million claimants in 1980 and 3.5 million claimants in 1988.[138] As shown in later chapters, means-testing in Britain intensified in the 1980s and 1990s under the New Right Conservative selectivist policy of 'targeting' benefits on those regarded as being in the greatest need and, under a controversial reform, is set for a further extension via the means-testing of an insurance benefit—incapacity benefit—under the Welfare Reform and Pensions Act 1999 (see Chapter 12).

With unemployment benefit being of limited duration and insurance benefits in general set at below subsistence levels in 1946, it was inevitable that increased demand would come to be placed by claimants on the means-tested benefits intended as the 'poverty safety net'. As shown above, the inadequacy of pensions, for example, led to widescale reliance on assistance. The development of means-tested benefits after the Second World War began with national assistance.

(i) National Assistance

National assistance was paid from 1948 until 1966, when it was replaced by supplementary benefit. National assistance was, as noted earlier, intended by Beveridge to meet the needs of those (expected to be a small minority of claimants) who did not satisfy contribution or other conditions for insurance benefits or who required sup-

[135] For discussion of residual and institutional models of welfare, see Chapter 1. For the contrasting central position of means-tested benefits in the Australian social security system, see P. Carney and T. Hanks, *Social Security in Australia* (Melbourne: Oxford University Press, 1994), ch. 6.

[136] See P. Alcock, 'Social Insurance in Crisis?' (1992) *Benefits* 6.

[137] G. Room, R. Lawson, and F. Lackzko, '"New Poverty" in the European Community' (1989) 17(2) *Policy and Politics*, 165–76.

[138] M. Wilson, 'The German Welfare State: A Conservative regime in crisis', in A. Cochrane and J. Clarke (eds) *Comparing Welfare States* (London: Sage, 1993), 149. Social assistance in Germany is a locally administered form of means-tested assistance, and it technically lies outside the social security system, which revolves around the nationally administered Social Insurance scheme.

plementation. The National Assistance Board, established under the National Assistance Act 1948, had a duty to 'assist persons in Great Britain who are without resources to meet their requirements, or whose resources . . . must be supplemented to meet their requirements'.[139] Regulations[140] set out in more detail how the Board was to compute requirements and resources. Rent was treated as a separate item of requirement: householders would generally receive their net rent in full, whilst non-householders would receive a 'reasonable share' of the rent paid by the householder, subject to upper and lower limits. The scheme also allowed for discretionary weekly additions to meet special circumstances such as laundry expenses and diets. Many of these were paid to pensioners. 'Exceptional needs grants'—lump sum payments to meet expenditure arising from special categories of need—were also available, at the discretion of the Board.[141]

The scale rates of assistance introduced under the 1948 regulations were more generous than unemployment assistance had been.[142] However, adult assistance rates made no ground on the gross and net earnings of male manual workers throughout the 1950s (although there were some gains in the mid to late 1960s).[143] The incomes of those in receipt of national assistance rose in real terms between 1948 and 1961 but by less than the rise in incomes for the population as a whole.[144] By the early 1960s the problems of stigma and lack of take-up were becoming more evident, especially among pensioners.[145] The incoming Labour Government in 1964 proposed an 'income guarantee' for pensioners and widows, but this non-means-tested payment proved to be unaffordable, unless it would be set at a very low level, and the Government instead concentrated on a new supplementary benefit scheme, to replace national assistance, as the centrepiece of its social security reforms.[146]

(ii) Supplementary Benefit

The Ministry of Social Security Act 1966 dissolved the National Assistance Board and gave its functions to the new Ministry of Social Security (which subsumed the Ministry of Pensions and National Insurance) and a Supplementary Benefits Commission (SBC). One of the aims of merging the administration of contributory and non-contributory benefits was to remove the stigma attached to claiming the latter. Claims certainly did increase, although rising levels of unemployment and increases in its duration were the major reasons. Between 1965 and 1971 weekly claims for the basic social assistance payment increased by one million.[147]

---

[139] Section 4.
[140] National Assistance (Determination of Needs) Regulations 1948 (S.I. 1948 No. 1334), Schedule.
[141] Ibid., reg. 6.
[142] See the Explanatory Memorandum to the 1948 Regulations, op. cit., para. 8.
[143] SBC, *Annual Report 1975* (London: HMSO, 1976) Table 7, 35.
[144] T. Lynes, op. cit., n. 84 above, 45.
[145] A. Deacon and J. Bradshaw, *Reserved for the Poor* (Oxford: Martin Roberton, 1983), 13–15.
[146] N. Timmins, *The Five Giants. A Biography of the Welfare State* (London: Harper Collins, 1995), 226–7.
[147] Ministry of Social Security, *Annual Report 1966* (London: HMSO, 1967), 173, Table 34; DHSS, *Supplementary Benefits Handbook* (London: HMSO, 1972), 2.

The 1966 Act in fact made few changes of substance to entitlement. Some areas of discretion were, however, replaced by prescription. For example, the policy that claimants who had deliberately deprived themselves of resources for the purpose of acquiring or increasing entitlement to benefit should be treated as still possessing those resources, was embodied in a legal rule.[148] But in essence the scheme retained its predominantly discretionary characteristics:

The distinctive feature of the Supplementary Benefits Scheme is its discretionary element, those powers vested in the Commission which enable it to consider the claims of individual circumstances. By definition, no one can claim as of 'right' that a particular discretionary power should be exercised in his favour.[149]

Discretion was defended by the SBC as the only effective way of directing benefit towards areas of the greatest need and enabling the system to be 'humanly responsive'.[150] It argued that the lack of precision in the law had 'not . . . diminished the social acceptability of supplementary benefits'.[151]

During the 1970s, debate on the role which discretion should be permitted to play in the benefits system gathered momentum. As noted in Chapter 1, Richard Titmuss was perhaps the most forthright advocate of individualised justice within a discretion-based system in which individuals' variable needs would be catered for adequately.[152] However, the then chairman of the SBC, David Donnison, argued that a discretion-based system was, *inter alia*, expensive to administer, conflict-producing, burdensome for officials, and unable to offer claimants clearly-defined entitlement to benefits.[153]

The key areas of discretion at the time were in the legislation permitting exceptional needs payments (ENPs) and exceptional circumstances additions (ECAs). ENPs were lump sum payments awarded to meet the cost of particular items—notably clothing and footwear, bedding, furniture, household equipment, removal expenses, household decorations and repairs, and so on. Prior to 1980, when discretion was much reduced, payments were available at the discretion of the SBC in any case where it appeared 'reasonable in all the circumstances' to make an award.[154] ECAs consisted of weekly additions to the scale rates, paid in 'exceptional circumstances' and covering such expenses as heating costs, laundry bills and the cost of special diets. A further area of discretion was the overriding power, often exercisable in cases where the claimant was otherwise disqualified from benefit (for example, for being in full-time education of a kind given in schools), to pay benefit in an 'urgent case'.[155]

---

[148] Ministry of Social Security Act 1966, Second Schedule, para. 27.

[149] DHSS, *Supplementary Benefits Handbook* (London: DHSS, 1972), 1.

[150] Ibid.   [151] Ibid., 1–2.

[152] R. Titmuss, 'Welfare "Rights" Law and Discretion' (1971) 42 *Pol Q* 113–32.

[153] D. Donnison, 'Dear David Bull, Frank Field, Michael Hill and Ruth Lister' (1976) 6 *Social Work Today*, No. 20, January 8; id., 'Supplementary Benefits—Dilemma and Priorities' (1976) 5 *J. of Social Policy*, 337; id., 'Against Discretion' (1977) *New Society*, 15 September.

[154] Supplementary Benefit Act 1976, s. 3(1) (formerly s. 7 of the Ministry of Social Security Act 1966).

[155] Ibid., s. 4(1) (formerly s. 13 of the 1966 Act).

The power to award (and in some cases withdraw) benefit was very wide indeed. To guide local offices on the exercise of this power the SBC prepared policy guidelines which were set out in the 'A Code' and 'AX Code'. These documents were never published, although many areas of policy were disclosed in the published *Supplementary Benefits Handbook*, which was revised periodically but did not purport to offer definitive statements as to whether a particular set of circumstances would necessarily prompt a decision to award a discretionary payment.[156] Ultimately, the criterion for awarding an ENP was 'whether the need is *essential*, that is, whether there would be hardship if it were not met', although it was said that 'there can be no simple and uniform definition of hardship . . . each claimant has to be dealt with individually'.[157] A similar approach was adopted by the courts. In *Supplementary Benefit Commission v Clewer*, for example, Stabb J, in dismissing an appeal by the SBC against an appeal tribunal's decision to award an ENP for the cost of an HGV licence course, said that 'there is no precise definition of the word "need" but plainly "exceptional need" must be a need which must be met to avoid hardship, which must involve consideration of the particular circumstances of the applicant'.[158]

While the secrecy of the policy rules was a problem for claimants and their advisers, the main difficulty faced by the supplementary benefit appeal tribunals was how to exercise the discretionary power not only to confirm the SBC's decision or to refuse to review a determination, but also to 'substitute for any determination appealed against any determination which the Commission could have made'.[159] In each year between 1976 and 1979 over 44 per cent of appeals concerned ENPs.[160] Both the SBC[161] and the DHSS Review team[162] considered the number of ENP appeals to be disproportionately large relative to the subsidiary place of ENPs within the supplementary benefit system as a whole. In 1979, 1,134,000 ENPs were awarded to the 2,855,000 claimants who received weekly supplementary benefit.[163] However, the number of appeals concerning ENPs might have been expected to be this high. For one thing, the fact that ENPs were, in the SBC's terms, for near emergencies in itself made an appeal against refusal far more likely. Furthermore, cases concerning general entitlement to benefit, including the amount of benefit, could often be dealt with without recourse to a tribunal; but ENP and ECA matters were 'more likely to need the lodging of an appeal or a tribunal hearing before they are resolved'.[164]

Appeals concerning ENPs and ECAs achieved quite a high success rate for

---

[156] DHSS, *Supplementary Benefits Handbook*, Foreword to the editions published (London: DHSS) in 1972, 1977, and 1979.

[157] Ibid., 1972 edn, para. 88, original emphasis.   [158] QBD, 17 May 1979 (SB 20).

[159] Supplementary Benefit Act 1976, s. 15(3).

[160] SBC, *Annual Report 1977* (1978), *1978* (1979) and *1979* (1980) (London: HMSO).

[161] Ibid., 1977 report, para. 13.7.

[162] DHSS Review Team, *Social Assistance* (London: DHSS, 1978), para. 9.52.

[163] SBC *Annual Report 1979*, op. cit., para. 16.14.

[164] R. Lawrence, *Tribunal Representation—The Role of Advice and Advocacy Services* (London: Bedford Square Press, 1980), 65.

claimants[165] and this was clearly one reason why it was proposed that the right of appeal should be largely discontinued in cases involving discretion.[166] The SBC, however, defended the right of appeal, even though appeal decisions were said to be something of a 'lottery'.[167] Appeals against discretion-based decisions in supplementary benefit cases also added to the strains under which the scheme was operating, caused by the increasing numbers of claimants of supplementary benefit and especially discretionary payments: 'In hard-pressed inner city offices, phones were taken off hooks, claimants were told that files had been lost, or giro cheques were "in the post" just to deter claims and limit the workload. The system, in the days when little of it was computerised, was at risk of collapse.'[168]

A review of the supplementary benefit system was instituted by the DHSS in 1977–8. The Review Team's report, published in July 1978, in effect backed the SBC's chairman's call for clearly defined areas of legal entitlement. It said, in relation to additional payments, that the law should specify those expenses for which additional help should be available and recommended that the overriding discretion of the SBC to award or withhold benefit should be similarly replaced.[169] The report commented that discretionary additions complicated the assessment of benefit and were an element of the scheme that was 'open to exploitation and pressures' in addition to overloading the appeal system.[170] One alternative (not subsequently adopted) was for regular six-monthly payments of lump sums to supplement weekly benefit, providing 'greater equity among claimants than the present system of ENPs "on demand"'.[171] The Review did accept the need to retain a small amount of discretion, recognising that a 'fully comprehensive list of all exceptional circumstances which could arise would be clearly impossible'.[172] The discretion that the Review wanted to preserve was 'officer discretion', exercised by the individual officer at the local office, as opposed to 'Commission discretion' based on the guidance provided for staff on the exercise of discretionary powers.

The SBC was broadly supportive of the recommendations, especially those concerning the discretionary elements of the scheme.[173] The Commission agreed that the fact that the administration of the scheme required 'more than half of the DHSS local office staff to pay out less than 15% of the total benefit expenditure' was undesirable,

[165] H. Dean, *Social Security and Social Control* (London: Routledge, 1991), 129–30.
[166] DHSS Review Team, n. 162 above, para. 9.52.
[167] SBC, *Response of the SBC to 'Social Assistance . . .'* (London: HMSO, 1979), para. 5.32. Critics of supplementary benefit appeal tribunals at this time pointed to their failure to exercise discretion effectively in meeting the demand for individualised justice. Many tribunals treated departmental policy as law. See M. Herman, *Administrative Justice and Supplementary Benefits* (London: Bell, 1972); N. Lewis, 'Supplementary Benefit Appeal Tribunals', [1973] *P.L.* 257–84; H. Calvert, 'Appeal Structures of the Future', in M. Adler and A. Bradley (eds), *Justice, Discretion and Poverty* (Abingdon: Professional Books, 1976), 183–207; K. Bell, *Research Study on Supplementary Benefit Appeal Tribunals* (London: HMSO, 1975).
[168] N. Timmins, *The Five Giants. A Biography of the Welfare State* (London: Harper Collins, 1995), 351.
[169] DHSS, n. 162 above, paras 9.45, 9.46, and 9.53.
[170] Ibid., para. 9.10.   [171] Ibid., para. 9.43.   [172] Ibid., para. 9.48.
[173] SBC, n. 167 above.

and that basically the scheme was out of date.[174] Under the Social Security Act 1980 and ensuing regulations, the precise circumstances in which weekly additions to benefit and 'single payments' (which replaced ENPs) could be made were prescribed, although a small amount of residual discretion remained—in the scope for interpretation of the regulations[175] and the need for individual judgment by benefit officers.[176] The rules set out in the regulations were adapted from SBC policy:[177] but the Commission itself was felt to be no longer needed. Its role in advising the Government on social security matters was taken over by the new independent SSAC.[178]

The Government was unafraid in the 1970s to amend the supplementary benefit scheme to nullify the effect of a court ruling that would result in greater entitlement for particular groups of claimants. Once the scheme became regulation based in November 1980, frequent and regular amendment to its legal structure became the norm in any event. It was inevitable that a scheme as legally complex as the regulation-based supplementary benefit scheme[179] would need amending from time to time, whether to remove anomalies or errors, or to effect policy changes. But it became clear that the Government could also be expected to use its legislative powers to reverse more speedily court or Social Security Commissioner decisions which confirmed entitlement where the Government did not support it.[180]

The Social Security Act 1986 replaced supplementary benefit with income support and, in the case of payments to meet particular exceptional needs, the social fund.[181] The background to these reforms is discussed in the next chapter.

(iii) Rent and Rate Rebates and Housing Benefit

Until the introduction of the housing benefit scheme in 1983 tenants could obtain financial assistance in respect of rent or rate charges through local authority

---

[174] SBC, *Annual Report 1979* (London: HMSO, 1980), para. 16.5. See also the White Paper, *Reform of the Supplementary Benefits Scheme*, Cmnd 7773 (London: HMSO, 1979).

[175] Regulation 30 of the Supplementary Benefit (Single Payments) Regulations 1980 (S.I. 1980 No. 985), which enabled a single payment to be made where it would offer the 'only means' of avoiding a 'serious risk to the health or safety' of the claimant and his/her dependants, provided the most discretion under the reformed supplementary benefit scheme.

[176] See M. Partington, 'Supplementary Benefits: Interpretation and Judgment' (1981) 131 *N.L.J.* 547–8.

[177] As Alcock explains, 'much of the old SBC guidance in the A Code was drafted into regulations and rushed, largely unexamined, through Parliament': P. Alcock, *Poverty and State Support* (London: Longman, 1987), 89. The rules on single payments are discussed more fully at pp. 129–132 below.

[178] Under the SSA 1980. See now SSCBA 1992 ss170, 172–4, Scheds 5 and 7; Ogus (1998) *J.S.S.L.* 156–74.

[179] This complexity was a major cause of claimants' difficulty in understanding how their benefit entitlement was arrived at under the new system, which was a widespread problem: R. Berthoud, *Reform of Social Security. Working Papers* (London: Policy Studies Institute, 1984).

[180] As in the response to the *Cotton* case on board and lodging payments in 1985: *R v Secretary of State for Social Services ex p Cotton* (1985) *The Times*, 14 December (CA). See N. Harris, *Social Security for Young People* (Aldershot: Avebury, 1989), 81–3. See also the response to the *Atkinson* case (*R v Barnsley Supplementary Benefit Appeal Tribunal ex p Atkinson* [1977] 1 WLR 917) on students' benefits in the 1970s: T. Prosser, 'Politics and Judicial Review: The *Atkinson* case and its aftermath' [1979] *P.L.* 59–83.

[181] The 'non-discretionary' part of the social fund covering maternity and funeral expenses payments was in fact introduced a year earlier than the rest of the social fund, on 6 April 1987: Social Fund Maternity and Funeral Expenses (General) Regulations 1987, SI 1987 No. 481. (Subsequently 'cold weather' payments were introduced: see pp. 440 and 443 below.)

administered rent and rate rebate schemes or, in the case of rent, through the rent allowance in supplementary benefit. So far as the latter was concerned, it was often advantageous for claimants of national insurance benefits to claim supplementary benefit, or national assistance before it, because of the more generous assistance available. It will be recalled that Beveridge had set the rent element of social insurance at the national average, whereas rent allowance in means-tested benefit could meet the actual cost of rent payable.

Rent rebates had first been offered to local authority tenants in the 1930s. They were intended to help those facing higher rents when moving from slums, which were being cleared, into new homes. There were further permissive powers before the war, enabling rent rebates to be extended to all tenants, on satisfaction of a means-test, although they did not develop on a wide scale.[182] Upward pressure on rents in the 1950s and 1960s led to greater Government encouragement of rent rebate schemes. By 1970 well over half of local authorities operated such schemes.[183] A national rate rebate scheme was introduced under the Rating Act 1966, although the scheme was not permanent. The Conservative Government's Housing Finance Act 1972 was designed to end the practice of local authorities using the generalised housing subsidy to depress council rent levels and/or administer a local rent rebate scheme. What was introduced was a national rent rebate scheme, administered as before by local authorities, which was extended to private tenants as well. The Government took the credit for an egalitarian reform: relatively well-off council tenants lost the advantage of subsidised rents, while poorer tenants had the guarantee of a rebate. Nevertheless, 'the price of switching subsidies from buildings and from all council rents was to put many more people on means-tested benefits in order to help them pay the higher rents being introduced'.[184] So far as rates were concerned, the Rate Rebate Act 1973 established a new rebate scheme from 1975, doubling the numbers receiving assistance.[185]

Meanwhile, rent allowances continued to be available within supplementary benefit. Those receiving national insurance benefits who wanted to maximise their rent support found themselves faced with a complex choice between switching to supplementary benefit or remaining on national insurance benefit or pension and claiming rent rebate. The case for a unified benefit seemed strong; but the Government went only part of the way. Support with housing costs for owner occupiers (mortgage interest payments, insurance, and so on) was left in the supplementary benefit scheme (apart from help with general rates), while rent allowances were taken out of supplementary benefit and merged with the rent rebates scheme to form a new, unified housing benefit scheme, administered by local authorities. The reform was intended to proceed on a nil-cost basis.

---

[182] Housing Act 1936. See Ogus, Barendt, and Wikeley (1995), 536.
[183] Ogus, Barendt, and Wikeley, ibid.
[184] N. Timmins, *The Five Giants. A Biography of the Welfare State* (London: Harper Collins, 1995), 304.
[185] Ogus, Barendt, and Wikeley (1995), 537.

The housing benefit scheme was fully introduced in April 1983, under the Social Security and Housing Benefits Act 1982. It was intended to provide assistance with rent and rates on premises occupied as a home. Claimants who were in receipt of supplementary benefit qualified for housing benefit automatically, receiving 'certificated' housing benefit. Other claimants would receive 'standard' housing benefit, subject to a means-test. Where a recipient of either form of housing benefit had a working son or daughter living with him or her, a 'non-dependant deduction' was made, since it was assumed that such a wage earner would make a weekly contribution towards housing costs. 'Housing benefit supplement' (HBS) (strictly part of supplementary benefit, but administered by the local authority) was paid where a standard housing benefit recipient who had not received complete assistance towards rent and rates found that his expenditure on these charges brought his income below the supplementary benefit threshold. HBS brought with it entitlement to various 'passported' health benefits, such as free prescriptions and dental treatment available to those on supplementary benefit.

The level of housing benefit payable to a claimant was related to his or her weekly income, which was compared with a notional 'needs allowance'.[186] Changes to the taper (which determined the basis on which benefit was increased or reduced on account of income) in 1984 meant that the maximum qualifying income for a couple with two children, who were being charged an average rent, declined relative to average earnings. However, those who qualified for certificated housing benefit received, subject to certain deductions, the full amount of their rent and rates.[187]

The new scheme did not fully achieve all the advantages which had been hoped for. Above all, it was complicated and costly to administer and did not remove all the anomalies between those who were in receipt of supplementary benefit and those who were not.[188] The scheme was reviewed as part of the 1984-5 reviews of social security. The reform proposals and the replacement housing benefit scheme, which came into operation in 1988, are discussed in the next chapter.

(iv) Supplementation of Low Wages: Family Income Supplement

Family income supplement (FIS) was devised by the 1970–4 Conservative Government as an alternative to raising family allowances. FIS had the same basic aim as family credit which later replaced it. It was a benefit designed to supplement the income of families with dependent children on a low income derived from full-time employment. It was described as 'a new form of family allowance subject to a means-test';[189] but, unlike the other principal means-tested benefit at the time, supplementary benefit, there was to be no discretionary element in its administration.

Raising family allowances significantly would not have benefited those working families with one child, because the allowance was only paid for the second child and

---

[186] See the Housing Benefits Regulations 1985 (S.I. 1985 No. 677), reg. 15.
[187] Ibid., reg. 9.   [188] See Ogus, Barendt, and Wikeley (1995), 539–40.
[189] M. Wynn, *Family Policy: A study of the economic costs of rearing children and their social and political consequences* (Harmondsworth: Penguin, 1972), 328.

subsequent children. Moreover, it would have been an extremely expensive way of providing the help that was needed.[190] A further problem was that falling tax thresholds had meant that much of the advantage gained by poor families would be lost through tax clawed back.[191] FIS was seen by the minister responsible for presenting it, Keith Joseph, as a more effective and less problematic way of helping poor families. Nevertheless, Joseph had to defend it against the criticism that it heralded a return to the 'Speenhamland' system,[192] via state subsidy of employers who paid low wages, and would benefit only 160,000 families (and then only if take-up levels were very high, which proved not to be the case: see below).[193]

Under the Family Income Supplement Act 1970 FIS was payable where the family's normal gross weekly income fell below the appropriate prescribed amount. Although the needs of the first child as well as those of subsequent children were taken into account[194] there was no differentiation between children's ages. It was argued that families with older children would be in a less favourable position, because teenagers cost more to feed (and clothe) than younger children.[195] The flat rate additions for children were not replaced by age-related scales until November 1985.[196] There had previously been resistance to such a reform, in an effort to maximise the scheme's simplicity.[197] FIS was paid at the rate of 50 per cent of the difference between the claimant's gross weekly income and the appropriate prescribed amount (based on family size and, latterly, on children's ages).[198] At first, benefit was awarded for twenty-six weeks once the claim had been accepted, but this was later increased to fifty-two weeks.[199]

FIS was dogged by two major problems. First, take-up was relatively low: in 1972 and 1973 it was an estimated 50 per cent and 67 per cent respectively, rising to an estimated 75 per cent in 1974.[200] Later, however, the SBC commented that the take-up rate was comparable with that for supplementary benefit or rent rebates and that 'no means-tested benefit can ever be free of take-up problems. There will always be some who fail to claim through ignorance or fear of stigma.'[201] The SBC's estimates

---

[190] R. M. Moroney, *The Family and the State* (London: Longmans, 1976), 200.

[191] See N. Timmins, *The Five Giants. A Biography of the Welfare State* (London: Harper Collins, 1995), 282.

[192] See Chapter 3.   [193] N. Timmins, op. cit., 283–4.

[194] There was a basic prescribed amount for a one-child family, with increases (or 'steps') for subsequent children. But FIS was structured in such a way that the first child was in effect more highly rated than the second and subsequent children: National Consumer Council, *Of Benefit to All* (London: NCC, 1984), para. 7.24. See also A. W. Dilnot, J. D. Kay, and C. N. Morris, *The Reform of Social Security* (Oxford: Clarendon Press, 1984), 122.

[195] Wynn, n. 188 above, 328–9.

[196] Three age bands were introduced: under 11; 11–15; and 16 or over. The differences between the rates (£11.50, £12.50, and £13.50) were not great and barely reflected the much greater costs of maintaining older children.

[197] See, for example, SBC, *Annual Report 1977* (London: HMSO, 1978), para. 14.11.

[198] Family Income Supplement Act 1970, s. 3.

[199] Pensioners and FIS Payments Act 1972.

[200] SBC, *Annual Report 1975* (London: HMSO, 1976), para. 12.8.

[201] SBC, *Annual Report 1979* (London: HMSO, 1980), para. 17.7.

were in fact unreliable. By 1984 the Government was admitting that only 50 per cent of those entitled to FIS were in fact claiming it.[202]

The other significant problem with FIS was the poverty trap.[203] A small rise in wages could take the claimant's income above the prescribed amount, or remove a considerable proportion of his or her entitlement. Moreover, FIS was a passport to other benefits, such as free dental treatment and health prescriptions, so reinforcing the effect of the poverty trap for those on low wages.[204] It was argued that Government fears of harming work incentives through closing the gap between low family wages and the 'official poverty line' were one of the reasons that it offered 'negligible and minimum' support for the family.[205] Like other means-tested benefits FIS also had the drawback of being fairly complex (especially as regards the calculation of income) and quite expensive to administer. It was also clear that women sometimes lost out, because the benefit was often paid to a male wage earner and in consequence women (and children) might remain poor 'because of the unequal intra-household distribution of income'.[206]

Despite the problems, after ten years FIS was regarded by the Social Security Advisory Committee as 'a crucial integral part of the social security safety net'.[207] FIS had originally been conceived of as a temporary measure. It had never been expected to be a long-term solution to the problem of income deficiency among poor working families. Indeed there were plans, soon after FIS was introduced, to abolish it as part of the Chancellor of the Exchequer's proposed (but never implemented) tax credits system. Now, it seemed, FIS had become firmly established in the benefits system. But problems, discussed above, remained and these were examined as part of the Fowler reviews of social security in 1984–5, discussed in the next chapter.

The legacy of FIS was in part its replacement benefit, family credit (recently itself replaced by working families tax credit). But, perhaps more significantly, it was also 'the psychological effects (for government) caused by its low take-up and its worsening of the poverty trap'.[208] The experience of this benefit had a broader effect on policy, as it raised 'fresh doubts about the merits of means-testing into Tory ranks to the point that no new means-tested benefit of any significance was introduced for twenty years, even if the boundaries of existing ones at times shifted'.[209]

---

[202] Hansard, Official Report H.C. Vol. 61 col. 460w, 12 June 1984. The problems in relation to take-up of FIS were analysed by A. Carden, *Taking Up a Means-tested Benefit: The process of claiming FIS* (London: HMSO, 1983).

[203] See Chapter 2.

[204] See R. Lister, *Moving Back to the Means-test* (London: CPAG, 1980), 9–14; National Consumer Council, n. 194 above, ch. 7; Dilnot, Kay, and Morris, n. 194 above, 55 *et seq*; SBC, *Annual Report 1979* (London: HMSO, 1980), para. 17.8; D. W. W. Williams, 'Poverty and Unemployment Traps and Trappings' [1986] *J.S.W.L.* 96–107.

[205] V. George, *Social Security and Society* (London: Routledge and Kegan Paul, 1973), 125.

[206] CPAG, *CPAG's Evidence to the Social Security Reviews 1984. Changed Priorities Ahead?* (London: CPAG, 1984), para. 1.4.

[207] SSAC, *Annual Report* 1981 (London: HMSO, 1982), para. 3.24.

[208] N. Timmins, *The Five Giants. A Biography of the Welfare State* (London: Harper Collins, 1995), 284.

[209] Ibid.

4. CONCLUSION

By the early 1980s the social security system in Britain retained the broad structures (and indeed the underlying gender discrimination: see Chapter 9) that were the product of the Beveridge plan. Nevertheless, in many respects it failed to reflect Beveridge's vision of a comprehensive, universal scheme of insurance against want by having become a massive and complex system in which means-tested social assistance was becoming the dominant form. It rested on a huge and expensive-to-operate administrative structure. The failure to provide proper subsistence level support and to maintain the value of insurance benefits in line with inflation, the withdrawal of earnings-related supplements, and the various rationalisations of benefits (e.g. the phasing out of child dependency additions), all contributed to increasing reliance on means-tested benefit at a time of rapidly rising levels of unemployment. Indeed, tracing the history of the welfare state after the Second World War, one can see that the decade from 1973–83 marks a sharp decline in the Beveridge-based social security system. Following the 1973 Western oil crisis the British welfare state became the casualty, under both Labour and Conservative governments, of the need for a more intense national economic management, particularly monetary control, in times of recession. According to Fraser, the consensus of social democracy which the adoption of the main strands of the Beveridge plan represented gave way to a new consensus of retrenchment in response to economic crisis.[210] Thus the welfare state, which had 'matured in the universalism of the 1940s and flowered in full bloom in the consensus and affluence of the 1950s and 1960s', was by the 1970s 'in its decline, like the faded rose of autumn'.[211] Most of the improvements in social security provision in the 1960s and 1970s were, as in the case of the earnings-related supplements to insurance benefits, too generous to survive the pressure to rein-in public expenditure thereafter. (Expenditure on social security rose from less than 10 per cent of government spending at the time of the 1946 Act to approaching one third of it by the early 1980s, when it was targeted for cutbacks.) Others, such as family income supplement, were far less effective and more problematic than anticipated.

In terms of social security law, the development of means-tested benefits post-Beveridge gave rise to increasing complexity in the legislative framework. Developments occurred piecemeal, adding new legislative provisions to an increasingly labyrinthine structure. Child benefit, FIS, and the revised supplementary benefit scheme after 1980 were characterised by a legalism which had intensified within the social security system, particularly as a result of the sets of regulations which replaced the policy basis for decisions on various additions to or elements within supplementary benefit. As Lister commented, although these regulations were SBC policy in legal form, 'SBC policy is pretty complex and when translated into legal language it becomes more so, as the DHSS lawyers attempt to dot all the "i"s and

---

[210] D. Fraser, *The Evolution of the British Welfare State*, 2nd edn. (Houdmills: Macmillan, 1984), 251.
[211] Ibid., 253.

cross all the "t"'s'.[212] According to Lustgarten, the law on supplementary benefit rivalled revenue law 'in its complexity and incomprehensibility to the ordinary person'.[213] Moreover, social security, which had its own appeal system as well as being a potential area of judicial review, was increasingly the subject of legal challenges of one kind or another. Case law was becoming increasingly important, particularly when the right of appeal to the Social Security Commissioners was extended to supplementary benefit from 1980.[214]

The Conservatives' 1985 Green Paper proposals were at least right about one thing: the social security system of the mid 1980s was ripe for reform. The next chapter discusses the case for change presented by the Conservatives and the reforms which, while certainly not on the scale of those from 1945–8, and not altering the broad structure of the benefits system as devised by Beveridge, have had a fundamental effect on some of the main areas of provision down to the present day.

---

[212] R. Lister, 'The New Supplementary Benefit Regulations—Comment' (1980) *J.S.W.L.* 341–3, 341.
[213] L. Lustgarten, 'The New Legislation II: Reorganising Supplementary Benefit' (1981) 131 *N.L.J.* 96.
[214] See Chapter 7.

5

Widening Agendas: the Social Security Reviews and Reforms of 1985–8

NEVILLE HARRIS

1. INTRODUCTION

The Social Security Act 1986 was an important landmark in the post-war development of social security in Britain. It is true that the reforms did not result in a complete restructuring of the benefits system and its legal framework; indeed, the Government acknowledged that its proposals, published in 1985, were 'not based on a grand design for a new state system'.[1] Nevertheless, the Act produced highly important changes—the introduction of income support, the social fund and family credit, and a revised housing benefit scheme—all of which are, over a decade on, still key elements of the present social security system. Among other reforms were the scaling down of the state earnings-related pension scheme (SERPS), the abolition of death grant and the restructuring of widow's pension. Just as significantly, the reforms produced gains for some client groups and losses for others—most notably, in the case of the latter, young people, families, and the unemployed. The reforms are also significant for their entrenchment of prevailing New Right principles of reduced state welfare provision, increased self-reliance and greater private provision. The Government postulated that while state provision had an important role to play, 'it should not discourage self-reliance or stand in the way of individual provision and responsibility'.[2] Social security provision should be based on 'a partnership between the individual and the state—a system built on twin pillars'.[3] In this sense, the reforms were setting an agenda for the future direction of social security policy in Britain. For all these reasons, this period of reform warrants careful examination. This chapter also provides an opportunity to discuss the background to the income-related benefits which today form the core of state social security provision.

The Conservative Government announced its review of social security in the spring of 1984. The Secretary of State for Social Services, Norman Fowler, claimed it would involve 'the most substantial examination of the social security system since the Beveridge Report'.[4] Four separate reviews were initiated—on supplementary benefit, housing benefit, provision for retirement, and benefits for children and young persons. There then followed a period of consultation, which was

---

[1] Green Paper (1985) Vol. 1, para. 1.14.   [2] Ibid., para. 1.7.   [3] Ibid., para. 1.5.
[4] Hansard, H.C. Debs, cols 652–60, 2 April 1984.

subsequently criticised for being too short and based on hopelessly vague consultation papers.[5] There was also criticism of the Government's failure to heed calls for a more wide-ranging review of tax and benefits.[6] Little secret was made of the fact that reform would have to occur within the existing level of public expenditure on social security. For example, the housing benefit review aimed to 'see if better use can be made of resources and staff within the present overall level of social security expenditure',[7] while the proposed income support scheme would 'use the same resources—I emphasise that—in a better way to help those in the most need'.[8] This nil-cost basis, it has been argued, conditioned the review process and the proposals themselves.[9]

2. THE REFORM PROPOSALS AND REACTION TO THEM

A. The General Objectives and Approach

The Government's proposals for reform of social security in 1985 began with the assertion that 'the British social security system has lost its way'.[10] In what sense was this the case? First, according to the Government it was costing too much to meet the demand for social security: since the Second World War the cost had grown disproportionately, five times faster than prices and twice as fast as the economy as a whole, and it was 'set to rise steeply for the next forty years'.[11] Secondly, resources had not always been directed at those in the greatest need, it was claimed. Finally, the system had become too complex, largely as a result of its piecemeal development with 'a multitude of benefits with overlapping purposes and differing entitlement conditions'.[12] This complexity was said to be hindering the efficient administration of the system and rendering it incomprehensible to many claimants.

The Green Paper put forward three main objectives for reform of social security.[13] First, the system should be capable of meeting genuine need. In this context it was suggested that families with children faced the greatest difficulties. Secondly, reform had to be consistent with the Government's overall objectives for the economy: thus, the tax burden caused by social security expenditure would have to be contained to

---

[5] See, for example, National Council for One Parent Families, *The Insecurity System* (London: National Council for One Parent Families, 1985), para. 2.1.

[6] See A. W. Dilnot, J. D. Kay, and C. N. Morris, *The Reform of Social Security* (Oxford: Clarendon Press, 1984). According to Timmins, Treasury ministers would not agree to taxation being considered by the DHSS, and the Chancellor, Nigel Lawson, was not convinced of the benefits of tax credits (sometimes called 'negative income tax'), basic income guarantees or similar schemes: N. Timmins, *The Five Giants. A Biography of the Welfare State* (London: Harper Collins, 1995), 400.

[7] *Housing Benefit Review (Request for Evidence)* (London: Department of the Environment, 1984), para. 3.

[8] Hansard, H.C. Debs, col. 193, 18 June 1985, *per* Mr N. Fowler.

[9] R. Lister, 'The Politics of Social Security: An Assessment of the Fowler Review' in A. Dilnot and I. Walker (eds), *The Economics of Social Security* (Oxford: Oxford University Press, 1989), 200–23.

[10] Green Paper (1985), Vol. 1., para. 1.1. [11] Ibid., para. 1.2. [12] Ibid.

[13] Ibid., para. 1.12.

avoid the risk of damaging the prospects for economic growth 'on which the real alleviation of poverty depends', and benefit provision would have to be set at a level which preserved and reinforced individual work incentives. Finally, the complexity in the system would have to be addressed; thus reform should be aimed at simplification.

In putting forward its programme of reforms, the Government indicated its intended approach.[14] First, future problems had to be avoided by immediate action, especially the future cost of pensions. Secondly, the Government would 'target the resources we have more effectively'.[15] As we shall see, this was and remains one of the most contentious aspects of the reforms, not least because, as the Government admitted, 'this involves some redistribution between different groups of people'.[16] Thirdly, the system would be simplified, with clearer rules of entitlement and less duplication between benefits. An emphasis would be placed on 'reasonable support for all with the minimum of complication' rather than on 'detailed needs-testing'.[17] Fourthly, there should be improved administration of the system, involving, for example, extensive computerisation.[18] Finally, the Government intended to create a system based on the notion of partnership between individual and state, as noted above. This, it was asserted, was the most important of all of the issues.

We now turn to the distinct areas of entitlement to see how these principles were to be applied, beginning with pensions, where the individual–state partnership was a dominant theme.

B. Pensions

The two related issues addressed in the proposals on pensions[19] were the enormous future cost implications for the state earnings-related pensions scheme (SERPS), the extent of which had not been anticipated when the scheme was established in 1978 (see Chapter 4), and the case for private provision to meet individual need, through an expansion of occupational pension arrangements.

The Government argued in the Green Paper that SERPS would at the very least need to be restricted in view of the expected increase in the size of the population of pension age set against broadly unchanged numbers of working population, over the following fifty years.[20] The cost of providing the state pension was expected to increase by 40 per cent over this period, if its value was unchanged, and by substantially more if the value was increased in line with increases in earnings over the period. The Government concluded that the full effects of the extra entitlements and expenditure consequent on the introduction of SERPS would not begin to be felt until after 2000 but that the future of the scheme could not be ignored and had to be addressed immediately. It wanted ideally to replace SERPS with new arrangements based on a partnership between public provision (in the form of basic state

---

[14] Ibid., ch. 6.   [15] Ibid., para. 6.3.   [16] Ibid.   [17] Ibid., para. 6.4.
[18] Ibid., para. 6.5.   [19] Ibid., ch. 7.   [20] Green Paper (1985), Vol. 2, paras 1.22–1.30.

pension) and occupational and personal provision.[21] However, concern over the cost of mandatory occupational pensions—in terms of additional tax relief and the cost of employers' contributions—forced the Government to back down from a compulsory scheme.

Those who had been paying into SERPS since its inception in 1978 and who were within fifteen years of retirement would still be able to derive the full benefit from it. However, the Green Paper envisaged a phasing out of SERPS over a period of just three years for men aged under fifty and women aged under forty-five, although those within ten years of these upper age limits were to be protected from a sharp differential between their rights and those of slightly older people by being credited with extra years of SERPS rights. For younger people, employee and employer contributions would be directed into occupational or personal pension schemes. The national insurance contribution rates for contracted-out and non-contracted-out pensions would be harmonised. There was a commitment to equalise the male and female pension retirement age in respect of occupational and personal pensions, but equalisation of the male/female differential in the general state retirement age was rejected on cost grounds.[22]

The Government claimed that the reforms would produce savings which would give it more flexibility in meeting future expenditure priorities and would complement other planned reforms on pensions (such as those on greater portability of pension rights between employments). Later, the White Paper announced incentive arrangements to encourage the spread of private and occupational pensions via an extra rebate.[23] At the same time it was reported that the Government had decided to bow to the pressure from the CBI and others to take a less drastic step than phasing out SERPS. It was clear that the political and economic costs of compulsory occupational pensions schemes, for both the Government and private and public sector employers, were prohibitive to complete abolition.[24] Instead, it was proposed that SERPS be modified by basing pension on the whole lifetime's employment rather than the best twenty years of earnings, which the Government said had been 'over generous'.[25] However, such a change would discriminate against those with fluctuating incomes or those who spent periods out of the workforce, many of whom were women. Moreover, the new arrangements as a whole would reduce the redistributive aspect of the state pension scheme.[26] The Government offered special arrangements to protect women and disabled people (plus those taking time out from work to look after disabled people): years without earnings due to incapacity or home responsibilities would not be counted when average lifetime earnings were calculated. However, spouses would only be able to inherit one half of the state pension rather than the full

[21] Green Paper (1985), Vol. 2, para. 1.40.   [22] Ibid., paras 1.54 and 1.70–1.75.
[23] White Paper (1985), para. 2.31.
[24] N. Timmins, *The Five Giants—A Biography of the Welfare State* (London: Harper Collins, 1995), 402.
[25] White Paper (1985), para. 2.15.
[26] N. Barr, *The Economics of the Welfare State*, 2nd edn. (London: Weidenfeld and Nicholson, 1993), 234–5.

amount. This would have adverse consequences for women in particular. Land commented: 'It weakens the extent to which women may acquire rights to a pension through their husband's contributions.'[27] Pensions would be calculated on the basis of 20 per cent of earnings rather than 25 per cent, a change which would be phased in over ten years (i.e. at the rate of 0.5 per cent per year), starting in 2000–1.

The Government had backed down from its original plan to dismantle SERPS, but had not altered its basic doctrinaire approach: state provision would be eroded, and there would be greater reliance on private provision.[28] Whether this undermining of a promise given by a previous Government as to future entitlement was justifiable remained a matter of some debate. Some commentators were in any event unconvinced by the financial evidence and the Government was accused of basing its claims that reform was a matter of economic imperative on unreliable economic and demographic projections. For example, it was argued that account appeared not to have been taken by the Government of the way in which, under the existing system, public expenditure savings would arise from reduced demand for means-tested benefits as SERPS entitlement accrued.[29] Some have even questioned the accuracy of predictions that future generations would not have been able to bear the extra cost of the full implementation of SERPS.[30]

C. Child/Family Benefits

The Government's principal objective as regards reform in the area of child and family benefits[31] was to lessen the effects of the poverty and unemployment traps.[32] Although these traps could be largely removed through increasing child benefit by a substantial amount, such a reform was rejected on the grounds of cost and failure to target those in the greatest need. Both means-testing and taxation of child benefit were felt to work against the concept of universality in relation to family support and to produce an unacceptable degree of 'churning' ('where the same people receive money through the benefit system and pay it back through the tax system').[33] The 'basis' of child benefit was to continue. However, despite this commitment the rate of the benefit was in fact frozen in each of the following three years.

The poverty and unemployment traps were to be tackled via a new in-work benefit for families, family credit, which would replace family income supplement (FIS).[34]

---

[27] H. Land, 'The social construction of dependency', conference on *The Goals of Social Policy: Past and Future*, LSE, 17–18 December 1987. This change is due in 2000—but see p. 181 n. 134 below.

[28] See S. Ward, 'Pensions', in R. Silburn (ed.), *The Future of Social Security* (London: Fabian Society, 1985), 22–41.

[29] J. Cullen and R. O'Kelly, 'The cost of pensions and the myth of funding', in R. Silburn (ed.), ibid., 42, 44.

[30] See J. Creedy and R. Disney, 'The New Pension Scheme in Britain', in A. Dilnot and I. Walker (eds), *The Economics of Social Security* (Oxford: Oxford University Press, 1989), 224–38, 226.

[31] Green Paper (1985), Vol. 1, ch. 8.

[32] The poverty and unemployment traps are discussed in Chapter 2.

[33] Green Paper (1985), Vol. 1, para. 8.8.   [34] For the structure of FIS, see Chapter 4.

FIS had long been criticised for its complexity and disproportionate administrative costs, in addition to its failure to overcome the poverty and unemployment traps, and its low take-up rate.[35] Initially it was anticipated that family credit would be 'paid' via the wage packet.[36] This was seen as a step towards integration of benefits and taxes, in the sense that for a majority of claimants the credit would merely have the effect of offsetting tax and national insurance deductions from earnings. The Government preferred this to what happened under FIS, where 'one member of a family may be paying tax and contributions *to* the state while another member of the family is in receipt of FIS *from* the state'.[37] This proposal was, however, later abandoned as there were fears that if family credit were paid through the wage packet it might not, in some cases, reach or be expended on those it was intended to help.[38] There was a particular concern that some mothers would be deprived of the benefit because their male partners would have control of it.

Family credit was to be set at a more generous level than FIS, partly to offset the loss of entitlement to free school meals and welfare foods.[39] Under family credit the family would be credited with an amount which was adjusted to take account of family size and which, together with child benefit entitlement, would ensure that 'at earnings above the income support level for a couple, a family with children should not be worse off in work'.[40] If the family's net income was above the prescribed threshold, the maximum credit would be reduced by a percentage (the 'taper') of the amount by which that net income exceeded the threshold. Below the threshold the family would receive 'maximum credit'. But net rather than gross income would be taken into account, so that benefit could not be reduced by an amount greater than any increase in earnings. Another important difference between family credit and FIS lay in the number of hours of work per week needed to qualify for it. Under FIS, a claimant had to be working for a minimum of thirty hours per week, or twenty-four hours if he or she was a lone parent. Under family credit, the threshold was to be twenty-four hours for all claimants. The capital rules were also to be more generous. The cut-off point was to be raised: a claimant could have capital of up to £6,000 and still be entitled to family credit as opposed to the £3,000 limit for FIS. A further difference was that the award would be assessed on the previous thirteen weeks' earnings (it was the previous five weeks under FIS) and entitlement would run for twenty-six weeks instead of fifty-two.[41]

The Government estimated that twice as many families would be entitled to fam-

---

[35] See pp. 114–5 above.   [36] Green Paper (1985), Vol. 1., para. 8.10.

[37] White Paper (1985), para. 3.78.

[38] House of Commons Social Services Committee: *First Report, Session 1985/86, Reform of Social Security*, HC 180 (London: HMSO, 1986), paras 28 and 32.

[39] White Paper (1985), para. 3.87. FIS was a passport to these; family credit would not be. The average cost of school meals across the country, rather than the actual amount in the particular locality, was to be taken into account in setting the rate.

[40] Green Paper (1985), Vol. 2, para. 4.47.

[41] See SSAC, *Fourth Report, 1985* (London: HMSO, 1985), para. 5.5.

ily credit as compared with FIS.[42] However, the opportunity had not been taken to develop a fully integrated benefit credit system, as had been proposed by the Institute for Fiscal Studies,[43] or a universal child benefit based scheme, as proposed by CPAG.[44] Both schemes were claimed to be potentially more effective in supporting families with children, overcoming the poor take-up problem which affected means-tested benefits, whilst preserving work incentives and weakening the poverty/unemployment traps. But the Government felt that both of these alternative schemes would be impracticable.[45] The House of Commons Social Services Committee wanted to see an integrated system of tax and child credits, and it accused the Government of 'procrastination' over what it saw as a logical reform.[46] Furthermore, some commentators doubted the Government's claims that the worst effects of the poverty trap would be removed. It was suggested that while a reduction in the numbers actually better off out of work would occur, many more families would be pushed onto the 'poverty plateau', losing over 80 per cent of any additional earnings.[47] The complicated system for assessment of income, including the administrative arrangements for certification of income by employers, was also criticised as involving considerable additional burdens on the DHSS and employers.[48] There were also doubts about whether take-up rates would be better. Even though the Government's plan to assess earnings over a thirteen-week period was dropped (it would be five weeks instead), there were still several disincentives to claim, including a reduction in the period for which benefit was awarded (from fifty-two to twenty-six weeks, as noted above) and the fear that the administrative burden on the employer might rebound against the employee through loss of employment. Nevertheless, despite these criticisms there was unanimous agreement that family credit would at least be a significant improvement on FIS, and it was broadly welcomed by the SSAC.[49]

D. Income Support

The proposals concerning a new benefit, 'income support', were part of a package of reforms to the benefits 'safety net'. Income support would replace weekly supplementary benefit (outlined in Chapter 4). Single payments for the cost of furniture, bedding, utensils, clothes, redecoration costs, and other items would be covered by a new 'social fund' (see section E below).

---

[42] White Paper (1985), para. 1.24.

[43] See A. W. Dilnot, J. D. Kay, and C. N. Morris, *The Reform of Social Security* (Oxford: Clarendon Press, 1984), 122.

[44] CPAG, *1984—Changed Priorities Ahead? Evidence to the Social Security Reviews* (London: CPAG, 1984).

[45] White Paper (1985), paras 3.67 and 3.68.   [46] N. 38 above, para. 32.

[47] National Council for One Parent Families, *The Insecurity System* (London: NCOPF, 1985), para. 3.5; IFS, *1985 Benefit Reviews: The Effects of the Proposals* (London: IFS, 1985), Table 1.10; R. Berthoud, *The Examination of Social Security* (London: PSI, 1985), 76 and 123 and *Selective Social Security* (London: P.S.I., 1986), 21–3.

[48] R. Berthoud, *Selective Social Security*, op. cit., 19–20.

[49] N. 41 above, ch. 5.

The Government claimed that there was 'widespread dissatisfaction' with the supplementary benefit scheme and that it was complex, making it difficult for claimants to understand, hindering administrative efficiency, and leading to errors by benefit staff.[50] It was clear that the reforms of November 1980, when regulations had replaced much of the discretion in the system (see Chapter 4), were seen as a contributing factor:

There are over 500 pages of law on the scheme. The rules on single payments alone run to over 1,000 lines of law: one regulation alone contains 20 separate categories of essential furniture and household equipment even before rules are set on which claimants are eligible for them. The result is extremely complicated instructions for staff and a further literature of case law.[51]

The overall experience of establishing a rule-based system in 1980 had demonstrated how difficult it was to 'administer provisions on a mass scale, both responding to individual need and avoiding cumbersome and controversial rules on the limits to help'.[52]

It was clear that in many cases operational considerations rather than matters of principle were foremost in the Government's thinking. (One exception was the proposal to raise the capital cut-off; set at £3,000 under supplementary benefit, the existing limit was said to penalise elderly claimants who had built up their savings over the course of their lifetime and, at the same time, encouraged others with capital sums to run down their assets quickly in order that entitlement be secured.[53]) Generally, the Conservatives wanted a means-tested form of assistance which was far easier to administer. For example, the Green Paper referred to the weekly special additions to benefit ('additional requirements') paid to some claimants for heating costs, dietary needs, laundry costs, or other expenses. They involved 'considerable investigation into the details of claimants' circumstances',[54] which was intrusive but above all very expensive. To take another example, the householder/non-householder distinction, which was important in determining the level of support (householders received a higher rate of weekly benefit because of their responsibility for various housing costs and living expenses), had become difficult to apply as a result of the increasing incidence of shared households.[55] Yet any reform which aimed to absorb additional payments into basic benefit rates could lead to some averaging out of support, inevitably resulting in the most needy receiving less help than before. Many welfare rights groups argued that unless overall benefit rates were increased, complexity was inevitable if resources were in effect to be rationed in accordance with need. The Government nevertheless wanted a simpler, clearer scheme—one which would be easier to operate but also one which would target resources on needs more effec-

---

[50] Green Paper (1985), Vol. 2, para. 2.27 and 2.29. The Government cited two PSI Research Papers (84/5.1 and 84/5.2), entitled *The Reform of Supplementary Benefit* (1984), which showed widespread ignorance among claimants as to how their entitlement was calculated.
[51] Green Paper (1985), Vol. 2, para. 2.28.   [52] Ibid., para. 2.64.   [53] Ibid., para. 2.41.
[54] Ibid., para. 2.56.   [55] Ibid., para. 2.34.

tively. Income support would, it was claimed, also seek to achieve greater fairness as between those on benefit and those in low-paid employment and would provide a base for calculating entitlement to other income-related benefits.[56]

The level of income support entitlement would be determined 'essentially by age and family responsibilities'.[57] What this meant was that there would be broad categorisations based on very wide assumptions about differing levels of need, rather than an attempt to relate entitlement to actual requirements. Thus, for example, while the separate heating cost additions to weekly benefit would be discontinued, pensioners, the disabled and those with young children (most likely to qualify for those additions in the past) would simply benefit from a premium in their income support. There would also be an age-twenty-five dividing line in the basic rates in place of the householder/non-householder distinction. Child additions to the basic age-related allowance (which also took account of marital or relationship status) would be paid as before; the Government initially proposed a restructuring of the age bands (set at ages 0–10, 11–15, and 16–17 from 1980), but later changed its mind. There was some disappointment that the extra costs of the under-fives had once again not been acknowledged.[58]

There had been various hints that the Government had it in mind to end the *independent* entitlement of sixteen to seventeen year olds, particularly with the development of its Youth Training Scheme, which aimed to guarantee a place on a training course for all school leavers. There was fierce opposition to this from the SSAC, CPAG and Youthaid, amongst others.[59] In the event, the Government decided not to change young people's eligibility to benefit,[60] and the minister confirmed that sixteen to seventeen year olds would be eligible for income support in their own right.[61] A proposed amendment to the Social Security Bill, to set the minimum age of entitlement to income support at eighteen, was defeated in Standing Committee by twenty-five votes to one. Nevertheless, in June 1987, following the General Election, plans for removing most under-eighteen year olds' independent entitlement were announced in the Queen's Speech and brought into effect in 1988 via amendments to the Social Security Act 1986.[62]

The Government proposed that help would be directed towards families with children through the payment of a standard *family premium*. Lone parents would

---

[56] Ibid., para. 2.70.   [57] Green Paper (1985), Vol. 1, para. 9.6.
[58] Recognition of those costs had been urged by the SBC in *Response of the Supplementary Benefits Commission to 'Social Assistance'* (London: HMSO, 1979), para. 6.4.
[59] See SSAC, *Second Report 1982/83* (London: HMSO, 1983), para. 4.16 and *Third Report 1984* (London: HMSO, 1985), para. 6.19, which stated: 'Given the fact that 16 year olds are considered old enough to marry, start their own families, pay national insurance contributions and taxes if they are working, and leave their parents to set up an independent existence, we think it would be hard to justify depriving them of a right to supplementary benefit if they are out of work.' See also CPAG, *1984: Changed Priorities Ahead? CPAG's Evidence to the Social Security Reviews* (London: CPAG, 1984), Part I, para. 7.4–7.9 and C. Horton, *Nothing Like a Job* (London: Youthaid, 1985), 43.
[60] *Green Paper* (1985), Vol. 1, para. 9.27.
[61] *Hansard*, HC Debs, Vol. 89, col. 434w, 20 December 1985.
[62] See p. 146 below.

receive, in addition, a *lone-parent premium* and would also qualify for the age twenty-five-plus personal allowance even if aged twenty-four or younger.[63] There would also be standard premiums for pensioners (the *pensioner premium*, with a *higher pensioner premium* for those aged eighty and over or those pensioners with disabilities who met prescribed conditions). There was also to be a *disability premium*, paid automatically to those who received various prescribed disability benefits (such as attendance allowance, mobility allowance, and severe disablement allowance). Other changes, relating to capital and income, included the raising of the capital cut-off level to £6,000, a new earnings disregard of £15 for lone parents, and the removal of water charges and certain residual housing costs from benefit (claimants would be expected to budget for these but account would be taken of this extra liability in fixing the level of income support)[64]. Although the reason for the scrapping of the long-term rate of benefit (paid to those who had been on benefit for not less than fifty-two weeks and who were not required to be available for work) was not really explained, the implication was that it failed to target needs effectively and contributed additional complexity to the system. Its abolition was supported by the House of Commons Social Services Committee.[65] Transitional protection arrangements were promised.

The absence of illustrative figures in the Green Paper made it difficult to determine the precise effect that the proposals would have on claimants' benefit levels. Nevertheless, it was clear that there would be losers, such as young people, and gainers, such as families with children. One of the main concerns was that the move to broad categories of entitlement, such as that arising from the age-twenty-five dividing line or those resulting from the introduction of the various premiums—especially pensioner, family, lone parent, and disability premiums—would make the system less responsive to individual needs, even if administration became easier.[66] Even allowing for the fact that standard rates of benefit were low, some claimants would undoubtedly receive extra help that they might not need.[67] The inflexibility of the proposed arrangements was demonstrated by the plan for only one level of disability premium irrespective of the degree of disability (although there was to be at least some recognition of severe disability through the continuing disregard, for benefit assessment purposes, of mobility allowance and attendance allowance). The Government referred to the difficulties in relating disability to financial needs but said it was keeping this matter under review in the light of its survey of disability.[68]

---

[63] Berthoud argued that the lone-parent premium was unjustifiable because, among those out of work, there was 'no evidence at all that lone parents have any needs not shared by couples with children': R. Berthoud, *Selective Social Security* (London: PSI, 1986), 6.

[64] Green Paper (1985) Vol. 2., para. 2.93.

[65] *Seventh Report, Session 1984/85, The Government's Green Paper 'Reform of Social Security'* (London: HMSO, 1985), para. 34.

[66] Ibid.

[67] See R. Berthoud, *Selective Social Security. An Examination of the Government's Plan* (London: PSI, 1986); M. S. Rowell and A. M. Wilton, 'Supplementary Benefit and the Green Paper' [1986] *J.S.W.L.*, 14–31.

[68] White Paper (1985), para. 3.23.

Later, provision was made in the Social Security Bill for an additional, *severe disability premium* (see below).

The House of Commons Select Committee supported abolition of the house-holder/non-householder distinction but was particularly worried about the effect of the age-twenty-five dividing line. The Government's argument was that a majority of young people in the eighteen to twenty-four age group were not independent, and were assessed as non-householders for benefit purposes, while a majority of those aged twenty-five or over were.[69] The Select Committee regarded the age-twenty-five dividing line as being 'inevitably arbitrary' and pointed to the fact that some 176,000 under twenty-five year olds (representing 30 per cent of all claimants in this age group) received the householder rate of supplementary benefit.[70] Indeed, some 58 per cent of twenty-four year olds were receiving supplementary benefit as house-holders.[71] There was widespread concern that the effect of the reform would be to prolong a young person's period of dependence on his or her family, which was unrealistic.[72] The Government accepted that 'all age dividing lines are . . . open to argument at the margin', but refused to abandon this structural change, arguing that the saving arising from it would enable the Government to target resources more effectively.[73] Concessions were, however, introduced in respect of young couples.[74]

Overall, while there was widespread agreement that the supplementary benefit scheme was urgently in need of reform and that the proposed income support scheme represented an overall improvement, there was concern about the potential impact of the reforms on particular claimant groups.

E. The Social Fund

The social fund was one of the most radical of the Fowler social security reform proposals, not least because much of the available support would take the form of loans rather than grants and because the fund would be cash-limited. It was intended to replace the supplementary benefit single payments system which ministers regarded as virtually out of control. This chapter discusses the background to the introduction of the fund and explains the rationale behind its constituent elements. The current operation of the fund is examined in depth by Simon Rahilly in Chapter 14.

(i) Background: Single Payments

From November 1980 regulations, revised in 1981,[75] specified the items for which a payment (a 'single payment', previously an 'exceptional needs payment') could be made and whether the payment would cover a new or second-hand item. The

[69] Green Paper (1985), Vol. 2, para. 2.73.   [70] N. 65 above, para. 35.
[71] SSAC, *Fourth Report, 1985* (1985), para. 3.8.
[72] See, e.g., House of Commons, Official Report, Standing Committee B, Social Security Bill, 6 March 1986, col. 679, *per* Mrs Margaret Beckett MP and SSAC, *Fourth Report*, op. cit., para. 3.11.
[73] White Paper (1985), para. 3.13.   [74] Ibid., para. 3.10.
[75] Supplementary Benefit (Single Payments) Regs 1981 (S.I. 1981 No. 1528).

regulations were highly technical and were frequently amended. Most claims for single payments were in respect of furniture, clothing, or household equipment. Certain items were excluded (e.g. anything arising from an educational or training need, sports clothes, or a television); and the regulations provided that others were only available in prescribed circumstances (e.g. a payment for the cost of a vacuum cleaner was only available if the claimant was allergic to house dust). To qualify for a payment a claimant had to 'need' the item: for this purpose he or she had not to be in possession of it nor have a suitable alternative available, and must not have unreasonably disposed of an item to be replaced.[76] As part of the general tightening up of the regulations in 1986 (see below), a further test of 'need' was that the claimant had not 'failed to exercise reasonable care to preserve or protect' the item which he or she wished to replace.[77] Payments for clothing and footwear were barred if the need had arisen through 'normal wear and tear', which did not include 'rapid weight loss or gain' or 'the accidental loss of, or damage to, or destruction of an essential item'.[78] As noted in Chapter 4, a small discretionary element was retained in the form of regulation 30, which provided for entitlement where a payment was necessary to avoid serious risk to the health or safety of the claimant or another member of the 'assessment unit' (i.e. all those whose needs were intended to be met by the claimant's supplementary benefit). All such provisions, aimed at defining need for the purposes of these payments, gave fairly wide scope for interpretation. Benefit officers relied on official guidance on these matters in the 'S' Manual. Thus, for example, the guidance suggested that rapid weight gain would not include 'growth spurts' by children.[79]

The introduction of the regulations at first achieved the Government's objective of reducing the number of payments. In 1980–1 there were 26 per cent fewer single payments than the number of exceptional needs payments (ENPs) in the previous year.[80] The SSAC suggested that the decline might have been due to claimants' unfamiliarity with the new regulations; whatever the reason it was only a temporary fall.[81] The overall number of single payments awarded in 1985 was four times greater than the number of ENPs awarded in 1979–80, although the pattern of demand had changed, with claims for clothing grants falling whilst furniture grant applications were rising dramatically.[82]

There is no doubt that the administrative and operational difficulties presented by the growth in single payment claims were the prime reasons behind the restrictions in 1986. Although expenditure on single payments amounted to only 4.4 per cent of

[76] Supplementary Benefit (Single Payments), reg. 3(2).
[77] Ibid., as amended by the Supplementary Benefit (Miscellaneous Amendments) Regulations 1986 (S.I. 1986 No. 1259).
[78] N. 75, reg. 27.   [79] DHSS, 'S' Manual, para. 7471.
[80] See generally J. Allbeson and R. Smith, *We Don't Give Clothing Grants Anymore* (London: CPAG, 1984).
[81] SSAC, *Second Report, 1982/83* (London: HMSO, 1983), para. 9.26.
[82] They rose from 135,000 in 1979 to 947,000 in 1984; and the proportion of claimants in receipt of furniture payments increased from 47 per 1,000 in 1979 to 205 per 1,000 in 1984: SSAC/Secretary of State for Social Services, *The Supplementary Benefit (Miscellaneous Amendments) Regulations (Etc)* Cmnd 9813 (London: HMSO, 1986), para. 29.

all supplementary benefit expenditure in 1985–6, single payments accounted for 48 per cent of all decisions in that period (and 49 per cent of appeals in 1985).[83] The Government claimed that a major reason for the growth in single payments was the 'open-ended nature of the regulations'.[84] This is highly contentious; as the previous discussion has shown, entitlement to a single payment was already subject to satisfaction of numerous conditions. The Government also argued that single payments had assumed a different role to that which had originally been intended; rather than being wholly exceptional they had become part of a claimant's expected entitlement.[85] The SSAC reported that the overall growth in single payments was, however, attributable both to increasing awareness among claimants of their rights (an awareness fuelled by pressure groups' take-up campaigns) and more particularly to the existence of an unmet need.[86] The Committee argued that the Government's tightening up of the rules sought to 'attack the symptoms (increased public expenditure) without fully analysing the causes ...' and could result in widespread hardship amongst claimants who were already living at the poverty level.[87] But the Government remained convinced that operational and financial considerations compelled change.

The 1986 changes[88] tightened up considerably the conditions which had to be satisfied for furniture, household equipment, and bedding payments. Also among the changes was the omission of several items from the previous list of 'essential' items of furniture, although a small lump-sum payment to cover 'miscellaneous' items of furniture became available, subject to extremely strict conditions.[89] Accidental damage to or loss of clothing ceased to be an exception to the general rule that a clothing need arising from 'normal wear and tear' to garments would not be recognised;[90] ministers had acted on advice that the exemption had encouraged claimants to dispose of or damage unwanted clothing and then seek a single payment to replace it. The qualifying period (on benefit) for some single payments was extended from six to twelve months and payment was barred for any item for which a payment had been made in the previous three years. Payments for 'miscellaneous' items were excluded from this bar, but were subject to an even more restrictive one—that once such a payment had been received, another one was not possible (above). There were several and somewhat inconclusive test cases over the question whether the new miscellaneous items payments were within, or excluded from, the scope of the residual

---

[83] SSAC, *Fifth Report, 1986/87* (London: HMSO, 1987) para. 2.3.3.

[84] N. 82 above, para. 28.   [85] Ibid., paras 30 and 31.

[86] As the SBC had noted, 'scale rates of benefit cannot be expected to cover the cost of furniture and larger items of household equipment': SBC, *Annual Report 1978* (London: HMSO, 1979), para. 15.6.

[87] N. 82 above, SSAC's comments, para. 45.

[88] Under the Supplementary Benefit (Miscellaneous Amendments) Regulations 1986 (S.I. 1986 No. 1259).

[89] Buck comments that the introduction of the new 'miscellaneous items' provision presaged the social fund reforms concerned with 'community care': T. Buck, *The Social Fund: Law and Practice* (London: Sweet and Maxwell, 1996), 40.

[90] N. 88, reg. 12.

discretion to make a payment to avoid serious risk to health and safety under regulation 30 (above).[91]

The Government said nothing to indicate that the 1986 single payment reforms were part of the preparation for the social fund changes. However, the rationale for the social fund (see below) was based on similar arguments to those underpinning the 1986 single payments reforms and many observers regarded the Government's real purpose in making the 1986 cutbacks to single payments as being 'to work towards the Social Security Bill's planned abolition of single payments, in advance, by the back door'.[92]

(ii) The Social Fund: General Features

By the time the 1986 single payments restrictions had begun to bite the legislation was already in place for the introduction of the social fund. As noted above, many of the payments under the fund would take the form of loans, repayable out of weekly benefit. The fund itself would be limited in size; it would have an 'annual budget'.[93] Instead of the kind of complex regulation-based legal structure that bedevilled the single payments system, much of the social fund would be administered through the exercise of discretion, to enable 'appropriate and flexible help to be given to those in genuine need'.[94]

It was planned that the fund would have a number of separate elements. One part would be concerned with community care needs: payments, in the form of grants (later classified as 'community care grants'), would be available for items needed or expenses incurred to help people in institutional care to re-establish themselves in the community, or to avert the need for residential care, or ease exceptional family pressures (see Chapter 14). Secondly, funeral and maternity expenses would, as under supplementary benefit, be met via grants, although changes would be made; it later became clear that this was to be one part of the system replacing single payments which would continue to be governed by regulations. Thirdly, payments would be available to help claimants who faced particular difficulty in meeting certain of the costs which they would normally be expected to budget for out of their weekly income, such as replacement of major household items, home repairs, large bills and debts, and the cost of accommodation moves.[95] These became known as 'budgeting loans', and as with community care grants they were to be administered on a discretionary basis. The fact that these payments were to be recoverable would, it was argued, mean the removal of an 'inequity' between the unemployed and those in work—arising from the fact that the former received a grant whilst the latter had to borrow privately if they were unable to meet their needs through budgeting from their wages.[96] Finally, there would be emergency help where the claimant had, for

---

[91] See J. Mesher, *CPAG's Supplementary Benefit and Family Income Supplement: the Legislation* (London: Sweet and Maxwell, 1987).
[92] *Welfare Rights Bulletin* No. 72, June 1986, 2.   [93] Green Paper (1985), Vol. 1., para. 9.8.
[94] Ibid.   [95] Ibid., Vol. 2., para. 2.104.   [96] Ibid.

example, lost possessions through fire or flood. As under the urgent needs payments available through the supplementary benefit system,[97] these payments would be possible irrespective of whether weekly benefit was in payment. It later became clear that these emergency payments would take the form of loans—'crisis loans'. The fund as a whole would be administered by specialist officers in local DHSS offices.

The three most controversial aspects of the proposals for the social fund were: (a) the majority of payments would be subject to the *budget limit* imposed by the Secretary of State; (b) decisions on payments would be based on *discretion* rather than defined legal entitlement; and (c) a high proportion of the payments would take the form of repayable *loans*.

(a) The Budget Limit

It was clear that the Government's intention was to limit the overall amount spent on extra payments to meet exceptional needs. As Timmins says, 'the Social Fund's primary aim was to cap a budget which had ballooned from £44 million in 1981 to £220 million by 1984 as the system sprung leaks at the hands of claimants and welfare rights groups'.[98] The experience of supplementary benefit single payments had been that demand was in effect impossible to control. The Government argued that all social security expenditure was in a sense limited, and there was no reason for the fund to be any different.[99] Yet capping the amount allocated to a particular area of social security expenditure had never occurred in this way before.

As the overall amount available to meet demand was to be limited by the fixed budget, the Government planned to prioritise claims. Priority would be judged with reference to the circumstances in which the need arose (for example, those leaving institutional care would have higher priority than those simply setting up home in the ordinary course of events) and the precise nature of need (so that, for example, a need for a bed would be a higher priority than a need for an armchair). It later became clear that the chances of success might also be affected by the way the particular local office managed its budget, the time of year in which the claim was made, and other variable factors (see further Chapter 14).

In neither the Green Paper nor the White Paper did the Government give any indication of the size of the fund and how it would be allocated to local offices. It was also unclear how the system would be made 'flexible enough to ensure that payments should not cease because a local office had run out of money before the end of the financial year'.[100] The SSAC regarded the whole scheme as 'dominated by the need to keep within the budget' and was anxious lest the budget would result in unmet need,[101] a fear which appeared to be realised by 1990, when it described the budget

[97] Supplementary Benefit (Urgent Cases) Regulations 1981 (S.I. 1981 No. 1529).
[98] N. Timmins, *The Five Giants. A Biography of the Welfare State* (London: Harper Collins, 1995), 403. Timmins was referring, *inter alia*, to the take-up campaigns of CPAG and others.
[99] Green Paper (1985), Vol. 2, para. 2.112.
[100] White Paper (1985), para. 4.38.
[101] SSAC, *The Draft Social Fund Manual Report by the SSAC* (London: SSAC, 1987).

for the first two years of the scheme as having been inadequate.[102] Single payments expenditure payments totalled £370.3 million in 1986; but in its first two years the fund's budget was set at £203 million.[103] Early experience suggested that pressure on local budgets was having the kind of deleterious impact that some had been feared: 'those whose applications are considered of lesser importance may be refused help. At other times of the year or in another area, the same application may have been accepted. This helps explain why the term "lottery" has been applied by some critics to the fund.'[104] The concern was not merely that needs would go unmet through exhaustion of the budget, but also that the budget would 'act as a real constraint on the exercise of creative discretion'.[105] Discretion was, after all, to be a key feature of the new system.

(b) Discretion

It has been argued that 'the decision to move away from regulation towards discretion was very largely to turn the clock back to before 1980'.[106] However, while officers were indeed being given a broader discretion to decide whether the circumstances of the case justified a payment from the fund, in a way that was broadly comparable with the power of benefit officers in the pre-1980 supplementary benefit scheme, there were important differences. First, there was the budget limit, which was of course unprecedented and was certain to limit discretion, as noted above. As Mullen argued, 'caution, not discretion, will be the watchword of (social fund officers)'.[107] A further important difference lay in the legal structure of the fund. In the pre-1980 supplementary benefit scheme, officers' discretion, which enabled them to take account of 'all the circumstances of the case', was constrained only by a limited amount of case law and the secret departmental codes (the 'A' Code and 'AX' Code) (see Chapter 4). The social fund, on the other hand, not only has a more specific set of statutory criteria as a framework within which discretion may be exercised,[108] but also has a set of directions, laid down by the Secretary of State. Officers must act in accordance with them when determining an application.[109] In

[102] SSAC, *Seventh Report, 1990* (London: HMSO, 1990).

[103] In fact, the 1989/90 total was increased to £206 million in the course of the year: see Secretary of State for Social Security, *Annual Report by the Secretary of State for Social Security on the Social Fund 1989/90* Cm 1157 (London: HMSO, 1990), para. 3.7.

[104] SSAC, *The Social Fund—A New Structure* (London: HMSO, 1992), para. 13. Simon Rahilly discusses the current operation of the budget in Chapter 14 below.

[105] R. Walker and D. Lawton, 'The Social Fund as an exercise in resource allocation' (1989) 67 *Public Administration*, 295–317, 300.

[106] Ibid., at 299.

[107] T. Mullen, 'The Social Fund—Cash-Limiting Social Security' (1989) 52 *M.L.R.* 64–92, 85.

[108] See SSCBA 1992, s. 140(1). See the changes to budgeting loans made by the SSA 1998 discussed in Chapter 14.

[109] Ibid., s. 140(2). See further J. Mesher, 'The Legal Structure of the Social Fund', in M. D. A. Freeman (ed.), *Critical Issues in Welfare Law* (London: Stevens, 1990), 35–57; and *R v Secretary of State for Social Services and the Social Fund Inspectors ex p Stitt, Sherwin and Roberts* (1990) CO/1026/89, CO/536/89, and CO/1901/89, *The Times*, 23 February (QBD) and 5 July (CA) (*Stitt*) only.

practice the directions have operated rather like regulations[110] by setting quite firm limits to officers' discretion—for example, prohibiting the award of a social fund payment to an applicant within twenty-six weeks of a previous award save in exceptional prescribed circumstances and excluding a list of expenditure needs from the scope of budgeting loans.[111]

The White Paper also explained that officers would receive guidance to 'set out the purposes for which the fund is intended and the factors to be taken into account' and to indicate the 'broad approach to be followed, leaving the decision to the officer on the spot in the light of the circumstances of each case and the spirit of the guidance'.[112] This guidance, set out in the *Social Fund Guide*, has been used to establish priorities for various payments. It also explains, for example, the factors which would determine the extent of the applicant's ability to repay a loan.[113] The potential of the Secretary of State's guidance to constrain the exercise of discretion has become clear: officers (and inspectors) are obliged to take account (one might add, close account) of it.[114] This issue is discussed further by Simon Rahilly in Chapter 14.

For the exercise of discretion to operate meaningfully would demand that officers be able to take close account of individual circumstances. In the case of community care grants, directed at claimants facing 'particular pressures' and 'special needs', it was envisaged that officers might need to have a much less impersonal relationship with applicants to enable them to respond more effectively to their circumstances. The Green Paper suggested that the role demanded of officers might approximate to that of social workers or other care professionals and that in the longer term officers might need to work jointly with such professionals to respond effectively to needs.[115] Such an initiative was linked in the Green Paper to the development of the 'care in the community' policy. However, this kind of co-ordinated approach involving the social fund has not really developed: 'As events turned out the more ambitious ideas for the social fund did not materialise, partly thwarted by widespread opposition [by these professional groups] to the whole idea of a discretionary social fund . . .'[116] Indeed, the fact that discretion was returning to displace rules on entitlement was not welcomed universally. Although merit was seen in the greater flexibility which was promised, there was concern lest the inconsistency and arbitrariness which characterised some of the decision-making in the supplementary benefit

---

[110] See R. Drabble and T. Lynes, 'The Social Fund—Discretion or Control?' [1989] *P.L.* 297–322.

[111] Social Fund Directions 7 and 12: But see now the changes made by the SSA 1998, discussed in Chapter 14 below.

[112] White Paper (1985), para. 4.42.

[113] An ability to repay the loan was a factor to be taken into account in determining whether a budgeting loan should be granted: see below.

[114] SSCBA 1992, s. 140(2). See also *R v Independent Review Service ex p Connell* (1994) CO/1811/94, 3 November 1994, *per* Brooke J.

[115] Green Paper (1985), Vol. 2, para. 2.100.

[116] M. Huby and R. Walker, 'Adapting to the social fund' (1991) 25(4) *Social Policy and Administration* 329–49, 331.

scheme prior to 1980 would be repeated.[117] A further concern was that there would be many unsuccessful applicants whose dissatisfaction could manifest itself in anger and abuse directed at administrators.[118]

(c) Loans

A uniform system of loans was to replace a more diverse system of grants to meet ordinary budgeting needs, but grants were to be available in cases of particular difficulty. The rationale for this was essentially that budgeting needs were something which all households faced, whether their members were dependent on benefit or not (as noted above), while expenses arising from crises or other dramatic changes in circumstances (such as leaving institutional care or experiencing the break-up of a cohabitational relationship) hit those on benefit particularly hard and warranted special help. The Government proposed that payments to assist with budgeting requirements would take the form of an advance—an interest-free loan—recovered by regular deductions from benefit.[119] The concept of an 'advance' was consistent with the Government's analogy with a 'banking service'.[120] The proportion of weekly benefit which could be used for repayment purposes would, however, be subject to a limit. Moreover, as the payment would take the form of a loan, decisions on applications would be based not merely on whether it was reasonable to meet the claimant's need but also on the claimant's ability to repay.[121] There would be a capital rule (based on a threshold of £500, or £1,000 for a couple). Payments would be subject to a maximum and a minimum (later prescribed by directions).

There were two major disadvantages to the loan arrangements. First, claimants who had too many existing financial commitments might be denied help because of their inability to repay the loan (a likely ground for refusal), leading to the criticism that one could be, in effect, too poor to be eligible for help. Secondly, the fact that loans had to be repaid from basic weekly benefit raised concerns about the resultant additional financial pressures on successful claimants. The SSAC felt that unless basic benefit increased it was not reasonable 'in all the circumstances where single payments are currently available, and which cannot be described as community care, to expect claimants in future to meet the cost from within their weekly income'.[122] The Committee advocated grants rather than loans for specific items of furniture and equipment, including beds, cookers, and heaters, in specific circumstances.[123]

---

[117] SSAC, *Fifth Report, 1986/87* (London: HMSO, 1987), para. 2.3.8. Note also Mullen's comment that inconsistencies and arbitrary decision-making are likely consequences of the pressure of the cash limit and anomalies in office allocations: T. Mullen, 'The Social Fund—Cash-Limiting Social Security' (1989) 52 *M.L.R.*, 64–92, 92.

[118] N.U.S., *Response of the National Union of Students to the Green Paper 'Reform of Social Security'* (London: N.U.S., 1985), para. 3.6.

[119] Green Paper (1985), Vol. 2, para. 2.105.   [120] White Paper (1985), para. 4.28.

[121] Ibid., para. 4.27.

[122] SSAC, *Fourth Report, 1985* (London: HMSO, 1985), paras 3.55 and 3.56.

[123] SSAC, *Fifth Report, 1986/87* (London: HMSO, 1987), para. 2.3.7.

(iii) Appeals and Reviews

A new system of reviews would, for most payments, replace the independent right of appeal to a tribunal which had been available in all single payment cases. The Government argued that the existing appeal arrangements[124] had proved unsuitable, as small sums were involved (there was thus a 'sledgehammer effect') and the formal appeals machinery was 'too slow, too cumbersome and too inflexible'.[125] There would only be an internal review procedure instead.[126] Essentially, initial decisions would be reviewed by the officer who made them and, if the claimant remained dissatisfied, by senior management in the local office. Regard would have to be had to the directions and guidance on the social fund issued by the Secretary of State.[127] It was argued that a review would be more likely to result in a 'sensible' outcome the nearer the review was to the original judgment, both in terms of locus and time.[128] 'Sensible' was perhaps a euphemism for 'less generous': 'It is difficult to avoid the impression that Ministers' impatience with appeal tribunals is as much caused by the obligation imposed on the Department to pay money it would prefer to withhold, as by the triviality of the nuts cracked by the sledgehammer.'[129]

As noted above, nearly all appeals to SSATs at this time related to single payments (and one in four single-payments appeals succeeded).[130] Thus this change to long established appeal rights would affect a substantial number of claimants. Nevertheless, such a reform was perhaps inevitable given the shift to a cash-limited social fund scheme. As Dean argues, it might have been seen as undermining the credence of the independent appeal system if a tribunal's decision-making had to be subject to the constraints of the local office budget; while at the same time if the tribunal was able to ignore such budgets it would 'dilute the potentially punitive impact of the social fund'.[131] The Government also argued that another feature of the social fund—discretion in a considerable part of it (above)—made decisions unsuitable to be dealt with by appeal tribunals: 'Decisions which turn on whether it is reasonable to give or deny help in a particular case lend themselves far less readily to a separate, external assessment than do matters which turn on more specific criteria.'[132] There certainly had been criticism in the past of the way that tribunals had exercised discretion (in particular, supplementary benefit appeal tribunals[133]); but the judicialising reform of

---

[124] Social security appeals are discussed further by Roy Sainsbury in Chapter 7.
[125] Green Paper (1985), para. 2.110.
[126] Ibid., para. 2.111. Social fund appeals to a tribunal were to be limited to maternity, funeral, and (later) cold weather payments.
[127] Ibid., para. 4.51.   [128] Ibid.
[129] R. Berthoud, *The Examination of Social Security* (London: P. S.I., 1985), 113.
[130] See N. Wikeley, 'The Future of Social Security Appeal Tribunals' (1987) 17 *Family Law* 133–5.
[131] H. Dean, *Social Security and Social Control* (London: Routledge, 1991), 168.
[132] White Paper (1985), para. 4.50.
[133] Bell found that in supplementary benefit appeal tribunals (SBATs) 'a disciplined and systematic approach to the exercise of discretion' had not evolved: K. Bell, *Research Study on Supplementary Benefit Appeal Tribunals. Review of Main Findings. Conclusions. Recommendations* (London: HMSO, 1975), 13. Adler et al. found SBAT members unwilling 'to exercise discretion . . . in a creative manner': M. Adler, et al., 'The

the tribunals in 1984 had seemed to promise considerable improvement in the quality of tribunal adjudication under the existing benefits structure.[134] Some argued that the element of discretion in the social fund made it particularly important for there to be an independent right of appeal (see below).[135] Indeed, the Council on Tribunals, in an unprecedented special report,[136] expressed its deep concern that a right of appeal which could be traced back over fifty years was being abolished. It found the reasons put forward by the Government for reform as seriously lacking. For example, it pointed out that discretion-based decisions had always been challengeable before tribunals under the pre-1980 supplementary benefit scheme. It regarded tribunals as having played a vital role in checking incorrect DHSS decisions, as demonstrated by the relatively high success rate for appeals (above).

In the event, the Social Security Bill was amended to provide for a third level of review by a 'social fund inspector',[137] who would be a member of a body of such inspectors (later part of the Independent Review Service) appointed by the new Social Fund Commissioner.[138] Despite the assertion that the inspector would be independent,[139] critics remained unconvinced of the case for the reduction in the appeal tribunals' jurisdiction.[140] The applicant would not have an opportunity to present and argue his or her case in person before the inspector, although would be able to attend an interview at the previous level, when the decision was reviewed by the social fund officer.[141] Thus it has been argued that 'the design of the procedure with the personal hearing in one stage and the independence in another stage means that neither stage fully meets the requirement of a personal hearing before an independent arbitrator'.[142] Various proposals were presented for ensuring at least some traditional independence to the adjudication process, such as by using tribunals in cases where the decision seemed to disclose an error of law, breach of natural justice or failure to state adequate reasons,[143] or establishing adjudicative bodies combining independent members with perhaps DSS officials. However, there is some force to

---

conduct of tribunal hearings', in M. Adler and A. Bradley, *Justice, Discretion and Poverty* (Abingdon: Professional Books, 1976), 109–129, 117. See also *R v West London SBAT ex p Wyatt* [1978] 1 WLR 240 and *Wald v SBC* (1980), 9 October QBD (unreported).

[134] N. Harris, 'Reform of the Supplementary Benefit Appeal System' [1983] *J.S.W.L.* 212–27.

[135] See M. S. Rowell and A. W. Wilton, 'Supplementary Benefit and the Green Paper' [1986] *J.S.W.L.* 14–31, 30 and 31.

[136] *Social Security—Abolition of independent appeals under the proposed Social Fund*, Cmnd. 9722 (London: HMSO, 1986).

[137] SSA 1986, s. 34.   [138] Ibid., s. 35.

[139] For discussion of the question of independence, see T. Buck, *The Social Fund: Law and Practice* (London: Sweet and Maxwell, 1996), 108–11.

[140] See M. Partington, 'Adjudication and the Social Fund: Some preliminary observations' (1986) *Legal Action*, April; SSAC, *Report on the Draft Social Fund Manual* (London: SSAC, 1987), para. 45; and H. Bolderson, 'The Right to Appeal and the Social Fund' (1988) 15 *J.L.S.* 279–92.

[141] See Social Fund Direction 33.

[142] G. Dalley and R. Berthoud, *Challenging Discretion—The Social Fund Review Procedure* (London: P. S.I., 1992), 148.

[143] M. S. Rowell, 'The Social Fund—Transitional Measures and Possible Alternatives' [1987] *J.S.W.L.* 137–49; M. Partington, n. 140 above.

Howells' argument[144] that such departures from the traditional tribunal model could have caused confusion and added to the complexity of the adjudication system—although the same could be said of the social fund review arrangements themselves. Later, as Sainsbury shows in Chapter 7, the social fund review model seems to have influenced the reforms to social security adjudication in general under the Social Security Act 1998.

(iv) The social fund: comment

As structured, the social fund was from the outset perceived to be one of the most problematic of the reforms emanating from the Fowler reviews of social security. Much of the concern which was expressed at the time was about matters of principle. For example, basing entitlement on the exercise of discretion was a further retreat from the rights-based notion of universalism associated with Beveridge. Moreover, repayable loans were seen as reasserting the notion of the deserving and undeserving poor and effecting social control: those who acted responsibly by avoiding too many financial commitments were more likely to be helped. Cash-limiting only the part of the social security system that catered for the most needy claimants could be regarded as further marginalising the poor. Removing the right of independent appeal constituted an assault on one of the cornerstones of administrative justice.

There were several unique features which gave the fund an experimental character, both in terms of the fund's legal structure and some of its key substantive areas. The experience of the first decade of the social fund has shown many of the fears about administrative difficulties and hardship expressed at this time to be justified. The way the fund has been operating and its present legal structure are discussed by Simon Rahilly in Chapter 14.

F. Housing Benefit

As noted in Chapter 4, a new housing benefit scheme was introduced in 1983. By 1984–5, one in three households (an average of 7.5 million households each week) was receiving housing benefit: a 'sharp increase in expenditure and caseload' was said to have resulted from the impact of the early 1980s recession on employment and in some cases from local authority rating policy (which the Government was in fact seeking to constrain further through its new rate capping powers).[145] Yet not only was the benefit widely received, it was also a widespread cause of dissatisfaction. Claimants were said to find it difficult to understand as a result of its complexity. It was said to be a cause of inequity between those on benefit and those in low-paid work. Local authorities had experienced an increasing administrative burden,

---

[144] G. G. Howells, 'Social Fund Budgeting Loans—Social and Civil Justice?' (1990) 9 *C.J.Q.* 118–38, 135.

[145] Green Paper (1985) Vol. 2, paras 3.29, 3.34, and 3.35.

inadequately compensated for by the Government.[146] The appeal system was criticised by lawyers for lacking independence and offering poor standards of justice (see below). Thus, as David Donnison commented, there was widespread agreement that a solution to the problems afflicting the housing benefit scheme called for 'radical reform'.[147] The review team examining housing benefit, whose report to the Secretary of State was published,[148] had, as its terms of reference: 'To examine the structure and scope of the (housing benefit) scheme to ensure it is as simple as possible, and that help is concentrated on those in most need; and to improve its administration by local authorities.' The review was limited in scope (failing to look at housing support in general) and was, as mentioned above, to assume a nil-cost basis to reform.[149] Nevertheless, the review did attempt to tackle some of the key problems with the housing benefit scheme as it then existed.

As noted in Chapter 4, the introduction of unified housing benefit in 1983 had not gone smoothly, with confusion, problems over delayed and inaccurate assessments and unjustifiable variations in provision.[150] The review team noted that the scheme had had 'an exceptionally difficult start'.[151] But the team concluded that administration of housing benefit, while in need of improvement, should remain with local authorities. It advocated internal and external monitoring of administration; and it wanted a central subsidy of less than 100 per cent to provide an incentive for local authorities to 'curb abuse, particularly in relation to unjustified rent increases and upmarketing, and to restrict unreasonably high expenditure'.[152] As regards appeal and review arrangements, the review team preferred to continue with the system of housing benefit review boards, for the time being at least, despite the criticism of their lack of independence, training, and legally qualified chairs.[153]

The review team recommended alignment of the separate income tests within the housing benefit scheme, to avoid inequities in the treatment of persons under them.[154] The supplementary benefit scale rates (which determined entitlement to 'certificated' housing benefit) and the housing benefit needs allowances (in 'standard' housing benefit) could, they believed, be brought into line if the additions made to

---

[146] See the comments of the Association of District Councils, in P. Kemp and N. Raynsford (eds), *Housing Benefit: The Evidence* (London: Housing Centre Trust, 1984), 14.

[147] 'Introduction', in Kemp and Raynsford, ibid., p. vi.

[148] Housing Benefit Review Team, *Housing Benefit Review: Report of the Review Team*, Cmnd 9520 (London: HMSO, 1985).

[149] For criticism, see for example the evidence presented by the Association of Metropolitan Authorities, in Kemp and Raynsford (eds), op. cit., 1; and CPAG, *1984: Changed Priorities Ahead?* (London: CPAG, 1984), Appendix.

[150] R. Walker, *Housing Benefit: the Experience of Implementation* (London: Housing Centre Trust, 1985); P. Kemp, 'The reform of housing benefit' (1987) 21(2) *Social Policy and Administration* 171.

[151] N. 148 above, para. 1.11.

[152] Ibid., para. 5.21. Subsidy is discussed by Simon Rahilly in Chapter 13.

[153] M. Partington, H. Bolderson, and K. Smith, *Housing Benefit Review Procedures* (Brunel: Brunel University, Department of Law, 1984). For the review team's rationale see n. 148 above, paras 5.28 and 5.29. Roy Sainsbury discusses housing benefit review boards in the broader context of reform of adjudication in Chapter 7 and Simon Rahilly explains the current arrangements in Chapter 13.

[154] N. 148 above, para. 2.6. See further Chapter 4.

supplementary benefit for heating and other 'additional requirements' disappeared under the restructuring of that benefit. Those whose income was at or below the supplementary benefit level would receive 100 per cent of their rent and rates. Where income was above this level, rent and rates support could be reduced in accordance with a 'single taper' scheme.[155] What this meant was that the claimant would have to meet a fixed proportion of his or her housing costs where income exceeded the supplementary benefit scale rates. Such a reform would meet the objective of greater simplicity and would obviate the need for housing benefit supplement (HBS). As noted in Chapter 4, HBS was at that time paid by the DHSS to those receiving 'standard' housing benefit if their contribution towards rent and rates left them with a residual income that was below the supplementary benefit scale rate. Around 200,000 households were receiving HBS. The review team acknowledged that the new single taper structure would lead to some redistribution of support in favour of those with higher costs and against those with below average costs.[156]

The team also recommended that the measures to prevent unreasonable exploitation of the scheme by landlords or tenants be more widely and effectively utilised.[157] It also noted that claims for housing benefit by students had proved particularly problematic, because benefit had to be reassessed at regular intervals throughout the year, and recommended that students should (subject to reform of the grants system) in the long term be excluded from housing benefit and in the short term be excluded during the grant-aided period each year (so they would qualify only during the long vacation).[158] This issue is discussed further in Chapter 11. Another important area which was examined was the 'non-dependant deduction'—a fixed-rate reduction in a person's housing benefit where he or she had a non-dependant (typically the claimant's adult child, brother/sister, or parent[159]) living with him or her, based on the assumption that a non-dependant could and should make a contribution towards housing costs. In April 1984 the deduction in respect of non-dependants in work stood at £8.20, or £3.30 for sixteen to seventeen year olds.[160] It was estimated that there were 850,000 households whose benefit was subject to a deduction in respect of a non-dependant.[161] In practice, however, parents were frequently reluctant to ask their children for the full rate of the deduction.[162] Evidence to the review suggested that the deduction was unfairly high.[163] The deduction was also regarded as complicating the administration of the scheme and causing an unfair disparity between

[155] Ibid., paras 2.22–2.27.   [156] Ibid., para. 3.22.   [157] Ibid., ch. 3.
[158] Ibid., paras 4.8 and 4.9.
[159] S. Witherspoon, C. Whyley, and E. Kempston, *Paying for Rented Housing*, DSS Research Report No. 43 (London: HMSO, 1996), para. 1.6.1.
[160] S.I. 1984 No. 103. This level was criticised by the SSAC as being excessive: *Report on the Draft Housing Benefit Amendment Regulations 1984*, Cmnd 9150 (London: HMSO, 1994), para. 28.
[161] Green Paper (1985), Vol. 2, para. 3.22.
[162] R. Cusack and J. Roll, *Families Rent Apart* (London: CPAG, 1985); also Kemp and Raynsford, op. cit. n.146 above, 5 and 12. This reluctance was because of the young persons' generally very low earnings.
[163] Kemp and Raynsford, op. cit., n. 146 above, 91 and 98; and CPAG, *Evidence to the Housing Benefit Review* (London: CPAG, 1984), paras 2.5 and 3.6.

owner-occupiers, who suffered no such deduction from mortgage tax relief, and those renting on housing benefit.[164] But the review team felt that the principle behind the deduction was right and noted that the cost of abolishing it would be £350 million per annum.[165] The review team nevertheless accepted that changes should be made to the structure of the deduction.[166]

The Government announced that to achieve the review team's objectives of greater equity, simplicity, efficiency, and effectiveness, housing benefit, which would remain under the administration of local authorities but would be subject to stricter controls, would be restructured.[167] Benefit would be assessed using the same scales as the proposed income support scheme, and those households who received income support or who had an equivalent level of income would automatically be eligible for maximum assistance with rent and rates. Benefit for households above this level of income would be reduced under a single taper; and all claimants would have to make some contribution (probably 20 per cent) to their domestic rates, ostensibly to bolster 'local accountability' of authorities to users of their services, but clearly aimed also at saving expenditure. Other recommendations of the review team, relating to control of excessive expenditure (including new subsidy arrangements, with the Government's initial subsidy to be set at 80 per cent but capable of variation), long-term removal of student support from the housing benefit system, and reform of the non-dependant deduction,[168] were also accepted. Water charges were to be absorbed into the income support scheme. The review team's response to the criticism of review boards was endorsed by the Government; there would be no change, but the matter would be reviewed.

The single taper was, however, thought likely to cause hardship for low-income owner-occupiers in particular.[169] This was because it had the effect of reducing rates support for those who paid rates only.[170] The Government therefore announced in the White Paper that it had decided to retain separate tapers for rent and rates.[171] Nevertheless, there was concern that hardship would result from the insistence that claimants should make at least a 20 per cent contribution to their rates.[172] Furthermore, although the combination of income tests was welcomed for improving simplicity and consistency, there was concern that inequities in the income support personal allowances would be replicated in housing benefit. Young people in particular would lose out, because of the income support age-twenty-five split (see section D above); the rate of housing benefit for the 200,000–250,000 under twenty-

[164] Kemp and Raynsford, op. cit., 5, 19, 24, 61, and 87.   [165] N. 148 above, para. 4.12.

[166] Ibid.   [167] Green Paper (1985) Vol. 2, ch. 3.

[168] In the event the Government opted for a fixed-rate deduction, but with account taken of income above or below a prescribed level (set at £49.20 in 1988–9).

[169] This was the view of the SSAC: see White Paper (1985), para. 3.58; see also House of Commons Social Services Committee, *First Report 1985–86. Reform of Social Security*, HC 180 (London: HMSO, 1986), para. 34.

[170] R. Berthoud, *The Examination of Social Security* (London: P.S.I., 1985), 55.

[171] White Paper (1985), para. 3.58.

[172] R. Berthoud, *Selective Social Security* (London: PSI, 1986), 18.

five year olds who received standard housing benefit in any week would be lower.[173] The Government acknowledged that there would be changes in the level of entitlement for a large number of households as a result of the proposed reforms. It subsequently emerged that the reforms had not only reduced entitlement for some claimants but had also had the effect of making 13 per cent fewer claimants eligible for the benefit than would previously have been the case.[174]

Leaving aside these criticisms, the general attempt to simplify housing benefit and remove some of the administratively awkward aspects, such as the housing benefit supplement, were widely welcomed. Nevertheless, local authorities still faced a considerable burden in implementing the new arrangements.

G. Maternity, Death, and Widowhood

The maternity benefits available at this time were the flat-rate universal maternity grant (see Chapter 4), which had been fixed at £25 since 1969, and the contributions-based maternity allowance, fixed in 1984–5 at £27.25 but with a reduced rate for those unable to meet the contribution conditions in full. The Government argued that the grant had 'outlived its usefulness' and proposed its abolition, on the grounds that to restore its value (to £125) would have cost an extra £70 million per annum and that removing it would enable extra help to be given to low-income families, via the new social fund.[175] The social fund maternity payment would be set at £75: it was increased slightly, to £80, when it came into operation, but was still regarded by the SSAC as 'insufficient to cover all maternity needs for the poorest mothers'.[176] The overall effect was a cut in support, as average single payments for maternity needs in 1983 were £60 and such women also received the £25 maternity grant.[177]

As regards the contributory maternity allowance, paid for eighteen weeks (see Chapter 4), it was proposed that the qualifying test should be changed to put more emphasis on recent work. Under the arrangements then in force, it was possible for someone to qualify for the benefit even where they had not worked for two or more years before the expected week of confinement. It was also proposed that women should be given more choice as to the period for which they received the allowance. As things stood, every week a woman worked beyond the eleventh week before her baby was due meant a week's less benefit.[178] For the most part these changes to maternity allowance were welcomed. In announcing that they would go ahead, the Government also indicated that the new statutory maternity allowance would be paid by employers and recovered from the state in the same way as statutory sick pay—

---

[173] P. Lewis and I. Willmore, *The Fowler Review: Effect on Young People* (London: Youthaid, 1985), 9–10.
[174] S. Witherspoon, C. Whyley, and E. Kempston, *Paying for Rented Housing*, DSS Research Report No. 43 (London: HMSO, 1996), para. 1.5.
[175] Green Paper (1985), Vol. 2, paras 5.17–5.19 and 5.23.
[176] SSAC, *Fifth Report, 1986/87* (London: HMSO, 1987), para. 2.3.16.
[177] National Council for One Parent Families, *The Insecurity System* (1985), para. 2.3.
[178] Green Paper (1985), Vol. 2, para. 5.21.

offering women a 'simpler and more convenient' way of receiving assistance. But a residual state maternity allowance scheme would continue to provide payments for some women.[179] Maternity benefits are discussed further by Gillian Douglas in Chapter 9.

Death grant, then paid at five different rates, but with a maximum of £30, was also recommended for abolition. The grant covered less than one-tenth of the average cost of a simple funeral and thus almost all of the cost was already met out of private resources. As a universal payment, it also failed to meet the Government's objective of effective targeting of help towards the most needy. As with the maternity grant, it was to be replaced by help under the social fund.[180]

The case for reform of widow's benefits[181] was based on the need for the benefits to reflect more accurately the changed social circumstances of women, and, in particular, the increasing number of women who worked, headed one-parent families, or were protected financially by occupational pensions. Widow's allowance, which was paid for the first twenty-six weeks after bereavement at a flat rate of £51.10 plus child additions (£7.65 per child), was to be replaced with a single lump sum of £1,000. The Government argued that a lump sum at this time would help bereaved women to cope with the immediate financial worries facing them at a difficult time.[182] The widowed mother's allowance (£35.80 plus £7.65 per child at that time) was to become payable from the date of bereavement rather than after six months, but the personal extension (for widows who had a non-dependent sixteen to nineteen year old living at home for whom child benefit was not payable) was to be ended. The reduced rate of widow's pension would apply to those aged forty-five to fifty-five rather than aged forty to fifty, in order to target help on older women, who were less likely to resume a career following their bereavement. The changes would not affect the benefit already in payment to existing widows.[183] The National Council for One Parent Families argued that the proposals were 'not designed to improve the circumstances of widowed families, but rather to make cuts and achieve large savings for the social security budget'.[184]

The Government's proposals on widow's benefits certainly did not represent an attempt at comprehensive reform, nor were they based on a comprehensive review, despite the fact that one had been recommended a couple of years earlier.[185] The Government ignored war widows' pensions and the consequences of separation and divorce for women later widowed. It also avoided opening up the issue of a possible benefit for widowers. The proposals, although welcome, were said to have worn 'an air of expediency'.[186]

---

[179] White Paper (1985), paras 5.20–5.25.   [180] Green Paper (1985), Vol. 2., paras 5.25–5.37.
[181] Their development post-Beveridge is discussed in Chapter 4 at p. 103.
[182] Ibid., paras 5.45–5.51.   [183] Ibid., paras 5.53 and 5.55.
[184] National Council for One Parent Families, op. cit., para. 10.
[185] House of Commons Social Services Committee, *Third Report 1981–82*, HC 26–I (London: HMSO, 1982), para. 198.
[186] House of Commons Social Services Committee, *Seventh Report, Session 1984/85, The Government's Green Paper 'Reform of Social Security'* (London: HMSO, 1985), para. 83.

The reforms on maternity, death, and widowhood were undoubtedly an attempt to modernise these areas of provision, but subject to the Government's nil-cost basis of reform and exploiting the convenient rationalisation—'targeting'. The latter was certainly the proposed basis for the abolition of the death grant and maternity grant, which meant that two further elements of the universalist welfare state planned by Beveridge were to disappear.

3. THE SOCIAL SECURITY ACT 1986 AND ITS AFTERMATH

The Social Security Act 1986 provided the broad framework for the changes outlined above. In the case of the income-related benefits, the basic conditions of entitlement (the claimant had to be in Great Britain, available for work, not in 'relevant education', have no income or one which did not exceed a prescribed amount, and so on) were set out in the Act. The definitions and exceptions, and the criteria for calculating income, capital, and eligible rent and for assessing entitlement to income support premiums, were all set out in regulations.[187] In some cases amendments were made even before the schemes came into operation.[188] The pattern of piecemeal and frequent amendment of the regulations which has continued ever since then was thus established: key changes over the years have included the introduction of a carer's premium in income support in 1990 and the reduction in the minimum qualifying hours for family credit to sixteen per week in 1992. The Secretary of State's directions and guidance on the social fund were also issued. There were also important transitional arrangements which in the short term cushioned some claimants against immediate reductions in benefit resulting from the reforms.[189]

The various proposals emanating from the Fowler reviews had been taken through Parliament with little amendment.[190] There were, however, a small number of significant changes, including a key reform to unemployment benefit (a benefit which had not directly been within the scope of the reviews), involving an increase in the maximum disqualification period from six weeks to thirteen,[191] and a new third stage of review in the social fund and an office of Social Fund Commissioner,[192] as noted above. Another important amendment was the introduction of a 'severe disability premium' in the income support scheme.[193]

The 1986 Act was the first major piece of primary legislation on social security for

---

[187] See SSA 1986, ss 20–22; Family Credit (General) Regulations 1987 (S.I. 1987 No. 1973); the HB(G) Regs 1987; and the IS(G) Regs 1987.

[188] For example, the Income Support (General) Amendment Regulations 1988 (S.I. 1988 No. 663).

[189] See, for example, the Income Support (Transitional) Regulations 1987 (S.I. 1987 No. 1969).

[190] R. Lister, 'The Politics of Social Security: An Assessment of the Fowler Review', in A. Dilnot and I. Walker (eds), *The Economics of Social Security* (Oxford: Oxford University Press, 1989), 200–23.

[191] SSA 1986, s. 43(2)–(3). The Secretary of State in fact acquired a power to effect further changes to the limit by statutory instrument, exercised in 1988 in extending the limit to 26 weeks: Unemployment Benefit (Disqualification Period) Order 1988 (S.I. 1988 No. 487).

[192] SSA 1986, ss. 34 and 35.   [193] Ibid. s. 22. See Chapter 12 below.

a number of years. After it, however, but not necessarily because of it, a new Social Security Act became almost an annual event. One measure that was passed almost straight away was the Social Fund (Maternity and Funeral Expenses) Act 1987, which gave the Secretary of State the power (omitted from the 1986 Act as originally enacted) to prescribe amounts of social fund funeral and maternity expenses payments and the items which they covered.[194] The Social Security Act 1988 came next. It received the Royal Assent only four weeks before many of the Fowler reforms came into effect and it built, in part, on them. In particular, it amended the 1986 Act to raise the minimum age of entitlement to income support from sixteen to eighteen.[195] Provision was made for exception to this general rule under regulations[196] and via a general discretion to pay income support to a sixteen or seventeen year old where 'it appears to the Secretary of State that severe hardship will result to that person unless income support is paid to him'.[197]

There were also less significant, tidying-up reforms to the income support scheme and some technical changes to the family credit scheme.[198] Changes were also made to contribution conditions for national insurance benefits and to the night rate of attendance allowance.[199] The Secretary of State was required to review the rate of child benefit annually (in April) taking account of the RPI and other relevant external factors.[200] Changes were also made to the social fund. A power was added enabling cold weather payments to be brought within the scope of the non-discretionary social fund and the Secretary of State was required to prepare an annual report to Parliament on the social fund as a whole.

By this time, the Fowler reforms were largely in place. Mr Fowler himself had been replaced by John Moore. Emphasis now began to shift further towards a New Right agenda of tackling 'welfare dependency'.[201] The Social Security Act 1989 tightened up the availability for work test, as the Government turned its attention towards the 'voluntarily unemployed'. Further piecemeal reforms followed, including changes to pensions, some of which aimed to give effect to Council Directive 86/378 on equal treatment for men and women under occupational pension schemes and others of which freed persons above retirement age to work whilst drawing a state pension.[202]

---

[194] SSA 1986, s. 32(2)(a), as amended by the 1987 Act. These payments formed the basis of the non-discretionary social fund, which actually came into operation in April 1987, a year before the rest of the fund: see the Social Fund Maternity and Funeral Expenses (General) Regulations 1987 (S.I. 1987 No. 481).

[195] SSA 1986, s. 20(3)(a), as amended by the SSA 1988, s. 4. See N. Harris, 'Raising the Minimum Age of Entitlement to Income Support: Social Security Act 1988' (1988) 15 *J. of Law and Society*, 201–15.

[196] IS(G) Regs 1987, as amended by the Income Support (General) Amendment No. 3 Regulations 1988 (S.I. 1988 No. 1228).

[197] SSA 1986, s. 20(4A), as amended by SSA 1988, s. 4.

[198] See N. Wikeley, 'Training, Targeting and Tidying Up: The Social Security Act 1988' [1989] *J.S.W.L.* 277–92, at 287–8.

[199] SSA 1988, s. 1, amending the SSA 1975, s. 35. The AA reform aimed to cancel out the effect of *Moran v Secretary of State for Social Services*, Reported as appendix to *R(A)1/88*. See Chapter 12 below.

[200] See Wikeley (1989), n. 198 above.

[201] C. Oppenheim and R. Lister, 'Ten years after the 1986 Social Security Act' , *Social Policy Rev.* 8 (1996) 84–105, 87.

[202] See Ogus, Barendt, and Wikeley (1995), 221.

Changes to the administration of the system, including the establishment of 'Next Steps' Agencies—such as the Benefits Agency and Contributions Agency (both established in 1991)[203]—and computerisation of benefits (aided by a new Information Technology Services Agency), were still underway but were soon completed.

Following reforms of disability benefits in 1991–2,[204] the Social Security Act 1986 was, together with the provisions on means-tested benefits and appeals, consolidated within the Social Security Contributions and Benefits Act 1992 and Social Security Administration Act 1992. By this time the community charge (or poll tax) (later itself replaced by council tax) had replaced the domestic rates system, leading to the introduction of a new means-tested benefit (community charge benefit, later replaced by council tax benefit). The introduction of jobseeker's allowance (JSA) in 1996[205] established a new unified benefit for the unemployed, with a contribution-based six months of entitlement in place of unemployment benefit and thereafter an entitlement on the basis of a means-test. As discussed in Chapter 6, income-based JSA is also available from the start of unemployment (but not the first seven days) to those who do not satisfy the contribution conditions. For many claimants, income-based JSA has taken the place of income support: but it is based on more or less the same means-test. Income support has remained for those not required to enter the jobs market, such as those who are retired or caring for children. Thus the central elements of the Fowler reforms have continued. The introduction of working families tax credit in place of family credit[206] marks the first radical departure from the Fowler scheme; but even here the new form of assistance has the same role as its predecessor (and similar features).

4. CONCLUSION

If the Fowler reforms were a genuine attempt to simplify parts of the social security system they were only a partial success. The rules governing basic entitlement to income support were complex from the start. The single payments regulations were swept away, but no one pretends that administering the social fund is any easier. Indeed, administrative costs involved in the social fund were equivalent to 61 per cent of the total expenditure on this benefit in 1989[207] and were still nearly 50 per cent in 1997–8.[208] In fact, the overall financial savings for the Government from the

---

[203] The Contributions Agency has since been discontinued, its functions being subsumed within the Inland Revenue: see Chapter 6.

[204] Disability Living Allowance and Disability Working Allowance Act 1991; see Chapter 12.

[205] Under the Jobseekers Act 1995.

[206] See Chapter 9.

[207] D. Piachaud, 'Means Testing and the Conservatives' (1996) *Benefits* No. 15, 5 at 7, quoted DSS figures. The equivalent percentage in respect of income support is 10 per cent.

[208] Based on figures in the Secretary of State for Social Security, *Annual Report of the Secretary of State for Social Security on the Social Fund 1997/98,* Cm 4003 (London: The Stationery Office, 1998).

reforms as a whole were extremely modest.[209] The reforms also failed to conquer the evil of the poverty trap, even though its effects were ameliorated by the use of net income to calculate entitlement to means-tested benefits, particularly family credit.[210] The numbers who experienced marginal tax rates in excess of 60 per cent increased, mainly due to increased dependence on income support: 'so the intensity of the poverty trap has been reduced at the expense of increasing its extensiveness'.[211]

Clearly the reforms were not comprehensive in their coverage and left the basic characteristics and, indeed, much of the existing structure of the benefits system, intact. Two of the key contributory benefits, unemployment benefit and sickness benefit, were barely touched,[212] and benefits for the disabled (other than premiums in income support) were deferred pending the outcome of a major survey of disabled people and their needs being conducted by OPCS for the DSS, which was published in stages between September 1988 and June 1989. The scope of the reforms was also narrowed by the failure to examine the 'fiscal welfare state'—the various tax allowances and reliefs—and, indeed, the ways in which the tax and benefit systems might be integrated.[213]

Despite these limitations, the Fowler reforms were of great symbolic importance. The reform of SERPS paved the way for a more fundamental shift towards occupational pensions (for example with the automatic indexation of occupational pension payments under the Social Security Act 1990), with greater diversity and, inevitably, more private pensions arrangements. The principle that help outside the social security system should be sought before assistance from the social fund is made available also demonstrated the shifting balance between public and private provision of social security.[214] The social fund helped to tighten the Government's control of benefit expenditure and, through the loans element, reinforced the notion of personal responsibility and reciprocity. As noted above, there was even some broader

---

[209] See N. Timmins, *The Five Giants. A Biography of the Welfare State* (London: Harper Collins, 1995), 404–5: 'Fowler emerged with his £40 bn budget largely intact . . . All (he) agreed to was a £450 million cut in housing benefit, barely 1 per cent of the social security budget.'

[210] Lister, however, comments that the use of net income in fact 'creates a new tax trap for the poor: a tax cut now has virtually no effect at all on the income of someone claiming means-tested benefits': R. Lister, 'Social Security', in M. McCarthy (ed.), *The New Politics of Welfare* (London: Macmillan, 1989), 104–31, 117. See also R. Lister, 'The Politics of Social Security: An Assessment of the Fowler Review', in A. Dilnot and I. Walker, *The Economics of Social Security* (Oxford: Oxford University Press, 1989), 200–23.

[211] J. Bradshaw, 'Implementing Thatcherite Policies: Audit of an Era', in D. Marsh and R. A. W. Rhodes, *Implementing Thatcherite Policies: Audit of an Era* (Milton Keynes: Open University Press, 1992), 81–93, at 93. See also D. Piachaud, 'Means Testing and the Conservatives' (1996) *Benefits* No. 15, 5–7 at 7. Piachaud quotes DSS figures (in DSS, *Social Security Departmental Report*, Cm 2813 (London: HMSO, 1995), fig. 17) showing that the numbers facing marginal net income deduction rates of 60 per cent and over increased from 450,000 in 1985 to 620,000 in 1994–5, although the reforms meant that no-one experienced a rate of 100 per cent or greater.

[212] But both were reformed in the mid-1990s when JSA (above, and see especially Chapter 10) and incapacity benefit (see Chapter 12) were introduced.

[213] R. Lister in McCarthy (ed.) (1989) op. cit., n. 210 above, 118; M. Hill, 'The 1986 Social Security Act: Ten Years On' (1996) *Benefits* No. 15, 2, 4.

[214] R. Lister, 'Social Security in the 1980s' (1991) 25(2) *Social Policy and Administration*, 91–107, 104.

significance to the abolition of both the maternity grant and the death grant. Timmins comments that they 'ended the "cradle to grave" span of the social security system'.[215]

The reforms also demonstrated particularly powerfully that the post-1979 Conservative Governments' economic or political agendas could override the needs of particular social groups (see Chapter 2). For example, it will be clear from the discussion of income support above that young unemployed people were one of the most disadvantaged groups under the Fowler reforms, following on earlier assaults on their benefits entitlement.[216] Young people were seen by the Government as an 'easy political target'[217] and as 'the most convenient group from which . . . money could be extracted with the least political pain'.[218] The Government argued that these changes affecting young people enabled it 'to concentrate more resources on older people—including pensioners and disabled persons living in other people's households'.[219] Of course, the fact that the reviews were conducted on a nil-cost basis made it inevitable that any attempt to target state welfare differently would necessitate a redistribution of support between existing client groups. Thus, Dilnot and Walker conclude that: 'One clear lesson (from the 1986 Act reforms) is that structural change without some spare money to protect potential losers is difficult to achieve.'[220]

There was much talk during the consultation period and while the legislation was being debated in Parliament of the likely losers and gainers under the reforms. DHSS estimates published in the Technical Annex to the White Paper in 1985 showed that the biggest gainers would be the sick or disabled (+£3.95 per week) and in-work couples with children (+£4.30 per week), while the biggest losers would be single people in work (−£3.49 per week). Figures calculated by the PSI, issued in March 1988, showed the pattern displayed in Table 5.1. These figures are clearly based on rates for new claims, and ignore the effects of transitional protection which enabled many existing claimants to maintain their previous rate of benefit when the changes came in, at least for a time.[221] It is clear that while families in work benefited from the reforms (mostly as a result of the more generous provision of family credit compared with FIS), non-working families with children appear to have been the major losers. The sick and disabled benefited from the new disability premiums in

---

[215] N. Timmins, *The Five Giants. A Biography of the Welfare State* (London: Harper Collins, 1995), 404.

[216] See N. Harris, *Social Security for Young People* (Aldershot: Avebury, 1989).

[217] J. Allbeson, 'Seen but not heard: young people', in S. Ward (ed.), *D.H.S.S. in Crisis* (London: CPAG, 1985), 98.

[218] Hansard, H.C, Standing Committee B, Social Security Bill, col. 677, 6 March 1986, *per* Mr A. Kirkwood MP.

[219] White Paper (1985), para. 3.10.

[220] A. Dilnot and S. Webb, 'The 1988 Social Security Reforms', in A. Dilnot and I. Walker, *The Economics of Social Security* (Oxford: Oxford University Press, 1989), 239–67, 267.

[221] One-third of income support claimants received transitional protection in the first year of the scheme: M. Evans, D. Piachaud, and H. Sutherland, *Designed for the Poor—Poorer by Design? The Effects of the 1986 Social Security Act on Family Incomes*, Discussion Paper WSP/105 (London: Suntory-Toyota International Centre for Economics and Related Disciplines, 1994), 35.

Table 5.1. Gainers and losers from the structural reforms of welfare benefits
(under the Social Security Act 1986): Policy Studies Institute calculation[222]

	Gain 50p-plus	No change (+/−50p)	Lose 50p-plus
Pensioners	26%	26%	48%
Sick/disabled	66%	17%	17%
Working families with children	61%	5%	34%
Non-working families with children	25%	12%	64%
Other non-workers	38%	17%	46%
OVERALL	32%	20%	48%

particular. But there were twice as many losers as gainers among pensioners. Above all, the PSI figures show that only a minority of claimants were unaffected one way or another by the reforms.

A more detailed assessment of winners and losers, over the period 1987–8 to 1990–1 (and thus going well beyond the period of transitional protection for over 95 per cent of claimants) has since been carried out at LSE.[223] The researchers have found that while average income across the population over this period rose by 5 per cent, those on means-tested benefits experienced a 9 per cent fall in real terms and a 13 per cent fall relative to all. There were variations across the different claimant groups. For example, across the older section of the population, pensioners' incomes rose by 10 per cent, but claimants aged over sixty receiving income support saw their income fall by 7 per cent in real terms. Couples with children receiving family credit gained on average, both in real terms and relative to the population as a whole, whilst the sick and disabled did not. Those who were out of work and did not have children saw their incomes fall by 24 per cent in real terms. However, the researchers regard these shifts as only partly attributable to the 1986 Act reforms, because demographic changes, employment patterns, and changes to housing costs also had an effect. They undertook a modelled assessment of gainers and losers under the reforms, and the key results are shown in Table 5.2.

Although there are variations, these LSE figures confirm the broad pattern of gains and losses in the PSI study and in the DHSS projections. The LSE researchers also calculated that the reforms hit hardest those in the bottom decile group, in terms of income: overall, 49 per cent of them lost income as a result of the reforms.[224] The reforms as a whole, particularly relating to the social fund and housing benefit, left some claimants on incomes below even the official poverty line. Thus targeting of the poorest has 'not happened unreservedly',[225] but of course targeting was not only

[222] P.S.I., Press Release 21 March 1988, *Government social security reforms 'ignore independent research'* (London: P.S.I., 1988).
[223] Ibid.
[224] Ibid., Table 24 at 80.
[225] Ibid., 90.

Table 5.2. Gainers and losers from Social Security Act 1986 reforms, to 1990–1: LSE model [226]

	Overall weekly gain (+) or loss (−)	Losers (%)	Gainers (%)	No change (%)
Over 80s	+£2.46	27.5%	66.4%	6.1%
60–79s	+£0.63	32.4%	49.4%	18.2%
Sick and disabled	+£1.83	31.8%	49.8%	18.4%
Lone-parent families	+£0.17	44.6%	46.5%	8.9%
Couples with children (if in receipt of family credit +£13.50)	+£2.18	37.1%	57.5%	5.4%
Others (singles or couples out of work, no children and not disabled)	−£3.43	73.4%	13.5%	13.0%

concerned with this but also with creating work incentives and achieving various political objectives.

As noted above, many other important social security reforms have followed the Fowler reforms of the 1980s. In particular, new benefits have been introduced—disability living allowance, disability working allowance, incapacity benefit, and job-seeker's allowance—in place of others. In many cases entitlement has become further restricted, although in some areas, provision has become a little more generous in order to encourage the take-up of employment (such as the 'back to work bonus' introduced in 1997: see Chapter 10). The Fowler reforms in a sense paved the way for these changes by precipitating something of a cultural shift.[227] The principles on which the Fowler reforms were said to be based, such as targeting and self-reliance, together with the reforms' economic objectives, have had a continuing influence on the development of social security since that time.[228] Social security reform above all came to be viewed as a tool of economic policy, for example in terms of minimising public expenditure (although social security expenditure has actually risen continually over the past decade) and maximising take-up of employment, rather than a means to ever greater levels of social protection.[229]

[226] Ibid., adapted from Table 26 at 83.

[227] In this respect they represent a 'watershed', according to R. Walker: 'Social Security Reform—Ten Years On' (1996) *Benefits* No. 15, 1.

[228] See, for example, the reform of widow's benefits to target support on those with children still at school or in further education (to age 19), while reducing support for those without dependent children, who might be expected to work after 52 weeks: Welfare Reform and Pensions Act 1999, s.55. See further Chapter 6, n. 14.

[229] M. Hill, 'The 1986 Social Security Act Ten Years On' (1996) *Benefits* No. 15, 2, 4; R. Lister and C. Oppenheim, 'Ten years after the 1986 Social Security Act', *Social Policy Rev.* 8 (1996), 84–105, 99–101.

Part 3

The Modern Framework

6

The Shape and Characteristics of Social Security Today (including Insurance, Pensions, and Means-tests)

NEVILLE HARRIS

1. INTRODUCTION

The British social security system is today based on a tangle of complex, often interrelated, benefit schemes whose structures are subject to frequent amendment. These structures are based on an even more intricate legal framework. This chapter aims to map out the current framework of social security provision and to draw some conclusions about the system's shape and principal characteristics. It examines various ways of classifying social security benefits for the purposes of such a map. It also explores the contrast between contributory and income-related benefits, including the principles on which each of these broad categories is based. The functions of the various benefits are also briefly referred to, whilst an examination of their legal basis and an evaluation of their role mostly occurs in later chapters. However, the national insurance contributions system and two major means-tested income-replacement benefits—income support and income-based jobseeker's allowance—are such core or pivotal areas of social security law that it is necessary to examine their structure in detail here. Income support in particular is referred to extensively in other chapters—for example those on housing, education, and families. In the course of discussing core areas in this chapter it has also been possible to examine some issues not fully covered elsewhere in the book, in particular the income support 'habitual residence test' and provision for those in hospital and residential care, and to bring the development of the retirement pension, covered in Part 2 of the book, up to date. As noted above, the structure of other benefits mentioned in this chapter, such as those concerned with disability or housing, is covered by later chapters.

2. CLASSIFICATION OF BENEFITS

The classification of benefits, which occurs for both theoretical and practical purposes, aids an understanding of the structure of the social security system and its legal context. Classification provides a code for reading the benefits 'map' and establishes terms of reference or a form of shorthand in respect of groups of benefits. If, to take one of the most obvious examples, there is a reference to a 'contributory' social security benefit, it is clear that the benefit is insurance based and that entitlement will depend, *inter alia*, on the claimant having paid or been credited with sufficient social security contributions. However, none of the classification methods is perfect and the colours on the benefits map are not always easily distinguishable.

Different methods of classifying benefits were examined by the Commission on Social Justice as part of its review of the welfare state. It was felt, in particular, that one could best construct a typology of benefits with reference to either their purpose or the basis on which they were awarded.[1] These and other methods of classification are discussed below.

A. Classification by Purpose

One advantage of using the purpose of a benefit to classify it is that this purpose is generally well understood and using it as the reference point facilitates the making of links between different benefits. For example, one can identify benefits whose central purpose is to assist those in low-paid employment and to encourage those on long-term benefits to enter work: benefits in this category until recently included family credit[2] and disability working allowance[3] and now include in their place working families tax credit and disabled person's tax credit respectively (under the Tax Credits Act 1999). They also include earnings top-up,[4] back-to-work bonus,[5] and child maintenance bonus.[6] Another group of benefits is, for example, concerned with providing specific financial support for disabled people through basic income assistance (income support, inclusive of a disability premium) or via assistance with the cost of help with their physical, or in some cases mental, needs (disability living allowance (DLA), care and mobility components).[7]

The Commission on Social Justice based its classification of benefits according to purpose with reference to: earnings replacement; meeting extra costs; and relief of poverty (see Table 6.1).

The earnings replacement benefits set out in part A of Table 6.1 opposite are not income-related.[8] As the Commission explains, they are distinguishable from benefits concerned with helping people to meet extra costs associated with particular cir-

---

[1] Commission on Social Justice, *Making Sense of Benefits* (London: I.P.P.R., 1993).

[2] This means-tested benefit supplements the low wages of families: see Chapter 5 for background and Chapter 9 for the structure of this benefit.

[3] This means-tested benefit supplements the low wages of disabled people: See Chapter 12.

[4] This operates on a pilot basis only at present in certain areas. It has a similar function to family credit, but is available only to claimants without children.

[5] This is based on credits accumulated by working part-time while receiving income support or JSA and is paid as a lump sum on entry to full-time employment or to waged employment under the New Deal: Jobseekers Act 1995, s. 29 and the Social Security (Back to Work Bonus) (No. 2) Regulations 1996 (S.I. 1996 No. 2570). See Chapter 10.

[6] This operates in a similar way to back-to-work bonus (above), but the credits are based on child maintenance and entitlement is based on the taking up of full-time work by either member of a couple: Social Security (Child Maintenance Bonus) Regulations 1996 (S.I. 1996 No. 3195).

[7] See Chapter 12.

[8] Contribution-based JSA is paid for a maximum of 6 months.

Table 6.1. Classification of benefits based on purpose[9]

A. *Earnings replacement*
   Jobseeker's allowance (contribution-based)
   Incapacity benefit
   Maternity allowance and statutory maternity pay
   Invalid care allowance
   Severe disablement allowance
   Retirement benefit*

B. *Meeting extra costs*
   Child benefit
   Disability living allowance and attendance allowance
   Industrial injuries benefits
   Widowed mother's allowance
   War pensions

C. *Relief of poverty*
   Income support/jobseeker's allowance (income-based)
   Family credit (working families tax credit)
   Disability working allowance (disabled person's tax credit)
   Earnings top-up
   Housing benefit
   Council tax benefit
   Widow's payment and pension*

* Probably belongs in more than one category

cumstances, such as child rearing (child benefit) or disability (DLA, attendance allowance, or industrial injuries benefit). The benefits which are intended to provide that additional help can be paid on top of benefits designed to replace earnings or those to relieve poverty (such as income support and housing benefit). Thus, for example, DLA is generally ignored in the calculation of income for the purposes of income support entitlement.[10] The earnings replacement benefits take account of the particular circumstances which prevent the individual from working: mental and/or physical incapacity (incapacity benefit or, in the case of severe disability which has prevented one from working on a long-term basis, severe disablement allowance),[11] unemployment (JSA), maternity (statutory maternity pay and maternity allowance), caring for an infirm relative (invalid care allowance), or advanced age (retirement pension).

[9] Adapted from Commission on Social Justice, n. 1 above.
[10] IS(G) Regs 1987, Sched. 9, paras 6 and 9.
[11] Severe disablement allowance (SDA) is payable to people who became incapable of work before the age of 20, or who are classed as 80 per cent disabled, or who were receiving the non-contributory invalidity pension which SDA in effect replaced. It is being abolished, for new claimants, under the Welfare Reform and Pensions Act 1999: see Chapter 12.

Although the examples of benefits concerned with the relief of poverty (part C of Table 6.1) are all income-related benefits, the Commission argues that some of the non-means-tested benefits paid to retired people—in particular the basic state retirement pension and the non-contributory pension for people aged eighty or over with no other retirement pension (who often live on very low incomes)—are also concerned with poverty relief.[12] The Commission also brings private benefits within the scope of its classification. Thus, for example, occupational pensions and employers' sick pay may provide replacement of earnings, while household or disability insurance may cover needs arising in special situations. The Commission also notes that charity may assist in the relief of poverty.[13]

This classification according to purpose is quite useful in deconstructing the benefit system for analysis purposes. However, it ignores the fact that a failure of benefits concerned with earnings replacement or extra needs to fully meet their intended objective means that an individual need for basic poverty relief benefits frequently arises. Furthermore, classifying some benefits in this way leads to ambiguities. For example, what is the principal purpose of the widow's benefit? Is it primarily concerned to replace a partner's earnings, or to relieve poverty *per se*, or to meet extra needs? Given the fact that it is taken into account in full when income support is assessed, it is most probable that poverty relief is its principal objective; but, on the other hand, widowed mother's allowance (see pp. 103 and 144 above) is also intended to offer special help to those now bringing up children on their own. The proposed reforms to widow's benefits announced at the end of 1998 and included in the Welfare Reform and Pensions Act 1999 are aimed at concentrating help on those unable to work and thus more likely to be poor.[14] It is also clear that the purpose of some poverty relief benefits—notably family credit/working families tax credit and disability working allowance/disabled person's tax credit—is also to encourage the take-up of full-time work.

B. Classification with Reference to the Basis on Which Benefit is Paid

Using the basis on which benefit is paid to classify the payment concerned (see Table 6.2) involves looking at the key factors which determine and restrict entitlement. Thus benefits may be 'contributory' (in the sense explained above) or 'means-tested' (nowadays more commonly referred to as 'income-related'). Contributory benefits are often referred to as 'insurance' benefits, because they derive from the national

---

[12] N. 1 above, at 14.

[13] Ibid., 15.

[14] The pre-1999 Act benefits are explained at pp. 103 and 144 above. The 1999 Act makes provision (via s. 55, inserting SSCBA 1992, ss 39A-39C) for a new non-means-tested 'bereavement allowance', payable for 52 weeks, for those who become widows or widowers when aged 45 or over and who do not have dependent children (replacing the widow's pension, but only for new claimants). A new 'widowed parent's allowance' replaces widowed mother's allowance. See Green Paper, *A New Contract for Welfare: Support in Bereavement*, Cm 4101 (London: The Stationery Office, 1998).

Table 6.2. Classification of benefits based on entitlement conditions

A. *Income-related*
    Income support/income-based jobseeker's allowance
    Social fund (where linked to income support entitlement)
    Family credit (working families tax credit)
    Earnings top-up
    Back-to-work bonus*
    Child maintenance bonus*
    Housing benefit
    Council tax benefit
    Disability working allowance (disabled person's tax credit)
    Health benefits
    Free school meals

B. *Non-means-tested benefits*
    i. *Contributory benefits*
    Jobseeker's allowance (first six months)
    Incapacity benefit
    Maternity allowance
    Statutory maternity pay
    Retirement pension
    Widow's benefits

    ii. *Non-contributory*
    Industrial injuries benefit
    Attendance allowance
    Disability living allowance
    Child benefit
    Guardian's allowance
    Invalid care allowance
    Severe disablement allowance
    War pensions

* These benefits are only partly income-related: see discussion below

insurance system, described later in this chapter. As the concept of insurance implies, they are generally contingency-based benefits, designed to meet needs arising in mostly unpredictable circumstances (unemployment, sickness, bereavement, and so on, the exception being retirement). Where, on the other hand, benefits are means-tested or income-related, entitlement depends on having an income (and/or capital) at or below a prescribed level. As discussed in Chapter 4, since the 1960s increasing numbers of claimants have had to rely on means-tested benefits such as income support and housing benefit. There are also benefits which are neither income-related nor contributory, and these are often referred to as simply 'non-contributory' benefits. Many disability benefits, such as DLA, fall into this category (see Table 6.2). The common theme to the non-contributory benefits is that they are paid in particular circumstances where a certain degree of additional need is assumed (and, as noted above, the benefit is often disregarded when the claimant's entitlement to an income-related benefit is assessed). One benefit which is difficult to classify under this system is back-to-work bonus (see pp. 316–7 below), included with the income-related benefits in Table 6.2. A credit, on which the bonus is based, accrues if a person is working part-time and receiving JSA or income support—so entitlement to the credit is clearly income-related. However, the bonus itself is paid (as a lump sum) when the claimant enters full-time work and at this point there is no means-test. A similar problem arises with the classification of child maintenance bonus.

Entitlement to some types of benefit is not as conditional as it is in the case of income-related or contributory benefits. These benefits are neither means-tested nor insurance-based and, because of the far less restrictive entitlement conditions than for other benefits, they are often referred to as 'universal' benefits—universal in the sense that all (or at least very many) are entitled. Universal benefits are seen as having a number of advantages over the 'selective' alternative, in that they are simpler and cheaper to administer and more likely to be taken up.[15] In fact, it is more accurate to refer to universal benefits as 'categorical', because they are always restricted to persons falling within a particular category.[16] Child benefit, generally paid to any person who has primary responsibility for the care of a 'child',[17] is often described as 'universal' but is in fact categorical. Categorical benefits mirror various tax reliefs which are themselves categorical: for example, an element of the reform of family allowances into child benefit itself was the abolition of child tax allowances. Social security systems are themselves categorical in the sense that schemes target particular categories of the population and direct particular types of support only at those who fall within the defined class. As Saunders, referring to the Australian social security system, explains, 'The basic categories may be defined in a number of ways, for example, on the basis of age (the elderly, dependent children), health status (the sick, invalids), economic status (the unemployed), or family status (sole parents)'.[18]

Grouping benefits with reference to their underlying basis is the most common method of classification. There is a degree of artificiality to this, particularly in view of the shift away from insurance-based social security, which has occurred on a much greater scale in Britain than elsewhere in the European Union[19] and which has led to increasing numbers of claimants requiring income-related benefits, whilst in some cases also being supported simultaneously by non-means-tested benefit. On the other hand, the development of common means-tests following the Fowler reforms

---

[15] On take-up see below and also Chapter 2.

[16] The Commission on Social Justice explained that 'Categorical benefits are paid to people in certain defined circumstances, without a test of previous contributions or means': n. 1 above, 8.

[17] See Chapter 9.

[18] P. Saunders, 'Selectivity and Targeting in Income Support: The Australian Experience' (1991) 20 *J. of Social Policy,* 299–326, 306.

[19] Commission of the European Union, *Social Protection in Europe 1993* (Luxembourg: Office for Publications of the European Communities, 1994), 38.

of the mid to late 1980s[20] has at least strengthened the ties between the various benefits which make up one distinctive category, income-related benefits.

One reason why benefits are often classified with reference to their underlying basis is that this method reflects the historical development of the welfare state itself, which was described in Chapters 3, 4, and 5. For example, a line can be traced through the Poor Law, transitional payments and unemployment assistance in the inter-war period, and, post-1945, national assistance, supplementary benefit, and income support. Basic means-tested benefits have mostly represented a safety net for the poor, or at least, for those assessed as having an income below a certain threshold. This basis of support evolved for the most part quite separately from the insurance system, particularly post-Beveridge.[21]

Benefits are sometimes also categorised with reference to whether they are primarily discretionary or based on defined entitlement. This dichotomy has already been explored (Chapters 1 and 4). As we have seen, income-related poverty relief is today available as of right in defined circumstances and there is only a limited range of broadly discretion-based benefits, such as: the social fund's budgeting loans, crisis loans, and community care grants; JSA/income support 'severe hardship' payments made to young people aged sixteen or seventeen; and discretionary maintenance awards and certain other education benefits.

C. Other Classifications

Other classifications which are used include 'in-work' and 'out-of-work' benefits, reflecting in particular the preoccupation of the present Labour Government, and the post-1979 Conservative Governments before it, with linking the benefits system to employment. This is premised on the basis that the relevant claimants are either in work or (should be) seeking it. In-work benefits refer to all those for which persons qualify only when in employment (such as family credit/working families tax credit, disability working allowance/disabled person's tax credit, earnings top-up, back-to-work bonus and statutory sick pay), while the latter comprise the benefits on which non-working claimants in particular place reliance (JSA or income support). Such classification is clearly inappropriate in the case of benefits paid to those for whom employment status may not be relevant, such as the severely disabled or the retired or elderly. Moreover, as the *Welfare Benefits Handbook* explains, the distinction between in-work and out-of-work benefits 'is not absolute . . . For example, you may fail to qualify for [income support] because you are found to be in full-time work, yet still fail to qualify for [family credit] because the work is held not to be the work you normally do.'[22]

[20] See Chapter 5.
[21] There were links, of course. For example, transitional payments were intended to meet the needs of those who had, *inter alia*, exhausted their entitlement to insurance-based unemployment benefit: see Chapter 3.
[22] C. George et al., *Welfare Benefits Handbook, Vol. 2.* (London: CPAG, 1999), 13.

Some classifications bring under one umbrella all the benefits concerned with the needs of a broad group, such as the disabled ('disability benefits') or families ('family benefits'). The problem with such classifications is that there is often such a diversity of schemes falling within them but so few common features across the class. Nevertheless, this is broadly the approach followed by the DSS statistics branch, which uses 'broad customer groups' in showing annual expenditure on social security: the elderly; the long-term sick and disabled; the short-term sick; families; the unemployed; widows and others (see Table 6.3). Benefits which are available to more than one group, principally the main income-related benefits, have to be listed in several places.

Table 6.3 Classification of benefits by broad customer groups[23]

A. Elderly
  Retirement pension
  Non-contributory retirement pension
  Christmas bonus
  Pension and other non-disability benefits
  Income-related benefits and social fund payments

B. Long-term sick and disabled
  Incapacity benefit
  Attendance allowance
  Mobility allowance
  Disability living allowance
  Disability working allowance (disabled person's tax credit)
  Industrial injuries benefits
  Severe disablement allowance
  Invalid care allowance
  War pensions
  Independent Living Fund
  Motability
  Christmas bonus (paid with disability benefits)
  Income-related benefits and social fund payments

C. Short-term sick
  Statutory sick pay
  Incapacity benefit
  Income-related benefits and social fund payments

D. Families
  Child benefit
  Family credit (working families tax credit)

[23] Taken from DSS, *Social Security Statistics 1998* (Leeds: DSS Corporate Document Services, 1998), which excludes back-to-work bonus and child maintenance bonus.

Statutory maternity pay
Maternity allowance
Social fund maternity payments
Income-related benefits and social fund payments

E. *Unemployed*
   Jobseeker's allowance (up to 6 months' unemployment)
   Income-related benefits and social fund payments

F. *Widows and others*
   Widow's benefit
   War widows' pension
   Guardian's allowance
   Child's special allowance
   Industrial death benefit
   Social fund funeral payments
   Income support

Some benefits are classified as 'passported' because they are only available to persons who have qualified for another benefit, especially income support. Examples include free school meals and health benefits such as free prescriptions available to those in receipt of income support and their dependants.

Finally, the European Commission uses its own classification of benefits. This is designed to facilitate comparison of social protection across Member States. The Commission's typology, showing the relevant UK social security benefits, is shown in Table 6.4 (over).[24] It involves a combination of benefit customer groups (such as 'survivors') and purposes (such as 'maternity' and 'guaranteeing sufficient resources'). It does not correspond with distinctions in EC law, however, such as that between 'social security', 'special non-contributory benefits', and 'social assistance' in relation to EC Regulation 1408/71 on free movement of workers (see Chapter 8 by Tamara Hervey).

The European Commission's classification of benefits may well facilitate international comparisons, but it clearly results in a degree of overlap. The DSS's categorisation of benefits, shown in Table 6.3 (above), provides a more coherent breakdown for UK analysis purposes.

D. Does it Matter which Classification System is Used?

The different methods of classifying benefits for the most part reflect the diversity of purposes for which benefits are categorised. For analytical purposes, and

---

[24] The table is adapted from the tables in the *MISSOC* handbook published by the European Commission.

Table 6.4 European Commission Social Protection typology of benefits

---

A. Sickness—Cash benefits
　Incapacity benefit*
　Statutory sick pay

B. Maternity
　Maternity allowance
　Statutory maternity pay

C. Invalidity
　Incapacity benefit*
　Severe disablement allowance*
　Attendance allowance*
　Disability living allowance*
　Invalid care allowance

D. Old age
　Retirement pension*

E. Survivors
　Widow's benefits

F. Employment injuries and occupational diseases
　Industrial injuries benefit
　War pensions

G. Family benefits
　Child benefit
　Social fund maternity payment
　Family credit (working families tax credit)
　Guardian's allowance

H. Unemployment
　Jobseeker's allowance (contribution-based)

I. Guaranteeing sufficient resources
　Income support and jobseeker's allowance (income-based)
　Housing benefit
　Council tax benefit
　Social fund payments
　Earnings top-up
　Retirement pension*
　Severe disablement allowance*
　Disability working allowance (disabled person's tax credit)
　Disability living allowance*
　Attendance allowance*

---

* Listed in more than one category

especially for the purposes of legal analysis, the most commonly used classification relates to the basis on which the benefit is paid, since it links the benefit most closely to the principal factors, often common to the class of benefit involved, on which legal entitlement will depend. Until recently the Child Poverty Action Group divided its authoritative annual welfare rights guidance on social security into two separate guides, one focusing on means-tested benefits and the other on benefits which are non-means-tested. This categorisation is still broadly adopted by the guidance, although it is now published as one integrated guide in two volumes.[25] The annually updated annotated legislation currently retains its division into two main volumes on income-related and non-means-tested benefits respectively.[26] The rest of the chapter adopts this broad categorisation and examines some of the key elements of each of these categories. Nevertheless, when discussing the role of benefits in their social and economic contexts it is also appropriate to link benefits together with reference to client groups or the purpose for which the benefits are paid (e.g. work incentives), as happens throughout most of the later chapters. Nick Wikeley, for example, uses a typology which corresponds to the Commission on Social Justice's purposes model (see section A above) in analysing provision in respect of disability in Chapter 12.

3. INSURANCE

A. Introduction: Values and Functions of Insurance

As we saw in Chapter 4, the Beveridge reforms to social security saw insurance benefits at their peak, but over the past two decades the insurance system has been in decline and has been eclipsed by means-tested benefits. Presented alongside the panoply of other social security benefits in Table 6.2 above, the list of contributory benefits is seen to represent only a minority form of social security provision today, as reflected in the relatively small numbers now receiving them (apart from retirement pension and incapacity benefit).[27] Increasing numbers of claimants have been forced to rely on income-related benefits as a result of high levels of long-term unemployment and cutbacks to the insurance benefits themselves over recent years (such as the reduction from twelve to six months in the duration of contributory benefit for unemployment—now the jobseeker's allowance—and abolition of the

---

[25] C. George et al., *Welfare Benefits Handbook, Vols 1 and 2* (London: CPAG, 1999), replacing the *National Welfare Benefits Handbook* and the *Rights Guide to Non-means Tested Benefits*. The new handbook also incorporates the former *Jobseeker's Allowance Handbook*.

[26] J. Mesher and P. Wood, *Income-Related Benefits: The Legislation* (London: Sweet and Maxwell, 1998); D. Bonner, I. Hooker, and R. Smith, *Non-Means Tested Benefits: the Legislation* (London: Sweet and Maxwell, 1998).

[27] In 1997 10.6 million were receiving state retirement pension, 5.2 million income support or income-based JSA, 4.5 million housing benefit, 5.4 million council tax benefit, and 3 million DLA or attendance allowance: DSS, *Social Security Statistics 1998* (Leeds: Corporate Document Services, 1998) 4. Statistics on recipients of other benefits are cited in the relevant chapters.

earnings-related supplement and child additions, as noted in Chapter 4). The concept
of insurance has been heavily weakened, not least in the minds of ordinary citizens.
Most people today understand social security contributions to be little more than
another form of taxation rather than the basis of a contractual guarantee of state
support at an adequate level. Nevertheless, it is worth noting that the largest number
of recipients of any one benefit is the approximately 10.6 million who receive contributory retirement pension[28] (although many pensioners depend also on income-
related benefits) and that over half of all benefit expenditure goes on contributory
benefits.[29]

The virtues of insurance have been proclaimed with increasing regularity over
recent years, largely because of increased dissatisfaction with means-testing as a
result of what (as noted in Chapter 4, at pp. 105–106) are seen as its stigmatising effects,
its complexity (despite attempts to simplify the benefits concerned), its reinforcement of the poverty trap,[30] its possible encouragement of dependency or dishonesty,
and its relatively poor take-up levels in some cases.[31] In some cases such problems
are interrelated: for example, the complexity of family credit seems to have deterred
take-up.[32] Means-testing also offers, through its rules on capital limits, a disincentive
to save (the 'savings trap', referred to in Chapter 2). Beveridge, referring to disadvantages of means-tested benefits, cited popular 'resentment at a provision which
appears to penalise what people have come to regard as the duty and pleasure of
thrift'.[33]

Insurance, on the other hand, is said to have the major advantage of wide public
acceptance, a factor which was identified specifically by Beveridge ('benefit in return
for contributions, rather than free allowances from the state, is what the people of
Britain desire').[34] Recent research on the attitudes of persons of pensionable age to
social security shows that there is a continuing resistance to claiming means-tested
benefits.[35] In this survey, a majority of the persons questioned regarded the state
retirement pension as something to which they were entitled and which was central
to their finances. But they were often unhappy about claiming additional income-
related benefits such as income support, unless in effect forced to do so when faced
with a significant change of circumstances such as where their husband/wife was
admitted to hospital on a long-term basis. This was not only a moral issue for some,

[28] See DSS, *Social Security Statistics 1998* (Leeds: Corporate Document Services, 1998) 4.
[29] See J. Creedy and R. Disney, *Social Insurance in Transition* (Oxford: Oxford University Press, 1985),
21–2. This figure may be contrasted with Beveridge's projections for 1965 (Beveridge Report (1942), para.
199), which were social insurance benefits, £553 million; children's allowances, £103 million; and national
assistance, £32 million.
[30] See Chapter 2, at 48–51.   [31] Ibid, at 63–4.
[32] A. Corden, *Changing Perspectives on Benefit Take-up* (London: HMSO, 1995), 14, citing previous research
by Corden herself on take-up of family income supplement and family credit. See further p. 64 above.
[33] Beveridge Report (1942), para. 21.
[34] Ibid.
[35] H. Finch and G. Elam, *Managing Money in Later Life*, DSS Research Report No. 38 (London: HMSO,
1995), referred to briefly in Chapter 2, at p. 63.

who saw means-tested benefits as 'unearned', but also a reflection of a traditional dislike of the invasion of privacy, reinforced in some minds by association with the pre-war household means-tests.[36] In any event, as Alcock comments, 'although in practice the link between contributions paid and benefits received is somewhat tenuous and often arbitrary, the notion of a right to such benefits remains a widely held and popular one'.[37]

Insurance benefits tend to be more easily and thus less expensively administered. Figures published in the 1980s showed that administration costs were equal to 3–4 per cent of total national insurance benefit payouts, compared with 11 per cent in the case of supplementary benefit and 15 per cent for local authority-administered housing benefits.[38] More recent figures reveal that the equivalent rate of administrative costs for retirement pension is 1 per cent, compared with 10 per cent for income support and 46 per cent for the social fund.[39] The fact that people contribute to pay for national insurance benefits obviously also makes it more cost-effective, although this is partially offset by the cost of administering the contributions system.

Although this does not happen in Britain, insurance benefits can be designed to ease the transition from one economic status (employment) to another (unemployment) by protecting income through setting the level of the unemployment benefit at a relatively high proportion of income, at least for the first twelve months or so. In Britain, most insurance benefits are now flat rate, which means that they are ineffective at targeting needs.

A further problem with insurance benefits in practice flows from the way that contribution conditions operate. In principle, insurance benefits will protect against lack of income when economic inactivity results from any of the insured contingencies, such as unemployment, sickness, or maternity. Nevertheless, the national insurance contribution conditions have the effect of excluding considerable numbers of workers from protection. Self-employed persons' contributions do not count towards contribution-based JSA. Undercollection of contributions from the self-employed (which count towards other contributory benefits such as incapacity benefit, retirement pension, and widow's benefit) is in fact a significant problem.[40] Indeed, nearly three million self-employed and employed workers pay either no or inadequate contributions, with the result that they fail to qualify for short-term contributory

---

[36] See Chapter 3.

[37] P. Alcock, 'The advantages and disadvantages of the contribution base in targeting benefits: A social analysis of the insurance scheme in the United Kingdom', (1996) 49(1) *International Social Security Review*, 31–49, 37.

[38] Creedy and Disney, n. 29 above, 24, citing figures quoted in Hansard.

[39] Secretary of State for Social Security and Chief Secretary to the Treasury, *Social Security Departmental Report, The Government's Expenditure Plans 1996–97 to 1998–99*, Cm 3213 (London: HMSO, 1996), Fig. 28, at 59 (but see p. 440 n. 62 below). See also R. Cohen et al., *Out of Pocket: The failure of the Social Fund* (London: The Children's Society, 1996).

[40] A. Corden, 'Self-employed people in the United Kingdom: Included or excluded?' (1999) 52(1) *I.S.S.R.* 31–47 and idem, *Self-Employed People and National Insurance Contributions*, DSS Research Report No. 84 (Leeds: Corporate Document Services, 1998).

benefits in particular.[41] Furthermore, a considerable growth in the numbers of part-time workers in the economy, a majority of whom are women earning, in some cases, insufficient to make them liable to contribute, is one of the social and economic changes which has seen increasing numbers, including many of the young unemployed and lone parents, lying outside the scope of insurance protection.[42]

The insurance principle is nevertheless also consonant with the notion, apparently supported by both centre-left and right-wing political thought, of reciprocity and social responsibility (now incorporated into the concept of stakeholderism)[43]—'social insurance is a contract between individuals and society'.[44] Indeed, given the fact that the insurance concept is ever more firmly embedded in the public conscience, not least because of the expansion of the insurance industry to meet consumer needs (such as holidays and, with increased owner-occupation, house insurance), there seems to be some political capital to be gained from reviving it in the social security context. The Commission on Social Justice has led the way by presenting the case for a 'new social insurance system', emphasising that social insurance is 'a contract between individuals and society',[45] and Field, seeking to weaken the hold of means-testing and provide for individual 'ownership' of the welfare system, published plans for a stakeholder's national insurance scheme.[46] Commentators see no signs that the Labour Government's policy on welfare reform will embrace any extension of the insurance principle, particularly following a further tightening up of national insurance contribution conditions under the Social Security Act 1998[47] and (in the case of incapacity benefit: see Chapter 12) the Welfare Reform and Pensions Act 1999. A possible exception is pensions, although any further element of insurance may well depend upon private schemes (see pp. 182–184 below).

B. Insurance Contributions

(i) Introduction

Although, as we have seen, the principle of insurance continues to have significance, contribution conditions (and rates) have been made more onerous in recent years as a means of recouping some of the spiralling costs of the social security system. This

---

[41] Commission on Social Justice, *Social Justice—Strategies for National Renewal* (London: Vintage, 1994), 227–9.

[42] P. Alcock, n. 37 above, 40. See also S. Webb, 'Social insurance and poverty alleviation: An empirical analysis', in S. Baldwin and J. Falkingham (eds), *Social Security and Social Change: New Challenges to the Beveridge Model* (Hemel Hempstead: Harvester Wheatsheaf, 1994), 11–28.

[43] F. Field, *Stakeholder Welfare* (London: IEA, 1996). See further Chapter 1.

[44] Commission on Social Justice, *Social Justice—Strategies for National Renewal* (London: Vintage, 1994), 231.

[45] Ibid.

[46] F. Field, *Making Welfare Work* (London: Institute of Community Studies, 1995) and *How to Pay for the Future* (London: IEA, 1996).

[47] See N. Harris and N. Wikeley, 'The strange death of national insurance?', editorial in (1998) 5(4) *J.S.S.L.* 147–8.

has re-emphasised the way that national insurance contributions have become, in reality, just a form of 'hypothecated taxes', although accounted for separately.[48] The contributions system is one of the most complex and obscure areas of social security law, and it is not proposed to examine it in complete detail here.[49] Nevertheless, the basic framework and some of the key rules will be addressed, together with some brief historical background.

(ii) From Flat-Rate to Earnings-Related Contributions

The flat-rate contributions system based on the Beveridge proposals and incorporated into the National Insurance Act 1946 remained the basis of the insurance scheme for nearly thirty years. Nevertheless, its duration was not so much a reflection of its suitability but rather of the difficulty of devising an appropriate alternative. It became clear that a flat-rate contributions system limited too severely the Government's ability to fund insurance benefits, because contributions could not be raised significantly without imposing an unjustifiable burden on the majority of workers, who were relatively lowly paid.

There were various moves towards an earnings-related scheme before wholesale reform in the 1970s. When a graduated pensions scheme was introduced in 1959, a contribution of 4.5 per cent of earnings within the range £9–£15 was required, 'buying' earnings-related additions to pensions, although the amounts were small.[50] The earnings-related supplement to sickness and unemployment benefit introduced in 1966[51] was supported by an additional graduated contributions system (both employers and employees contributed). Meanwhile, the basic flat-rate contributions system continued.[52] By 1967, the flat-rate contribution for workers aged eighteen or over had been increased on fourteen occasions (twelve times in the case of the under eighteens).

Although both the Labour Party (in 1969) and the Conservatives (in 1973) had attempted to extend earnings-related contributions, it was not until the Social Security Act 1975 that a wholesale shift to them was effected, together with the introduction of SERPS in 1978 via separate legislation.[53] The new contributions scheme adopted features of income taxation, with which it was to some extent harmonised. Thus there was a lower income threshold, below which no contributions were payable, although there was also an upper threshold, which is not a feature of income

---

[48] P. Alcock, op. cit., n. 37 above, 42. N. Barr, *The Economics of the Welfare State*, 2nd edn. (London: Weidenfeld and Nicolson, 1993), 179.

[49] See generally, Ogus, Barendt, and Wikeley (1995), 42–72, although note that there have been recent changes to the system.

[50] A. I. Ogus, 'Great Britain', in P. A. Kohler et al. (eds), *The Evolution of Social Insurance 1881–1981* (London: Frances Pinter, 1982), 150–264, 201. Ogus explains that the scheme was 'almost a complete failure', offering claimants a 'poor return for money contributed'.

[51] See Chapter 4, at p. 99.

[52] National Insurance Act 1965, ss 3–7 and Sched. 2, para. 1.

[53] The Social Security and Pensions Act 1975. See p. 103 above. Those who contracted out of this scheme paid a reduced contribution. The scheme became operational in 1978.

taxation. In the case of self-employed contributors, liability was for these purposes based on calculations of their profits. Another change made in 1975 was classification according to contributions rather than persons. Class 1 contributions were those made by those who were 'employed', Class 2 were paid by the self-employed, Class 3 comprised voluntary flat-rate contributions from earners and others, and Class 4 were paid on the basis of profits or gains arising from a trade, profession, or vocation and were earnings-related (unlike Class 2 contributions, which were flat-rate). Workers aged under sixteen were exempt from contributing.[54]

As under previous arrangements, the Social Security Act 1975 enabled crediting of contributions for certain categories of persons who were unable (for the most part temporarily) to contribute.[55] However, the initial contribution condition to establish oneself in the national insurance scheme could only be satisfied by contributions actually paid. For short-term benefits, such as unemployment and sickness benefit, the initial condition under the 1975 Act was that during any one tax year since the age of sixteen the claimant had paid contributions the 'earnings factor' for which was not less than twenty-five times the lower earnings limit in force for that year.[56] Credited contributions could, however, count towards the second qualifying condition, which required an earnings factor of fifty times the lower limit.[57]

A new system of differential contribution rates was introduced under the Social Security Act 1985.[58] Prior to this there was one rate. The new system differentiated on the basis of earnings. There were three bands: the first applied to those earning between the lower earnings limit (£35.50) and £54.99, where the contribution rate was set at 5 per cent. This was a lower rate than the previous general rate (6.5 per cent) and, as employer and employee paid the same rate, was intended to reduce employers' costs of employing young people and those who were to be paid low wages. There were, in fact, doubts about the potential of this change to reduce levels of youth unemployment, because the overall fall in employers' costs was only 6.45 per cent as compared with a wages subsidy of 50 per cent under the Government-funded Young Workers' Scheme which had had little impact.[59] The other two bands were for earnings of £55–£89.99, where the contribution rate was 7 per cent, and £90–£265 (the upper earnings limit), where the rate stood at 9 per cent (although the employer paid 10.45 per cent in respect of earnings above £130). This scheme was scrapped in 1989

---

[54] SSA 1975, ss 4(2)(a), 7(1), 8(1), and 9(8).

[55] For example, students: Social Security (Credits) Regulations 1975 (S.I. 1975 No. 556), regs 7 and 8. See also, National Insurance Advisory Committee, *Report on Unemployment Benefit for Students*, Cmnd 7613 (London: HMSO, 1979).

[56] SSA 1975, Sched. 3, paras 1–4. The pre-1975 rule was that at least 26 Class 1 contributions had to be paid since entry into insurance. 'Earnings factor' is explained in n. 81 below.

[57] Prior to April 1975, 50 Class 1 contributions had to be paid or credited. Reduced benefit was payable to those who had paid, or had been credited with, between 26 and 49 contributions.

[58] SSA 1985, s. 7.

[59] P. Lewis, 'Less Work, Less Money, Less Hope', *Poverty*, No. 62, Winter 1985/86, 18. Unemployment among under 18 year olds increased from 107,800 to 197,700 between 1979 and 1985: *Youthaid Bulletin*, No. 23, October 1985, 12.

because of fears that it acted as a disincentive to individual effort by discouraging employees from seeking a higher employment status (and thus remuneration).[60]

(iii) The Present Contributions Scheme

(a) Classes of Contribution

Class 1 Contributions There are 'primary' and 'secondary' contributions. 'Primary' contributions are paid by 'employed earners'[61] aged sixteen or over and under pensionable age.[62] As liability under this class hinges primarily on whether the person concerned is employed under a 'contract of service', reference must be made to the now substantial body of case law on its definition.[63] The employment must be in Great Britain.[64] The amount payable by way of contribution depends on the level of gross earnings.[65] There is a *lower earnings limit*[66] (which for the year to April 2000 stands at £66 per week, but which will be raised to £76 in April 2000 and £87 in April 2001—having the effect of bringing employees' contributions into line with the single person's tax allowance[67]) and an *upper earnings limit* (currently £500 per week). (Note that new thresholds are to be introduced under the Welfare Reform and Pensions Act 1999, Sched. 9.) The standard Class 1 contribution rate today for employees is 10 per cent,[68] assessed on gross earnings between the lower and upper earnings limits from all employments.[69] 'Secondary' contributions[70] are those which are made by the employer or other person who pays earnings. Secondary contributions liability begins once earnings reach the

[60] Ogus, Barendt, and Wikeley (1995), 52.
[61] Defined as 'a person who is gainfully employed in Great Britain either under a contract of service, or in an office (including elective office) with emoluments chargeable to income tax under Schedule E': SSCBA 1992, s. 2(1)(a); see also *Vandyk v Minister of Pensions and National Insurance* [1955] 1 QB 29, *per* Slade LJ at 38. Emolument holders here would include trustees and executors and NHS consultants: Ogus, Barendt, and Wikeley (1995), 49.
[62] SSCBA 1992, s. 6(1) and (2). The upper age limits give rise to gender discrimination, but this is not contrary to the EC Equal Treatment Directive 79/7/EEC as there is a derogation in respect of retirement ages: see Art. 7(1), *Equal Opportunities Commission v Secretary of State for Social Security* Case C-9/91 [1992] 3 CMLR 233. See Chapter 8.
[63] See Ogus, Barendt, and Wikeley (1995), 44–9.
[64] Special rules apply to determine when a person who is working in Great Britain is normally resident abroad, or where a person normally resident here is working abroad: see the Social Security (Contributions) Regulations 1979 (S.I. 1979 No. 591), regs 119 and 120.
[65] On the income included for this purpose, see S.I. 1979 No. 591, op. cit., regs 18 and 19, as amended.
[66] SSCBA 1992, s. 5(1) and S.I. 1979 No. 591, reg. 7, as amended by the Social Security (Contributions and Credits) (Miscellaneous Amendments) Regulations 1999 (S.I. 1999 No. 568). The Social Security Contributions (Transfer of Functions etc) Act 1999 (Sched. 3 para. 5) will transfer the power to prescribe this limit from the Secretary of State to the Treasury.
[67] This follows a report commissioned by the Chancellor of the Exchequer which recommended this alignment in order to prevent the current distortion of the labour market: M. Taylor, *The Modernisation of Britain's Tax and Benefits System—2. Work Incentives* (London: HM Treasury, 1998), para. 2.07.
[68] SSCBA 1992, s. 8, as amended. Social Security (Contributions) Act 1994, s. 1, increased it by 1 per cent from 9 per cent. The 2 per cent contribution payable on earnings below the lower earnings limit was abolished by the SSA 1998.
[69] SSCBA 1992, s. 3 and Sched. 1.
[70] Ibid., s. 1(2)(a)(ii). See Ogus, Barendt, and Wikeley (1995), 53–4.

'earnings threshold', which corresponds to the single person's income tax allowance (£83 per week, from April 1999). These contributions are assessed at 12.2 per cent of earnings in excess of that level.[71] There are separate rules relating to those contracted out of the SERPS scheme.[72] Satisfaction of Class 1 contributions provides entitlement to JSA, incapacity benefits, statutory maternity pay, and other national insurance benefits, including state retirement pension.

Note that the Jobseekers Act 1995 introduced a national insurance 'holiday' period.[73] The employer's contribution was abated for employers who provided employment for a person who had been unemployed for at least six months.

Class 1A Contributions   The purpose of this class of contributions, introduced under the Social Security (Contributions) Act 1991, is to ensure that payments in kind, specifically the private use and fuelling of company cars, are also reflected in contributions liability. The contributions are applicable where these car benefits are enjoyed by those in employed earner's employment. Only if these benefits are chargeable against Schedule E income tax will Class 1A apply; and no Class 1A contribution is payable in respect of the availability of a car if Class 1B contributions (see below) are payable in respect of it.[74] The contributions are currently payable at the rate of 10 per cent of the cash value, in the relevant tax year, of the relevant car benefits. They do not give rise to any benefit entitlement.

Class 1B Contributions   These are paid by employers on small non-cash payments which are dealt with under a pay-as-you-earn (PAYE) settlement arrangement. They were introduced in April 1999 under SSCBA 1992, section 10A. Under an amendment included in the Welfare Reform and Pensions Act 1999 (s. 77) they will be paid at the same rate as Class 1 secondary contributions.

Class 2 Contributions   This class is paid by the self-employed[75] aged sixteen to retirement age,[76] who may also pay Class 4 contributions (see below). The requirement only applies to those who are ordinarily resident in Great Britain or who resided there for twenty-six of the fifty-two contribution weeks immediately preceding the week in question. The rate of contribution is considerably lower than for Class 1 contributors, although Class 4 contributions will also be payable in most cases (see below). The flat-rate contribution for 1999–2000 stands at £6.55 per week, but is set for reduction to £2 per week from April 2000. If annual net earnings are below a cer-

---

[71]   SSCBA 1992, s. 9(1), as substituted by s. 51(4) of the SSA 1998. The calculation of secondary Class 1 contributions is transferred to the Treasury by Sched. 3 para. 9 to the Social Security Contributions (Transfer of Functions etc) Act 1999.

[72]   In particular, the rate of contribution is currently set at 8.4 per cent.

[73]   JS Act 1995, s. 27. The 'holiday' scheme ended on 31 March 1999.

[74]   See SSCBA 1992, ss. 1(2)(b) and 10; SSA 1998, Sched. 7; S.I. 1979 No. 591, op. cit., regs 22A–22G.

[75]   Defined as 'a person who is gainfully employed in Great Britain otherwise than in employed earner's employment (whether or not he is also employed in such employment)': SSCBA 1992, s. 2(1)(b).

[76]   SSCBA 1992, s. 11.

tain level (currently £3,770) there may be a certificate of exemption and no liability to pay; but a voluntary contribution may be made. Class 2 contributions will 'buy' entitlement to incapacity benefit and other contributory benefits but not contribution-based JSA, as noted above.

Class 3 Contributions These are flat-rate voluntary contributions by non-employed persons or those in Classes 1 or 2 who want to rectify a gap in their contributions record (for example, to bolster retirement pension entitlement).[77] They are currently set at £6.45 per week. Class 3 contributions count towards retirement benefit and widow's benefit only. The age requirements are the same as for Class 1 and 2 contributions. There is a residence requirement.[78]

Class 4 Contributions The purpose of Class 4 contributions is to ensure that the self-employed contributor aged sixteen or over and below pensionable age pays an appropriate 'earnings-related' contribution, fixed with reference to business profits as determined under Schedule D of the Income Tax Acts for the relevant tax year, subject to certain non-applicable tax reliefs which are prescribed.[79] There is one rate of contribution, standing at 6 per cent at present, payable on the relevant aggregate profit and gains of at least the prescribed lower limit (currently £7,530 per annum), but with amounts above the upper limit (currently £26,000 per annum) ignored. Class 4 contributions will be linked to those made under Classes 1, 2, or 3 for the purposes of entitlement to benefit. In the case of those also liable to make Class 1 contributions, the contribution is the maximum that would be paid under *one* of the classes.[80]

(b) Contribution Conditions

There are two separate sets of conditions: initial conditions and continuing conditions. Over recent years the contribution conditions have become more onerous.

Under the 1975 Act the initial or first condition for short-term benefits, such as unemployment and sickness benefit, was (as noted above) that during any one tax year since the age of sixteen the claimant had paid contributions the 'earnings factor'[81] for which was not less than twenty-five times the lower earnings limit in force for that year (or twenty-five flat-rate contributions were paid before April 1975). Credited contributions did not count towards the initial condition. The initial condition for

---

[77] Ibid., s. 13(1) and (2).   [78] S.I. 1979 No. 591, above n. 64, reg. 119(1)(e).
[79] SSCBA 1992, ss 15 and 17 and Sched. 2, para. 3(2).
[80] S.I. 1979 No. 591, above n. 64, reg. 67.
[81] The earnings factor was and is still used in the calculation of entitlement, including entitlement to state retirement pension (see below). The earnings factor for Class 1 contributions is simply the amount of earnings on which contributions have been paid (or treated under the rules as paid), whereas for Class 2 and 3 contributions it is the lower earnings limit multiplied by each contribution made in the relevant tax year. See the Social Security (Earnings Factor) Regulations 1979 (S.I. 1979 No. 676), as amended, Sch. 1. See further Ogus, Barendt, and Wikeley (1995), 64.

contribution-based JSA is now that the required contributions (the same as under the 1975 Act) must have been paid in either of the two immediately preceding tax years.[82] Again, credited contributions will not count. For incapacity benefit and widow's payment, payment of the required contributions in any single tax year will suffice[83] although the Welfare Reform and Pensions Act 1999 will amend this so that the claimant will have to have actually paid contributions of the relevant class in respect of one of the last three complete years before the beginning of the relevant benefit year.[84] The initial condition is most tough in respect of longer-term benefits—such as category A and B retirement pensions or widowed mother's allowance (to be replaced by widowed parent's allowance: see p. 158 n. 14)—where contributions the qualifying earnings factor of which is fifty-two times the lower earnings limit for the year in question must have been paid.[85]

Once the initial condition is satisfied, a further, continuing or second condition, must also be met. For the short-term benefits, such as contribution-based JSA, the condition is that contributions, including those which are credited (see below), sufficient to produce an earnings factor which is fifty times the lower earnings limit must have been made in each of the preceding two tax years (or, in the case of widow's payment, twenty-five times that limit in any tax year before the benefit year in question).[86] Separate, rather more complicated, rules apply to long-term benefits such as pensions.[87] Here it will be necessary for contributions with an earnings factor of at least fifty-two times the lower earnings limit for the required number of years (calculated with reference to the length of a person's 'working life' as prescribed) to have been paid or credited.[88]

(c) Credits and Home Responsibilities Protection

Crediting of contributions, which occurs in prescribed circumstances,[89] is designed to assist those with an overall attachment to the labour market but who are unable to contribute for various reasons, including the unemployed, sick (incapable of work), disabled people receiving disability working allowance (disabled person's tax credit) not earning enough to pay Class 1 or 2 contributions, those receiving invalid care allowance

[82] SSCBA 1992, Sched. 3, para. 1. 25 Pre-April 1975 flat-rate contributions will also still satisfy the requirement.
[83] SSCBA 1992, Sched. 3 para. 2. Note that the concession, under which those whose incapacity for work was the result of an industrial accident or disease but who were unable to satisfy the contribution conditions for sickness benefits were deemed to do so (SSCBA 1992, s. 102), which was introduced in 1983 when injury benefit was scrapped, was abolished by the Social Security (Incapacity for Work) Act 1994: for discussion, see D. Bonner, 'Incapacity for work: a new benefit and new tests' (1995) 2(2) *J.S.S.L.* 86–112, at 93–4.
[84] s. 62.   [85] SSCBA 1992, Sched. 3, para. 5(2).
[86] Ibid., paras 1(3)(b), 2(3)(b), and 4(3). The SSA 1988 tightened up these conditions: see N. Wikeley, 'Targeting, Training and Tightening Up: the SSA 1988' [1989] *J.S.W.L.* 277–92. See also SSA 1989, s. 11.
[87] See C. George et al., *Welfare Benefits Handbook Vol. 2* (London: CPAG, 1999), 275–6.
[88] SSCBA 1992, Sched. 3, para. 5.
[89] Social Security (Credits) Regulations 1975 (S.I. 1975 No. 556), as amended.

or statutory maternity pay, and students.[90] Also, since 1978 it has been possible for a person's contributions record to be protected where they have been away from work while caring for children or a sick or disabled relative. This is known as 'home responsibilities' protection, and it will be particularly important for those (often women) who have a gap in paid contributions but who later wish to claim a state retirement pension (although it will only count for this purpose if the relevant earnings factor in the year in question is at least fifty-two times the lower earnings limit).

(d) Administration and Adjudication of Contributions

From 1991 individual contribution records were maintained by the Contributions Agency at Longbenton in Newcastle. The Social Security Contributions (Transfer of Functions, Etc) Act 1999 transfers formally the Agency's work to the Inland Revenue, thereby streamlining the administration of contributions records. Most contributions were already collected by the Inland Revenue even though the Contributions Agency, on behalf of the Secretary of State, had ultimate responsibility for ensuring that payments were at the correct level. Section 3 of the 1999 Act puts contributions 'under the care and management' of the Commissioners of Inland Revenue (referred to as 'the Board'). Various questions, such as whether a person falls within a particular class for contribution purposes, or whether there is liability to make contributions, or whether contributions have been paid, are referred to the Revenue which, under amendments made by the new Act, now has the power previously held by the Secretary of State to make regulations on these matters and on contributions rates and thresholds.[91] What the 1999 Act has done is to incorporate within the contributions system a division of regulation-making powers that reflects such a division in relation to taxation, where the Treasury has powers that relate to the size of a tax liability and the Board of Inland Revenue is empowered to make regulations on administrative matters. The Act has also changed the decision-making structure. Decisions on home responsibilities protection and contribution credits are made by the Secretary of State but under the management of the Inland Revenue as agents for him or her.[92] Other decisions on contributions, many of which were previously the Secretary of State's decisions under the Social Security Administration Act 1992, such as whether a person is or was in employed earner's employment and whether contributions have been paid or are due, are now to be made by the Board.[93]

---

[90] Ibid. See also, National Insurance Advisory Committee, *Report on Unemployment Benefit for Students*, Cmnd 7613 (London: HMSO, 1979).

[91] See the list of powers and amending provisions in the Social Security Contributions (Transfer of Functions etc) Act 1999, Sched. 3.

[92] Ibid., s. 17.

[93] Social Security Contributions (Transfer of Functions etc) Act 1999, s. 8. Transitional arrangements are made by s. 15. The Board has regulation making powers in relation to decisions: ibid., s. 9. Note that issues arising on, for example, consideration of a claim or on an application for revision of a decision within the Decisions and Appeals framework for social security (see Chapter 7), may also be referred to the Board where they require the Board's determination: Social Security and Child Support (Decisions and

Provision is made for variation or supersession of decisions and for appeals.[94] The new appeal arrangements are significant. Previously there was no right of appeal (to an independent tribunal) over these decisions on contributions, although a person aggrieved (or the Secretary of State himself) could refer a question of law to the High Court, or, in Scotland, the Court of Session, for a determination. Reform could have involved the complete integration of contributions appeals within the tax appeals system for income tax, which would have been consonant with the broader transfer of responsibility under the Act. The 1999 Act in fact largely takes this course, but enables the rules on appeals to be modified to reflect the material differences between tax and contributions (and statutory sick pay and statutory maternity pay liability, also covered by these provisions). Appeal against a decision or superseded decision lies to the tax appeal commissioners (the General and Special Commissioners for income tax), who sit as an independent tribunal. The 1999 Act also contains enforcement and recovery powers and penalties for non-compliance.[95]

C. Retirement Pensions

(i) Introduction

In statistical terms the state retirement pension is the most important of all the insurance-related benefits: as noted above, 10.6 million people (two-thirds of them women) received the basic retirement pension in 1997, at a cost (for 1996–7) of over £30 billion.[96] Receipt of the pension also brings entitlement to the Christmas bonus of £10.[97] The issue of pensions reform has become a matter of serious debate in recent years as the projected cost of future funding of pensions as a result of demographic changes and the maturity of SERPS—already a factor behind the changes made under the Social Security Act 1986 discussed in Chapter 5—has established an economic imperative to avoid a potentially crippling financial burden on the state and thus future generations. Even allowing for the equalisation of the state retirement age at 65 by 2020, which will delay access to retirement pension for a significant number of women employees, projections indicate that the ratio of pensioners to those of working age will fall from 1: 3 to 1: 2 between 2000 and

Appeals) Regulations 1999 (S.I. 1999 No. 991), regs 11A and 38A added by (the same) (Amendment) (No. 3) Regulations 1999 (S.I. 1999 No. 1670), reg. 2. Partington examined the Secretary of State's jurisdiction: M. Partington, *The Secretary of State's Power of Adjudication in Social Security Law* (Bristol: SAUS, 1991).

[94] 1999 Act, ibid., ss 9–13 and Sched. 7, and the Social Security Contributions (Decisions and Appeals) Regulations 1999 (S.I. 1999 No. 1027), Parts II and III.

[95] 1999 Act above n. 93, Scheds 4, 5, and 6 and the various statutory provisions referred to therein.

[96] DSS, *Social Security Statistics 1998* (Leeds: Corporate Document Services, 1998), Tables B1.01 and B1.03.

[97] SSCBA 1992, ss 148–50; see also SSA 1998, s. 33. Free prescriptions and eye tests are, *inter alia*, age-related (60–plus) rather than passported via retirement pension. There are alternative qualifying benefits for the Christmas bonus, such as invalid care allowance and disability living allowance.

2030.[98] There will be 10.5 million pensioners in 2000 but 14.3 million in 2050.[99] The Government's 1998 Green Paper on pensions reform[100] has been followed by legislative change, under the Welfare Reform and Pensions Act 1999. The Green Paper recognises that reform of pensions must be seen in the context of general levels of income among those in retirement. In this regard, the Government has also implemented a minimum income guarantee to assist the poorest pensioners who are most reliant on income support (see below).

(ii) The Basic State Retirement Pension

Current state pensions provision is structured around a basic retirement pension and earnings-related schemes—SERPS (save for those who are contracted out of the scheme)[101] and a graduated pensions scheme. The basic retirement pension is flat rate and payable on reaching state retirement age (currently sixty-five for a man and sixty for a woman, but the retirement age for women will be progressively raised over a ten-year period from 2010). There are three main categories (A, B and D). Category A pension[102] is based on the insured's contributions (above) while Category B[103] is based on a spouse's contributions and is payable to a widow or widower. If contribution conditions are not fully met the basic pension will be paid at a reduced rate: the minimum pension payable will be 25 per cent of the standard rate. Those who are widowed may elect to pay Class 3 contributions (above) to bolster entitlement to Category B pension. Persons aged eighty or over (male or female) are entitled to a Category D pension[104] if they are not entitled to any other retirement pension or their existing pension provides them with less than the current rate of a Category D pension. For 1999–2000 a Category A pension is paid at the rate of £66.75 for the claimant, with additions for an adult dependant (£39.95), the elder/eldest or only child (£9.90) and other children (£11.35 per child). The basic rate for a widow or widower receiving Category B pension is the same as for Category A claimants, including the child dependency additions. Those who have (or whose husbands/wives had) deferred their retirement for more than forty-two days will get increments of approximately 7.5 per cent of the basic rate per year of deferred retirement.[105] All those aged over eighty receive an addition of 25 pence per week on the basic rate of pension.

The flat-rate pension has been increased only in line with prices since 1980 and this has resulted in a serious erosion in its value. For example, in 1993 the basic retirement pension was £56.10 for a single person and £89.80 for a couple whereas if the previous link with earnings had been preserved the amounts payable would have

---

[98] DSS, *A New Contract for Welfare: Partnership in Pensions*, Cm 4179 (London: The Stationery Office, 1998).

[99] Ibid.   [100] Ibid.   [101] See Ogus, Barendt, and Wikeley (1995), Ch. 5.

[102] SSCBA 1992, s. 44.   [103] Ibid., s. 49.

[104] Ibid., s. 78. There is also a Category C pension, now virtually obsolete: see n. 101.

[105] Ibid., Sched. 5, paras 1 and 2 and the Social Security (Widow's Benefit and Retirement Pensions) Regulations 1979 (S.I. 1979 No. 642).

been £74.55 and £119.30 respectively.[106] In April 1995 the respective basic retirement pension rates would need to have been £20.30 and £33.05 per week higher.[107]
The basic state pension is currently worth approximately 15 per cent of average male
earnings, compared with 20 per cent two decades ago.[108] One of the effects of this
relative devaluation of the basic retirement pension has been to increase reliance on
means-tested benefit to supplement income.[109] In November 1997 1.5 million persons
aged over sixty were receiving income support on top of state retirement pension.[110]
Conservative Governments increased the amount allocated to pensioners in means-
tested benefit by £1.2 billion between 1988 and 1994[111] and the Labour Government
has made a significant (three times the normal) increase in income support rates for
pensioners in April 1999—although, as discussed in Chapter 2, take-up of means-
tested benefits is low among older people relative to others. The Government's Green
Paper on pensions published in late 1998 promises that the basic state retirement
pension will henceforth be increased 'at least in line with prices',[112] thus suggesting a
higher increase than the present norm. However, the increases in income support
rates for the over-sixties in 1999 (see below), while preventing any increase in
inequality among the elderly resulting from the future increases in the basic pension,[113]
recognise that means-tested top-ups remain necessary for many.

(iii) Earnings-related Additions and Second Pensions

Turning to the earnings-related element of state pensions, we saw in Chapter 4 how a
graduated pension was introduced in 1961 under the National Insurance Act 1959 to
supplement the basic retirement pension. Although this was subsequently replaced by
SERPS, there is still accrued entitlement in respect of contributions made before April
1975. The graduated pension,[114] entitlement to which is not dependent upon being
entitled to the basic retirement pension (above), is currently paid at the rate of £8.67
per week (or half that rate in the case of a widow claiming by virtue of her husband's
contributions) for every £9.00 contributed by a woman or £7.50 by a man between
April 1961 and April 1975. As at 30 September 1997, 77 per cent of pensioners were
receiving graduated pension, but the weekly average was only £2.36.[115]

---

[106] SSAC, *State Benefits and Private Provision: The Review of Social Security Paper 2* (Leeds: BA Publishing
Services Ltd, 1994), para. 5.5.
[107] C. Oppenheim and L. Harker, *Poverty: The Facts*, 3rd edn. (London: CPAG, 1996), 61.
[108] J. McCormick, 'Prospects for Pensions Reform', in J. McCormick and C. Oppenheim (eds), *Welfare
in Working Order* (London: I.P.P.R., 1998), 175–251, 184.
[109] SSAC, n. 106 above, para. 5.6.
[110] DSS, *Social Security Statistics 1998* (Leeds: Corporate Document Services, 1998), Table A2.24.
[111] Ibid.
[112] DSS (Green Paper), *A New Contract for Welfare: Partnership in Pensions*, Cm 4179 (London: The
Stationery Office, 1998), ch. 4, para. 12.
[113] McCormick makes the point that a substantive increase in the basic pension would widen inequality because the increase would be offset against benefit for those on income support, whereas those not
on means-tested benefits would benefit in full: J. McCormick, op. cit., n. 108 above, 191.
[114] National Insurance Act 1965, s. 36.
[115] DSS, n. 110 above, Table B1.11.

Earnings-related additions to pension are also paid to those covered by SERPS. The calculation of SERPS entitlement is very complex, particularly in the case of persons who reach pensionable age between 6 April 1999 and 5 April 2009.[116] The basic system for a Category A pension involves identifying the years for which contributions were paid and multiplying the earnings factor (see p. 173 n. 81 above) for each year by a prescribed percentage for that year (intended to revalue the earnings factor in line with earnings increases which have occurred up to the year before pensionable age)—for example, 140.2 per cent for 1984–5, 92.9 per cent for 1987–8. This calculation produces what is known as the excess (or surplus) income. The lower earnings limit for the year before the claimant's pensionable age is then multiplied by fifty-two and the product of this sum is deducted from the excess income. The calculation then proceeds as follows:

In the Case of Someone Retiring Before 5 April 1999 the resulting figure for each year is aggregated and deducted from the aggregated excess or surplus income in respect of the years in question; the weekly SERPS figure is determined by multiplying the resulting sum by 1.25 and then dividing by fifty-two.

In the Case of Someone Retiring After 5 April 1999 the revalued earnings factors (as in the pre-6 April cases) are divided up into two groups—one relates to the years 1978–9 to 1987–8 and the other to the years 1988–9 onwards—and they are aggregated within each period. The aggregate figure for the first period is then multiplied by 25 per cent and divided by the number of years in the period concerned. This also happens in the case of the second period, save that the multiplier is a prescribed figure between 20 and 25 per cent, depending on the retirement date, and the resulting figure for this second group is divided by the total number of years between 1978 and 1979 and the end of the last year before retirement. The overall figures for each of the two groups of years are added together and the total is divided by fifty-two to determine weekly SERPS entitlement, which is then the basis for a periodic uprating.

Although it is not immediately apparent from these formulae, the overall effect of the post-5 April 1999 rules is that there will be a reduction in the accrual rate from 1/80th of eligible earnings for someone retiring in 1998 to an eventual 1/244th of earnings within thirty years.[117] This principally reflects the scaling down of SERPS entitlement following the Social Security Act 1986 (see Chapter 5). Overall, those who remain within SERPS today (fewer than 20 per cent of employees) are likely to be in lower-paid employment;[118] around three-quarters of those earning £15,000 or

---

[116] SSCBA 1992, ss. 44 and 45. The basic rules are described in detail in Ogus, Barendt, and Wikeley (1995), 242–5, which also discusses in more detail the method of calculating earnings-related pension for persons retiring on or after 6 April 2009.

[117] J. McCormick, 'Prospects for Pensions Reform', in J. McCormick and C. Oppenheim (eds), *Welfare in Working Order* (London: I.P.P.R., 1998), 175–251, 202.

[118] P. Johnson, *The Pensions Dilemma* (London: I.P.P.R., 1994), 10.

more have an occupational or personal (private) pension.[119] As McCormick points out, however, this does not mean that SERPS is redistributive, because the average benefit paid will be low, especially for those who have had interruptions to employment (thus particularly disadvantaging women, compounding the discriminatory effect of lower wage levels): 'Most beneficiaries will not receive enough to float them above the Income Support line.'[120] For McCormick, therefore, the choice for a government serious about reforming the system would be to improve SERPS for those who remain within it or devise a better second pension system.[121]

Those not covered by SERPS include persons contracted out of the scheme under a salary-related or money-purchase occupational pension scheme or those who are members of an appropriate personal pension scheme.[122] Salary-related occupational pensions schemes relate pensions entitlement to final salary; an advantage of these schemes is that entitlement is defined and the employer takes on most of the cost of running the scheme, but the down side is that contributions are expensive and there can be problems for those who leave employment early.[123] Contracted-out money purchase schemes (or COMPS) require a defined contribution in return for investment in a pension fund whose level of pension will be far less certain, although these pensions have the advantage of portability. Both sets of scheme will reinforce the gender discrimination resulting from differences between male and female average earnings and gaps in contributions due to maternity and child-rearing.[124] Moreover, retired males are twice as likely as females to have been in an occupational scheme.[125] Today, among full-time employees, approximately 86 per cent of males and 77 per cent of females are contributing to an occupational or personal pension scheme.[126]

Occupational schemes have been popular, and they have contributed to above-average increases in income for persons of pensionable age since 1979 (around 50 per cent greater than that of the population as a whole).[127] In the 1998 Green Paper on pensions[128] the Government argued that the development of occupational pen-

---

[119] J. McCormick, op. cit., 202.   [120] Ibid.   [121] Ibid.

[122] To count, these schemes must be certificated by the Occupational Pensions Board under the Pensions Schemes Act 1993. Those persons who are contracted out pay lower national insurance contributions rates.

[123] J. McCormick, n. 117 above, 215.

[124] See E. Whiteford, *Adapting to Change: Occupational Pension Schemes, Women and Migrant Workers* (The Hague: Kluwer Law International, 1997). On the issue of sex equality within the terms of occupational pensions schemes, and the effect of *Barber v Royal Exchange Assurance Group*, C-262/88 [1991] 1 QB 344 (which held that the principle of equal treatment in Article 119 of the EEC Treaty was applicable to employer-based occupational pension schemes), see Whiteford, op. cit. and Ogus, Barendt, and Wikeley (1995), 260–3. See further pp. 236–8 below.

[125] R. Disney, E. Grundy, and P. Johnson, *The Dynamics of Retirement*, DSS Research Report No. 72 (London: The Stationery Office, 1997), para. 5.1.

[126] Hansard, H.C. Debs, 23 February 1999, col. 221, *per* Mr A. Darling, Secretary of State for Social Security.

[127] Green Paper (1998), ch. 4, para. 11.

[128] DSS, *A New Contract for Welfare: Partnership in Pensions*, Cm 4179 (London: The Stationery Office, 1998).

sions schemes might have peaked, particularly given the decline in employments where the tradition of such schemes is strong, such as parts of the public sector. Moreover, changes in the pattern of employment were felt to be affecting the capacity for employees to build up pension rights, with a greater number and variety of employment contracts and levels of income experienced over the course of a working life. A further problem for second pensions has been mistrust and confusion among workers. Participation in private pensions was encouraged via the Social Security Act 1986 (see Chapter 5). But the mis-selling of these pensions and the affair of the Maxwell pensioners, while resulting in additional safeguards via greater regulation of funded (non-state) pension schemes,[129] made many employees remain understandably cautious. Private schemes in any event tend to be very expensive relative to the benefits that accrue: 'contributions of around 15% of income over a working life may be needed to provide a reasonable pension'.[130]

Government policy of facilitating the development of second pensions outside the state system has meant that 'pension provision has been privatized significantly ... by stealth'.[131] However, the SSAC concluded from its review of pensions provision that:

While it is clear that private provision for retirement will have a continuing and increasingly important role for the future, ... for some people it can never provide more than part of the answer to ensuring a reasonable level of income. State provision will continue to be needed for people who have been unable to make their own provision, or adequate provision, for their retirement—for example, those whose opportunities to earn have been limited or disrupted by disability, unemployment or caring responsibilities.[132]

The Committee acknowledged that, given the decline in the state retirement pension and the phasing out of SERPS, most pensioners would in the future either be in receipt of an occupational or personal pension, or would depend on income support.[133] The Labour Government has responded to this prediction by planning increases in the basic pension (as noted above), reform of second pensions, and the introduction of the minimum income guarantee for pensioners on income support (below). The main structural changes proposed concern second pensions, including SERPS.[134]

---

[129] See R. Goode, *Pension Law Reform—the Report of the Pension Law Review Committee* (London: HMSO, 1993) and the Pensions Act 1995 which, amongst other things, introduced new offences in connection with the management of occupational pensions schemes.

[130] SSAC, *State Benefits and Private Provision: The Review of Social Security Paper 2* (Leeds: BA Publishing Services Ltd, 1994), para. 5.8. This would mean that employees would generally need to make full additional voluntary contributions.

[131] R. Hemming, 'Should pensions be funded?' (1999) 52(2) *I.S.S.R.* 3–29, 25.

[132] SSAC, op. cit., para. 5.9.

[133] Ibid., para. 5.11. The background to the introduction of SERPS was described in Chapter 4.

[134] An immediate problem which has arisen, resulting from the past failure to warn SERPS contributors of the 50 per cent reduction in SERPS entitlement from 2000 for those inheriting it from a spouse (see *The Times*, 12 October 1999, 60), has led to a new power to establish (for a prescribed period) a scheme under which those given incomplete or incorrect information can claim exemption from the reduction and their surviving spouse would not be affected by it: Welfare Reform and Pensions Act 1999, s. 52.

(iv) Reform, Including the Introduction of Stakeholder Pensions

A discussion of all the potential options for change in relation to pensions provision cannot be accommodated here;[135] and in any event the Government has already made moves to reform the state pensions system, following the publication of a Green Paper at the end of 1998.[136] The pay-as-you-go element of state pensions (whereby pensions are paid for by contributions from current taxpayers) will remain central to provision, but the Government has acknowledged the importance of funded pensions (i.e. those, such as occupational or personal pensions which are supported by an accumulated fund rather than by current contributions) for support in retirement. A key objective of any reform of pensions, must be to ensure that low earners are adequately protected in retirement while, at a time when the number of people, and proportion of the population, of retirement age is set to increase steadily (noted above), keeping public expenditure within reasonable bounds. The Green Paper notes that the gap between the best-off and worst-off pensioners has been increasing. It estimates that within twenty-five or so years over half of those reaching state retirement age would have to rely on income-related benefits. How could such reliance be minimised, when low earners find it difficult to save and generally cannot afford private pensions, when occupational pensions seem to be in decline, and when changes in the pattern of employment (with a greater number and variety of employment contracts and levels of income over a working life) are adversely affecting the capacity to build up pension rights?

   The Green Paper hints, but offers no firm commitment, that increases in the basic retirement pension will be earnings-linked in future. Without such an increase it is entirely likely that there will be a further erosion in its value relative to incomes in the population as a whole. Income support rates are being more substantially increased, however. The proposed 'minimum income guarantee' referred to in the Green Paper has already seen a substantial rise in the income support pensioner premium in April 1999 (by over 17 per cent in one year), leading to an overall annual increase in income support for this age group three times higher than would normally be expected. The Green Paper says that the minimum income guarantee will be increased year by year as resources allow and that the long-term aim is to align the increase with that of earnings. Winter fuel payments, originally introduced on a short-term basis (in 1998–9 paying £20 or, in the case of couples, £10 per person, or £50 for pensioners on income support), will be continued and the minimum payment per household has been increased for the winter of 1999/2000 onwards (to £100, £50, and £100, respectively) (see p. 443 below). These changes will improve income levels for the very worst-off pensioners argues the Government.

---

[135] For discussion, see, for example, McCormick, n. 117 above, 203 ff; F. Field, *How to Pay for the Future: Building a Stakeholders' Welfare* (London: ICS, 1996); P. Lilley, *Providing for Pensions* (London: Politeia, 1996); and P. Johnson, *The Pensions Dilemma* (London: I.P.P.R., 1994).

[136] DSS, *A New Contract for Welfare: Partnership in Pensions* (Green Paper) Cm 4179 (London: The Stationery Office, 1998).

Workers earning less than around £9,000 will also see improvements with the introduction of a 'state second pension' in place of SERPS. The Government claims that this new scheme will offer double the value of SERPS. It is claimed that 'moderate' earners (described as those earning £9,000–£18,500) will experience a similar increase for the first £9,000 of their income and will receive a boosted contributions rebate to encourage them to take out a funded second pension. One of the second pensions that is contemplated is the 'stakeholder pension'—a new form of 'low-cost, value-for-money' private second pension.[137] Stakeholder pensions are expected to be attractive to those on moderate and higher earnings, particularly where an occupational scheme is not available. The expectation is that, in time, funded pensions would replace state second pension entirely for moderate and higher earners and state second pension would then become a flat-rate scheme, utilised by lower earners. The overall effect of the changes, it is claimed, will be increased levels of pension for those earning below £18,500, with higher earners no worse off than at present.[138]

Inevitably, however, a question arises as to whether private insurance companies will be able to provide second pensions of sufficient value and affordability (and also meeting the new minimum standards which the Government will require).[139] There is also a doubt over whether employers will perceive sufficient incentives to expand provision of occupational schemes (incentives to be offered include a reduced regulatory burden). A further problem will be the inherent complexity of the system. The Green Paper acknowledges that people find pensions very confusing. It will be vital that the Government's commitment to 'an education philosophy'[140] results in clear and coherent information being available, given the important individual choices to be made.

Elements of the new pensions system are being put in place via the Welfare Reform and Pensions Act 1999. Stakeholder pension schemes providing money purchase benefits will be able to be established, subject to conditions, as occupational or personal pensions schemes for the purposes of the Pension Schemes Act 1993. The 1999 Act provides for registration of stakeholder pension schemes by the Occupational Pensions Regulatory Authority. The Government has explained that the 1999 Act represents only the start of the process of pensions reform:[141] it does not provide for implementation of the state second pension proposals (above), which are to be included in a new Bill.[142] The new system, when fully

[137] Ibid., ch. 6. See also DSS, *Helping to Deliver Stakeholder Pensions* (London: DSS, 1999). On EC implications, see pp. 251–2 below. The author discusses the concept of stakeholderism at pp. 29–30 above.
[138] *Partnership in Pensions*, op. cit., ch. 6, para. 16.   [139] Ibid., ch. 7.   [140] Ibid., ch 10.
[141] Hansard, H.C. Debs, 23 February 1999, cols 215 and 230, *per* Mr A. Darling, Secretary of State for Social Security. The Act makes provision (in Parts I and II) for stakeholder pension schemes and the additional safeguards for personal and occupational pensions schemes. It also (in Parts III and IV) makes provision for pension sharing on divorce and generally.
[142] Disney, Emmerson, and Tanner note that in any event the long transition period from SERPS to state second pension that is contemplated means that the full benefit of this reform will not be felt until well into the next century: *Partnership in Pensions: An Assessment* (London: Institute for Fiscal Studies, 1999).

implemented, will not mark a return to the universalist insurance-based model con-templated by Beveridge. None the less, there is a recognition in the Green Paper of the principle of universal *security* for pensioners. Although there is no guarantee to eliminate poverty among this age group, the minimum income guarantee (above) and plans to improve savings incentives (via higher disregards in income-related benefits) are intended to ensure that 'all can face retirement in security'.[143] The Green Paper also proposes contributions credits for those unable to contribute due to being engaged in domestic caring responsibilities, which has been a major gap in insurance provision in the past.[144] Whether the planned reforms will achieve the measure of social justice expressed in the 1997 Labour general election manifesto—'we believe all pensioners should share fairly in the increasing prosperity of the nation'[145]— remains to be seen.

4. MEANS-TESTED OR INCOME-RELATED BENEFITS: CORE PROVISIONS

A. Introduction

General policy issues relating to means-tested benefits were discussed above. We now turn to the basic structure of these benefits. Provision is made by statute[146] for the following income-related benefits: *income support* or *income-based jobseeker's allowance*, which are intended to cover basic living costs, with certain exceptions such as hous-ing costs for those in rented accommodation and council tax liability; *housing benefit*, which covers up to 100 per cent of the rent payable to a private or public sector land-lord; *family credit* (or now *working families tax credit* (WFTC)), and *disability working allowance* (DWA) (or now *disabled person's tax credit* (DPTC)), which are intended to supplement the income from full-time (16 hours or more per week) employment of, in the case of family credit/WFTC, those who are responsible for a child, and in the case of DWA/DPTC, those who are at a disadvantage in getting a job; and *council tax benefit*, which in some cases meets up to 100 per cent of the claimant's council tax liability. The legal structure of many of these benefits is referred to variously in other chapters. For the purposes of clarity, and to illustrate the complexity of modern means-testing under regulations, this chapter outlines some of the common rules relating to these benefits and explains the basis of entitlement to income support and income-based JSA as the basic assistance benefits.

---

[143] N. 136 above, ch 4.

[144] Ibid., ch. 6. One possibility considered has been the introduction of a 'Citizenship Pension' for car-ers: Green Paper (1998), ch. 4, para. 14.

[145] The Labour Party, *New Labour—because Britain deserves better* (London: The Labour Party, 1997), 26–7.

[146] SSCBA 1992, s. 123(1), which states that 'prescribed schemes shall provide for' each of the listed benefits, and JS Act 1995, ss 1 and 3.

B. Common Rules

Although these benefits are separate in substance and in their administration, one of the outcomes of the reform of income-related benefits under the Social Security Act 1986 was provision for a common basis of assessing a claimant's means across diverse schemes. Thus the rules have been harmonised, although not consolidated into one set of provisions. There are also common conditions of entitlement, such as being 'in Great Britain'.[147] Specific conditions of entitlement, such as those relating to the work test (availability for employment, etc) and not being in certain forms of education are covered in later chapters.[148] The citations below include references to DWA and family credit regulations, which have been amended to cover the tax credit schemes (above) (see further Chapters 9 and 12 respectively). Council tax benefit has similar rules but these have not been included.

Both the size and nature of family relationships have long been important determinants of the level of need which social security should meet. In particular, the social security system embodies a number of dependency assumptions about family relationships and marks out particular family groups as a unit for benefit assessment purposes. The income-related benefits are subject to common provisions on, for example, the treatment of couples (married or unmarried but living together as husband and wife)[149] and children and young people within families. If the claimant is a member of a married or unmarried couple, his or her partner's income will be aggregated with that of the claimant for the purposes of assessing the claimant's entitlement.[150] In contrast, although the income of his or her child will generally be aggregated with that of the claimant, any capital will not.[151] Dependency assumptions also underlie the rules governing the age at which independent entitlement shall start (basically eighteen, with limited access at sixteen or seventeen see below)—on the basis that below a particular age a young person, if not in employment, is deemed to be dependent on his or her parents for support. This assumption also affects the age twenty-five divide in the income support, jobseeker's allowance, and housing benefit rates.[152] Family relationships are also reflected in the family premium and disabled child premium, discussed below.

There is also a broadly common approach to the calculation of the claimant's income and capital, although the upper capital limits are lower in the case of income

---

[147] See SSCBA 1992, ss 124(1), 128(1) and 129(1), and the JS Act 1995, s. 1(2). See the discussion of the habitual residence test below.

[148] The work test conditions are covered by Lundy in Chapter 10. The education restrictions are covered by the author in Chapter 11.

[149] See Chapter 9.

[150] SSCBA 1992, s. 136(1); JS Act 1995, s. 13(2).

[151] Ibid. and IS(G) Regs 1987, regs 44(5) and 47; JSA Regs 1996, regs 106(5) and 109; FC(G) Regs 1987, regs 27(2) and 30; DWA Regs 1991, regs 30(3) and 33; HB(G) Regs 1987, regs 36(2) and 39. Nevertheless, the effect of the child having capital in excess of £3,000 is that there can be no child allowance for that child in the assessment of the claimant's benefit (see, for example, IS(G) Regs 1987, reg. 17(1)(b)).

[152] IS(G) Regs 187, Sched. 2; JSA Regs 1996, Sched. 1; HB(G) Regs 1987, Sched. 2. For discussion of this reform, see Chapter 5 above.

support, income-based JSA, and family credit (maximum of £8,000)[153] than they are for DWA, housing benefit, and council tax benefit (maximum of £16,000). As income-related benefits, these forms of social security payment are intended to be tailored to the particular circumstances of the claimant in determining the level of support needed. If the claimant's income exceeds the relevant applicable amount—calculated with reference to circumstances such as the claimant's age, family circumstances, physical or mental capacity, etc—there will be no entitlement to benefit.[154] As noted in Chapter 5, an important step towards a common approach was the change in 1988 to using net income in calculating both income support and family credit entitlement, as well as entitlement to other income-related benefits.

In broad terms income refers to net income from employed earner's employment or calculated with reference to the net profits of self-employed earners, in either case subject to disregards.[155] Complex rules determine how the calculations are to be made, including those designed to measure a net weekly income.[156] Income other than earnings must also be factored in: this time it is *gross* income (or 'receipts') which counts.[157] Again there are disregards.[158] In some cases capital received is treated as income.[159] Among the other complicated rules on the calculation of income are those designed to ensure that income which the claimant ought reasonably to have available to him or her but which is no longer in his or her possession is taken into account, as 'notional' income. This includes income of which the claimant has deprived him or herself in order to secure or boost entitlement to benefit.[160] A further type of resource which affects entitlement to income-related benefit is 'tariff' income.[161] The assumption underlying this is that if the claimant's capital is above a certain threshold, there are, in effect, resources which are available to the claimant which it would be reasonable to expect him or her to use to defray living expenses. Tariff income of £1 per week is assumed for each £250 by which the claimant's capital exceeds £3,000.[162]

Although there are differences in upper capital limits between some of the benefits (see above), there are common approaches to the determination of capital. In fact, the term 'capital', which includes that of the claimant and his or her partner aggregated, is not in itself defined in the various regulations, but there is a consider-

---

[153] It is £16,000 in the case of income support where a claimant lives permanently in certain forms of residential care: see below.
[154] See, for example, SSCBA 1992, ss. 124(1)(b) and 128(1)(a) and JS Act 1995, s. 3.
[155] JSA Regs 1996, regs 94 and 95 and Sched. 6; IS(G) Regs 1987, regs 36 and 38 and Sched. 8.
[156] IS(G) Regs 1987, regs 28–39; JSA Regs 1996, regs 100–102.
[157] IS(G) Regs 1987 reg. 40; JSA Regs 1996, reg. 103.
[158] IS(G) Regs 1987, Sched. 9; JSA Regs 1996, Sched. 6.
[159] IS(G) Regs 1987, reg. 41; JSA Regs 1996, reg. 104. An example is a payment under an annuity.
[160] IS(G) Regs 1987, reg. 42; JSA Regs 1996, reg. 105.
[161] IS(G) Regs 1987, reg. 53; JSA Regs 1996, reg. 116; FC(G) Regs 1987, reg. 36; DWA Regs 1991, reg. 40; HB(G) Regs 1987, reg. 45.
[162] Note that there are special rules on tariff income for those living permanently in certain forms of residential care or other specified accommodation: see below.

able body of case law on the subject.[163] Moreover, it is clear that amounts held as savings will count, including cash amounts, savings certificates and premium bonds, as will various forms of property, such as choses in action, and sums available from a trust in the claimant's favour (but not a trust set up from personal injury compensation).[164] The various regulations list the types of capital to be disregarded for the purposes of the capital rule, including the value of the dwelling the claimant occupies as his or her main home, personal possessions (except those acquired with a view to reducing capital in order to guarantee or improve the level of entitlement), and the surrender value of a life assurance policy.[165] There is also a 'notional capital' provision, so that capital parted with in order to avoid the effects of the capital rules, for example savings transferred into the name of a relative, will be treated as though still belonging to the claimant, even if there was an additional motive.[166] Although payment for an expensive holiday might be an obvious example of notional capital, it seems that the test is principally whether the claimant *intended* to avoid the capital rule rather than the kind of expenditure involved.[167]

C. Income Support and Income-based Jobseeker's Allowance

Since the introduction of jobseeker's allowance (JSA) in October 1996 there have been two forms of basic means-tested benefit: income support for people who are not required to be available for employment as a condition of receiving benefit; and income-based JSA for others.[168] The eligibility rules governing entitlement to JSA are discussed in Chapter 10. They include a requirement that the claimant (or jobseeker) enters into a 'jobseeker's agreement' as a condition of entitlement to benefit, in addition to conditions of being in Great Britain, available for and actively seeking employment, not in 'relevant education',[169] and not, nor having a partner who is, engaged in remunerative work.[170] JSA is aimed at the unemployed, so there is no entitlement to this benefit for a person who is of pensionable age.[171] The minimum age of entitlement to income support or JSA is

---

[163] See J. Mesher and P. Wood, *Income-Related Benefits: the Legislation* (London: Sweet and Maxwell, 1998), 218–22.

[164] See, for example, JSA Regs 1996, Sched. 8 para. 17.

[165] IS(G) Regs 1987, Sched. 10; JSA Regs 1996, Sched. 8; FC(G) Regs 1987, Sched. 3; DWA Regs 1991, Sched. 4; HB(G) Regs 1987, Sched. 5. On the position where ownership takes the form of a beneficial joint tenancy, see *Chief Adjudication Officer v Palfrey* (1995) *The Times*, 17 February.

[166] See *CIS/40/1989*; *CIS/621/1991*; and *R(SB) 38/85*.

[167] C. George et al., *Welfare Benefits Handbook 1999/2000 Vol. 2* (London: CPAG, 1999), 456.

[168] A person is not eligible for income support if they are entitled to jobseeker's allowance: SSCBA 1992, s. 124(1)(f), introduced by JS Act 1995, Sched. 2 para. 30(5).

[169] IS(G) Regs 1987, reg. 12 and CB(G) Regs 1976, reg. 5(2). See Chapter 11 for an explanation.

[170] JS Act 1995, ss 1(2)(a), (c), (e), and (i) and 3(1)(e); SSCBA, s. 124(1)(c). Remunerative work is basically work of at least 16 hours per week for which payment is made or in the expectation of payment: IS(G) Regs 1987, reg. 5(1). The calculation of hours of work is governed by reg. 5(2). See also *R(IS)15/94*. In prescribed circumstances a person must be deemed not to be in remunerative work: reg. 6.

[171] JS Act 1995, s. 1(2)(h).

set at eighteen although, as noted above, exceptional entitlement for sixteen and seventeen year olds arises in tightly defined circumstances[172] and in addition provision is made for discretionary severe hardship payments for those aged under eighteen who would otherwise not qualify for the benefit concerned. A severe hardship payment will be payable where the Secretary of State makes a direction under section sixteen of the Jobseekers Act 1995.[173] The rules on income support and JSA also contain special restrictions on eligibility for particular groups, such as strikers, persons in residential care, and (following much criticised changes to the rules in 1996) asylum seekers (see below).

If the claimant's income[174] is less than the 'applicable amount', he or she may be entitled to income support or income-based JSA. In the case of both of these benefits the applicable amount is determined with reference to the prescribed personal allowances and the various premiums, as noted above.

(i) Personal Allowances

The structure is broadly the same for both of the benefits.[175] There is one weekly rate for single under eighteen year olds who qualify, although in some circumstances (for example, where the disability premium is payable or the claimant has to live away from his or her parent for various prescribed reasons, such as to avoid physical or sexual abuse or because the parent is in custody), a higher rate is payable.[176] Single persons aged eighteen to twenty-four (inclusive) will also be entitled to the higher rate, and those aged twenty-five or over will qualify, at present rates, for approximately £10 per week more than this.[177]

The rules governing the rate of personal allowance available to couples are complex. Broadly speaking, where one or both are under eighteen, the rate depends on such factors as whether or not both are eligible for income support or income-based JSA and the age of a partner if over eighteen. The highest rate[178] is paid if one member is eighteen or over and the other member is under eighteen and is eligible for income support or JSA (including where a direction under section 16 has been made in the case of the latter).[179] The next highest rate[180] applies where *both* partners are under eighteen; if they are married they will receive this rate provided they are both registered for work or youth training or meet certain prescribed conditions, whereas if they are not married they must both be eligible for income support or JSA (or be the subject of a section 16 direction), or one of them must be responsible for a child. In other circumstances where both are aged under eighteen, one of two lower rates

---

[172] SSCBA 1992, s. 124(1)(a); IS(G) Regs 1987, reg. 4ZA and Sched. 1B; JS Act 1995, s. 3(1)(f); JSA Regs 1996, ss. 57–68.

[173] On the way that claims from 16–17 year olds are to be dealt with, see Mesher and Wood, n. 163 above, 58–9.

[174] See pp. 185–6 above.

[175] See JSA Regs 1996, Sched. 1 para. 1; IS(G) Regs 1987, Sched. 2 para. 1.

[176] The higher rate is £40.70 in 1999–2000, while the standard rate is £30.95.

[177] £51.40 at 1999–2000 rates.   [178] Currently set at £80.65.   [179] See above.

[180] £61.35 in 1999–2000.

will be payable.[181] Where the under eighteen year old claimant is not eligible for income support or JSA (and there has not been a section 16 direction in respect of him or her), the rate will depend on whether his or her partner is aged twenty-five or over or aged eighteen to twenty-four.[182] Where both members of a couple are aged at least eighteen, the highest couples rate (above) applies.

The adult personal allowances are supplemented by dependant additions in respect of children and young persons. Prior to April 1997 there were four ascending age-related rates (under 11, 11–15, 16–17- and 18-plus). However, the age bands are now basically 0–11, 11–16, and 16–18 (inclusive).[183] Despite some transitional protection, this change has had a negative impact on entitlement for some.[184]

Finally, there are special rates of additional allowance, towards accommodation costs, for persons living in certain forms of residential care and nursing homes who receive 'personal care' there.[185] They only apply to persons entering such accommodation after March 1993 (and thus who do not have 'preserved rights' under the previous benefit regime), when the new Community Care arrangements were introduced: see below.

(ii) Premiums

When the proposed Fowler reforms were announced in 1985 the Government said it had committed itself to recognising the needs of the disabled, elderly, and families. The various premiums built into the income support scheme (and now also income-based JSA) were intended to reflect the needs of these groups. However, as we saw in Chapter 5, there was criticism at the time of their introduction that the broad categorisation of groups with assumed levels of need was actually a rather crude way of targeting additional support.

Family Premium The family premium is payable to any family one of whose members is a child or young person or, in the case of a polygamous marriage, where either partner is responsible for a child or young person who is a member of the same household.[186] For income support purposes, a 'child' is a person under the age of

---

[181] £40.70 if one partner is eligible for IS at the higher under-18s rate, or £30.95 if that partner is eligible for the lower rate instead.

[182] In 1999–2000 the rates are £51.40 (age 25 or over) and £40.70 (aged 18–24).

[183] IS(G) Regs 1987, Sched. 2 para. 2; JSA Regs 1996, Sched. 1 para. 2. The rates stand at £20.20 (£24.90 from October 1999: S.I. 1999 No. 2555), £25.90, and £30.95 respectively. Under these arrangements, there is now a link to the start of the school year. This is the cause of the overlaps in the age bands shown. Thus, for example, a child falls within the middle band until the first Monday in September following his or her 16th birthday: see the Income-related Benefits and Jobseeker's Allowance (Personal Allowances for Children and Young Persons) (Amendment) Regulations 1996 (S.I. 1996 No. 2545).

[184] See the SSAC's report on the proposed regulations Cm. 3393 (London: HMSO, 1996).

[185] IS(G) Regs 1987, Sched. 2 para. 2A; JSA Regs 1996, Sched. 1 para. 3. The rates are currently £59.40 outside the Greater London area and £66.10 within it.

[186] IS(G) Regs 1987, regs 17(1)(c) and 18(1)(d) and Sched. 2 para. 3; JSA Regs 1996, regs 83(d) and 84(1)(e) and Sched. 1 para. 4. The rate for 1999–2000 is £13.90 and the lone-parent rate (see below) is £15.75.

sixteen[187] and a 'young person' is a person aged sixteen to eighteen who is treated as being a child for child benefit purposes, provided he or she is not in 'advanced' education or entitled to income support or JSA in his or her own right.[188] For a child to be a member of a 'family', it is necessary for a person who is 'responsible' for the child to be living in the same 'household' as him/her.[189] For income support or JSA purposes a person is treated as being responsible for a child if he or she is receiving child benefit for the child.[190] If this condition is satisfied it follows that they must for income support or JSA purposes be treated as living in the same household save in exceptional cases (for example where a child or young person is placed in the residential care of the local authority or is being held in custody pending trial).[191]

There is only one family premium payable per family, irrespective of its size. In the case of a lone-parent family, additional support has traditionally been provided but is being phased out.[192] Under previous rules, a lone-parent premium was available.[193] In April 1996 the lone-parent premium was frozen at its 1995 rate. The Government questioned the need for the premium to continue at its higher rate and believed it might be undermining work incentives for lone parents. It announced an intention to merge the family premium and lone-parent premium.[194] This happened and the family premium became payable at two rates, with the higher rate going to lone parents. However, from July 1998 lone parents only receive the higher rate if they received it on 5 April 1998. This higher rate was in any event frozen with effect from April 1999. These changes to lone-parent premium have been accompanied by changes to child benefit.[195]

Pensioner Premium The rules governing the pensioner premium differ as between IS and JSA,[196] because there is no entitlement to JSA if the claimant is of pensionable age. For both benefits the basic condition is that the claimant is aged sixty or over or has a partner of this age.[197] For IS purposes, once the claimant or his/her partner is seventy-five there is entitlement to the higher-rated *pensioner premium for persons seventy-five and over*.[198] JSA entitlement does not continue to this age, where the claimant is concerned, as noted above. Therefore, this special rate is only available as a pensioner

---

[187] SSCBA 1992, s. 137(1); JS Act 1995, s. 35(1).

[188] IS(G) Regs 1987, reg. 14(1) and (2); JSA Regs 1996, reg. 76(2). For the meaning of 'advanced' education, see IS(G) Regs 1987, reg. 12(2) and JSA Regs 1996, reg. 1(3). A course of advanced education is broadly speaking one which is above 'A' level and is of at least first degree or higher national diploma level. See further Chapter 11 at p. 344.

[189] SSCBA, s. 137(1); JS Act 1995, s. 35(1).

[190] IS(G) Regs 1987, reg. 15; JS Regs 1996, reg. 77.

[191] IS(G) Regs 1987, reg. 16; JSA Regs 1996, reg. 78.

[192] Lone parents aged 18–24 still receive the over-25 standard rate of personal allowance however.

[193] IS(G) Regs 1987, Sched. 2 para. 8; JSA Regs 1996, Sched. 2 para. 9.

[194] DSS, *Restructuring Benefits for Lone Parents, Note to the SSAC* (1996), para. 2.

[195] See Chapter 9 (at pp. 266 and 268) by Gillian Douglas.

[196] IS(G) Regs 1987, Sched. 2, para. 9; JSA Regs 1996, Sched. 1, para. 10.

[197] The rates for 1999–2000 are £23.60 for a single person and £35.95 for a couple.

[198] IS(G) Regs 1987, Sched. 2 para. 9A. The 1999–2000 rates are £25.90 single or £39.20 for a couple.

premium in JSA where the claimant's partner has attained the age of seventy-five.[199] Pensioner premium rates were increased by over 15 per cent in April 1999 as part of the Government's 'minimum income guarantee' for poorer pensioners. This is discussed in the section on pensions above (see p. 182).

Higher Pensioner Premium[200]

For the purposes of income support,[201] the claimant or his/her partner must be aged eighty or over or, alternatively, must be not less than sixty and satisfy a disability test (the relevant 'additional condition')[202] or must have qualified for the disability premium (see below) in the eight weeks before their sixtieth birthday and been continuously entitled to it since then (disregarding any period of disentitlement to income support of up to eight weeks). Where the higher pensioner premium is paid the claimant will not receive the pensioner premium.[203]

Disability Premium The disability premium (discussed by Nick Wikeley in Chapter 12) is payable at two rates, one for a single person or lone parent aged under sixty who receives one or more of prescribed disability benefits or is, for example, registered blind,[204] and a higher rate for couples, where the claimant or his/her partner is aged less than sixty and meets similar conditions.[205]

Severe Disability Premium[206] The rules governing entitlement to severe disability premium (SDP) have been the subject of several important legal challenges in recent years and, largely as a consequence of the various judicial rulings, have been amended on several occasions.[207] The purpose of the premium is to acknowledge the additional costs facing a severely disabled person who is living independently or with a partner who is him/herself severely disabled. Entitlement is restricted to persons who have no non-dependants aged eighteen or over normally residing with them[208] and, in the case of a single person, no-one is receiving invalid care allowance for

---

[199] JSA Regs 1996, Sched. 1 para. 11.

[200] The 1999–2000 rates are £30.85 (single) and £44.65 (couple).

[201] IS(G) Regs 1996, Sched. 2 para. 10.

[202] See ibid., para. 12(1)(a) and (c). The test would, for example, be satisfied by receipt of a qualifying benefit (e.g. disability living allowance, long-term incapacity benefit or severe disablement allowance (in the case of the last two of these, it must be the claimant who qualifies for them) or being registered blind.

[203] IS(G) Regs 1987, Sched. 2 paras 5 and 6; JSA Regs 1996, Sched. 1 paras 6 and 7.

[204] IS(G) Regs 1987, Sched. 2 paras 11(a) and 12; JSA Regs 1996, Sched. 1 paras 13(a) and 14(1)(a), (c), (e), (f), or (h). The rate for 1999–2000 is £21.90.

[205] IS(G) Regs 1987, Sched. 2 paras 11(b) and 12(1)(a), (b), or (c); JSA Regs 1996, Sched. 1 paras 13(b) and (c) and 14. The rate for 1999–2000 is £31.25.

[206] This is discussed by Nick Wikeley in Chapter 12 at 391–2. It is governed by: IS(G) Regs 1987, Sched. 2 para. 13; JSA Regs 1996, Sched. 1 para. 15. The rate for 1999–2000 is £39.75 for a single person and £79.50 for a couple who both qualify, unless there is someone in receipt of invalid care allowance for one of them, in which case it will be £39.75.

[207] These developments are discussed by Nick Wikeley in Chapter 12.

[208] The definition of 'non-dependant' in reg. 3 of the IS(G) Regs 1987 (see also JSA Regs 1996, reg. 2) has also been amended in the light of the relevant cases noted in Chapter 12.

looking after him/her, or, in the case of a couple, such an allowance is not in payment or is only in payment in respect of one of them. The test of severe disability *per se* is receipt of attendance allowance or the care component of the disability living allowance at the highest or middle rate.[209] The fact that a parent is paid attendance allowance or disability living allowance on behalf of a child does not make the parent 'in receipt of' that benefit for the purpose of being able to qualify for the severe disability premium.[210] Clearly, the conditions of eligibility are strict.[211]

Disabled Child Premium To qualify for the disabled child premium[212] the claimant or his/her partner must be responsible for a disabled child or young person who is a member of the claimant's household and who has either no capital or capital not exceeding £3,000. A child or young person is disabled for this purpose if: (i) they are in receipt of disability living allowance (DLA); or (ii) they are no longer in receipt of DLA because they are a patient, provided that they are still a member of the claimant's family; or (iii) they are blind or treated as blind.[213] A person is 'in receipt of' these benefits for the purposes of these rules 'if, and only if, it is paid in respect of him'.[214]

Carer Premium The carer premium was not in the original list of income support premiums planned for introduction in 1988. It was proposed in the 1990 white paper on disability benefits and was introduced in October of that year.[215] It was seen as one of the reforms that was needed to support the Conservative Government's Community Care policy under which there was an emphasis on keeping disabled persons out of institutional/residential care—a policy which of necessity has put an additional care burden on families. It is paid to persons entitled to invalid care allowance (ICA) and is intended to provide additional assistance to those who are caring for an infirm or disabled relative. Entitlement continues for up to eight weeks after the claimant ceases to be entitled to ICA.[216]

Overlap and entitlement to premiums The general rule is that where the claimant satisfies the conditions of entitlement in respect of more than one premium there is entitle-

---

[209] See below.
[210] IS(G) Regs 1987, Sched. 2 para. 14B. On the pre-April 1990 situation, see *Rider v Chief Adjudication Officer*; *Palmer v (Same)*; *Doyle v (Same)*, *The Times*, 30 January 1996 (CA).
[211] See further p. 391 below.
[212] IS(G) Regs 1987, Sched. 2 para. 14; JSA Regs 1996, Sched. 1 para. 16. The 1999–2000 rate is £21.90 in respect of each disabled child or young person.
[213] A person who was registered blind is treated as registered blind for 28 weeks after regaining their eyesight: IS(G) Regs 1987, Sched. 2 para. 12(2); JSA Regs 1996, Sched. 1 para. 14(2).
[214] IS(G) Regs 1987, Sched. 2 para. 14B; JSA Regs 1996, Sched. 1 para. 19. See also *Rider and Others v Chief Adjudication Officer* (1996) n. 210 above.
[215] DSS, *The Way Ahead—Benefits for disabled people* Cm 917 (London: HMSO, 1990), para. 7.3; Income Support (General) Amendment No. 3 Regulations 1990 (S.I. 1990 No. 1776), reg. 8.
[216] IS(G) Regs 1987, Sched. 2 para. 14ZA; JSA Regs 1996, Sched. 1 para. 17. The weekly rate from April 1999 is £13.95.

ment to only one—whichever involves the higher/highest amount.[217] The family premium is not caught by this general rule. Furthermore, three of the premiums— the severe disability premium, the disabled child premium, and the carer premium— are payable in addition to any other premium.[218]

(iii) Housing Costs[219]

The only housing costs which are met through the income support or income-based JSA schemes today are those relating to owner occupation. The rules are analysed by Simon Rahilly in Chapter 13.

(iv) Trade Disputes

Particularly harsh rules apply to strikers. The restrictions on entitlement are based on the principle that union strike funds can and should assist strikers and that the social security system should not be used as a means of subsidising employees in dispute with their employers. The basic rule is that entitlement is lost or reduced in any week where the claimant is disqualified from JSA either by reason of there being a stoppage of work due to a trade dispute at his or her place of work, in which he has a direct interest, or because he or she has withdrawn his/her labour in furtherance of a trade dispute.[220] The claimant is treated as being in remunerative work for the first seven days and so there would be no entitlement to income support or JSA.[221] Thereafter the applicable amount of a single claimant is withdrawn. If the claimant is a member of a married or unmarried couple the applicable amount for the couple is halved, but it will be nil if they are both involved in the dispute. There will be no premium payable in respect of the claimant or partner (if they are also involved in the dispute), but otherwise there is entitlement to premiums as well as child additions. Payments made to a member of the family in the form of income tax refunds shall be treated as income when benefit is assessed as shall payments made because the claimant is out of work for the relevant period.[222] Also taken into account in full as income is actual strike pay above a prescribed figure (currently £27.50), but alternatively benefit is reduced by a notional prescribed amount (again £27.50) for assumed strike pay (whether or not that amount of strike payment is made).[223] On return to work the claimant is entitled to benefit for fifteen days, unless his or her partner is in full-time work.[224] The position of strikers is considered further by Laura Lundy in Chapter 10 at pp. 312–14.

---

[217] IS(G) Regs 1987, Sched. 2 para. 5; JSA Regs 1996, Sched. 1 para. 6.
[218] IS(G) Regs 1987, Sched. 2 para. 6; JSA Regs 1996, Sched. 1 para. 7.
[219] The rules are contained in the IS(G) Regs 1987, Sched. 3 and the JSA Regs 1996, Sched. 2.
[220] SSCBA 1992, s. 126: JS Act 1995, s. 15.
[221] JS Act 1995, s. 14(1); IS(G) Regs 1987, reg. 5(4).
[222] SSCBA 1992, s. 126(5)(a): JS Act 1995, s. 15(2)(c).
[223] SSCBA 1992, s. 126(5)(b): JS Act 1995, s. 15(2)(d).
[224] SSCBA 1992, s. 127(b): JS Act 1995, s. 15(4).

(v) Reductions for Voluntary Unemployment, etc

A claimant who becomes unemployed for various prescribed reasons or who fails to comply with a jobseeker's direction or who refuses to join, or unjustifiably leaves, the New Deal may be subject to a sanction which may take the form of disqualification from benefit. These sanctions and the circumstances in which they may be imposed are discussed in detail by Laura Lundy in Chapter 10 (at p. 307 ff.).

(vi) Persons in Hospital

Patients in hospital do not normally qualify for JSA because they are incapable of work or unavailable for it. However, they could receive income support at the full rate provided their stay does not exceed six weeks; the severe disability premium will, however, cease after four weeks, because the claimant's entitlement to the benefits which provide a 'passport' to the premium—attendance allowance and disability living allowance care component—will lapse.[225] (The entitlement of those who were in a residential home immediately before entering hospital is governed by separate rules.[226]) After six weeks in hospital, income support is reduced.[227] Benefit will continue at this rate until the claimant has been in hospital for fifty-two weeks, when it will be further reduced.[228] However, a lesser amount will, in some cases, be paid if the claimant is incapable of managing his own affairs[229] (on the basis that, because of his/her condition, the full rate would not be needed by the claimant). If the claimant is not a patient but his or her child is and has been for more than twelve weeks, the child allowance will be reduced.[230]

The circumstances in which a person is to be classed as a 'patient' for benefit purposes are not always clear. 'Patient' is defined for income support purposes as 'a person (other than a prisoner) who is regarded as receiving free in-patient treatment within the meaning of the Social Security (Hospital In-Patients) Regulations 1975'.[231] A person is normally regarded as receiving such treatment when he or she is or has been maintained free of charge while undergoing 'medical or other treatment as an in-patient' in a 'hospital or similar institution'.[232] In some cases persons in nursing

---

[225] IS(G) Regs 1987, Sched. 2 para. 13(3A). See p. 192 above.

[226] These are set out in ibid., Sched. 7 para. 18 and JSA Regs 1996, Sched. 5 para. 16.

[227] The applicable amount of a single person falls to £16.70 (at 1999–2000 rates) (often referred to as the 'higher hospital personal allowance'). Housing costs may be payable in addition: see above. The entitlement of couples is also reduced by a prescribed amount if only one is a patient; if both are patients a prescribed rate is paid: IS(G) Regs 1987, Sched. 7 and JSA Regs 1996, Sched. 5 para. 2 (applies only where one member of a couple who is not the claimant is in hospital for over 12 weeks).

[228] IS(G)Regs 1987, reg. 21 and Sched. 7 para. 2(b) (£13.35 for 1999–2000). This is often referred to as the 'standard hospital personal allowance'. By virtue of reg. 16(2)(b) a member of a couple would be treated as a single person if his or her stay in hospital is expected to be substantially more than fifty-two weeks.

[229] The amount paid will be 'such amount (if any) not exceeding £13.35 as is reasonable having regard to the views of hospital staff, the patient's relatives if available as to the amount necessary for his personal use': IS(G) Regs 1987, Sched. 7 para. 2(a).

[230] The prescribed amount is currently £13.35: ibid., para. 3. If the claimant is also a patient, his/her personal allowance will be unaffected: ibid.

[231] IS(G) Regs 1987, reg. 21(3), referring to S.I. 1975 No. 555.   [232] S.I. 1975 No. 555, ibid., reg. 2(2).

homes (see below) will be classed as receiving 'medical or other treatment' in a 'similar institution' to a hospital. In *Botchett v Chief Adjudication Officer*,[233] nursing staff cared for a resident of a home who suffered from a mental difficulty which the court regarded as an 'illness' such as to bring the institution close to the statutory definition of a hospital ('any institution for the reception and treatment of persons suffering from illness')[234] and thus able to be classed as a 'similar institution'. A more clear-cut case is *White v Chief Adjudication Officer*.[235] Mentally ill residents of a nursing home received medication and other nursing care from nurses under arrangements with the health authority made on behalf of the Secretary of State; for the purposes of the Social Security (Hospital In-Patients) Regulations 1975 (above) the home was a 'hospital or similar institution'.

(vii) Persons in Residential Care and Nursing Homes

Nearly 500,000 people aged sixty-five or over (approximately one in twenty of this age group) are currently in care homes.[236] The rules governing entitlement, which cover accommodation provided on a commercial basis and other than by a close relative, changed in line with the Conservatives' Community Care reforms. These reforms led to new arrangements from 1 April 1993, although with 'preserved rights' for those who had remained in their accommodation since before that date. Those who do not have 'preserved rights' will have entered a nursing or residential home for the first time from 1 April 1993 onwards or will have lost their preserved rights because they were absent from that home for, in the case of a temporary resident, more than four weeks or, in the case of a permanent resident, thirteen weeks, or in any case they were a hospital patient for more than fifty-two weeks.[237]

Persons with 'preserved rights' who live in an independent residential care or nursing home[238] are entitled to an applicable amount which comprises, in aggregate, the 'weekly charge' for their accommodation (less any amount of housing benefit to meet any part of this charge), a weekly amount for personal expenses, any housing costs to which they are entitled in respect of their dwelling (only applicable to persons temporarily in the nursing home, etc) and any transitional payments to which they are entitled.[239] The 'weekly charge' element can be increased to take account of certain separate charges made by the home (for

---

[233] (1996) *The Times*, 8 May 1996 (CA).
[234] National Health Service Act 1977, s. 128.
[235] (1983) *The Times*, 2 August (CA). See also *R(IS)7/92*.
[236] Royal Commission on Long Term Care, *With Respect to Old Age: Long Term Care—Rights and Responsibilities*, Cm 4192–I (London: The Stationery Office, 1999), para. 2.5.
[237] IS(G) Regs 1987, reg. 19(1ZB)(b); JSA Regs 1996, reg. 86(2).
[238] Basically, this generally means a privately run home or one run by a voluntary body as opposed to a local authority home. See *Chief Adjudication Officer v Quinn; Chief Adjudication Officer v Gibbon* [1996] 4 All ER 72 (HL).
[239] IS(G) Regs 1987, Sched. 4; JSA Regs 1996, Sched. 4. The transitional payments are those designed to preserve a particular level of entitlement which was threatened by the introduction of income support: see IS(G) Regs 1987, reg. 17 and JSA Regs 1996, reg. 87(3).

example, charges for heating, laundry, and special diets or separate meals charges, subject to prescribed maxima); but it normally cannot exceed the prescribed maximum.[240] The maximum will vary according to the kinds of need being met in the home; for example, the standard residential care home rate for old age stands (in 1999) at £218, whilst the rates payable in respect of nursing homes are higher— up to more than £367 in the case of physical disablement.[241]

Those without 'preserved rights' who live in an independent home will be entitled to benefit calculated in the standard way (personal and child allowances plus premiums), save that the housing costs in respect of their own property will not be met once their stay in the home ceases to be classed as temporary. The home's charges will be met by the local authority and not by income support or income-based JSA. Local authorities use a means-test for them based on the income support scales, including the capital limit of £16,000.[242] Tariff income accrues at the rate of £1 for every £250 of capital above £10,000. The local authority could sell the claimant's own home if necessary to recover expenditure on residential home charges.[243] The Royal Commission on Long Term Care has recommended that because 'people are often placed permanently into care away from their own homes when there is a chance of possibly returning' the value of the claimant's home should be disregarded for up to three months while the claimant's need for long-term care is assessed.[244] The claimant is entitled to a residential allowance (currently £59.40 per week outside London and £66.10 in the capital) in income support if he or she is aged sixteen or over and requires and receives 'personal care' in the home, as long as the accommodation and any meals are provided on a commercial basis and no part of the weekly charge for the accommodation is met by housing benefit.[245] The Royal Commission on Long Term Care has recommended the abolition of the allowance which, it claims, 'serves no useful purpose and adds to the arcane nature of the current system'.[246] It proposes instead that the resources which underpin the allowance should be reallocated to local authorities to meet needs more effectively.

Separate rules govern the entitlement of those in local authority homes. The

[240] IS(G) Regs 1987, Sched. 4 para. 2; JSA Regs 1996, Sched. 4 para. 2.

[241] IS(G) Regs 1987, Sched. 4 paras 6–10; JSA Regs 1996, Sched. 4 paras 5–8.

[242] The Royal Commission (n. 236 above, at para. 6.20) recommends that the limit should be raised to £60,000 because the current limit penalises those with modest savings and encourages 'cheating the system' among vulnerable people and their families, and because 'to force the means test on [people] when they are old, when many of them have sought to avoid it during their working lives, is particularly insidious and unfair' (ibid. para. 6.13).

[243] Health and Social Services and Social Security Adjudications Act 1983, s. 22.

[244] Royal Commission on Long Term Care, *With Respect to Old Age: Long Term Care—Rights and Responsibilities*, Cm 4192–I (London: The Stationery Office, 1999), para. 6.3. The overall estimated cost of this, which would benefit 40–50,000 claimants per annum, is put at £90 million.

[245] IS(G) Regs 1987, Sched. 2 para. 2A; JSA Regs 1996, Sched. 1 para. 3. 'Personal care' means 'care which includes assistance with bodily functions where such assistance is required'. For the background to the introduction of the allowance, see Royal Commission on Long Term Care, *With Respect to Old Age: Long Term Care—Rights and Responsibilities*, Cm 4192–I (London: The Stationery Office, 1999), para. 4.28.

[246] Ibid.

claimant receives an applicable amount at a special rate.[247] There will be a means-tested charge by the local authority for residence in the home.[248]

(viii) Prisoners

A prisoner is not entitled to income support,[249] but a person who is detained in custody pending trial or for sentence to be determined following conviction may be entitled to have his or her housing costs met.[250] While in custody the claimant and his/her partner clearly cannot be members of the same household, and, for the purposes of income support, this means that the claimant's partner can be entitled to benefit as a single person or lone parent (as appropriate).[251] In *Chief Adjudication Officer v Carr*[252] the Court of Appeal held by a majority that a person who was on home leave from prison (in this case for five days) was not in custody or under the control of a prison officer and so should not be classed as a prisoner. Nevertheless, the Court concluded that the particular claimant would have to show that he was available for and actively seeking employment as conditions of entitlement to income support.

(ix) Students

Most students are not entitled to income support while attending their course (including during all vacation periods). Some part-time students may be entitled. The rules are discussed in Chapter 11.

(x) Persons from Abroad, Including Asylum Seekers

The rules affecting persons from abroad are complex and entitlement depends, *inter alia*, on immigration status, place of habitual residence (under the 'habitual residence test') and other factors. The entitlement of persons from abroad to income-related benefits in general has been progressively restricted under a number of legislative changes aimed, in ministers' rhetoric, at curbing 'benefits tourism'.[253]

The basic rule states that where a claimant is a 'person from abroad' he or she is not entitled to income support/income-based JSA; and if he or she has a partner who is not a person from abroad, that person will not be entitled either.[254] The

---

[247] IS(G) Regs, Sched. 7 paras 10A–10C; JSA Regs 1996, Sched. 5 paras 7–9.

[248] The charge is made under the National Assistance Act 1948. The scales are laid down in the National Assistance (Assessment of Resources) Regulations 1992 (S.I. 1992 No. 2977).

[249] IS(G) Regs 1987, Sched. 7 para 8. See *R(IS)1/94*. This does not apply where the claimant is merely required to live in a bail hostel, because he is 'basically at liberty, and in particular . . . free to carry on his normal employment': *R(IS)17/93, per* Commissioner Rice.

[250] Under reg. 17(1) of IS(G) Regs 1987.

[251] Ibid., reg. 16(3)(b).

[252] (1994) *The Times*, 2 June. For analysis of this decision, see P. Rowe, 'Case Analysis' (1994) 1 *J.S.S.L.* 133–8.

[253] See M. Adler, 'The habitual residence test: a critical analysis' (1995) 2 *J.S.S.L.*, 179–95.

[254] IS(G) Regs 1987, Sched. 7 para. 17; JSA Regs 1996, Sched. 5 para. 14. If the claimant is not a person from abroad, but his or her partner is, then the claimant may be entitled to IS for himself/herself. Note that the rules make special provision where the claimant is a member of a polygamous family.

claimant may, however, be eligible for an urgent cases payment.[255] 'Person from abroad' is defined in the regulations. Falling within the definition are, subject to certain exceptions, persons with limited leave to enter or remain in the UK which has been given (under the immigration rules) on condition that there would be no recourse to or charge on public funds (including the various income-related benefits and housing provided under statute for homeless people).[256] Those who have remained in the UK without further leave once their limited leave has expired are also 'persons from abroad'.[257] Also included are those subject to a deportation order under the Immigration Act 1971, those adjudged to be illegal entrants who have not been granted leave to enter and remain, those allowed temporary admission to the UK under certain provisions of the 1971 Act, and those whose immigration status has not been determined by the immigration authorities.[258] Members of EU Member States, indeed members of the wider group of states in the European Economic Area (EEA), do not require leave to enter or remain in the United Kingdom provided they are exercising Community rights concerning freedom of movement.[259] Nevertheless, they may be denied entitlement to benefit under the habitual residence test (below). In any event, where a national of an EU Member State is required by the Secretary of State to leave the UK they will be classed as a person from abroad.[260]

The 'habitual residence test' is a device introduced in 1994[261] to quell apparent (but unquantified) 'public anxiety' about alleged abuses of the right to draw benefit in the UK by non-UK citizens and to bring rules of entitlement to benefit for such citizens into line with the more restrictive rules operating in other countries.[262] If a person is 'not habitually resident' in the UK, the Republic of Ireland, the Channel Islands, or the Isle of Man he or she is a 'person from abroad' for income support or income-based JSA purposes.[263] There are some exceptional categories, however: refugees; persons granted 'exceptional leave' to remain in the UK by the Secretary of State;

[255] IS(G) Regs 1987, reg. 70(3); JSA Regs 1996, reg. 147. For the purposes of an urgent cases payment, the personal allowance is 90 per cent of the normal rate: IS(G) Regs 1987, reg. 71(1)(a)(i) and JSA Regs 1996, reg. 148(1)(a)(i).

[256] IS(G) Regs 1987, reg. 21(3) and (3)(a); JSA Regs 1996, reg. 85(4)(a).

[257] IS(G) Regs 1987, reg. 21(3)(b); JSA Regs 1996, reg. 85(4)(b).

[258] IS(G) Regs 1987, reg. 21(3)(c)–(g); JSA Regs 1996, reg. 85(4)(c)–(g).

[259] Immigration Act 1971, s. 7(1); Immigration (European Economic Area) Order 1994 (S.I. 1994 No. 1895).

[260] IS(G) Regs 1987, reg. 21(3)(h); JSA Regs 1996, reg. 85(4)(h). On the rights of EU citizens to remain in the UK while looking for work, see *R* v *Immigration Appeal Tribunal ex parte Antonissen* [1991] I ECR 745 and *R v Secretary of State of the Home Department ex parte Vitale and Do Amaral* [1995] NLJ 631 (discussed by P. Twomey, 'Case Analysis' (1995) 2 *J.S.S.L.* 208–14).

[261] Those who were entitled to income support on 31 July 1994 and who have continued to receive the benefit since then are not subject to the habitual residence test. If at any time they cease to be entitled to the benefit and subsequently make a fresh claim they will be caught by it: Income-related Benefits Schemes (Miscellaneous Amendments) (No. 3) Regulations 1994 (S.I. 1994 No. 1807), reg. 4(2).

[262] DSS, *The Income-Related Benefits Schemes (Miscellaneous Amendments) (No. 2) Regulations 1994, Note for the Social Security Advisory Committee* (London: DSS, 1994). For discussion of the evolution of the test and a general critique of it, see M. Adler, n. 253 above.

[263] IS(G) Regs 1987, reg. 21(3); JSA Regs 1996, reg. 85(4).

and persons who are workers for the purposes of EC Regulations 1612/68 or 1215/70 or who have a right of residence under EC Directives 68/360 or 732/48.[264]

'Habitual residence' is not defined in the regulations. It is, however, a concept embodied in EU Law on migrant workers' rights.[265] The phrase has also been considered in a number of unemployment benefit cases.[266] A test of 'habitual residence' is arguably a more stringent one than that of 'ordinary residence' found in other areas of family and welfare law.[267] Benefits Agency and other official guidance on habitual residence refers to such factors as: the claimant's centre of interest (the country in which are his home, family, friends, etc); stable employment in a particular country; length and continuity of residence in a country; reasons for coming to the UK; and future intentions,[268] although in a recent decision in a case where the rule was applied, Commissioner Howell said that the most important factors were 'the length, continuity and general nature of his or her *actual* residence here, rather than his or her intentions as to the future'. However, he also said that there should be a 'settled intention' to remain in the country.[269]

The period of residence required has been held in two Commissioners' decisions to be 'an appreciable period of residence', which is to be determined as a question of fact in each case, although there is no minimum period.[270] This view was upheld in *Nessa v Chief Adjudication Officer*,[271] an appeal from the second of these decisions, leaving the habitual residence test as a major obstacle for immigrants in the early part of their residence in the UK. The House of Lords has dismissed an appeal in *Nessa*. Lord Slynn said that the claimant must have 'taken up residence and lived here for a period', the required length of which would depend upon a range of factors in any given case.[272]

The test of an 'appreciable period of residence' has in any event been called into question, at least in its application to EU citizens, by the decision of the ECJ in *Swaddling*.[273] The Advocate General had advised that having to serve an appreciable

---

[264] The provisions apply to all EEA nationals. The exception of all EEA workers from the habitual residence test was made in order to avoid a possible charge of indirect discrimination under EC Law.

[265] See EC Regulation 1408/71, Art. 1(h). See also the discussion of *Swaddling v Adjudication Officer* (ECJ) Case C-90/97, *The Times*, 4 March 1999, below and in Chapter 8. See also *Di Paolo v Office National de L'Emploi* [1977] ECR 315; *Perry v Chief Adjudication Officer and the Secretary of State for Social Security* (1998) *The Times*, 20 October (discussed at pp. 245–6 below); N. J. Wikeley, 'Migrant Workers and Unemployment Benefit in the European Community', [1988] *J.S.W.L.* 300–15, 306–8.

[266] *R(U)7/85*, *R(U)4/86*, and *R(U)8/88*. For discussion, see N. J. Wikeley, n. 265 above at 308.

[267] See, for example, *Kapur v Kapur* [1984] FLR 920; *Shah v Barnet London Borough Council* [1983] 2 AC 309; *Castelli and Tristan-Garcia v Westminster City Council* (1996) *The Times Law Report*, 27 February (CA).

[268] AOG 20747; *Habitual Residence Test Income Support Procedures*, IS Circular ISG 15/94; CAS, Guidance for Adjudication Officers: Income Support: Habitual Residence Test, Memo AOG Vol. 3, July 1994.

[269] *CIS/1067/1995*, at para. 20.

[270] Ibid., and *CIS/2326/1995*, *per* Commissioner Mesher. See also *CIS/15927/1997*.

[271] [1998] 2 All ER 728 (CA).

[272] *The Times*, 27 October 1999, also to be reported at [1999] 2 FLR 1116. The factors would include having a right of abode, bringing possessions, and seeking to bring family.

[273] N. 265 above. For the background to this case, which was brought by CPAG, see 131 *Welfare Rights Bulletin* at 13. For discussion of the broader implications of *Swaddling*, see Chapter 8 (at pp. 241–6) below by Tamara Hervey. See also *CIS/15484/1996* (starred decision 48/99).

period of residence might be in conflict with EU law on migrant workers' rights. From 1980 the applicant worked mainly in France and returned to the UK only for occasional visits. In January 1995 he returned to the UK after being made redundant in France and applied for income support. The Commissioner held that he could be regarded as having an appreciable period of actual residence in the UK, such as would, together with a settled intention, constitute 'habitual residence', only after eight weeks (that is, in March 1995). The matter was referred to the ECJ to determine whether a different conclusion might result under EU law, which also provides for entitlement under social security schemes (including, for this purpose, income support) for migrant workers (including the self-employed) who 'reside'—meaning to have habitual residence—in the territory of the Member State concerned.[274] The Court held that account would need to be taken of certain factors in determining whether the person was habitually resident in the state and whether the 'habitual centre of his interests' was there. The factors were: the person's family situation; the reasons which had led him to move; the length and continuity of his residence; any evidence of stable employment; and his intention as inferred from the circumstances. These mirror the criteria already used by the Benefits Agency, cited above. However, the Court stated that in this context the length of residence in the Member State could not be regarded as an intrinsic element to the concept of residence and that by virtue of the Council Regulation the state could not make it a condition that one had to complete an appreciable period of residence there.

The difficulty of determining whether there is habitual residence in any particular case, which clearly involves consideration of a wide range of factors and circumstances, was specifically referred to by the Social Security Advisory Committee as one of the test's major drawbacks.[275] There are more fundamental concerns, however, relating to the fairness of the test. The regulations which introduced the habitual residence test survived a legal challenge in 1995[276] when it was alleged that they were *ultra vires* section 124 of the SSCBA 1992, which purports to confer a right to income support on any person who is 'in Great Britain'. This argument was, in essence, rejected on the grounds that the section imposed a necessary but not a sufficient condition. A further argument that was rejected was that the regulations were not compatible with EU Law on the grounds that the legal status of Irish nationals under the habitual residence test was the same as UK nationals and thus there was discrimination against *other* Member States' nationals.[277] By October 1995, over 30,000 claimants had failed the habitual residence test.[278] The effects of the test have been

---

[274] Regulation (EEC) 1408/71, Articles 1(h) and 10a(1).

[275] SSAC, *Report on the Income-Related Benefit Schemes (Miscellaneous Amendments) (No. 2) Regulations 1994*, Cm 2609 (London: HMSO, 1994).

[276] *R v Secretary of State for Social Security ex parte Sarwar, Getachew and Urbanek*, 11 April 1995 (QBD).

[277] See M. Adler, n. 253 above, at 190.

[278] Approximately 25 per cent of those who have failed the test so far have been UK nationals. The Government announced that savings from the application of the test to the end of November 1995 were an estimated £37 million: Hansard, H.C. Debs, Vol. 269, col. 573w, 16 January 1996.

monitored closely by the National Association of Citizens' Advice Bureaux (NACAB) which, in a report recommending the test's withdrawal, has concluded that it is proving 'expensive, unfair and unworkable'.[279]

One group of persons from abroad whose benefit entitlement has been particularly restricted is asylum seekers. Further restrictions are set to occur under the Labour Government's Immigration and Asylum Act 1999. The last Conservative Government tightened up the rules in February 1996, arguing that reform was necessary to prevent abuse of the system by 'bogus' asylum seekers.[280] Under the current benefit rules, an asylum seeker—a person who has entered the UK and claims refugee status which is under consideration by the Home Office—is excluded from income support and is entitled to an urgent cases payment[281] only in specific circumstances: where he was so entitled before that date; or where asylum was applied for, and officially recorded, upon arrival in the UK;[282] or, if the Secretary of State declares formally that there has been such a change of circumstances in the claimant's country of origin (of which he is a national) of the kind that would normally result in no order for him or her to return and asylum is applied for after entry to the UK and within three months of the declaration.[283] A person ceases to be an asylum seeker when, *inter alia*, the Secretary of State records the decision concerning the claim for asylum on or after 5 February 1996.

There was and continues to be serious opposition to these rules. Amnesty International, for example, drew attention to the fact that over 70 per cent of those granted asylum between 1992 and 1995 had applied for it after entering the country, which for that majority would now mean being deprived of benefit.[284] The SSAC recommended that a window of eligibility should be permitted on entering the country.[285] Several legal challenges to the rules have been brought, including an important action by the Joint Council for the Welfare of Immigrants.[286] Here the Court of Appeal ruled, by a majority, that the rules were *ultra vires* in their draconian effect

---

[279] NACAB, *Failing the Test: CAB clients' experience of the habitual residence test in social security* (London: NACAB, 1996).

[280] See DSS, *Explanatory Memorandum to the Social Security Advisory Committee*, Cm 3062 (London: The Stationery Office, 1996).

[281] IS(G) Regs 1987, re.g.. 70; JSA Regs 1996, reg. 147(3)(b). For the rate of an urgent cases payment, see n. 255 above.

[282] The application for asylum must be 'on his arrival'. The scope for flexibility is more limited than might be supposed (see, for example, *CIS/4117/1997*, noted at (1999) 6(1) *J.S.S.L.*, D38–9) and this provision has been interpreted strictly as meaning before leaving the port of arrival and possibly within a short time of arrival (perhaps the first 24 hours): see *CIS/2719/1997* and *CIS/3231/1997*, noted at (1998) 5 *J.S.S.L.* D136–9, *CIS/143/1997* noted at ibid., D38 and *CIS/2809/1997*, noted at ibid., D89–91. See also *CIS/4341/1998* (starred decision 50/99)

[283] IS(G) Regs 1987, reg. 70(3A), as amended by the Social Security (Persons from Abroad) Miscellaneous Amendments Regulations 1996 (S.I. 1996 No. 30).

[284] Cited in M. Carter 'The squeeze on asylum seekers' (1996) *Poverty*, No. 94, 9–11, 10.

[285] See SSAC, *The Social Security (Persons from Abroad) Miscellaneous Amendments Regulations*, Cm 3062 (London: HMSO, 1996).

[286] *R v Secretary of State for Social Services ex p Joint Council for the Welfare of Immigrants and Another* [1996] 4 All ER 385. For analysis, see J. Scoular, 'Case Analysis' (1997) 4 *J.S.S.L.* 86–90.

which Parliament would not, it was felt, have sanctioned, in that most of those who applied for asylum after arriving in the UK would not be eligible for benefit. However, this ruling only had a short-term effect on the rights of asylum seekers. Persons caught by the February 1996 reform were able to qualify for benefit under the old rules, but only until 24 July 1996, when the Asylum and Immigration Act 1996 modified the regulations, thereby restoring the restrictions currently in operation.[287]

It is estimated that each month around 2,000 people who require benefit will fail to qualify for it because of these restrictions, which some (including the United Nations Commission of Human Rights) have argued are in breach of some of the UK's international human rights obligations.[288] While the overall numbers of asylum seekers continue to rise—from 4,000 in 1988 to 32,500 in 1997 and an estimated 38,000 in 1998[289]—the numbers receiving income support are falling. There were 42,000 asylum seekers in receipt of the benefit in February 1998 compared with 45,000 in May 1997.[290] The Labour Government regards these numbers as still too high and, following White Paper proposals in July 1998,[291] announced in the Queen's Speech in November 1998 plans to reform the immigration system and at the same time introduce a new system of support for asylum seekers in the form of food and clothing vouchers rather than access to the social security system. The Immigration and Asylum Act 1999 introduces a framework for a new system of support, with detailed provision to be made via regulations.

The Act empowers the Secretary of State to provide support for asylum seekers who, for example, cannot meet their 'essential living needs' (which may be determined under criteria laid down in regulations).[292] Under the Bill as originally drafted there was a general presumption that such support would not take the form of payments, although it was planned that cash allowances of £1 per day for adults and 50p per day for children would be available to cover telephone calls, nappies, bus

---

[287] Asylum and Immigration Act 1996, s. 11 and Sched. 1. See generally, F. Nicholson and P. Twomey, *Current Issues of Asylum Law and Policy* (Aldershot: Ashgate, 1998). On the effect of the transitional arrangements, see *R v Secretary of State for the DSS, President of the Social Security Appeal Tribunal, ex p. Vijekis and Vijeikeine; R v DSS ex p Adioy Okito; R v The Benefits Agency ex p Mohammed Zaheer*, unreported, 10 July 1997. The 1996 Regulations (see n. 283 above) also affected entitlement to disability living allowance: see *R v Chief Adjudication Officer ex p B*, 9 December 1998 (CA), discussed in P. Billings, 'Case Analysis' (1999) 6 *J.S.S.L.* 137–144. Child benefit was also excluded, subject to transitional protection: SSCBA 1992, s. 146A, inserted by s. 10 of the 1996 Act; Child Benefit (General) Regulations 1976 (S.I. 1976 No. 965), reg. 14B, as amended: see *R v Adjudication Officer and Chairman of the Sutton Social Security Appeal Tribunal ex p Velasquez* (1999) 17 March (unreported) (CA).

[288] For example, the U.N. Convention on the Rights of the Child, Art. 2, which requires states to ensure that children are free from discrimination irrespective of their parents' status. See B. Lakhani, 'Asylum seekers on the streets' (1996) *Poverty*, No. 93, 7–9.

[289] *The Times*, 25 November 1998.

[290] Hansard, H.C. Debs (web), col. 393w, 2 November 1998. This notes that the average monthly payment was £255.90.

[291] Home Office, *Fairer, Faster and Firmer: a modern approach to immigration and asylum*, Cm. 4018 (London: The Stationery Office, 1998).

[292] ss 95 and 96. There is a gateway criterion of current or impending destitution. See also s. 122 (support for children). Accommodation may also be provided (s. 96(1)(a)).

fares, and other incidental expenses, as part of an overall support package which was to be worth £90.80 per week for a family of two adults and two children. Following a threatened backbench revolt in the House of Commons, the Government made a concession by promising an increased cash allowance of £10 per week per adult and child, although the overall level of support would remain the same.[293] The Secretary of State will thus be able to set up a scheme for this purpose, with prescribed rules about claiming procedures and various other matters. Appeals against refusals of support will be heard by new asylum support 'adjudicators' (under s. 103). Asylum seekers will be excluded from a long list of social security benefits,[294] although the Act also enables provision to be made (via social security regulations) for backdating of benefits where a person is later granted refugee status.[295]

The rights of asylum seekers to general assistance from local authorities and in respect of housing and housing benefit, are outside the scope of this chapter.[296] However, it should be noted that the Act, while giving local authorities a general power to provide support (under arrangements made by the Secretary of State for the purposes of s. 95: see ss. 99 and 100), will not only exclude asylum seekers from entitlement to housing benefit or council tax benefit but also from the scope of the duty of a local authority in section 21(1) of the National Assistance Act 1948 to provide residential accommodation—if the need has arisen because they are 'destitute' or because of the physical effects, or anticipated effects, of being destitute.[297]

5. CONCLUSION

The modern social security system's complexity, which is partly the result of its piecemeal development and continual amendment, is reflected in its elaborate legislative framework, parts of which were illustrated above in the discussion of

---

[293] A. Travis, 'Straw moves to quell asylum bill rebellion', *The Guardian*, 9 June 1999. Note that 'unless the circumstances of a particular case are exceptional, support . . . must not be wholly or mainly by way of payment': s. 96(3). On limits, see s. 97(5).

[294] s. 115. Those listed are JSA, attendance allowance, severe disablement allowance, invalid care allowance, DLA, income support, working families tax credit, disabled person's tax credit, social fund payments, child benefit, housing benefit, and council tax benefit.

[295] s. 123. At present, an income support payment would be backdated but would be paid at the urgent cases rate (which means that the personal allowance is, as noted above, 90 per cent of the ordinary rate): IS(G) Regs 1987, regs 21ZA(1) and (2) and 71(1)(a)(i). An argument that the reduced rate unlawfully discriminated against non-UK nationals contrary to EC Regulation 1408/71 (see Chapter 8) failed in *Krasniqi v Chief Adjudication Officer and the Secretary of State for Social Security* (1998) 10 December (CA). See T. O'Neill, 'Case Analysis' (1999) 6(2) *J.S.S.L.* 93–8.

[296] Housing benefit is dicussed by Simon Rahilly in Chapter 13. See also, S. Cox et al., *Migration and Social Security Handbook* (London: CPAG, 1997) and C. Hunter, 'Asylum seekers' rights to housing: New recipients of the Old Poor Law', in Nicholson and Twomey, n. 287 above at 329–49.

[297] Immigration and Asylum Act 1999, s. 116. This exclusion will also apply in respect of others who are subject to 'immigration control'. The Court of Appeal confirmed the duty to provide residential accommodation under the 1948 Act in relation to asylum-seekers in *R v Hammersmith and Fulham L.B.C. ex p M; R v Lambeth L.B.C. ex p A; R v Westminster City Council ex p A; R v Lambeth LBC ex p X* (1997) 1 CCLR 85; *The Times*, 19 February. An appeal before the House of Lords in *ex p A* is pending. In *R v Secretary of State for Health and Hammersmith and Fulham LBC* (1998) *The Times*, 9 September, the Court of Appeal held that a local authority may not hand over cash or vouchers to asylum seekers to spend themselves. On destitution, see for example *R v Croydon LBC ex p Gou* (1998) 21 August (CO/2142/98) (QBD) and cases referred to therein by Ognall J.

pensions and income-related benefits. British social security law is by no means unique in this respect, perhaps demonstrating that a high degree of intricacy and complexity is inherent in any modern system of social security law. For example, as in Britain, social security law in both the United States and Australia is widely acknowledged to be very technical and inaccessible.[298] Attempts in the latter jurisdiction to codify legislation and in so doing use less technical language appear not to have alleviated the problem. According to the Full Court of the Federal Court of Australia, the replacement legislation (introduced in 1991) consists of 'a maze of provisions made the more complex by prolix definitions, provisos and exceptions. Both those who claim entitlements under it and those responsible for its administration will not always find it easy to discover whether or not a benefit is payable.'[299] This closely echoes judicial comment in the UK that: 'The rules and regulations which govern entitlement to welfare benefit in a modern state are necessarily numerous, highly complex and subject to frequent variation and amendment ... those whom they are designed to benefit are among the least able to unravel their mysteries.'[300]

The present Government's plan to structure the social security system around the unifying concept of access to work (see Chapter 10) is, irrespective of the administrative effects of the 'gateway to work' concept in practice, in many ways merely a symbolic gesture to make diverse claimants confront the common issue of work at the outset of a claim (and at certain points thereafter) without any accompanying harmonisation of the basis of support. Irrespective of any streamlining of individual benefits and modernisation of delivery methods, there is nothing in any of the recent Green Papers on social security to indicate that the legislative basis to social security will be any less complex in the future. Indeed, none of the Government's principles of welfare reform specifically addresses this issue.[301] Instead, there are merely promises of better advice for claimants. Recent reforms—the working families tax credit and disabled person's tax credit in particular—have not made the system and its legislative basis any simpler.

No-one can predict with absolute certainty which method of classifying benefits will be most appropriate for mapping out the system in the future. Indeed, the different methods examined above can in many ways be regarded as having equal validity and relevance. Nevertheless, the present Government's preoccupation with welfare to work focuses particular attention on the distinction between in-work and

---

[298] See F. Bates, 'Social Security Law and Children with Disabilities: Change and Decay in Australian Statute Law' (1998) 18(3) *Statute Law Rev.*, 215–34. As regards Britain, note the comment by Glidewell LJ in the Court of Appeal in *Bate v Chief Adjudication Officer* (1994) 23 BMLR 155, 158: 'it is deplorable that legislation which affects some of the most disadvantaged people in society should be couched in language which is so difficult for even a lawyer trained and practising in this field to understand'.

[299] *Re Blunn v Cleaver* (1993) 111 ALR 65 at 82, cited in F. Bates, op. cit., 217.

[300] *R v Legal Aid Board ex p Bruce* [1992] 1 FLR 324, *per* Ld Donaldson MR at 324.

[301] See DSS, *New ambitions for our country: a new contract for welfare*, Cm 3805 (London: The Stationery Office, 1998) and DSS, *A new contract for welfare: principles into practice*, Cm 4101 (London: The Stationery Office, 1998). The former promises 'fairer gateways for eligibility' (ch. 9) but relates this principle entirely to the question of fraud, as does the latter (ch. 2, para. 14).

out-of-work benefits. Support for part-time and more flexible patterns of working, and the Government's drive to improve work opportunities for disabled people and other groups, might increase the centrality of work status or potential to the whole shape and classification of social security. At the same time, it seems that with the continuing decline of contributory benefits and the likely extension of private sector involvement there will be a particularly strong case for constructing the social security system, and classifying its various benefit schemes, primarily with reference to social groupings rather than on the basis of entitlement. Indeed, the general elements of income-related schemes have been partly structured in this way since the Social Security Act 1986. For example, as we have seen in relation to income support, there are specific premiums for particular groups such as the elderly and disabled; and these are mirrored in the housing benefit and council tax benefit schemes. All of the chapters in Part 4 of this book are concerned with the impact of social security law on various key social groups who are the subject of specific areas of social security provision.

7

Social Security Decision Making and Appeals

ROY SAINSBURY

1. INTRODUCTION—WHY IS DECISION MAKING IMPORTANT?

In 1998, a new Social Security Act was passed which, among other things, established a new framework for decision making and appeals for large parts of the social security system. It has to be said that this barely provoked a flicker of interest in the media or among the public at large. Perhaps this should not surprise anyone. How decisions are made, who makes them, and how appeals are handled seem to be dry administrative details compared with important issues such as the cuts to benefits for lone parents, also contained in the Act. And yet, decision making *is* important. The rules of decision making and the way they are used in practice will have a direct bearing on the outcome of a claim for benefit.

Imagine you are a social security claimant. You are unemployed and think that in your particular circumstances you should be entitled to, say, income support. You dutifully fill in a claim form supplied by the Benefits Agency and wait. While you are waiting your claim is in the hands of one or more people working in one of the hundreds of Benefits Agency offices across the country. These people will decide whether you are indeed entitled to benefit and if so the amount of your award. Your financial well-being depends on them getting the decision right. That is why the processes of decision making that go on thousands of times a day in every benefit office are important. If everything goes smoothly you will soon receive the amount of money that current social security legislation decrees that someone in your circumstances should receive. (You might be disappointed with what you get, but that is another story, and nothing to do with the processes of decision making.)

But can you, sitting at home, be confident that the unknown officials working on your claim will actually produce the correct decision? You may think that because your entitlements are laid down in legislation, it should be a simple matter of applying the appropriate social security law to your specific circumstances (clearly set out by you on the claim form). From that process a single, unequivocal decision should surely result. And for most people it does. However, there is a considerable body of evidence that in a large number of cases the processes of decision making do not produce correct decisions. (For example, in 1996–7, the Chief Adjudication Officer[1] found deficiencies in decision making in 45 per cent of income support claims.)

---

[1] The statutory official who, since 1984, has provided independent monitoring of the standards of decision making on social security claims. The role of the CAO is discussed in more detail later in the chapter.

Every year many thousands of people will either not be awarded a benefit to which they are actually entitled or will receive a level of award that is wrong. Although random checks are carried out within social security offices and may reveal individual cases that are wrong, the onus for identifying a potentially incorrect decision and doing something about it lies with you, the claimant. And again you might feel reassured to know that there are mechanisms in place (procedures to review the decision and tribunals to hear appeals) which allow you to challenge decisions and to obtain redress. Are you right to be confident? Some of the evidence suggests that even when you have a valid and legitimate claim that should entitle you to benefit, the review and appeal system is not guaranteed to produce the correct decision either. For example, in 1997 social security appeal tribunals overturned 35 per cent of appeals against adverse decisions that had already been reviewed by Benefits Agency officials.[2]

By this point, the argument that decision making is important should be convincing. People who make claims for social security benefits are generally in some degree of financial need (which sometimes will be acute and urgent). If the social security system is to serve the interests of such people, its systems for deciding claims and for handling appeals need to be as robust and as effective as possible. Those systems are currently in a state of transition following the enactment of the Social Security Act 1998, making this an opportune time to reflect on the developments in decision making over the course of this century (and particularly in the last twenty years) and to consider the impact of the latest changes and the more general issues they raise.

2. SCOPE AND AIMS OF THE CHAPTER

The social security system is never static and what comes within its definition ebbs and flows. An administrative definition might be 'everything that comes within the auspices of the Department of Social Security'. Using such a definition would bring national insurance contributions within the scope of this chapter, but they are now the responsibility of the Inland Revenue (see p. 175 above). The administration of child support through the Child Support Agency of the DSS would also now be included, although it would not have been before 1991 when the courts had prime responsibility for such matters. War pensions, which the Department of Social Security administers through the War Pensions Agency, are not defined officially as a social security benefit[3] though sharing many common features with other benefits and generally included within its classification of benefits.[4]

For the purposes of this chapter, however, the analysis of social security decision

[2] Department of Social Security, *Social Security Statistics 1998* (Leeds: Corporate Document Services, 1998), Table H3.05.
[3] Department of Social Security, *Improving Decision Making and Appeals in Social Security*, Cm 3328 (London: HMSO, 1996).
[4] See Chapter 6.

making will be restricted to benefits administered by the range of DSS agencies and local authorities. I will stretch this meaning to include the social fund, which, inter alia, provides loans rather than benefits to income support recipients, but which has a different and interesting model of decision making and appeals. National insurance, child support, and war pensions are, however, not covered in the description and analysis that follows.[5]

The overall aim of this chapter is to present the reader with an understanding of how the decision making and appeals system (or systems in the plural to be accurate) have developed over the course of this century, and a critical assessment of the latest round of changes that will flow from the Social Security Act 1998. The discussion that follows is in two parts, beginning with an historical overview of decision making and appeals up to but not including the most recent changes. This first part (section 3 below) sets out to describe the principal features of what might be considered two distinct phases of development:[6] the period up to 1983 when the Health and Social Services and Social Security Adjudications Act was passed; and the period 1983 to 1998 when the Social Security Act 1998 was passed. The second part of the chapter (section 4 below) looks in more, and critical, detail at the latest developments, most of which are contained in the Social Security Act 1998, though some pre-date the Act slightly.

It should be made clear that this chapter is not intended to be an exposition of the current black letter law relating to social security decision making and appeals.[7] Rather, the intention is to provide a discussion of the pertinent issues around the subject. In particular, it is salutary to think about the part that administrative arrangements play in the successful delivery of social security to those entitled to it. The sorts of questions that I will address will include the following: Why do we have such a range of diverse models of decision making? What were the reasons behind the latest round of reforms in the 1998 Social Security Act? What are likely to be the effects of the new changes?

3. A SHORT HISTORY OF DECISION MAKING AND APPEALS TO 1998

A. Decision Making and Appeals Before 1983

(i) The Origins of Social Security Decision Making

For the purposes of understanding the long and complicated history of social security adjudication in the UK it is important to grasp the legacy of the development of

---

[5] Appeals with regard to national insurance contributions are covered by Neville Harris at p. 176.

[6] These phases have been identified to suit the purposes of this chapter. It is certainly possible to define other periods that would be equally as valid.

[7] See further chapters 16 and 17 of Ogus, Barendt, and Wikeley (1995) for the position before the latest legislation, and N. Wikeley, 'Decision making and appeals under the SSA 1998' (1998) 5 *J.S.S.L.* 104–17.

social security and its associated decision making arrangements from its early days to the important year of 1983 when the Health and Social Services and Social Security Adjudications Act (HASSASSA) changed the basis of decision making in important ways. In brief the most important parts of this legacy are:

- the establishment of the principle of independent adjudication
- the establishment of the principle of a claimant's right to appeal
- the dominance of practical and political factors in the design of decision making arrangements for different benefits.

We can begin the story of social security decision making and appeals with the passage of the first wave of social security legislation under the Lloyd George government before the First World War. The details of the administrative arrangements for the new sickness and unemployment benefits need not overly concern us here, but some of the principles established then are important and have had a far-reaching effect down the years.

One important principle was the separation of responsibilities for making decisions under the law from the administrative tasks associated with the processing of claims. The formation of a new corps of civil servants whose political head was a Government minister created a link between claimants of benefits and ministers. However, the last thing Government ministers wanted was to be held accountable for every one of the hundreds of thousands of decisions made on social security claims. The prospect of having to stand up in the House of Commons to explain why Mr Smith had been denied unemployment benefit could not be tolerated; ministers had to be protected. Thus was born the notion of *independent adjudication*. Although they were civil servants, insurance officers who made, for example, decisions on unemployment benefit claims, assumed the status of *independent statutory authorities* when carrying out the task of decision making. They therefore had a responsibility to make decisions in accordance with the law only; they were not bound by administrative or managerial constraints or pressures. As we shall see later, this principle endured until 1998 when independent adjudication was abolished.

Another important principle established in the early years of the social security system was the right of claimants to appeal against adverse decisions by officials. Under the forerunner of the modern social security system, the Workmen's Compensation scheme,[8] aggrieved workers had recourse only to the civil courts if they wanted to challenge decisions. This was not only time-consuming and expensive but resulted in difficulties for the court system in coping with the number of cases. Under the early social security legislation, other non court-based appeal mechanisms were introduced,[9] but by the early 1930s the familiar tribunal model had emerged as the preferred means of dealing with administrative appeals.

To cut a long story very short, the result of the piecemeal and incremental devel-

---

[8] Workmen's Compensation Act 1897. See Chapter 15 at pp. 463–4.

[9] R. E. Wraith and P. G. Hutchesson, *Administrative Tribunals* (London: Allen & Unwin, 1973) has a detailed account of the early evolution of appeals structures.

opment of the social security system and its decision-making arrangements was that, in the early 1980s, there was diversity, confusion, and dissatisfaction with the benefit system itself (which was not particularly new) and with decision-making and appeals structures and practices as well (which *was* new).[10]

The diverse range of decision making arrangements at the time can be attributed primarily to pragmatism. In deciding what decision making arrangements to introduce for new elements of the social security system, policy makers and politicians have been more influenced by practical and political considerations than by any guiding principles derived, for example, from natural justice or administrative law. As the social security system expanded both before and after the Second World War,[11] new decision making arrangements and new appeals mechanisms were introduced, for example, in connection with war pensions, national assistance and its successor supplementary benefit, industrial injuries benefit, and the range of disability benefits created in the 1960s and 1970s. What informed the design of the decision-making arrangements for each new or reformed benefit was usually the nature and structure of the benefit itself and the type of people who would be making claims. Hence, in the early 1980s we see separate and distinctive decision-making structures for different benefits.

(ii) Decision Making and Appeals in the Early 1980s

Immediately prior to the HASSASSA reforms in 1983 there was a distinction between the administration and adjudication of supplementary benefit and national insurance benefits. Decisions under the national insurance scheme lay with the statutorily independent insurance officer in the first instance, and to the national insurance local tribunal (NILT) on appeal. From there, there was a further right of appeal on a point of law to the Social Security Commissioner (described later in the chapter). In contrast, initial decisions on the main means-tested benefit, supplementary benefit, were made by officials (benefit officers) of the Department of Health and Social Security (the DHSS, the predecessor of the DSS). Appeals were possible to supplementary benefit appeal tribunals (SBATs) with (from November 1980) a right of appeal to the Social Security Commissioner.

There were also separate arrangements for the range of disability-related benefits, such as industrial disablement benefit, attendance allowance, and mobility allowance. Under the industrial injuries scheme, 'disablement questions' were (until 1983) decided by a medical board of two doctors, from which an appeal was possible to a medical appeal tribunal (MAT)[12] comprising a legally-qualified chairman and two

[10] For an excellent account of the history of social security adjudication over this period, see A. W. Bradley, 'Recent Reform of Social Security Adjudication in Great Britain' (1985) 26 *Les Cahiers de Droit*, 403–49.

[11] See Chapters 3 and 4.

[12] Special arrangements exist for hearing cases which involve serious chest diseases such as pneumoconiosis and asbestosis. See N. Wikeley, 'Social Security Adjudication and Occupational Lung Diseases' (1988) 17 *I.L.J.* 92.

doctors of consultant status. Medical boards also heard appeals on mobility allowance on medical questions and further appeal was allowed to the MAT. A separate government body, the Attendance Allowance Board, had responsibility for attendance allowance decisions and appeals through a network of 'delegated medical practitioners' who in practice were salaried medical officers of the DSS.

During the 1970s the social security appeal system had become the focus of concerted criticism because of the perceived incompetence and inconsistency of SBATs.[13] (In contrast, NILTs were generally regarded as working satisfactorily.[14]) The strong current of dissatisfaction with SBATs led the DHSS to commission research into their operation[15] which confirmed the shortcomings in the SBAT system. Tribunal chairmen, most of whom were not legally qualified, were found to have a limited knowledge and understanding of supplementary benefits; proceedings were unsystematic; there was an over-reliance on the clerk (an official seconded from the DHSS); decisions were not recorded satisfactorily; and discretion was not exercised in a disciplined or systematic way. Bell concluded that a comprehensive review was required as a matter of urgency and proposed a number of reforms to be achieved in three stages. Immediate improvements could be secured by providing training for chairmen and members. Some changes would take longer to implement (such as the introduction of legally-qualified chairmen), whilst others would be structural in nature, such as the provision of a further stage of appeal after the SBAT, and the merging of SBATs with NILTs.

Changes within the existing SBAT structure began to be implemented in 1977. More legal chairmen were appointed, training was instigated, a procedure manual produced, and (from 1978–80) a right of appeal from SBATs to the High Court in England and the Court of Session in Scotland was provided. Later, in the Social Security Act 1979, full-time (legally qualified) Senior Chairmen were introduced, to have some responsibility for organising tribunals in addition to hearing cases.

B. From HASSASSA 1983 to SSA 1998

(i) The Health and Social Services and Social Security Adjudications Act 1983 ('HASSASSA')

In 1980 the supplementary benefit scheme, which until then was based largely on administrative discretion, was replaced by a scheme based on legal entitlement to benefit.[16] The case for introducing independent adjudication into supplementary

[13] See, for example: N. Lewis, 'Supplementary Benefit Appeal Tribunals' [1973] *P. L.* 257–84; J. Farmer, *Tribunals and Government* (London: Weidenfeld and Nicolson, 1974); and J. Fulbrook, *Administrative Justice and the Unemployed* (London: Mansell, 1978).

[14] See K. Bell, P. Collinson, S. Turner and S. Webber, 'National Insurance Local Tribunals' (1974) 3(4) *J. of Social Policy* 289–315.

[15] K. Bell, *Research Study on Supplementary Benefit Appeal Tribunals: Review of Main Findings; Conclusions; Recommendations* (London: HMSO, 1975).

[16] See Chapter 4 at pp. 110–11.

benefit and for merging SBATs and NILTs therefore became stronger, and the desirability for change was accepted by the Government.

In 1983 HASSASSA was passed marking a break with the past and putting decision making and appeals on a new footing. In some ways HASSASSA marks the zenith for independent adjudication. For the next fifteen years or so it provided the principal model for social security decision making, although as we shall see there were important departures from the model which would prove to have a crucial influence on the provision made by the Social Security Act 1998. HASSASSA introduced a unified three-tier adjudication system comprising adjudication officers (replacing insurance officers and supplementary benefit officers), a unified social security appeal tribunal (the 'SSAT', replacing SBATs and NILTs), and the Social Security Commissioner (whose jurisdiction continued to be restricted to appeals on a point of law). Thus we see an important development in the extension of the principle of independent adjudication to the main means-tested (though no longer discretionary) social assistance benefit. The new SSAT system was brought within a presidential organisation similar to those for other tribunals.[17] The President, a circuit judge, was appointed by the Lord Chancellor, and became responsible for the management of tribunals and for the training of tribunal chairs and members.

In addition, HASSASSA established the post of Chief Adjudication Officer who, as a statutorily independent official, was given the job of advising adjudication officers and monitoring their standards of decision making (tasks previously carried out by DSS officials). The principle of independent adjudication was therefore further strengthened and promoted. The Act also made changes to the medical adjudication system. Medical boards comprising two doctors were, except in specified instances, replaced by a single doctor, now called an 'adjudicating medical practitioner', but they continued to hear appeals against mobility allowance decisions. Whilst the constitution of MATs remained the same they became part of the presidential system alongside SSATs.

The Attendance Allowance Board retained its responsibilities for both initial decision making and appeals until the benefit was replaced in 1992 by disability living allowance (DLA), which also subsumed mobility allowance. The appeal arrangements for DLA were something of a hybrid. A new tribunal—the Disability Appeal Tribunal—was established along the lines of SSATs and MATs but with a different membership, became part of the existing Presidential system, and came under the jurisdiction of the Council on Tribunals. However, an appellant had also to go through an earlier stage of compulsory internal administrative review (similar to that for housing benefit described below) before having the opportunity of an independent consideration of their case.

Not everything moved towards the model of decision making embodied in

---

[17] Presidential systems operate in connection with, *inter alia*, Lands Tribunals, Mental Health Review Tribunals, Industrial Tribunals, Immigration Tribunals, and VAT Tribunals.

HASSASSA, though. Two developments in the 1980s bucked the trend and were effectively the beginning of the end for independent adjudication.

(ii) The Retreat from Independent Adjudication: Housing Benefit and the Social Fund

The decision making and appeal arrangements for housing benefit reflect the tensions inherent in the administration by autonomous local authorities of a national social security benefit. Housing benefit was established in 1982 replacing locally-based rent rebate and rent allowance schemes with a unified benefit.[18] It would have been possible (and probably rational) to transfer responsibility for the benefit from the 400 or so local authorities in Great Britain to the DSS (or DHSS as it was then), but local authorities were unwilling to relinquish what they saw as part of the delivery of services to their communities. The decision to leave housing benefit with local authorities is thus an example of pragmatism and politics over the desirability of extending independent adjudication. Initial decisions became therefore the responsibility of council officials, who did not have the status of independent statutory authorities and did not come under the scrutiny of the Chief Adjudication Officer.

The passage of the Social Security and Housing Benefits Bill through Parliament in 1981 and early 1982 is well documented by Partington and Bolderson[19] and reveals how the appeal rights of housing benefit claimants were only considered late in the parliamentary process. The arrangements which eventually emerged were an attempt to reconcile pressure for housing benefit appeals to be brought within the jurisdiction of the then SBAT structure, and local authority arguments that an independent body would be an infringement of local democracy because their decisions would affect council expenditure for which they were accountable. What emerged was a two-tier system of internal administrative review by local authority officers, followed by a hearing before a review board comprising local authority councillors but with no right of appeal to the Social Security Commissioner. Aggrieved review board appellants had instead to rely on seeking judicial review in the High Court (or Court of Session) restricted to points of law only. Unlike the mainstream social security tribunals, housing benefit review boards did not come within the jurisdiction of the Council on Tribunals, the statutory body set up to monitor the operation of administrative tribunals across all areas of government.

The social fund was also taken out of the social security tribunal system.[20] Applicants dissatisfied with the decision of a social fund officer were given the right to an internal administrative review of the decision in the first instance.[21] This review system is described more fully elsewhere.[22] The social fund officer who made the

[18] See Chapter 4 at pp. 111–13.

[19] M. Partington and H. Bolderson, *Housing Benefit Review Procedures: A Preliminary Analysis* (Uxbridge: Brunel University, 1984).

[20] The purpose of the social fund and the background to its introduction and to its exclusion from the tribunal-based appeal system are discussed by Neville Harris in Chapter 5. For the current operation of the fund, see Chapter 14 by Simon Rahilly.

[21] SSAA 1992, s. 66(1).

[22] See Chapter 13 and T. Buck, *The Social Fund: Law and Practice* (London: Sweet and Maxwell, 1996).

original decision will either grant the appeal in full or invite the claimant for an inter-view, at which the decision will be explained to them. If the social fund officer is still not prepared to change the decision the case is passed to a senior member of the local office management who will again review the original decision. Applicants who are still dissatisfied may then request a further review by a social fund inspector based in a central office in Birmingham.[23] The inspectors can substitute their own decision, uphold the original decision or refer the decision back to the social fund officer, but there is no right of appeal against their decisions to the Social Security Commissioner. The work of social fund inspectors is monitored by the Social Fund Commissioner, who reports annually to the Secretary of State.[24] Taking the social fund out of the mainstream of social security decision making provoked consider-able opposition at the time,[25] but as we shall see later, the system of independent review not only remains in place ten years later but has had an important influence on the 1998 Social Security Act.

C. Summary of the Principal Features of Decision Making and Appeals before the 1998 Social Security Act

Before embarking on a critical discussion of the most recent changes to decision making and appeals, it is worth summarising the principal features of decision making and appeals pre-Social Security Act 199218. At the time of writing they are in the process of being replaced or amended as the provisions of the 1998 Act are gradu-ally implemented.

(i) Making a Claim

To make a claim for any social security benefit a claimant must usually complete the appropriate claim form. This sounds somewhat obvious but it is an important step because the date at which a claim is received by one of the DSS agencies is usually the date from which any payment will be made if the eligibility criteria for the bene-fit is satisfied. In some circumstances (Social Security (Claims and Payments) Regulations 1987, reg . 19) payments can be backdated beyond the date of the claim. The rules concerning the valid date at which a claim starts have endured for many years, although were tightened up in 1997, and reflect the principle that a person should be entitled to receive a benefit from whenever he or she satisfies the conditions of the benefit. The rules at least to some extent assist claimants by recognising that some people do not always act in their own best interests by delaying when they make a claim. The message implicit in the rules is that the benefit system is adaptable to the realities of human nature and will not penalise people who, for some good reason, do

---

[23] SSAA 1992, s. 66(3) and (4).   [24] Ibid., s. 65.
[25] Particularly vehement was the Council on Tribunals who took the unusual step of publishing a special report on the subject: Council on Tribunals, *Social Security—Abolition of independent appeals under the proposed Social Fund*, Cmnd. 9722 (London: HMSO, 1986). See Chapter 5 by Neville Harris at pp. 137–9.

not act in the most administratively convenient way.[26] Once a benefit is in payment, the recipient has a duty to inform the relevant agency of any change in circumstances so that the benefit can be revised if necessary. Again, the principle behind this rule is simply that the amount of an award should be an accurate reflection of a person's circumstances at all times.[27]

Decisions about entitlement to most benefits and, if applicable, the level of award payable are made by independent adjudication officers in one of the DSS agencies. Some decisions, about the validity of claims for example, are assigned to officials acting in the capacity of representative of the Secretary of State. In practice, one individual can act in both capacities during the processing of a claim. (Again the Social Security Act 1998 changes this, by abolishing the status of independent adjudication officer.) The arrangements for housing benefit and for the social fund depart from this model of independent adjudication as described earlier.

(ii) Bringing Appeals

As explained earlier, it is a principle that people who are the recipients of decisions from the social security system have a right to challenge decisions they disagree with. The short history of adjudication presented earlier gives an idea of how the various appeal structures have developed along different paths over the years. However, by the mid 1990s, there were basically three models of appeal that had emerged:

- the tribunal-based, two-tier, one appeal system
- the tribunal-based, three-tier, two appeal system
- the review-based system.[28]

In the *tribunal-based, two-tier, one appeal* model, a social security claimant can lodge an appeal directly to the appropriate tribunal. The adjudication structure can therefore be described as having two tiers: initial adjudication and appeal to a tribunal. In practice, once an appeal has been lodged, the Benefits (or other) Agency will examine the case and review the decision if the appeal falls within one of the three prescribed grounds for review.[29] A new decision is substituted and the appeal proceeds

---

[26] See further p. 434 n. 22 above. It is interesting that the Bill that preceded the SSA 1998 contained provisions to limit the period of backdating to one month only. This was a deeply unpopular measure which was strongly opposed at the time (see R. Sainsbury, *Consultation on Improving Decision Making and Appeals in Social Security: Analysis of responses* (London: Department of Social Security, 1997)) and which was withdrawn only at a late stage in the Bill's passage through the Lords.

[27] It should be noted here that the requirement to report changes in circumstances is a major source of difficulty for the Benefits and other agencies. Benefit recipients do not report changes reliably or quickly (R. Sainsbury, S. Hutton, and J. Ditch, *Changing Lives and the Role of Income Support,* DSS Research Report No. 45 (London: HMSO, 1996) with the result that overpayments and underpayments frequently arise which require administrative action to put right. Not reporting changes in circumstances is also thought to be a significant source of benefit fraud: Benefits Agency, *Benefit Review—Income Support and Unemployment Benefit* (Leeds: Benefits Agency, 1995).

[28] These models are compared in more detail in R. Sainsbury, 'Internal Reviews and the Weakening of Social Security Claimants' Rights of Appeal' in G. Richardson and H. Genn (eds.), *Administrative Law and Government Action* (Oxford: Clarendon Press, 1994), 287–307.

[29] The three main grounds are: (i) that there has been a mistake in, or ignorance of, a material fact; (ii) that there has been a mistake in law; and (iii) that there has been a relevant change in circumstances (see

no further if all aspects of the appeal can be settled in the claimant's favour. Before the 1998 Social Security Act the *tribunal-based, two-tier, one appeal* model was used for most social security benefits, including income support, child benefit, and retirement pensions.

In the *tribunal-based, three-tier, two appeal model*, the internal review of the appealed decision described above is part of the formal appeals structure. In practice this means that when the Benefits (or other) Agency has reviewed the case it notifies the claimant of the outcome and explains that a further right of appeal lies to a tribunal. To access the tribunal stage, however, the claimant must lodge another (i.e. second) appeal. The adjudication structure can therefore be described as having three tiers: initial adjudication, internal administrative review, and appeal to a tribunal. This model is used for a number of benefits, in particular for some introduced since HASSASSA (above), including disability living allowance and attendance allowance. Appeals against decisions of the Child Support Agency also follow the model, and a variant operates for housing benefit appeals.[30]

In the *review-based* model, which exists only for the social fund, a two-tier review is used in place of appeal to a tribunal. The first review is undertaken within local Benefits Agency offices by social fund officers and the second by centrally-based social fund inspectors under the management and control of the independent Social Fund Commissioner.[31]

Principal Features of Tribunals

Before the Social Security Act 1998, there were a number of separate tribunals which heard appeals by claimants against the decisions of adjudication officers. Table 7.1 sets out the basic features of the main tribunals.

We have already described how housing benefit represents a departure from the mainstream model of adjudication. Table 7.1 below shows that the review board also departs from the model of independent tribunal managed by a central body. Nevertheless, across all the tribunals described there are structural features and aspects of procedure which are common, and which are subject to change by the provisions of the 1998 Act.

The model of the *three-person* tribunal is well-established. It has the advantages that different perspectives can be brought to bear on individual cases, the merits of each case can be fully explored, and the dangers of prejudice or bias are minimised.

in particular Social Security Administration Act 1992, s. 25, repealed by the SSA 1998: see below). The regulations concerning reviews of decisions (Social Security (Adjudication) Regulations 1995 (S.I. 1995 No. 1801), revoked by S.I. 1999 No. 991) are primarily intended as an administrative means of correcting errors and dealing with changes in circumstances without the need for the claimant to submit a fresh claim or lodge an appeal.

[30] R. Sainsbury and T. Eardley, *Housing Benefit Reviews. An evaluation of the effectiveness of the review system in responding to claimants dissatisfied with housing benefit decisions*, DSS Research Report No. 3 (London: HMSO, 1991).

[31] See above and Chapter 13. The social fund system of reviews has been the subject of evaluative research by Dalley and Berthoud: G. Dalley and R. Berthoud, *Challenging Discretion: The Social Fund Review Procedure* (London: Policy Studies Institute, 1992).

Table 7.1. The main social security tribunals, pre-Social Security Act 1998

Name of tribunal	Benefits covered	Membership	Managed by
Social Security Appeal Tribunal (SSAT)	All those not covered by other tribunals (principally, income support, incapacity benefit, jobseeker's allowance)	3 members: legally-qualified chair, plus 2 'wing' members. (A 'medical adviser' assists the tribunal on incapacity benefit cases but does not take part in decision making.)	Independent Tribunal Service (ITS)
Medical Appeal Tribunal (MAT)	The medical questions relating to industrial injuries disablement benefit and severe disablement allowance	3 members: legally-qualified chair, plus 2 medical practitioners of consultant or equivalent status	ITS
Disability Appeal Tribunal (DAT)	The medical questions relating to disability living allowance and attendance allowance	3 members: legally-qualified chair, plus a medical practitioner of general practitioner status, and a person having experience of disability (either directly as a disabled person or indirectly as, for example, a carer)	ITS
Housing Benefit Review Board	Housing benefit and council tax benefit	At least three members drawn from, and appointed by, the elected members of the council. No requirement for chair to be legally qualified	Individual local authorities

Access to the tribunals described is equal and unrestricted. All appellants have the right to have their appeal dealt with and heard in the same way as other appellants regardless of its substance or financial value. This includes the right to appear and be represented in person before the tribunal.

(iii) Further Appeals: the Social Security Commissioners and Beyond

Appellants dissatisfied with the decision of a SSAT, MAT, or DAT have a right of appeal to a Social Security Commissioner but only on the grounds that the tribunal's decision was erroneous in law,[32] with leave from the tribunal chair or from the Commissioners. Adjudication officers and some other people affected by benefit

---

[32] SSAA 1992, s. 23, and the Social Security Commissioners Procedure Regulations 1987 (S.I. 1987 No. 214). See N. Harris, 'The Social Security Commissioners' (1993) 22(3) *Industrial Law J.* 222–6.

decisions can also appeal against tribunal decisions. Further appeal, to the Court of Appeal, on a point of law lies against a Commissioner's decision (with leave of a Commissioner or the court).[33]

Social Security Commissioners must be barristers (or advocates in Scotland) or solicitors of at least ten years' standing.[34] The Commissioners' decisions constitute the case law of social security. The more important of them are published as 'reported' decisions. Under certain circumstances (on a point of law only) there lies a further right of appeal to the Court of Appeal or the Court of Session in Scotland.[35] There is no comparable appeal in housing benefit cases. Dissatisfied appellants in those cases can only pursue their challenges to review board decisions by way of judicial review.[36]

Having set out the principal features of the decision-making and appeal arrangements for the main social security benefits prior to the Social Security Act 1998, we can turn to the next part of the chapter which will firstly present an analysis of a minor but significant change to tribunal hearings introduced in 1996, and secondly provide a critical account of the provisions of the Social Security Act 1998 as they affect decision making and appeals.

4. DECISION MAKING AND APPEALS: ALL CHANGE

A. The Case for Change in the Mid-1990s

The picture presented in the earlier part of this chapter is one of piecemeal development over the course of a century which has resulted in a diverse range of decision-making and appeal arrangements across the social security system. But how was it doing? In 1996 the Conservative Government clearly thought the answer was 'not very well' and set in train, with the publication of a consultative Green Paper,[37] the policy-making process that would culminate in the Social Security Act 1998. Although the Green Paper formed part of a wider Government strategy to cut radically the cost of administering social security (by 25 per cent of the current £4 billion bill in a three-year period) it also contained arguments that the way in which decision making and appeals were carried out were flawed and had shortcomings that together justified a serious overhaul.

The Green Paper identifies a number of problems with the initial adjudication and subsequent maintenance of social security claims:

- incomplete claim forms, which require officials to chase up missing information before a claim can be adjudicated;

---

[33] SSAA 1992, s. 24. [34] Ibid., s. 52. [35] n. 33 above.
[36] See Ogus, Barendt, and Wikeley (1995), ch. 17 and M. Partington, 'Judicial review and Housing Benefit', in T. Buck (ed.), *Judicial Review and Social Welfare* (London: Pinter, 1998), 182–201. See further Chapter 13.
[37] Department of Social Security, *Improving Decision Making and Appeals in Social Security*, Cm 3328 (London: HMSO, 1996).

- other unnecessary administrative work, caused, for example, by claimants failing to notify the authorities of changes in circumstances in time, so that overpayment and recovery action may become necessary;
- complexity and confusion, for claimants and for benefit staff, caused by staff having two roles, i.e. as independent adjudication officers and as representatives of the Secretary of State.

The handling of appeals was also seen to have a number of shortcomings and deficiencies:

- tribunals wasting time by hearing cases which have no possibility of succeeding, the so-called 'hopeless' cases;[38]
- tribunals having to deal with new facts which could have been dealt with by the Benefits Agency under existing review provisions;
- tribunals having to address changes in circumstances which had taken place between lodgement of the appeal and the hearing, again, which could have been dealt with by the Benefits Agency;
- claimants getting drawn in to the appeals process when an explanation of their original decision would have satisfied them;
- the statutory requirements placed on tribunals (for example, that they have three members including a legally-qualified chair, and that in some cases members must hold specified professional qualifications) which are too formal and inflexible, and may not be cost-effective;
- deficiencies in the service provided by the Independent Tribunal Service (particularly in the time taken to clear cases) and in the accountability of its judicial head, the President, for performance and efficiency.

This analysis of the problems with the decision-making and appeal arrangements was not convincing to many of the people and organisations who responded to the Green Paper[39] but most of the proposals which were derived from it survived the consultation process and reappeared in the 1998 Act.

In the remainder of this part of the chapter I will set out, and critically examine, the principal changes to decision making and appeals which have either been introduced recently or will be put in place as part of the implementation of the Social Security Act 1998.

---

[38] In Parliamentary and press reports at the time, reference was repeatedly made to '20,000 hopeless Income Support cases' per year to illustrate the extent of the problem. Where this figure came from though remains a mystery.

[39] R. Sainsbury, *Consultation on Improving Decision Making and Appeals in Social Security: Analysis of responses* (London: Department of Social Security, 1997) and idem 'A Critique of the Case for Change' in M. Adler and R. Sainsbury (eds.), *Adjudication Matters: Reforming Decision Making and Appeals in Social Security*, New Waverley Papers SP14 (Edinburgh: Department of Social Policy, University of Edinburgh, 1998), 23–9.

B. Initial Adjudication Following the 1998 Act

The Social Security Act 1998 does away with independent adjudication for all social security benefits[40] (and also child support). So, the independence of decision makers which was initially introduced before the First World War will no longer be a feature of social security decision making. The change will remove the confusion about the roles of social security officials which undoubtedly existed before,[41] though the extent to which this was the cause of serious difficulty for claimants is largely unknown. It could be argued, of course, as Partington has done,[42] that the confusion could have been dealt with by transferring all decision-making powers to adjudication officers, but this option was never considered in the Green Paper nor in subsequent official documents.

Perhaps, as Lynes has commented,[43] not much will be lost if initial decisions are taken by the same officials acting in the capacity of representatives of the Secretary of State. However, another change is linked to abolition of independent adjudication in the Act which might prove more detrimental to the quality of decision making and in turn may prove to be to the serious disadvantage of social security claimants. Section 1 of the 1998 Act also transfers the duties of the Chief Adjudication Officer (CAO) for providing advice and guidance to adjudication officers and for monitoring their standards of adjudication to the Chief Executives of the various DSS agencies. The post of the CAO will therefore cease to exist.

The role of the CAO has probably barely, if at all, touched the consciousness of the average social security claimant but since the post was established as part of the HASSASSA reforms in 1984, the CAO has been something of a thorn in the side of the Benefits Agency and the DSS. The persistent deficiencies in adjudication (particularly on benefits such as income support, and procedures such as preparing appeal submissions) have been made public through the publication of annual reports. That improvements, where they have been achieved, have been slow and incremental cannot be a criticism of the CAO, who has used his monitoring and reporting powers to press continuously for poor standards of decision making to be tackled. In the future Chief Executives will be held to account for standards to the Secretary of State, who him/herself will publish reports on the standards being achieved.

The new arrangements have failed to convince some critics[44] who suspect that

---

[40] That is, where it existed in the first place. Housing benefit, for example, is unaffected by this change. The operation of the present housing benefit review system is discussed by Simon Rahilly in Chapter 13.

[41] See, for example, J. Baldwin, N. Wikeley, and R. Young, *Judging Social Security* (Oxford: Clarendon Press, 1992).

[42] M. Partington, *Secretary of State's Powers of Adjudication in Social Security Law* (Bristol: School for Advanced Urban Studies, 1991).

[43] T. Lynes, 'The End of Independent Adjudication?' in M. Adler and R. Sainsbury (eds.), *Adjudication Matters: Reforming Decision Making and Appeals in Social Security*, New Waverley Papers SP14 (Edinburgh: Department of Social Policy, University of Edinburgh: 1998), 30–3.

[44] For example: Lynes, 'The End of Independent Adjudication?', op. cit., 30–3; and N. Wikeley, 'Decision making and appeals under the SSA 1998' in (1998) 5 *J.S.S.L.* 104–17.

Chief Executives will not be as outspoken and comprehensive as the CAO and, in contrast, have every interest in playing down deficiencies in their Agency's standards. A further fear is that the advice provided to adjudication officers could reflect political and managerial concerns, such as smooth administration or cost-cutting, rather than be strict interpretations of social security law. As Lynes points out: 'Rightly or wrongly, when legal issues arise, the Chief Executive will be accused of bias and the charge will be difficult to refute.'[45]

C. Dealing with Changes in Circumstances

Section 10 of the Act allows the Secretary of State to supersede a decision made under section 8 or section 9. Wikeley[46] suggests that this power will be used when there has been ignorance or mistake as to a material fact, an error of law, or a change in circumstances since the original decision (as such it resembles closely previous powers to review decisions under the Social Security Administration Act 1992).[47] What is new, however, is the timing of a revised award. If a claimant reports a change within a month of it occurring then the revised decision will normally take effect from the date of change of circumstances. But if the claimant takes longer to report the change the new award will not be backdated to the date of change but only to the date when it was reported.[48]

Compared with previous regulations (under which benefits could be backdated up to a year in some circumstances) claimants will lose out. The exception to this is where the reported change results in a reduction of benefit, in which case the reduction will take effect from the date of change. So, essentially a case of double standards has been introduced. If the claimant has received an overpayment, then repayment of the full amount is required, but if the claimant has been underpaid, he or she can only receive a backdated award up to a maximum of one month. Any money that they were entitled to before then will not be paid.

It is clear that this particular change in social security legislation does nothing to benefit claimants but is aimed at reducing the administrative work (and therefore the cost) of maintaining claims in payment.

D. Unification of the Range of Social Security Tribunals

Section 4 of the 1998 Act transfers the functions of existing social security tribunals (including child support appeal tribunals and vaccine damage appeal tribunals) to a new 'unified appeal tribunal'. This change may have some minor advantages by

[45] Lynes, 'The End of Independent Adjudication?', op. cit.
[46] N. Wikeley, n. 44 above.
[47] See now the Social Security and Child Support (Decisions and Appeals) Regulations 1999 (S.I. 1999 No. 991), regs 6 and 7, as amended by (the same) (Amendment) (No. 2) Regulations 1999 (S.I. 1999 No. 1623).
[48] S.I. 1999 No. 991, ibid., reg. 7.

allowing all tribunal members to hear any type of case, but in practice it was always likely that members would continue to be restricted in what cases they could hear, simply because it would not be feasible for them to acquire the requisite detailed knowledge to be able to hear all types of case. The type of person sitting on DATs hearing disability living allowance cases was unlikely to be willing or able to hear, for example, income support appeals. Tribunal membership is discussed in section G (pages 225–6) below. Whether the new unified tribunal will provide the more 'modern and efficient structure' that the Government envisages remains to be seen (see below).

E. Access to a Tribunal

When a claimant gets a decision at the start of a claim or a new decision (based for example on a change in circumstances) he or she will have a month (called the 'dispute period') to seek a revised decision. No formal grounds need to be established, the claimant need only invoke his or her right to have their decision looked at again.[49] The Secretary of State can also invoke the same provisions on his or her own initiative. The rationale for this power is that it creates flexibility for the Secretary of State to change decisions quickly and with the minimum of fuss. Claimants also have the opportunity for their case to be examined a second time without getting drawn in to any formal appeal procedures.

There are several possible outcomes of the review. The original decision could be found to be correct and therefore confirmed, or a new, revised decision could be made superseding the original. In both of these instances the claimant has a further month to take matters further by lodging an appeal.[50] Another possible outcome is that the Secretary of State deems the challenge to the original decision to be without foundation and refuses to act upon it, thus dealing with the problem of so-called 'hopeless cases' referred to earlier.[51]

On the face of it, there seems little exceptionable about these arrangements: challenges will get dealt with quickly and without fuss, and hopeless appeals will be prevented from clogging up the system. However, the introduction of a new stage in the decision making arrangements was met with opposition when the idea was first floated in the Green Paper.[52] Concerns were expressed that some claimants, particularly those without professional representation, could lose out. For example, during the second look at the case an unrepresented claimant would be at a disadvantage if they did not have the requisite knowledge to make judgments about the definitions or relevance of facts or issues concerning the case. They might therefore come to

---

[49] SSA 1998, s. 9 and the Decisions and Appeals Regulations (n. 47 above), regs 3 (as amended by S.I. 1999 No. 1623) and 4.

[50] SSA 1998, s. 12 and the Decisions and Appeals Regulations, op. cit., reg. 30.

[51] There would be no right of appeal in such a case: see N. Wikeley (1998), n. 44 above, 107.

[52] See R. Sainsbury, *Consultation on Improving Decision Making and Appeals in Social Security: Analysis of responses* (London: Department of Social Security, 1997).

some form of settlement which did not reflect the merits of their case and therefore deny themselves the opportunity of a tribunal finding in their favour.

The power to identify and dismiss 'hopeless' cases where there is no possibility of the decision being changed (see above) or to strike out an appeal on the basis that it is 'misconceived' for being 'obviously unsustainable and [having] no prospect of success'[53] could also lead to claimants being denied their proper entitlements. Many tribunal members who responded to the Green Paper were able to cite instances of cases which, on an examination of the tribunal papers only, had initially appeared to be without merit, turned in the claimant's favour when the tribunal was able to investigate the case further directly with the claimant. It is also arguable whether any case in which issues of *fact* were relevant could ever be considered 'hopeless'.

F. New 'Streamlined' Appeal Procedures

Section 12 of the 1998 Act introduces a radical restriction on what a tribunal can consider in the course of hearing a case. Under the Act, tribunals need only consider issues that are raised as points of appeal by the appellant and should not consider any changes in circumstances that occur between the lodgement of the appeal and a hearing. Hence, there will be a greater degree of clarity in the role of the tribunal which will in future provide a genuine appeal solely against a prior decision of an adjudication officer. In future, therefore, there should be no problem of new issues arising during the course of a hearing or of tribunals having to deal with changes in circumstances as well as judging the initial decision.

However, looked at from the perspective of an appellant, the service provided by the tribunal will be much reduced. Regardless of the change in the law, appellants will no doubt continue to introduce new issues at a hearing and will describe changes in circumstances to the tribunal. Before the 1998 Act, the tribunal would have dealt with these and provided the appellant not only with a decision on the appeal but also an up-to-date assessment of their entitlements. In so doing it may have been stepping beyond what might be considered an appeal in a judicial sense, but it was substituting decisions which were correct at the time of the hearing. Appellants could leave a tribunal knowing exactly what their benefit was going to be. In future, many appellants will leave, in their eyes, with only a partial resolution of their appeal. They may have raised issues that the tribunal had been obliged to dismiss because they had not been raised at the outset of the appeal, and they may have reported changes in circumstances that the tribunal would have been obliged to refer back to the Benefits Agency to deal with.

It is possible, and probably likely, that for some appellants the appeal process will continue beyond the tribunal hearing and that the Benefits Agency will find itself

---

[53] Social Security and Child Support (Decisions and Appeals) Regulations 1999 (S.I. 1999 No. 991), regs 46(4) and 48. The definition of 'misconceived appeal' is in reg. 1(3). It also includes an appeal which is considered 'frivolous or vexatious'.

dealing with changes in circumstances referred back from tribunals. The stated aim of speeding up and streamlining the appeal process could, therefore, be considerably undermined.

G. Tribunal Membership

The proposals in the Green Paper to reform the membership of tribunals were far-reaching. In place of the statutory requirement that tribunals should sit with three members headed by a legally-qualified chair, the Green Paper proposed that tribunals should operate with one or two members in most cases and only comprise three members for the more difficult cases. Furthermore, it proposed that tribunal members, even when sitting alone, need not be legally qualified. The idea, as it was put forward in the consultation document, was to introduce flexibility and increase efficiency. The proposals surprised many and seemed to have been made in ignorance of the HASSASSA Act and its history. One of the major, and damning, criticisms of the supplementary benefit appeal tribunals in the 1970s, as discussed above (see section 3.A), was their lack of a legally-qualified chair which had led to poor standard of procedure and decision making.

The opposition to these proposals was vociferous and sustained with the result that the provisions of the 1998 Act were less extreme though still controversial. Section 7 of the Act allows tribunals to consist of up to three members, thus admitting the prospect of the single-person tribunal, but also contains the provision that every tribunal must have a qualified lawyer sitting as one of the members.[54] The regulations[55] require the panel to comprise a legally-qualified member and medical member in certain instances (for example, appeals on the 'all work' test or industrial injuries benefit) or a legally-qualified and a financial member where it is a child support or other relevant benefit case involving complex financial matters and accounts. Legal, medical, and disability members would be needed for a DLA case and three-person panels would also be needed in certain other prescribed cases, but the default position is that the tribunal would comprise a legally-qualified member alone.

How these arrangements operate in practice and whether all prove acceptable to appellants remains to be seen. It is possible already for a two-person tribunal to hear cases (with the agreement of all the parties) and there are many instances in the British judicial system of decision makers sitting alone. The success or otherwise of the arrangements will depend on a number of factors, including the way in which cases are allocated to one-, two- or three-person tribunals, the quality of their decisions, and the quality of the experience for the appellants and their representatives. The outcomes of the differently constituted tribunals (i.e. the comparative success

---

[54] The Decisions and Appeals Regulations, op. cit., reg. 35 and Sched. 3, provide for the appointment to panels of legally-qualified, medical, financial, and disability members. SSA 1998, s 7(2) requires an appeal tribunal to include or comprise a legally-qualified member.
[55] Ibid., reg. 36.

rates for appellants) will provide revealing evidence of the effect of these controversial changes.

H. Paper and Oral Hearings

Another controversial change to social security appeals in recent years actually preceded the 1998 Social Security Act. In October 1996 regulations[56] were introduced which required tribunal appellants to opt specifically for an oral hearing if they wanted to attend their hearing. If they did not so opt, a tribunal would consider the case 'on the papers' with no-one present. Before 1996 the policy direction was to get more people to attend tribunals rather than reducing their numbers. There was a clear presumption that an oral hearing was the preferred and most effective method of dealing with an appeal (and was therefore to be encouraged), but that appellants could opt for a hearing on the papers if they wished.

Though there is nothing new about hearings which are dealt with on the papers alone—there have always been appellants who do not appear and who are not represented—there is clear research evidence[57] that an appellant's chances of success are significantly increased if they attend their hearing and even better if they are also represented. Appeal success rates derived from official statistics demonstrate the same point. In 1997, the success rate of appellants who attended their tribunal hearing alone was 48 per cent. If they attended with a representative, their success rate was 65 per cent. In stark contrast, only 12 per cent of cases decided on the papers went in the claimant's favour.[58]

The change in the regulations was referred to in the Green Paper, but more for information than for consultation since the regulations were already due to come into force before the end of the consultation period. Nevertheless, they attracted a huge negative response.[59] The regulations were generally seen as an attempt to cut government expenditure by increasing the number of cases that tribunals could deal with at a single sitting, at the expense of social security claimants. What critics feared was that many appellants who were apprehensive about appearing before a tribunal would opt for a paper hearing without understanding the implications for their chances of success. The aggregate effect of an increase in 'paper' hearings would therefore be a decrease in the number of successful appeals. At the time of writing, the available official statistics for social security appeal tribunals for the year follow-

---

[56] Social Security (Adjudication) and Child Support Amendment (No. 2) Regulations 1996 (S.I. 1996 No. 2450). See now reg. 39 of the Decisions and Appeals Regs, op. cit.

[57] H. Genn and Y. Genn, *The Effectiveness of Representation at Tribunals* (London: Lord Chancellor's Department, 1989).

[58] Department of Social Security, *Social Security Statistics 1998* (Leeds: Corporate Document Services, 1998), Table H5.03.

[59] See R. Sainsbury, *Consultation on Improving Decision Making and Appeals in Social Security: Analysis of responses* (London: Department of Social Security, 1997) and T. Lynes, 'Not seen and not heard', (1998), *The Guardian,* 7 January.

ing implementation of the regulations, appear to confirm these fears. Tables 7.2 and 7.3 (below) show the relative changes between oral and paper hearings.

Table 7.2 shows that the change of policy has had a sharp and dramatic effect on the balance between attended and unattended hearings. As feared by critics and presumably intended by policy makers, paper hearings are increasing. In the space of twelve months from the change in regulations the proportion of appellants attending tribunals fell by 18 per cent to 44 per cent, though it is possible that this figure will continue to decline.

The effect on overall success rates for appellants can be seen in Table 7.3, which shows that the success rates of appellants at both attended and paper hearings has not changed in the period since the regulations changed. However, whereas about four in ten of appeals were successful before October 1996, only three in ten were successful a year later. It is inconceivable that in the time the new regulations have been in force the proportion of meritorious appeals has simultaneously dropped by about a quarter. What the figures confirm is that a paper hearing is, in general, an

Table 7.2. Comparison of SSAT hearings attended and those decided on the papers

Quarter ending	Total number of cases dealt with	% of cases heard orally with claimant and/or representative present	% heard on the papers
31.12.96	28,048	62	38
31.3.97	25,586	62	38
30.6.97	31,507	54	46
30.9.97	36,053	44	56

Source: House of Commons, *Hansard*, col. 59, 27 April 1998

Table 7.3. Success rates of claimants at attended and unattended ('paper') tribunal hearings

Quarter ending	% success rate for attended hearings	% success rate for paper hearings	% of all cases that were successful
31.12.96	55	12	39
31.3.97	55	12	39
30.6.97	56	13	36
30.9.97	55	13	31

Source: House of Commons, *Hansard*, col. 59, 27 April 1998

unsatisfactory means of dealing with social security appeals from the viewpoint of the appellant.

I. Summary of the Principal Features of Decision Making and Appeals after 1998

In section 3.C of this chapter the decision-making and appeal arrangements for the range of social security benefits were set out using three basic models and could be characterised as diverse and targeted (to be generous) or as confused and confusing (to be less generous). The Social Security Act 1998 changes the picture again.

The *tribunal-based, two-tier, one appeal* model has become the dominant model with the addition of a formal (but optional) 'second look' procedure. Claimants will be able to lodge an appeal directly to a tribunal but will be encouraged to avail themselves of the opportunity of settling the dispute without the need to invoke the full tribunal procedures. The model can no longer be labelled 'independent adjudication', however, since all decisions will be made by representatives of the Secretary of State in future. The new model will apply to all social security benefits administered by the DSS and its agencies.

The *tribunal-based, three-tier, two appeal model* survives only for housing benefit and council tax benefit which will continue to be administered by local authorities. Housing benefit is unaffected by the 1998 Act (despite arguments that it should be consistent with other benefits).[60]

Similarly, the specialised arrangements for the social fund, the *review-based* model, are untouched by the Act. The roles of social fund officers, inspectors, and the Social Fund Commissioner will continue as before.

Table 7.4 summarises the simplified tribunal structure that will emerge when the relevant provisions of the Social Security Act 1998 have been fully implemented.

The Social Security Commissioners (and the right of appeal to the Court of Appeal, with leave, against their decisions) have also survived,[61] though a change in the powers of tribunals means that the Commissioners are likely to hear fewer cases in future. Under the 1998 Act appeals against tribunal decisions can, at the discretion of the chair, be referred to another tribunal for a re-hearing where an error of law has been made or the parties agree that such an error has been made by the tribunal. Alternatively, a tribunal chair could, on a leave to appeal application, set aside a decision that is erroneous in law.[62] Previously, errors of law would have been identified by the Commissioners themselves whose usual course of action was to refer the case back to a tribunal for a re-hearing. This time-consuming procedure should now become largely redundant. While this may be a welcome development for some individual appellants, Wikeley[63] points out that the development of case law may become

---

[60] See R. Sainsbury (1997), op. cit.
[61] SSAA 1992, ss 23 and 24, and the Social Security Commissioners (Procedure) Regulations 1999 (S.I. 1999 No. 1495).
[62] SSA 1998, ss 13 and 14.
[63] N. Wikeley, 'Decision making and appeals under the SSA 1998' in (1998) 5 *J.S.S.L.*104–17.

Table 7.4: The main social security tribunals, post-Social Security Act 1998

Name of tribunal	Benefits covered	Membership	Managed by
Unified Appeal Tribunal	All those administered by the DSS and its agencies	1, 2, or 3 members, of whom one must be legally qualified	New executive agency for day-to-day administration of appeals. The Appeals Service (TAS) for judicial matters
Housing Benefit Review Board	Housing benefit and council tax benefit	At least three members drawn from, and appointed by, the elected members of the council. No requirement for chair to be legally qualified	Individual local authorities

restricted if the Commissioners hear significantly fewer cases. A reduction in the time within which leave to appeal must normally be sought from a Commissioner where a chair refuses it —from forty-two days to four weeks[64]—may also have an effect on the number of appeals heard.

5. CONCLUSION: AN UNCERTAIN FUTURE

The intention behind this chapter was to provide the reader with a critical discussion of the issues surrounding the development of social security decision making and appeals over the course of this century, and in particular in recent years when decision making has featured strongly in governments' thinking about the future of social security. The recent debates about how to deliver social security policy reveal that the subject of decision making and appeals is indeed important, but is also inherently political. Questions such as how much of the country's resources should be devoted to social security administration, the degree of independence that should be granted to decision makers, who should monitor standards on decision making, and how appeals should be handled, are all political questions. Hence they have no single answer. How they are resolved is subject to political, social, and economic forces as much as any other area of government policy.

---

[64] S.I. 1999 No. 1495, n. 61 above, reg. 9. The appellant has a maximum of thirteen months from the date that the tribunal's decision and/or reasons were sent to him or her in which to plead special reasons for a late appeal.

On one level, it is entirely understandable that a government should take an interest in the cost of administering the social security system—after all, it does consume somewhere in the region of £4 billion a year (although as a percentage of the overall £100 billion annual social security bill, it might be considered reasonable value for money). However, as the driving force for reform, a dominant concern for cutting costs effectively precludes a more open and wide discussion about the problems and shortcomings of decision making and appeals and constrains thinking about the range of options that might address them.

How one views the recent changes, most of which are contained in the 1998 Act, depends very much on the perspective one chooses to adopt. From a perspective which promotes costs and organisational convenience as the principal concerns, the new measures stand up very well. Administrative costs should fall because the amount of work involved in making initial decisions and maintaining claims should be reduced. Fewer cases should proceed to tribunal hearings because many will be dealt with by officials. Tribunal costs will fall as more cases are heard on the papers. There are other perspectives, however.

From the perspective of the social security claimant, the future is more uncertain. Features of the new arrangements may appear attractive on the surface but may ultimately mean that claimants have less chance of receiving their full entitlements. The opportunity for your case to be looked at again by officials may be reassuring and for many who are really only seeking clarification of their benefit decision it may be all that is needed. However, it is far from certain that the quality of the 'second look' will be sufficient to ensure that most errors or misinterpretations are identified and put right. The old adjudication system which guaranteed that cases not changed on review (equivalent to the new 'second look') would be considered by a tribunal may have drawn some claimants a little unwillingly into appeal processes that they might find daunting or difficult, but they were more likely to emerge at the other end with the correct decision on their claim. Similarly, it might be a relief to appellants frightened of appearing before a tribunal to be offered a paper hearing and might seem to add legitimacy to their decision not to attend, but appellants making that choice reduce dramatically their chances of succeeding with their appeal.

Concern over the impact of the recent and imminent reforms to social security decision making and appeals may yet prove to have been unfounded. However, being aware of the potential dangers and disadvantages that could befall claimants will help us to evaluate the impact of the changes when it becomes apparent. Claimants may well enjoy quicker and simpler administration of their claims and appeals but the early evidence concerning paper hearings should alert us to the need for constant vigilance.

8

Social Security: the European Union Dimension

TAMARA K. HERVEY*

1. INTRODUCTION

As was noted briefly in Chapter 2, there is no European Union-level 'welfare super-state'. Social security and social welfare remain largely within the competence of the governments of the Member States of the European Union (EU), and are governed mainly by national rules and policies. However, social security and social welfare systems of the Member States of the EU no longer operate in isolation from the obligations in Community law of those Member States. Some EU-level legal norms have implications for the operation of such national social welfare systems. Thus in the EU, social security and welfare might be described as a field of 'multi-level governance',[1] in which rules, principles, and norms emanating from EU, national, and indeed sub-national levels interact to create the overall picture of law and policy. This chapter is concerned with the interactions between the law of the European Union and that of the United Kingdom in the field of social security and social welfare.

There are four basic 'modes of interaction' between the EU and national levels relevant to social security and social welfare law.[2] These are the regulatory co-ordination by the EU of national social security systems in respect of migrant workers; the relatively rare phenomenon of EU-level harmonised regulatory social security norms; the promotion of harmonisation or convergence through soft law[3] norms and financial support; and modified deregulation in the context of the EU's law of the internal market. Concentrating on the 'hard law' modes of interaction, this chapter aims to show that the impact of Community law means that governments of

* I am grateful to Neville Harris and to Philip Rostant for their very helpful comments and suggestions on earlier drafts, and to the participants at the SPTL EC law subject session, Oxford, March 1999 and SLSA, Loughborough, April 1999 for their views on the 'social solidarity' material.

[1] S. Leibfried and P. Pierson, *European Social Policy: Between Fragmentation and Implementation* (Washington DC: Brookings, 1995).

[2] See T. Hervey, *European Social Law and Policy* (London: Longman, 1998), 31–40.

[3] 'Soft law' measures are non-binding measures which neither place legally enforceable obligations on Member States or individuals, nor grant enforceable rights to individuals. However, their significance in EU policy-making processes should not be underestimated. Soft law measures may provide interpretative guidance with respect to 'hard law' measures (Case C-322/88 *Grimaldi v Fonds des Maladies Professionelles* [1989] ECR 4407); may constitute a statement of 'best practice'; may carve out areas of 'Community concern' as opposed to formal competence; and may pave the way for future hard law action at EU level. See T. Hervey, n. 2 above, 49–53; N. Wellens and D. Borchardt, 'Soft Law in European Community Law' (1989) 14 *ELRev.* 267–321.

Member States no longer maintain total control over the terms on which social security benefits are given, and in particular access to those benefits. Thus the UK's social security law must now be viewed in its European Union context.

Among the main preoccupations of Community law are the creation of the 'internal market' (an area in which free movement of goods, persons, services, and capital is ensured)[4] and ensuring that competition within that internal market is not distorted.[5] Community internal market and competition law is supreme and directly effective within the Member States. Thus, to the extent to which measures of national social security law, and mechanisms for provision of social security benefits, fall within the scope of such Community law, national social security systems may be affected by it. The main thrust of this aspect of Community law may be considered to be deregulatory: its aim is to remove obstacles to free movement and to promote free competition.[6] However, as we will see below, the impact of Community internal market and competition law is not wholly deregulatory. In the context of interactions between Community internal market and competition law, and national social security law, the legitimate aims of national social policy provisions may be protected through the application of legal concepts developed at EU level, in particular the notion of 'social solidarity'.

Before turning to a more detailed examination of these various modes of interaction, the chapter sets the developing EU-level norms in their historical context.[7] This is followed by a very brief overview of the legal and institutional structure of the EU dimension of social security and social welfare law.

2. HISTORICAL CONTEXT

After an early period of relative inaction in the social field, the EU's involvement in social security and social welfare policy has been characterised by tensions between competing models justifying such action.[8] Broadly speaking, there are four such models.[9] According to the neo-liberal market model, it is undesirable for the

[4] Article 14 (ex 7a) EC.
[5] Article 3(g); Articles 81–9 (ex 85–94) EC.
[6] On the nature of Community internal market and competition law generally, see for instance S. Weatherill, *Law and Integration in the European Union* (Oxford: Clarendon Press, 1995); D. Chalmers and E. Szyszczak, *European Union Law volume 2: Towards a European Polity* (Aldershot: Dartmouth, 1998) and M. P. Maduro, *We the Court: The European Court of Justice and the European Economic Constitution* (Oxford: Hart, 1998).
[7] See further T. Hervey, n. 2 above, ch. 2; H. Mosley, 'The social dimension of European integration' (1990) 129 *International Labour Rev.* 147–63; R. Nielsen and E. Szyszczak, *The Social Dimension of the European Union* (Copenhagen: Handelshojskolens Forlag, 1997), 16–64; D. O'Keeffe, 'The Uneasy Progress of European Social Policy' (1996) 2 *Columbia J. of European Law*, 241–63.
[8] See further Hervey, n. 2 above, 6–11. As *models* these positions are simplified versions of 'real-life' policy orientations, reflecting neither objective reality, nor the position of a particular institution, government of a Member State, or other actor.
[9] See Hervey, n. 2 above, ch. 1.

European Union to operate any significant social policy, save for those few measures necessary to ensure effective functioning of the EU's single internal market. The convergence model holds that interventionist EU social policy is superfluous. The economic and political forces of the internal market will encourage a tendency towards convergence of national social welfare standards. According to the conservative social cohesion model, social policy measures at EU level are justified by the need to maintain the established social order. The unimpeded functioning of the internal market will produce social 'dislocation', as competitive pressures brought about by European economic integration, with the restructuring of European industries, will have an uneven impact across geographical or social groupings within the European Union. EU-level social policy intervention is therefore justified to correct these market inefficiencies and to promote effective competition. Finally, the social justice model holds that principles of distributive justice necessitate EU-level social policy, in order to 'humanise' the operation of the market.

During certain periods of time, one model or another seems to gain predominance, and consequently different types of EU-level action are promoted. In the early days of the EEC, neo-liberal and convergence models held sway. The conservative social cohesion and social welfare models gained some influence during the1970s, during which time for instance the European Community's first 'Social Action Programme'[10] was established. A brief period in the early 1980s in which neo-liberal ideas of 'flexibility' and 'deregulation' prevented regulatory action at EU level followed. However, the Delors Commission[11] and the Single European Act effectively revitalised EU-level social policy. Although the main aim of the Single European Act was to complete the internal market by 31 December 1992, the social dimension of this was also given prominence, most famously in Delors' speech concerning the '*Espace Sociale Européenne*',[12] in which the Commission President expressed a social justice model as underpinning the EU's activities in the social sphere:

The creation of a vast economic area, based on the market and business co-operation, is inconceivable—I would say unattainable—without some harmonisation of social legislation. Our ultimate aim must be the creation of a European social area.

More recently, the tensions between such social justice models and other models have been given expression even in Treaty provisions. The Treaty of Amsterdam amends the Treaty of Rome to include new Articles 2 and 136 EC, which appear to express contradictory intentions:

The Community shall have as its task . . . to promote . . . a high level of employment and social protection . . . a high degree of competitiveness and convergence of economic performance . . . (Article 2 EC)

---

[10] OJ 1974 C 13/1; EC Bulletin 2/74.
[11] On the Delors administration generally see G. Ross, *Jacques Delors* (Cambridge: Polity, 1995).
[12] European social area.

The Community and the Member States, having in mind fundamental social rights . . . shall have as their objectives . . . proper social protection . . . with a view to the combating of exclusion. To this end the Community shall . . . take account of . . . the need to maintain the competitiveness of the Community economy . . . (Article 136 EC)

This curious combination of social justice and social cohesion models sits well with the views of current centre-left governments in a number of key Member States[13] and also appears to be the current conception of the 'European social model' adopted by the European Commission.[14] Thus we might expect new EU-level initiatives in terms of policy and regulation over the next few years to reflect some kind of balance between these two competing models.

3. LEGAL AND INSTITUTIONAL STRUCTURES

The EU's competence to regulate and make policy in the fields of social security and social welfare is limited (as in all fields)[15] to that granted to the institutions of the EU by the enabling 'legal basis' provisions of the Treaty of Rome.[16] A small number of specific legal basis provisions are relevant to the social security and welfare field, and these are complemented by more general legal basis provisions.[17] Specific legal basis provisions empower the Council of Ministers to 'adopt measures in the field of social security as necessary to provide freedom of movement for workers',[18] and, now that the Treaty of Amsterdam has entered into force,[19] Council is empowered to 'adopt, by means of directives, minimum requirements for gradual implementation' in order to achieve the aims of 'proper social protection' and 'the combating of exclusion', and may 'adopt measures designed to encourage co-operation between Member States . . . in order to combat social exclusion'.[20] The legal basis for running

---

[13] In particular, Germany, France, and the United Kingdom.

[14] Recently defined by Commissioner Flynn in a speech for the conference *Visions for European Governance*, Harvard University, 2 March 1999, as follows: 'The European social model spans many policy areas. Education and training. Health and welfare. Social protection. Dialogue between independent trades unions and employers. Health and safety at work. The pursuit of equality. The fight against racism and discrimination. It takes many forms—welfare systems, collective arrangements, delivery mechanisms. It has been conceived, and is still applied, in many different ways. By different agents. Under different public, private and third sector arrangements in different parts of Europe. It is a system steeped in plurality and diversity—reflecting our richness of culture, tradition and political development. All the variants reflect and respect two common and balancing principles. One is competition—the driving force behind economic progress—the other is solidarity between citizens.'

[15] See in general on competence, S. Weatherill, 'Beyond Preemption? Shared Competence and Constitutional Change in the EC', in D. O'Keeffe and P. Twomey (eds), *Legal Issues of the Maastricht Treaty* (London: Wiley Chancery, 1994), 13–33.

[16] For further discussion of the legal and institutional structure of EU social policy see T. Hervey, n. 2 above, chs 3 and 4.

[17] In particular Articles 95 (ex Art. 100a) and 308 (ex Art. 235) EC.

[18] Art. 42 (ex 51) EC.

[19] On 1 May 1999. The Treaty of Amsterdam will renumber the articles of the Treaty of Rome. For clarity, reference to both new and old numbers is made below.

[20] New Arts 136–7 EC.

the structural funds[21] (a modest means of redistribution of resources from richer to poorer groups in the EU, defined either geographically or socially)[22] is found in Articles 161 and 162 EC.[23]

Legal basis provisions not only provide the source of the EU's competence to make law and policy, but also set out the procedural terms according to which that policy is to be made. There are many different legislative procedures set out in the Treaty of Rome,[24] but the general rule is that the Commission proposes new law or policy, and the Council of Ministers and European Parliament decide. It is easier for new measures to be enacted if the relevant procedure is one which provides for voting in the Council of Ministers by qualified majority,[25] rather than unanimity, as otherwise the opposition of the government of just one Member State is sufficient to block the proposal. Before the Treaty of Amsterdam, however, virtually all social measures had to be enacted by unanimity in Council, and even after Amsterdam the unanimity procedure remains for various social security and social welfare measures.[26]

Thus the EU's activities in terms of enacting EU-level law or policy measures which are *directly* concerned with social security or social welfare are limited. However, an appreciation of the effect that membership of the European Union may have on national social security or welfare policies must also consider the impact of more general policies of the EU, and the legally enforceable rules and principles effecting those policies, on national welfare systems. Chief among the EU's policies is the 'creation of the internal market', defined in the Treaty as 'an area without internal frontiers in which the free movement of goods, persons, services and capital is ensured'.[27] The EU institutions have extensive powers to enact legislation in order to bring about the internal market, and many relevant Treaty provisions have been held by the European Court of Justice to be 'directly effective', that is, enforceable at the suit of individuals before national courts. The final part of this chapter will consider the impact or potential impact of such litigation on national social security and

---

[21] The European Regional Development Fund, the European Social Fund, and the European Agricultural Guidance and Guarantee Fund (Guidance Section): Arts 158–162 (ex 130a–130e) EC. See further J. Scott, *Development Dilemmas in the European Community: Rethinking Regional Development Policy* (London: Open University Press, 1995); J. Kenner, 'Economic and Social Cohesion: The Rocky Road Ahead' (1994) *Legal Issues in European Integration*, 1–37; H. Armstrong, 'Community Regional Policy', in J. Lodge (ed.), *The European Community and the Challenge of the Future* (London: Pinter, 1993), 131–51; G. Marks, 'Structural Policy in the EC', in A. Sbragia (ed.), *Euro-Politics* (Washington DC: Brookings, 1992), 191–224. The European Investment Bank and the Cohesion Fund also operate as redistributive financial mechanisms in the EU: Articles 266–267 (ex 198d–198e) EC. See further D. Allen, 'Cohesion and Structural Adjustment' in H. Wallace and W. Wallace (eds), *Policy-making in the European Union* (Oxford: OUP, 1996), 157–84.

[22] See Commission, *First Cohesion Report* COM(96) 452 final.

[23] Ex Arts 130d and 130e EC.

[24] For details see P. Craig and G. de Búrca, *EU Law: Text, Cases and Materials* (Oxford: OUP, 1998), 129–50.

[25] Such as Art. 251 (ex Art. 189b) EC.   [26] See for instance Art. 137(3) EC.

[27] Art. 14 (ex 7a) EC.

welfare systems. First, however, we turn to other modes of interaction between EU-level and national-level measures in the social security and social welfare fields.

4. EU-LEVEL HARMONISATION AND REGULATORY CO-ORDINATION

The main impact of EU-level regulation on the UK's social security system in terms of harmonisation and regulatory co-ordination has been in two substantive areas: entitlements of migrant workers and sex equality.

A. Sex Equality

In the sex equality field, harmonised EU-level rules give directly effective rights to individuals within the Member States. This is probably the most obvious field in which Community law has affected UK social security law.[28] Much of the litigation in this area has concerned pensions. The relevant provisions of Community law are Directive 79/7/EEC[29] on sex equality in state social security; Article 141 (ex 119) EC on equal pay, in terms of its application to pensions; Directive 86/378/EEC,[30] as amended by Directive 96/97/EC[31] on sex equality in occupational social security schemes; and Directive 92/85/EEC[32] which makes some provision for maternity benefits.[33]

Article 141 (ex 119) EC provides that 'each Member State shall ensure that the principle of equal pay for male and female workers for equal work or work of equal value is applied'. On a literal interpretation, this measure would not seem to apply in the context of social security benefits. However, the concept of 'pay' in this context has been construed generously by the European Court of Justice to include access to occupational pensions,[34] contributions made by employers[35] and employees[36] to occupational pension schemes, and benefits[37] paid to members of occupational

---

[28] J. Ditch and P. Spicker, 'The impact of European law on the development of social security policies in the United Kingdom' (1999) 52 *I.S.S.R.* 75–90, 76.

[29] OJ 1979 L 6/24.   [30] OJ 1986 L 225/40.   [31] OJ 1997 L 46/20.

[32] OJ 1992 L 348/1.

[33] See further C. Hoskyns, *Integrating Gender* (London: Verso, 1996); J. Sohrab, *Sexing the Benefit: Women, Social Security and Financial Independence in EC Sex Equality Law* (Aldershot: Dartmouth, 1996); T. Hervey and J. Shaw, 'Women, Work and Care: Women's Dual Role and Double Burden in EC Sex Equality Law' (1998) 8 *J. of European Social Policy,* 43–63; C. Hoskyns and L. Luckhaus, 'The European Community Directive on Equal Treatment in Social Security' (1989) 17 *Policy and Politics,* 321–55; J. Steiner, 'The principle of equal treatment for men and women in social security' in T. Hervey and D. O'Keeffe (eds), *Sex Equality Law in the European Union* (Chichester: Wiley, 1996), 111–36.

[34] Case 170/84 *Bilka-Kaufhaus v Weber von Hartz* [1986] ECR 1607.

[35] Case 192/85 *Newstead v Department of Transport* [1987] ECR 4753; but see Case C-152/91 *Neath v Hugh Steepner* [1993] ECR I-6935 (noted T. Hervey *C.M.L. Rev.* 31 (1994), 1387–97) and Case C-200/91 *Coloroll Pension Trustees v Russell and others* [1994] ECR I-4389 concerning the use of actuarial tables differentiating between women and men in this context.

[36] C-200/91 *Coloroll Pension Trustees v Russell and others* [1994] ECR I-4389.

[37] Case C-262/88 *Barber v Guardian Royal Exchange* [1990] ECR I-1889.

pension schemes.[38] This provision applies to all employees and beneficiaries of occupational pension schemes in the European Union.

Directive 79/7 has the aim of the progressive implementation of sex equality in state social security schemes. It applies to workers and the self-employed, those who are no longer able to work due to 'illness, accident or involuntary employment', work-seekers, and retired workers.[39] The interruption of employment need not be due to the risk covered by the Directive befalling the worker; for instance, a woman whose work is interrupted by her mother's invalidity falls within the scope of the Directive.[40] The test is whether a person was a member of the working population at the time the risk arose.[41] The Directive applies to statutory social security schemes protecting against the 'classic risks' of sickness, invalidity, old age, accidents at work and occupational diseases, unemployment, and 'social assistance, in so far as it is intended to supplement or replace' those schemes.[42] 'Social assistance' is a Community law concept, denoting elements of social welfare schemes under which entitlement is determined not through membership of, or insurance under, a social security scheme, but, for instance, through means-testing.[43] Social assistance schemes are covered by the Directive only to the extent that they are 'directly and effectively linked' to one of the enumerated risks.[44] Thus, for example in the UK context, sex equality is required by Community law in the provision of family credit[45] (recently replaced in the social security system: see p. 285 below), but not income support;[46] and in NHS prescription charges,[47] but not transport concessions.[48]

That Directive 79/7 is only a step towards the *progressive* implementation of sex equality in state social security is illustrated by the relatively generous exemption provisions it contains. The most significant of these is Article 7 (1)(a), which permits Member States to exclude from its scope 'the determination of pensionable age for the purposes of granting old-age and retirement pensions and the possible consequences thereof for other benefits'. This provision permits derogations for discriminatory measures in benefit schemes which are 'necessarily and objectively linked' to different state pensionable ages.[49] In determining whether the link is necessary and

---

[38] See further E. Whiteford, 'Occupational Pensions and European Law: Clarity at Last?' in T. Hervey and D. O'Keeffe (eds), *Sex Equality Law in the European Union* (Chichester: Wiley, 1996), 21–34; D. Curtin, 'Occupational Pension Schemes and Article 119: beyond the fringe?' (1987) 24 *C.M.L.Rev.* 215–57; D. Curtin, 'Scalping the Community Legislator: Occupational Pensions and *Barber*' (1990) 27 *C.M.L.Rev.* 475–506.

[39] Directive 79/7/EEC, Art. 2.

[40] Case 150/85 *Drake* [1986] ECR 1995.

[41] Case 48/88 *Achterberg-te Riele* [1989] ECR 1905; Case C-31/90 *Johnson v Chief Adjudication Officer* [1991] ECR I-3723; Case C-77/95 *Züchner* [1996] ECR I-5689.

[42] Directive 79/7/EEC, Art. 3. Survivors' benefits and family benefits (save those granted by means of increases to benefits for the listed risks) are excluded by Art. 3 (2).

[43] See below, text accompanying n. 65.

[44] Case C-243/90 *Smithson* [1992] ECR I-467.   [45] Case C-116/94 *Meyers* [1995] ECR I-2131.

[46] Cases C-63 & 64/91 *Jackson and Cresswell* [1992] ECR I-4737.

[47] Case C-137/94 *Richardson* [1995] ECR I-3407.   [48] Case C-228/94 *Atkins* [1996] ECR I-3663.

[49] Case C-328/91 *Thomas* [1993] ECR I-1247.

objective, the European Court of Justice considers the financial equilibrium and the coherence of social security schemes. Thus for instance, in Case C-92/94 *Graham*,[50] concerning invalidity benefit, the Court held that the necessary link was *present*, therefore the UK could lawfully continue to discriminate in the provision of invalidity pensions. The Court's reasoning appears to have been that, as the purpose of invalidity benefit was to replace income from work, the UK might cease to provide that benefit at state pensionable age. By way of contrast, in Case C-137/94 *Richardson*,[51] the Court held that there was *no* necessary link between the UK's rules on free provision of medical prescriptions and state pensionable ages. The removal of the discrimination would produce no consequences for the financial equilibrium of the (non-contributory) scheme, as persons claiming free prescriptions would no longer be liable for national insurance contributions. Therefore, in those circumstances, the UK could not rely on the exclusion in Article 7 (1)(a), but was required to grant free NHS prescriptions to men and women on an equal basis.

The main purpose of the Pregnancy and Maternity Directive 92/85/EEC is to ensure the health and safety at work of pregnant women and women who have recently given birth.[52] However, the Directive contains some provision on maternity leave and maternity benefits. Pregnant workers are to be guaranteed a period of at least fourteen weeks maternity leave,[53] during which time they are to be entitled to either 'maintenance of a payment' or 'an adequate allowance' or both.[54] An allowance is adequate if it is at least equivalent to statutory sick pay.[55] Compliance with the Pregnancy and Maternity Directive required the UK to amend the Employment Rights Act 1996 to include the right to fourteen weeks maternity leave,[56] but the existing provisions on statutory maternity pay already met the (limited) requirements of Community law in terms of maternity benefits. The equal pay provision of Article 141 (ex 119) EC does not apply in the context of a comparison between maternity pay and ordinary pay.[57]

Community sex equality law is one of the few fields in which harmonised EU-level regulatory measures have required significant alteration of national social security laws. The relevant measures of Community law are directly effective, so the interaction between these EU-level norms and provisions of UK law has largely been through private litigation. Such litigation promotes changes in national legislation.

B. Migrant Workers

Interaction between UK law and Community law concerning the rights of migrant workers has been in accordance with both harmonised regulation and regulatory co-

---

[50] [1995] ECR I-2521. [51] [1995] ECR I-3407.
[52] See further C. Barnard, *EC Employment Law* (Chichester: Wiley, 1996), 204–8; N. Burrows and J. Mair, *European Social Law* (Chichester: Wiley, 1996), 159–72.
[53] Directive 92/85/EEC, Art. 8. [54] Directive 92/85/EEC, Art. 11 (2).
[55] Directive 92/85/EEC, Art. 11 (3). [56] Employment Rights Act 1996, ss 71–85.
[57] See Case C-342/93 *Gillespie* [1996] ECR I-475; discussed in C. McGlynn, 'Equality, Maternity and Questions of Pay' (1996) 21 *ELRev.* 327–32.

ordination. Creation of the internal market, one of the central aims of the European Union, requires provisions ensuring mobility of labour. If people are to move around the European Union in order to work, then provision must be made for their protection in the event of the traditional social security risks (illness, invalidity, industrial accidents, unemployment, old age, death, and family needs). Yet responsibility for such protection remains with the Member States, and there is no EU-level social security system. However, if no EU-level provision were made, potential migrant workers might be dissuaded from moving on the grounds that they would lose social security entitlements if they did so. The EU's answer to this problem is the system of regulatory co-ordination of national social security systems, set out in Regulation 1408/71/EEC,[58] as amended,[59] and supporting legislation.[60]

The technical operation of this system is the subject of many detailed rules and numerous interpretative rulings of the European Court of Justice.[61] Broadly, the system established by Regulation 1408/71 is based on four basic over-arching principles. These are the principle of non-discrimination on grounds of nationality; the principle of aggregation or apportionment of benefit rights; the exportability of benefits from Member State to Member State; and the 'single state' rule in terms of affiliation, liability to contribute, and benefit entitlement.[62] The personal scope of the Regulation is governed by Article 2 (1): it extends to employed or self-employed persons, who are citizens of the European Union,[63] or stateless persons or refugees resident in a Member State, and their families[64] and survivors. The concept of 'employed or self-employed' in this context is not a Community law concept, but is defined by reference to affiliation to and insurance under a national social security scheme.

The material scope of the Regulation is governed by Article 4. This draws a broad distinction between national social *security* benefits—which are covered by the Regulation—and 'social and medical *assistance*'—which is not. The traditional social security benefits of incapacity benefits, maternity benefits, old-age benefits, survivors' benefits, benefits in respect of accidents at work and industrial diseases, unemployment benefits, death grants, and family benefits are all covered. The test for whether a benefit constitutes 'social or medical assistance' has been developed by the European Court of Justice. The Court considers whether the benefit accrues as of right, consequent upon a period of employment or affiliation under a social security

---

[58] OJ 1971 L 149/2; OJ Sp Ed 1971 II p 416.

[59] Regulation 1408/71/EEC is amended regularly. Readers are referred to CELEX, the online source of EU legislation, for the latest text.

[60] Regulation 574/72/EEC, OJ 1972 L 74/1.

[61] See for instance L. Luckhaus, 'European Social Security Law' in Ogus, Barendt, and Wikeley (1995), ch. 18; C. Barnard, n. 52 above, 139–57 and the regular reviews of case law on Regulation 1408/71 in the *Common Market Law Review.*

[62] Regulation 1408/71/EEC, Articles 3, 18(1), 38, 45, 64, 67, 72; 10(1), 12(1), and 46(3).

[63] That is, hold the nationality of a Member State of the European Union; Art. 17 (ex 8) EC.

[64] But see Case 94/84 *Deak* [1985] ECR 1873.

scheme (more likely to constitute 'social security'), or whether there is an element of means-testing (more likely to constitute 'social assistance').[65]

The EU-level system of regulatory co-ordination of national social security systems operates not only within the context of national social security laws, but also within the context of relevant provisions of *harmonised* EU-level laws. In particular, the Treaty of Rome in Article 18 (ex 8a) provides that citizens of the EU shall have the right to move and reside freely within the territory of the EU,[66] and Article 39 (ex 48) provides that freedom of movement for workers shall be ensured within the territory of the EU. Such freedom of movement is effected, *inter alia*, by application of the principle of non-discrimination on grounds of nationality.[67]

The provisions on free movement of EU citizens are elaborated in secondary legislation. For instance, the 'residence directives'[68] grant EU citizens a right of residence in Member States other than that of which they are a national, provided that they have sufficient resources to avoid becoming a burden on the social and medical assistance schemes of the host Member State. Particularly relevant for our purposes is the provision in Regulation 1612/68/EEC,[69] Article 7 (2) which applies the principle of non-discrimination in provision of 'social and tax advantages' to migrant (EU citizen) workers and members of their families. Thus migrant workers from other Member States (and their families) may impose burdens on national social welfare systems. Generally, this is not problematic, as workers by definition will also be contributing to such national systems. However, in this context, 'worker' is a concept defined by European Community law, and has been construed broadly by the European Court of Justice.[70] It is not necessary to earn more than is needed to subsist in a Member State in order to be classified as a 'worker' for these purposes. Moreover, the position of work-seekers is one that has exercised the EU legislature and the European Court of Justice alike.[71]

Even this brief introduction serves to illustrate that the interaction between EU-level regulatory co-ordination, harmonisation, and provision made by national legal systems in respect of social security and welfare entitlements is not straightforward. The position of individuals in practice, in terms of their rights under the different systems, may not always be easy to determine. In order to appreciate this interaction in the UK context, a detailed examination of some recent litigation concerning receipt of

---

[65] See, for instance, Case 139/82 *Piscitello v INPS* [1983] ECR 1427.

[66] This is not an absolute right, but is 'subject to the limitations and conditions laid down by this Treaty and by the measures adopted to give it effect'.

[67] Regarded as a 'general principle' of Community law by the European Court of Justice, see for example Case 152/73 *Sotgiu v Deutsche Bundespost* [1974] ECR 153; and given expression in the Treaty in Art. 12 (ex 6) EC.

[68] Directive 90/366/EEC OJ 1990 L 180/30 (replaced by Directive 93/96/EC OJ 1993 L 317/59); Directive 90/365/EEC OJ 1990 L 180/28; and Directive 90/364/EEC OJ 1990 L 180/26.

[69] OJ Sp Ed 1968 II p 475.

[70] Case 53/81 *Levin* [1982] ECR 1035; Case 66/85 *Lawrie-Blum* [1986] ECR 2121; Case 139/85 *Kempf* [1986] ECR 1035; Case 196/87 *Steymann* [1988] ECR 6159; Case C-357/89 *Raulin* [1992] ECR I-1027.

[71] See Regulation 1408/71/EEC, Article 69; Case 316/85 *Lebon* [1987] ECR 2811 and Case C-292/88 *Antonissen* [1992] ECR I-745.

income support by free movers is presented below. This analysis aims to show the ways in which EU-level norms interact with national law in the social security field, and thus illustrates the importance of the EU dimension in UK social security law.

C. Income Support: a Case Study

The stark distinction between social security and social assistance provisions drawn by Regulation 1408/71 became problematic during the 1980s and early 1990s, as Member States' social security and welfare systems altered to deal with changing patterns of employment, and in particular increasing levels of unemployment. For instance, new benefits, which provide supplementary protection against the risks listed in Regulation 1408/71, but are means-tested, such as the UK's income support, were introduced. To respond to these developments, Regulation 1408/71 was amended[72] to include within its scope (see Article 4 (2a)) a new category of benefits: 'special non-contributory benefits', which supplement, substitute for, or provide ancillary cover against the listed risks. However, the rules on these 'special non-contributory benefits' do not fit easily with the established scheme under the Regulation, a point which is explored below in the context of discussion of the application of Community law to UK rules on income support.[73]

The UK Regulations governing entitlement to income support provide that the applicable amount of the benefit is nil where the claimant is a 'person from abroad'.[74] A 'person from abroad' is defined as someone 'not habitually resident in the UK', except in the case of a 'worker' in the terms of Regulation 1612/68/EEC.[75] In practice, habitual residence for these terms was defined as an intention to remain in the UK *plus* at least eight weeks' actual residence. Thus a 'person from abroad' could not claim income support for the first eight weeks of their residence in the UK.[76] The consistency of these rules with Community law was explored by the European Court of Justice in Case C-90/97 *Swaddling v Chief Adjudication Officer.*[77]

---

[72] By Regulation 1247/92/EEC OJ 1992 L 136/1.

[73] The introduction, in 1996, of jobseeker's allowance (JSA) in the UK restricted income support to those who do not have to register their availability for work, as they are assumed to be outside the labour market: see further Chapters 6 and 10. Income-based JSA has partially replaced income support for those who are unemployed in the 'traditional' sense. The analysis below concerning the application of Community law to income support would also apply to income-related JSA, which meets the criteria for a 'special non-contributory benefit' in the sense of Regulation 1408/71.

[74] IS(G) Regs 1987, reg. 21. See further Chapter 6.

[75] Further exceptions are given for workers in terms of Regulation 1251/70/EEC OJ Sp Ed 1970 II p 402 on the right of workers to remain in the host state; for persons with the right to reside under Directive 68/360/EEC OJ Sp Ed 1968 II p 485 on the abolition of restrictions on movement and residence within the Community for EU citizen workers and their families; or Directive 73/148/EEC OJ 1973 L 172/14 on the abolition of such restrictions with regard to establishment and the provision of services; for refugees; and for persons with exceptional leave to remain in the UK.

[76] It appears that the 'habitual residence test' was introduced in response to the perceived problem of 'benefit tourism'. See pp. 198–201 above; J. Ditch and P. Spicker, n. 28 above; M. Adler, 'The habitual residence test: a critical analysis' (1995) 2 *J.S.S.L.* 179–95; R. White, 'Editorial' (1999) 24 *ELRev.* 119–20.

[77] Judgment of 25 February 1999.

Robin Swaddling is a UK national. He worked in France from 1980–8, but paid UK national insurance contributions. In 1988 he worked for six months in the UK; then he held fixed-term jobs in France until 1994. In 1994 he was made redundant when his employer's business failed. In January 1995, Swaddling returned to the UK. He applied for income support, but was refused on the grounds that he did not meet the habitual residence test. He appealed the adjudication officer's decision, and the matter came before the Social Security Commissioner, who sought a preliminary ruling from the European Court of Justice on the interpretation of Article 48 EC in relation to the habitual residence test. Essentially, the national court wished to know whether the habitual residence test was lawful in Community law.

The Advocate General (Saggio) took the view that, although the reference was made in terms of Article 48 EC (a measure of EU-level regulatory harmonisation), the question raised by the national court could not be answered without taking into account the provisions of Regulation 1408/71 (the regulatory co-ordination system set up by Community law). In general, any residence requirement imposed in respect of a benefit falling within the material scope of that Regulation, on a person falling within its personal scope, would breach the non-discrimination principle,[78] as such a rule would be indirectly discriminatory on grounds of nationality, because it is more difficult for a non-national to meet a residence requirement than a national. However, 'special non-contributory benefits' are subject to special rules. If such a benefit is listed by a Member State in Annex IIa of the Regulation, that state may reserve such benefits to those resident within its territory. The Advocate General took the view that, as it is listed in Annex IIa, income support is a 'special non-contributory benefit' in terms of Regulation 1408/71, Article 4 (2a),[79] providing supplementary support in respect of the risk of unemployment. Thus the habitual residence requirement stems not only from national law, but also from Community law. In this context then, the state of 'habitual residence' is a Community law concept, meaning the state to which the person concerned has formed 'a social attachment which is stronger and more stable than any links he may have with other Member States'[80] or the 'place where the person concerned has established the permanent centre of his interests'.[81] By definition, then, the length of stay in a particular Member State could not, in and of itself, be determinative of habitual residence.

The European Court of Justice followed its Advocate General in holding that the application of Regulation 1408/71 to Swaddling's situation should be considered before turning to Article 48 EC.[82] Likewise, the Court held that income support is a 'special non-contributory benefit', in terms of Article 4 (2a) of the Regulation.[83] Such benefits are only for persons resident in the territory of the state granting the

---

[78] See Regulation 1408/71/EEC, Article 10: '… benefits… shall not be subject to any reduction … or withdrawal … by reason of the fact that the recipient resides in the territory of a Member State other than that in which the institution responsible for payment is situated'.
[79] See Case C-20/96 *Snares* [1997] ECR I-6057.   [80] Opinion of the Advocate General, para. 18.
[81] Opinion of the Advocate General, para. 19.   [82] Case C-90/97 *Swaddling*, para. 21.
[83] Ibid., para. 24.

benefit. Residence is a Community law concept, referring to the habitual centre of a person's interests.[84] However, the length of actual residence 'cannot be regarded as an intrinsic element of the concept of residence within the meaning of Article 10a'.[85] The habitual residence test, as applied to income support by the UK authorities, was inconsistent with Regulation 1408/71.[86] Thus the Court concluded that there was no need to consider Article 48 EC.

In reaching their conclusions, both the Advocate General and the Court relied on a comparison between the provisions for special non-contributory benefits and those for unemployment benefits. Dealing with unemployment in the context of the free movement of persons within the EU is a sensitive issue for Member States and the institutions of the European Union alike. On the one hand, a single market in persons would seem to imply that work-seekers, like workers, should be permitted (or even encouraged) to move to a Member State other than that of which they hold nationality, in order to find employment. On the other hand, practical encouragement of such cross-frontier work-seeking would require receipt of unemployment benefits in the state in which the work-seeker is looking for work. However, if the work seeker had not paid contributions to the social security system of that state, then this would impose an unfair burden on the host state. Underlying this problem are the high levels of unemployment across the EU, the increased instability (or 'flexibility' depending upon one's view) of working patterns, and (at least to some extent) the increasing mobility of workers within the EU. No Member State is keen to pay benefits to unemployed persons who are not 'its own'. Nor would a Member State be keen to pay unemployment benefit to someone who is looking for work in another Member State, and thus is unlikely to 'repay' the benefit by working again in the former Member State. But neither is there any enthusiasm for transferring responsibility for unemployed persons to the EU level.

The EU has resolved this by differentiating 'work-seekers' from 'workers' in the terms of its regulatory harmonisation provisions. Work-seekers do fall within the personal scope of Article 48 EC, and thus must be permitted to enter and reside in the host Member State for the purposes of looking for work. However, significantly, the Court has held in Case C-292/88 *Antonissen*[87] that national rules requiring work-seekers to leave if, after a period of six months, they have not found work and cannot show that they have a reasonable prospect of finding work in the near future, are compatible with Community law. Moreover, Regulation 1612/68/EEC, Article 7 (2) does not apply to work-seekers.[88] Therefore, work-seekers cannot claim unemployment benefits in the host state on the grounds that those benefits constitute a 'social advantage' to which they are entitled, in accordance with the principle of non-discrimination, on the same terms as national work-seekers.

In terms of the regulatory co-ordination provisions of Regulation 1408/71/EEC, the EU makes some special provision for unemployment benefits. The general rules

---

[84] Ibid., para. 29.　　[85] Ibid., para. 30.　　[86] Ibid., para. 33.　　[87] [1992] ECR I-745.
[88] Case 316/85 *Lebon* [1987] ECR 2811.

on aggregation apply, in that all periods of employment in any Member State are to be taken into account in determining entitlement to unemployment benefit, and in calculating the amount of benefit due.[89] The general rule is that the Member State responsible for payment ('the competent Member State') of employment benefits is that state in which the individual was last employed. Benefits are paid to the competent Member State by each of the Member States in which the recipient of the benefits has been employed. Unlike other benefits covered by Regulation 1408/71, unemployment benefits are not fully 'exportable' to other Member States. Article 69 of the Regulation provides that an unemployed person who goes to a Member State other than the competent Member State to look for work only retains entitlement to unemployment benefit for three months, after which time the work-seeker must return to the competent Member State, or lose all entitlement to unemployment benefits in that state. Thus in effect Member States may impose residence requirements on recipients of unemployment benefit; a situation which offends the general principles of non-discrimination and exportability of benefits. As the Advocate General in *Swaddling* pointed out, the limitations placed on the concept of non-discrimination by the rules in Articles 67 and 69 of Regulation 1408/71/EEC are justified only by the special nature of unemployment benefits, and 'the fact that unemployment benefits are paid on the basis of the social legislation of [the state of last employment], which must reimburse them to the competent institution of the state to which the unemployed person has gone to find work'.[90] However, it should be pointed out that this 'fact' is a result of the details of the system of regulatory co-ordination in respect of unemployment benefits agreed by the Member States. In reality, it is underpinned by the justification that unemployed persons are to be encouraged to seek work in the state in which they were last employed, not anywhere in the European Union. This is in order to ensure that the competent state, which is paying for the unemployment benefits, stands the greatest chance of gaining any future contributions made by the work-seeker when (or if) he or she finds work. Residence tests fulfil that purpose. This reasoning was applied by analogy in *Swaddling* to the special non-contributory benefit of income support.

In holding in *Swaddling* that Article 48 EC does not apply to the habitual residence test as applied to income support in the UK, but that Regulation 1408/71 does, the Court is leaving it open for the UK to continue to apply residence tests for receipt of such benefits. It is true that such tests cannot lawfully operate on the basis of such crude formulae as 'so many weeks actual residence', but the essence of the principle—that a benefit such as income support can lawfully be reserved for those whose social attachment and the centre of whose interests is located in the state concerned—remains.

However, this conclusion need not necessarily operate to the detriment of recipients of income support. The concept of habitual residence, as applicable to special non-contributory benefits, is a matter of *Community* law: the place of habitual

---

[89] Regulation 1408/71/EEC, Art. 67–68.   [90] Opinion of the Advocate General, para. 23.

residence is the habitual centre of a person's interests. Actual presence at a particular point in time is not necessarily required to meet this habitual residence test. This analysis does not sit comfortably with the 1998 ruling of the Court of Appeal in *Perry v Chief Adjudication Officer.*[91]

Anthony Perry, a UK national, resident in the UK, who suffers from incapacitating disabilities, is normally in receipt of income support. In the winters of 1991, 1992, and 1993, Perry spent time in Portugal, for therapeutic reasons. On each occasion, he was temporarily absent from the UK for periods of time exceeding four weeks. Accordingly, following the provisions of the Social Security Contributions and Benefits Act 1992 and the Income Support (General) Regulations 1987, Perry's income support was withdrawn during those periods of absence from the UK. Perry claimed that this was incompatible with Community law, in particular Regulation 1408/71.

With respect to the 1991 absence, Regulation 1408/71 did not apply, as the amendments bringing 'special non-contributory benefits' such as income support within its scope did not enter into force until 1 June 1992.[92] As regards the 1992 and 1993 absences, both the social security appeal tribunal and the Social Security Commissioner took the view that the amended Regulation 1408/71 did not assist Perry either, as the amended Article 10a permitted the application of a residence requirement for receipt of special non-contributory benefits. Perry appealed this conclusion, on the basis that he was still 'habitually resident' in the UK during the periods of absence. He claimed that at no time did he become 'resident' in Portugal: 'habitual residence' in the sense of Article 10a does not necessarily mean actual presence. Thus he argued that he was not asking to 'export' income support, and so the exclusion in Article 10a did not apply.

The Court of Appeal did not agree, but upheld the conclusions of the lower courts. Mummery LJ held that 'Article 10a does not confer on Mr Perry a positive right to income support claimed by him so as to displace the requirement of presence under the domestic income support system'. He noted that Article 10a provides that special non-contributory benefits are to be granted in accordance with the legislation of the state of residence. Here, that legislation required actual presence in the UK. This, he concluded, was consistent with the co-ordination system of Regulation 1408/71.

In the light of *Swaddling* (decided after *Perry*), this conclusion must be viewed with some caution. The European Court of Justice in *Swaddling* made it clear that 'habitual residence' is to be determined in accordance with Community law. The Community law definition of habitual residence refers to the centre of interests of the claimant. It follows that it does not necessarily mean actual presence in the territory of the state granting the benefit. In particular, a crude (though convenient) indicator such as periods of absence over four weeks seems as unlikely to satisfy the Community law test for habitual residence as the eight-week rule at issue in *Swaddling*.

---

[91] 15 October 1998; SSTRF 97/0866/1.   [92] Regulation 1247/92/EEC OJ 1992 L 136/1.

Moreover, the policy arguments outlined above with respect to the rationale for limiting receipt of unemployment benefits and special non-contributory benefits for the
unemployed such as income support to those satisfying a residence requirement do
not apply in a situation such as Perry's. Perry was in receipt of income support
because of his disability, not through 'ordinary' unemployment. There was no suggestion that he was seeking work in Portugal; rather he was there for therapeutic reasons (presumably because the winter months are rather warmer in the Algarve than
in Lancashire). Thus, were Perry to find work again, this would be in the UK, and so
the UK would gain any further national insurance contributions Perry made. In any
event, at the very least, the conclusion of Mummery LJ, to the effect that Community
law was so clear as to preclude the need for a reference to the European Court of
Justice on the point, cannot be regarded as appropriate.

In the absence of harmonisation in the social security field, each Member State is
competent to govern membership of and entitlements under its national social security scheme. However, the exercise of this competence may not lawfully undermine
the fundamental principles of freedom of movement found in Articles 18, 39, and
42 (ex 8a, 48, and 51) EC. In other words, *national* social security rules may not operate so that migrant workers lose benefits because they exercise their rights to freedom
of movement. Likewise, however, the *EU-level* system of regulatory co-ordination,
may not lawfully inhibit freedom of movement in an unjustified manner. Implicit in
the *Swaddling* ruling is the decision that the inhibitions on freedom of movement
imposed by residence rules in respect of unemployment benefits, and special non-
contributory benefits such as income support, are *justified* in Community law. However,
the application of residence tests is now a matter of Community, not national, law. The
income support litigation illustrates the interactions between UK law, EU-level regulatory co-ordination and EU-level harmonised regulation in the social security field.
The final part of the chapter considers interactions between the EU's internal market
and competition law, and provisions of national social security law.

5. THE INTERNAL MARKET AND 'SOCIAL SOLIDARITY'

As explained above, membership of the European Union requires Member States to
comply with Community internal market and competition law.[93] Internal market and
competition law may be an inhospitable environment for national social welfare entitlements, in particular because it is enforceable by individuals within the Member
States. The 'direct effect' of most Community internal market law means that it can
be used by individuals within the Member States to enforce 'free movement rights',
to ensure that goods and services may move freely around the EU and that the principle of non-discrimination on grounds of nationality applies. Community competition law is also directly effective, and operates to render unlawful anti-competitive

---

[93] Article 10 (ex 5) EC.

behaviour (of firms, but also in some circumstances of public authorities) which has an effect on the internal market.

Currently within the European Union, social security and welfare benefits are increasingly being provided not directly through state agents, but through market providers. In this situation, 'goods and services' in the context of the internal market rules in principle includes welfare goods and services. Individual litigation on provision of national welfare entitlements may have the effect of rendering some national laws and policies inconsistent with Community law, and therefore governments of Member States are precluded from pursuing those policies or maintaining in place those laws. Probably more importantly in practice, the dynamic of the impact and application of internal market or competition law may render some aspects of national welfare policies non-viable. This may arise for instance in terms of the financial drain placed on those policies by requiring non-discriminatory treatment of all citizens of the European Union (EUCs) or migrant EUC workers,[94] or because of the lack of control over supply implied by freedom to receive and provide welfare services across frontiers.[95] Thus, litigation processes may constrain policy options for national governments, not by making policies formally unlawful, but by rendering some options politically undesirable.

These matters are often expressed as social or welfare dumping, or 'the race to the bottom'. They may also be articulated as a threat to the 'European social model'.[96] There is, of course, a multiplicity of social models among the Member States of the EU.[97] A distinctively 'European' model is discernible only at a high level of abstraction. However, this does not mean that the values encapsulated in the phrase the 'European social model' are not worthy of protection. The concern is that Member States may be tempted to lower their levels of social welfare provision, or alter the principles upon which social welfare provision is based, in response (*inter alia*) to the competitive pressures of the internal market on such measures.[98] The chapter now

---

[94] For instance in the provision of educational maintenance grants to students in tertiary education.

[95] For instance if access to health care is limited through restrictive regulation of medical professional qualifications; see below the discussion of Case C-120/95 *Decker* and Case C-158/96 *Kohll*.

[96] See n. 14 above.

[97] See T. Hervey, n. 2 above, 57–61; G. Esping-Andersen, *The Three Worlds of Welfare Capitalism* (Cambridge: Polity, 1990); N. Ginsburg, *Divisions of Welfare* (London: Sage, 1992); A. Cochrane, 'Comparative Approaches to Social Policy' and 'Looking for a European Welfare State' in A. Cochrane and J. Clarke (eds), *Comparing Welfare States: Britain in International Context* (London: Open University Press, 1993), 239–68; R. Gomà, 'The social dimension of the European Union: a new type of welfare system?' (1996) 3 *J. of European Public Policy*, 209–30; M. Rhodes and Y. Mény, 'Europe's Social Contract under Stress' and M. Ferrera 'The Four "Social Europes": Between Universalism and Selectivity' in M. Rhodes and Y. Mény (eds), *The Future of European Welfare: a new social contract* (Basingstoke: Macmillan, 1998), 1–19 and 81–96.

[98] Commentators do not agree over whether the phenomenon of welfare dumping really exists. For an overview, see C. Barnard, n. 52 above, 81–7. See also H. Mosley, n. 7 above; M. Kleinman and D. Piachaud, 'European Social Policy: Conceptions and Choices' (1993) 3 *J. of European Social Policy*, 1–19; S. Deakin, 'Labour Law as Market Regulation' in P. Davies et al. (eds), *European Community Labour Law: Principles and Perspectives* (London: Clarendon, 1996), 63–94. However, this in itself may not be particularly important: what matters is that policy makers and other institutional actors behave as if it might be a reality, and thus

explores, through the recent cases of Case 70/95 *Sodemare*,[99] Case C-67/96 *Albany International et al*,[100] Case C-120/95 *Decker*, and Case C-158/96 *Kohll*,[101] the ways in which internal market law may place pressures on national welfare systems. In these cases, the European Court of Justice appears to be responding explicitly to these problems, through articulation and application of the concept of 'social solidarity', as a modification of the deregulatory thrust of internal market law.

Case 70/95 *Sodemare* concerned the provision of social welfare services of a health-care character in residential homes for the elderly in the region of Lombardy in Italy. The region of Lombardy subsidised through its social welfare and health-care budgets provision of such services by licensed non-profit-making homes. As such non-profit-making homes were almost exclusively Italian, the exclusion of commercially operated homes from receipt of public funds for provision of these health-care benefits was indirectly discriminatory on grounds of nationality. A Luxembourg company and its Italian subsidiaries challenged the national legislation on this basis. Questions were asked by the national court in respect of the impact of Articles 52, 58, and 59 EC[102] on national legislation which hampers the pursuit of business activity of a company exercising its rights of freedom of establishment in Community law, by imposing on that company the condition either that it carries out its activities on a non-economic basis, or that it takes upon itself the burden of services which should be provided at the expense of the public health service.

The Advocate General (Fennelly) was of the view that the Treaty rules on freedom of establishment would apply in such circumstances. Relying on earlier jurisprudence of the Court,[103] the Advocate General set forth as a general proposition of Community law that where sufficient elements of 'social solidarity' were present, measures of national social security law would fall outside the scope of Community internal market law:

. . . the existence of systems of social provision established by Member States on the basis of the principle of solidarity does not constitute, as such, an economic activity, so that any inherent consequent restriction on the free movement of goods, services or persons does not attract the application of Treaty provisions. Social solidarity envisages the inherently uncommercial act of involuntary subsidisation of one social group by another. Rules closely connected with financing such schemes are more likely to escape the reach of the Treaty provisions on establishment and services. Thus, pursuit of social objectives on the basis of solidarity may lead Member States to withdraw all or part of the operations of social security schemes from access by private economic operators.[104]

However, where only limited elements of solidarity were present, such as was the

---

seek to protect 'European' national welfare provision from such regulatory competition within the EU which might place the values implicit in European welfare models in jeopardy.

[99]　[1997] ECR I-3395.

[100]　Not yet decided; Opinion of the Advocate General, 28 January 1999.
[101]　Both of 28 April 1998.　　　[102]　New Articles 43, 48, and 49 EC.
[103]　Case 238/82 *Duphar* [1984] ECR 523 and Case C-159/91 *Poucet and Pistre* [1993] ECR I-637.
[104]　Case 70/95 *Sodemare*, Opinion of the Advocate General, para. 29.

case in *Sodemare*, then Community law would apply.[105] The Court, however, did not follow its Advocate General. Rather than making a distinction between this case and the earlier cases, as the Advocate General had done, the Court simply reasserted the principle, articulated in those cases, that 'Community law does not detract from the powers of the Member States to organise their social security systems'.[106] For the Court, the relevant comparison was between profit-making companies established in Italy and profit-making companies established in other Member States. Here there was no discrimination.

There appears to be a contradiction in these two statements of the Court. Member States may organise their social security systems without the impact of Community law, *but only so long as they do so without the involvement of 'economic operators'*. Thus it follows that if a Member State opts to keep its system of provision sufficiently 'public' to satisfy the Court's definition of 'solidarity', then it will escape the rigours of internal market law. However, a Member State may *not* choose to 'privatise' aspects of its social welfare system without subjecting its providers to competition from other Member States. Therefore, a Member State cannot operate a 'privatised' social welfare policy without taking into account the possibility (or perhaps likelihood) of interaction with non-national providers. This means that in the UK context if, for instance, social security provision is moved onto a more private footing, as suggested in the recent Green Paper on welfare reform,[107] this will require that the 'market' in the UK for social security provision is opened up to competition from providers established in other Member States, and subject to their regulatory controls. In such circumstances, the UK will not be able to maintain regulatory control over all providers of social security benefits or services within its territory. Thus, as much as the Court may assert that 'Community law does not detract from the powers of the Member States to organise their social security systems', Member States cannot be said to maintain complete control over such systems.

Sodemare illustrates the possibility of introduction of competition from providers of social welfare benefits established in *another* Member State. The application of Community competition law in the field of social welfare may raise the possibility of increased competition from other *internal* providers. This is illustrated by Case C-67/96 *Albany International et al*,[108] not yet decided by the Court, concerning the Dutch system of compulsory affiliation to sectoral pension funds. Albany International (and the other litigants) were ordered to pay contributions to sectoral pension funds. They refused, on the grounds *inter alia* that their own supplementary pension scheme was more generous than the sectoral scheme. Albany took the view that the national system of compulsory affiliation breached Community competition law in a number of respects, in particular that it constituted an 'abuse of a dominant position' by the

---

[105] Case C-244/94 *Fédération Française des Sociétés d'Assurance (FFSA)* [1995] ECR I-4013.
[106] Case 70/95 *Sodemare*, para. 27.   [107] Green Paper (1998).
[108] Case C-67/96 *Albany International*; Case C-115–7/97 *Brentjens'*; Case C-219/97 *Drijvende Bokken*. Not yet decided; Opinion of the Advocate General, 28 January 1999.

sectoral pension funds, contrary to Article 86 EC.[109] According to Article 90 (1) EC,[110] public undertakings and 'undertakings to which Member States grant special or exclusive rights' are required to comply with Community competition law. Where such an undertaking is entrusted with the provision of a 'service of general economic interest', those rules apply only in so far as their application does not obstruct the performance of the particular tasks assigned to it.[111]

The Advocate General (Jacobs) rejected the contention made by the Funds, the Commission, and the governments of intervening Member States (Netherlands, France, and Sweden) to the effect that there is a general exception from Community competition law for the social field.[112] The Advocate General found that, within the meaning of the competition law provisions of the Treaty, the sectoral pension funds constitute 'undertakings', carrying out economic activities, irrespective of their social objectives, and the elements of sector-wide solidarity present within them.[113] According to the Advocate General, 'the decisive factor is whether a certain activity is necessarily carried out by public entities or their agents'.[114] Therefore if pension provision is made through redistribution, for instance whereby this generation's working population finances the pensions of the previous generation, this by definition is not being carried out by an 'undertaking'. The concept of generational solidarity implies state activity, not the 'economic' activity of an undertaking. In the pension funds at issue here, there were some elements of 'solidarity', but not enough to deprive the funds of their economic nature.[115]

Having decided that the pension funds were undertakings, the Advocate General turned to the issue of whether there was a breach of Articles 90 (1) and 86 EC.[116] In view of the compulsory nature of affiliation, the pension funds held exclusive rights (in the sense of Article 90 (1)) to collect and administer the contributions. The funds

---

[109] New Article 82 EC. This provides that: 'Any abuse by one or more undertakings of a dominant position within the common market or a substantial part of it shall be prohibited as incompatible with the common market in so far as it may affect trade between Member States.' The text is unchanged by the Treaty of Amsterdam.

[110] New Article 86 EC.

[111] Article 86 (2) (ex 90 (2)) EC. Article 86 (ex 90) provides: '(1) In the case of public undertakings and undertakings to which Member States have granted special or exclusive rights, Member States shall neither enact nor maintain in force any measure contrary to the rules contained in this Treaty, in particular to those rules provided for in Article 12 and Articles 81–89. (2) Undertakings entrusted with the operation of services of general economic interest or having the character of a revenue-producing monopoly shall be subject to the rules contained in this Treaty, in particular to the rules on competition, insofar as the application of such rules does not obstruct the performance, in law or in fact, of the particular tasks assigned to them. The development of trade must not be affected to such an extent as would be contrary to the interests of the Community.'

[112] Case C-6/96 *Albany*, Opinion of the Advocate General, para. 23. See Case C-41/90 *Höfner and Elser* [1991] ECR I-1979; Case C-55/96 *Job Centre* [1997] ECR I-7119; Cases C-159 & 160/91 *Poucet and Pistre* [1993] ECR I-637; Case C-244/94 *Fédération Française des Sociétés d'Assurances (FFSA)* [1995] ECR I-4013.

[113] Case C-6/96 *Albany*, Opinion of the Advocate General, paras 306–48, distinguishing Cases C-159 & 160/91 *Poucet and Pistre* and Cases C-430 & 431/93 *Van Schijndel* [1995] ECR I-4705; and following Case C-244/94 *FFSA*.

[114] Case C-6/96 *Albany*, Opinion of the Advocate General, para. 330.

[115] Ibid., para. 343.   [116] Ibid., paras 349–468.

held the further exclusive right to decide on applications for individual exemptions. In applying Article 90 (1), the Advocate General adopted what he termed the '*Corbeau*-type approach',[117] according to which Article 90 (1) must be read together with Article 90 (2), concerning the permissibility of conferral of exclusive rights on undertakings providing a service of general economic interest. The pension funds did provide a service of general economic interest, that of securing supplementary pension income for a large proportion of the population. In assessing whether the exclusive rights—that is, the compulsory affiliation—are necessary to achieve the objective of providing an adequate level of protection, national courts must assess in detail all relevant economic, financial, and social matters: 'Accordingly, compulsory affiliation as such infringes Articles 90(1) and 86 only where by reason of the Netherlands' regulatory framework the funds are manifestly not in a position to satisfy demand, and where abolishing compulsory affiliation would not obstruct the performance of the services of general interest assigned to the funds'.[118] The funds' exclusive right to decide on individual exemptions,[119] however, was incompatible with Articles 90 (1) and 86 EC.

If the Court follows its Advocate General in *Albany*, then this will confirm that, in principle, social insurance schemes may be subject to Community competition law. Thus, it will be possible for undertakings administering social insurance schemes to 'abuse their dominant position', which would be in contravention of Article 82 (ex 86) EC. Such undertakings would almost certainly be granted 'special or exclusive rights', as otherwise they would not be able to provide the service of universal social insurance, and thus are likely to occupy a dominant position. This is all the more likely if the relevant market is restricted to provision of social insurance of a particular type (for instance, as in *Albany*, retirement pensions) to those working in a particular Member State, or a particular economic sector within a Member State.

These rules may become relevant in the UK, for instance in the provision of pensions. If the UK's current proposals to reform state pension provision to promote occupational, personal, and in particular the new 'stakeholder' pensions[120] provided by private pension funds go ahead,[121] the principles illustrated by *Albany* would apply. Provision of pensions in the UK would be subject not only to Community internal market law, thus opening up the market to 'non-UK' providers, as noted above in the discussion on *Sodemare*, but also to Community competition law which affects the position of providers even without any cross-border elements being present. One

[117] Following Case C-320/91 *Corbeau* [1993] ECR I-2533, a case concerning postal services—a subject-matter not in the social security field—in which the Court held that the provision of special (postal) services could be lawfully prohibited only where the existence of those special (postal) service providers would compromise the economic basis and general equilibrium of the general (postal) service.

[118] Case C-6/96 *Albany*, Opinion of the Advocate General, para. 440.

[119] Subject only to marginal judicial review.

[120] These are discussed by Neville Harris at pp. 182–4 above. Promotion of such pensions would be by means of rebates as incentives: see the Green Paper DSS, *A New Contract for Welfare: Partnership in Pensions* Cm 4179 (London: Stationery Office, 1998).

[121] See further N. Harris and N. Wikeley, 'Editorial' (1998) 6 *J.S.S.L.* 1–3.

potential effect of the application of Community competition law in such a case may be an increased risk of 'cream-skimming' activities in the UK pensions market. Private pensions providers must have a sufficient incentive to make a profit. Notwithstanding the possibility of profit-making through increased efficiency, there must be at least a possibility that such providers will seek to enter only the more lucrative parts of the pensions market, for instance by restricting access to lower risk groups. The UK may impose regulatory standards on providers of 'stakeholder' pensions, in order to counteract such behaviour. But these regulatory standards will be subject to Community competition law. 'Special' pension provision (in the sense of *Corbeau*) may be restricted only to the extent that it would compromise the economic basis and equilibrium of the general service.

In addition to the *Sodemare* situation of cross-border provision of social welfare by providers established in another Member State, Community internal market law may also have an effect on cross-border *receipt* of social welfare goods or services by individuals. This is illustrated by Case C-120/95 *Decker v Caisse de Maladie des Employés Privés* and Case C-158/96 *Kohll v Union des Caisses de Maladie*, involving requests to the Luxembourg social security funds for reimbursement for medical goods or treatment. In *Decker*, the issue concerned a Luxembourg national who bought, on a prescription given by an ophthalmologist established in Luxembourg, a pair of prescription spectacles from an optician established in Belgium. According to national law, treatment abroad would be reimbursed by the social security fund only where prior authorisation had been granted. That was not the case in Decker's circumstances, and so authorisation was refused. Decker challenged the refusal on the grounds that it breached Article 30 EC,[122] in that it constituted a hindrance to the free movement of goods within the internal market. The national court took the view that this case fell within Regulation 1408/71/EEC, not Article 30. Article 22 of Regulation 1408/71 provides that *authorised* individuals may go to another Member State to receive medical treatment. It does not impose any duty on a Member State to grant authorisation to receive medical treatment, at the expense of the responsible Member State's public health funds, in another Member State, except in the unusual situation in which the treatment sought is not available in the responsible Member State.[123]

The Court repeated its established formula that 'according to settled case law, Community law does not detract from the powers of the Member States to organise their social security systems', citing *Sodemare*.[124] However, the Court went on to note that 'the Member States must nevertheless comply with Community law when exer-

---

[122] New Article 28 EC.

[123] See Case 117/77 *Pierek No 1* [1978] ECR 825 and Case 182/78 *Pierek No 2* [1979] ECR 1977. The responsible Member State is normally the state of residence of the person in receipt of the social security benefit. See further A. P. Van der Mei, 'Cross-border access to Medical Care within the EU', (1998) 5 *Maastricht J. of European and Comparative Law*, 277–97; T. Hervey, 'Buy Baby: The European Union and the Regulation of Human Reproduction' (1998) 18 *O.J.L.S.* 207–33, 215–16.

[124] Case C-120/95 *Decker*, para. 21.

cising those powers'.[125] The Court found that the fact that the national rules at issue fell within Regulation 1408/71 did not exclude the application of Article 30.[126] This is in stark contrast to *Sodemare* where the rules at issue were found to be outside the scope of internal market law. Therefore, the Court had little difficulty in finding that the rules of the Luxembourg social security scheme, by requiring a prior authorisation to purchase spectacles from an optician established outside Luxembourg, but no prior authorisation to purchase spectacles from an optician established in Luxembourg, constituted a barrier to the free movement of goods as the national rules are liable to curb the import of spectacles assembled in other Member States.[127] Moreover, with regard to Luxembourg's submission that the national rules were justified by the need to control health expenditure—an argument based on the 'social solidarity' concept—the Court accepted that as spectacles were reimbursed only at a flat rate, the financial burden on the social security funds was the same as it would have been had the spectacles been bought in Luxembourg. In general, the risk of seriously undermining the financial balance of a national social security system could constitute a justification, but here that risk was not present.[128] The Court therefore found that the national rules requiring prior authorisation breached Articles 30 and 36 EC.

In *Kohll*, decided on the same day, the Court was faced with a very similar issue, only this time concerned with receipt of services. Kohll (a Luxembourg national) challenged the refusal of authorisation for his daughter to receive dental treatment in Trier, Germany. Kohll's doctor recommended treatment by an orthodontist established there, but the social security medical supervisors refused to authorise payment for the treatment from the social security fund. Only one orthodontist established in Luxembourg would have been able to give the treatment, thus the daughter would have had to wait much longer if she were to receive treatment there, rather than in Germany.

The text of the judgment in *Kohll* is very similar to that in *Decker*. The Court held that the 'special nature of certain services does not remove them from the ambit of the fundamental principle of freedom of movement'.[129] Treatment was to be provided for remuneration by an orthodontist, established in another Member State 'outside any hospital [i.e. public] infrastructure'.[130] Thus the application of Articles 59 and 60 EC[131] on provision of services was not excluded in this case. Luxembourg again raised as justification the need to control health expenditure. The Court accepted the argument of Mr Kohll, that he was asking for reimbursement only at the Luxembourg rate, and so application of the free movement rules presented no threat to the financial stability of the social security scheme.[132] Justification was not established.

---

[125] Ibid., para. 23.   [126] Ibid., para. 25.
[127] Ibid., para. 36, following Case 8/74 *Dassonville* [1974] ECR 837.
[128] Ibid., paras 39–40.   [129] Case C-158/96 *Kohll*, para. 20.   [130] Ibid., para. 29.
[131] New Articles 49 and 50 EC.   [132] Case C-158/96 *Kohll*, para. 37.

The *Decker* and *Kohll* cases establish that, provided that no direct threat is posed to the financial stability of the social security funds, individuals may receive health or welfare benefits from providers in another Member State, and require that their national social security funds meet the cost, at least at the rate at which they would be reimbursed if the benefit were received in the home Member State. Of course, this principle applies only in the case of benefits or social services provided through the mechanism of cash benefits to be spent in the market of social service providers. The principle would not apply where, as in the case of most UK NHS services, a Member State makes provision through publicly funded services, and health or welfare benefits are free at the point of receipt.

Two distinct pressures on national health systems may arise from the rulings. Difficulties experienced by those Member States whose nationals go elsewhere to receive medical treatment or purchase medical goods[133] are unlikely to affect a Member State such as the UK, where health services are not, in the main, financed through a mechanism of cash benefits. However, the UK might find itself becoming a 'host state', to which patients go to receive medical goods or services, especially in areas such as dental treatment where professionals have both NHS and privately funded patients. Such host states may experience an unpredictable influx of patients. This may have an impact on national health-care provision for nationals, for instance longer waiting lists. Nothing in the *Decker* or *Kohll* judgments appears to provide a mechanism by which such host states may protect the stability of their health service systems, as they may not lawfully refuse treatment to non-nationals as to do so would be discriminatory, contrary to Articles 49 (ex 59) and 12 (ex 6) EC. Moreover, a Member State that provides a higher standard of service, better value for money, or a greater choice for medical 'consumers' is likely to attract more free movers to receive these services. Perhaps, for instance, Decker wanted to go to Belgium to purchase spectacles because the choice of frames and lenses was greater there. Or perhaps the amount of reimbursement would purchase a higher quality of spectacles on the Belgian market than in Luxembourg. The high reputation of the British NHS and of medical professionals in the UK may attract free movers seeking treatment here. As a worst case scenario, if such pressures reached extreme levels, there might be a temptation on the part of the UK authorities to reduce the quality of service provided, in order to discourage such 'medical tourism'.

An examination of the potential effects of the principles established in these 'social solidarity' cases illustrates that the application of Community internal market and competition law, through individual litigation, may have not insignificant effects on the organisation, financing, and delivery of social welfare in the Member States of the EU. The examples outlined above on possible pressures on the UK's social welfare system are illustrative only; other examples could be envisaged.[134] The Court's mantra to the effect that 'according to settled case law, Community law does

---

[133] In particular, loss of control over supply as a cost containment measure.
[134] For instance, the possibility of a privatised industrial injuries benefit scheme, discussed in Chapter 15.

not detract from the powers of the Member States to organise their social security systems' does not hold true.

However, the deregulatory thrust of the application of internal market and competition law to welfare provision in the Member States is not absolute. It at least appears to be held in check by the application by the European Court of Justice of the concept of 'social solidarity'. Social solidarity may in effect *justify* measures of national social welfare systems which *prima facie* breach Community law. Social solidarity thus preserves at least some elements of national regulatory autonomy in the social welfare field. However, the question of justification through social solidarity (and indeed the concept itself) are now matters of *Community*, not national, law.

6. CONCLUSION

The aim of this chapter was to outline the importance of the European Union dimension in the context of social security provision in the UK. In some areas, notably rights of migrant workers and sex equality, the interaction of EU-level regulatory norms with UK social security provision is relatively well known. Community law on free movement of persons and sex equality has had a fairly significant impact on some aspects of UK social security law. However, though the effect of Community law is without doubt crucial for those whose benefit entitlements in the UK are improved by the application of such EU-level norms, these areas remain relatively small corners of the totality of social welfare provision in the UK. Much of the UK's social security and welfare regime—an area of national competence—has remained untouched by Community law.

However, an appreciation of the interactions between EU and national regulation in the social welfare field is incomplete without consideration of the potential impact of Community internal market and competition law on national social security systems. If cases such as *Sodemare*, *Albany*, *Decker*, and *Kohll* continue to come before national courts and the European Court of Justice, Community internal market and competition law look set to exert an increasing influence over national social welfare regimes in the Member States more generally. Such an impact is only possible where social security or welfare is provided in some way through 'market' mechanisms, with the involvement of market providers. The UK, along with other Member States,[135] is showing an increasing interest in such mechanisms.

There is no suggestion that the European Union is simply promoting a model in which social security and welfare is left entirely (or even largely) to a deregulated

---

[135] M. Rhodes and Y. Mény, n. 97 above; V. George, 'Political Ideology, Globalisation and Welfare Futures in Europe' (1998) 27 *J. of Social Policy*, 17–36; V. George, 'The Future of the Welfare State' and P. Taylor-Gooby, 'The Response of Government: Fragile Convergence?' in V. George and P. Taylor-Gooby (eds), *European Welfare Policy: Squaring the Welfare Circle* (Basingstoke: Macmillan, 1996), 1–30 and 199–218; P. Taylor-Gooby, 'Paying for Welfare: The View from Europe' (1996) 67 *Pol.Q.* 116–26; G. Esping-Andersen, *Welfare States in Transition: National Adaptations in Global Economies* (London: Sage, 1996).

market. On the contrary, the articulation by the EU institutions of the elements of the 'European social model' seems to reflect a desire, among other things, to preserve what are perceived as 'European' values of universal social solidarity. Social solidarity in this context appears to be concerned with (cross-generational or cross-class) subsidisation, on a 'not-for-profit' basis, through public, or at least highly regulated, bodies. While there may be some problems with the current conception of social solidarity,[136] its underlying function appears to be to protect national regulatory autonomy in the social security and welfare field. However, this is of course only to the extent to which such national regulatory autonomy does not interfere disproportionately with the functioning of the internal market. Thus the European Union's conception of 'social solidarity' looks set to become the means through which the balancing of 'social' and 'economic' goals is effected across the European Union's unique system of governance.

---

[136] For instance, it does not seem to take account of voluntary sector welfare provision.

Part 4

Specific Issues

9

The Family, Gender, and Social Security

GILLIAN DOUGLAS

1. INTRODUCTION

The social security system since the Beveridge Plan[1] has shown ambivalence and uncertainty in its treatment of the family and of women and children. As Ogus, Barendt, and Wikeley comment, 'family provision has developed on the periphery of the mainstream social security schemes'.[2] This stems from underlying assumptions about the role of women and the place of the family within the social structure. The keys to these assumptions are the patriarchal ideology of the traditional family and the liberal creation of a private sphere—the family—within which women and children are confined.

This chapter outlines these assumptions and illustrates their influence upon the development of the social security system from Beveridge to the New Labour proposals of the late 1990s. It will be seen that the search to 'fit' women and children into the system has required consideration of whether financial responsibility for them should rest with (a) the family and especially the male breadwinner in that family; (b) the state; or (c) women themselves.

2. THE INSURANCE PRINCIPLE AND ITS PROBLEMS FOR WOMEN AND CHILDREN

The underpinning principle of the social security system since Beveridge has been that of paying insurance premiums, through national insurance contributions made while in paid work or self-employment, against certain 'contingencies' which prevent a person from working.[3] Thus, unemployment or sickness interrupt earning; disability or old age make working difficult or impossible.

A. Children

Children, of course, are not expected to engage in paid work and hence cannot make insurance contributions themselves. Ways must therefore be found either to build

---

[1] Beveridge Report (1942). See further Chapter 4 by Neville Harris.

[2] Ogus, Barendt, and Wikeley (1995), 427.

[3] The main feature of the Beveridge plan was 'a scheme of social insurance against interruption and destruction of earning power and for special expenditure arising out of birth, marriage and death': n. 1 above at para. 17. Of course, national insurance is only another form of taxation—but the ideology is of insurance. See further Chapter 6.

components within an insured person's benefits to cover the needs of any children for whom they are responsible or for the state to assume the responsibility. Beveridge proposed a combination of these approaches. He considered that, in principle, the responsibility for supporting children should be shared between their parents and the community.[4] However, he recognised that wages are based on the rate for the job, not the size of a person's family. To ensure that a family has enough to live on, and that the family was not better off when the father was out of work and claiming benefits than when he was in work but on an inadequate wage, it was therefore necessary to pay allowances in respect of the children, to supplement the father's earnings.[5] Since the allowance would be paid regardless of earnings or financial circumstances, it should come, not from the National Insurance fund, but out of the Exchequer through general taxation.[6] To reflect the principle that family and community share the burden, no allowance would be paid in respect of the first child—which might also have the effect of encouraging larger families, an objective of importance to Beveridge.

B. Women

The needs of women—that is, married women and mothers—have proved much more problematic for the system. The Beveridge Report, reflecting no doubt the views of its time, and also articulating a clear pro-natalist policy, envisaged that *married women*, at least, would generally not be engaged in paid work. For Beveridge, 'maternity is the principal object of marriage'.[7] The 'fact' was that 'the great majority of married women must be regarded as occupied on work which is vital though unpaid, without which their husbands could not do their paid work and without which the nation could not continue.'[8] Furthermore, he was anxious that the declining birth rate in the UK should be addressed: 'In the next thirty years housewives and mothers have vital work to do in ensuring the adequate continuance of the British race and of British ideals in the world.'[9]

The role of married women (and most women did marry, though the issue of separated, divorced, and single mothers raises separate problems which have come to dominate the debate on social security and the family, as is discussed below) was therefore clear. They were expected to be at home, having as many children as possible, and enabling their husbands, as heads of the household, to go out to work. They were thus clearly to be placed within the private sphere, first, because by not engaging in paid work they were not entering the public sphere of the market, and secondly, because they would be at home making and maintaining a family life for their husbands and children. If such women were not going to be in paid employ-

---

[4] N. 1 above at para. 417.
[5] A more direct subsidy of low earnings was later introduced, through family income supplement and then family credit, discussed below.
[6] Beveridge Report (1942) at para. 415.   [7] Ibid., para. 109.   [8] Ibid., para. 107.
[9] Ibid., para. 117.

ment, then they, like children, could not be expected (and indeed, as explained below, were to be positively discouraged) to make contributions to insure against future loss of employment. Once again, therefore, provision would have to be made for them in some other way.

Beveridge's answer was to include them within the husband's insured risks, treating the couple as a 'team, each of whose partners is equally essential'.[10] If the husband became unemployed, the presence of the wife would be recognised through the rate of benefit paid to him. When the husband retired, he and his wife would receive a married couple's pension based on his contributions. If the husband died, some provision would be made, through widow's pension, etc, for the wife, again thanks to the contributions he would have made during his lifetime.

Married women would be exempt from making contributions to the Fund. It was assumed that if they did work, this would be a matter of choice, because married women's earnings were regarded as supplementary to those of the husband, being intended to enhance the family standard of living, or to give the wife 'pin money' rather than to meet subsistence.[11] Even if they worked, they would therefore be able to choose to be exempt from paying national insurance contributions. Indeed, there was no point in paying the full rate for a single man or woman, because a married woman, by virtue of her status, would not be entitled to claim full amounts of benefit if she *did* become unemployed, etc. The reasoning behind this approach was that married women make a trade-off on marriage: they acquire a new economic and social status with risks and rights different from those of the unmarried. For example, a married woman has a right to maintenance from her husband[12] but runs the risks of separation and widowhood.[13] Married women's essential role as *mothers* would be recognised (and incentivised) by paying them a maternity grant, and, if they had been working prior to the birth, maternity benefit at a rate *higher* than the benefit paid to single men and women for unemployment or disability. This would encourage them to give up work, in good time, to have the baby.[14] However, the trade-off required that their accrued benefits from past contributions would be lost on marriage, and if they did carry on working but became unemployed or disabled, they would receive a lower rate than the single person's rate—to offset the higher rate they would receive on maternity.[15]

Such a regime was predicated on certain assumptions which were dubious.[16] First, it assumed that married women's paid work is only intended as a supplement to that of the husband whereas, certainly now, and probably then, it is needed to provide

---

[10] At para. 107.   [11] At para. 108.

[12] At common law, this was not reciprocal, but by statute each spouse is now required to support the other: Matrimonial Causes Act 1973 s. 27; Domestic Proceedings and Magistrates' Courts Act 1978 s. 1; SSAA 1992 ss 78(6) and 105(3) discussed further below.

[13] Beveridge Report (1942), at para. 107.   [14] At para. 19.   [15] At para. 109.

[16] See the discussion by M. Finer and O. McGregor, 'The History of the Obligation to Maintain', Appendix 5 in M. Finer, *Report of the Committee on One Parent Families* Cmnd 5629 (London: HMSO, 1974), 2, paras 102–3; M. Hill, *Social Security Policy in Britain* (Aldershot, Edward Elgar, 1990) at 32–6 and 153–7.

adequate support for a family.[17] Secondly, it assumed that all members of a family share in the standard of living enjoyed by the breadwinner, whereas research now shows that 'the patriarchal structuring of conjugal relationships means that within the family or household men are . . . likely to exercise a greater command over those resources'.[18] In other words, men expect and consume the larger share of the resources they bring into the family, and women expect and are prepared to go without rather than let their husbands or children suffer deprivation. Thirdly, and most importantly, it assumed that marriages would generally endure. Although Beveridge did contemplate the possibility of separation and divorce, his proposals for these were unconvincing in tone. He argued that, since one cannot insure against events which occur through one's own fault or with consent, husbands could not insure against the risk of divorce through their contributions, and wives who were at fault or consented to divorce should not receive benefits either. But he recognised that 'innocent' wives (assuming that blame for the marital breakdown could be correctly attributed)[19] might be placed in a difficult predicament, and proposed for them a temporary separation benefit, modelled upon widow's benefit and intended, like that, to last only for thirteen weeks (ironically, the same period as maternity benefit) as a period in which they could adjust to finding employment.[20] The payments would be recoverable from the husband. If the separated wife or divorcee had children, she would receive, like a widow, a guardian's allowance for their care, but otherwise she, like a widow,[21] was expected to go out to work. This, in turn, assumes that work can be found even where the woman has, as Beveridge expected of her, been out of the labour market raising her family, and ignores the pay differentials (legitimate at the time of the Beveridge Report) between men and women.

In any case, no such 'separation benefit' was introduced[22] and, as Spicker has commented, the real reason behind the uncertainty regarding divorce (and even more so the position of unmarried mothers) was moral disapproval.[23]

For those, including deserted married women or single mothers who found themselves unable to work and uninsured, the safety net of national assistance would be available, as a means-tested benefit, but Beveridge envisaged that only a limited number of such cases would exist.[24] National assistance was intended to provide enough,

---

[17] See E. Ferri and K. Smith, *Parenting in the 1990s* (London: Family Policy Studies Centre, 1997), ch. 2, especially at 16.

[18] J. Millar and C. Glendinning, 'Gender and Poverty' (1989) 18 *J. of Social Policy*, 363–81 at 366.

[19] Beveridge Report (1942) at para. 347.

[20] The concept is similar to 'rehabilitative' fixed-term maintenance on divorce, though most courts would regard 13 weeks as somewhat short! See Matrimonial Causes Act 1973, s. 25A(2), and note the Family Law (Scotland) Act 1985, s. 9(1)(d), which provides for a usual maximum of 3 years' rehabilitative maintenance.

[21] The husband could always take out life assurance if he wanted to provide permanently for the widow: Beveridge Report (1942), para. 156.

[22] Finer and McGregor, n. 16 above, paras 109–11.

[23] P. Spicker, *Poverty and Social Security: Concepts and Principles* (London: Routledge, 1993) at 155; for the problem of unmarried mothers, see Beveridge Report (1942) at para. 261.

[24] At para. 19(x). See Chapter 4 by Neville Harris.

but no more, for subsistence, since otherwise there would be no gain from paying insurance contributions.[25]

C. After Beveridge: Changes in Family and Social Structure

Beveridge's assumptions both as to the future of the economy and the stability of the family structure, proved false. In particular, as far as women are concerned, he failed to foresee the growth of women's employment, especially in part-time, low-paid, and insecure jobs, which cause particular problems so far as building up an adequate contributions record is concerned. He also did not foresee the increasingly high rates of breakdown of marriage, cohabitation, and births outside wedlock. As Kiernan, Land, and Lewis have documented,[26] it was only in the 1970s and thereafter that lone motherhood became perceived as a social 'problem'. During this time, there was a seemingly ever-increasing number of lone mothers, who were also increasingly likely to claim means-tested benefits[27] and to remain dependent upon them for long periods. Families headed by a lone mother increased from 7.5 per cent of all families with dependent children in 1971, to 21 per cent by 1994. The majority of these were separated or divorced but a striking feature of the 1980s and 1990s was the increase in never-married mothers, from 1.2 per cent of heads of families in 1971 to 8 per cent by 1994. The number of children living in households dependent upon means-tested benefits rose from one in ten to one in three between 1979 and 1993. By that time, some one and three-quarter million children were in families dependent upon income support.[28]

Beveridge's assumption that married women, as mothers, and their children, would be adequately covered by the earnings, or benefits, of the husband/father of the family, was clearly falsified by such numbers. Further, their lack of recourse to other forms of support meant that they were likely to be permanently dependent upon what had been intended only as a safety-net subsistence allowance to last for a short period while earnings were interrupted. Changes therefore needed to be made to cater for this situation. There are three options open: (1) accept that the burden of support must fall upon the state, perhaps as part of its responsibility to children as the next generation of citizens, whose upbringing needs to be supported as far as possible; (2) try to avoid, or recover, as much state expenditure as possible by fixing liability to support on the husband/father; (3) encourage, or even compel, lone mothers to take paid work and support themselves and their families. We can see all three options in the present social security system. The following discussion explains this and also traces, briefly, the historical background.

---

[25] Ibid., para. 369.
[26] K. Kiernan, H. Land, and J. Lewis, *Lone Motherhood in Twentieth-Century Britain* (Oxford: Oxford University Press, 1998). See also H. Land and J. Lewis, *The Emergence of Lone Motherhood as a Problem in Late Twentieth Century Britain*, Discussion Paper WSP/134 (London: Toyota Centre, LSE, 1997).
[27] First as 'national assistance' then supplementary benefit and now income support; see further below.
[28] Land and Lewis, n. 26 above at Tables 1 and 17.

3. RELIANCE UPON THE STATE

A. Child Benefit

We have seen that 'family allowances' were introduced in 1945 as one of the underlying 'assumptions' of Beveridge's scheme. The idea came originally from Eleanor
Rathbone, who argued that society has an interest in ensuring that its children are
adequately clothed and fed.[29] Her efforts resulted not only in the passage of the
Family Allowances Act 1945, but also in an amendment requiring payment of the
allowance to be made to the mother rather than the male head of the household.[30]
However, Beveridge was firm that the financial burden of raising children is one to
be shared between state and parents—not cast entirely onto the state. This reasoning reflects the liberal view of the family as being in the private sphere—the decision
to have children is a personal and private one (especially now that contraception is
fully accepted in society—a position not true at the time Beveridge was reporting).
This ideological stance has allowed successive governments to pay limited attention
to the size or effectiveness of family allowances. Thus, they were not uprated in line
with inflation.[31] They also operated alongside child tax allowances, which were paid
in respect of the first child as well as subsequent children, and which, of course,
reduced the main breadwinner's (i.e. usually the father's) tax liability rather than put
cash into the hands of the mother. Concern that the benefit of the tax allowance was
not filtering through to the mothers and children it was intended to support, and that
the tax allowance did nothing for children of the lowest wage earners, since these did
not pay tax and therefore could not claim the allowance, led to moves to phase out
the tax allowance and raise the amount of benefit paid to the main carer of the
child—the mother. The result was the Child Benefit Act 1975.

Child benefit,[32] like its forerunner, is a flat-rate non-contributory benefit, but now
paid in respect of each child, and a higher amount is paid for the first child, to reflect
added expenses accrued in providing for the first child in a family (such as baby
equipment, clothes, etc). However, the validity of this differential is open to question. It has been calculated that child benefit rates assume that a second or subsequent child in a family costs 19 per cent less than the first but that, in fact, the
difference is no more than 10 per cent.[33] It is payable to a 'person who is responsible for one or more children' in any given week.[34] A person is treated as responsible

---

[29] E. Rathbone, *The Disinherited Family* (London: Allen and Unwin, 1924).

[30] Ogus, Barendt, and Wikelely (1995), at 429.

[31] Townsend reported that their value increased by 25% over a period in which average money incomes
increased by more than 50%: cited by Hill, n. 16 above, at 41.

[32] An additional benefit, guardian's allowance, is payable where a person is looking after a child whose
parents are dead, or one is dead and the other missing or in prison. For details, see Ogus, Barendt, and
Wikeley (1995), 287–92.

[33] See S. Middleton, K. Ashworth, and I. Braithwaite, *Small Fortunes: Spending on Children, Childhood Poverty
and Parental Sacrifice* (York: Joseph Rowntree Foundation, 1997), 40; and see also the criticisms by Ogus,
Barendt, and Wikeley (1995), at 432–3.

[34] SSCBA 1992, s. 141.

for a child if she has the child living with her, or is contributing to the cost of providing for the child at a rate not less than the weekly child benefit payable for that child. Where care of a child is shared between parents—for example, where there is a shared residence order—they may agree between themselves who is to receive the benefit, with the Secretary of State deciding in default. The carer need not be a parent, or even a relative of the child, so long as she fulfils the responsibility test. Where there are competing claims, the person having the child living with her takes priority over a person contributing to the child's financial support; a parent takes priority over a non-parent; and a wife or mother takes priority over a husband or unmarried father where they reside together.[35] Section 142 defines a child in respect of whom the benefit may be paid as a person under the age of sixteen, or under the age of nineteen and receiving full-time non-advanced education either in a recognised educational establishment or elsewhere, or a person under eighteen who has recently ceased full-time education, and is in what is called the 'extension period' (i.e. effectively in transition from education to work or training).[36]

When child benefit was introduced, an additional amount was given to lone parents. This 'one-parent benefit', according to Ogus, Barendt, and Wikeley,[37] was probably a response to the recommendation of the Finer Committee on One Parent Families[38] that a guaranteed maintenance allowance be introduced for lone parents with young children. The Finer Committee[39] examined the question whether lone-parent families have greater or lesser expenses than two-parent families. On the one hand, there is only one adult to support, but on the other, the Committee received evidence that lone parents may face higher housing costs because of their difficulties in finding suitable accommodation, and there might be additional costs incurred because of the lack of another adult to take on certain tasks, such as DIY or housekeeping, which must therefore be paid for. Their examples were as gender-stereotyped as Beveridge had been thirty years earlier; if there is no man in the house, the woman incurs extra expense in decorating and repairs; if no woman, how are sewing, cooking, ironing to be accomplished? Such arguments would carry limited weight today. However, Finer was on firmer ground perhaps, in noting that childcare costs—not simply during a parent's working hours, but at other times when the parent needs to leave the children—may be greater. The Committee concluded that:

there are many families where the lone parent is forced into substantial extra expenses . . . It is not infrequent for this expenditure to equal or even exceed the saving to the household of not maintaining the other parent.[40]

When the 'problem' of the lone mother, especially the unmarried mother, became demonised in the 1990s (see pp. 53–5 above), and caught up in the new Right's moral crusade to save the traditional family, an obvious target was the payment of an extra

---

[35] Sched. 10 para. 5.
[36] Child Benefit (General) Regulations 1976 (S.I. 1976 No. 965), reg. 7D.
[37] Ogus, Barendt, and Wikeley (1995), at 449.   [38] N. 16 above (discussed further below).
[39] At paras 5.40–5.48.   [40] At para. 5.48.

benefit, at the cost of the taxpayer, to 'subsidise' the lifestyle choice of lone parenthood. The Conservative Government therefore replaced the separate 'one-parent benefit' with a 'lone-parent rate' for the eldest child, which was in fact equivalent in amount to the combination of the eldest child rate and the former additional benefit.[41] The aim was to allow the higher rate for lone parents to wither away through inflation, and to bar new claimants from receiving it. The incoming Labour Government confirmed this stance in its Green Paper, *New Ambitions for Our Country: A New Contract for Welfare*:[42]

We believe that additional support should be provided for children in poorer families on the basis of the identifiable needs of children, not on whether there happens to be one parent or two. So there is no case for a one-parent benefit, and the Government will not return to that approach.

The Social Security Act 1998, section 72, gave power to revoke the relevant regulations prescribing a higher rate of child benefit in the case of a lone parent, and after 5 July 1998, no lone parents can receive the lone-parent rate unless they were receiving it already, or were lone parents receiving income support or income-based jobseeker's allowance before that date and have started work.[43] To compensate for the loss, it was proposed to increase child benefit for all children under age eleven by £2.50 per week (but only from April 1999) and to implement 'working families tax credit' (discussed below, at pp. 285–6) from October 1999. The increase in benefit for younger children would have gone part way to meeting the criticisms, noted above, of the lack of recognition of the costs of younger and subsequent children in the current benefit system. As it happened, there was instead an increase across the board of £2.95 per week for the oldest or eldest child, in April 1999.

The rates of child benefit from this date are as follows:

lone-parent rate	£17.10
standard rate, only/eldest child	£14.40
standard rate, other child(ren)	£ 9.60

It has been estimated[44] that child benefit meets about one-fifth of average spending on children (21 per cent for oldest children and 19 per cent for others). This can be regarded, of course, as woefully inadequate—but as Middleton et al. point out, any withdrawal or further erosion of the value of the benefit would be highly detrimental to the financial circumstances of children, especially in poor families. The existence of child benefit is symbolically important in asserting the state's concern

---

[41] See the discussion by Kiernan, Land, and Lewis, n. 26 above, ch. 6, and the Child Benefit and Social Security (Fixing and Adjustment of Rates) Regulations 1976 (S.I. 1976 No. 1277), reg. 2(1), as amended by the Child Benefit, Child Support and Social Security (Miscellaneous Amendments) Regulations 1996 (S.I. 1996 No. 1803), reg. 5.
[42] Green Paper (1998), 57.
[43] Child Benefit and Social Security (Fixing and Adjustment of Rates) (Amendment) Regulations 1998 (S.I. 1998 No. 1581).
[44] Middleton et al., n. 33 above.

for the well-being of children and it reasserts the Beveridge partnership principle. The symbolism, as opposed to the substance, will be made even more significant when, as has been proposed, child benefit becomes taxable for higher rate taxpayers, just as the old family allowances were.[45]

B. Income Support

Beveridge recognised that 'deserted' wives and mothers might have to have recourse to national assistance to secure them a safety net from destitution. As already noted, he recommended a 'separation allowance' of limited duration, though without much obvious enthusiasm, and this proposal was not adopted. The growth in family instability has led to a burgeoning in the numbers of such parents indefinitely reliant upon means-tested benefits, most notably income support. It was the Finer Committee[46] which drew the most detailed picture of the financial circumstances of lone parents and their reliance upon what was then supplementary benefit. From fewer than a quarter of a million such families receiving the benefit then, the number had climbed to around a million by 1993.[47] Income support remains the key benefit available to lone parents.[48]

The Social Security Contributions and Benefits Act 1992, section 124, provides that to be eligible for income support, a claimant must be habitually resident in the United Kingdom[49] and at least sixteen years old. A claim is made on behalf of the family unit, so that the income and capital of all members of that unit are 'aggregated'.[50] This means that maintenance paid by an absent parent for a child will be regarded as part of the assets of the claimant and thus reduce the amount of income support she can receive, even though the money is not intended for her benefit.[51] Where a couple live together outside marriage, they are assumed to support each other financially, even though they have no legal liability to do so. This 'cohabitation rule' caused particular annoyance and controversy in the 1970s, though seems to have become less problematical more recently, perhaps because the stigmatic associations of cohabitation have disappeared. In determining whether a couple are 'living together as husband and wife' for the purposes of social security, specific factors to be considered are spelt out in the Adjudication Officer's Guide (taken from the approval given by Woolf J in *Crake v Supplementary Benefits Commission*):[52] membership of the same household; stability; financial support; a sexual relationship; the presence of children; and public acknowledgement. In addition, according to the Social Security Commissioner in *Re J (Income Support: Cohabitation)*,[53] the parties' 'general

---

[45] Department of Social Security, n. 42 above at 58.   [46] N. 16 above, Part 5.

[47] Land and Lewis, n. 26 above, Table 7.

[48] Jobseeker's allowance is less crucial, because lone parents are not required to be available for work. IS(G) Regs 1987, reg. 4ZA and Sched. 1B para. 1.

[49] See pp. 197–201 above.   [50] SSCBA 1992, s. 136.

[51] *Supplementary Benefits Commission v Jull, Y v Supplementary Benefits Commission* [1981] AC 1025, [1980] 3 All ER 65, HL. See below for consideration of child support.

[52] [1982] 1 All ER 498.   [53] [1995] 1 FLR 660 (Commissioner Rowland).

relationship' must be considered, to obtain a full picture of their circumstances. Thus, notwithstanding concerns regarding individual privacy, it may be necessary to question claimants closely as to the presence of a sexual relationship, but the absence of such a relationship will be potent (although not conclusive) ground for determining that the couple are not living together.[54]

The claimant must have no income, or income below an applicable amount; have no capital, or capital below a prescribed amount;[55] not be engaged in remunerative work; not be entitled to a jobseeker's allowance; and not be receiving relevant education. A claimant may still be eligible if working for fewer than sixteen hours per week,[56] though any earnings above £15 (in the case of a lone parent) will reduce the benefit awarded.[57]

The amount of income support payable[58] to an eligible claimant depends upon her family circumstances. A personal allowance is paid for each member of the unit: from April 1999 this is £51.40 per week for a single person aged twenty-five or over (or lone parent aged over eighteen); £80.65 per week for a couple aged eighteen or over (see variations in the case of younger couples, noted in Chapter 6); and amounts for children aged under eleven (£20.20 rising to £24 from October 1999); eleven to fifteen (£25.90) and sixteen to eighteen (£30.95). Middleton et al.[59] estimated that income support allowances for children in 1997 would meet between 50 and 70 per cent of average spending on all children. As was the case for child benefit, they found that the rates payable for younger children underestimated the amounts needed for their support, though again the change to the rate for under-elevens introduced in 1998 will go some way to meeting this shortfall.

In addition to these allowances, premiums are paid to reflect the particular circumstances of the claimant. Thus, a family premium (worth £13.05 per week from April 1999) is paid where the claim is made on behalf of a family unit. Before 6 July 1998, a higher-rate family premium was paid to lone parents (akin to the lone parent rate added to child benefit), worth an additional £4.70 per week. This higher rate remains payable to lone parent claimants in receipt of it on 5 April 1998.[60]

A claimant's housing costs may be met through income support (if they consist of mortgage payments) or housing benefit (if they consist of rent) (see Chapter 13). At one time, mortgage interest payments were met in full, immediately the claim was payable, regardless of the size of the mortgage. This possibility could be turned to

---

[54] For a full discussion of this issue, see N. Harris, 'Unmarried Cohabiting Couples and Social Security in Great Britain' (1996) 18 *J. of Social Welfare and Family Law*, 123–46.

[55] Currently £8,000: benefit is reduced for capital between £3,000 and £8,000. See further Chapter 6.

[56] Or more, if the work is as a childminder. Income Support (General) Regulations 1987 reg. 6.

[57] IS(G) Regs 1987 Sched. 8 para. 5. For a single claimant who is not a lone parent, £5 is disregarded; for a couple, £10.

[58] The rates of income-based jobseeker's allowance are identical.   [59] N. 33 above, at 41.

[60] With some provision made for persons who were not receiving benefit on that actual date but had been doing so within 12 weeks of that date; or who take work and cease to claim, but re-claim within 12 weeks: IS(G) Regs 1987, Sched. 2 para. 3 (as amended by Social Security Amendment (Lone Parents) Regulations 1998 (S.I. 1998 No. 766), regs 11, 12).

considerable mutual advantage when couples were negotiating a financial settlement on divorce. Consistently with the increasing preference in the divorce law for a 'clean break' settlement, whereby the parties cut all financial ties with each other,[61] an arrangement could be made whereby the husband (usually) would transfer to the wife his share in the matrimonial home, enabling her to remain there with the children[62] in return for her agreeing to forgo any claim against him for maintenance either for herself, or for her children.[63] The wife could then claim income support to meet the ongoing needs of herself and the children; the DSS would pay the mortgage instalments, thus freeing the husband to take on a new mortgage and re-house himself. Indeed, not only would the DSS undertake the interest payments on an existing house mortgage. It would also meet the payments on a second mortgage taken out to provide a lump sum with which the wife could part-compensate the husband for transferring his share to her.[64] This state-financing of divorce settlements very dramatically shifted the 'burden' of supporting a family from the private sphere—the husband/father—to the public—the DSS. However, it has been curtailed or at least restricted by a number of measures intended, in fact, primarily to reduce the burden on the DSS of meeting mortgage payments at a time of very high house price inflation, and which was seen as resulting in a work disincentive, rather than specifically to tackle the 'welfare benefit clean break' divorce. From 1995, the mortgage debt which can be met from income support was limited to £100,000.[65] Even if the mortgage debt is below this limit, housing costs may be restricted if they are deemed excessive, for example, because the home is too big for the claimant and her family, or the area is too expensive and cheaper alternative accommodation could reasonably be obtained.[66] In determining whether it is reasonable to expect the family to move, consideration may be taken of effects on the children—for example, of a change of school—and of the fact that the house is too big because a spouse has left.

Of greater significance to the majority of claimants, one would expect, is the period of 'waiting time' which is imposed before mortgage instalments will be met. The general rule is that, where a loan was taken out after 1 October 1995, no help with the payments is given for the first thirty-nine weeks of the claim to income support. However, if the claimant is a lone parent whose partner has left or died, she will receive no help for the first eight weeks of claim; half the payments will be met for

---

[61] See the Matrimonial Causes Act 1973, s. 25A.

[62] Thus fulfilling the statutory requirement to give first consideration to their welfare—Matrimonial Causes Act 1973, s. 25(1).

[63] The latter was contrary to the terms of s. 23 of the 1973 Act and disapproved in successive precedents (see, e.g. *Minton v Minton* [1979] AC 593, [1979] 1 All ER 79, HL; *Dipper v Dipper* [1981] Fam 31, [1980] 2 All ER 722, CA), but appears to have been widely practised.

[64] For a full discussion of this mechanism, see G. Davis, S. Cretney, K. Bader, and J. Collins, 'The Relationship between Public and Private Financial Support following Divorce in England and Wales' in L. Weitzman and M. Maclean (eds) *Economic Consequences of Divorce: The International Perspective* (Oxford: Clarendon Press, 1992).

[65] IS(G) Regs 1987, Sched. 3 para. 11(4), (5).   [66] Ibid., Sched. 3 para. 13.

the following eighteen weeks and thereafter the full costs will be paid.[67] The claimant is expected to rely upon savings, mortgage protection insurance, or a sympathetic lender, to meet or defer the shortfall. It should also be noted that the rate of interest paid through income support is standard, and may be lower than that incurred by the mortgagor.[68] If so, she must again meet the difference herself or negotiate an arrangement with the lender. The extent of hardship which these measures have caused, and how far they have prevented couples reaching divorce settlements which were highly beneficial both to them and their children, are as yet unknown. While it can be argued that there was no reason for the state to subsidise divorce to the extent that it was doing, the potential detriment to children if they are forced to move home and school because of financial hardship at a time of emotional upheaval argues for a more generous approach to couples' attempts to minimise harm and disruption.

C. A Guaranteed Maintenance Allowance?

Income support is state support for families where no-one else is able or willing to support them. It thus operates as the measure of last resort (albeit that in practice the benefits office is likely to be the first port of call for a deserted parent). A more ambitious proposal to provide a special one-parent family allowance was made by the Finer Committee in 1974.[69] Although not adopted, it is important to understand the proposal since it can be seen as the high-water mark of preparedness to impose the *primary* obligation, at least in the case of one-parent families, of family support upon the state (and of course, for that very reason, it failed to find favour with government). As the Finer Committee put it:

The fact has to be faced that in a democratic society, which cannot legislate . . . different rules of familial and sexual behaviour depending on the ability to pay for the consequences, the community has to bear much of the cost of broken homes and unmarried motherhood.[70]

It can be seen that, of necessity, given their terms of reference, the focus of the Finer Committee was on the needs of 'broken' families with children, rather than, as in the Beveridge Report, the importance of support for all children.

Finer's recommendation essentially entailed the payment of a non-contributory benefit to all one-parent families, made up of a childcare allowance for the adult, and a separate allowance for each child. Eligibility would be established after a three-month waiting period to ensure that the husband/partner was not going to return to the family. The amount would be 'linked quite closely to supplementary benefit [now income support] payments, but the operation and administration . . . devised to meet specific problems in the one-parent family situation'.[71] It would be means-tested and the adult allowance extinguished by the point at which the carer's income reached the

---

[67] Ibid., Sched. 3 paras 1(2), 6, 8.   [68] Ibid., Sched. 3 para. 12.   [69] N. 16 above, para. 5.104ff.
[70] Ibid., para. 4.224.   [71] Ibid., para. 5.115.

level of average male earnings. However, the child allowances would be paid regardless of the carer's income.

These proposals were not adopted, but they both built on what had gone before and have provided models for what has followed. The continuation of means-testing shows the similarity with national assistance, supplementary benefit, and now income support, while the payment of child allowances regardless of adult income is akin to the universal family allowance and now child benefit. A key feature of the allowance, which will be discussed in greater depth below, would have been the recoupment of the cost, where possible, from the non-resident parent, a feature (albeit an ineffectual one) of national assistance and supplementary benefit, and which underpins the child support scheme. Further similarities with that scheme were the assessment of the amount of allowance by reference to supplementary benefit levels, and the use of a formula to determine the amount of maintenance required from the non-resident parent.

It has clearly proved politically unacceptable to require the state to provide the primary source of support for families—or at least to require it to do so openly. Instead, the history of income support and its forerunners shows that the state will make a contribution—more or less grudgingly—through some form of child allowance, and will pick up the bill when there is no alternative—but the search continues for the alternative. One answer is to place the family, women, and children squarely back in the private sphere by imposing and enforcing the responsibility to support them on the other partner/parent, and we explore this dimension next.

4. RELIANCE UPON THE LIABLE RELATIVE

A. Background

Financial support of members of a family has always rested primarily upon other family members. It is part of the social fabric and culture to assume that kin relationships carry with them obligations and expectations of care in the widest sense, though it by no means follows that the extent and scope of these is unproblematic.[72] While the common law was ineffectual in its enforcement of the husband's duty to maintain his wife, and was slow to develop a legal duty on a parent to support his child,[73] the Elizabethan Poor Law established a national system (building upon earlier provisions) putting 'legal sanctions behind the observance of what were then regarded as the ordinary obligations of kinship'.[74] The Poor Relief Act of 1601

---

[72] Janet Finch and her colleagues have explored this question in a series of research studies: see J. Finch, *Family Obligations and Social Change* (London: Polity Press, 1989); J. Finch and J. Mason, *Negotiating Family Responsibilities* (London: Tavistock/Routledge, 1993); J. Finch, J. Mason, L. Wallis, and L. Hayes, *Wills, Inheritance and Families* (Oxford: Clarendon Press, 1996).
[73] See J. Eekelaar and M. Maclean, *Maintenance after Divorce* (Oxford: Clarendon Press, 1986), ch. 1.
[74] M. Finer and O. McGregor, n. 16 above, para. 51.

provided that a destitute person unable to work could obtain relief from his or her parish, but it also imposed a legal duty to maintain such a person on the parents, grandparents, and children of that person. In the case of an illegitimate child, only the mother and putative father were obliged to support. The Justices of the Peace of the parish where the destitute person was present would order the relative to support that person, on pain of fine, and to repay any public expenditure already incurred. A parish was only required to support a destitute person belonging to that parish (see Chapter 3)—if the person had wandered to another place, they would be sent back to their home parish, or at least moved on. As Finer and McGregor comment: 'Thus was established the national system by which the public supported those who were unable to support themselves, but sought reimbursement by imposing a legal liability upon financially able relatives.'[75]

The harsh reforms of the Poor Law enacted in 1834 were intended mainly to reinforce the principle of 'less eligibility' (i.e. that any relief should leave a pauper at a standard of living worse than that of the poorest labourer: see Chapter 3). However, the Commissioners who proposed the reforms argued also that an unmarried mother should not be able to charge the putative father with liability to support his child; rather, the shame of her offence should fall solely upon her (or her parents) thus rapidly deterring such practices on the part of women, it being accepted by the Commissioners that 'all punishment of the supposed father is useless'.[76] This particular example of the sexual double standard of the nineteenth century was soon repealed and replaced by a dual system—the mother could obtain a civil order against the father from the justices, who could order the payments to be made to the parish.[77] The relief afforded to the unmarried mother was the workhouse and separation from her child, however, whereas for widows and deserted wives, outdoor relief (i.e. financial support to remain in their own home) was the norm. Any amelioration of the position of unmarried mothers, or any equity between them and 'respectable' lone parents, was seen as a threat to the institution of marriage—an argument still heard and, indeed, employed in the 1990s debate surrounding the lone parent's child benefit addition and income support premium discussed above.

We have seen that the Beveridge Report was tentative in its proposals for separated wives, suggesting a temporary benefit and accepting that the primary recourse should be to the husband through the court maintenance system or, failing this, reliance upon national assistance, in which case the Ministry of Social Security would seek recoupment from the husband of its expenditure.[78] In the case of unmarried mothers, maternity benefit payments could perhaps be recovered from the putative father.[79]

When the Poor Law was abolished by the National Assistance Act 1948, the oblig-

---

[75] M. Finer and O. McGregor, n. 16 above, para 52.
[76] Quoted by Finer and McGregor, n. 16 above, at para. 56.   [77] Poor Law Amendment Act 1868.
[78] Beveridge Report (1942), para. 347.
[79] But Beveridge really did not know what to do in such cases, and did no more than raise the issue: see paras 263–4.

ation to support was limited to husbands and wives, and parents of children. With the absence of any 'separation benefit', the only way in which this obligation could be enforced was where national assistance was paid to the family member and the money sought to be recovered from the 'liable relative'. The National Assistance Board (and its successors) was given the right to take either civil or criminal proceedings against the liable relative. It may be noted that the Act itself did not make the support obligation conditional upon the 'good behaviour' of a spouse (an issue which had concerned Beveridge), but it was held, in *National Assistance Board v Wilkinson*, that where the claimant was an adulterous or deserting spouse there could be no recovery of national assistance from the innocent party.[80]

Even though such powers were given to the social security authorities, it was recognised early on that they were likely to be of limited effect. As the Finer Committee noted, where, for example, a man has left his wife and family, and formed a new relationship, he will support the second and leave the State to support the first:

> It is the almost inescapable consequence of the principles [of the system] that wherever there is not enough money for the husband to support two women, it is the one with whom he is not living who has to resort to [benefits].[81]

Finer reported that, when receiving a new claim for support from a lone parent, the social security authorities would attempt to reach an agreement with the liable relative to make a contribution to the cost,[82] applying a liable relative 'formula' to arrive at what was seen as an appropriate and fair amount. This would be fixed by asking him to pay the balance remaining after deducting from his net income an amount set according to the prevailing (income support) rates for the liable relative and any second family dependent upon him, a housing allowance, plus a margin of £5 or a quarter of his net earnings to encourage him to remain at work. This was not the approach adopted by the courts when making maintenance orders, who were encouraged to leave both families at roughly equal levels, even if this meant the liable relative would be no better off than if out of work.[83] The formulaic approach was adapted by Finer for the ill-fated guaranteed maintenance allowance, and bears similarities with aspects of the later child support formula discussed below.

When the problem of the number of lone parents dependent upon income support became the subject of renewed attention at the start of the 1990s, greater emphasis was placed upon the possibility of recovering public expenditure from the liable relative. Bradshaw and Millar found that only 22 per cent of lone parents received any maintenance, down from around a half ten years earlier.[84] The

---

[80] [1952] 2 QB 648. No longer good law because the concept of the 'matrimonial offence' is not part of family law and matrimonial misconduct is only a fact to be taken into account where it would be inequitable to disregard it. See also *National Assistance Board v Parkes* [1955] 2 QB 506 (separation agreement whereby wife agreed not to seek maintenance no bar to pursuit of husband as liable relative).

[81] N. 16 above, at para. 4.182. The National Assistance Board had reached the same conclusion in 1953, quoted ibid.

[82] Paras 4.184–4.202.   [83] Paras 4.203–4.205 and cases cited therein.

[84] J. Bradshaw and J. Millar, *Lone-parent Families in the UK*, DSS Research Report No. 6 (London: HMSO, 1991).

Government's response was to embark upon a fundamental reform of the assessment, collection, and enforcement of the *parental* support obligation, and in so doing, to shift the emphasis, probably permanently, away from a concern to support women—or even mothers—towards a concentration upon *children*. However, before discussing this, we first outline the remaining provisions regarding 'liable relatives'.

B. The Present 'Liable Relative' Provisions

Notwithstanding the child support system, there remain other opportunities for the Department of Social Security to seek a contribution from a liable relative where a claim is made for income support.[85] Under the Social Security Administration Act 1992, ss 78(6) and 105(3):

(a) a man shall be liable to maintain his wife and any children[86] of whom he is the father; and

(b) a woman shall be liable to maintain her husband and any children of whom she is the mother.

The spousal liability terminates on divorce, but the liability to support one's children applies regardless of the parent's marital status, and cannot be excluded.[87] On the other hand, only a person who is legally the parent is liable to support a child; unlike matrimonial law, there is no concept of a 'child of the family' whereby a step-parent may be made liable to pay maintenance.[88] In any case, the DSS does not invoke these provisions to deal with the support of children, but applies the Child Support Act 1991 instead (discussed below).

The liable relative formula remains in existence, though with some variations, and it is uncertain how much it is actually used in practice. It appears[89] that where the claimant has taken court proceedings for maintenance, no approach to the liable relative will be made. The amounts in the formula are as described above, except that apparently only a 15 per cent margin is now allowed. The sum arrived at is a negotiating figure, and where the liable relative has other essential expenses, the DSS may agree to a lower amount being paid. It would still be open to the claimant to bring court proceedings for a higher amount of maintenance.[90] Where the liable relative declines to contribute, the DSS may take proceedings. Civil proceedings may be taken under section 106 of the Social Security Administration Act 1992. A complaint may be made by the Secretary of State to the magistrates, who may order the liable

---

[85] Strangely, criminal, but not civil, proceedings—see below—may be taken against a *spouse* of a recipient of income-based jobseeker's allowance: SSAA 1992, s. 105(4).

[86] A child includes a person who has attained the age of 16 but is under 19, in respect of whom the claimant is receiving income support or income-based jobseeker's allowance: ibid. s. 78(6)(d).

[87] *Hulley v Thompson* [1981] 1 All ER 1128.

[88] See the discussion in N. V. Lowe and G. Douglas, *Bromley's Family Law*, 9th edn. (London: Butterworths, 1998), 764–72.

[89] This discussion is taken from J. Mesher and P. Wood, *Income-Related Benefits: The Legislation* (London: Sweet & Maxwell, 1997), 1106.

[90] Except if she is seeking child support maintenance: see below.

relative to pay such sum, weekly or otherwise, as they consider appropriate. In cases of persistent refusal or neglect to maintain, criminal proceedings may be taken under section 105.[91]

Given that the focus of Government attention has moved to support for children, it seems likely that minimal if any use is made of these provisions by the Benefits Agency. Where the claimant is a lone parent, the child support assessment against the absent parent takes into account the amount of income support she receives for herself so that there is no need to rely on the liable relative provisions.[92] Where the claimant has no dependent children, she is required to register for work (unless she comes under one of the other exempt categories based on age, incapacity, etc) and claim jobseeker's allowance, and these provisions[93] cease to be relevant. In any case, once she is divorced, the former spouse ceases to be liable to support her under the social security legislation. However, he might still be liable to support her by virtue of a periodical payments order made under the Matrimonial Causes Act 1973. Where this is the case, and she is receiving income support and *does* have dependent children, the Secretary of State may enforce that order with or without the recipient's consent.[94] Since there is no particular incentive for her to do so (her income support currently being reduced by any amount of maintenance received), the onus is squarely on the DSS to take action if it wishes to recoup expenditure in such a case.

C. Child Support

It was noted above that fewer than a quarter of lone parents receiving income support also received maintenance at the start of the 1990s. The Government's concern to reduce public spending on social security led it to review the system then in place, which revealed fundamental problems with the maintenance system operated by the courts. Amounts of maintenance were low in comparison with the real costs of child-rearing, and courts had a discretion to set levels of maintenance which resulted in wide variations in the amounts ordered even where the payers' circumstances appeared identical. Uprating of orders to take account of inflation, and enforcement of the obligation to pay, were haphazard and ineffectual.[95] Building upon the Finer Committee's work, the liable relative formula, and developments of similar schemes in Australia and the United States, the Child Support Act 1991 was enacted to put in place an administrative, rather than judicial, system of assessing and collecting child maintenance. The provenance of the scheme was the Department of Social Security and its driving force the desire to cut the net income support bill. The child support scheme can therefore be seen as belonging firmly to the social security system;

---

[91] There are no recent statistics available on the number of proceedings taken under either section.
[92] A stop-gap provision to enable the same effect to be achieved within the court maintenance system was introduced by the Social Security Act 1990 and remains as s. 107 of the SSAA 1992, see Mesher and Wood, n. 89 above at 1107–11, but it is doubtful if it is used.
[93] Except s. 105.   [94] Section 108.
[95] Department of Social Security, *Children Come First*, Cm 1264 (London: HMSO, 1990), I, ch 1.

indeed, over 90 per cent of applicants using the system are benefit recipients. Although, in one sense, the system can be described as 'privatising' the support obligation, because it attempts to reimpose liability on absent parents, the close attention paid by the state to the circumstances of families caught up in the system and its insistence on setting the amount of money to be paid for child maintenance hardly reflect a withdrawing of the state from a private sphere—rather the reverse.

In order to ensure that a more realistic level of maintenance is levied on the absent parent, and to obtain consistency of awards, the assessment of the maintenance bill under the Child Support Act is determined by means of a formula. To enhance the rate of collection and enforcement of maintenance, these tasks are carried out by the Child Support Agency, which was intended to be proactive in its work in contrast to the stance of courts, which act only upon application to them.

As with liability under the social security legislation, only parents are required to support a child under the child support system,[96] leaving the court system still available where maintenance is sought from a step-parent. There are two classes of applicant for child support. Under section 4, a person[97] with care of a qualifying child[98] or the absent parent[99] may apply, provided that no maintenance agreement made before 5 April 1993, or child maintenance order, is in force, and the applicant is not receiving income support, family credit (now WFTC: below), disability working allowance (now disabled person's tax credit—see Chapter 12), or income-based JSA.[100] Under section 6, a *parent* (i.e., *not* a non-parent) with care of the child in receipt of one of these benefits is *required* to authorise the Secretary of State to carry out and collect a child support assessment. Where such a parent does not wish to give this authorisation, she must show reasonable grounds for believing that her compliance in identifying or helping to trace the absent parent would lead to a risk of her, or any child living with her, suffering harm or undue distress as a result. In the absence of such grounds, her benefit may be reduced by 40 per cent of the income support adult personal allowance (£20.64 per week at 1999–2000 rates) for three years in the first instance, and then renewable.[101] The aim of this penalty, which was increased in 1996 from a 20 per cent deduction for a maximum eighteen-month period when the legislation was originally enacted, is to deter parents from colluding to prevent the Child Support Agency from carrying out an assessment. The Labour Government's Green Paper proposing reforms to the child support scheme[102] stated that 'over 70% of lone mothers on Income Support seek to avoid making a child support application'. However, it is not clear how this statistic is arrived at or whether it refers

---

[96] Child Support Act 1991, ss 1(1) and 3.

[97] Note that a non-parent can apply, if he or she has the care of the child, but only a parent can be liable to pay.

[98] A child under the age of 16 or under 19 who is receiving full-time non-advanced education (s. 55) in respect of whom at least one parent is 'absent' (s. 3(1)).

[99] Or in Scotland, also the child if aged 12 or over: s. 7.   [100] Section 4(10).

[101] Section 46 and Maintenance Assessment Procedure Regulations 1992 (S.I. 1992 No. 1813), Part IX.

[102] Department of Social Security, *Children First: a new approach to child support*, Cm 3992 (London: The Stationery Office, 1998), 12.

specifically to parents claiming 'good cause' for refusing to co-operate. What is clear is that the task of satisfying the Agency of reasonable grounds has become harder during the scheme: in the first year of operation, good cause was accepted in 49 per cent of cases where it was raised; by 1997, the proportion had fallen to 14 per cent.[103]

As an equal incentive upon absent parents (overwhelmingly male) to co-operate with the Agency in providing financial details to enable an assessment to be calculated, a failure to comply by completion of the appropriate forms may result in an 'interim maintenance assessment'.[104] This levies a penal rate of maintenance upon the absent parent until compliance is forthcoming. It seems that much of this money is never collected. In 1997, £869 million was regarded as 'uncollectable' and most of this figure related to interim assessments.[105]

(i) Assessment under the Formula[106]

Although the imposition of a 'reduced benefit direction' upon lone mothers was highly controversial before the Act came into force, it was the impact of the scheme upon prospective payers which has caused the most difficulty. The child support formula requires the child support officer to compare the amount deemed necessary for the qualifying children in the applicant's family to live on, with the amount which the absent parent can afford to pay.

The appropriate income support allowance for each child, according to age, plus a proportion up to 100 per cent of the adult single allowance to reflect the care given by the person with care,[107] plus the appropriate premiums for the family, are added together. Child benefit is deducted since this will be paid regardless of income. The resulting figure is the children's 'maintenance requirement'. In assessing how much of this requirement the absent parent should pay, a calculation similar to the liable relative formula is then carried out. Where both parents are working, their resulting 'assessable incomes' are added together and then halved. However, in practice, as we have seen, nearly all applicants are on benefit, and in such a case, they are deemed to have no assessable income. If the result is a sum equal to, or less than, the children's maintenance requirement, the absent parent must pay half of his assessable income, subject to ensuring that not more than 30 per cent of his net income can be taken from him as child support. Where the result is greater than the maintenance requirement, he is required to pay an additional proportion of his remaining income to reflect his greater wealth. Absent parents who are themselves in receipt of benefit can be required to pay the 'minimum amount'—10 per cent of the adult single

---

[103] Child Poverty Action Group, *Child Support Handbook*, 6th edn. (London: CPAG, 1998), 93.

[104] Child Support Act 1991, s. 12.

[105] House of Commons Select Committee on Public Accounts, *21st Report: Child Support Agency, Client Funds Account 1996/97* (London: House of Commons, 1998), para. 40.

[106] For details, see E. Jacobs, and G. Douglas, *Child Support: The Legislation*, 3rd edn. (London: Sweet & Maxwell, 1997), *passim*.

[107] The proportion depends on the age of the youngest child in the family; 100% is included where this child is under 11, and none where the child is over 16.

person's allowance—as a token of their obligation of support, although this is not required where the absent parent has a child to care for.

There are several problems with this approach, although a number of them are deliberate choices intended to reinforce the symbolic message that a parent's first priority must be the support of his children. First, the adult carer's allowance in the maintenance requirement has proved deeply controversial, since it appears to require the payer to meet the maintenance need of the carer, to whom he may owe no duty of support, for example, because they are divorced or were never married.[108] Secondly, the presence of the absent parent's second family is only partially taken into account. If he has had a child of his own with a new partner, an allowance will be made for that child's support in the assessment, but if he has step-children, then even if he is fully supporting them (perhaps because their own parent is dead) this is only taken into account when ensuring that no more than 30 per cent of his net income is taken as child support. Thirdly, the formula takes no account of many out-goings which form part of modern consumerism, such as hire purchase debts, car expenses, and credit card bills. Fourth, and again highly controversially, it makes no automatic[109] allowance for the fact that an absent parent may have given up his share in the capital value of the former home to the parent with care, perhaps to offset his maintenance liability to her and/or the children.

Coupled with the facts that first, because liability to pay may arise before the assessment has actually been completed,[110] the delay in carrying out the assessment will very often mean that the absent parent is in arrears before he can start paying, and secondly, that the final assessment is often much higher than he has anticipated, the resultant shock to absent parents has resulted in the largest protest of middle-class and 'respectable' working-class men since the revolt against the poll tax. Unlike the poll tax, however, both the Conservative and succeeding Labour Governments have attempted to keep the basic child support system while softening its hardest edges. Yet ironically, when one examines the actual amounts being assessed under the scheme, there is not a great deal of difference overall with the old court system. In 1997, nearly 40 per cent of absent parents had a nil liability (because they were dependent on benefit themselves or on low incomes and not required to pay the min-imum amount); a further 15 per cent were assessed to pay the minimum amount. The average assessment (excluding interim assessments) was £39 per week, falling to £23.72 for the self-employed.[111] Of course, these averages conceal very wide varia-tions, but given that an assessment is made for *all* qualifying children in a family, these figures are not wildly higher than the average child maintenance order in 1990 for *one child*, which was £18 per week.[112]

---

[108] In this respect, it is directly comparable with s. 107 of the SSAA 1992, discussed above.
[109] A 'broad brush' allowance may be given if claimed; see below.
[110] Maintenance Assessment Procedure Regulations 1992 (n. 101 above), reg. 30.
[111] E. Knights, 'Child Support Update' [1997] *Fam Law* 559–63.
[112] Department of Social Security, *Children Come First*, n. 95 above, at para. 1.5.

(ii) Reform of the System

Reform of the child support scheme has gone through three stages. In the first, the former Government made some relatively minor adjustments to the formula and the administrative regulations; for example, allowing absent parents to claim their travel to work costs as essential expenses which must be deducted from their income assessable for maintenance,[113] and enabling them to receive a 'broad brush' allowance for any property or capital transfer made on divorce and intended to offset their maintenance obligation to the qualifying child.[114]

In the face of continuing criticism that the formula was too rigid, primary legislation was then enacted to permit 'departures' from the formula in certain, carefully defined circumstances.[115] Sections 28A to 28I of the 1991 Act (inserted by Child Support Act 1995), permit either party to apply for a 'departure direction' relaxing the formula, on the basis of 'special expenses' such as the cost of travel to have contact with the qualifying child, or debts incurred before the parents split up, or the cost of supporting step-children; property or capital settlements not adequately recognised in the 'broad brush' allowance; or claims that the other party has an extravagant lifestyle inconsistent with his or her declared income.

It will be seen that the first category is intended to address the argument, mainly of absent parents, that their inescapable expenses are not catered for within the constraints of the formula; the second relates more to arguments that the formula's failure to recognise the sacrifice made in divorce settlements was unjust; the third category of cases reflects concern that it has proved easy for absent parents to conceal their true financial circumstances from the Child Support Agency in order to reduce the size of the assessment.[116]

Where a claim for a departure is made out, an appropriate alteration will be made to the assessment. This alteration is itself circumscribed, but in determining whether to give it, consideration must be given to whether it would be 'just and equitable' to do so. This interpolation of discretion into what was intended to be an automatic formulaic exercise fundamentally weakens the basis of the child support system, and although it appears to have quietened complaints (though there are as yet no published statistics on the success rates of applications for departures, or the extent of 'gains' made by successful applicants), the incoming Labour Government proposed a more thorough revision of the system.

Thus, for the second time since 1991, primary legislation will be enacted to change the child support scheme. The key concern of the new proposals appears now to be

---

[113] Only expenses incurred in journeys exceeding 150 miles per week are allowed: Maintenance Assessments and Special Cases Regulations 1992 (S.I. 1992 No. 1815), Sched. 3B, inserted in 1995.

[114] Ibid., Sched. 3A.

[115] See J. Priest, 'Departure directions in the Child Support scheme' (1998) 5 *J.S.S.L.* 104–38.

[116] The most dramatic example of this was shown in *Phillips v Peace* [1996] 2 FLR 230: the absent parent, a self-employed businessman, lived in a house worth £2.6 million and owned cars worth £190,000, but was assessed as having nil income by the Child Support Agency. In proceedings brought by the mother of his child for a *capital* settlement for the child, he was ordered to pay £90,000.

that 90% of staff time is spent in calculating the assessment and keeping cases up to date, leaving only 10% for ensuring that maintenance is actually paid.[117] It is indeed scandalous that in 1997, £1,127 million was owed by absent parents to the Child Support Agency.[118] In so far as the Government is therefore seeking to ensure that more money is actually collected, its concern is the same as that of the Conservative Government when it originally proposed the scheme—to reduce the burden on the taxpayer and place it back on the shoulders of the liable relative. The means of achieving this is going to be by greatly simplifying the formula, replacing it with a simple requirement that the absent parent[119] pay a fixed percentage of his net income, ranging from 15 per cent where there is one qualifying child, to 25 per cent where there are three or more. The consequence of such simplicity is, in the majority of cases, to reduce the amount the absent parent must pay—it is estimated that 70 per cent will be better off under this revision and that the average assessment will be £29 per week.

This reduction represents an acceptance[120] that absent parents *will not* pay sums they deem unacceptable for their children, no matter how unrealistic their views on the costs of bringing up a child may be.[121] The shortfall, therefore, will have to come from elsewhere. The state will pick it up in most cases. To provide an incentive to co-operate with the Child Support Agency, up to £10 per week of any maintenance paid will be kept by a parent with care on income support as a 'child maintenance premium', so even the partial recoupment by the state of the costs of paying benefit will be further reduced. In the remaining cases, it will be for the parent with care to find the difference. This leads to the final avenue of support for families and children—women's earnings. If, contrary to the pattern of policy and culture which has previously operated, women can be increasingly pushed into the *public* sphere of the market and the world of work, they can, first, be more or less self-supporting and thus reduce the 'burden' on others to meet their particular needs and, secondly, they can meet the remaining cost of their children which the other parent, or the state, is either unable or unwilling to pay. This approach is clearly fundamentally at odds with the patriarchal conception of women's 'role' in society.

5. WOMEN AT WORK

As has been extensively documented[122] the proportion of women, and in particular married women and mothers, in the working population, was higher than Beveridge

[117] Department of Social Security, Cm 4349 (London: The Stationery Office, 1999), 3.

[118] House of Commons Select Committee on Public Accounts *21st Report*, n. 105 above, para. 40.

[119] To be called, apparently less pejoratively, the 'non-resident' parent.

[120] Department of Social Security, *Children First*, n. 102 above, at 48.

[121] Middleton et al., n. 33 above, calculate average spending on a child of £57.01 per week: Table 6.

[122] Kiernan, Land, and Lewis, n. 26 above; R. Lister, '"She has other duties"—Women, citizenship and social security', 31–44; H. Land, ' The Demise of the Male Breadwinner—In Practice but not in Theory: A challenge for social security systems', 100–15; H. Joshi and H. Davies, 'The Paid and Unpaid Roles of Women: How should social security adapt?' in S. Baldwin and J. Falkingham (eds.), *Social Security and Social Change* (Hemel Hempstead: Harvester Wheatsheaf, 1994), 235–54.

assumed in the 1940s, and has grown ever since. Kiernan, Land, and Lewis show that 25 per cent of married women were economically active in 1951, and by 1995, 75 per cent of *mothers* were in paid work.[123] Women's employment pattern is, of course, different from that of men, because of their childcare and other domestic responsibilities. Joshi, Davies, and Land comment that the increase in 'working women' during the post-war era was due largely to a reduction in the length of the gap before they re-enter the labour market. However, even with greater opportunities for maternity leave and return to one's former job (outlined below), they suggest that: 'Most of the new mothers of the 1990s still experience some degree of employment disruption, as did almost all of those who had become mothers earlier.'[124] Added to the break from continuity of employment or career progression caused by child-bearing, there are significant features of women's employment opportunities which render them more vulnerable to poverty, especially in old age. Since social security policies are intended to impact upon poverty, these may have a greater impact upon them than upon men.

The features of women's activity in the market are well known. They earn, on average, less than men, receiving hourly rates 72 per cent of men's in 1995 for manual work, and 68 per cent for non-manual work;[125] and they are much more likely to be working part-time in order to fit their employment around their domestic commitments.[126] Social security measures aimed at supplementing low wages are therefore potentially of major significance to them. This will be particularly so for lone parents: where there are two parents in the household, their employment situations are related, so that an employed father is more likely to have an employed wife, and a professional husband working full-time is more likely to have a professional wife working full-time. Where there is only a lone parent, she is much less likely to be working at all, although the differential between part-time and full-time work is less marked.[127]

It is therefore necessary to outline the ways in which the social security system seeks to encourage women, and especially lone parents, to take or remain in paid employment.

A. Maternity Benefits

Since interruption of employment due to child-bearing has a significantly detrimental effect on women's ability to have a full contribution record and satisfactory earnings over their lifetime,[128] measures aimed at enabling women to maintain their income after having a child, and to return to work, may be crucial.

---

[123] N. 26 above at 244 and Table 8.1.

[124] H. Joshi, H. Davies, and H. Land, *The Tale of Mrs Typical* (London: Family Policy Studies Centre, 1996), at 9.

[125] G. Pascall, *Social Policy: A New Feminist Analysis* (London: Routledge, 1997), 49.

[126] See E. Ferri and K. Smith, *Parenting in the 1990s* (London: Family Policy Studies Centre, 1996), ch. 2.

[127] Kiernan, Land, and Lewis, n. 26 above, Table 5.3.

[128] See Joshi, Davies, and Land, n. 124 above at 13, who estimate that 'Mrs Typical' foregoes £230,000 or 55% of earnings she would have made after age 25 if she has two children.

Ironically, the development of maternity benefits stemmed from a very different concern. Because of his desire to encourage larger families, Beveridge was anxious that women should be assisted to have healthy babies and should not be deterred from giving up work in good time for the birth, nor compelled to return to the labour market too soon afterwards. Accordingly, he proposed (as had in fact been in existence since 1911 for insured women) a maternity grant to go towards the costs of the birth and a maternity benefit payable for thirteen weeks to those women giving up work, paying a rate of benefit 50 per cent higher than the unemployment benefit rate.[129] The maternity grant was originally intended to cover medical costs in the days before the National Health Service but thereafter it was regarded as helping with the 'layette'. Rather like family allowances, its value was allowed to be eroded by inflation. The Beveridge preference for increasing the population was no longer fashionable, and, after an interim period in the 1980s when the grant became non-contributory, it was abolished and replaced by a maternity expenses payment available only to a woman in receipt (or whose partner is in receipt) of income support, income-based jobseeker's allowance, family credit, or disability working allowance.[130]

As Ogus, Barendt, and Wikeley[131] explain, the payment of a maternity allowance through the benefits system has been largely integrated with employment protection measures giving a statutory right to maternity pay. European legislation in particular has enhanced the rights of women workers in this regard. The position now is that 'statutory maternity pay' (SMP) is payable where a woman has been working for an employer for at least twenty-six weeks before the 'qualifying week' (which is the fifteenth week before the expected week of the childbirth),[132] and her average weekly earnings are at least the lower earnings limit for national insurance contributions. The payment is made by the employer, who recoups the bulk (or, if a small employer, the whole sum plus an allowance for administrative expense) from the Government. The payments last for up to eighteen weeks; for the first six weeks, the amount is 90 per cent of the claimant's average weekly earnings, and thereafter, £59.55 per week (the April 1999–2000 rate).[133] The current system has been criticised, both for excluding some 50,000 women whose earnings are below the national insurance threshold,[134] and for enabling very high-earning employees to take maternity leave and receive 90 per cent of their salaries courtesy of the taxpayer. In fact, about two-thirds of recipients of SMP were earning no more than the average full-time women's wage in 1995–6, and only 5 per cent were earning double or higher.[135] The Government

---

[129] Beveridge Report (1942), paras 113, 342, 348(iii). See pp. 92–3 above.

[130] Social Fund Maternity and Funeral Expenses (General) Regulations 1987 (S.I. 1987 No. 481), reg. 5. The value of the payment is £100 at time of writing. See further Chapter 14. Family credit and disability working allowance are being replaced under the Tax Credits Act 1999: see below.

[131] (1995), 268–70.   [132] SSCBA 1992, s. 164.

[133] Many employers have more generous arrangements as a result of collective agreements.

[134] Department of Trade and Industry, *Fairness at Work*, Cm 3968 (London: The Stationery Office, 1998), ch. 5.

[135] Figures taken from Hansard, H.C. Debs, col. 314, 15 January 1998.

announced a full review of maternity provision in 1998, to enable it to deal with such issues and also to ensure compatibility with European requirements.[136]

The earliest that payment can be made is eleven weeks before the expected week of childbirth, and the latest the beginning of the week after that in which the child is born. This provides flexibility to enable the woman herself to choose when she wishes to take her maternity leave.

For women ineligible for statutory maternity pay, it may still be possible to claim 'maternity allowance'. This is payable where the woman gave up work during pregnancy or changed jobs and so cannot satisfy the twenty-six-week qualifying period of employment, or is self-employed, but has paid national insurance contributions for at least twenty-six weeks in the year ending with the qualifying week (see above). If the claimant was working in that week, she will receive £57.50 per week (the same rate as for SMP after the first six weeks); otherwise the payment is £50.10 per week. The duration of payments is the same as for SMP.

Clearly the rate of allowance paid may be significantly lower than the woman's earnings level. For women in large enterprises with fully-developed maternity leave and pay agreements, there may be relatively little detriment, but for others, the drop in income may be substantial and force a return to work sooner than the woman might have chosen. The decision to return will itself depend upon the availability of childcare provision.

B. Childcare Provision

If the place of mothers was traditionally in the home, the place of their young children was with them there. The provision of day-care facilities for pre-school children was not regarded as a priority once the war was over (even then, the number of nursery places created was relatively small).[137] As Pascall points out,[138] traditional ideology was reinforced by Bowlby's 'maternal deprivation' thesis and the Conservative Government of the 1980s and 1990s did its best to resist calls for an expansion of childcare places. However, a right-wing Government which is in thrall to the market and concerned to encourage flexible working practices, as the Thatcher and Major Governments were, and at the same time keen to cut welfare spending, cannot completely ignore the demands of employers simply to pay lip-service to New Right family ideologues. By the end of the Conservative period of government, plans to give 'childcare vouchers' to the parents of all four year olds had been implemented. The new Labour Government put forward a National Childcare Strategy in 1998 replacing the voucher scheme and planning expansion of provision for both pre- and school-age children, it finally dawning on politicians that there are insufficient jobs to fit the school-day or school-terms nor sufficient partners,

---

[136] Department of Trade and Industry, n. 134 above, para. 5.13.
[137] Land and Lewis, n. 26 above, 19.   [138] N. 125 above, ch. 3.

grandmothers, or other relatives available to care for children outside these times when mothers have to work.

The Government also signed the Working Time and Parental Leave Directives, which it claimed as 'support for working parents'.[139] The first of these limits the hours employers can require their employees to work; however, it is possible to be opted out of these limits, and workers in the United Kingdom already work longer than anyone else in Europe, so the opportunity to 'spend more hours with their children' is likely to be limited. The latter enables parents to take unpaid leave from work. For low-paid workers this will also have minimal impact since they cannot afford to take much time off to be with young children. As yet, few employers have sophisticated paternal or parental leave arrangements, but implementation of the Directive by December 1999 will require them to offer up to three months' leave to both men and women on the birth or adoption of a child.[140]

C. Supplementing Low Earnings

For all families dependent upon low wages, the possibility of enhancing earned income through social security benefits may be vital. As a cure to the growth in the number of lone-parent families dependent upon income support, it is particularly useful to governments. And those politicians who might still, in their heart of hearts, prefer mothers to stay at home with their children, at least for a while, may see supplementing the male breadwinner's paypacket as an incentive to women to do so. Wage supplements can therefore fulfil a variety of family policy objectives.

We have seen that Beveridge recognised that wages may be insufficient to meet the needs of a family. His answer was family allowance but we have also seen that benefits of this type have been of limited, though useful, effect. Rather than raise family allowances, a new benefit, called family income supplement (FIS), was introduced in 1970, enabling a family with one child or more to gain an extra cash sum each week where their gross income fell below a 'prescribed amount'.[141] Alongside the cash benefit, FIS operated as a 'passport' to other benefits, such as free school meals. However, as noted in Chapter 5, the take-up rate of FIS was low, and it entailed sizeable poverty and unemployment traps rendering it unattractive to potential recipients. In 1988, it was replaced by family credit which, although basically similar in outline, sought to address some of the worst disincentives of FIS. As the spotlight moved to lone parents in the 1990s, further attempts were made to encourage lone parents to move off income support and into work by boosting the attractiveness of family credit.

(i) Family Credit (pre-October 1999)

The claimant for this benefit had to be present and ordinarily resident in Great Britain and, in the case of a couple, was usually the woman, and had to be responsible for—

---

[139] Green Paper (1998), 59.   [140] Department of Trade and Industry, n. 134 above, para. 5.5.
[141] See Chapters 4 and 5. See also Ogus, Barendt, and Wikeley (1995), 518–22.

that is, have normally living with her—a child under sixteen, or under nineteen and still in full-time, non-advanced education.[142] She, or her partner, had to be working for sixteen hours a week or more. However, where either worked for thirty hours or more, an additional 'credit' was payable, worth £11.05 per week from April 1999. To calculate a person's entitlement, a credit was given for each member of the family, plus the thirty-hour credit if applicable. The total was the 'maximum family credit' payable. The family net income was then calculated (deducting any childcare costs up to £60 per week for one child, or £100 per week for two or more and ignoring up to £15 per week maintenance). If this was the same as or below the 'applicable amount', £80.65 per week from April 1999, the family received the maximum family credit. If it was higher, the family received the maximum family credit less 70 per cent of the difference.

Interviews with a representative sample of 900 lone mothers between 1991 and 1995 found that family credit was successful in increasing the chances of lone mothers obtaining paid work, and in reducing the chances of them leaving employment. For an added 10 per cent of family credit entitlement, the probability of being employed in a job of more than sixteen hours per week increased by 5 per cent. It can thus be said that family credit indeed encouraged mothers back to work, although it was found that many mothers preferred to work shorter hours to spend more time with their children, thus reducing their childcare costs, rather than maximise their earnings.[143] If this strategy reflects a positive choice to be with the children, one might conclude that family credit enabled some lone mothers to have the best of both worlds—to work and achieve a higher standard of living thereby, but not to be forced to work full-time. The state was offering them a positive choice.

(ii) Working Families Tax Credit and Childcare Tax Credit (from October 1999)[144]

None the less, the incoming Labour Government considered family credit to have been unsuccessful in 'making work pay' for low wage-families, although three-quarters of a million families were receiving it in 1998. In particular, the childcare disregard had been claimed by only 32,000 families.[145] Instead, drawing upon the American 'Earned Income Tax Credit', it proposed a tax allowance, called 'working families tax credit' (WFTC) reducing the earner's tax liability, and paid through the wage packet. The credit, introduced from October 1999 (under the Tax Credits Act 1999), is payable to low-income families with at least one child under the age of eighteen, where the main earner works more than sixteen hours per week. Such a

---

[142] Social Security (Claims and Payments) Regulations 1987 (S.I. 1987 No. 1968), reg. 4(2).

[143] A. Bryson, R. Ford, and M. White, *Making Work Pay: Lone mothers, employment and well-being* (York: Joseph Rowntree Foundation, 1997). See further below for findings concerning the New Deal initiative for lone parents.

[144] Tax Credits Act 1999; and Tax Credits Schemes (Miscellaneous Amendments) Regulations 1999 (S.I. 1999 No. 2487). See HM Treasury, *The Modernisation of Britain's Tax and Benefit System: Number 3, The Working Families Tax Credit and work incentives* (London: The Stationery Office, 1998); HM Treasury, *Work Incentives* (London: The Stationery Office, 1998).

[145] Green Paper (1998), 29 and 58.

family will receive a basic tax credit plus additions depending upon the number and age of the children in the family. Where the family's net income exceeds £90 per week, the credit will be progressively withdrawn at a taper of 55 per cent for each extra £1 (compared with 70 per cent for family credit). There is an equivalent 'thirty-hour' credit to that introduced in family credit.

For families receiving WFTC, it will also be possible to claim an additional child-care tax credit, worth 70 per cent of eligible childcare costs up to £100 per week for one child and £150 for two or more.[146] This is obviously required to replace the child-care disregard in family credit, though it has been pitched at a slightly higher level. Although it is intended to reflect average costs of childcare and to provide 'an incentive to "shop around" to find good value',[147] it is unlikely to cover the full costs of a nursery place or nanny for a pre-school child.

The virtue of moving to a tax credit system is primarily presentational. There appears much less public, or political, resistance to granting generous tax allowances which increase a person's take-home pay, than to 'paying out' benefits in cash, even though the net cost to the state may be exactly the same. There are some problems however. According to the former Minister for Welfare Reform, Frank Field MP,[148] there is potential for collusion between employers and employees whereby the employer keeps wages low knowing that the worker will have them supplemented by the state. This, of course, has always been recognised—and exploited to employers' advantage. It also has the effect of encouraging entry to, and remaining in, jobs at lower rates of pay than the worker's qualifications and experience should command.[149] This will have long-term consequences for the worker's standard of living in old age. Furthermore, tax credits directly benefit the wage-earner, while cash benefits are redistributive. For this reason, the new system may be more advantageous to lone mothers than to women whose partners are the main or sole breadwinner. Although it is possible, if both parties are earning, to choose which will receive the credit, this of course cannot otherwise be the case. The old problem which prompted the withdrawal of child tax allowances may therefore be repeated.

D. The New Deal for Lone Parents

All governments have baulked at the idea of *compelling* lone mothers to seek work. This is a bridge too far in terms of prevailing family ideology. Instead, measures must *encourage* the motivation and opportunity to go into the market place. Notwithstanding the apparent willingness of single parents to work[150] it is clear from

[146] HM Treasury, *Work Incentives* (n. 144 above), para. 3.05. See the Tax Credits Act 1999.
[147] Department of Social Security, *New Ambitions for Our Country*, n. 42 above, 58.
[148] Speech to the Social Market Foundation, 6 August 1998.
[149] Bryson, Ford, and White, n. 143 above.
[150] Department of Social Security, *Children Come First* (n. 95 above) para. 1.5; Bryson, Ford, and White (n. 143 above).

the growth in the number on income support that such encouragement has so far been inadequate. The Labour Government therefore introduced a 'New Deal for lone parents' in July 1997 on a pilot basis, and nation-wide from April 1998, under which lone parents whose youngest child is aged five or more are targeted for 'help'. Such parents are invited to contact a local New Deal adviser in the Job Centre, followed up by a specific interview invitation. This adviser provides advice on job vacancies, in-work benefits, childcare arrangements, and training opportunities to update skills, etc. He or she can also assist in the preparation of job applications and help the parent develop a 'Personal Plan'. The Government reported that, in the first year of the pilot scheme, lone parents moving into work with family credit had seen their incomes rise by £39 per week, but a more detailed analysis of statistics in individual areas painted a less positive picture. For example, in the Cardiff pilot area, of nearly 4,000 lone parents initially contacted, only 531 attended an initial interview and only 196 had obtained jobs.[151]

It is still too soon to tell whether such initiatives can make a significant impact upon the majority of lone mothers in Britain who continue to remain out of work. If the analysis of Bryson et al. (above) is correct, this will only come about if considerably greater opportunities are given for improving qualifications and experience, coupled with affordable childcare. But instead, the Government appears to favour greater degrees of compulsion. Under its proposals to introduce a single 'gateway' into the benefit system for all claimants, it has resolved to *require* (and not merely *invite*) lone parents, like other applicants,[152] to attend a discussion about opportunities for work and training along with advice on available benefits. In the new welfare philosophy:

it is reasonable to ask those who seek the support of the state to take part in a discussion about the different kinds of help on offer … [and] to make it a condition of benefit that, when asked to do so, people take part in an interview with a personal adviser.[153]

By equating lone parents with all other claimants in this way (albeit still stopping short of requiring them to sign a jobseeker's agreement), the Government reinforces the trend towards downgrading the importance of family responsibilities in order to encourage women into the public sphere of work.

6. CONCLUSION—CAN'T PAY, WON'T PAY

This survey of the social security mechanisms intended to support families—effectively women and children—has demonstrated a reluctance on the part of either the state or men to foot the bill. In an age of formal equality, the refusal of men to take

---

[151] Department of Social Security, Press Release 98/211, 21 July 1998 and 98/080, 31 March 1998.
[152] See Chapter 10 by Laura Lundy for discussion of the 'gateway to work' and New Deal in general.
[153] Department for Education and Employment and Department of Social Security, *A New Contract for Welfare: The Gateway to Work*, Cm 4102 (London: The Stationery Office, 1998), ch. 3, para. 22.

full responsibility for the costs of families can hardly be criticised. Their earnings would in any event be inadequate to do so in the majority of cases, which is why so many married or cohabiting women are working in the first place. The state *could*, of course, meet the cost if it chose, but only through higher taxation and redistribution, which are deemed politically unfeasible in a post-Thatcher age where poverty can be safely regarded as caused, and remedied, by individual rather than structural factors.[154]

The result is a continuation of the 'traditional' situation of women and children— they are more likely to be living in poverty than men, but, because they live their lives in the private sphere, their poverty is revealed only by the consequential drain on the social security budget. The likelihood of their experiencing poverty becomes greater when the family relationship has broken down and there is no male earner in the household. Compounding their difficulties, women's disadvantages will follow them down the years, in the shape of inadequate pension provision and insecurity in old age.[155]

All of the three possible sources of support for women and children have been tried and found wanting in the welfare state era. The national insurance system was predicated on assumptions about women's lives and working patterns which rapidly turned out to be false, or falsified by changes in family relationships, and which there-fore had to be supplemented by inadequate safety-net benefits never intended to pro-vide long-term support. Attempts to encourage liable relatives—in most cases men—to contribute to the maintenance of their first families have failed, both through lack of rigour in enforcement and through over-ambition in the amounts of money asssessed for collection. In any case, it is unrealistic and unfair to place the 'burden' of support upon individual men, who may themselves be facing hardship. The payment of in-work benefits to families demonstrates the realisation that prob-lems of low pay and poverty cannot in fact be redressed by individual effort alone. It cannot therefore sensibly be left to divorcing husbands, or absent parents, to make up for the structural inequalities in society. But encouraging (or coercing) women back into the workplace will not provide the solution to the conundrum. It may be desirable to shatter the stereotyped role of women, but this will be as unfair to them as are the assumptions about the responsibility of men to support their families, so long as women's earnings continue to be lower than those of men and subject to greater disruption through childcare responsibilities. And after all, if men cannot comfortably support their families on one wage, how can women be expected to do so?

The current system therefore falls far short of removing 'want' among families, as Beveridge had hoped. In March 1999, the Prime Ministr, Mr Blair, said of his Government that

---

[154] See B. Jordan, *The New Politics of Welfare* (London: Sage, 1998), *passim*.
[155] See, on pensions, Chapter 6 by Neville Harris (at pp. 176–84).

Our historic aim will be for ours to be the first generation to end child poverty, and it will take a generation. It is a 20 year mission but I believe it can be done.[156]

But apart from the important recognition of the role of education (of both parents and children) in raising aspirations and achievements, the strategy for achieving this aim relies largely on the same potential sources of support that have been discussed above. The state may continue to help—but only through residual support in the form of top-ups of low wages and, if necessary, through the safety-net of income support or its equivalent. Men and women are to be encouraged and helped back to work so that they can directly support their children (with state aid in the form of tax credits to meet the inevitable shortfall). Parents who have separated from their families will be expected to make a contribution, even though for many this can only be a token gesture. It is clear from the history discussed in this chapter, however, that none of these mechanisms will do more than provide partial solutions to the fundamental problem facing women and children in poverty—the continuing refusal to address the underlying assumptions and values relating to their place within society.

---

[156] Beveridge Lecture, Toynbee Hall, London, 18 March 1999.

10

From Welfare to Work?
Social Security and Unemployment

LAURA LUNDY

1. INTRODUCTION

This chapter focuses on a dilemma which is as old as welfare itself—how to ensure that the provision of relief by the state does not remove the incentive for the recipient of assistance to find or retain employment. The New Poor Law provides an illustration of what is perhaps the crudest weapon in the arsenal of measures which might be employed to achieve this objective, that is to make the relief conditional upon institutionalised work. The legal provisions which determined entry into the workhouse in the nineteenth century were simple since: 'the instrument of relief was itself the test of relief'.[1] In modern social security systems, a workfare programme of such a kind would be unacceptable. However, the dilemma remains current and recent years have witnessed a set of increasingly sophisticated measures which strive to link entitlement to social security to the quest for work. The focus of this chapter is to examine the ways in which the Government is currently attempting to ensure that unemployed recipients of social security continue to look for work. The chapter concentrates on jobseeker's allowance (JSA), which is the main income replacement benefit for those who are unemployed but capable of work.[2] JSA was introduced with the express intention of reinforcing the link between the receipt of social security and the search for work. Its title symbolises the transition from the perception of social security as a form of 'benefit', 'assistance', or 'support' to those in need into a permitted allocation to those *en route* to employment or as it was described in 1995: 'a means of support while a person looks for work, not an income from a lifestyle divorced from work'.[3] The objective of all the provisions which are examined in this chapter is clear: to encourage unemployed people to work and *ergo* to stop them from claiming benefit or to ensure that they claim less benefit. The analysis is divided into three sections. The first section examines the reasons why

---

[1] G. Himmelfarb, *The Idea of Poverty*, (London: Faber and Faber, 1985), 165.

[2] JSA was introduced in 1996 as an amalgamation of the contribution-based unemployment benefit and means-tested income support. There are consequently two types of JSA, contributory and income-based. Income support, discussed more fully by Neville Harris in Chapter 6, continues to be paid to unemployed people who are not expected to seek work on account of their illness or age or care responsibilities.

[3] Department of Employment/DSS, *Jobseeker's Allowance*, Cm 2687 (London: HMSO, 1995), para. 2.5. The placing of the apostrophe before the 's' may also have been a deliberate strategy to focus responsibility for the search for work firmly on the individual recipient of the benefit.

social security systems endeavour to encourage unemployed claimants to find work; the second section analyses the current provisions which are designed to achieve this objective; and the final section considers the implications of the Government's proposals for reform.

2. WHY MAKE SOCIAL SECURITY CONDITIONAL UPON WILLINGNESS TO WORK?

The Beveridge Report stipulated that social assistance should be subject to 'any conditions as to behaviour which may seem likely to hasten restoration of earning capacity'.[4] This chapter proceeds on the assumption that it continues to be appropriate to make the receipt of social security conditional upon the claimant satisfying work-focused obligations. If pressed as to why assistance to the unemployed should be made conditional upon a willingness to work, most would instinctively point out that it is not morally justifiable to pay social security to those who are able to work but choose not to. For instance, the classic theory which is usually cited in this context is the voluntary unemployment principle, which defines the purpose of social security as 'to provide against the misfortune of unemployment happening against a person's will'.[5] The corollary of this is that benefits should not be provided to those who are unemployed through their own fault. The voluntary employment principle is most commonly advanced to justify benefit disqualifications for actions inconsistent with a willingness to work.[6] None the less, the notion extends to situations where a claimant has failed to take sufficient positive steps to secure employment or to improve his or her employability. The difficulty is that the principle, while encapsulating to some extent the essence of the labour market rules, does not address satisfactorily the underlying rationale. It provides a basic definition but no explanation as to why entitlement should be confined to those whose unemployment is considered unavoidable.

The argument which is most in vogue currently is based on what has been described as a contractarian approach to welfare.[7] Social contract theorists advocate a theory of justice which places emphasis on the reciprocity of obligations between the citizen and the state. In social security, this translates into the notion that the receipt of benefits should be conditional upon the claimant's readiness to (take reasonable steps to find) work. Work-related conditions are seen to be an essential aspect of a welfare package which is founded on the assumption that entitlement is dependent on the claimant's willingness to work. The approach was apparent in the Beveridge Report where it was stated that the correlative of the state's undertaking to ensure adequate benefit was 'enforcement of the citizen's obligation to seek and

---

[4] Beveridge Report (1942), para. 369.   [5] *R(U) 20/64*, para. 8.

[6] See, generally, K. Kempfer, 'Disqualifications for Voluntary Leaving and Misconduct', (1945) 55/134 *Yale Law J.* 147–66.

[7] See A. Deacon, *Benefit Sanctions for the Jobless: Tough Love or Rough Treatment* (London: Employment Policy Institute, 1997).

accept all reasonable opportunities of work'.[8] However, while evident in the 1940s, the overtly contractual nature of the relationship has come to the fore more recently. Since the mid 1990s the language of social security has been imbued with contractual terms: from the Conservatives' jobseeker's *agreement* to Labour's New *Deal*. It is at its most explicit in the 1998 Green Paper, *A New Contract for Welfare,* in which the movement declared its intention to bring about a fundamental change in the relationship between the Government and claimants to a 'new welfare contract between the citizen and Government, based on responsibilities and rights'.[9] This emphasis on the contractual entitlement might be seen to have developed out of traditional notions of citizenship as guaranteeing individuals minimum levels of income to a more active form of citizenship where the receipt of assistance places obligations on the recipient.[10] For those who advocate this approach, the responsibility to seek work does not have to be justified outside this framework since it is an inherent part of the claimant/state relationship.

From a more pragmatic point of view, the key reasons which are advanced to support work-related conditions are related to the economics of unemployment. It is generally regarded that the cost of unemployment includes not just the actual payments of social security but the other losses to the public purse from taxes and national insurance which might have been paid along with the indirect costs arising from the poor health and increased criminal activity which are associated with long-term unemployment.[11] It is in the public's interest that the social security rules should be used to reduce such expenditure. In addition, the costs of unemployment have to be met from the national insurance fund and/or the Exchequer, a position which is considered to be unfair on those who contribute to these funds. When JSA was introduced, the Government justified new benefit sanctions on the basis that they 'protect the taxpayer and National Insurance contributor from subsidising people who have no good reason to be, or to remain unemployed'.[12] The same argument has been underlined in the case law,[13] and has been reiterated time after time in Parliament and acknowledged by bodies such as the Social Security Advisory Committee.[14] It is widely accepted that it is not fair to those who fund the benefit system through work to pay benefits to those who choose not to work.

Other arguments focus on the benefits for claimants themselves, asserting that work-focused obligations are in the claimant's long-term interest. Work is considered to be good for the individual not only on account of its income-generating capacity

---

[8] Beveridge Report (1942), para. 130.   [9] Green Paper (1998), 3.

[10] For further discussion of this, see Chapter 1.

[11] See generally, The Employment Committee, Second Report, *The Right to Work/Workfare,* HC 82 Session 1995–96, (London: HMSO, 1996), paras 64–9.

[12] Department of Employment/DSS, *Jobseeker's Allowance,* Cm 2687 (London: HMSO, 1995), para. 4.35.

[13] One Commissioner compared a claim for unemployment benefit after the loss of a job to a person who throws their bags overboard on a boat and then tries to claim for the loss on their travel insurance. *R(U) 4/87,* para. 9.

[14] See for instance, the Social Security Advisory Committee, *Sixth Report* (London: HMSO, 1988).

but also because it reinforces the individual's autonomy and self-esteem.[15] It is there-fore considered appropriate for the state to use the social security system to reinforce societal values about the work ethic. The social security rules are considered to have an important role both in discouraging unemployment and in reinforcing incentives for unemployed people to take the right steps to get back into work.[16] Since work is the individual's best route out of poverty, work-focused obligations are in the claimant's own interest. A variation of this argument is based on the benefit which claimants are thought to derive from the effect of labour market rules on the pub-lic's perception of the unemployed. For instance, in 1923, the Minister of Labour justified tough new labour market conditions on the basis that: 'the administration of benefit should not be allowed to fall into disrepute owing to benefit being paid to persons who are not really doing their utmost to secure work'.[17] There is also a modern view that: 'a system with no incentive to work legitimises the accusation that all claimants are feckless'.[18] It may be of little consolation to the individual claimant faced with a barrage of labour market conditions that they are doing their bit to maintain the general reputation of the unemployed. None the less, without such rules, accusations that the system places a bounty on idleness would be easy to make and difficult to defend.

Whatever the reason which one finds most convincing, the fact that the system should encourage claimants to work is uncontroversial. Two assumptions underpin the rules. These are that claimants who are capable of work should attempt to find work and that the state should restrict assistance to those who are unemployed through no fault of their own. There is nothing new or startling in these assump-tions. They have cross-party political support. When JSA was introduced, the Conservative Government emphasised that: 'those who can play an active part in the labour market should receive support when they are genuinely unable to find a job, but not when they have no intention of looking for one'.[19] In a similar vein, one of Labour's key principles is that: 'The new welfare state should help and encourage people of working age to work where they are capable of doing so',[20] a sentiment since condensed into the motto 'work for those who can, security for those who can-not'.[21] Such party political differences as exist (and these are increasingly difficult to discern) emerge only in an analysis of the strategies adopted within the social secu-rity system to reinforce the obligation to seek work.

---

[15] See, S. Sayers, 'The need to work: a perspective from philosophy', in R. E. Pahl (ed.), *On Work* (Oxford: Basil Blackwell Ltd., 1988), 722–41.

[16] *Jobseeker's Allowance* (1995), n. 3 above, para. 2.4.

[17] *Per* T. Shaw, Minister for Labour, cited in A. Deacon, *In Search of the Scrounger* (London: G. Bell and Sons, 1976), 36.

[18] Social Security Advisory Committee, *Sixth Report* (London: HMSO, 1988), para. 3.2.

[19] *Jobseeker's Allowance* (1995), n. 3 above, para. 1.6.   [20] Green Paper (1998), 20.

[21] DSS, *A New Contract for Welfare: The Gateway to Work*, Cm 4102 (London: The Stationery Office, 1998), ch. 1, para. 7.

3. WORK-RELATED SOCIAL SECURITY PROVISIONS

The policy intention of encouraging claimants to look for work and restricting assistance to those unavoidably unemployed must be translated into workable legal provisions. A key problem is that claimants' attitudes towards employment cannot be pigeon-holed into one simple category. It is widely accepted that few people are completely work-shy.[22] However, some claimants face structural or personal barriers to employment such as a lack of childcare or suitable education or training. Other claimants may have become disillusioned by their failure to obtain employment (a group referred to by Mead as the 'dutiful but depressed').[23] The legislative approaches adopted need to reflect the different reasons why people are unwilling or unable to find work. At one end of the spectrum, policy makers might employ a scheme which simply requires claimants to declare an intention to make themselves available for work. At the other end, governments can impose time-limited periods of claim, for example, by removing benefit from all claimants if they have not found work within six months of the initial claim. In between, responses vary from obligations to engage in active work-search to disqualifications for those who have deliberately refused an opportunity to work or failed to participate in work-related training. Most systems employ a mixed strategy which balances conditions with disqualifications and incentives with penalties. For the purposes of this chapter, the analysis of current United Kingdom provision is divided into three categories: conditions of entitlement; sanctions for failure to meet appropriate labour standards; and incentives to work.

In the discussion which follows, the work-related provisions will be analysed individually. However, at the outset, it is worth bearing in mind the impact which the rules will have cumulatively. One of the most interesting facets of the law in this area has been that it has developed incrementally with reform coming on top of reform. Provisions in the Jobseekers Act 1995 can be traced directly to the National Insurance Act 1911. Moreover, measures which were vigorously opposed by the Labour Party in opposition have been adopted and even enhanced when it assumed power.[24] Welfare history in this context is not characterised by party-political swings but by a steady tightening of the rules which reinforce the obligation to seek work. The end result has been a layering of conditions which over time has built into a considerable wall which has to be surmounted by those who are capable of work yet wish to claim assistance from the state. The volume and complexity is somewhat ironic given that one of the key objectives behind the introduction of JSA was to

---

[22] See for instance, Department of Employment/DSS, *Jobseeker's Allowance* (London: HMSO, 1995), Cm. 2687, para. 4.35, where the Conservative Government acknowledged that: 'The overwhelming majority of people who become unemployed make every effort to find employment at the earliest opportunity.'

[23] L. Mead, *The Politics of Poverty* (New York: Basic Books, 1992), 170–2.

[24] This was regularly commented upon in Parliament during the debates on the Welfare Reform and Pensions Bill 1999. See for instance, Mr I. Duncan Smith, Hansard, H.C. Debs, Vol. 326, col. 234, 23 February 1999.

provide simpler and clearer rules.[25] With few exceptions, JSA has produced a 'legislative swirl of social security sections',[26] which might not only reduce claimants' understanding of their rights and obligations, but also increase the scope for error in decision making. Successive annual reports of the Chief Adjudication Officer have been scathing about the quality of decision making, most recently in relation to the labour market conditions.[27] It will be apparent from a consideration of the rules below that the consequence of error is significant since a mistake will lead not to a miscalculation but to a denial of assistance.

A. Labour-market Conditions

JSA has a number of provisions which make the receipt of relief conditional upon the claimant engaging in behaviour which will improve his or her prospects of finding work. Each of the conditions considered requires a claimant to take some form of action to prove his or her willingness to work. In the contractarian analysis, these conditions might be considered to be the fundamental terms of the contract, since breach of these conditions entitles the state to rescind. In each case, a failure to satisfy the condition of entitlement will result in benefit being withdrawn.[28] The labour market conditions are detailed in the chronological order in which they appeared in the statute books, namely, availability (1946), actively seeking work (1989), the jobseeker's agreement (1996), and New Deal (1997). It is notable that, after a forty-year lull there has been a veritable flurry of legislative activity in the past ten years and that the recent changes mark a significant shift along the workfare spectrum.

(i) Availability for Work

In order to qualify for JSA a claimant must be available for employment.[29] Until 1989 this was the only provision which required the claimant to do something positive to find work.[30] To comply with it, all a claimant had to do was to appear in person at the benefit office, 'sign on', and thus register as available for employment should an opportunity arise. The claimant's physical presence was the proof that he or she was available for work. Although claimants were asked at the first interview to complete a questionnaire as to their availability, a government review in 1988 considered that

---

[25] *Jobseeker's Allowance* (1995), n. 3 above, para. 3.7.

[26] J. Fulbrook, 'The Jobseekers Act 1995: Consolidation with a Sting of Contractual Compliance' (1995) 24 *I.L.J.* 395–401, 395.

[27] Chief Adjudication Officer, *Annual Report of the Chief Adjudication Officer 1997–1998* (London: The Stationery Office, 1998), 64–5, where the CAO noted his disappointment with the 61 per cent comment rate for labour market decisions taken by front-line adjudication officers.

[28] In a small number of exceptions, claimants may receive hardship payments. See the discussion of hardship payments at 309 below.

[29] JS Act 1995, s. 1(1).

[30] This condition formed part of the basic conditions of entitlement to unemployment benefit: National Insurance Act 1946, s. 11.

this was easily circumvented by those who wished to abuse the system.[31] As a result, a new more detailed questionnaire designed 'to ensure that claimants are really looking for work and are not restricting their choice of jobs' was introduced for both initial claims and six-month reviews.[32] A similar form is now part of the process leading to the construction of the jobseeker's agreement which is considered later in the chapter.[33]

A person is considered to be available for employment if he or she is 'willing and able to take up immediately employed earner's employment'.[34] A claimant can be treated as being available for work in a number of situations (for instance, where they are engaged in emergency work).[35] Other categories of claimant are deemed unavailable in all instances.[36] If a claimant does not fall within one of these exceptional categories, the focus will be on his or her availability for work and not the actual availability of jobs.[37] A claimant has to be available for work even if there is no work to do. Availability is determined in the context of a fictitious rather than the prevailing labour market. In contrast, it will be seen that when a claimant attempts to place restrictions on the work which they are prepared to do, reality re-emerges and a claimant may be considered to have jeopardised his or her prospect of employment in the light of the actual industrial conditions.[38]

The availability condition is an attempt to gauge the answer to a relatively simple question: is the claimant willing to work? The problem lies in finding a suitable way to ascertain the required degree of willingness since 'availability is to a very real extent a state of mind'.[39] What a person thinks can only practically be measured by what they do and this is also the case in determining availability. The administrative guidance states that whether or not a claimant is available depends on his or her 'intentions and attitude towards employment' and suggests that the following might act as proof: the claimant says they are available and does all that is required to prove it; the claimant gives promises that are normally accepted as proving availability; and there is nothing in their statements or actions to suggest that they are not available.[40] In practice, doubts about availability will normally arise where the claimant has

---

[31] Department for Education and Employment, *Training for Employment*, Cm. 316 (London: HMSO, 1988), para. 7.14

[32] Ibid.　　[33] *Helping You Back to Work*, ES. 2.

[34] JS Act 1995, s. 6(1). Some claimants such as carers and voluntary workers do not have to be available immediately but can expect 24 or 48-hours' notice. JSA Regs 1996, reg. 5.

[35] JSA Regs 1996, reg. 14.

[36] Ibid., reg. 15. The largest single category of excluded claimants is students. See generally Chapter 11. However, prisoners on temporary release and women receiving maternity pay or allowance are also deemed unavailable.

[37] *R(U) 1/55.*

[38] Adjudication officers will look at the type and number of vacancies within daily travelling distance of the claimant's home in determining whether he or she has a reasonable prospect of securing employment. See JSA Regs 1996, reg. 10(1)(b).

[39] National Insurance Advisory Committee, *The Availability Question* (London: HMSO, 1953), Cmd. 8894, para. 12.

[40] *Adjudication Officers' Guide*, para. 26200.

restricted the work which they will accept with the result that their chances of obtaining employment were seriously prejudiced. In view of this, regulations prescribe the work which a claimant has to be prepared to accept and limit the restrictions which a claimant might put on that work. Not all restrictions are rendered unacceptable in the legislation. The overarching test is that a claimant has not put so many restrictions on his or her availability that he or she has no reasonable prospect of obtaining employment.[41]

In terms of the hours worked, a claimant must be prepared to take a job which would involve at least forty hours work per week. The hours (and the spread of the hours across the day) can be restricted where it is reasonable to do so in the light of the claimant's physical or mental condition or where the claimant has certain care responsibilities, provided the claimant is still available for at least sixteen hours per week and has a reasonable chance of finding a job in spite of the restricted hours.[42] On the other hand, claimants must be prepared to be available for jobs of under forty hours per week although in practice no-one is expected to work less than twenty-four hours.[43] The expectations are quite extensive. An unwary claimant who declares that he or she is prepared to work the society norm of thirty-five hours a week from 9–5 p.m. would almost certainly be considered to be unavailable for work and, as Fulbrook points out: 'Appropriate warnings from employment officers, of the Judges Rules or Fifth Amendment variety, are unlikely in the Jobcentre.'[44]

A thorny issue in the context of acceptable restrictions is the issue of pay. The general rule is that claimants must not place any restrictions on the rate of pay which they are prepared to receive once they have been unemployed six months.[45] One of the questions asked in the process leading up to the compilation of the jobseeker's agreement is: 'What is the lowest wage you are willing to accept?'[46] Leaving aside the disheartening impact that this 'how low will you go?' approach might have on a new claimant, high expectations about prospective wages can lead to benefit being refused. This is in spite of the fact that the evidence shows that most claimants are ultimately prepared to take employment at levels below their reservation wage.[47] Some protection has been afforded by the introduction of the minimum wage since it should now be unreasonable to expect claimants to work for an unlawful level of pay. Moreover, in-work benefits provide families with a minimum wage guarantee

---

[41] The JSA Regs 1996, reg. 10.

[42] All claimants may restrict their hours of availability to 40 or more if this is in their jobseeker's agreement and does not considerably reduce their prospects of employment: ibid., reg. 6(1).

[43] Ibid., reg. 6(2).

[44] J. Fulbrook, 'The Jobseekers Act 1995: Consolidation with a Sting of Contractual Compliance', (1995) 24 *I.L.J.* 395–401, 400–1.

[45] JSA Regs 1996, reg. 9. An exception is made where the restriction is because of a physical or mental problem: reg. 13(3).

[46] Employment Service, 'Helping you back to work', Form ES2, Q. 10.

[47] H. Trickey, K. Kellard, R. Walker, K. Ashworth, A. Smith, *Unemployment and Jobseeking: Two years on*, DSS Research Report No. 87 (London: The Stationery Office, 1998), 85.

which should avoid a situation where they end up worse off in work.[48] However, claimants aged over twenty-five without children could be expected to work for twenty-four hours a week at the minimum wage of £3.60 per hour, giving them a current total of £86.40. This could leave a claimant with a considerable shortfall between income and expenditure if he or she has a partner and/or housing costs which are not catered for outside the benefit system.[49]

Claimants may also wish to place restrictions on the nature of the work which they are prepared to accept. This is acceptable in situations where the restrictions are reasonable in view of their physical or mental condition or if a particular job is in contravention of a religious belief or a conscientious objection.[50] However, a key issue is how long a claimant may insist on looking for the type of work in which he or she has previously engaged. The regulations provide that a jobseeker's agreement may include a permitted period up to a maximum of thirteen weeks during which a claimant may restrict his or her availability to their normal occupation or normal pay.[51] When the employment officer is deciding whether to allow a permitted period and/or how long that should be, he or she will have regard to what the normal occupation is, relevant skills or qualifications, the length of time spent training or working in that occupation and the location and availability of jobs in that field. There is a difficulty in balancing these factors since a person with a highly specialised skill may be considered unlikely to be able to get any employment in his or her field and therefore not allowed any permitted period. In any event, the rules classify all claimants as in the same position after three months of unemployment. There is no social hierarchy of unemployment. The graduate who trained for five years and worked for ten must be available for the simplest manual work if he or she cannot find work in their normal line after thirteen weeks. When a person is unemployed for three months, they are uniformly expected to 'broaden their horizons',[52] (or, more prosaically, lower their sights). This might be considered to be a waste of that person's skills which could lead to a general dampening of ambition. On the other hand, the well-qualified person is still making the same drain on the fund or exchequer as the person with no qualifications and little employment experience.

It has been pointed out that there is a difficulty in formulating sufficiently precise guidelines for those administering the availability test yet retaining an approach which is flexible enough to take account of the individual characteristics of the claimant.[53] In attempting to address the issues, the foundational labour market condition has spawned a series of increasingly detailed regulations which seek to define the appropriate degree of willingness. One wonders whether it is necessary to have this level of detail when in practice much of it is gathering dust or performing an

---

[48] Family credit is available where the claimant or his or her partner is working over 16 hours a week. From October 1999 it will be replaced by the working families tax credit. See Chapter 9.
[49] Housing Benefit does not cover mortgage interest costs.
[50] JSA Regs 1996, reg. 13.   [51] Ibid., reg. 16.
[52] *Per* Mr P. Lilley, Hansard, H.C. Debs, Vol. 264, col. 632, 24 October 1994.
[53] See Ogus, Barendt, and Wikeley (1995), 104.

unnecessary task. For instance, there are detailed exceptions which allow certain claimants to have a period of notice for employment of twenty-four or forty-eight hours even though few immediate chances of employment are likely to occur. Moreover, since a large proportion of claimants get work during the first three months of unemployment, it seems wasteful to spend time determining which claimants should be allowed to look for a particular type of work or pay during that period.[54] When the actively-seeking-work condition was introduced (see below), some commentators argued that this newcomer to the rules was unnecessary.[55] The converse may also be true. The actively-seeking-work test could be reformulated to take into account the essential aspects of availability.[56] Moreover, when presented with tests of availability—the offer of a job or even a place on a scheme—the claimant can be disqualified under other provisions of the legislation. If the availability condition were to be removed, its more robust offspring could well get on with the task of testing willingness to work.

(ii) *Actively Seeking Work*

In order to qualify for JSA, a claimant must be 'actively' seeking work.[57] The requirement was introduced in 1989 (in the unemployment benefit scheme) to remedy perceived gaps in the availability condition, namely that there was no requirement for the unemployed to look for a job actively (as opposed to passively waiting for work to be offered to them) and that this encouraged claimants to abuse the system. Evidence was presented of claimants who had lost the desire to work.[58] The statistical basis for this has been disputed.[59] However, whether or not the problem had increased, the actively-seeking-work test was not completely new in 1989. For a start the existing case law on availability for work had emphasised that there was a responsibility on claimants to take active steps to obtain work.[60] Moreover, claimants were routinely questioned at the time of claim on the steps they would take to find work. None the less, the introduction of the obligation as a separate statutory requirement was controversial, being hailed by many as a return to the 'genuinely seeking whole time employment' condition of entitlement which had been in operation in the 1920s.[61] The condition was repealed in 1930 in the wake of a government report

---

[54] H. Trickey, K. Kellard, R. Walker, K. Ashworth, A. Smith, *Unemployment and Jobseeking: Two years on,* DSS Research Report No. 87 (London: The Stationery Office, 1998), ch. 9, 151–63. The research shows that about half of all jobseekers found employment within the first 12 weeks of claiming and two-thirds within 6 months.

[55] See for instance, T. Buck, 'Actively Seeking Work', (1989) 18 *I.L.J.* 258–65, 259.

[56] The 'work' which a claimant is required to actively seek could be defined in such a way as to prohibit excessive restrictions being imposed by claimants.   [57] JS Act 1995, s. 1(2)(c).

[58] Department for Employment, *Training for Employment,* Cm 316 (London, HMSO, 1988), ch. 7, 33–6; and Department for Employment, Cm 540, *Employment for the 1990s* (London, HMSO, 1988), 54–8.

[59] See N. Wikeley, 'Unemployment Benefit, the State and the Labour Market', (1989) 16(3) *J. of Law and Society,* 290–309, 298–300; T. Buck, 'Actively Seeking Work', (1989) 18 *I.L.J.* 258–65, 263–4.

[60] See for instance *R(U)5/80,* para. 14 where a Commissioner stated that: 'availability implies some active step by the person concerned to draw attention to his availability'.

[61] Unemployment Insurance Act 1921, s. 3(3)(b).

which concluded that the test was not working.[62] Beveridge is often quoted as expressing the hope that it would never arise from 'its dishonoured grave'.[63] None the less, in 1989 it was revived by the Conservatives and has subsequently been adopted by the Labour Government in spite of vociferous opposition at the time it was first proposed.

The requirement to actively seek work is the *actus reus* (just as availability is in some senses the *mens rea)* of the obligation to seek work. Active job search can only be established through proof of things which have actually been done. A person is considered to be actively seeking work if he or she takes 'such steps as he can reasonably be expected to take in order to have the best prospect of securing employment'.[64] Steps are defined by the regulations to include: oral and written applications; seeking information from advertisements, employers, and employment agencies; registration with an employment agency; and the appointment of a third party to assist.[65] No account is taken of informal networks in spite of the fact that many claimants hear of jobs through word of mouth from friends.[66] Generally speaking a claimant must take more than one step on one occasion per week.[67] However, there may be occasions where one step on one occasion is all that is reasonable for the person in question to do that week. The decision as to whether a claimant has taken sufficient steps is a question of fact to be determined by the adjudication officer who will have regard to all the circumstances of the case and in particular: the claimant's skills, qualifications, abilities, and physical or mental limitations; the person's work experience and the duration of his or her unemployment; any steps taken in previous weeks; the availability and location of vacancies; and engagement in activities or training which may enable the claimant to be deemed to be available for employment.[68]

The test was given further bite in 1996 when it was merged into JSA. One of the key criticisms of the condition was that it was wide open to abuse by the genuinely work-shy claimant. There were ways in which a person who wished to avoid work could comply with the test 'by adhering to the letter of the law'[69] but effectively spoil their chances of obtaining employment (anti-social behaviour at interview or coffee rings on application forms). The Government was alive to these possibilities and, in an attempt to clamp down on tactics which would undermine the individual's job prospects, introduced a number of provisions under which a claimant's acts will be disregarded.[70] Each of these is intended to remove entitlement where the

---

[62] *Report of the Committee on the Procedure and Evidence for the Determination of Claims of Unemployment Insurance Benefit*, Cmnd 3415 (London: HMSO, 1929), paras 35–44.
[63] W. Beveridge, *Unemployment—A Problem of Industry* (1930) 280, cited in N. Wikeley, 'Unemployment Benefit, the State and the Labour Market' (1989) 16(3) *J. of Law and Society*, 309–90, 307.
[64] JS Act 1995, s. 7(1). Certain categories of claimant are deemed to be actively seeking work. The JSA Regs 1996, regs 19–21.
[65] JSA Regs 1996, reg. 18(2).
[66] H. Trickey, K. Kellard, R. Walker, K. Ashworth, A. Smith, *Unemployment and Jobseeking: Two years on*, DSS Research Report No. 87 (London: The Stationery Office, 1998), 142.
[67] JSA Regs 1996, reg. 18 (1).   [68] Ibid., reg. 18(3).
[69] Department of Employment/DSS, *Jobseeker's Allowance*, Cm 2687 (London: HMSO, 1995), para. 4.13.
[70] Ibid., reg. 18(4).

unemployed person's behaviour is such that it 'actively militates against finding work'.[71] The first of these is where he or she has acted in a violent or abusive manner. The second is where they have deliberately spoiled an application form. The final and perhaps most controversial instance is where 'by his behaviour or appearance he otherwise undermined his prospects of securing the employment in question'. The White Paper had suggested that claimants could be directed 'to present themselves acceptably to employers'.[72] This gave rise to concern about the limits of the state in policing such issues and the possibility of claimants being subjected to conditions which might be inherently racist or sexist. In the end, the legislation adopts a narrower restriction which requires the appearance or behaviour to constitute a deliberate attempt to undermine job chances. Nevertheless, the rules send out an unsavoury message about the personal appearance and behaviour of unemployed people and reinforce the notion that unemployment is the claimant's own fault rather than due to the unavailability of suitable jobs.[73]

Everyone would accept that unemployed people should be taking active steps to look for work. The problem is that a legal requirement to actively seek work remains difficult to police. Decision makers cannot properly judge the claimant's efforts without being at the job interview or seeing the actual application form submitted. It is costly and time consuming to review each individual's efforts and, at the end of the day, it will simply allow them to disregard one 'step'. If there are a number of others, the claimant may well be considered to have actively sought work. Moreover, if the claimant loses entitlement for having failed to satisfy the condition, there is nothing to stop him or her claiming again the next week (unless disqualified under another head). The 1920s genuinely-seeking-work condition was dropped because proving 'genuineness' was considered to be 'an impossible task'.[74] An effective legislative means of policing 'activeness' is similarly elusive.

Claimants' attitudes towards employment fall roughly into one of three categories: work-shy, looking for work, and waiting for work (i.e. those who want to work but who have given up an active search). Even with the requirement to actively seek work, it remains possible for work-shy claimants to remain on benefit. Moreover, claimants who are actively seeking work are doing what the law requires anyway. On this basis, the requirement to prove active work search should have its greatest impact on the third category of claimant—those who want to work but have become disillusioned by their lack of success in obtaining work. Unfortunately, while the labour market rules may sustain the pressure on such claimants to look for work, they also provide a setting in which the award of entitlement is an acknowledgment of

---

[71] N. 69 above.   [72] Ibid., para. 4.18.

[73] For a critique of this provision, see N. Wikeley, 'The Jobseeker's Act 1995: What the unemployed need is a good haircut . . .' (1995) 25 *I.L.J.* 71–6.

[74] *Report of the Committee on the Procedure and Evidence for the Determination of Claims of Unemployment Insurance Benefit*, Cmnd 3415 (London: HMSO, 1929), para. 41. The Committee suggested that adequate protection to the fund was afforded by a disqualification for those refusing offers of suitable employment (para. 43).

failure. If claimants are confronted with their inability to obtain employment once a fortnight, this might compound their sense of inadequacy and lead to further demoralisation. There is also a danger that genuine claimants will spend their time complying with the test rather than doing the most effective things to get work. Although claimants are aware of the need to provide proof of jobsearch, few believe that their efforts in this regard will secure employment.[75] Proving may well hinder doing, if claimants' time is skewed towards convincing benefit officers rather than following their instincts about the things which give them the best chance of obtaining work.

(iii) The Jobseeker's Agreement

In order to qualify for JSA a claimant must have entered into a written jobseeker's agreement with an employment officer (EO).[76] The agreement was intended to 'build on the strengths' of the administrative 'back to work' plan which had been used by the Employment Service from 1990.[77] Aside from personal information, the agreement must contain the following information: the hours the claimant is available for work per week including a breakdown per day (unless the claimant says that they are available to work any time); any restrictions placed on the work the claimant is prepared to do; the types of jobs sought; the steps which will be taken to actively seek work; and the details of any permitted period if there is one. To be effective, the agreement must be signed by the permitted period.[78] The EO will sign the agreement if satisfied that there is no dispute and that the claimant is available for and actively seeking work.[79] If the EO is not satisfied, he or she will pass the proposed agreement to an AO (or, post-SSA 1998, the Secretary of State's official) who will decide if it is reasonable for the claimant to agree to it or, if the claimant is proposing something different, whether the claimant would qualify as available and actively seeking work.[80]

The EO will conduct a short review of the claimant's compliance with the agreement each fortnight when the claimant is signing on. In addition there are full advisory interviews after thirteen weeks where the agreement will be reviewed.[81] When reviewing the claimant's progress the EO is assisted by a computer database called the 'Labour Market System' (LMS) which not only records the interviews but can also be used to match claimants to suitable vacancies in their area. If the EO is not happy with the claimant's progress, he or she may issue a jobseeker's direction, specifying that a claimant must take a particular course of action to increase his or her chances of employment.[82] This might include a direction to apply for a particular job, send a curriculum vitae to a particular employer, or take steps to improve appearance

---

[75] H. Trickey, K. Kellard, R. Walker, K. Ashworth, A. Smith, *Unemployment and Jobseeking: Two years on,* DSS Research Report No. 87 (London: The Stationery Office, 1998), 149.
[76] JS Act 1995, s. 1(2)(b).   [77] N. 69 above, para. 2.11.   [78] JSA Regs 1996, reg. 31.
[79] JS Act 1995, s. 9.
[80] The AO/official must normally make a decision within 14 days. If the claimant is dissatisfied with the outcome of this, he or she can ask for it to be reviewed by a different AO/official, after which there is a right of appeal to a tribunal: JS Act 1995, s. 9(6)–(7).
[81] There are also restart interviews at 6, 12, 18, and 24 months.   [82] JS Act 1995, s. 19(10)(b).

or behaviour. A direction can also require the claimant to sign up for specified training and employment programmes. A direction can be made at any time but is intended to operate as a last resort and is likely only to be issued where the claimant has persistently not taken a particular action or blatantly ignored an obvious route to employment.[83] The directions are the teeth of the jobseeker's agreement since a failure to comply with a direction may result in a benefit sanction being imposed.

The jobseeker's agreement is a tangible manifestation of the contractarian approach to welfare. By signing an agreement, the claimant is providing written evidence of his or her side of the bargain. However, it has been pointed out that the term 'agreement' is something of a euphemism in this context, given the associated notions of partnership, free choice, and equality of bargaining power. As Fulbrook has observed: 'There seems little leeway here for a "meeting of the minds" but rather more the concept of "take it or leave it".'[84] One of the most vociferous opponents of the agreements asserted in Parliament that he had 'never heard, however, of an agreement or contract that falls to be arbitrated by one of the parties to it and under which one party may impose penalties. In such circumstances, to talk of a jobseeker's agreement is an abuse of language in an abuse of power.'[85] The official's hand which shakes on this agreement is truly a glove of velvet masking a fist of steel, since failure to sign the agreement will result in the claimant being denied benefit. The possible loss of entitlement undoubtedly has the capacity to affect the claimant's approach to the issue, a situation which is tantamount to duress but on the other hand might be interpreted as a fundamental element of the overall welfare package which demands co-operation on the road to employment.

The jobseeker's agreement provides a new mechanism for monitoring the labour market conditions of entitlement. The agreement and attendant reviews provide a new means of policing the claimant's availability and active work search. However, it was envisaged that the agreement would do more than this. In particular, it was seen as an opportunity to provide the claimant with information and guidance as to how to get back to work.[86] Its forebear, the Back to Work Plan, appears to have had limited success in this respect.[87] Moreover, the compulsory nature of the agreement may not be conducive to the type of relationship envisaged by the policy makers. Much depends on its implementation and in particular on the relationship between the claimant and EO. The latter has a difficult job in finding the right balance between facilitator and enforcer. Rigid enforcement of the directions will undoubtedly jeopardise the advisor/counsellor role, yet a softly, softly approach might prove ineffective. Buck anticipated that this dilemma might lead to the decision makers and claimants colluding to produce a 'bureaucratic exercise which bears little relevance to

---

[83] *Employment Service Guidance, Interviewing Policy Volume*, ch. 5, para. 4.

[84] J. Fulbrook, 'The Jobseekers Act 1995: Consolidation with a Sting of Contractual Compliance' (1995) 24 *I.L.J.* 395–401.

[85] *Per* Mr A. Howarth, Hansard, H.C. Debs, Vol. 262, col. 600.   [86] N. 69 above, para. 4.18.

[87] A. Nove and N. Smith, *The Employment Service National Customer Satisfaction Survey 1994*, ES Research and Evaluation Report No. 103 (London: HMSO, 1995).

the economic realities of the job market'.[88] There is some evidence that this is the case, since the majority of claimants have noticed little or no difference in the procedure for 'signing on' since the implementation of JSA.[89] Those claimants who have noted changes commented upon the more rigorous checking and the active role in presenting job opportunities.[90] Since the introduction of New Deal, considered next, the guidance and counselling function has become an integral part of the gateway period for some claimants, leaving the jobseeker's agreement to police the tougher condition-based part of entitlement.

(iv) New Deal

New Deal was introduced by the Labour Government as a strategy for getting certain categories of claimants, namely eighteen to twenty-four year olds, lone parents, the disabled and those over twenty-five who have been unemployed for two years, back into work. New Deal is the flagship of Labour's Welfare to Work policy which was a cornerstone of the Labour Party's 1997 election manifesto. The schemes were funded initially by a one-off windfall levy on the profits of private companies. The title, while echoing the Roosevelt reforms in the United States in the 1930s, reflects the modern British emphasis on the 'rights and responsibilities' of claimants. The focus of New Deal is to get claimants into work, an objective emphasised in its public sound bite: 'as more sign up, fewer sign on'. The New Deal requirements are not classified officially as separate labour market conditions since they were bolted in to the existing provisions on training and employment programmes. None the less, those who are required to participate face a significant additional obligation which must be complied with if the claimant is to continue to receive assistance.

There are a number of New Deal schemes, two of which are directed at the traditional unemployed—that is, young people and the long-term unemployed.[91] New Deal is compulsory for all those aged between eighteen and twenty-four who have been unemployed for six months and those aged over twenty-five who have been unemployed for two years. New Deal for Young People is the largest and most ambitious of all the New Deal programmes.[92] Its first stage is known as the 'gateway' period, which is intended to provide claimants with an intensive period of counselling advice and guidance. During this time the claimant is allocated a personal adviser who will carry out an interview and draw up a New Deal action plan. This will set out realistic job goals. Claimants are not required to sign the plan but the jobseeker's agreement will be brought into line with the plan and failure to comply with

---

[88] T. Buck, 'Jobseeker's Allowance: policy perspectives', (1996) 3 *J.S.S.L.* 149–64, 157.

[89] H. Trickey, K. Kellard, R. Walker, K. Ashworth, A. Smith, *Unemployment and Jobseeking: Two years on*, DSS Research Report No. 87 (London: The Stationery Office, 1998), 136–7.

[90] Ibid.

[91] Other New Deal schemes include New Deal for Lone Parents (discussed by Gillian Douglas in Chapter 9), New Deal for the Disabled and, more recently, New Deal for the Partners of the Unemployed, New Deal for Communities, and New Deal for the over 50s (announced in the March 1999 budget).

[92] New Deal for the over 25s does not have a 'gateway' period although it begins with an intensive period of guidance. The options are limited to education and training and subsidised employment.

an aspect of the jobseeker's agreement can result in a sanction. The intention is that claimants will have found employment or entered a New Deal option before the end of the gateway period. If not, the claimant will be required to participate in the option which the personal adviser considers most appropriate.[93] There are four New Deal options: full-time education or training for up to twelve months during which the participant receives an allowance equivalent to JSA; a job with an employer who will be subsidised for six months; voluntary work for six months during which the participant receives a wage or allowance equivalent to JSA along with a grant of £400; and finally work with the Environment Taskforce for six months during which the participant receives a wage or allowance equivalent to JSA along with a grant of £400. At the end of the option, if the claimant has not found a job, they can re-claim JSA, but will normally participate in a 'follow-through' period.

The Government has emphasised that there is no 'fifth option'. Participation in one of these options is effectively compulsory since a failure to participate will result in a sanction. The sanctions are not, however, different from the sanctions that have been in place since the introduction of JSA. In fact, New Deal did not require primary legislation, simply a set of regulations to amend the list of compulsory training and employment programmes.[94] New Deal's novelty lies in its scale and style rather than its substance, a fact which explains why it was possible to slot it into the existing statutory framework. However, a key difference between New Deal and other compulsory training programmes is that claimants who refuse to participate in the New Deal for Young People have a more restricted access to hardship payments than is usual.[95] This clearly increases the pressure to participate, since the alternative to New Deal is not a reduction in benefit but no benefit at all. Furthermore, the Government has recently announced an intention to introduce regulations which would enable those who refuse to participate in a New Deal option three times to be sanctioned for six months.[96]

New Deal was given a cautious welcome by groups working with the unemployed. It has attractive features in that there is an emphasis on individual support and training and that extra money has been pumped into the scheme to counteract some of the problems associated with earlier training schemes. There is also a new emphasis on partnership with employers and many high-profile companies have signed up to participate. The financial incentives for employers are balanced with labour market protections for existing workers.[97] Moreover, employers must promise to treat those on the New Deal schemes the same way as they treat other employees and give a commitment to retaining them at the end of the subsidised period, subject to their competence and commitment. In this way New Deal avoids some of the key criti-

[93] JSA Regs 1996, reg. 75(1)(a)(ii) (for the Employment Option, Voluntary Sector Option, and Environment Task Force Option) and reg. 75(1)(b)(ii) (for the Full-Time Education and Training Option).
[94] Social Security Amendment (New Deal) Regulations 1997 (S.I. 1997 No. 2863).
[95] Claimants subject to New Deal sanctions can only claim hardship payments if they fall into a specified category of claimants considered to be vulnerable: JSA Regs 1996, reg. 140(4A).
[96] See J. Sherman, 'Workshy to lose six months' cash' (1999) *The Times*, 19 May, 2.
[97] Existing workers must not be dismissed or made redundant to create New Deal jobs.

cisms of its predecessors such as the Youth Training scheme which was considered to be inadequately resourced and open to employer exploitation.[98]

New Deal has not been in existence long enough for a proper evaluation of its impact. None the less, a number of criticisms are emerging. For a start, recent research has cast doubt upon the value of both voluntary work for the unemployed and obtaining qualifications while on benefit as stepping stones to employment.[99] This would suggest that the most valuable of the New Deal options is direct contact with employers in the subsidised employment option. However, apart from the general arguments about the negative impact of employment subsidies on labour market efficiency, it has been suggested that there are not enough young people signing up to employer schemes, and that employers are not honouring their New Deal pledges by using subsidised labour in jobs which would not otherwise attract a subsidy.[100] For its part the Government is upbeat about its success, so much so that most of its proposals for the future in this area either build upon or extend key elements of New Deal. In March 1999, the Government indicated that 249,200 people had entered the New Deal for Young People; that it had secured 61,380 sustained jobs; and had a further 58,000 participating in the options.[101] New Deal for the over twenty-fives had just 104,800 people participating.[102] Evaluations on the success of the New Deal options are due in April 2000. The ultimate test of its worth will be whether the people who graduate from New Deal move into permanent employment or revert to the traditional rank of jobseekers. At the present time it is just too early to say.

B. Sanctions and Disqualifications

Social security legislation not only requires claimants to comply with positive conditions to seek work, it also imposes financial penalties when people engage in behaviour which is seen to be inconsistent with a willingness to work. Some consider that the sole purpose of social security is to provide assistance to the needy and that, once a claimant can show that he or she is in need, how they arrived on benefit and why they remain there is irrelevant. Perhaps the best-known proponent of that view was Winston Churchill who, when asked for an opinion on proposed labour market

---

[98] See, e.g., N. Harris, *Social Security for Young People* (Aldershot: Avebury, 1989), ch. 7.

[99] H. Trickey, K. Kellard, R. Walker, K. Ashworth, A. Smith, *Unemployment and Jobseeking: Two years on,* DSS Research Report No. 87 (London: The Stationery Office, 1998), 116. The research did not look at New Deal programmes which may be qualitatively different and therefore have greater success as stepping stones to employment.

[100] Per Q. Davies, *House of Commons Second Standing Committee for Delegated Legislation, Session 1997–1998,* 17 November 1998, in the discussion of the Draft Social Security (New Deal Pilot) Regulations 1998.

[101] DfEE Press Release, 19 March 1999, per A. Smith. Of those gaining employment, 48,870 had entered sustained unsubsidised jobs and 12,510 had started sustained subsidised jobs. The following numbers have participated in the work experience and training options: 11,400 in the voluntary sector, 10,700 on the Environment Task Force, and 36,000 on the full-time education and training option.

[102] Ibid.

disqualifications, remarked that he did not like: 'mixing up moralities with mathe-
matics . . . Our concern is with the evil, not with the causes, with the fact of unemployment, not with the character of the unemployed.'[103] Others argue that sanctions
are difficult to apply on the facts and that the costs of administering them outweigh
the sums saved from the withdrawal of benefit.[104] However, it is apparent that the
sanctions are designed to do more than make cost savings: they are intended to have
a general deterrent effect to dissuade claimants from engaging in behaviour which
undermines job prospects. This has been described as part of the industrial discipline
function of social security.[105] The concept of industrial discipline ensures that
employees behave according to certain accepted labour standards which the social
security rules clearly emulate.[106] However, where the social security rules depart from
recognised notions of industrial discipline is that the employment rules place emphasis on correction and warning. In employment law a person who misbehaves will usually get a series of warnings before dismissal; in social security, the removal of benefit
is automatic on a first offence. The approach seems harsh, particularly in the light of
the fact that most claimants are unaware of the rules until they lose benefit.[107]

The removal of benefit for actions inconsistent with a willingness to work has
always been part of the law. However, the scope and effect of the rules has changed
in recent years. So too has the terminology. Until 1996, there was a set of traditional
'disqualifications'.[108] With the introduction of JSA, these were renamed sanctions
while the trade dispute disqualification became a cause for 'disentitlement'. The reason for the change in terminology is not apparent—although it is possible that the
word sanction has more of a punitive ring to it. In any case, the end result is the
same—the claimant is denied benefit. Essentially there are two types of disqualification (to use the old term for want of something all-encompassing): sanctions and the
rules on trade disputes.

(i) Sanctions

A claimant can be sanctioned (i.e. denied benefit) for behaviour which is considered
inconsistent with a willingness to work. During a period of sanction a claimant will not

---

[103] W. Churchill, Internal Memorandum to H. Llewelyn Smith, *Notes on Malingering,* 6 June 1909, cited
in D. Lewis, 'Losing Benefits Through Misconduct: Time to Stop Punishing the Unemployed?' [1985]
J.S.W.L., 145–50, 149. Churchill's comments were made when he was a Liberal backbencher in advance
of the National Insurance Act 1911. When he became Prime Minister, he took no action to reverse the
disqualification for voluntary unemployment.
[104] R. Hasson, 'Discipline and Punishment in the Law of Unemployment Insurance—a Critical View
of Disqualifications and Disentitlement' (1987) 25(3) *Osgoode Hall Law J.* 615–37.
[105] See N. Wikeley, 'Unemployment Benefit, the State and the Labour Market' (1989) 16(3) *J. of Law
and Society,* 290–309, 300.
[106] Department of Employment, *In Working Order: A Study of Industrial Discipline* (London: HMSO,
1973).
[107] D. Bottomley, S. McKay, and R. Walker, *Unemployment and Jobseeking,* DSS Research Report No. 62
(London: The Stationery Office, 1997), 55–67.
[108] For losing a job through misconduct, voluntary leaving without just cause, refusing to take up an
opportunity for employment, and the trade dispute disqualification.

receive any contributory JSA. If a claimant is entitled to income-based JSA, he or she may apply for hardship payments.[109] These will only be given where the claimant can show that he or she, or his or her partner, will suffer hardship if no payment is made.[110] Consideration will be given to whether a member of the family is ill or qualifies for a disability premium; the resources available to the household; and whether there is a risk that the claimant will be unable to buy essential items of food, clothing, heating and accommodation, and, if so, for how long. Generally speaking, a claimant is not entitled to any hardship payments during the first two weeks of entitlement unless the claimant or the claimant's partner is pregnant, responsible for a child under eighteen, qualifies for a disability premium, suffers from a serious chronic medical condition, or is caring for someone who is disabled.[111] The actual rate of hardship payment is calculated in a similar way to the disqualifications in income support operating prior to 1996, in that the claimant's personal allowance is reduced by 40 per cent.[112] The key difference is that there is now no automatic right to payment. These are discretionary and subject to the key hurdle of proving hardship.

There are two types of sanction: those lasting up to twenty-six weeks and fixed-period sanctions. The sanctions which last up to a maximum of twenty-six weeks are all connected to a failure to keep work or to take up an opportunity for employment. The fixed-period sanctions cover a range of behaviour, including failure to comply with a jobseeker's direction, a New Deal requirement, or to undertake training. It is interesting that there is a two-tier system for offences which places a harsher penalty on actions associated with real chances of employment as opposed to the less direct opportunities created through participation in training and employment schemes. In some ways, it might seem unfair to impose a harsher punishment on the person who has lost a job through error than the person who has been unemployed for some time yet is not willing to take interim steps to improve his or her employability. On the other hand, it may be acceptable to show greater disapprobation of behaviour which undermines a real job than the more nebulous links which arise from workfare schemes.

(a) Losing/refusing Employment

A claimant will be sanctioned for a minimum of one week and a maximum of twenty-six weeks in circumstances where he or she loses a job or refuses an opportunity connected to employment. The first instance in which a sanction will be applied is where he or she loses his or her employment through 'misconduct'.[113] Misconduct has been defined as conduct which 'can fairly be described as blameworthy, reprehensible and wrong'.[114] In practice the sanction covers dishonesty,

---

[109] If the claimant or his or her partner is entitled to income support, he or she cannot claim hardship payments: JSA Regs 1996, reg. 140(3). They will receive a reduced amount of income support which would be equivalent to that received in hardship payments.

[110] Ibid., reg. 140(2).

[111] Ibid. Only claimants in these groups can receive a hardship payment after a New Deal sanction.

[112] Ibid., reg. 145. The deduction is 20 per cent if a member of the family is pregnant or seriously ill.

[113] JS Act 1995, s. 19(1).   [114] *R(U) 2/77*, para. 1.

violence, drunkenness, and poor punctuality. Claimants may also be sanctioned
where they leave a job voluntarily 'without just cause'.[115] The meaning of voluntarily
is not defined in the legislation. However, it extends to situations where the employee
acts in such a way as to leave the employer no choice but to terminate the contract
of employment.[116] To establish 'just cause' the claimant must show that in leaving he
or she acted reasonably in circumstances that make it just that the burden of his or
her unemployment should be cast on those who provide funding for the system.[117]
Claimants have been considered to have just cause where they leave to look after a
sick relative[118] or where the employer is in breach of a fundamental term of the contract of employment.[119] Finally, a claimant may be sanctioned if he or she fails without 'good cause' to take up a job opportunity notified to him or her or fails to act
upon a reasonable opportunity of getting a job.[120] It is interesting that a claimant will
be considered to have automatic good cause if he or she refuses to take a job which
the claimant has found out about for themselves.[121] It seems strange that the actively-
seeking-work condition requires jobseekers to be autonomous in their efforts to find
work yet does not penalise them if they refuse to take the job once their efforts bear
fruit.

All of these sanctions can be traced to the origins of unemployment benefit and
to the Beveridge Report. The key difference is that they originally attracted a disqualification period of six weeks. The maximum period of disqualification was extended
during the 1980s to thirteen weeks and then to twenty-six weeks.[122] The increase to
twenty-six weeks was justified on the basis that there were growing numbers of people leaving work voluntarily at a time when the total number of people claiming benefit was decreasing.[123] The minimum period of sanction has also been extended.
Prior to 1996, the disqualification could have been imposed for one day. It is now
one week in line with the fact that JSA is calculated on a weekly basis.[124] Moreover,
while previously the disqualification period did not affect the period of entitlement
to unemployment benefit, since contribution-based JSA was introduced, the sanction
periods runs during the entitlement period. This means that a claimant sanctioned
for twenty-six weeks will not receive any contribution-based JSA. Moreover, even if
the claimant breaks the causal link with the first loss of employment (opportunity)

---

[115] JS Act 1995, s. 19(6).
[116] See, for instance, *R(U) 16/52* where a claimant who was employed as a canteen assistant subject to
a medical examination and who refused to have an X-ray test was disqualified.
[117] *Crewe v Social Security Commissioners* [1982] 2 All ER 745.   [118] *R(U) 14/52.*
[119] *R(U) 18/57.*
[120] JS Act 1995, s. 19(5)(b)(ii). Prior to 1989, a claimant could only be disqualified for failure to act upon
'suitable' opportunities for employment.
[121] JSA Regs 1996, reg. 72(8).
[122] Unemployment Benefit (Disqualification Period) Order 1988 (S.I. 1988 No. 487). See generally, N.
Wikeley, 'Unemployment Benefit, the State and the Labour Market' (1989) 16(3) *J. of Law and Society*,
290–309, 300–4.
[123] *Per* N. Scott, Hansard, HC Written Answers, Vol. 122, Col. 154, 10 November 1988.
[124] Although the sanction must be for a minimum of one week, periods of sanction over and above
this can be for part weeks: JSA Regs 1996, reg. 150.

by securing a job and then returning to benefit, they will serve out the rest of their disqualification period.[125]

When the twenty-six-week period was introduced, the Social Security Advisory Committee branded it a 'harsh penalty' and advocated that it would be applied with care.[126] In practice there was a lot of discretion given to decision makers and evidence that the maximum sanction was being applied routinely.[127] Regulations now require those determining the period of disqualification to take into account all the circumstances of the case, including the length of time the job would have lasted, any mitigating circumstances of physical or mental stress with the job, and the rate of pay and hours of work in the job if it was for less than sixteen hours a week.[128] The problem is that the regulations still require quite subjective judgments, and advice agencies continue to report dubious disqualifications and periods of sanction. The seeming arbitrariness is worrying since the overall impact of these sanctions can be tremendous. They can wipe out an entire claim to contribution-based JSA and can severely affect the income of a person relying on means-tested assistance.[129] Although many appeals about the length of sanctions are upheld, there can be a long delay before money is received. The impact of the rules seems particularly unfortunate when few claimants appear to be aware of the sanctions until they fall foul of them.[130] Moreover, research suggests that the levels of both voluntary leaving and dismissals vary according to labour market conditions.[131] In view of the fact that some claimants may be disqualified for a standard of behaviour which might be acceptable in a different economic climate, it has been argued that the legislation should adopt the approach favoured by some American states and only penalise those who have 'wilfully' lost employment.[132]

(b) Fixed-Period Sanctions

Fixed-period sanctions will be imposed in a number of instances: where a claimant fails to comply with a jobseeker's direction; where he or she fails to comply with a requirement of New Deal; or where he or she in some way loses or fails to take up an opportunity for training or an employment scheme.[133] In the latter case the sanctions apply where the claimant: loses a place on a training scheme or employment programme (including New Deal) through misconduct; gives up or fails to attend

---

[125] For a critique of this approach, see K. Kempfer, 'Disqualifications for Voluntary Leaving and Misconduct' (1945) 55/134 *Yale Law J.* 147–66.

[126] SSAC, *Sixth Report* (London: HMSO, 1988), para. 3.16.

[127] See J. Jacobs, *Benefit of the Doubt* (London: NACAB, 1994), 37–40.   [128] JSA Regs 1996, reg. 70.

[129] For an account of the impact of disqualifications on claimants, see D. Byrne and J. Jacobs, *Disqualified from Benefit: the operation of benefit penalties* (London: Low Pay Unit, 1988), 21–37.

[130] D. Bottomley, S. McKay, and R. Walker, *Unemployment and Jobseeking*, DSS Research Report No. 62 (London: The Stationery Office, 1997), 55–67.

[131] See P. Fenn, 'Sources of Disqualification for Unemployment Benefit, 1960–76' (1980) XVIII *British J. of Industrial Relations*, 240–53.

[132] D. Lewis, 'Losing Benefits Through Misconduct: Time to Stop Punishing the Unemployed?' [1985] *J.S.W.L.*, 145–50, 149.

[133] JS Act 1995, s. 19(5).

without good cause; does not apply or does not accept a place on a compulsory scheme which has been notified to him or her; or neglects to avail him or herself of a reasonable opportunity of a place on a scheme. A claimant will be considered to have good cause automatically in certain instances such as where they are suffering from a disablement, have a religious or conscientious objection, the travelling time would be excessive, or they have other responsibilities which excuse them from participation.[134] The normal sanction period is two weeks (in line with the fact that claimants sign on fortnightly). However it is increased to four weeks if the claimant has been sanctioned within twelve months of a previous fixed-period sanction.[135] The fixed-period sanctions are akin to the kind of short, sharp shock such as those associated with fixed penalties for minor motoring offences. Although the periods are potentially shorter than the employment-related sanctions, the fixed-period sanctions can be applied time and time again for the same basic problem, leaving a claimant facing an indefinite period of benefit loss.

The element which is common to all the fixed-period sanctions is that they are deliberately intended to bolster the various 'welfare to work' policies in operation since 1996. Each of the sanctions is used to impose a penalty for behaviour not connected to a specific job but to non-participation in the various government initiatives which are intended to improve employability. It has been queried whether such strategies should be backed up by sanctions. Some consider that voluntary schemes will be more successful because participants are more disposed to take advantage of what is offered than conscripts. Others think that mandatory schemes have a wider impact because they reach people who would benefit but who would not choose to participate otherwise. Research from the United States, where various voluntary and mandatory programmes have been in operation for some years, is inconclusive as to whether compulsion is more effective than voluntary participation.[136] The evaluations which will be undertaken into the various types of New Deal programmes will eventually shed more light on this issue in the United Kingdom context.

(ii) Trade Disputes

As noted in Chapter 6 in the discussion of income-related benefits, a person is not entitled to JSA where he or she is unemployed for any day where there is a stoppage of work due to a trade dispute at his or her place of work.[137] The definition of trade dispute extends not just to strikes but also to lock-outs. Moreover, the merits of the dispute are irrelevant.[138] The key way in which disqualification can be avoided is where the claimant can show that he or she does not have a direct interest in the dis-

---

[134] JSA Regs 1996, reg. 72.

[135] A claimant will only be sanctioned for 2 weeks for a first New Deal 'offence' even if he or she has had another non-New Deal sanction in the previous 12 months. It is proposed that those who refuse to participate in a New Deal option 3 times will receive an extended sanction period of 6 months. See, J. Sherman, 'Workshy to lose six months' cash' (1999) *The Times*, 19 May, 2.

[136] J. M. Gueron and E. Pauley, *From Welfare to Work* (New York: Russell Sage Foundation, 1991), 243.

[137] JS Act 1995, s. 14(1).   [138] R(U) 17/52.

pute.[139] For a long time, this provision had the inglorious reputation of being one of the most convoluted of all the social security provisions (which is, of course, no mean feat). This claim was borne out by a spate of Commissioners' decisions stretching from the 1950s to the 1980s.[140] Its current incarnation in the jobseeekers legislation is a relative model of simplicity and has certainly proved less contentious in recent times in line with the general decrease in industrial action.

A provision of this kind has always formed part of social security law.[141] However, it is now very much *sui generis* in the battery of labour market conditions. Until 1996 it was formulated as a disqualification alongside the other traditional labour market disqualifications. However, since the introduction of JSA, the trade dispute provision stands alone in the legislation as a reason for 'disentitlement' rather than a reason for imposing a sanction.[142] The decision not to employ sanctions for loss of employment due to a trade dispute is probably related to the historically distinct financial consequences of this head of disqualification. Where the provision applies, the person involved in the dispute may not claim JSA but can claim income support for his or her family.[143] However, no benefit will be paid for the first seven days of the strike and, as noted in Chapter 6, the amount of income support received will be reduced by an assumed strike pay of £27.50.[144] This deduction occurs whether or not any strike pay is actually received. In fact it will be assumed even where the claimant is in non-unionised employment and therefore not in a position to receive strike pay. During a trade dispute a family's income is severely reduced in a way that goes well beyond the normal hardship payments received following the other sanctions and this position continues for as long as the strike/lock-out persists. The severe restrictions on entitlement have been used explicitly for the purposes of deterring strike action,[145] in spite of the fact that the research evidence suggests that the rules do not have a deterrent effect,[146] and may even, in certain instances, strengthen strikers' resolve to pursue the dispute.[147]

Various reasons have been advanced to justify the rules on trade disputes. Chief

---

[139] Ibid. See *Presho v Insurance Officer* [1984] 1 All ER 97.

[140] For an analysis of these cases see K. D. Ewing, *The Right to Strike* (Oxford: Clarendon Press, 1991), 76–87.

[141] It can be traced to *Attorney General v Guardians of the Poor of the Merthyr Tydfil Union* [1900] 1 Ch. 516, where the Court of Appeal was clear that it was unlawful to pay relief to strikers but that relief could be given to their families. For a discussion of this, see W. I. Jennings, 'Poor Relief in Industrial Disputes' (1930) 46 *Law Quarterly Rev.* 225–34.

[142] JS Act 1995, s. 14.

[143] The claimant will receive nothing for his or her needs but may claim for his or her partner (provided that he or she is not involved in a dispute) and his or her children (SSCBA 1992, s. 126). Alternatively, the partner of the person involved in the trade dispute may claim income-based JSA, in which case similar rules are applied to calculate entitlement (JS Act 1995, s. 15(2)(d)).

[144] SSCBA 1992, s. 126(7); IS(G) Regs 1987, Sched. 3.

[145] See, *Financing Strikes* (London: The Society of Conservative Lawyers, 1974).

[146] See J. W. Durcan and W. E. J. McCarthy, 'The State Subsidy Theory of Strikes: An Examination of the Statistical Data for the period 1956–1970' (1974) 12 *British J. of Industrial Relations*, 26–47; J. Gennard and R. Lasko, 'Supplementary Benefits and Strikers' (1974) 2 *British J. of Industrial Relation*, 1–25.

[147] See L. Lundy, 'Income support during a strike' (1995) 2 *J.S.S.L.* 129–41 at 138.

among these has been the fact that this type of unemployment is seen to be a clear infringement of the voluntary unemployment principle. In the words of one Minister for Social Security: 'there is the choice not to strike, to go back to work and earn the living that is available'.[148] Quite how this applies to lock-outs is difficult to gauge. Moreover, there is a general argument that those who take strike action as a last resort are not truly acting voluntarily.[149] However, it has also been argued that to provide assistance to strikers would result in the state adopting a non-neutral approach to trade disputes by, in effect, subsidising strikes.[150] This too has been criticised by those who consider that the inequality of bargaining power in trade disputes is such that the state would only be adjusting the unequal balance if it gave strikers full and generous benefits.[151] Such criticisms are particularly cogent in situations where the stoppage of work cannot be considered to be the claimant's fault.[152] None the less, removing entitlement to benefit from a person who has walked away from a job which continues to be available to him or her is perhaps the greatest manifestation of an infringement of the labour-market principles which underpin benefit entitlement.

4. INCENTIVES TO WORK

When discussing the legal provisions which are designed to encourage claimants to work, it would be misleading to give the impression that the rules are all vinegar and no honey. People respond to incentives as much if not more than they respond to sanctions since it is human nature to act in positive self-interest. The two main incentives discussed in this section (earnings disregards and the back-to-work bonus) apply to income-based JSA. In the context of income-based JSA, incentives to work have to be financial given that the purpose of the system is to ensure that the claimant is getting sufficient money to cover his or her needs The problem is that there is a tricky tightrope between encouraging people to leave benefit and maintaining differences in wage levels so others do not find themselves better off unemployed. In Field's view the nature of means-testing is such that: 'Hard work is penalised by loss of entitlement. Incentives reinforce dependency.'[153] The need for incentives in the means-tested system is an inevitable consequence of means-testing itself. The solution advocated by Field and others is a move towards insurance, a strategy which seems unlikely in view of the ongoing erosion of contributory benefits. Since most

---

[148] *Per* R. Prentice, Hansard, H.C. Debs, Vol. 982, col. 1144, 15 April 1980.

[149] See L. Lesser, 'Labor Disputes and Unemployment Compensation' (1945) 55 *Yale Law J.* 167–201, 171.

[150] Memorandum of the Ministry of Social Security submitted to the *Royal Commission on Trade Unions and Employers' Associations 1965–1968*, Cmnd. 3623 (London: HMSO, 1968).

[151] See H. Fierst and F. Spector, 'Unemployment Compensation in Labor Disputes' (1940) 49 *Yale Law J.* 461–80, 465.

[152] See L. Lundy, 'Unemployment Benefit after a withdrawal of labour' (1994) 23 *I.L.J.* 127–40.

[153] *Stakeholder Welfare* (London: IEA, 1996), 20.

claimants remain dependent on means-tested assistance, policy makers have been struggling to find ways of accommodating work-related self-interest.

The current incentives tend to operate in one (or both) of two ways. The first is to encourage claimants to undertake part-time work while on benefit in the hope that this will act as a springboard to full-time employment. The idea is that participation in some form of work will keep the claimant's desire to work alive, give them experience which will enhance their future employability and expose them to full-time positions should they arise. The second is to encourage claimants to move off benefit through financial assistance with transitional costs or at the very least protected entitlement to social security in the event that the move does not work out. The three main incentives which have a statutory basis—earnings disregards, the back-to-work bonus, and employment on trial—are considered separately below.

A. Earnings Disregards

The obvious way to encourage claimants to engage in part-time work is to allow them to keep some of those earnings on top of their benefit. JSA claimants are able to work up to sixteen hours a week and are given a number of 'earnings disregards', that is amounts which a claimant is allowed to earn without it affecting benefit entitlement. A single person has a disregard of £5 and a couple has a total disregard of £10.[154] Specified categories of claimants such as lone parents, the disabled, carers, and those engaged in emergency work can claim £15.[155] All earnings above the disregard are subtracted pound for pound from the benefit payment. This means that a single claimant working five hours per week at £4 per hour would receive an extra £5 but lose £15 in benefit entitlement. The problem with the disregards is apparent: few people are encouraged to work for such meagre financial returns with the result that many choose not to work or to work and not declare their income.[156] There is also evidence that many claimants believe that you cannot engage in any paid work while on benefit, a perception which may be directly related to the levels of the disregarded earnings.[157] While working on benefit is not unlawful, pound-for-pound deductions undoubtedly create a perception that it is taboo or, at the very least, not encouraged.

The current rates of disregard have not been raised since 1988. Once the minimum wage is factored into this, people will be able to undertake much less part-time employment without affecting their benefit entitlement than was the case a decade ago. In 1948, a couple could earn the equivalent of 75 per cent of their national

---

[154] JSA Regs 1996, Sched. 6.

[155] Ibid., paras 5–10. Couples who have been claiming for over 2 years may also claim a higher disregard of £15.

[156] DSS, *Beating Fraud is Everyone's Business*, Cm 4102 (London: The Stationery Office, 1998), para. 5.16, where the earnings disregards were identified as one of the key rules which contribute to fraudulent claims.

[157] D. Bottomley, S. McKay, and R. Walker, *Unemployment and Jobseeking*, DSS Research Report No. 62 (London: The Stationery Office, 1997), 123.

assistance without affecting their claim.[158] In spite of this, calls to raise the disregards have been continually resisted by Government. Increasing the disregards would certainly encourage more people to work part-time. The problem is that it might also create a disincentive to obtain full-time employment because it reduces the differential between benefit and earnings. It also has the effect of drawing more people into the benefit system and consequently the poverty trap which the disregards are intended to alleviate. For this reason, the Social Security Advisory Committee has endorsed governmental concerns about the raising of disregards.[159] In 1996 the Government chose to 'square the circle'[160] created by disregards by introducing the back-to-work bonus, considered next. No consideration appears to have been given to the possibility of allowing unused disregards to be accumulated, to allow people to engage in seasonal work or other short bursts of work without losing or disrupting their benefit entitlement.[161]

B. The back-to-work bonus

The back-to-work bonus was introduced in 1996 alongside JSA.[162] The bonus was hailed as a 'springboard to full-time employment' which would 'provide financial help at a crucial time and greatly ease the transition into full-time work'.[163] It is a tax-free lump sum to which a claimant can build entitlement through part-time work when they are claiming JSA or income support. The sum will only begin to accrue if the claimant has been in receipt of JSA or income support for ninety-one consecutive days.[164] It can be claimed when the claimant is no longer in receipt of JSA or income support, that is, he or she returns to work full-time or is earning enough money to disentitle them from claiming benefit.[165] Claimants can build up credits of fifty pence for every pound earned above their normal earnings disregards up to a maximum of £1,000. Thus in order to qualify for the maximum bonus a claimant would have to have earned £2,000 over their earnings disregards. Studies have shown repeatedly that one of the major factors which discourages claimants from taking work is worry about how they will manage financially.[166] Particular concerns have been expressed about the delays in receiving wages in the first few weeks of work.[167]

---

[158] An unemployed couple received £2.00 National Assistance and could earn up to £1.50 between them. This is cited in the SSAC, *Sixth Report* (London: HMSO, 1988), para. 3.5.

[159] SSAC, *Sixth Report* (London, HMSO, 1988), para. 3.6

[160] *Per* Mr E. Forth, Hansard, H.C. Debs, Vol. 288, col. 752, 17 January 1996.

[161] This was suggested in J. Brown, *Escaping From Dependence, Part-time Workers and The Self-Employed: The Role of Social Security* (London: IPPR, 1994), 32; see also the Commission on Social Justice, *Social Justice: Strategies for Renewal* (London: Vintage, 1994), 251.

[162] JS Act 1995, s. 26.

[163] Department of Education/DSS, *Jobseeker's Allowance*, Cm 2687 (London, HMSO, 1995), paras 2.15 and 2.16.

[164] The Social Security (Back to Work Bonus) (No. 2) Regulations 1996 (S.I. 1996 No. 2570), reg. 6.

[165] Ibid., reg. 7.

[166] See E. McLaughlin, J. Millar, and K. Cooke, *Work and Welfare Benefits* (Aldershot: Avebury, 1989).

[167] D. Bottomley, S. McKay, and R. Walker, *Unemployment and Jobseeking*, DSS Research Report No. 62 (London: The Stationery Office, 1997), 141.

This fuels concern about paying ongoing expenses such as mortgage costs, council tax, and other debts and loans.[168] The bonus offers claimants a concrete reward for moving off benefit which should help to cover some of these transitional costs. The problem is that, as a financial incentive, it is quite thin.[169] Moreover, a person's sense of personal investment will undoubtedly be coloured by their assessment of their prospects of obtaining full-time work. While the bonus might provide help in the early stages of work, it does nothing to counteract claimants' concerns about how they will manage on wages in the longer term. Claimants are more likely to be influenced by their 'replacement ratio' (the comparison between the amount received out of work and in earned employment) than a short-term lump sum.

C. Employment on Trial

The regulations make provision for claimants who take a new job but find that it does not work out and wish to return to benefit. In normal instances a claimant who gives up a job will be considered to be voluntarily unemployed and will be sanctioned (see above). Claimants would undoubtedly have to be cautious about any work attempted for fear of exposing themselves to that penalty. However, in 1989 provision was made for claimants unemployed for twenty-six weeks or more not to be disqualified where they take a new job and leave that job after four and before twelve weeks of work.[170] In 1996 the qualifying period for this exception was reduced from twenty-six to thirteen weeks.[171] The rationale is clear: to protect claimants who take the risk of a new job from financial loss should the return to employment not work out. The need for such a protection cannot be disputed. However, it is very much an *ex post facto* protection rather than an incentive to try something new. In practice, worry about disqualification does not seem to be the key factor which discourages claimants from trying out new lines of work. The reality is that few claimants are aware of the sanction for voluntary unemployment.[172] Instead, the factor which most discourages claimants from trying out new employments is the concern that the employment will be short-lived and that they will have the 'hassle' of reapplying for benefit.[173] In view of this, it has been suggested that a better incentive would be to allow claimants to reactivate a previous claim rather than requiring them to go

---

[168] A. Shaw, R. Walker, K. Ashworth, S. Jenkins, and S. Middleton, *Moving off Income Support: Barriers and Bridges*, DSS Research Report No. 53 (London: HMSO, 1996), 117.

[169] It would take quite some time before a claimant would earn anything really worthwhile. For instance, a single person aged 25 in receipt of wages of £4 per hour would have an earnings disregard of £5. If he or she worked 10 hours per week at £4 per hour, he or she would be storing up a bonus of £17.50 per week. It would take 10 weeks of working 10 hours a week for a £5 advantage before he or she would be able to claim £175 on leaving benefit.

[170] SSA 1989, s. 12(4).   [171] JS Act 1995, s. 20(3); JSA Regs 1996, reg. 74.

[172] In one survey in 1995, only 2.9 per cent of claimants knew that they could lose benefit if they left work voluntarily: D. Bottomley, S. McKay, and R. Walker, *Unemployment and Jobseeking*, DSS Research Report No. 62 (London: The Stationery Office, 1997), 57.

[173] A. Shaw, R. Walker, K. Ashworth, S. Jenkins, and S. Middleton, *Moving off Income Support: Barriers and Bridges*, DSS Research Report No. 53 (London: HMSO, 1996), 126.

through a process of reapplication if they leave employment within the trial period.[174]

D. Encouraging Work?

There has been a series of research studies examining the difficulties experienced by unemployed people attempting to reintegrate into the labour market and some imaginative solutions have evolved.[175] Many of these incentives do not feature in the legislation, but instead are available at the discretion of the Employment Service.[176] However, in addition to the statutory incentives already discussed, in recent times the rules have been changed to allow claimants to claim housing benefit and council tax benefit for up to four weeks on return to work.[177] There has also been a number of financial incentives aimed directly at employers.[178] Although the impact of all these provisions has been hampered by a lack of claimant or employer awareness, it is clear that the rules which seek to ease the transition into full-time employment have the potential to be more effective than those which aim to encourage claimants to undertake work while on benefit.

Most claimants believe that part-time work will help them to get a full-time job.[179] Moreover, the value of part-time work as a stepping stone to full-time employment is also borne out by the research which has been conducted on the operation of JSA.[180] In spite of this, there is little incentive for claimants to undertake part-time work while on benefit.[181] The earnings disregards are too small to be meaningful. And although the back-to-work bonus is intended to get more claimants to take part-

---

[174] Above n. 173, 155.

[175] See ibid.; D. Bottomley, S. McKay, and R. Walker, *Unemployment and Jobseeking,* DSS Research Report No. 62 (London: The Stationery Office, 1997); D. Snape, *Recruiting Long-term Unemployed People,* DSS Research Report No. 76 (London: The Stationery Office, 1998); B. Stafford, C. Heaver, N. Croden, A. Abel Smith, S. Maguire, J. Vincent, *Moving into Work: Bridging Housing Costs,* DSS Research Report No. 79 (London: The Stationery Office, 1998).

[176] For details on the various schemes which provide claimants with help in order to get into work see, C. George et al., *Welfare Benefits Handbook Vol. 2* (London: CPAG, 1999), ch. 35. These include schemes such as Work Trial (15 days' work experience while on JSA), the Jobfinder's grant (a one-off grant to assist with the expenses of returning to work) and Jobplan (5 days of work-focused workshops).

[177] HB(G) Regs 1987, Sched. 5A, para. 1 and reg. 62A(2); Council Tax Benefit General Regulations 1992 (S.I. 1992 No. 1814), Sched. 5A, para. 1 and reg. 52A(2) and (3). For an analysis of the impact of this provision see, B. Stafford, C. Heaver, N. Croden, A. Abel Smith, S. Maguire, J. Vincent, *Moving into Work: Bridging Housing Costs,* DSS Research Report No. 79 (London: The Stationery Office, 1998) and N. Harris, 'Research reveals problems with HB and CTB extended payments scheme' (1998) 5(4) *J.S.S.L.,* 154–5.

[178] These include the New Deal subsidies and the newly introduced national insurance holiday when an employer employs someone who has been unemployed for at least 2 years.

[179] Shaw, Walker, Ashworth, Jenkins, and Middleton, above n. 173, 101.

[180] H. Trickey, K. Kellard, R. Walker, K. Ashworth, A. Smith, *Unemployment and Jobseeking: Two years on,* DSS Research Report No. 87 (London: The Stationery Office, 1998), 6. However, the people who were able to make the transition from part-time work to full-time work tended to be younger, healthier, and more literate than those remaining on part-time work.

[181] One exception to this is a discretionary scheme called 'Jobmatch' which provides certain claimants participating in New Deal options with a grant of £50 per week if they are taking a job of at least 16 but less than 30 hours per week.

time work, claimants are more likely to be persuaded to take part-time work if it presents an opportunity to enjoy the fruits of their labour when they most need it. The bonus was specifically chosen instead of raising earnings disregards which were considered to reduce the incentive for full-time work.[182] However, it is likely that claimants would resent the lack of any real financial reward for their efforts in return for the prospect of a lump sum in the uncertain event of them finding a job. It is only when claimants see a real benefit weekly in their pockets that they will feel that they are truly benefiting from their work: an ongoing top-up is better than a one-off lump sum without the safety net.

Likewise the rules do little to encourage claimants to undertake casual or temporary work. Means-tested benefits 'assume stable earnings from employment, in defiance of a labour market which frequently offers insecure, unpredictable and fluctuating earnings'.[183] There are linking rules (usually set around twelve weeks) which allow claimants to re-qualify for certain benefits previously enjoyed after a short spell of employment.[184] The 'employment on trial' rules also offer some claimants protection for spells of employment lasting under three months. However, claimants may be discouraged from taking work of a longer duration such as six months. This is in spite of the fact that recent research shows that claimants who are prepared to take temporary work are more likely to find stable employment.[185] Although temporary work would undoubtedly improve their chances of obtaining permanent employment, it would jeopardise their entitlement on a return to social security. One of the biggest risks would be for those with mortgage debt who may have to pay all their mortgage costs themselves for the first thirty-nine weeks of a fresh claim if they take temporary work which lasts longer than twelve weeks.[186] Many claimants are rightly concerned about the impact on their income after a short spell of employment.[187] If a person has previously been entitled to full housing costs, there is a direct and significant barrier to work which is either temporary or insecure.

Successive governments have emphasised the importance of having a supply of workers to support the demands of the modern 'flexible' labour market.[188] They have

---

[182] *Per* E. Forth, Hansard, H.C. Debs, Vol. 288, Col. 752, 17 January 1996.

[183] Commission on Social Justice, *Social Justice: Strategies for National Renewal* (London: Vintage, 1994), 249.

[184] For instance, claimants do not have to serve 3 'waiting days' if they claim within 12 weeks of a previous period of entitlement to JSA: JSA Regs 1996, reg. 48.

[185] H. Trickey et al., n. 180 above, 115.

[186] JSA Regs 1996, Sched. 2, para. 13. This applies to new housing costs, i.e. where the mortgage is taken out after 2 October 1995. Claimants who entered into loans before this date will normally receive nothing in the first 8 weeks of the claim, half the eligible costs in the next 18 weeks and the full amount thereafter. See Chapter 13 by Simon Rahilly. See further, N. Wikeley, 'Income support and mortgage interest: the new rules', (1995) 2 *J.S.S.L.*168–78; L. Lundy, 'State Assistance with House Purchases—Mortgage Interest and Social Security' [1997] *The Conveyancer and Property Lawyer*, 36–46.

[187] See, for instance, A. Shaw, R. Walker, K. Ashworth, S. Jenkins, and S. Middleton, *Moving off Income Support: Barriers and Bridges*, DSS Research Report No. 53 (London: HMSO, 1996).

[188] When JSA was introduced the Conservative Government emphasised the importance of 'removing restrictions which impede the response of labour supply and demand': Department of Employment/DSS, *Jobseeker's Allowance*, Cm 2687 (London: HMSO, 1995), para. 2.1.

also recognised the benefit of part-time and temporary employment, not only because it provides claimants with valuable experience, but also because it counteracts some of the 'employer chill' which faces the long-term unemployed. In spite of this, the system declines to offer claimants meaningful encouragement to take part-time or temporary work. It is ironic that the Government is currently spending millions in subsidies to employers through the New Deal programmes when many claimants could gain direct employment at no cost (or indeed some gain) to the Treasury. While concerns about the impact on the 'poverty trap' must be heeded, the problems are not insurmountable. Incentives could be targeted (for example, to those unemployed over two years). Not only do such claimants face considerable obstacles in obtaining full-time employment, they are also the group who would most benefit from an increased income at a time when their savings will be exhausted and household goods will have to be replaced.[189] Enabling the long-term unemployed to benefit from part-time or casual work while claiming would be a significant anti-poverty strategy. Moreover, the disincentive effect of higher disregards could be counteracted to some extent by time restrictions (for example, generous disregards could be limited to six or twelve months). If a period of profitable part-time work were to be combined with a revamped back-to-work bonus, the result could be a genuine spring-board to full-time permanent work.

5. THE FUTURE OF WELFARE AND WORK

Although the social security system is a mixed bag of work-related rules, the incentives to work are vastly overshadowed by the labour-market obligations and sanctions. On the face of it, the legislation has the makings of a very strict labour-market regime. If rigorously implemented, a claimant could find life on benefit extremely arduous. When JSA was introduced commentators warned of the dangers of such a strategy, arguing that a heavy-handed approach would have serious consequences for the claimant/adviser relationship and could in the long term seriously impact on the claimant's motivation to work.[190] The research which has been conducted in the first two years of JSA points to a different picture. Essentially, this shows that officers have been doing little more than giving each claimant's jobsearch efforts a cursory scan at the fortnightly interviews. In fact, most claimants notice little difference from the situation pre-JSA, although a minority comment on the need to provide evidence of jobsearch and a more pro-active role on the part of benefit advisers.[191] It would appear that there is more form-filling than brow-beating going on. The reasons for

---

[189] C. Oppenheim and L. Harker, *Poverty: The Facts*, 3rd edn. (London: CPAG, 1996), 49.
[190] See for instance, T. Buck, 'Jobseeker's allowance: policy perspectives' (1996) 3 *J.S.S.L.* 149–64.
[191] H. Trickey et al., n. 180 above, ch. 8. 76 per cent of respondents considered the procedure to be broadly similar to that for unemployment benefit or income support (at 135). The 23 per cent of respondents who considered that it was different indicated that there were more checks on jobsearch activity (at 137).

the less than rigorous implementation have not been explored. However, it is probably due at least in part to the sheer amount of work which would face the front-line decision makers if the jobseeking of each individual claimant were to come under very strict scrutiny.

Few claimants believe that compliance with the labour-market rules will enhance their chances of employment, an indictment which strikes at the heart of JSA.[192] However, this fact has to be balanced with the more positive finding that the vast majority of unemployed people were actively looking for work prior to the introduction of JSA and that this continues to be the case.[193] Moreover, as noted above, most claimants find work within the first three to six months on benefit, after which the chances of finding employment decrease significantly.[194] Faced with such evidence as to the operation of JSA, those seeking to use the social security rules to get more unemployed people into work have two choices: to step up the enforcement of the existing rules (particularly in relation to the long-term unemployed) or to change tack. The Labour Government appears to have chosen the latter.

The first key change has been a shift in emphasis from coercion and penalty to guidance and support. This is typified by the various New Deal strategies described earlier in the chapter. In these the emphasis is on helping people who are assumed to want to work rather than on coercing those perceived as work-shy out of a state of idleness. The Conservative reforms of the 1980s and 1990s portrayed an image of unemployment which perpetuated the notion that failure to obtain work could be attributed to claimants' attitudes (the 'scroungers' syndrome') rather than the lack of suitable opportunities for employment. In contrast, the Labour Government's focus is on working with the individual to improve his or her employment prospects. For instance, Frank Field summarised the Labour Party's pre-election vision for the unemployed somewhat idealistically as: 'This is the first day of the rest of your lives; how can we make the rest of your lives as happy and constructive as possible'!'[195] The shift from punishment and deterrence to support and guidance is to be welcomed if it boosts claimants' self-perception and improves the perception of employers and the general public. Although New Deal requirements carry the possibility of new sanctions, these sanctions are not qualitatively different from those which were previously in operation. In fact, the labour-market conditions cannot go much deeper than they already do without the imposition of time-limited assistance. This is perhaps why the Government has chosen the second sea-change which is to extend the application of the existing rules.

The second change in strategy has been towards widening the scope of the rules rather than tightening the rules further for the traditional categories of unemployed. The net has been spread to include those who have not traditionally been expected to work. The Government's intention is to encourage all claimants (not just those able and available) to work rather than 'writing them off and consigning them to

---

[192] Ibid., 149.   [193] Ibid.   [194] Ibid., 151.
[195] F. Field, Hansard, H.C. Debs. 23 February 1999, Vol. 326, col. 247.

economic failure'.[196] From the beginning, categories of claimants like lone parents and the disabled were included in the New Deal strategy. The Government is now taking steps to offer work-incentives in areas not previously associated with such things such as benefits for the long-term sick.[197] The Welfare Reform and Pensions Act 1999 has two reforms which take this a stage further in relation to partners of the unemployed and the extension of the gateway concept.

A. Partners of the Unemployed

In 1999, the Government introduced a New Deal for Partners of the Unemployed which offers guidance and training to partners of existing claimants.[198] The Welfare Reform and Pensions Act 1999 will extend the scope of the labour-market rules for partners of the unemployed through the introduction of joint-claim JSA. Currently, one partner in a couple claims JSA, but only the person claiming is subject to the labour-market conditions. Claimants aged eighteen to twenty-four who do not have children will be required to claim JSA jointly.[199] The labour-market conditions will apply to both partners and both will be required to participate in the New Deal for Young People. In certain circumstances (for instance, where one partner is disallowed or sanctioned) the other partner will be able to make a single claim for his or her own needs.[200] In the long term the requirement will eventually extend to all partners of the unemployed who are aged twenty-four or under at the date of implementation. The Government's stated intention is to allow the partners of the unemployed 'to have access to support and advice from the Employment Service'.[201]
The change was recommended by the Taylor Report, which stated that the presumption that the partners of the unemployed do not want to work was a relic of the days when men worked and their wives did not and was inappropriate for a time when 47 per cent of employees were women.[202] Furthermore, research in the area indicated that the reform would be positively received by the persons who would be affected by it.[203] The relevant clause received little commentary in Parliament, an indication that it was uncontroversial.[204] In truth, it is difficult to see why the rules should not be applied to both partners if they are capable of working,

---

[196] DSS, *A New Contract for Welfare: The Gateway to Work*, Cm 4102 (London: The Stationery Office, 1998), ch. 4, para. 2.

[197] The Welfare to Work Regulations 1998 (S.I. 1998 No. 2231) introduced a series of measures designed to encourage the long-term sick into work through the extension of linking periods.

[198] DfEE Press Release, *New Deal £60m jobs boost for partners of the unemployed*, 5 January 1999.

[199] Welfare Reform and Pensions Act 1999, s. 59 and Sched 7.

[200] Income and capital will continue to be jointly assessed.

[201] *Per* Mr A. Darling, Hansard, H.C. Debs, Vol. 326, col. 220, 23 February 1999.

[202] M. Taylor, *The Modernisation of Britain's Tax and Benefit System, Number Two: Work Incentives* (London, The Stationery Office, 1998).

[203] K. Woodfield and H. Finch, *Unemployed Couples: attitudes towards proposals affecting partners of jobseekers*, DSS Research Report No. 47 (London: The Stationery Office, 1997).

[204] The lack of criticism of this provision might also be related to the level of controversy which attached to some of the other major reforms in the Bill in the area of pensions and incapacity benefits.

especially given that single mothers with children of school age are expected to work. Leaving aside general objections to the labour-market rules, it is difficult to see why they should not apply with parity in such instances.

B. Widening the Gateway to Work

The Government's plans for social security centre round the notion of a 'gateway to work'. The concept, which is integral to the New Deal for Young People, is to be extended to all people claiming income-replacement benefits. The Government has stated that the gateway represents a fundamental shift away 'from merely asking *"What money can we pay you?"* to *"How can we help you become more independent?"*'[205] The intention is that all benefit claimants will be able to find information on work, benefits, tax credits, and other services from one source (one of the reasons for the recent re-classification of the single gateway to work as 'ONE'). The key change in the law will be that all claimants will be required, if asked, to take part in an interview to talk about their prospects of finding work.[206] While such requirements previously only applied to claimants of JSA and those in the New Deal categories, the gateway to work will apply to all those claiming a number of income-replacement benefits including income support, incapacity benefit, and housing benefit.[207] Although only claimants of JSA will be required to take subsequent courses of action such as training or job search, a failure to co-operate at the initial interview may result in a sanction being imposed. Moreover, the explanatory notes to the Welfare Reform and Pensions Bill suggest that simply attending the interview may not be enough if a claimant does not provide sufficient information to help gauge his or her employability.[208]

The proposed extension of the gateway has given rise to a number of concerns. In the Commons debates, one of the main problems identified was the lack of detail in the legislation about those who will be exempt. It is thought that this might be unduly stressful on those with genuine excuses and abused by those who have not.[209] More generally, there is concern about the fact that a failure to comply can result in benefit withdrawal. Some view its compulsory nature sceptically, arguing that people would attend voluntarily if it is truly worth while and that claimants will be suspicious that 'more compulsion will follow'.[210] Others expressed concerns about the resource implications of such a time-intensive process, warning that it might become a 'bottleneck' which would result in gatekeepers using their discretion liberally and thus

---

[205] DSS, *A New Contract for Welfare: The Gateway to Work*, Cm 4102 (London: The Stationery Office, 1998), Summary, para. 6.

[206] Welfare Reform and Pensions Act 1999, s. 47 which inserts a new section 2A into the SSAA 1992 giving the Secretary of State the power to make regulations requiring claimants to take part in an interview.

[207] It also extends to claimants of council tax benefit, widows' benefits, severe disablement allowance, and invalid care allowance.

[208] Welfare Reform and Pensions Bill—Explanatory Notes, 76.

[209] *Per* R. Berry, Hansard, H.C. Debs, 23 February 1999, Vol. 326, col. 264.

[210] *Per* A. Wise, Hansard, HC Debs, 23 February 1999, Vol. 326, col. 269.

defeating the purpose of the regulations.[211] Thus, while the Government considers that attendance at an interview is a 'modest and reasonable requirement', the Shadow Secretary for Social Security considers it to be no more than an expensive 'chat'.[212] It remains to be seen whether it will be effective in encouraging categories of people who are not expected to work to think positively about their employment potential or whether it represents the thin end of a wedge which will eventually push open the door to additional labour-market obligations.

6. CONCLUSION

Social security has a labyrinth of rules which are designed to coax, coerce, or cajole people to take employment. The ability of social security to influence claimant behaviour is open to doubt generally.[213] In this context too it is not altogether clear whether or not the rules are effective in encouraging people to work. The value of the rules which are designed to monitor active jobsearch is questionable in the light of the evidence that most claimants are quite effectively doing what the law wants them to do of their own volition; sanctions do not appear to have a general deterrent effect; and the jury is out on the rules which require claimants to participate in programmes which improve employability, until New Deal has been properly scrutinised. It may be that the major input of the law in this context is symbolic rather than practical. The value of the rules may lie in the general message which they transmit about the importance of work rather than in their effectiveness in getting claimants off benefit and into employment. The reality is that the key factor which will encourage the unemployed to take employment is completely external to the social security system. Time and time again, research shows that most claimants want to work and are not unrealistic in their expectations about the nature of that employment, provided that it meets their needs and that of their families. The challenge for Government is to provide such opportunities for employment. For the Conservatives, the key to this lay in job creation on the back of a healthy economy. Labour's approach is different. Its strategy appears to be proceeding on the assumption that there are appropriate jobs available but that people need to be trained to do them and then paid enough to make it worth their while.

The Government has stated that its priority is to 'forge an entirely new culture which puts work first'.[214] In many respects, unemployment has fallen prey to Labour's famous 'spin'. There is little talk of unemployment which is now referred to as 'worklessness' or 'detachment from the labour market'. One of its key policies is 'making work pay', a twentieth-century twist on the Poor Law notion of less-

---

[211] *Per* I. Duncan Smith, Hansard, HC Debs, 23 February 1999, Vol. 326, col. 235.

[212] I. Duncan Smith MP, 'They talk tough, they act weak', *Daily Telegraph*, 12 February 1999.

[213] See Chapter 2 at pp. 57–61.

[214] DSS, *A New Contract for Welfare: The Gateway to Work*, Cm 4102 (London: The Stationery Office, 1998), ch. 1, para. 3.

eligibility. There have been a number of reforms designed to increase the income of those in low-paid work.[215] Although these changes are external to the social security system, the battle to make employment financially viable is played out at the frontier between work and social security, involving a complex interaction between tax and benefits. While the Government is grappling with measures to get claimants into full-time work, little is being done to 'make work pay' while a claimant remains on social security benefits. The Government is concentrating on strengthening in-work benefits, yet there continue to be few incentives for on-benefit work. In the course of the twentieth century governments came to accept that full employment was no longer a realistically attainable objective. The twenty-first century may witness a similar change in attitude towards full-time/permanent employment. Employers' demands for a more flexible labour force may yet result in a rethink of the work/welfare interface which acknowledges the need for some to survive on a combination of employment and benefit. If so, the challenge for social security in the early stages of the next millennium will be to determine what constitutes an acceptable mix of work and welfare—even if what transpires is that the social security system should both encourage and enable claimants to do as much (or as little) work as they can get when they can get it.

[215] For instance, April 1999 witnessed the implementation of the national minimum wage alongside a new 10 pence rate of income tax. The working families tax credit (an in-the-wage packet benefit) replaced family credit in October 1999: see Chapter 9 by Gillian Douglas at pp. 285–6.

11

Social Security and Education

NEVILLE HARRIS

1. INTRODUCTION

Since the late 1980s successive governments have adopted a policy of seeking to widen access to and participation in further and higher education. The present government endorses the philosophy of a 'learning age' and recognises a need for 'lifelong learning'.[1] Indeed, enhanced educational opportunity is one of the Government's principal policy goals and is seen as the key to future economic prosperity and social cohesion. The Government wants to increase by 500,000 the number of students with places in further and higher education. At the same time, there is a background of spiralling costs of student support which has led to reforms designed to shift the burden of financial responsibility away from the state and firmly towards young people and their families, a trend maintained under the new student support system introduced under the Teaching and Higher Education Act 1998. Students have also been squeezed by the social security system: student hardship or poverty is not seen as a matter for the benefits system and full-time students have been progressively excluded from it. For part-time students a highly complex series of rules has attempted to distinguish between those who are usefully filling their time while seeking work by adding to their qualifications and those who have detached themselves from the labour market and need to be directed back towards it.

This chapter explores the complex and evolving relationship between social security and education. It seeks a rationale for the present position of students as regards entitlement to benefit in the context of the current financial support arrangements for entrants to higher education, particularly following the implementation of Part II of the Teaching and Higher Education Act 1998, and the changing and more flexible patterns of participation in further and higher education. The position of students in higher education has always been different to that of further education students[2] and each area is analysed separately. The position of school pupils, who have long been excluded from social security entitlement in their own right, is covered in the discussion of further education below.

---

[1] See especially, DfEE, *The Learning Age: A new renaissance for a new Britain*, Cm 3790 (London: The Stationery Office, 1998), and, DfEE, *Learning to Succeed: A new framework for post-16 learning*, Cm 4392 (London: The Stationery Office, 1999).

[2] See further N. Harris, *Social Security for Young People* (Aldershot: Avebury, 1989), 31–2 and 115–42.

2. THE DEVELOPMENT OF STUDENT SUPPORT AND
SOCIAL SECURITY IN HIGHER EDUCATION

A. Before the Introduction of Student Loans

Students were entitled to supplementary benefit when it was first introduced in 1966 as the principal means-tested benefit in place of national assistance.[3] They could qualify for benefit during university vacations provided they were available for work.[4] The Supplementary Benefits Commission (SBC), which administered what was a largely discretion-based benefit pre-November 1980, took the view that so far as students were concerned there was 'no justification for excluding them from a right that is available to others'.[5] Claims from students increased dramatically in the 1970s: during Easter vacations, for example, the number of students receiving benefit increased from 48,000 in 1973 to 90,000 in 1975; and in the Easter vacation in 1976 there were 182,000 student claims, 174,000 of which were successful.[6] However, changes to the student grant later in 1976 meant that students received a greater element in their grant to cover the short (Easter and Christmas) vacations.[7] Benefit entitlement thereby became reduced and, indeed, most students only received benefit during the long (summer) vacation. Only 23,000 students received benefit in the Christmas vacation in 1976 compared with 155,000 the previous year.[8]

Student entitlement survived the reforms to the supplementary benefit scheme in 1980.[9] Although changes to the treatment of the student grant as income under the scheme resulted in further reductions in entitlement, a significant number of claims were made. In 1985 around half the student population were receiving supplementary benefit during the long vacation.[10] A similar proportion were receiving housing benefit in 1986 during term-time and short vacations.[11]

The post-1983 Conservative Government, which had already set in train a review of means-tested benefits aimed at rationalising provision through greater selectivity ('targeting') and at streamlining administration,[12] was concerned at what it saw as the disproportionate cost of administering benefits to students.[13] In its 1985 Green Paper the Government gave a clear indication that it was considering a severe curtailment of students' benefit entitlement, saying it was 'right in principle to return to the situation which existed before the introduction of supplementary benefit in 1966 with students being helped through the grants system, by their families and by their own earnings in vacation'.[14] So far as unemployment benefit was concerned, the

---

[3] See Chapters 4 and 5 for discussion of the supplementary benefit scheme.
[4] Ministry of Social Security Act 1966, s. 11.
[5] SBC, *Annual Report 1976* (London: HMSO, 1977), para. 2.25.
[6] Cited in N. Harris, n. 2 above, at 31.   [7] For background, see ibid., at 119.   [8] Ibid., 32.
[9] See Chapter 4.   [10] Cited in N. Harris, n. 2 above, at 32.   [11] Ibid., 121.
[12] See Chapter 5.
[13] For example, it cost £1 to pay each 65p to students during the short vacations: n. 2 above, 116.
[14] Green Paper (1985), Vol. 1, para. 9.28.

Government argued that students who claimed it were receiving double provision from public funds, as their maintenance grant did not offset entitlement to this non-means-tested benefit. The Government also wanted to cut back students' entitlement to housing benefit. Rents in the private sector (at a time of contraction in the supply of privately rented housing) were increasing at a much greater rate than the student grant (the value of the student grant actually fell in real terms between 1979 and 1986),[15] yet escalating hall fees were forcing more students to look for privately rented housing. Nevertheless, the Housing Benefit Review Team argued that reliance on housing benefit was 'both wrong in principle and unnecessarily complicated in practice'.[16] Students' housing benefit entitlement normally had to be reassessed at least six times per year[17] and it cost £3 to deliver each £5 in benefit.[18] Although the Green Paper indicated that reform of student benefits would have to await the introduction of a revised or new system of student support, the Government moved quickly to change the rules in relation to unemployment benefit, supplementary benefit, and housing benefit.

The principal means by which student entitlement was curtailed was via amendment of the various sets of regulations to redefine 'student'. Under the supplementary benefit provisions at this time a person was a student and thus disentitled to benefit where he or she was engaged in a full-time course (in the case of a person aged under nineteen the course had to be 'advanced', namely degree or higher diploma level);[19] but he or she was not deemed to be a student when not *attending* the course nor engaged in a programme of studies.[20] Thus, as Mesher pointed out at the time, 'a person is not a student ... during vacations'.[21] Amendment of the regulations in 1986 resulted in 'student' being redefined in order to remove short-vacation entitlement: a person was normally deemed to be on his or her course, and thus a student, throughout the period spanned by it, other than during the long vacation.[22] (This change was also incorporated into the new income support scheme when it replaced supplementary benefit in 1988: see below.) A House of Commons Select Committee felt that adequate compensation for loss of benefit entitlement was necessary, via an increase in the student grant.[23] But the annual grant increased by just £36 in 1986–7. The Social Security Advisory Committee (SSAC) also expressed

[15] SSAC, *The Supplementary Benefit (Conditions of Entitlement) Amendment Regulations 1986, Report by the SSAC*, Cmnd 9813 (London: HMSO, 1986), para. 64.
[16] Housing Benefit Review Team, *Report of the Review Team*, Cmnd 9520 (London: HMSO, 1985), para. 4.8.
[17] Ibid., para. 4.6.
[18] House of Commons, Standing Committee B, Social Security Bill, col. 1906, 30 April 1986.
[19] The meaning of 'full-time' at the time is discussed in N. Harris, n. 2 above, at 118. See below.
[20] Supplementary Benefit (Conditions of Entitlement) Regulations 1981 (S.I. 1981 No. 1526), reg. 2(1), as amended by the Supplementary Benefit (Miscellaneous Amendments) Regulations 1984 (S.I. 1984 No. 938), reg. 4(2).
[21] J. Mesher, *Supplementary Benefit and Family Income Supplement: the Legislation* (London: Sweet and Maxwell, 1984), 148.
[22] Supplementary Benefit (Conditions of Entitlement) (Amendment) Regulations 1986 (S.I. 1986 No. 1010).
[23] Cited in N. Harris, n. 2 above, 120.

concern at the loss of benefit entitlement for students where grant levels were inadequate.[24]

There was a corresponding change to the unemployment benefit regulations, despite criticism from the SSAC that a denial of benefit earned through the national insurance system represented a 'violation of the contributory principle'.[25] A day could not be a 'day of unemployment' (for which there might be entitlement to benefit) if it was a day on which a person was attending a full-time course of education; and a person would be treated as attending their course during the short vacations.[26] But in some ways the reform that had the most devastating impact was the reduction in entitlement to housing benefit, aimed at saving £16 million in public expenditure. Some of the reforms to this benefit were quite technical in nature and related to the treatment of grant income.[27] The most significant reforms[28] involved the disentitlement of most students in halls of residence, the offsetting against benefit entitlement of the accommodation element in the student grant (this change was phased in to avoid hardship), and the averaging of that accommodation element over the full grant-aided period of thirty-eight weeks rather than over term time only. From 1987 a student's eligible rent was reduced by a set amount (£17.80 in London and £13.60 elsewhere), subsequently increased annually.

B. The Introduction of Student Loans

Despite these significant cutbacks the Government had not taken students out of the social security system altogether; but this remained its long-term goal. In 1988 it announced in a White Paper the introduction of a new maintenance system for students based around top-up loans.[29] The plan was that the level of the student grant and parental contribution would be frozen from the start of the academic year 1990–1. Students would qualify for an interest-free top-up loan averaging £420; it would be uprated annually in line with prices. In addition, there would be 'access funds', administered by the universities and other higher education institutions, for students whose 'access to higher education might be inhibited by financial considerations, or where students, for whatever reasons, faced real financial difficulties'.[30] The Government hoped that institutions would offer additional assistance, such as helping students to find vacation employment.[31] Student loans would be repayable in the same way as a mortgage—over a number of years, depending on the students'

---

[24] SSAC, *The Supplementary Benefit (Conditions of Entitlement) Amendment Regulations 1986, report by the SSAC*, Cmnd 9813 (London: HMSO, 1986), para. 21.

[25] Ibid., para. 36.

[26] Social Security (Unemployment, Sickness and Invalidity Benefit) Regulations 1983 (S.I. 1983 No. 1598), reg. 7, amended by the Social Security (Unemployment, Sickness and Invalidity Benefit) Amendment (No. 2) Regulations 1986 (S.I. 1986 No. 1611).

[27] See N. Harris, n. 2 above, 121–4.

[28] See the Housing Benefit (Amendment No. 3) Regulations 1986 (S.I. 1986 No. 1009).

[29] Department of Education and Science, *Top-Up Loans for Students*, Cm 520 (London: HMSO, 1988).

[30] Ibid., para. 3.21.   [31] Ibid., para. 3.25.

circumstances—from the April following the end of the period of study. As far as social security was concerned, the White Paper cited a survey of student incomes (covering the year 1986–7) by the Department of Education and Science which showed that 77 per cent of students claimed benefits at some stage during the academic year; and 43 per cent of students living away from home received housing benefit. The Government reiterated its long-standing view that 'the benefits system is intended to serve social and not educational purposes' and that 'student dependence on benefits is inappropriate and undesirable'.[32] It argued that the new system of student support would 'make it possible to implement the Government's long-standing commitment to removing full-time students from dependency on social security benefits'.[33] Entitlement to income support (which replaced supplementary benefit in April 1988), housing benefit and unemployment benefit, was to cease, although the eligibility of partners of students would not be affected.[34] Figures for May 1988 show that 78,000 students were in receipt of housing benefit (around 12 per cent of the student population);[35] so the changes were certain to have a major impact.

The assumption that the loss of benefit would be more than compensated for by the availability of top-up loans and access funds was challenged. According to the White Paper the average total amount received in housing benefit was £211, or £296 in London, and the overall average in social security benefits was £249, compared to £420 in top-up loan. But these were *averages* and, as the White Paper acknowledged, some students received more than £1,000 in benefits. Some students clearly stood to lose a substantial amount overall. The National Union of Students (NUS) also criticised the basis on which the calculations were made, because many of the students surveyed lived in halls of residence and had lost entitlement to housing benefit in 1986, whereas those living out of hall faced a much greater loss of benefit.[36] Access funds might help some students, but payments would be discretionary as compared with a right to social security.

The student loans legislation was introduced in 1990.[37] The Government allocated £25 million for access funds and gave institutions considerable discretion as to their distribution.[38] Top-up loans were normally repayable over five years.[39] The loans scheme was administered partly by the Student Loans Company and partly by the higher education institutions, which were placed under a duty to assess students' eligibility, certify eligibility if established, and determine the level of entitlement in individual cases.[40] The planned social security changes, intended to remove students' entitlement throughout their course, including all vacations within it, were

---

[32] Ibid., para. 2.12.   [33] Ibid., para. 3.26.   [34] Ibid.

[35] SSAC, *Report of the Social Security Advisory Committee on the Social Security Benefits (Student Loan) Amendment Regulations 1990*, Cm 1141 (London: HMSO, 1990), para. 55.

[36] See N. Harris, 'Social Security, Student Loans and Access to Education' (1991) 54 *M.L.R.* 258–70 at 262.

[37] The Education (Student Loans) Act 1990 and the Education (Student Loans) Regulations 1990 (S.I. 1990 No. 1401).

[38] See N. Harris, above n. 36.

[39] Education (Student Loans) Regulations 1990, op. cit., reg. 7(2) and (5).   [40] Ibid., reg. 11.

introduced separately.[41] The changes made at this stage for the most part form the basis of the limited entitlement today.

The reforms to housing benefit were strongly resisted. The key amendment to the housing benefit regulations[42] provided that a claimant would remain a student throughout his or her course (including the long vacation, as with income support: see below). During this time he or she would not be treated as liable to make payments in respect of a dwelling and would not, therefore, be regarded as occupying that dwelling as his or her home, such as would trigger entitlement. There were exceptional categories, including certain disabled students and those responsible for a child. A dissenting minority of members of the SSAC argued that the changes would result in students' housing costs not being adequately met.[43] There were various unsuccessful Opposition attempts to amend the Social Security Bill, and challenges to the regulations in Parliament.[44] Furthermore, eight university Vice-Chancellors in the South of England wrote to *The Times* complaining about the difficulties which would face students in an area of the country where rent increases had far exceeded the national average.[45]

The principal change to the income support scheme was to extend the definition of full-time 'period of study', the period during which a person would be classed as a student and thus be ineligible for income support. This period was now the entire period of the course (or until the student abandoned it).[46] Student entitlement to benefit during the long vacation had survived the 1986–7 reforms; and in the summer of 1989, for example, 135,000 students had received income support.[47] Although the average period of payment had been only six weeks, there were fears that the loss of long-vacation entitlement could have a serious impact when combined with the loss of housing benefit.[48]

Student entitlement to unemployment benefit was also reformed. Following on from the 1986–7 reforms (above), the restriction on entitlement was extended to the long vacation. A person was a student throughout his or her course, including all vacations, unless and until he or she finished or abandoned it.[49]

It has rightly been argued that 'the reduction in the contribution of social security

[41] Via the Social Security Benefits (Student Loans and Miscellaneous Amendments) Regulations 1990 (S.I. 1990 No. 1549) and the Income-related Benefits Amendment Regulations 1990 (S.I. 1990 No. 1657).
[42] Housing Benefit (General) Regulations 1987 (S.I. 1987 No. 1971), as amended by S.I. 1990 No. 1549, op. cit. There was some transitional protection, however.
[43] N. 35 above, 'Note dissenting from the report' signed by 7 members of the Committee, para. 7.
[44] See N. Harris, n. 36 above, at 266.
[45] *The Times*, 1 October 1990.   [46] IS(G) Regs 1987, reg. 2(1), as amended.
[47] SSAC, *Report of the Social Security Advisory Committee made under section 10(3) of the Social Security Act 1980 on the Social Security benefits (Student Loan) Amendment Regulations 1990*, Cm 1141 (London: HMSO, 1990), para. 55.
[48] Ibid.
[49] Social Security (Unemployment, Sickness and Invalidity Benefit) Regulations 1983 (S.I. 1983 No. 1598), reg. 7(m), added by the Social Security Benefits (Student Loans and Miscellaneous Amendments) Regulations 1990 (S.I. 1990 No. 1549), reg. 6. There was an unsuccessful challenge to the *vires* of the amendment provisions: *R v Secretary of State for Social Security ex p Rouse; ex p Moore* (1993) *The Times* 1 February (QBD).

benefits to student incomes had a significant impact on young students'.[50] A Policy Studies Institute survey revealed that by 1995–6 only 9 per cent of all students, but less than 2 per cent of those aged twenty-five or under, were receiving any income by way of social security.[51] Among older ('mature') students the figure was much higher, at 51 per cent.[52] Mature students are more likely to be partners of claimants or to have dependent children and thus to be in a household receiving income-related benefits.[53] The average amount received in benefit by both groups of students had fallen markedly between 1988–9 and 1995–6: for example, in the case of young students it went down from £115 to £20.[54]

Given the Government's argument that the new student loans system would largely obviate the need for welfare benefits support, the impact of the considerable reductions in entitlement and the reduced reliance on benefits could only be judged by the actual effects of loans system. The first point to note is the relatively low take-up of loans. In 1994–5 only 53 per cent of students who were eligible for a loan were in receipt of one,[55] although there was an increase to 64 per cent in 1997–8.[56] The principal reason for this general reluctance to take out a loan appears to have been fear of future debt and a general cultural belief among their parents against incurring debt.[57] Indeed, in some cases parents were making increased contributions to students in order to avoid the need for a loan. A Barclay's Bank survey in 1997 calculated that nationally parents were contributing an additional £403 million in financial support for their children at university or college.[58] Yet at the same time many students (37 per cent of those eligible) were not receiving the full parental contribution.[59]

Access funds were, as noted above, intended to help those facing real hardship. By 1996 the total amount allocated to universities and colleges for this purpose had increased to £35 million. The general guidelines issued to universities made particular reference to the needs of students with dependants and those with unavoidably high housing costs. Universities also developed their own criteria, although a survey by the NUS found them to be vague and imprecise.[60] There were wide inconsistencies in the amount of support offered across universities, confirmed by a HEFCE

[50] K. Mullan and G. McKeown, 'Supporting full-time students in higher education—the role of social security benefits' (1999) 6 *J.S.S.L.* 56–78, 72.

[51] C. Callender and E. Kempson, *Student Finances: Income Expenditure and Take-up of Student Loans* (London: Policy Studies Institute, 1996), 42.

[52] Ibid.

[53] Note, however, that much of the student's grant will fall to be taken into account as income.

[54] C. Callender and E. Kempson, op. cit.

[55] NUS, *Value for Money Survey* (London: NUS, 1995). In the first year of the loans system only 28 per cent of students in Scotland applied for them, but this increased to 39 per cent the following year: see 'Students sued over loans', news item in (1992) *N.L.J.* 886.

[56] DfEE, Press Notice 555/98, 30 November 1998, *Student Support: Statistics of Student Loans*.

[57] See O. Swanton, 'Higher Education: Burden of debt' (1997) *The Guardian*, 3 June.

[58] Reported in NUS Press Release, 'Student hardship hits record high', 12 July 1997.

[59] N. Fenton, 'Higher Education—the writing is on the wall' (1998) *Poverty* No. 101, 12–14 at 14.

[60] NUS Access Funds Survey, cited in NUS, *Student hardship—the facts* (London: NUS, 1996).

survey.[61] The NUS described access funds as 'a lottery: whether a student receives assistance—and if so, how much—depends entirely upon where they happen to be studying'.[62] A survey by the Committee of Vice-Chancellors and Principals (CVCP) showed that in 1994–5 only an estimated 7.5 per cent of students received access funds.[63] Overall, it is not clear that the funds have had much of an impact on student hardship.

Meanwhile, there has been increasing concern about the problem of student debt, not least from students themselves. The Dearing Committee found that the fear of debt under the loan-based student support system was deterring participation of potential students from unskilled or semi-skilled family backgrounds.[64] In a survey of students by the NUS in 1995, 27 per cent of respondents had considered leaving their course because of financial difficulties and 54 per cent thought that their financial situation was adversely affecting their studies.[65] The fact that from September 1995 mature students were eligible for only the same level of support as younger students (following the abolition of the allowance for students aged twenty-six or over in the mandatory award), despite often having greater financial commitments, was almost certainly one reason for the higher drop-out rate among mature students compared to younger students noted by the CVCP.[66] A survey of student finances in 1994–5 showed that average student expenditure exceeded average student income.[67] Not surprisingly, many full-time students have had to take jobs to supplement their income. A joint survey by the NUS and the General, Municipal and Boilermakers' Union (GMB) in 1996 found that 40 per cent of students were employed during term time and that nearly half of them worked for between 12.5 and 20 hours per week. A majority (two-thirds) said their employment adversely affected their studies, for example causing them to miss lectures or fail to submit academic work.[68]

It seems reasonable to conclude that the level of student hardship has to some extent been attributable to the significant reductions in student entitlement to benefits from 1990. By 1998, the basic income of a person in receipt of a student loan was £800 a year less than the income of an unemployed single person in receipt of jobseeker's allowance (JSA) and housing benefit.[69] If students had retained entitlement to benefit the differential would be far smaller and in some cases would be zero.

[61] HEFCE, *Access Funds—monitoring information for 1994/95,* cited in NUS, *Student hardship—the facts* (London, NUS, 1996) at 10.
[62] NUS (1996), ibid.
[63] CVCP, *CVCP Survey of Student Financial Support 1995* (London: CVCP, 1996).
[64] National Committee of Inquiry into Higher Education, *Report of the National Committee* (London: DfEE, 1997), paras 20–37.
[65] NUS, *Value for Money Survey* (London: NUS, 1995).
[66] CVCP, *CVCP Survey of Student Financial Support 1995* (London: CVCP, 1996).
[67] E.g. C. Callender and E. Kempson, *Student Finances: Income Expenditure and Take-up of Student Loans* (London: Policy Studies Institute, 1996), 42 and 61.
[68] GMB/NUS, *Students at Work* (London: NUS, 1996).
[69] Hansard, H.C. Debs (web version), col. 814, 8 June 1998.

The current rules on entitlement, as affected by the further restrictions in 1995, are discussed below.

3. THE DEVELOPMENT OF FINANCIAL SUPPORT AND SOCIAL SECURITY FOR THOSE
REMAINING IN NON-ADVANCED EDUCATION BEYOND COMPULSORY SCHOOL AGE
AND FOR STUDENTS IN THE FURTHER EDUCATION SECTOR

We now turn to the position of those receiving education beyond compulsory school age (the upper limit of which was raised from fifteen to sixteen in 1972) who are not within the higher education system. A majority of those in this category needing social security will be students in colleges of further education.

A. Supplementary Benefit 1966–80

The minimum age of entitlement to supplementary benefit, introduced in 1966, was sixteen. However, those aged sixteen or over who remained in education were likely to be caught by the general rule that 'a person attending a school or receiving full-time instruction of a kind given in schools shall not be entitled to benefit'.[70] Regulations could specify the circumstances in which a person was or was not to be treated for this purpose as attending school or receiving analogous education, but the power was never exercised. Later, however, the Department of Health and Social Security (DHSS) explained that the latter included 'non-advanced courses at, for example, colleges of further education and technical colleges' and that the exclusion from benefit applied to 'term-time and holidays alike'.[71] The test of whether a course was or was not advanced was entirely a matter of SBC policy, which relied on the claimant's local authority's classification of the course for student grant purposes. This practice was declared illegal, however, on the grounds that a policy rule was being applied as though law.[72] Nevertheless, the SBC continued to exclude from benefit those on courses at or below A level or Ordinary National Diploma standard, believing that they were the responsibility of their parents who could claim child benefit for them.[73]

Once a young person left school he or she could claim benefit in the usual way. But policy was amended to restrict the right of school leavers to benefit. For example, in 1976, there was a massive increase in claims from school leavers resulting from changes in the permitted school leaving date[74] and so moves were made to prevent

---

[70] Ministry of Social Security Act 1966, s. 9(1). This section was later replaced by s. 7(1) of the Supplementary Benefits Act 1976.

[71] DHSS, *Supplementary Benefits Handbook* (London: HMSO, 1977), para. 6.

[72] *Sampson v Supplementary Benefit Commission* (1979) 123 *S.J.* 284.

[73] See J. Loosemore, 'Policy and discretion in supplementary benefit decisions' (1980) *N.L.J.* 495–6.

[74] *Department of Employment Gazette*, July 1977, 719. Young people had become entitled to leave school at any time from the Friday before the last Monday in May.

school leavers becoming entitled immediately they left school, to discourage premature school leaving and the 'socially undesirable trend for children to enter adult life
by moving straight from school onto benefit'.[75] The DHSS also became concerned
about sixteen or seventeen year olds who received benefit during the summer holiday when they actually intended to return to school or college after then but had not
disclosed this, which was regarded as an 'abuse of the system'.[76] The SBC had wondered whether benefit entitlement could be delayed 'until the end of the school holidays when it is clearer whether they [school leavers] are in the employment field'.[77]
The DHSS Review team supported this idea and proposed fixed dates for school
leavers' entitlement to supplementary benefit: the first or second Monday in May
or September for those who had last attended school in the spring or summer
terms respectively.[78]

B. Supplementary Benefit from 1980

The changes were included in the revision of the supplementary benefit scheme in
1980. The concept of 'relevant education' was introduced and it is still a key element
within the rules on entitlement (now in relation to income support and JSA). Persons
aged under nineteen and in receipt of relevant education, and those aged nineteen
who were to be treated as being in relevant education, were excluded from entitlement.[79] 'Relevant education' was defined in the 1980 Act as 'full-time' education at
an establishment recognised by the Secretary of State 'as being, or as being comparable to, a college or school'.[80] A person leaving school or college was to be treated as
though in 'relevant education' where child benefit was payable in respect of them.
The regulations governing child benefit were amended so that a school leaver was to
continue to be treated as a child for the purposes of this benefit until the first
Monday: in January; or after Easter Monday; or in September; or before the child
reached the age of nineteen.[81] (Later these 'terminal dates' were incorporated into
the income support scheme.)

The financial effect on households of the delayed entitlement of young people
was a reduction in overall potential income of £10.50 per week.[82] A further change,
in 1987, restricted the right of those who, having reached the age of sixteen, 'left'

---

[75] DHSS, *Social Assistance. A Review of the Supplementary Benefits Scheme* (London: DHSS, 1978), para. 4.4.
[76] Ibid., para. 4.6.
[77] SBC, *Supplementary Benefit Commission Annual Report 1976* (London: HMSO, 1976), para. 3.31.
[78] DHSS, *Social Assistance. A Review of the Supplementary Benefits Scheme* (London: DHSS, 1978), para. 4.9.
[79] SSA 1980, s. 6(2); Supplementary Benefit (Aggregation) Regulations 1981 (S.I. 1981 No. 1524), reg. 3(5).
[80] SSA 1980, s. 6(3). Persons aged 19 or over were not expressly excluded from this definition, but only
a person who had not attained the age of 19 could be in relevant education: *R(SB) 8/86*.
[81] Child Benefit (General) Regulations 1976 (S.I. 1976 No. 765), reg. 7, as amended by the Child Benefit
(General) Amendment Regulations 1980 (S.I. 1980 No. 1586). See also the Supplementary Benefit
(Conditions of Entitlement) Regulations 1981 (S.I. 1981 No. 1526).
[82] Representing the difference between a 16 year old's supplementary benefit of £15.25 (£13.10 basic
rate plus £2.15 non-householder's addition) less child benefit of £4.75.

school at Easter but who had an intention of returning to sit GCSE or other examinations in the early summer from qualifying for benefit until the next terminal date
(in September).[83] However, there was concern that these young people would face a
choice of abandoning examinations or taking them and losing a considerable total in
benefits.[84]

In order to distinguish between persons who were genuinely outside the labour
market and those who were undertaking a limited amount of study but were otherwise unemployed, 'relevant education' was defined in terms of a minimum number
of hours of study per week. Initially this definition was based on policy guidelines
and it referred to 'attendance of 15 hours per week including homework, of which
at least 7½ hours is spent at the establishment'.[85] The 'fifteen-hour rule', criticised for
its rigidity by a Social Security Commissioner[86] and problematic to administer
because inquiries tended to sour relationships between the benefits authorities and
schools and colleges,[87] was abandoned in 1984 when regulations provided for a
twelve-hour test under which private study was excluded from the calculation of a
student's hours.[88] This remains the basic test of 'relevant education' for income support and JSA claims (see below).

Linked into the fifteen- or twelve-hour basis to the definition of 'relevant' education was a concession for young people who 'had completed their formal education but wished to do some formal study or training while seeking work'.[89] This
began in 1971 as the 'three-day rule': claimants attending college for not more than
three days of the week could be awarded supplementary benefit provided they were
available for work in the sense that they were prepared to leave their course and take
up suitable employment if it was offered.[90] By 1979 the rule had evolved into the
'twenty-one-hour rule'.[91] The new regulation-based supplementary benefit scheme
introduced in 1980 incorporated this rule, which also applied to persons on training
courses. It also added further conditions: first, the claimant must not have deliberately given up a job or full-time course in order to study part-time, as this would have
involved a deliberate move to put oneself into reliance on benefit; and secondly, if
aged twenty-one or over (later this age limit was revoked) the claimant must have
been in receipt of benefit and unemployed for the previous twelve months.

On the face of it the twenty-one-hour rule was a fairly generous provision. Its

---

[83] Supplementary Benefit (Conditions of Entitlement) Amendment Regulations 1987 (S.I. 1987 No.
358). The complexity of the existing rules was commented upon by a Tribunal of Commissioners in
R(F)2/85(T).

[84] SSAC, *Proposals for Regulations Regarding Benefits for Children and Young People*, Cm 106 (London: HMSO,
1987), para. 18.

[85] Chief Supplementary Benefit Officer, *CSBO Memo No. 15* (London: SBC, 1982), para. 2(1).

[86] Commissioner Bowen in *CF/38/1983*.

[87] J. Pelican, *Studying on the Dole* (London: Youthaid, 1983), 53.

[88] Supplementary Benefit (Miscellaneous Amendments) Regulations 1984 (S.I. 1984 No. 938).

[89] DHSS, Memorandum submitted to the House of Commons Education, Science and the Arts
Committee, 1983, cited in N. Harris, *Social Security for Young People* (Aldershot, Avebury, 1989), 133.

[90] For further background, see N. Harris, ibid., 132–3.   [91] Ibid., 133.

development in the 1970s recognised the problem of increasing youth unemployment[92] and the need to encourage unemployed young people to improve their employment prospects by acquiring (further) qualifications. The DHSS was always keen to stress that benefit provision was primarily concerned with addressing social rather than specifically educational needs: 'we look after people between 16 and 19 as part of a family, when they are in education (. . . either by paying child benefit to their parents or dependency benefits if their parents are on some sort of social security benefit), but we do not provide student support as such'.[93] The benefit authorities wanted to make a clear distinction between the unemployed, including those studying while waiting for work, and those firmly and exclusively committed to the pursuit of education. It is the application of this distinction that has continued to present enormous difficulties for the benefits system and its clients.

The first problem to arise concerned the linking of the qualifying number of hours to attendance on the course.[94] After a Tribunal of Commissioners[95] ruled in 1982 that classroom hours plus compulsory fieldwork and timetabled hours of private study on the college premises were included, but other private study was not, the regulations were amended to exclude from the computation of the twenty-one hours time spent on meal breaks and any unsupervised study.[96]

A further and much more serious problem arose because of another change to the regulations. The Government had become concerned that the twenty-one-hour rule enabled young people to leave school and take an A level or Diploma course at college while receiving benefit. It argued that this was inconsistent with the principle that supplementary benefit was not intended as basic maintenance for those young people who were removed from the labour market.[97] It therefore introduced a qualifying period of three months for those seeking benefit under the twenty-one rule. The qualifying period meant that the claimant had to have been unemployed and in receipt of benefit for three months before being able to receive benefit and study for up to twenty-one hours per week. In effect, the claimant could study for up to twelve hours per week during the qualifying period, as by doing so he or she would not be in 'relevant education' (above) and could thus still be entitled to benefit. Thereafter he or she could increase the number of hours to twenty-one per week. The most problematic aspect of this reform, educationally, was the fact that the course of study of up to twenty-one hours had to be different from any course undertaken during the qualifying period. Those who left school in the summer and claimed ben-

---

[92] See N. Harris, 23–4.

[93] DHSS response to the House of Commons Education, Science and the Arts Committee, Minutes of Evidence, 20 April 1983, Q.730.

[94] Supplementary Benefit (Conditions of Entitlement) Regulations 1981 (S.I. 1981 No. 1526), reg. 7(2)–(4).

[95] *R(SB)26/82.*

[96] Supplementary Benefit (Miscellaneous Amendments) Regulations 1982 (S.I. 1982 No. 907).

[97] Secretary of State for Social Services, Annex to SSAC, *The Supplementary Benefit (Requirements and Resources) Amendment Regulations 1982 (Etc)*, Cmnd 8598 (London: HMSO, 1982)

efit in September would have to start a new course in December, which was rather late in the year to commence a GCSE or equivalent course.

The change was roundly criticised largely for this reason by both the SSAC and a report of a study commissioned by the Department of Employment, which recommended the discontinuance of the qualifying period requirement.[98] The 'different course' aspect of the rule proved difficult to apply and it was not in any event applied in a consistent manner. The Further Education Unit offered some guidance for colleges in 1984 on how to make the two courses demonstrably different while maintaining continuity and an element of progression between them.[99] It was desperately needed, as many colleges' provision structured around the old twenty-one-hour rule was now, in the light of the new qualifying period, unsuitable to students' needs. It was evident that the DHSS had not acted in co-ordination with the Department of Education and Science when revising the twenty-one-hour rule, indicative of a more general lack of coherence to policy development in this area. There was better co-ordination at a local level, with some LEAs (which, until 1992, were responsible for further education provision in colleges) concluding local agreements with the DHSS which eased some of the problems in administering the rule.

The changes to the twenty-one-hour rule had caused difficulties but did not, it seems, precipitate a reduction in the numbers receiving benefit under it.[100] However, at a time of rising youth unemployment an increase in the numbers receiving benefit under the rule might have been expected. It may be that a further amendment in 1983,[101] enabling time spent on a government youth training scheme to count toward the qualifying period, helped to prevent a fall in numbers. Nevertheless, there is some evidence that colleges of further education which formerly regarded the rule as creating opportunities to meet young people's educational needs now saw it rather more as a problem and were confused by it.[102]

In 1987 there were 30,000 sixteen and seventeen year olds studying and receiving benefit under the twenty-one-hour rule.[103] The whole situation changed dramatically, however, when the Social Security Act 1988 came into operation. The Government had been placing increasing emphasis on youth training initiatives to tackle or at least contain the problem of youth unemployment. Now it decided that the general minimum age of entitlement to income support (which had recently replaced supplementary benefit) should be increased from sixteen to eighteen (subject to certain exceptions).[104] It argued that it was necessary to discourage young people from moving from school to the dole and that because paid training places were guaranteed (a

---

[98] SSAC, ibid., para. 8 and J. Pelican, *Studying on the Dole* (London: Youthaid, 1983).

[99] Further Education Unit, *FEU Guidance Note No. 3, Curriculum Implications of the 12/21 hour rules* (London: FEU, 1984).

[100] See DES, *Administrative Memorandum 3/1984* (London: DES, 1984).

[101] Supplementary Benefit (Miscellaneous Amendments) Regulations 1983 (S.I. 1983 No. 1000).

[102] J. Allbeson, 'Seen but not heard: young people', in S. Ward (ed.), *DHSS in Crisis* (London: CPAG, 1985), 97.

[103] Cited in N. Harris, *Social Security for Young People* (Aldershot: Avebury, 1989), 137.

[104] See ibid., ch. 7.

fact which was hotly disputed in Parliament and by youth organisations) there was no need for benefit entitlement.[105] The effect of this change was to restrict the availability of the twenty-one-hour rule to those aged eighteen or over.[106] For those aged nineteen or over, however, the position was complex. Only if their course was in effect part-time and non-advanced could they be covered by the twenty-one-hour rule. If their course was 'full-time' they were 'students' and thus governed by separate provisions relating to those in higher education. Those aged nineteen or over in *part-time higher education* were not covered by the twenty-one-hour rule, but could qualify for benefit subject to the other tests relating to availability for work.

The development of the above rules was piecemeal. It did not take proper account of educational considerations bearing on the development of courses for young people and, indeed, for mature adults returning to learning. It is true that ministers had not sought to, more or less, wholly relinquish the role of the social security system in supporting such claimants while they were engaged in education, as had happened in the case of students (above). Nevertheless, difficulties were placed in the way of participants in further education and the institutions which were seeking to meet their educational needs. In the case of sixteen and seventeen year olds, public policy demonstrated a clear bias in favour of training rather than education. Training allowances on government schemes were paid at a rate that was on average one-third higher than the non-householder rate of supplementary benefit and generally far in excess of any support available from local education authorities (LEAs) via educational maintenance allowances and discretionary awards.[107] Indeed, these education grants were unevenly provided and many young people at college had little option but to use 'social security as student grants'.[108] A PSI study called for equalisation of the rate of these education awards with training allowances, and the payment of social security for those in part-time study but at a lower rate in order to encourage full-time education.[109] It favoured the introduction of a national scheme of educational allowances in place of discretionary awards. This did not happen, and the availability of discretionary awards declined as LEAs sought ways of reducing expenditure (see below). Moreover, the restriction of awards has not proved amenable to legal challenge in individual cases save in the case of a fairly extreme fettering of discretion.[110]

[105] Ibid. [106] IS(G) Regs 1987 (1988–9 version), reg. 9.

[107] Made at the time under the Education Act 1962 and Scholarships and Other Benefits Regulations 1977 (S.I. 1977 No. 1443).

[108] K. Roberts et al., *Youth Labour Markets: The Class of '83*, Department of Employment Research Paper No. 59 (London: Department of Employment, 1985). See also L. Burghes and R. Stegles, *No Choice at 16: a study of educational maintenance allowances*, Poverty Pamphlet No. 57 (London: CPAG, 1983).

[109] S. Cooper, *Family income support Part 2: the education and training benefits* (London: P.S.I., 1985), 108–10.

[110] See P. Diamond, 'The end of discretionary awards' (1996) 8(1) *Education and the Law*, 61–8.

4. SOCIAL SECURITY AND FURTHER AND HIGHER EDUCATION:
THE PRESENT LEGISLATIVE FRAMEWORK

A. The Basic Position

The introduction of JSA in 1996 has meant that most of those who seek benefit while in education or during periods of temporary absence from it will need to claim income-based JSA rather than income support, which is only available to those who because of a disability or particular personal circumstances are not required to register for and be available for work. The basic position of claimants who are in relevant education and those who are classed as students is discussed below.

(i) Relevant Education

In respect of both contribution-based and income-based JSA[111] a person is not entitled to benefit when in 'relevant education'. This concept has therefore had a continuous place in the legislation since the days of supplementary benefit (above). School leavers will normally remain in relevant education until the next terminal date or until their nineteenth birthday, whichever is the sooner.[112] The term 'relevant education' is defined in the regulations as being education which is full-time and not advanced.[113] Only a child or young person[114] can be a person in relevant education. Such a person is deemed to be in full-time education for the purposes of JSA if he or she is treated as being in full-time education under the child benefit regulations, which refer to the twelve-hour test discussed above. In other words, to be in relevant education the young person must be on a course involving contact hours (plus supervised study) of at least twelve hours per week; unsupervised study and meal breaks do not count towards the time.[115]

Those young persons who are part-time students on further education courses under learning agreements with the relevant funding council (in other words in the equivalent of 'non-advanced' education under the old arrangements for income support) and who are studying for *more* than twelve hours per week may still escape being classed as in relevant education for JSA purposes if they meet the current qualifying period condition. The qualifying period condition specifies that they must have spent the previous three months, or three months in aggregate over the previous six months, on JSA, incapacity benefit, or income support where incapable of work or on a 'course of training'.[116] This is similar to the position under income support prior

---

[111] Note that in the remainder of this chapter all references to JSA are to income-based JSA, unless stated otherwise.

[112] Child Benefit (General) Regulations 1976 (S.I. 1976 No. 965), reg. 7. The 'terminal dates' are unchanged from previously: see above.

[113] JSA Regs 1996, reg. 54(1); IS(G) Regs 1987, reg. 12.

[114] A young peson is broadly someone aged at least 16 but under 19: JSA Regs 1996, reg. 76; IS(G) Regs 1987, reg. 14.

[115] JSA Regs 1996, reg. 54(2) and Child Benefit (General) Regulations 1976 (S.I. 1976 No. 965), reg. 5.

[116] JSA Regs 1996, regs 11 and 54(3).

to the introduction of JSA, save that a part-time student here is essentially someone whose course of study involves not more than sixteen hours per week of 'guided learning hours' rather than twenty-one hours inclusive of tuition time, supervised study time, examinations, and practical work.[117]

The changeover from the old twenty-one-hour rule to the sixteen-hour test in 1996 was intended to reflect changes in educational practice: 'Instead of people being made to turn up and sit behind desks so that the number of hours can be measured, they now follow modules and have guided learning hours.'[118] Although the DSS also claimed that the effect on claimants would be 'neutral',[119] the definitions are very similar in effect and it seems likely that this change represented little more than a tightening up on eligibility. Indeed, the choice of sixteen hours is significant, as the definition of being in remunerative work (which, if applicable, denies a JSA claimant entitlement) is based on this number of hours of employment per week. Thus it seems that the intention was probably to align the two tests in order to have a consistent and more coherent distinction between those who are or are not in the labour market rather than to reflect changes in educational provision. It might have been difficult for the Government to admit this without also acknowledging that a cut was being made. To Frank Field, then an Opposition spokesperson, the effect of the reform was clear: 'The regulations tighten controls on those who spend their time profitably while they are unemployed by undertaking courses: the 21-hour rule becomes a 16-hour rule.'[120] There are suggestions that the change from twenty-one to sixteen hours has operated as a discouragement for unemployed people to study.[121]

There are also exceptions to the general rule that those in 'relevant education' would not be entitled to income support.[122] The list of categories of persons eligible includes, broadly: persons responsible for a child; severely mentally or handicapped persons facing difficulty securing employment; those living away from their parents or guardian and estranged from them or in various forms of physical, moral, or mental danger or risk; those leaving residential care with no family home to go to; and those whose parent or person acting in place of a parent cannot, for specified reasons, support him or her financially. These categories have been in place for several years. A new exception is persons who are participating in the full-time education and training option of the New Deal (see below and Chapter 10).

---

[117] JSA Regs 1996, reg. 1(3). There are slight variations in Scotland. See also the 1995 version of the IS(G) Regs 1987, reg. 9, now revoked.

[118] Hansard, H.C. Debs, col. 791, 17 January 1996, *per* Mr R. Evans (Parliamentary Under-Secretary of State for Social Security), debate on the proposed JSA Regs 1996.

[119] Ibid.   [120] Ibid., cols 783–4.

[121] See A. Herbert and C. Callender, *The Funding Lottery: Student support in further education* (London: Policy Studies Institute, 1997).

[122] IS(G) Regs 1987, reg. 13. As briefly noted above, income support rather than JSA would only be available to persons who because of a disability or personal or family circumstances are excused from having to be registered for, available for, and actively seeking employment.

(ii) Students

Despite the introduction of JSA there has been no change since the 1990 reforms (above) to the general exclusion of persons classed as students from entitlement to means-tested benefit. The rules are very complex and technical. The general rule is that a full-time student is not to be regarded as available for work—a condition of entitlement to JSA—during his or her 'period of study' unless he or she has a partner who is also a full-time student and either or both of them are responsible for a child, in which case the student is capable of being available during the summer vacation only.[123] For the purposes of income support, a full-time student is not entitled to benefit during his or her 'period of study' unless he or she falls within one of the categories of exception, which include refugees, lone parents responsible for a child, disabled students (as defined), students who have been incapable of work for twenty-eight weeks, and (as a separate category) those suffering from deafness.[124] For the purposes of both JSA and income support, the student's 'period of study' runs from the start of the course to the last day of it; the period of study will, however, expire if before the expected end the student 'abandons' his or her course or is dismissed from it.[125]

The JSA regulations state that a full-time student will be deemed to be attending or undertaking his or her course until the last day of the course or his or her earlier abandonment or dismissal from it.[126] They also specify when a claimant will be classed as a 'full-time student': he or she must not be in receipt of a training allowance and must be (i) aged sixteen to eighteen and be undertaking a 'full-time course of advanced education'; or (ii) aged nineteen or over and either:

(a) attending a 'full-time course of study' which is not funded in whole or in part by the Further Education Funding Council (FEFC) or Secretary of State for Scotland at a college of further education; or

(b) attending a course which is so funded by the Secretary of State for Scotland and which is a course of higher education; or

(c) attending a course which is funded in whole or in part by the FEFC or Secretary of State for Scotland but basically involves more than 16 hours per week of guided learning hours in the week in question and, in the case of Scotland, is not a course of higher education.[127]

Overall, this definition preserves the essence of the restriction which dates back to the 1980s (above), with the exception of the sixteen-hour test applicable to those in category (ii). Although the scheme of the definitions is different in the case of income support, there are the same distinctions between claimants as under JSA,[128]

---

[123] JSA Regs, reg. 15.   [124] IS(G) Regs 1987, reg. 4ZA.

[125] JSA Regs, reg. 4 and IS(G) Regs 1987, reg. 2(1).

[126] JSA Regs 1996, reg. 1(3). The IS(G) Regs 1987 contain a similar abandonment/dismissal provision (reg. 61).

[127] JSA Regs 1996, reg. 1(3). Note the modification of the sixteen-hour test in Scotland when 'structured learning packages' are involved.

[128] IS(G) Regs 1987, reg. 61.

including a sixteen-hour test.[129] There is a common definition of 'course of advanced education', being a course leading to a postgraduate qualification, a degree or higher diploma, or a qualification above advanced GNVQ (general national vocational qualification) or equivalent.[130]

We have seen that to be a 'student' a person aged sixteen to eighteen must be on a 'full-time course of advanced education'. However, there is no definition of 'full-time course' in the case of 'advanced' courses.[131] The matter has been considered by the Commissioners, in several cases, and recently by the Court of Appeal, in *Denton*.[132] Here Henry LJ noted[133] (without citing any Commissioners' decisions although obviously guided by them) that the established principles were: (i) it is the course itself to which attention should be directed, not the claimant's diligence in attending or working on it;[134] (ii) the question whether a person is attending a full-time course depends on the circumstances of each case;[135] and (iii) account should be taken of the relevant education authority's description of the course, because a maintenance grant (and now a loan) would be payable only if the course was classed as full-time.[136]

The same basic definitions relating to students as those above are used in the regulations governing entitlement to housing benefit; they operate to restrict entitlement in the case of full-time students.[137] As in the past (above), the basic rule is that a full-time student is to be 'treated as if he were not liable to make payments in respect of a dwelling', with the result that there is no entitlement to housing benefit during the course of study.[138] There are some exceptions to this general rule, such as certain disabled students, those who have a partner who is also a student and either of them is responsible for a child or young person, certain persons who are (or to be treated as) incapable of work, and those aged under nineteen who are not in higher education.[139] Overall, the restrictions to housing benefit made in 1986–7 and in 1990 are having a continuing effect. There are also common rules governing the treatment

---

[129] The effect of this 16-hour rule for those aged 19 or over on non-advanced courses could have been to re-classify them as being in full-time rather than part-time study. There is, however, transitional protection for such students who were receiving income support but caught by the new rule when it was introduced in August 1996. They will be able to continue to receive income support until the end of their part-time course or their abandonment of or dismissal from it: Income-related Benefits Scheme and Social Fund (Miscellaneous Amendments) Regulations 1996 (S.I. 1996 No. 1944), reg. 8.

[130] JSA Regs 1996, reg. 1(3) and IS(G) Regs 1987, reg. 61. A pupil barrister is not on a 'course' (*R(SB) 25/87*), but a person attending a Bar Vocational Course is (*CIS/5035/1995*, to be reported as *R(IS) 5/1997*). See also *CIS/450/97* (starred decision *11/98*), where a student nurse on Project 2000 was held to be attending a course of study at a hospital because it was under the aegis of a university.

[131] See JSA Regs 1996, reg. 1(3)(a) and IS(G) Regs 1987, reg. 61.

[132] *Denton v Chief Adjudication Officer* [1999] E.L.R. 86.   [133] At 87–8.

[134] This reflects the view taken by the Commissioners in *R(SB) 40/83*, *R(SB) 41/83* and *CSB/176/1987*.

[135] In *CIS/152/1994* relevant circumstances were held to include the number of hours of study, the number of modules taken and how that number related to the overall completion period of the course, the fees payable and any information supplied or published by the college.

[136] This is consistent with the approach in *CIS/576/1994*, later appealed (on a different point) as *Webber*, op. cit. The college's view of the course was held to be material in *CIS/152/1994*, op. cit.

[137] HB(G) Regs 1987, regs 46 and 48A.   [138] Ibid., reg. 48A(1).   [139] Ibid., reg. 48A(2).

of student loans, covenanted income, disregards, and other matters for the purposes of calculating entitlement to JSA, income support, and housing benefit.[140]

Despite the technicality and complexity of the rules governing students' entitlement to benefit, the basic position for most students is fairly clear: there will be no entitlement to JSA, income support, or housing benefit if they (in the case of JSA) or their course is full-time until they leave the course, either by completing it or departing early from it (whether voluntarily or not). The student support and social security systems contemplate that a person will either: (i) start a full-time course and progress through it, collecting a degree after (normally) three years, having access to student support but not social security during this period; or (ii) enrol as a part-time student and be self-funded/supported or sponsored by an employer, and therefore not require public financial support, apart from limited access to social security. But the legislative scheme still leaves areas of uncertainty. For example, what is the position of a person who changes their mode of study part-way through their course? In what circumstances can a person who has had to interrupt their course and take time off from it be entitled to benefit? What is the position of a person who is unable to progress to the next year of their course due to examination failure and has to resit the failed examinations at the end of the next year (as an external or non-attending student)? These are questions that have confronted the Commissioners and courts in a number of key cases in recent years (see section B below).

B. Students: Problem Areas

As noted above, since 1990 the income support scheme has classed a person as a student if he or she is attending a full-time course of study, which must be 'advanced' if he or she is aged sixteen to eighteen; a student remains so throughout the period of study. The income support regulations were amended, however, and the revised definition incorporated also into the JSA regulations, following a decision of the Court of Appeal in *Chief Adjudication Officer v Clarke; Same v Faul (Clarke and Faul)* in 1995.[141] Despite subsequent changes to the legislation, the court's interpretation of various key aspects of the definition of student has had a continuing significance, particularly in respect of students forced to break from their expected pattern of studying due, for example, to examination failure or a need to intercalate as a result of personal circumstances.

Ms Clarke and Ms Faul were students at the University of East Anglia. Both had

---

[140] HB(G) Regs 1987, regs 53–60; IS(G) Regs 1987, regs 62–9; JSA Regs 1996, regs 131–9. Subject to disregards, new student loan is taken into account, during the 3/4 ths of the year it covers (eg 15(G) Regs 1987, reg. 66A, as amended). On the effect, see H. Swain, *Times Higher Educational Supplement*, 29 October 1999. It is the maximum possible loan that the student could receive if it were applied for that will be taken into account, whether or not that amount is claimed. On disregards for travel, books, and etc, see *CIS/497/1993* and *Alexander v Chief Adjudication Officer* [1998] E.L.R. 455.
[141] [1995] E.L.R. 259.

commenced three-year degree courses in 1989. Ms Clarke, who wanted to take some time off to consider whether to continue with the course, was granted permission by the university to intercalate the academic year 1991–2. Ms Faul had been ill during the first term of that year and was also granted permission to intercalate, in this case for the remaining two terms of the year. During these periods of intercalation neither student was entitled to a mandatory award or student loan. They each claimed income support but both were held by a Commissioner[142] to fall within the definition of student at the relevant time.

The definition at the time referred to persons:

attending a full-time course of study . . . and for the purposes of this definition—
(a) a person who has started on such a course shall be treated as attending it throughout any period of term or vacation within it, until the last day of the course or such earlier date as he abandons it or is dismissed from it.[143]

The crucial questions in determining whether the two appellants were students were, first, whether they could be said not to be 'attending' their course while intercalating, and, secondly, whether they should be treated as having 'abandoned' the course. The Commissioner had found the students not to be attending a course of study at the material time and regarded them as having abandoned their course during the intercalated periods. The Chief Adjudication Officer (CAO) argued that the Commissioner had been wrong because abandonment meant final abandonment, whereas in this case the students had had the option of returning to their course. The Court of Appeal unanimously supported the CAO's argument regarding abandonment. Hoffmann LJ said that: 'The context places the word in conjunction with two other events which are undoubtedly final, namely the end of the course and the student's dismissal from it. Furthermore, nothing short of total abandonment can make the definition work.'[144] Nevertheless, a majority of their Lordships (Hirst LJ dissenting on this point) considered that the references to attendance on a course 'throughout any period of term of vacation within it' meant that a person who was intercalating could not be in attendance.[145] As Glidewell LJ said: 'The fact that a reference is made to terms and vacations is an indication . . . that it is to those periods, and not to an intercalated year, that the extended definition applies . . .'.[146] The court therefore upheld the appeals on this point.

What was particularly interesting about the court's approach, and particularly that of Hoffmann LJ, to this issue was the way the court contextualised the position of students under the income support scheme. The court was mindful of the background to the bar on students' entitlement which accompanied the introduction of

---

[142] Commissioner's decisions *CIS/514/1992* and *CIS/413/1993*.
[143] IS(G) Regs 1987, reg. 61. Para. (a) is often referred to as the 'deeming provision' in this context.
[144] At 263.
[145] Hoffmann LJ was keen to point out (at 26–5) that that did not mean that a person could claim to be intercalating between the months of June and October each year in order to qualify for benefit!
[146] At 266.

student loans in 1990 (discussed above). Hoffmann LJ considered that in the light of Government assurances in 1989–90 that under the new student support arrangements students would not need social security, '[o]ne would ... expect that a student's exclusion from social security benefits would be mirrored by his entitlement to an education award and a student loan'.[147] If students did not have access to a grant or loan (as was the case here) 'there would be an anomalous class of people who for no obvious reason were left to destitution without State support of any kind'.[148]

This emotive argument apparently evoked little or no Government sympathy, for the regulations were swiftly amended in an undisguised attempt to negate the potential impact of *Clarke and Faul*. The words 'throughout any period of term or vacation within it' were removed from paragraph (a) of the definition (above).[149] The Court of Appeal had felt that if the CAO's view that an intercalating student was still attending his or her course was valid these words would have been superfluous. This offered a clear, if not particularly intended, signpost to the Government which it followed.

What was not altogether clear was the position of students whose studies were suspended or interrupted in some other way. In *Driver*[150] the claimant's industrial placement, forming part of a sandwich higher education course, had come to an end prematurely. The Court of Appeal had to determine whether she was then a student or alternatively was not, in which case she was entitled to income support during the remainder of the academic year. An additional provision fell to be considered—paragraph (b) of the regulation,[151] which stated that 'a person on a sandwich course shall be treated as attending a full-time course of advanced education or, as the case may be, of study . . .'. The decision was based on the same version of the regulations that had been considered in *Clarke and Faul*. Waller LJ, dissenting, felt that paragraph (b) (above) merely made it clear that a course with a placement element was still full time, provided paragraph (a) (above) also applied. He felt that irrespective of the fact that the placement period coincided with a period of term or vacation, if Miss Driver was not expected to attend for lectures at the university during the placement period then 'the term is a non-term so far as full-time education is concerned, and a vacation while she is on placement cannot be described as a vacation from such a term'.[152] The majority, however, distinguished (not wholly convincingly)[153] *Clarke and Faul*, holding that the work-experience period formed part of a university term (albeit that the university actually operated semesters) and that as a person was to be treated as attending his or her course throughout any term or vacation Miss Driver should be treated

---

[147] At 264.   [148] Ibid.
[149] Social Security Benefits (Miscellaneous Amendments) Regulations 1995 (S.I. 1995 No. 1742), reg. 2, in force 1 August 1995. The amendment reversed the effect of *Clarke and Faul: CIS/14477/1996* (Commissioner Rowland).
[150] *Driver v Chief Adjudication Officer and the Secretary of State for Social Security* [1997] E.L.R. 145.
[151] IS(G) Regs 1987, reg. 61, definition of 'student' with reference to attendance of a full-time course.
[152] At 154.   [153] See L. Lundy, 'Case Analysis' (1997) 4 *J.S.S.L.* 129–33.

as a student, irrespective of the apparent hiatus caused by the premature ending of the actual work experience.

Once again, therefore, the Court of Appeal had confirmed a gap in support for students. The court had not considered relevant to entitlement the issue of whether grants or loans might or might not have been available to the claimant. Although the assumption behind the exclusion of full-time students from benefit was, as noted earlier, that student support would normally be available, nothing turned on the fact that Miss Driver would have been eligible for a loan. However, Peter Gibson LJ was keen to express his sympathy with Miss Driver, who had unexpectedly lost paid employment on her placement and now had no grant or income support to fall back on. He opined that 'the social security system seems to me to be deficient in failing to meet the very real needs of a person in Miss Driver's position'.[154] The amendment of the regulations in 1995 in any event made it even more clear that someone in Miss Driver's situation would not be entitled to income support or, now, JSA. Nevertheless, as Lundy says, *Driver* was important in highlighting 'the hardship which can be caused by the blanket exclusion of students from social security'.[155]

The situation that resulted in Miss Driver having to claim social security arises fairly rarely. A much more common situation is where a student has embarked on a full-time degree course but has to take time out in order to resit examinations in the next examination period or to recover from illness. Often a student who is to resit examinations will not progress to the next year of his or her course and, unless repeating the year in attendance, will not be registered as a student with the university. In *Webber*,[156] however, the position was different. The claimant had been attending a course at Oxford Brookes University on a full-time basis. Despite failing some of his first-year modules, he was still able to progress to his second year (1993–4), but only as a part-time student (taking fewer modules). In fact, he did not take any modules in the final term of that year because none of his chosen modules was running then. In his final year (1994–5) he was a part-time student for the first term only, thereafter reverting to full-time. He claimed income support from October 1993. The university recognised three types of course: full-time; part-time; and 'mixed mode', where the students attended on a full-time or part-time basis at different stages of the course. The claimant had been denied benefit on the basis that he was deemed to be a full-time student at the material time. The court's decision was based on the pre-August 1995 version of the regulations.

Although the CAO's appeal was dismissed, the individual judgments diverged as regards the correct approach to resolving the question whether Mr Webber was covered by the deeming provision (regulation 61(a) (above)) and thus was a student at the material time. Hobhouse LJ found, as the Commissioner had done, that the course Mr Webber had embarked upon was a 'mixed mode' course which was of uncertain length and composition, enabling the transfer between full-time and part-time atten-

---

[154] At 150–1.   [155] N. 153 above, at 132.
[156] *Chief Adjudication Officer and the Secretary of State for Social Security v Webber* [1997] E.L.R. 404.

dance and vice versa.[157] He said that if the relevant course was not a full-time course then the student would 'not at any time be "attending a full-time course of study" and the problem posed by the deeming provision does not arise'.[158] Mr Webber therefore 'never was a "student" within definition in reg. 61'.[159] This fairly radical interpretation of the regulation has to be seen in the light of his Lordship's earlier percipient comment that the assumption underlying the definition of student—that a course is either full-time or part-time at the outset and remains so through to the last day of the course—did 'not accord with the practices of universities and other institutions of advanced education', which often included 'a large element of flexibility' as to the mode of study.[160] Peter Gibson LJ similarly wondered 'whether the draftsman of the regulations had properly in mind the wide variety of advanced education courses available to students today and the range of differing circumstances in which students who have embarked on such courses may subsequently find themselves'.[161] He felt that the 'period of term or vacation within it' (the course) referred to the full-time course: 'Plainly for the respondent's second year there was no period of term or vacation within any full-time course.'[162] Evans LJ considered, however, that Mr Webber's case did not turn on the deeming condition but on the overriding condition that someone was a full-time student: 'the deeming condition in reg 61(a) cannot be relied upon to create a status of full-time student which does not exist in fact'.[163] Echoing Hoffmann LJ's words in *Clarke and Faul*, his lordship was not prepared to support an interpretation of the regulations that would create 'for no apparent reason, "an anomalous class of people left in destitution without state support of any kind"'; he would 'require express words of the utmost clarity to persuade me that Parliament intended to produce that disgraceful result'.[164]

The Government's response to *Webber* was to propose further amendments to the regulations (with effect from April 1998). The amendments were also intended to clarify the situation concerning students in the relatively common situation, referred to above, of having to take time out in order to re-sit examinations. Before discussing the proposed amendments (which at the time of writing the Government appears to have put on hold) it is necessary to explain further the problems that had arisen in determining the status of these students under the regulations. In *CIS/13986/1996*[165] one such student had been attending the Nottingham Trent University on a full-time degree course but had failed his second-year examinations and had taken a year out in 1995–6 with a view to resitting his examinations in June 1996. He had managed to find temporary work during this year out but claimed income support for six days in October 1995. He was denied benefit on the grounds that he was deemed to be a student at the relevant time. But Commissioner Howell

---

[157] At 412. [158] At 413. [159] Ibid. See also *CIS/12823/1996* at para. 17. [160] At 407.
[161] At 413. [162] At 414. [163] At 416 [164] Ibid.
[165] Starred decision *24/97*. See also *CIS/595/1992*, where the claimant was expecting a child and took a year out from her studies; she had no guarantee of being re-admitted following her year away and it was held that she had abandoned or been dismissed from her course and that upon resuming her studies would be starting another course.

found in his favour, holding that the claimant had been 'dismissed' from his original course and had thus ceased to be a student.[166] The Commissioner explained that the 'actual programme of attendance and study' needed to be looked at because of its relevance to the 'temporal connotations' implicit in the references in regulation 61 to a period of study, the start of a course, and the last day of the course. The Commissioner held that there had been a break in the continuity of the claimant's original course and that this was final notwithstanding his option of returning to complete a degree if he succeeded in his examinations: 'In October 1995 when he claimed income support the claimant was no longer engaged on *that* course as a student, because his failure to get the required grades in his second year exams meant that he was no longer permitted to pursue it.'[167]

These arguments were rational but somewhat tenuous. They were not supported by Commissioner Mesher in *CIS/15594/1996*. In this case the claimant was enrolled at the University of Sheffield on a full-time degree course from 1993. He failed some of his second-year examinations in 1994–5 and after June 1995 he was away from the university. He was to retake his examinations as an external candidate in 1996. He claimed income support from December 1995. He was denied benefit but appealed successfully to the appeal tribunal. The Commissioner (who also dismissed an argument that the 1995 amendment regulations were *ultra vires*[168]) overturned the tribunal's decision. He specifically disagreed with Commissioner Howell's reasoning in *CIS/13986/1996*. In particular, he could not see why a person who resits should be regarded as being on a different course when readmitted to the university and why it mattered that he would complete his studies a year later than previously expected. He also rejected the view that there was a clear reason for distinguishing cases of intercalation (as per *Clarke and Faul*), where the claimants could always identify the last day of the course for which they were enrolled, and cases of examination failure, where the date depended on a decision yet to be taken by the university. In *Clarke and Faul*, the course had not been 'abandoned' by the intercalating students, because abandonment had to be final, and the Commissioner considered the position of the claimant who was resitting to be the same; he felt that to hold otherwise would undermine the distinction between final or total and non-final abandonment.[169]

Commissioner Mesher reiterated his view of *CIS/13986/1996* in *CIS/13276/1996* in June 1997, when he refused an appeal by a student who, after a car crash, had been given leave of absence from university from September 1995 until the following year and who was denied income support on the grounds that she was a student during this leave period.[170] The Commissioner's view was endorsed by Commissioner Rowland in a January 1998 decision (*CIS/14255/1996*), where the

---

[166] In an earlier decision (concerning an architecture student taking a year out on work placement) the Commissioner had held that a course was a 'unified sequence of study, tuition and/or practical training' which was 'intended to lead to one or more qualifications obtained on its completion': *CIS 179/1994*, now *R(IS)1/96*.

[167] Para. 14.   [168] See paras 6–15 of the decision.   [169] At para. 25.

[170] The appellant's challenge to the *vires* of the 1995 amendment regulations was also rejected.

facts were more or less identical to those in the first of the Mesher decisions (*CIS/15594/96* above). Mr Rowland went a little further, however, holding that the claimant was attending the course when he attended the university to resit his second-year examinations (at Aston University); it could not therefore be said that when he had failed the examinations first time he had been 'dismissed' from the course.[171] According to the Commissioner, it would, therefore, follow that, by virtue of the deeming provision (reg. 61(a) above), the claimant should be regarded as attending his course during the year out. The Commissioner distinguished the case from *Webber* (above) on the facts, on the basis that there had been no obligation on Mr Webber ever to resume full-time study in order to obtain his degree, whereas the present claimant's course 'was not modular and clearly had been full-time when he started it and would, if he passed the examinations, be full-time again'.[172] The Commissioner agreed with the approach adopted by Commissioner Mesher in *CIS/15594/1996* rather than Commissioner Howell's approach in *CIS/13986/1996*, which he found (along with the approach of Evans LJ in *Webber* (above)) to be inconsistent with *Clarke and Faul* (above).

The problematic post-August 1995 provisions reached the Court of Appeal again, in *O'Connor v Chief Adjudication Officer and the Secretary of State for Social Security*,[173] when the claimant appealed Commissioner Mesher's decision in *CIS/15594/1996* (above). Although there was unanimity in dismissing a challenge to the *vires* of the 1995 amendment regulations, the Court of Appeal was once again split on the question whether the claimant was a student during his year out of the university. The majority (Auld and Swinton Thomas LJJ, Thorpe LJ dissenting) considered that the purpose of the 1995 amendment had been, in the words of Auld LJ, to 'underline the deemed continuity of full-time student status even when interrupted, for whatever reason'.[174] The deeming provision sought to treat attendance on a course that was full-time at the start as 'continuing to be full-time even though there are breaks in it when the student does not follow the course full time'.[175] Auld LJ disapproved *CIS/13986/1996* and approved Commissioner Mesher's reasoning in the instant case and that of Hoffmann LJ in *Clarke and Faul*. He distinguished *Webber*: the course here was a standard three-year full-time course from the outset, not modular or flexible like Mr Webber's. His Lordship explained that the status of the student was to be determined by the nature of the course he started. If it was full-time at the start, the claimant fell to be treated as continuing to attend it until its last day or his or her earlier abandonment of or dismissal from it: 'Any other view would defeat the deeming provision, leaving the definition of full-time student to later events, notwithstanding the initial commitment of the student and the institution to its full-time nature.'[176] During his year off the claimant had not been dismissed from his course and had not abandoned it. However, if, at its start, the course could be followed full-time or part-time, according to the student's choice as it progressed, the position would be different. Thorpe LJ,

---

[171] At para. 7. [172] At para. 10. [173] [1999] E.L.R. 209. [174] At 217.
[175] At 218. [176] At 220.

dissenting, preferred the view of Evans LJ in *Webber*, who, it will be recalled, thought that regulation 61(a), as amended, did not apply to a person who had ceased to be a full-time student *in fact*, because he was no longer attending a course. He could find no rational basis for the distinction which resulted from the amended regulations between intercalating students and others who were not studying full-time and who were available for and actively seeking work, entitling them to income support.

The conflict between some of the Commissioners' decisions and the dissent in all of the key Court of Appeal decisions demonstrates the problematic nature of the definitions used to restrict students' entitlement. The weight of judicial authority now presents us with only a partially clear picture of the position of students who claim income support or income-based JSA and who spend some time away from the university in the situations discussed above or who change from full-time to part-time status. It is clear that, following the 1995 amendments, students who are on a full-time course and who are given leave from their course to intercalate will be regarded as still attending their course of study during the period of absence. It also seems clear that a person on a sandwich course will continue to be a student throughout the year of work experience, even if the work experience fails for whatever reason. But the position of students whose course has no one prescribed mode of study, as in *Webber*, is less clear because of the different approaches of the judges in that case. On one view, their 'course' is not full-time and so they could be eligible for benefit. Moreover, a Commissioner has recently argued that for JSA purposes a switch from full- to part-time study could put one on a part-time course (*CJSA/836/1999*).

This still leaves open the question of a person who switches from full-time attendance on a course offered by his university to part-time attendance leading to the same qualification. From the Government's point of view, there is a need to avoid the situation where, with courses becoming increasingly flexible and students' personal finances more and more tight, students do not switch to part-time study midway through a course in order to receive benefit. The effect of *Webber* (see also *CJSA/836/1999*) and *O'Connor* seems to be that full-time students who, at the start of their course, have the choice of switching to part-time study later when they wish, may qualify for benefit, whereas students embarking on what is clearly a full-time only course, but forced because of circumstances arising later to change their mode of attendance with the university's permission, remain barred from benefit throughout this period. What we see, therefore, is a benefits system that is making artificial distinctions and failing to relate entitlement to the actual needs of the claimant.

The Government's proposed solution to the difficulties involves amendment of the various definitions to reverse the effect of *Webber* and at the same time to make it clear that intercalating students and those retaking examinations as external students should be excluded from benefit.[177] The Government is unsympathetic to the problem confronting students who, for example, cannot progress to the next year of their course because they have failed examinations. In its view students themselves

---

[177] The draft Social Security Amendment (Students) Regulations 1998.

have brought about this situation and 'should take responsibility for their own actions'; the Government says it will 'not provide State support in these types of cases'.[178] It is proposed that a course of study will become one that the student is 'undertaking' rather than 'attending', which it is hoped will make it clear that one could still be on a full-time course of study without necessarily attending the institution on a full-time basis (although the Commissioners and courts have already acknowledged this to be the case, as noted above). An expanded definition of 'student' would therefore refer specifically to periods during which a person was to be undertaking a course of study, including days during periods of experience on a sandwich course (reflecting *Driver*, above) or when continuing the course as an external or part-time student with the university's permission.

The position of those undertaking postgraduate courses of study is also addressed specifically for the first time. This has been an area of uncertainty in the past, particularly in the case of those undertaking research-only degrees, although there is no legal reason why the restriction for attendance on a full-time course of study should not apply equally to them.[179] The proposed regulations would make it clear that, in relation to a postgraduate student, the last day of a person's course of study (after which they would cease to be a student) would be the date of the submission of the final piece of coursework required for the qualification concerned or the date of the final examination, whichever is later.

These proposed amendments were put on hold pending the reform of student support and perhaps also the Court of Appeal's ruling in *O'Connor* (above). Changes to support for students in further education (see below) may result in a further delay in their implementation, but it seems likely that they will re-surface in some form or other over the next couple of years, given the Government's continuing belief that most full-time higher education students should be excluded from the benefit system.

5. CURRENT FURTHER AND HIGHER EDUCATION POLICY

Before drawing some conclusions about the present and future role of social security in this field it is necessary to consider the broader context of current further and higher education policy, particularly as regards student access.

A. Further Education

In the case of further education (that is, basically sub-degree or sub-higher diploma academic or vocational education for those aged sixteen or over not provided at

---

[178] DSS, *Explanatory Memorandum to the Social Security Advisory Committee* (London: DSS, 1998), para. 5.

[179] See, for example, J. Mesher and P. Wood, *Income-related Benefits: The Legislation 1998* (London: Sweet and Maxwell, 1998), 257.

school),[180] the Government's policy is to raise participation, retention, and attainment in the education system. It has been particularly influenced by the report of the committee on widening participation in further education, chaired by Helena Kennedy QC, which highlighted the need to broaden access, particularly by encouraging more students from non-traditional backgrounds to enrol.[181] The Government has published a Green Paper on lifelong learning[182] and has supported an intiative entitled Investing in Young People (formerly 'Target 2000'). Both developments are aimed at encouraging more young people to take advantage of educational opportunities. Although the proportion of young people aged sixteen to eighteen in full-time education and training rose considerably in the decade from 1986–96 (from 57 per cent to 75 per cent of the age group), it has since levelled off. Participation rates are significantly lower among those from unskilled or semi-skilled family backgrounds (62 per cent) than among those from socio-economically more advantaged backgrounds, namely professional or managerial families (87 per cent).[183] Significant numbers of people also study part-time in further education, including (in 1997–8) 1.1 million people aged twenty-five or over.[184]

It is clear that the Government's goal of broadening access is to some extent dependent on the development of adequate systems of support for young people engaged in education. In early 1998 the Government announced in the welfare reform Green Paper that it was 'reviewing the current arrangements for financial support for students in further education, including adults, with a view to establishing a coherent system which is simpler, more equitable and better targeted on those most in need'.[185] For most young people entering full-time further education post-sixteen, the only independent support available has been a discretionary award from their LEA. Yet, as noted above, LEAs have been cutting back on these awards (due to be phased out from September 1999: see below). In 1994–5 discretionary awards in England and Wales were paid to 179,700 out of a total of three million further education students, but the total fell to 146,800 in 1995–6 (an 18 per cent drop in one year) and then to 135,500 in 1996–7.[186] Total LEA spending on discretionary awards to students in further education also fell dramatically from £244 million in 1992–3 to £108 million in 1996–7 and £89 million in 1997–8; and the average amount of

---

[180] See also the definition in the Education Act 1996, s. 2.
[181] H. Kennedy (QC) (Chair), *Learning Works: Widening Participation in Further Education* (London: FEFC, June 1997).
[182] DfEE, *The Learning Age: A new renaissance for a new Britain*, Cm 3790 (London: The Stationery Office, 1998).
[183] DfEE Press Notice 159/97 and Youth Cohort Study, England and Wales, cited in Further Education Student Support Advisory Group, *New Arrangements for Effective Student Support in Further Education* (London, DfEE, 1998), para. 1.11.
[184] Further Education Student Support Advisory Group, op. cit., para. 1.12.
[185] Green Paper (1998), ch. 5, para. 16.
[186] DfEE, *Statistics of Education: Student Support England and Wales 1996/97* (London: The Stationery Office, 1998), 18, Table 2a. There has been a similar decline in the number of pupils or students receiving educational maintenance allowances, from 39,800 in 1992–3 to 30,400 in 1996–7: ibid.

individual awards fell from £1,235 to £740 per student over this period.[187] By 1998, some LEAs had more or less stopped paying discretionary awards altogether.[188] In general, access to discretionary awards has, as with the award of access funds in higher education (above at pp. 333–4), been a lottery.[189]

Further evidence of the need for reform came from a report of the Further Education Student Support Advisory Group in 1998, which noted clear evidence that a lack of effective financial support can be a barrier to participation in education beyond the age of 16.[190] It also referred to a study in the United States which found that a lack of financial support was a significant factor in drop-out rates among further education students. The Advisory Group was particularly impressed by the AUSTUDY scheme introduced by the Australian Government in 1987. This provides a means-tested allowance to parents of young people aged sixteen or over remaining in full-time education,[191] which has led to an improvement in staying-on rates.[192] From 1 July 1998 AUSTUDY was replaced by a Common Youth Allowance, which is a generic form of means-tested income support payment available to those undertaking education or training and, in appropriate cases, to those who are sick or unemployed. The Advisory Group recommended that there should be a new student support system for those aged sixteen or over.[193] The House of Commons Education Select Committee also proposed a new support system for further education students, recommending that awards should take the form of grants for those aged under nineteen.[194]

The Government's response has been to reform the current system of LEA discretionary awards. A new legislative framework has been put in place. From September 1999 section 44 of the Teaching and Higher Education Act 1998 has (subject to transitional arrangements) replaced the power of LEAs to make discretionary awards.[195] LEAs will continue to have a power to provide scholarships, bursaries, and other allowances to persons over compulsory school age—a power which they are also authorised by new regulations *not* to exercise in any particular year.[196]

---

[187] Policy Studies Institute Press Release, 12 January 1998 and DfEE, *DfEE Departmental Report* Cm 3910 (London: The Stationery Office, 1998), Annex Bii.

[188] Hansard, H.C. Debs (web version), col. 429, 29 April 1998.

[189] See A. Herbert and C. Callender, *The Funding Lottery: Student support in further education* (London: Policy Studies Institute, 1997), commissioned by the FEFC.

[190] Further Education Student Support Advisory Group, above n. 183, para. 1.12.

[191] In 70 per cent of cases the payment is actually passed on to the young person.

[192] See Institute for Fiscal Studies, *Income Support and Staying in School: What can we learn from Australia's AUSTUDY Experiment?* (London: I.F.S 1995).

[193] Over the years others have also called for a comprehensive youth allowance: e.g. P. Cooper (1985) op. cit. and N. Pearce and J. Hillman, *Wasted Youth* (London: I.P. P. R., 1998), ch. 7.

[194] House of Commons Select Committee on Education and Employment, *Sixth Report, 1997–98, Further Education* (London: The Stationery Office, 1998), para. 89.

[195] Under ss 1(6) and 2 of the Education Act 1962. The transitional arrangements enable those receiving discretionary awards to continue to receive them until the end of their course: The Teaching and Higher Education Act 1998 (Commencement No. 2 and Transitional Provisions) Order 1998 (S.I. 1998 No. 2004).

[196] Education Act 1996, s. 518, as substituted by the School Standards and Framework Act 1998, s. 129; and the Local Education Authority (Post-Compulsory Education Awards) Regulations 1999 (S.I. 1999 No. 229), in force 1 March 1999. The Scholarships and Other Benefits Regulations 1977 (S.I. 1977 No. 1443) governing this power are revoked.

The regulations describe these awards as 'post-compulsory education awards' and enable individual LEAs to determine eligibility criteria for them, as under the old system. LEAs may therefore, for example, continue to award educational maintenance allowances (EMAs) for young people (aged sixteen to eighteen) who stay on in full-time education at school or college. Moreover, from September 1999 a new scheme of EMAs is being piloted in fifteen areas (selected because they have low post-sixteen participation rates). The award will amount to a maximum of £30 or £40 per week, depending on the area. It will be subject to a means-test,[197] but child benefit and other passported family benefits will be disregarded. These pilot schemes, which to some extent mirror the AUSTUDY scheme discussed above, will cost a total of £100 million and will run for three years. In view of the cost, it seems likely that if, in the future, the new EMA scheme were to be introduced on a national basis ministers might well perceive a case for the withdrawal of child benefit in the case of young people aged sixteen or over remaining in education, as proposed in 1998 by the House of Commons Education Select Committee when recommending new student grants.[198]

There will also be a new system of further education access funds. It seems that these will operate, for an initial period of three years, in rather the same way as the access funds in higher education have done in the past. The access funds will be administered by colleges, which will receive an allocation from the FEFC. At the time of writing, the criteria for determining the amount allocated to colleges have not yet been announced. For the first time, part-time students will also be eligible to apply for these funds. Although the Select Committee argued strongly that any new award introduced should be available as of right,[199] the new further education access funds will be discretionary. This is unfortunate, because in the past discretionary access funds have been unevenly distributed.[200] As noted above, the Government promised a more equitable system. Nevertheless, although making these funds available to part-time students, who were not eligible for discretionary awards, will help to achieve that, unevenness of provision may hinder significant progress.

So far as social security entitlement is concerned, it is still unclear whether in the longer term part-time students in further education, particularly those without dependent children, will continue to have access to income support or, more especially, JSA (there were some 281,000 JSA recipients studying part-time in further education in 1998[201]) where the relevant conditions are met. The Government has, for example,

[197] The parents' relevant income must not exceed £30,000 (or, in Greater London, £20,000): the Education Maintenance Allowance (Pilot Areas) Regulations 19999 (S.I. 1999 No. 2168).

[198] House of Commons Select Committee on Education and Employment, *Sixth Report, 1997–98, Further Education* (London: The Stationery Office, 1998), para. 89.

[199] Ibid. The Committee also favours means-tested maintenance loans for further education students who are studying work-related courses: ibid.

[200] See A. Herbert and C. Callender, *The Funding Lottery: Student support in further education* (London: Policy Studies Institute, 1997).

[201] Further Education Student Support Advisory Group, *New Arrangements for Effective Student Support in Further Education* (London: DfEE, 1998), Annex C.

raised concerns that the benefit concession for part-time students may not result in claimants following courses that 'maximize their prospect of improving their long term employability', and about problems faced by Employment Service staff in seeking to resolve 'the inevitable tensions in the current arrangements between an individual's wish to complete their course of study and the requirement to be available for work.'[202] One reform being considered is to require part-time students receiving JSA to enter into a 'personal action plan' agreed with their Employment Service personal adviser under the ONE programme (formerly the single 'gateway to work'). The plan would set out how the skills acquired through the course would improve the individual's employment prospects.[203]

Either way, claimants studying part-time are likely to find entitlement affected by the New Deal. Under the New Deal for Young People (aged eighteen to twenty-four—there is also a scheme for persons aged twenty-five plus) claimants who have been in receipt of JSA for six months or longer will be directed by the Employment Service into the New Deal programme (there are potential benefit sanctions for non-participation[204]). During a 'gateway' period of up to four months the claimant will, in effect, become a whole-time jobseeker and thereafter will have various options, including a period of subsidised employment or full-time education or training for twelve months. Those in receipt of JSA while studying part-time would, if they had been on benefit for at least six months by then, therefore face a loss of benefit if they did not abandon their studies and enter the New Deal.[205] It is true that some of those entering the New Deal could have an opportunity for full-time study while receiving benefit. Indeed, the New Deal can also pay certain expenses such as the cost of college fees, travel expenses, and the cost of materials. The education and training option seems to have proved attractive to ethnic minorities: they are considerably over-represented among those on this option, although this is possibly no more than a reflection of the adverse discrimination they often face in relation to employment, or the need to remedy educational disadvantage experienced at school.[206] But despite this option, the New Deal aims to find work for young people; thus once they enter the programme some would in effect be forced for financial reasons to take up employment when what they really want to do is study.

B. Higher Education

Like its policy on further education, the Government's higher education policy is also aimed at improving and widening access: 'We want wider participation in higher

---

[202] DfEE, *Learning to Succeed: A new framework for post-16 learning*, Cm 4392 (London: The Stationery Office, 1999), para. 7.45
[203] Ibid., para. 7.46.   [204] See further Chapter 10.
[205] See generally JSA Regs 1996, regs 69–75; JS Act 1995, s.19; and Chapter 10 above.
[206] Official New Deal figures show that at the end of January 1999 25 per cent of those within the New Deal for 18–24s were from ethnic minorities whereas the proportion was as high as 66 per cent among those taking the education and training option.

education, especially by those from semi-skilled and unskilled family backgrounds, or from disadvantaged areas, as well as people with disabilities, all currently under-represented in higher education.'[207] The Government has calculated that while full-time student numbers in higher education increased by 70 per cent between 1989 and 1995, 'the increase in participation in the 1990s amongst socio-economic groups A to C has been double that among groups D and E'.[208] The Government acknowledges that financial considerations can be a barrier to student participation in higher education; but it believes that most students should share some of the costs of their education in view of the long-term rewards they will derive from it. The new funding arrangements, including liability for tuition fees, under the Teaching and Higher Education Act 1998,[209] are based around the principle that 'on average, graduates earn more and have more secure jobs than non graduates . . . they should therefore share the cost'.[210] These are remarkably redolent of the Conservative statements in the 1980s seeking to justify student loans and reduced social security support, that 'most students are on their way to relatively prosperous careers'[211] and should not 'learn to depend upon a wrong understanding of the reciprocal obligations of the citizen and the state'.[212]

The new arrangements are being phased in.[213] Prior to 1991 students were eligible for an annually uprated mandatory grant; but since then the grant has not been increased and its value has therefore been continually eroded by inflation. The remainder of the support has taken the form of a student loan. In 1998 the maximum maintenance grant outside London stood at £1,755 and the maximum loan at £1,685. From the academic year 1999–2000 there will be no maintenance grants, only income-related loans (which will only be available to those aged under fifty-five).[214] Just as significantly, students' families are liable to meet up to £1,025 per annum in tuition fees at universities.[215] The extent of liability will be based on a means-test. The Government estimates that one-third of students' families

---

[207] Green Paper (1998), ch. 5, para. 11.

[208] DfEE, *Higher Education in the 21st Century* (London: DfEE, 1997), ch. 1, 1–2.

[209] Section 22–28 and the Education (Student Support) Regulations 1998 (S.I. 1998 No. 2003) and 1999 (S.I. 1999 No. 496).

[210] Green Paper (1998), para. 12. On average, graduates earn 20 per cent more than those without a degree within 10 years of graduation: DfEE, *Investing in the Future* (London: DfEE, 1997), 5.

[211] Hansard, H.C. Debs, col. 1002, 12 March 1986, *per* Sir Keith Joseph MP.

[212] Department of Education and Science, *Top-Up Loans for Students*, Cm 520 (London: HMSO, 1988), para. 2.12.

[213] Students with a firm offer of a place by 1 August 1997, or a provisional offer subsequently confirmed, can receive financial support under the old scheme until the end of their course, provided they took up the course in 1998–9. See S.I. 1998 No. 2003 op cit. and, from 1 September 1999, S.I. 1999 No. 496, op cit.

[214] S.I. 1999 No. 496, op. cit., reg. 17. Loans are paid for 3/4 ths of the year: ibid., reg. 24. Persons aged 50–4 (inclusive) will only qualify for a loan if they intend to enter employment or another higher education course after completing their present course.

[215] The imposition of fees by the universities is a condition of the grant made to the funding councils by the Secretary of State under s. 26(4) of the Teaching and Higher Education Act 1998. Those liable to pay fees are prescribed by the Education (Fees at Higher Education Institutions) Regulations 1999 (S.I. 1999 No. 603).

will not have to contribute towards the tuition fees, while another third will pay less than £1,025 and the final third (on a gross income of over £35,000 approximately) will be liable for the full £1,025. A non-means-tested grant of up to £10,250, at 1999–2000 rates, will be available for certain disabled students who need extra support because of their special needs.[216]

Like the old student support system the new system makes hardship provision, in the form of a 'hardship loan', but only students who have applied for a maximum student loan will be eligible. Only one hardship loan may be applied for and the maximum is £250.[217] Part-time students will not be eligible. Yet there are significant numbers of part-time students. In 1996–7 as a whole a total of nearly 2 million students attended part-time courses, and at any one time there were around 750,000 part-time students.[218] Although there was recognition of the importance of part-time study in its report, the Dearing Committee was wary of the cost of extending loans to part-time students and worried that any such support would undermine employers' contributions to part-time study. Yet there is evidence that no more than half of part-time students have their fees paid by employers.[219] Social security provision may continue to be important therefore in facilitating part-time study. Indeed, the Government somewhat belatedly acknowledged this when announcing (in September 1998) that from 1999–2000 no tuition fees would be charged for part-time students in receipt of social security benefits.[220] This was in line with a recommendation of the Dearing Committee, although the Committee wanted this reform to be introduced a year earlier.[221] The Committee also urged the Government to consider 'the interaction between entitlement to benefits and part-time study, with a view to ensuring that there are no financial disincentives to part-time study by the unemployed or those on low incomes'.[222] As yet, there is no indication that such a specific review of the eligibility of part-time students' entitlement has occurred or, if it has, of the outcome. Thus the current state of uncertainty concerning the future benefit entitlement of part-time students in higher education to some extent mirrors that relating to students in further education, noted above.

6. CONCLUSION

There are various ways of viewing the attempt to exclude those undertaking education courses from social security entitlement. At a time of increasing policy

---

[216] S.I. 1999 No. 496, op. cit., reg. 13. [217] Ibid., reg. 20. The minimum loan is £100.

[218] Hansard, H.C., Standing Committee F, Teaching and Higher Education Bill, 21 April 1998 (10.30 am) (no col. no.).

[219] Ibid.

[220] DfEE Press Release 431/98, 17 September 1998. Part-time students who lose their employment during the duration of their course will also be exempt from tuition fees.

[221] National Committee of Inquiry into Higher Education, *Report of the National Committee* (London: DfEE, 1997), paras 20.6–20.11.

[222] Ibid., Recommendation 76.

emphasis on work and reduced welfare dependency, the Government regards it as increasingly justifiable to reinforce the distinction traditionally made between, on the one hand, those who have entered, and have a primary attachment to, the employment market and, on the other, those who are making the normative transition from school to college or university and are still therefore primarily focused on education. Yet reflecting this distinction in social security law has proved problematic. As we have seen in the case of part-time students, the law attempts to make concessionary provision recognising the value of undertaking study as a means to improving one's long- or even short-term employment prospects. However, the position of part-time students receiving JSA, who may be directed into the New Deal on pain of withdrawal of benefit for non-cooperation, and who could in the future face the prospect of having their choice of course limited by the Employment Service (under a 'personal action plan'), demonstrates that any conflict been employment or education is resolved in favour of the former. Moreover, one of the consequences of the distinction to be drawn is a highly complex set of provisions which, in the case of those in further education in particular, have had a distorting effect on educational provision as colleges attempt to mould courses around limiting, and frequently amended, benefit rules.

Many have regarded the removal of benefit entitlement from full-time students as questionable when the student support system is, so the evidence seems to suggest, flawed. Student support is, however, an issue which the present Government is taking seriously and the new policy initiatives in this area, outlined above, do seem to be addressing the situation of the groups for whom social security would, in the past, have been so vital. Nevertheless, while there is a case for arguing, as the Government has done, that students should accept greater responsibility for their own financial situation (clearly part of the broader policy emphasis on moral responsibility discussed in Chapter 1), the more or less blanket exclusion of full-time students from social security would still seem to be premature, when it is still not clear that the new student support systems in further and higher education can respond adequately (and, in particular, with sufficient flexibility) to the problem of student hardship. Moreover, the displacement of rights to social security by access to discretionary payments represents a downgrading of status that some might see as an attack on the social citizenship of students. On a more pragmatic level, the SSAC has argued that the removal of social security entitlement was unnecessary, as any loans or grants derived from the student support system could simply be included in the assessment of income for benefit purposes in the usual way.[223] However, it was unlikely that any Government would have accepted this argument given the administrative costs that would be involved and the overriding objection in principle to social security support for those in education.

For full-time students, therefore, the present exclusion of most from benefit is

---

[223] SSAC, *Report of the SSAC on the Social Security Benefits (Student Loan) Amendment Regulations 1990*, Cm 1141 (London: HMSO, 1990).

unlikely to be reversed, although the present Government or a future one may well see a need to amend the legislation to clarify the restrictions. For part-time students the current role of social security remains important, but in the longer term the position is somewhat uncertain in the light of the developing employment and further education student support policies of the present Government.

12

Social Security and Disability

NICK WIKELEY

1. INTRODUCTION

Sickness and disability benefits constitute the second largest component of the social security budget, exceeded only by spending on pensions.[1] Thus more is spent on sick and disabled people[2] than on any other group of people of working age, including unemployed people and families.[3] Yet the system of benefits for sick and disabled people was described over twenty years ago as 'a ragbag of provisions based on differing, sometimes conflicting and anachronistic principles'.[4] This description remains equally valid today; as will be seen in this chapter, successive governments have resorted to a series of *ad hoc* changes to the benefits structure for disabled people.[5] In the 1990s alone there have been three major reforms of disability benefits: the introduction of disability living allowance and disability working allowance in 1992, the replacement of sickness and invalidity benefits by incapacity benefit in 1995 and the latest reforms signalled by the 1998 Green Paper, *A New Contract for Welfare: Support for disabled people,*[6] and in part enshrined in the Welfare Reform and Pensions Act 1999. Indeed, the current arrangements hardly merit being described as a system at all,[7] given the absence of internal 'fit' as between the various benefits available.

---

[1] K. Rowlingson and R. Berthoud, *Disability, Benefits and Employment*, DSS Research Report No. 54 (London: HMSO, 1996), 17.

[2] It has been estimated that there are about 8.6 million disabled adults living in private households: DSS, *First Findings from the Disability Follow-up to the Family Resources Survey*, Research Summary No. 5 (London: DSS, 1998), 5. This is a markedly higher figure than the 1985 OPCS Disability Survey estimate of 5.8 million; see ibid., 8–10, for a discussion as to the reasons for this disparity.

[3] DSS, *Social Security Departmental Report: The Government's Expenditure Plans 1999/2000*, Cm 4214 (London: The Stationery Office, 1999), 83. The disparity is especially acute when insurance-based benefits alone are considered: in 1997–8 expenditure on incapacity benefit amounted to £7,412 million, whilst just £474 million was paid out in contribution-based JSA: National Audit Office, *National Insurance Fund Account 1997–8*, H.C. 130, Session 1998–9 (London: The Stationery Office, 1999), 9.

[4] J. Simkins and V. Tickner, *Whose Benefit?* (London: Economist Intelligence Unit, 1978), 17. The origins of this incoherence can be traced back to the early years of the modern welfare state: see H. Bolderson, 'Compensation for Disability' (1974) 3 *J of Social Policy* 193–211 and *Social Security, Disability and Rehabilitation: Conflicts in the Development of Social Policy 1914–1946* (London: Jessica Kingsley, 1991).

[5] For a diagrammatic representation of the resulting complex interrelationship between different disability benefits, see SSAC, *Social Security Provision for Disability: A Case for Change?* (London: The Stationery Office, 1997), 33. See further P. Larkin, 'Social security provision for disability: a case for change?' (1998) 5 *J.S.S.L.* 10–17.

[6] Cm 4103 (London: The Stationery Office, 1998).

[7] A term which gives 'a false impression of coherence': Rowlingson and Berthoud (1996), n. 1 above, 19.

Disability benefits in the widest sense have three main objectives.[8] The first goal is as a means of earnings replacement in the traditional Beveridge model. This category covers statutory sick pay, incapacity benefit, and income support for disabled people. Secondly, attendance allowance and disability living allowance have been developed since the 1970s to meet the extra costs associated with living with a disability. Thirdly, the industrial injuries and war pensions schemes provide a degree of compensation by way of extra income for injuries and diseases sustained either at work or in the armed forces. The benefits in this last category are distinguished by the fact that access is determined uniquely by the origin of the incapacity or disability; moreover, they now account for a relatively small proportion of spending on disability benefits and so are not considered further in this chapter.[9]

In this chapter we start by exploring the concepts of disability and incapacity within the benefits system. The scope of benefits for sick and disabled people is then considered using a threefold typology of traditional earnings replacement benefits, extra costs benefits, and means-tested benefits respectively. This is followed by a discussion of the particular problems associated with mental health, incapacity, and disability before returning to some of the wider policy issues underpinning the debate on welfare reform. The principal focus is necessarily on the substantive eligibility rules for the various benefits concerned and their impact in practice. This should not obscure the fact that disabled people may also be able to access community care services, either in the form of direct cash payments or assistance in kind from local authority social services departments, or in the form of discretionary payments from the Independent Living Funds, established to assist the most severely disabled members of society.[10] These benefits, however, are available within a very different legal framework.[11] It is also important to bear in mind throughout this discussion that sick and disabled people may face particular difficulties in securing access to the benefits system, over and beyond the difficulties which claimants ordinarily encounter in their dealings with the Benefits Agency.[12]

[8] R. Berthoud, *Disability Benefits: A review of the issues and options for reform* (York: Joseph Rowntree Foundation, 1998), 2.

[9] In 1978–9 these benefits constituted the second largest category in terms of public expenditure on disability benefits (totalling about twice that devoted to extra costs benefits). Real expenditure on this category has remained virtually constant over the 20 years since; by 1996–7 expenditure on extra costs benefits was more than five times that on these special schemes (ibid., 11–12). See further Chapter 15 on the industrial scheme and Ogus, Barendt, and Wikeley (1995), chs 7 and 8.

[10] The interaction between the benefits system and community care is explored in A. Kestenbaum and H. Cava, *Work, Rest and Pay: The deal for personal assistance users* (York: Joseph Rowntree Foundation, 1998).

[11] See e.g. M. Mandelstam, *Community Care Practice and the Law* 2nd edn.(London: Jessica Kingsley, 1999) and *Equipment for Older or Disabled People and the Law,* (London: Jessica Kingsley, 1997).

[12] See A. Hedges and A. Thomas, *Making a Claim for Disability Benefits*, DSS Research Report No. 27 (London: HMSO, 1994).

2. DISABILITY AND INCAPACITY

An understanding of the concepts of disability and incapacity is crucial in developing a critique of the diverse range of social security benefits designed to deal with the problems of those who are disabled and incapable of work. According to Keeler:

There is no consistent use of the terminology of 'disability' and 'incapacity', but the most usual interpretations define disability as a loss or reduction of functional ability that results from an anatomic or functional abnormality or loss, and incapacity as the loss of capacity to earn money from work that arises from the disability.[13]

The concept of disability as 'a loss or reduction of functional ability' is located squarely within the medical model of disability, and is reflected in the standard World Health Organisation classification.[14] This approach views disabled people as suffering from an inherent disadvantage *caused* by their bodily impairment. This remains the dominant paradigm in legal discourse.[15] A radically different interpretation, the social model of disability, has been advanced by disability theorists. This regards disabled people as being disadvantaged by society's failure to accommodate them. As one of the leading exponents of this school of thought has argued, 'the disabled individual is an ideological construction related more to the core ideology of individualism and the peripheral ideologies related to medicalisation and normality'.[16] Adherents to this philosophy have accordingly questioned both the conceptual basis and the research methodology of the Office of Population and Census Survey studies which informed the introduction of disability living allowance in 1992.[17]

How are these concepts translated into social security law? One can search in vain in the legislation for an all-purpose definition of disability. The eligibility criteria for disability living allowance depend not on the severity of disability as such, but use a claimant's care and mobility needs as proxies for disability. As we shall see, the inevitable consequence is that there is no direct correlation between the degree of disability and entitlement to a particular rate of benefit. There is, quite separately, a methodology for assessing disablement on a sliding scale of up to 100 per cent which

---

[13] J. F. Keeler, 'Social Insurance, Disability and Personal Injury' (1994) 44 *Univ. Toronto L.J.* 275–352, 280. Thus, as Keeler notes, a blind person undoubtedly experiences a disability under this definition, but that by no means results in incapacity for work.

[14] See P. Wood, *International Classification of Impairments, Disabilities and Handicaps* (Geneva, World Health Organisation, 1980) cited in DSS, *The Way Ahead: Benefits for Disabled People*, Cm 917 (London: HMSO, 1990), 14.

[15] See, for example, the Disability Discrimination Act 1995, discussed in B. Doyle, 'Disabled Workers' Rights, the Disability Discrimination Act and the UN Standard Rules' (1996) 25 *I.L.J.* 1–14 and, more generally, J. Cooper and S. Vernon, *Disability and the Law* (London: Jessica Kingsley, 1996).

[16] M. Oliver, *The Politics of Disablement* (Basingstoke: Macmillan, 1990), 58. See further M. Sullivan, 'From personal tragedy to social oppression: the medical model and social theories of disability' (1991) 16 *N. Z. J. of Industrial Relations*, 255–72; M. Oliver, *Understanding Disability* (Basingstoke: Macmillan, 1996); and C. Barnes and G. Mercer (eds.), *Exploring the Divide: Illness and Disability* (Leeds: Disability Press, 1996).

[17] P. Abberley, 'Counting Us Out: a discussion of the OPCS disability surveys' (1992) 7 *Disability, Handicap and Society*, 139–55.

applies in the context of the industrial injuries scheme.[18] These processes of assessment are firmly rooted in the medical model of disability.[19]

The concept of incapacity is no less problematic. As Neville Harris notes in Chapter 4, the Beveridge scheme identified a series of causes of earning loss as the basis for the award of national insurance benefits: for example, unemployment, incapacity, and retirement. For many years the concept of incapacity for work remained ill-defined, turning in the individual case on whether it was reasonable to expect a person of the claimant's age, education, and health to be in employment.[20] The replacement of sickness and invalidity benefits by incapacity benefit in 1995 was accompanied by a fundamental change in the test for determining incapacity. For the first twenty-eight weeks of sickness, the claimant's capacity for work is assessed by their ability to do their usual work.[21] Thereafter—or from the outset for someone without a normal occupation—claimants are judged by reference to their score on the 'all work' test, which seeks to measure their ability to perform certain specified physical or mental functions.[22] This test also applies to other benefits where incapacity for work is in issue.[23]

The all work test was ostensibly introduced to provide a more objective foundation for determining incapacity.[24] However, the shift in both terminology and assessment methodology should not be allowed to disguise the common thread between the former test of 'reasonableness' for invalidity benefit, widely perceived to be more claimant-friendly, and the narrower all work test for incapacity benefit. The fundamental issue in the wider context of welfare policy has been identified by Handler:

Thus, the heart of poverty policy centers on the question of who is excused from work. Those who are excused are the 'deserving poor'; those who must work are the 'undeserving'. Ultimately, this is a moral distinction. It involves deciding the nature and significance of the work ethic, the causes and extent of disability, the impact, both real and perceived, of incen-

---

[18] SSCBA 1992, s. 103 and Sched. 6. This also applied to severe disablement allowance, which will be abolished for new claimants under the Welfare Reform and Pensions Act 1999; see below in section 3.B (pp. 368ff). Analogous provisions apply to war pensions: Ogus, Barendt, and Wikeley (1995), 362.

[19] The assessment is 'as compared with a person of the same age and sex whose physical and mental condition is normal': SSCBA 1992, Sched. 6, para. 1(a).

[20] SSCBA 1992, s. 57(1)(a), repealed by the Social Security (Incapacity for Work) Act 1994, s. 11(2) and Sched. 2. The original test in the 1992 Act reflected the traditional position of the DHSS, as set out by the National Insurance Advisory Committee in 1977: 'The Department have explained that from their long experience of the existing incapacity benefits . . . it has been found that leaving to the statutory authorities the interpretation of "incapacity" works well, enabling consistency to be achieved through the development of case law, while also providing a degree of flexibility to enable justice to be done in varying circumstances' (NIAC, *Social Security (Non-Contributory Invalidity Pension) Amendment Regulations 1977*, Cmnd. 6900 (London: HMSO, 1977), para. 10).

[21] The so-called 'own occupation' test: SSCBA 1992, s. 171B.

[22] Under the Welfare Reform and Pensions Act 1999 this is renamed the personal capability assessment; see further below in section 3.B.

[23] SSCBA 1992, s. 171A(1); but this does not apply to either SSP or the industrial injuries scheme: ibid., s. 171G.

[24] See N. Wikeley, 'The Social Security (Incapacity for Work) Act 1994' (1995) 58 *M.L.R.* 523–33.

tives and disincentives on human behavior, and the consequences to the individual, the family and the community of failing to abide by conventional norms.[25]

As Handler also notes, 'from at least the time of Henry VIII the overarching tension has been to balance the need to maintain labor discipline with the need to relieve misery'.[26] This ambivalence is inadvertently but unerringly echoed in the Labour Government's declaration of its key philosophy for welfare reform, namely 'work for those who can and security for those who cannot'.[27]

With this ideological debate in mind, we now turn to examine the range of benefits available for disabled people, categorising these according to whether they are designed as: first, earnings replacement benefits (statutory sick pay, incapacity benefit, and invalid care allowance); secondly, benefits to assist with extra costs (disability living allowance and attendance allowance); or, thirdly, means-tested benefits which make specific provision for disabled people (principally income support and disability working allowance, the latter now replaced by disabled person's tax credit).

3. EARNINGS REPLACEMENT BENEFITS

A. Statutory Sick Pay

The great majority of employees who fall sick and become incapable of work qualify for statutory sick pay (SSP) in the first instance. SSP is not paid for the first three days of sickness, but thereafter is paid at a flat rate, with no additions for dependants, for twenty-eight weeks.[28] Many larger employers will provide more generous cover through occupational sick pay schemes (both in terms of a proportion of normal pay, rather than as a flat rate, and for a longer period), but SSP remains a crucial legal minimum, especially in smaller companies.[29] Entitlement to SSP does not depend on the claimant having a contributions record and there is no means-test. Some employees are excluded from the ambit of SSP, for example because they are engaged on short-term contracts or have low earnings,[30] and so will be reliant on income support or, if they have an adequate contributions record, the lower rate of short-term incapacity benefit.[31]

---

[25] J. F. Handler, '"Constructing the Political Spectacle": The Interpretation of Entitlements, Legalization, and Obligations in Social Welfare History' (1990) 56 *Brooklyn L.R.* 897–974, 906.

[26] Ibid., 906.

[27] DSS, *A New Contract for Welfare: Principles into practice*, Cm 4101 (London: The Stationery Office, 1998), Prime Minister's foreword, 1.

[28] For 1999/2000 SSP was paid at £59.55 a week.

[29] In one study only 43 per cent of establishments employing fewer than 11 employees had formal occupational sick pay arrangements: S. Middleton et al., *Statutory Sick Pay: The response of employers to the 1991 changes*, DSS Research Report No. 24 (London: HMSO, 1994), 3.

[30] See further Ogus, Barendt, and Wikeley (1995), 160–4.

[31] This may, of course, be topped up by income support, as can SSP itself.

When SSP was first introduced in 1983,[32] employers became responsible for administering the benefit (essentially the former DHSS short-term sickness benefit under another name[33]) and were then reimbursed by central government. The scope and nature of SSP has since been radically transformed; by a series of incremental reforms, the duration of SSP was extended from eight to twenty-eight weeks in 1986 and the provision for reimbursement initially reduced to 80 per cent[34] and then abolished by 1994.[35] The benefit has therefore effectively now been privatised in terms of both its delivery and funding. This has, in theory at least, increased the incentives for employers to police their own employees in respect of claims for short-term sickness. As one study has noted, 'Direct scrutiny by an employer or line manager has thus replaced the scrutiny of medical certificates by remote and anonymous DSS officials.'[36]

B. Incapacity Benefit

Incapacity benefit was introduced in April 1995, replacing the former short-term sickness benefit and long-term invalidity benefit. The then Conservative Government had identified the increase in spending on invalidity benefit as one of the major factors driving the overall growth in social security expenditure.[37] However, the underlying reasons for the increasing numbers of invalidity benefit claimants were more complex.[38] Although the new benefit was still in the process of bedding down, the Labour Government declared its intention in the 1998 Green Paper on welfare reform to institute further changes in the structure of incapacity benefit.[39] These provoked the most serious challenge to the authority of the Blair Government in the form of a backbench revolt in both Houses in the course of the passage of the Welfare Reform and Pensions Act 1999.

Incapacity benefit comes in three different forms, depending on the length of time a person has been incapable of work.[40] In the initial period of sickness of up to

[32] See R. Lewis, 'The Privatisation of Sickness Benefit' (1982) 11 *I.L.J.* 245–54.

[33] This benefit remained in place for those not covered by SSP, e.g. the self-employed, but was subsumed into incapacity benefit in 1995; see below in section 3.B.

[34] Statutory Sick Pay Act 1991; small employers continued to receive 100 per cent reimbursement. These changes had very little impact on employers' policies or practices: S. Middleton et al. (1994), n. 29 above, 115.

[35] A modified version of the reimbursement arrangements for small employers was introduced by Statutory Sick Pay Act 1994, s. 3, inserting SSCBA 1992, s. 159A: see further Statutory Sick Pay Percentage Threshold Order 1995 (S.I. 1995 No. 512). DSS expenditure on SSP thus dropped from £659 million in 1993–4 to just £26 million in 1997–8: DSS (1999), n. 3 above, 99.

[36] H. Dean and P. Taylor-Gooby, 'Statutory Sick Pay and the Control of Sickness Absence' (1990) 19 *J. of Social Policy* 47–67, 64. See also P. Taylor-Gooby and S. Lakeman, 'Back to the Future: Statutory Sick Pay, Citizenship and Social Class' (1988) 17 *J. of Social Policy* 23–39.

[37] DSS, *The Growth of Social Security* (London: HMSO, 1993), 17.

[38] See e.g. R. Disney and S. Webb, 'Why are there so many long term sick in Britain?' (1991) 101 *Economic J.* 252–62 and P. Holmes, M. Lynch, and I. Mohlo, 'An Econometric Analysis of the Growth of Numbers Claiming Invalidity Benefit: An Overview' (1991) 20 *J. of Social Policy* 87–105.

[39] Green Paper (1998), ch. 6.

[40] See further D. Bonner, 'Incapacity for work: a new benefit and new tests' (1995) 2 *J.S.S.L.* 86–112.

twenty-eight weeks, as described above, the great majority of employees will qualify for statutory sick pay, which may of course be supplemented by more generous occupational sick pay provision.[41] During this period the test of incapacity is the so-called 'own occupation test' (effectively whether the person is capable of performing their normal work), typically satisfied on production of a sickness certificate from the claimant's GP.[42] Those workers who are ineligible for SSP,[43] but who have an adequate contributions record, may qualify for the lower rate of short-term incapacity benefit during this initial period.[44] This is paid at a flat rate (less than SSP)[45] but may be supplemented by an adult dependant increase in narrowly defined circumstances.[46] Both this benefit and SSP run out after twenty-eight weeks; at this point claimants who are still incapable of work, as determined by the 'all work test', transfer to the higher rate of short-term incapacity benefit,[47] which is in fact set at the same weekly rate as SSP. Unlike SSP, however, it may be supplemented by adult and child dependant increases.[48] After a year claimants move on to the long-term rate of incapacity benefit, at which point an age addition[49] may be payable as well as the dependant increases. In principle a claimant may then continue to draw incapacity benefit until retirement, assuming that they are found to be incapable of work on subsequent all work tests.[50]

Even before the 1999 changes, incapacity benefit was less generous than its predecessor, invalidity benefit, in a number of important respects. Most notably the long-term rate of incapacity benefit is only payable after twelve months of incapacity, whereas invalidity benefit was payable after just six months. In addition, the provisions governing adult dependant increases and age additions were made more stringent, the earnings-related additional pension abolished and the new benefit made taxable.

---

[41] In the event that an employee off sick only receives SSP, s/he may also be eligible for income support, depending on whether or not their income falls short of their applicable amount.

[42] SSCBA 1992, s. 171B and Social Security (Incapacity for Work) (General) Regulations 1995 (S.I. 1995 No. 311), regs 4–6.

[43] E.g. because they are self-employed or on a short-term contract.

[44] SSCBA 1992, s. 30B(2). This is the former sickness benefit by another name.

[45] For 1999/2000 SSP was paid at £59.55 per week and the lower rate of short-term invalidity benefit at £50.35 per week.

[46] SSCBA 1992, s. 86A and Social Security (Incapacity Benefit—Increases for Dependants) Regulations 1994 (S.I. 1994 No. 2945).

[47] SSCBA 1992, ss 30A(4) and 30B(2).

[48] Ibid., s. 80. Consequently for some claimants the increase in incapacity benefit pushes them off income support, so that they lose passported benefits and have to contribute to their rent and council tax, making them *worse off* in their second 6 months of incapacity: House of Commons Social Security Committee, *Incapacity Benefit*, Minutes of Evidence, H.C. 80, Session 1996–7 (London: The Stationery Office, 1997), memorandum submitted by CPAG, 177.

[49] These are only payable where the period of incapacity began either before the age of 35 (higher rate) or between 35 and 44 (lower rate): SSCBA 1992, s. 30B(7).

[50] 'Unless forced to take work, or assured of a permanent, well-paid job, there is every incentive for a beneficiary to "sit tight". The covert message conveyed by the benefit system—presumably unintentionally—has been that a disabled person receiving IB or SDA is quite incapable of work and need not consider working again. Effectively, for most people, IB is perceived as an early pension for those who have ceased work because of illness or disability': SSAC (1997), n. 5 above, 9.

However, the most significant difference between the two benefits is the test applied in assessing incapacity for work beyond the initial period of sickness. Entitlement to invalidity benefit turned on whether there was 'work which the person can reasonably be expected to do'.[51] Under these arrangements GPs effectively acted as reluctant and uncertain gatekeepers.[52] Long-term claimants on invalidity benefit would be periodically called in for review by a departmental doctor and, on appeal, tribunals would typically be faced with conflicting opinions from the claimant's own GP and the departmental doctor as to the claimant's fitness for work. The previous Conservative Government was convinced that this test had become too elastic, and that the prime reason for the underlying growth in invalidity benefit claims was malingering.[53] It therefore sought to tighten up the procedure for assessing incapacity.

A key feature of the introduction of incapacity benefit in April 1995 was thus the imposition of the all work test, from the outset of the claim for a person who had no usual occupation and after six months for all other claimants.[54] The all work test was purportedly designed to be a more objective test of incapacity, with the claimant first completing a questionnaire on his or her functional abilities and then being examined by a doctor on behalf of the Benefits Agency.[55] The all work test is focused purely on the specified physical and mental health (in)capabilities of the claimant, taking no account of age, work experience, or training. It is therefore firmly located within the medical model of disability. As regards the physical functions, each functional area is divided into a series of descriptors, specifying differing levels of capability, each of which is in turn allotted a certain number of points in the Schedule to the regulations. Thus an inability to walk more than fifty metres without stopping or severe discomfort rates fifteen points, whereas a limit of 200 or 400 metres qualifies for only seven or three points respectively.[56] A claimant is adjudged incapable of work on the physical descriptors alone if he or she reaches the threshold of fifteen points.[57] The mental health descriptors are organised differently, grouped into four broad functional areas, with each individual descriptor being valued at one or two points.[58] To qualify as incapable of work on the mental

[51] N. 20 above.

[52] J. Ritchie, *GPs and IVB: A Qualitative Study of the Role of General Practitioners in the Award of Invalidity Benefit*, DSS Research Report No. 18 (London: HMSO, 1993).

[53] R. Berthoud, *Disability Benefits: A review of the issues and options for reform* (York: Joseph Rowntree Foundation, 1998), 34.

[54] See Wikeley (1995), n. 24 above and R. Berthoud, 'The "medical" assessment of incapacity: a case study of research and policy' (1995) 2 *J.S.S.L.* 61–85.

[55] For criticism of the all work test, see S. Ward, *An Unfit Test: CAB clients' experience of the medical test for incapacity benefit* (London: National Association of Citizens Advice Bureaux, 1997). The work of the examining doctors has been contracted out to the private sector.

[56] Schedule to the Social Security (Incapacity for Work) (General) Regulations 1995 (S.I. 1995 No. 311), Part I, para. 1.

[57] Ibid., reg. 25(1)(a). This may be on the basis of 15 points under one function, or a combination of points for different descriptors.

[58] Namely completion of tasks, daily living, coping with pressure, and interaction with other people: ibid., Part II of the Schedule. Here separate descriptors within each functional area may be aggregated: ibid., reg. 26(4).

health descriptors alone, a claimant must reach ten points.[59] Where the claimant suffers from both physical and mental health problems, the threshold is fifteen but a convoluted scoring system operates to combine the points from each part of the Schedule.[60] A claimant who has failed to score enough points on the all work test may still be deemed to be incapable of work if certain special circumstances apply.[61] These exceptions were made significantly more restrictive by amendments to the regulations in January 1997.[62]

The assessment arrangements for incapacity benefit have been described by Berthoud as being based on two fundamentally flawed premises:

First, the so-called all work test is not directly about work at all: it is a test of impairment which does not assess the actual probability of employment faced by disabled people in particular circumstances. Second, it has entrenched the unrealistic assumption that capacity is an all-or-nothing question: you are either completely capable of work or utterly incapable.[63]

As regards the first of these points, the essential problem is that 'there is no objective way to measure the impact of a medical condition on an individual's ability to function in a work setting . . . the question of when pain or discomfort should be considered sufficient to render an individual "unable" to perform an activity requires a judgment about how much pain our society requires individuals to endure'.[64] The characterisation of such issues as a purely medical matter thereby side-steps this fundamental moral and political question.[65] Furthermore, as Diller notes, the more factors that a benefit system considers in assessing incapacity for work, 'the better the program will be able to gauge the actual impact of a medical impairment on an individual's ability to earn a living'.[66] Yet by the same token as more factors are considered so 'the category [of disability in the USA, or incapacity in the UK] begins to dissolve into the general rubric of unemployment'.[67]

The second fundamental problem with the all work test, as Berthoud identifies, is that it preserves incapacity benefit as an 'all or nothing' benefit.[68] The Welfare Reform and Pensions Act 1999 itself does nothing to address this problem. A claimant is either incapable of work, in which case she qualifies for incapacity benefit, assuming the other conditions are satisfied, or she is not, in which case she must

---

[59] Ibid., reg. 25(1)(b).   [60] Ibid., regs. 25(1)(c) and 26(1).   [61] Ibid., reg. 27.

[62] In particular, the catch-all exception for cases where 'there would be a substantial risk to the mental or physical health of any person if [the claimant] were found capable of work' was abolished. This substantially reduced the scope for taking full account of the situation of claimants with severe mental health problems, whose problems in functioning and behaviour management may not be adequately captured by the mental health descriptors: Social Security Committee (1997), n. 48 above, 232–3.

[63] R. Berthoud (1998), n. 53 above, 64.

[64] M. Diller, 'Entitlement and Exclusion: The Role of Disability in the Social Welfare System' (1996) 44 *U.C.L.A. Law Rev.* 361–465, 387.

[65] See further D. Stone, *The Disabled State* (London: Macmillan, 1985).

[66] M. Diller (1996), n. 64 above, 368.

[67] Ibid., 390–1.

[68] See SSAC, *Social Security Provision for Disability: A Case for Change?* (London: The Stationery Office, 1997), 0–12.

sign on as unemployed for JSA[69] or, if she falls within one of the prescribed categories (e.g. as a lone parent with a child aged under sixteen), rely on means-tested income support.[70] Although there are gradations of entitlement for disability benefits,[71] a *partial* incapacity benefit is conspicuous by its absence from the UK social security scheme. To some extent this may merely reflect the simplistic and bipolar perception within society that a person is either capable or incapable of work, without recognising the reality of a spectrum of (in)capacity.[72] A further reason for the absence of such a benefit may well be a concern on the part of policy makers to minimise the temptation for people to prefer benefits to any kind of work.[73] Consequently the United Kingdom is not alone is maintaining a fairly rigorous definition of incapacity which fails to accommodate the partially disabled.[74] On the other hand, a comprehensive comparative study has concluded that one of the advantages of a single system, permitting both full and partial awards, is that 'disabled people may move between full and partial benefits without the need to apply for a different benefit, and as, in principle, all partial benefits can be held in work they may also move in and out of work relatively easily'.[75] This is therefore highly relevant to the policy debate about helping disabled people into work. As we shall see, the route taken by the previous Conservative Government was to introduce in 1992 a further means-tested benefit, disability working allowance, modelled on family credit.[76] The Labour Government has abandoned this approach principally in favour of using tax credits.[77]

Meanwhile, the replacement of invalidity benefit by incapacity benefit failed to

---

[69] She must be capable of work to qualify for jobseeker's allowance (SSCBA 1992, s. 1(2)(a)), although she may still be allowed to restrict her availability for work in certain respects: see Jobseeker's Allowance Regulations 1996 (S.I. 1996 No. 207), reg. 13(3). In practice a claimant who is found to be not incapable of work under the all work test may well face difficulties in persuading the Employment Service that they are in fact fit for work: see Social Security Committee (1997), n. 48 above, 178.

[70] In the past she might have qualified for SDA (see above), but for a single claimant that would almost invariably have needed to be topped up by income support.

[71] Thus industrial disablement benefit is paid on a percentage basis (see Chapter 15), as are war pensions (see Ogus, Barendt, and Wikeley (1995), ch. 8). The care component of disability living allowance and attendance allowance is paid at a number of different rates, depending on the severity of the disabling condition (see below in section 4.A).

[72] As a respondent to one research study commented, 'You are either really, really deserving and half dead, and then you will be pitied and you will get [benefits], or you are treated as if there is nothing really wrong with you, and you should get off your backside and do things which, when you do that, you are really ill': K. Rowlingson and R. Berthoud, *Disability, Benefits and Employment*, DSS Research Report No. 54 (London: HMSO, 1996), 23.

[73] In other words, the Poor Law principle of 'less eligibility' continues to cast its long shadow.

[74] J. F. Keeler, 'Social Insurance, Disability and Personal Injury' (1994) 44 *Univ. Toronto. L.J.* 275–352, 303.

[75] P. Thornton, R. Sainsbury, and H. Barnes, *Helping Disabled People to Work: A Cross-National Study of Social Security and Employment Provisions* (SSAC Research Paper 8, 1997), 142.

[76] See further below in section 5.B. For a valuable critique, see L. Luckhaus, 'New Disability Benefits: Beveridge Turned Upside Down' (1992) 21 *I.L.J.* 237–44.

[77] In addition, a number of the work disincentives associated with the previous incapacity benefit regime have been modified (e.g. by extending the linking rule and abolishing the 16-hour-a-week limit on unpaid voluntary work); see also the provision for pilot schemes under SSA 1998, s. 77.

generate expenditure savings on the scale which had originally been anticipated.[78] Yet the 1995 changes undoubtedly had a dampening effect on this sector of the welfare state. Spending on invalidity benefit accounted for over 40 per cent of social security expenditure on disabled people in 1993–4; by 1998–9, the proportion devoted to incapacity benefit had fallen to below 30 per cent; over this five-year period the cost of this benefit fell by an average of nearly 3 per cent a year in real terms.[79] Notwithstanding this, the Labour Government swiftly concluded that further modifications were required. It argued that incapacity benefit was poorly targeted and had become a benefit-funded route to early retirement, in just the same way as had been asserted by the Conservatives in relation to invalidity benefit.[80] The Welfare Reform and Pensions Act 1999 has accordingly made a number of significant changes to the structure and process of claiming incapacity benefit. The four key changes comprise the rebranding of the all work test as the 'personal capability assessment', the narrowing of the contribution conditions for incapacity benefit, its partial means-testing, and the integration of some (but not all) severe disablement allowance recipients within the scope of the more generous incapacity benefit scheme.[81]

The first change is the replacement of the all work test with a so-called personal capability assessment. On one level this reflects minimal reform, or indeed no substantive change at all; on another it is indicative of a fundamental shift in the philosophy underlying the rules governing eligibility for benefits. As regards the former, the personal capability assessment mirrors the existing all work test in terms of access to benefit, so the scoring regime introduced in 1995 remains intact.[82] As regards the latter, this is inextricably bound up with the Government's ambition to create a 'single gateway' to enable claimants (whether disabled or otherwise) to access information on work, benefits, and government services in one place. The single gateway (or 'ONE') strategy includes a commitment to ensure that new claimants of

---

[78] The 1993 estimate was that savings for 1996–7 would be £1,185 million; by 1996 this had been revised downwards to £790 million: Social Security Committee (1997), n. 48 above, 10.

[79] DSS, *Social Security Departmental Report: The Government's Expenditure Plans 1999/2000*, Cm 4214 (London: The Stationery Office, 1999), 85. Future estimates for incapacity benefit are still subject to some uncertainty as the full effects of the all work test have yet to emerge: Government Actuary's Department, *Report by the Government Actuary on the drafts of the Social Security Benefits Up-rating Order 1999 and the Social Security (Contributions) (Re-rating and National Insurance Fund Payments) Order 1999*, Cm 4199 (London: The Stationery Office, 1999).

[80] The language was strikingly similar: compare 'Too many people regard invalidity benefit as a readily available supplement to their occupational pensions when they take early retirement' (Mr P. Lilley MP, Secretary of State for Social Security, Hansard, H.C. Debs. Vol. 236, col. 37 (24 January 1994) with 'for some people, [incapacity benefit] has become an alternative means of support in unemployment and for others, it acts as a supplement to income in early retirement' (DSS, *A New Contract for Welfare: Support for disabled people*, Cm 4103 (London: The Stationery Office, 1998), 5).

[81] The second and third of these changes are expected to save nearly £100 million in 2001–2002 rising to £650 to £700 million a year in the long run: ibid., 23.

[82] 'We do not intend to change the way in which the test acts as the gateway to benefit': ibid., 17. However, provision is made for the assessment process to begin earlier than is currently the case (SSCBA 1992, s. 171C(4), to be introduced by Welfare Reform and Pensions Act 1999, s. 61) and the Secretary of State's powers to initiate reviews of entitlement is made more explicit: ss 171A(3) and 171C(5) to be inserted by para. 23(3) of Sched. 8 to and s. 61 of the 1999 Act respectively.

incapacity benefits are assigned a 'personal adviser' whose role it will be to conduct an interview as early as possible and to discuss ways of helping them to become independent. Moreover, as from April 2000, incapacity benefit claimants will be required to attend such an interview as an integral part of their claim for benefit.[83] Thus the new assessment is intended to provide additional information,[84] beyond that needed to determine benefit entitlement: 'This information will be potentially helpful to claimants and their personal advisers, in combination with a wider assessment of the individual's employability, to decide what might be done to assist a return to work.'[85] According to the Government:

Our priority is to forge an entirely new culture which puts work first and is based on a modern, integrated, flexible service for all. This means a fundamental shift in the way we support people—away from merely asking *'What money can we pay you?'* to *'How can we help you to become more independent?'*[86]

The rhetoric behind these reforms is entirely consonant with the Government's determination to shift the focus of the benefit system from passive to active citizenship, to attack the scourge of dependency, and to generate a climate in which the individual's own commitment to improve their lot is seen as a necessary corollary of continuing receipt of state benefit. This has been characterised by Raymond Plant as the concept of 'supply-side citizenship'[87] or, in the soundbite of the modern Labour Party, a hand-up and not a hand-out. However, this new discourse of conditional citizenship rights cannot disguise the fact that similar strategies have been tried by the DSS in the past, principally with a view to enhancing customer service, but to no avail. It is true, however, that previous attempts have not been on the same scale and have lacked an equivalent degree of political will.[88] The quality of personal advisers will be crucial to the success of the gateway[89] and there is the potential for conflict given the dual purpose of the personal capability assessment.[90] It may be recalled that previous much-heralded reforms which have promised a personalised holistic service have singularly failed to deliver.[91] The success of the strategy, which will be

---

[83] This requirement was first introduced on a pilot basis in a number of areas: see DSS, *A New Contract for Welfare: The gateway to work*, Cm 4102 (London: The Stationery Office, 1998).

[84] The personal capability assessment is introduced by s. 61 (replacing SSCBA 1992, s. 171C) and para. 23 of Sched. 8 to the Welfare Reform and Pensions Act 1999.

[85] DSS, *A New Contract for Welfare: Support for disabled people*, Cm 4103 (London: The Stationery Office, 1998), 17.

[86] Ibid., 18 (original emphasis).

[87] R. Plant, 'Supply Side Citizenship?' (1999) 6 *J.S.S.L.* 124–36.

[88] See further C. Bellamy, 'Transforming Social Security Benefits' (1996) 74 *Public Administration*, 159–79.

[89] DIG, '*A New Contract for Welfare: support for disabled people*'; *response from Disablement Income Group* (1999), 2.

[90] 'The "nice" official who helps you to find work is also potentially the "nasty" official who reduces your benefit if you are judged capable of work': R. Berthoud, *Disability Benefits: A review of the issues and options for reform* (York: Joseph Rowntree Foundation, 1998), 65.

[91] The original plans for the social fund are a case in point, under which it was proposed that social fund officers would undertake a welfare advisory as well as a decision-making role. See further p. 135 above. The fund is discussed in Chapter 14.

immensely resource-intensive if the commitment is delivered, will also depend upon the overall state of the economy: a significant contraction in demand will ensure that gateway interviews with disabled people on the margins of, or excluded from, the labour market will become little more than a meaningless ritual.[92]

Secondly, the 1999 Act makes the contribution conditions for qualifying for incapacity benefit much tighter by aligning them with those for contribution-based JSA. Thus claimants would need to have actually paid the appropriate number of Class 1 or Class 2 National Insurance contributions in one of the last three tax years before the benefit year in which the claim is made, rather than in any one tax year, as has been sufficient.[93] The justification for this change is that entitlement to incapacity benefit for new claimants should be, as with JSA, 'on the basis of recent work and contributions'.[94] The difficulty with this rationale is that the analogy between incapacity benefit and JSA ignores a fundamental distinction: JSA, as the successor to unemployment benefit, has always been a short-term benefit; incapacity benefit, on the other hand, in its original manifestation as invalidity benefit, was always designed to provide long-term security. This original purpose, however, sits very uneasily with the emphasis in Labour Government rhetoric on welfare to work. The long-term effect of this change is estimated to be that the number of people on incapacity benefit will fall by 170,000, approximately 10 per cent of the caseload.[95] Many of these unsuccessful claimants will have no alternative but to depend on income support (or income-based JSA if they are found to be capable of work).

The third change involves the importing of means-testing into incapacity benefit. In future, where a new claimant is in receipt of an occupational or personal pension of £85 a week or more, 50 per cent of the excess income over that threshold is to be deducted from the relevant rate of incapacity benefit.[96] The justification for this change is put in terms of more effective targeting and ensuring 'a fairer balance between State and private provision'.[97] It represents a partial alignment with contribution-based JSA, where 100 per cent of a private pension of £50 or more a week is deducted pound for pound from benefit entitlement.[98] The new arrangements involve a marginal tax rate of about 60 per cent on occupational pensions of more than £85 a week, and fail to take account of the fact that many occupational and other private pension schemes incorporate an assumption that the individual is already receiving the basic state incapacity benefit.[99] More fundamentally, once

[92] The pre-eminence of the personal adviser in the new arrangements, with the implications of closer case management, also has important implications for the principles underlying adjudication processes: T. Carney, 'Merits review of contractual social security payments' (1998) 5 *J.S.S.L.* 18–43.
[93] SSCBA 1992, Sched. 3, para. 2, amended by Welfare Reform and Pensions Act 1999, s. 62.
[94] DSS (1998), n. 85 above, 20.   [95] Ibid., 21.
[96] SSCBA 1992, s. 30DD, inserted by Welfare Reform and Pensions Act 1999, s. 63.
[97] DSS (1998), n. 85 above, 21. Note that the threshold was raised to £85 from £50 in the Bill as drafted, in an attempt to head off a back-bench revolt.
[98] The more generous rule for incapacity benefit is in recognition of the fact that whereas contribution-based JSA is paid for only 6 months, incapacity may last for many years: ibid.
[99] DIG (1999), n. 89 above, 6–11.

means-testing begins to intrude on the structure of an insurance benefit, experience demonstrates (as with unemployment benefit, and now contribution-based JSA) that the insurance basis of the benefit is subsequently eroded by further incremental changes.

Finally, the Welfare Reform and Pensions Act 1999 creates a new category of incapacity benefit claimant, described as 'persons incapacitated in youth'.[100] At the same time section 65 of the 1999 Act abolishes severe disablement allowance (SDA), a benefit only introduced in 1984, which had itself replaced the former non-contributory invalidity pension (NCIP) and housewives' non-contributory invalidity pension (HNCIP). SDA was essentially a benefit for people who were incapable of work but who failed the contributions test for incapacity benefit. Reflecting its status as a non-contributory benefit, it was paid at a lower rate.[101] It was in effect the poor man's incapacity benefit; or, more accurately, the poor *woman's* incapacity benefit as some two-thirds of SDA recipients were female, whereas the proportions are reversed for incapacity benefit. SDA claimants had to be aged between sixteen and sixty-five when they claimed and must have *either* been incapable of work for at least twenty-eight weeks beginning on or before the claimant's twentieth birthday *or* been assessed as being at least 80 per cent[102] disabled for a minimum of twenty-eight weeks.[103] The effect of the 1999 Act is to transfer those incapacitated in their youth to the more generous incapacity benefit, but to withdraw entitlement altogether from new claimants over the age of twenty-five[104] who would previously have satisfied the 80 per cent disablement test. Those aged twenty and over who were in receipt of SDA on the basis of an 80 per cent assessment will continue to receive the benefit, but new claims will not be accepted from the point of change.[105]

The purported justification for the changes to SDA were two-fold: first, that the low rate of SDA meant that many claimants had to rely on income support in any event to top up their income and, secondly, that SDA was poorly targeted, in that two-thirds of new awards were made to those aged over twenty, many of whom lived in households 'which already have adequate resources'.[106] Moreover, the 1998 Green Paper on disability argued that this was inconsistent with the original policy intention of SDA as a benefit for people disabled from childhood. The difficulty with this official rationale is that it hardly reflects the true origins of the benefit as, in large measure at least, an acknowledgement of the discriminatory nature of

---

[100]   s. 64, amending SSCBA 1992, s. 30A.

[101]   As Berthoud (n. 90 above, 13) observes, the basic rates of both SDA and ICA 'are incredibly stingy'. In 1999–2000 the long-term rate of IB was £66.75 a week compared to £40.35 for SDA and £39.95 for ICA.

[102]   The principles governing the percentage assessment of disablement were the same as those applying under the industrial injuries scheme.

[103]   A third possible qualifying route was that the claimant had previously been entitled to a non-contributory invalidity pension. Some claimants were deemed to be 80 per cent disabled on the basis of their receipt of other benefits (e.g. the highest rate care component of DLA).

[104]   The original proposal was to retain the SDA age limit of 20, but this was raised to 25 following lobbying during the passage of the Act.

[105]   Regulations to be made under Welfare Reform and Pensions Act 1999, s. 85.

[106]   DSS (1998), n. 85 above, 9.

HNCIP and thus a response to the Equal Treatment Directive.[107] The Green Paper rather implied that SDA would be preserved as a separate benefit, but modernisation in the 1999 Act has actually involved abolition of the benefit. Given the confusing proliferation of disability benefits, this may on one level be no bad thing. Yet the 1999 changes raise a number of important issues. The incorporation within the mainstream incapacity benefit of those incapacitated in their youth implements a proposal first made by the SSAC in 1988.[108] However, the SSAC also recommended that the rate of SDA for other claimants should be progressively raised until it was equal with the then invalidity benefit, at which point the two benefits should be merged. Instead, SDA has been abolished for this group, which will inevitably have a disproportionate adverse effect on disabled women, and in particular on disabled married women.[109]

C. Invalid Care Allowance

Invalid care allowance is, as the name implies, a benefit for carers rather than disabled persons themselves.[110] It is a non-contributory benefit which, notwithstanding its modest rate,[111] is designated as an earnings replacement benefit[112] and hence is subject to the overlapping benefits rules.[113] The main qualifying condition[114] is that the claimant must be caring for a person who receives either attendance allowance or the highest or middle rate of the care component of disability living allowance.[115] The claimant must also be 'regularly and substantially engaged' in such caring (defined by regulations as at least thirty-five hours a week). In addition to presence and residence requirements, the claimant must not be gainfully employed,[116] nor receiving full-time education[117] nor aged under sixteen or over pensionable age. An income support claimant who qualifies for invalid care allowance will have that benefit fully taken into account for the purposes of assessing her applicable amount, but she will qualify for

---

[107] L. Luckhaus, 'Severe Disablement Allowance: The Old Dressed up as New?' [1986] *J.S.W.L.* 153–69.

[108] SSAC, *Benefits for Disabled People: A Strategy for Change* (London: HMSO, 1988), para. 11.20.

[109] DIG (1999), n. 89 above, 13–15.

[110] See generally Office for National Statistics, *Informal Carers* (London: The Stationery Office, 1998) and Department of Health, *Caring about Carers: National Strategy for Carers* (London: The Stationery Office, 1999).

[111] In 1999/2000 ICA is paid at £39.95 a week, with increases for dependants.

[112] And so ICA claimants are credited with Class 1 national insurance contributions.

[113] This means that a claimant cannot receive ICA at the same time as, for example, incapacity benefit or contribution-based JSA.

[114] The qualifying rules are set out in SSCBA 1992, s. 70 and the Social Security (Invalid Care Allowance) Regulations 1976 (S.I. 1976 No. 409). See generally Ogus, Barendt, and Wikeley (1995), 208–12.

[115] See below on the conditions for these benefits.

[116] This is defined by reference to a weekly earnings threshold, rather than a set number of hours: for 1999/2000 the earnings rule is set at £50 a week.

[117] Defined by regulations as 21 hours or more a week of class contact time; thus many full-time university students will *not* be excluded on this ground.

the carer's premium in the income support calculation.[118] Although entitlement to invalid care allowance has now been shorn of its sexually discriminatory qualifying criteria,[119] there is ample evidence that the benefit fails to reach the majority of carers and provides only token support to those whom it does reach.[120]

4. EXTRA COSTS BENEFITS

A. Disability Living Allowance

Disability living allowance (DLA) was introduced in April 1992, from the merger of the former mobility allowance and attendance allowance.[121] As with the creation of JSA,[122] DLA is essentially an amalgamated rather than an integrated or unified benefit. It comprises two freestanding components, for mobility and care needs respectively. A successful claimant may be awarded either or both components for either a fixed period of years or for life.[123] The most significant substantive reform of the 1992 changes was the introduction of a new lower rate for each component, designed to provide help to an estimated 290,000 moderately disabled people who fell outside the former arrangements for mobility allowance and attendance allowance. On the procedural level greater emphasis was placed on self-assessment, with a move away from reliance on 'snapshot' medical examinations.

The origins of DLA as two separate benefits are reflected in the age limits for each of the components.[124] Mobility allowance was only payable to disabled persons who made their claim after their fifth birthday but before reaching the age of sixty-five.[125]

---

[118] Consequently the person for whom she is caring would not be able to qualify for the severe disability premium as part of their own income support entitlement.

[119] Originally married and cohabiting women were precluded from claiming ICA, and there were separate age limits for men (65) and women (60). Both these conditions were struck down by the European Court of Justice as offending against the principle of equal treatment: see *Case 150/85, Drake v Chief Adjudication Officer* [1987] QB 166 and *Case C-328/91, Thomas v Chief Adjudication Officer* [1993] QB 747.

[120] See e.g. C. Glendinning, 'Dependency and Interdependency: the Incomes of Informal Carers and the Impact of Social Security' (1990) 19 *J. of Social Policy* 469–97; E. McLaughlin, *Social Security and Community Care*, DSS Research Report No. 4 (London: HMSO, 1991); and S. Baldwin and G. Parker, 'Support for Informal Carers—the Role of Social Security' in G. Dalley (ed.), *Disability and Social Policy* (London: PSI, 1991), 163–98.

[121] The reforms were originally embodied in the Disability Living Allowance and Disability Working Allowance Act 1991, but were subsequently consolidated in the SSCBA 1992.

[122] See Chapter 10.

[123] The legislation precludes the granting of two fixed-term awards of different lengths, although other permutations of life and fixed-term awards of both components are possible: SSCBA 1992, s. 71.

[124] It should be noted that some assimilation of the rules for the two components has taken place to the detriment of claimants. Historically, mobility allowance was unaffected by admission to publicly-funded care, e.g. hospital, whereas attendance allowance was withdrawn after 28 days. In 1996 the rules for the mobility component of DLA were aligned with those for the care component and attendance allowance.

[125] Thus a claimant who successfully claimed before reaching 65 would carry on receiving benefit after that age. The original relaxation at the margins, entitling a person to claim before their 66th birthday if the disabling condition was present before reaching 65, was abolished in 1997.

Attendance allowance, on the other hand, originally had a lower age limit of two and no upper limit. In 1990 very severely disabled children became eligible for attendance allowance. These rules were carried over into DLA in 1992, with claimants with care needs who made a claim for the first time after reaching the age of sixty-five being considered for the new attendance allowance. The Welfare Reform and Pensions Act 1999 makes three and four year olds eligible for the higher rate mobility component of DLA for the first time.[126] The exclusion of children under the age of five has always been difficult to sustain.[127] The new qualifying age limit of three years reflects the view of the Disability Living Allowance Advisory Board that 'by the age of 2½ years, the very great majority of children will be walking independently'.[128] At the other end of the age spectrum, there remains no assistance for those people with mobility problems who claim for the first time after attaining the age of sixty-five. There are probably three reasons for this. First, it becomes increasingly difficult with advancing years to distinguish between the effects of the aging process and disability respectively. Secondly, one of the rationales underlying the 1992 reforms was the perceived need to direct resources to the disabled of working age.[129] Thirdly, the cost implications of lifting the age cap on the mobility component would be enormous.[130]

(i) *The Mobility Component of DLA*

The mobility component is paid at one of two rates: a higher or lower rate. The higher rate mobility component is essentially a direct lineal successor to the old mobility allowance, although the qualifying routes have been extended at the margins in exceptional cases. The great majority of awards of the higher rate mobility component are made on the basis that the claimant's *physical* disablement is such that he or she is 'virtually unable to walk'.[131] There is no 'magic distance' beyond which a person is regarded as outwith the scope of the benefit. Indeed, adjudicators of higher rate mobility component claims, whether at first instance or on appeal, must exercise a considerable degree of judgement in fact-finding and in applying the law to those facts. The statutory test provides that in determining whether a person is virtually unable to walk the decision maker must have regard to the distance, speed, length of time, and

[126] Welfare Reform and Pensions Act 1999, s. 67(3), amending SSCBA 1992, s. 73(1). Buck's comment about the government strategy underlying the 1992 reforms is equally pertinent in the context of the 1999 changes: 'certain client groups are targeted for help (here mainly the young disabled), the proposals only take place amidst tight financial control, what is given with one hand is taken away with the other': T. Buck, 'The Way Ahead: Benefits for the Disabled' (1990) 19 *I.L.J.* 125–32, 132.

[127] See Ogus, Barendt, and Wikeley (1995), 195 and M. Howard, *Too Young to Count* (London: Disability Alliance, 1994).

[128] DLAAB, *Child Mobility and Disability Living Allowance* (London: DLAAB, 1998).

[129] DSS, *The Way Ahead: Benefits for Disabled People*, Cm 917 (London: HMSO, 1990).

[130] This has not stopped the Disability Living Allowance Advisory Board, in a submission which in other respects is highly critical of the perceived over-generosity of DLA, arguing the case for removing 'the present discrimination against elderly disabled people . . . as a result of a realignment of priorities': House of Commons Social Security Committee, *Disability Living Allowance*, Fourth Report, Minutes of Evidence, H.C. 641, Session 1997–8 (London: The Stationery Office, 1998), 4.

[131] SSCBA 1992, s. 73(1)(a).

manner of any walking.[132] No one factor carries any particular weight. Moreover, the criteria include reference to two matters on which human judgment is notoriously fallible: distance and speed.[133] Whilst such a test is therefore hardly transparent to start with,[134] it is made even more opaque by the statutory direction to disregard any walking which can only be achieved 'with severe discomfort', a factor which is simply not susceptible to clinical measurement.[135] Awards of the higher rate of the mobility component account for over one-quarter of all disability living allowance awards and almost a third of the life awards.[136] The Disability Living Allowance Advisory Board has expressed its concern at 'the large number of applicants who are currently awarded the higher rate mobility component inappropriately'.[137]

The other less common ways in which a person may qualify for the higher rate mobility component include several categories inherited from the former mobility allowance, covering claimants who are *actually* unable to walk, or for whom the exertion involved would constitute a risk to their life or health, or double amputees, or those who are both deaf and blind. When DLA was introduced the higher rate mobility component was also extended to a very narrow category of claimants with severe mental impairment and severe behavioural problems.[138]

An innovatory feature of the 1992 reforms was the introduction of a new lower rate mobility component. This rate is available to those who 'cannot take advantage of [their ability to walk] out of doors without guidance or supervision from another person most of the time'.[139] In making such an assessment, any ability to walk on familiar routes on their own must be disregarded. The lower rate component is available to those with a physical *or* mental disability. In practice the four types of disability which are significantly associated with lower rate mobility awards are those related to seeing, consciousness, intellectual functioning, and behaviour.[140] Originally it was estimated that some 150,000 people would qualify for assistance at this rate;[141] by 1997, however, there were 355,000 lower rate mobility awards in payment, of which nearly half were paid alongside the middle rate care component.[142]

---

[132] Social Security (Disability Living Allowance) Regulations 1991 (S.I. 1991 No. 2890), reg. 12(1)(a)(ii).
[133] In a typical appeal against the refusal of higher rate mobility component, the tribunal will have to decide between competing estimations of distance and time, provided by the claimant, their GP, and an examining medical practitioner.
[134] In this context note should be made of SSAC's fourth guiding principle for disability benefits, namely that 'benefit entitlement rules should be readily understandable': SSAC, *Social Security Provision for Disability: A Case for Change?* (London: The Stationery Office, 1997), 1.
[135] The same difficulty arises in the context of incapacity benefit and the all work test.
[136] Social Security Committee (1998), n. 130 above, Table G.3, 68.
[137] Ibid., 5.
[138] See N. Wikeley, 'Severe mental impairment and the higher rate mobility component of DLA' (1999) 6 *J.S.S.L.* 10–32.
[139] SSCBA 1992, s. 73(1)(e).
[140] R. Sainsbury, M. Hirst, and D. Lawton, *Evaluation of Disability Living Allowance and Attendance Allowance*, DSS Research Report No. 41 (London: HMSO, 1995), 51.
[141] DSS (1990), n. 129 above, 29.
[142] DSS, *Social Security Statistics 1997* (London; The Stationery Office, 1997), E2.06, 196.

(ii) The Care Component of DLA

The structure of the care component of DLA is more complex than the mobility component: there are three different rates (highest, middle, and lowest).[143] Entitlement to the highest and middle rates turns on the so-called day and night conditions, each of which has alternative qualifying routes based on personal care and supervision needs respectively. A claimant who meets both these conditions qualifies for the highest rate; a claimant who only meets one of these conditions—in practice usually the day condition[144]—is entitled to the middle rate care component. Eligibility for the lowest rate care component is also based on parallel tracks: in this instance either because the claimant has more limited day-time care needs or is unable to prepare and cook a main meal.

There are therefore two ways in which the day condition may be satisfied. The first is that the claimant reasonably requires 'frequent attention throughout the day in connection with his bodily functions'.[145] This formulation has been the focus of a series of test cases before the courts. For many years this phrase was interpreted by the courts in the context of attendance allowance in a relatively narrow fashion, which was entirely consistent with the construction advanced by the (then) Department of Health and Social Security. Thus 'bodily functions' included 'breathing, hearing, seeing, eating, drinking, walking' and so on, all of which, in Lord Denning's famous explanation, 'an ordinary person—who is not suffering from any disability—does for himself. But they do not include cooking, shopping or any of the other things which a wife or daughter does as part of her domestic duties'.[146] Whilst it is easy to criticise the sexist use of language, Lord Denning's dictum certainly had the virtue of emphasising (almost certainly inadvertently) the gendered nature of care in contemporary society. Lord Denning also held that attention was only 'in connection with' the claimant's bodily functions if it was 'out of the ordinary—doing for the disabled person what a normal person [sic] would do for himself—such as cutting up food, lifting the cup to the mouth, helping to dress or undress at the toilet'.[147] This also served to exclude 'ordinary domestic duties' such as shopping and cooking meals. The introduction of DLA in 1992 with the inclusion of a new lowest rate care component represented a departure from this restrictive approach. For the first time an inability to prepare and cook a main meal became an explicit basis for the award of a disability benefit. The potential scope of DLA was widened

---

[143] The highest and middle rates of the DLA care component are identical to the two rates of AA: see further below.

[144] This is for the simple reason that it is unusual for a person to have night-time care or supervision needs but not to require day-time attention. One study reported that 85 per cent of recipients of the middle rate care component satisfied a day-care need and just 14 per cent a night-time need: K. Swales, *A Study of Disability Living Allowance and Attendance Allowance Awards*, DSS In-house Report 41 (London: DSS Social Research Branch, 1998), 23.

[145] SSCBA 1992, s. 72(1)(b)(i). See further D. Pollard, 'Attention in connection with bodily functions' (1998) 5 *J.S.S.L.* 175–94.

[146] *R v National Insurance Commissioner, ex p Secretary of State for Social Services* [1981] 1 W.L.R. 1017.

[147] Ibid., 1022.

further by two House of Lords' decisions, *Mallinson* and *Fairey* and, to a much lesser extent, by the decision in *Cockburn*.

The appellant in *Mallinson v Secretary of State for Social Security*[148] was a blind man who claimed the lower rate of attendance allowance (equivalent to the middle rate of the DLA care component). The fundamental question for the courts was whether the help which he required when walking outdoors could be regarded as 'attention . . . in connection with his bodily functions'.[149] Both the Commissioner and the majority of the Court of Appeal took the view that the bodily function in issue was walking and that, as the claimant could physically walk, the day condition was not met. In addition, he did not need attention in connection with the bodily function of seeing precisely because he could not see at all. However, a majority of the House of Lords held that the bodily function involved *was* seeing; any assistance which he required with seeing (for example, whilst out walking) was to be aggregated to determine whether such care was frequent throughout the day.[150] The fact that the claimant could not see at all could not prejudice his claim; Parliament could hardly have intended that a person with a total disability should be in a worse position than one with a partial disability.

Yet it is not sufficient that the attention is frequent throughout the day; it must also be 'required'. It is well-established that this means reasonably rather than medically required.[151] In the post-*Mallinson* case of *Secretary of State for Social Security v Fairey*[152] the House of Lords unanimously upheld the decision of the Commissioner and the majority of the Court of Appeal that this concept included 'such attention as may enable the claimant to carry out a reasonable level of social activity'.[153] In *Fairey* the claimant was a young woman who had been born deaf; she was unable to communicate effectively with hearing people outside her family without the assistance of an interpreter. Lord Slynn, in a powerful judgment, confirmed that the test was 'whether the attention is reasonably required to enable the severely disabled person as far as reasonably possible to live a normal life'.[154] Moreover, 'social life in the sense of mixing with others, taking part in activities with others, undertaking recreation and cultural activities can be part of normal life'.[155] The courts' traditional approach to the interpretation of the statutory care criteria was firmly located in the medical model of disability; the construction advanced by Lord Slynn as to what is 'reasonable' represents an implicit recognition of the social model of disability. The extent to which these test cases have had a significant impact on decision making at first instance

---

[148] [1994] 1 W.L.R. 630; see N. Wikeley, 'Case Analysis' (1994) 1 *J.S.S.L.* 80–5.

[149] There was no dispute that on the introduction of DLA he qualified for the lower rate mobility component.

[150] The actual decision on the facts was remitted to an adjudication officer to determine in accordance with the principles set out by the House of Lords.

[151] *R v Social Security Commissioner, ex p Connolly* [1986] 1 W.L.R. 424.

[152] [1997] 1 W.L.R. 799; see N. Wikeley, 'Benefits, Bodily Functions and Living with Disability' (1998) 61 *M.L.R.* 551–60.

[153] *Per* Commissioner Sanders at first instance in *CA/780/1991* at para. 10.

[154] N. 152 above, 814.   [155] Ibid., 815.

remains uncertain. An internal DSS study estimated that the outcome of awards would have been different in only 13 per cent of cases involving a *Mallinson* or *Fairey* point, or in just two per cent of cases overall.[156] Yet the Disability Living Allowance Advisory Board, which appears wedded to the medical model of disability, has still argued that 'benefit entitlement has been stretched well beyond the original policy intention of the legislation by commissioners' decisions'.[157]

The outcome of *Fairey* stands in stark contrast to that in the conjoined appeal of *Cockburn v Chief Adjudication Officer*.[158] This case concerned an elderly woman suffering from both incontinence and arthritis who had claimed attendance allowance. The issue was whether the additional laundry arising from these complaints generated a requirement for attention in connection with her bodily functions. The majority of the House of Lords held that this was not so: the laundry did not need to be done in the presence of the claimant and, in any event, was not a bodily function which able-bodied persons would necessarily normally perform for themselves. As Lord Clyde observed, 'assistance would cover activities done for the person. Attention implies services done to the person.'[159] The fact that the claimant's daughter took the bedding away to be washed was apparently a critical consideration in their lordships' judgments; had all the activities been conducted at the claimant's home, it appears that a majority of the House might well have allowed the claim.[160] This seems, at best, a narrow distinction upon which a claim should succeed or fail.

The alternative means of satisfying the day condition, the supervision test, has been the subject of much less contention in the case law. To qualify on this basis, the claimant must need continual[161] supervision throughout the day in order to avoid substantial danger to themselves or others.[162] It is accepted that 'supervision' is a more passive concept than 'attention', and includes being in a position to intervene in an emergency if required.[163] Furthermore, the remoteness of the risk of substantial danger materialising must be weighed against the seriousness of the consequences should the risk actually arise.

The criteria for the night condition use some of the same concepts as for the day condition but modified to suit the different context. Thus the care requirement is that the claimant reasonably requires 'prolonged or repeated attention in connection with his bodily functions' at night.[164] As a general rule, adjudicative custom and practice has been to interpret 'prolonged' as meaning at least twenty minutes, whereas 'repeated' clearly means more than once. This test is therefore less onerous in terms of the time required than either the day condition or indeed the attention test for the lowest rate care component. The rationale for this is the more demanding nature of care provided at night.[165] The supervision requirement, however, is set at an

---

[156] Swales (1998), n. 144 above, 76.   [157] Social Security Committee, n. 130 above, 4.
[158] [1997] 1 W.L.R. 799.   [159] Ibid., 824.   [160] See further Wikeley (1998), n. 152 above, 553.
[161] Bot not *continuous* (see *R(A) 1/73*): accordingly limited breaks in the supervision required may not preclude entitlement.
[162] SSCBA 1992, s. 72(1)(b)(ii).
[163] *Moran v Secretary of State for Social Services*, reported as an appendix to *R(A) 1/88*.
[164] SSCBA 1992, s. 72(1)(c)(i).   [165] Ogus, Barendt, and Wikeley (1995), 200.

extremely high threshold, partly because of the passive nature of the concept itself. This requires that a carer must be 'awake for a prolonged period or at frequent intervals for the purpose of watching over' the claimant.[166] The great majority of claimants with night needs qualify on the basis of the attention requirement: 'very few satisfied the "watching over" entitlement condition, and virtually nobody satisfied this alone'.[167]

A claimant who fails to satisfy either the day or night conditions may still qualify for the lowest rate care component of DLA. Again, there are two means of establishing entitlement. The first, derived from the standard day-time personal care criterion, is that the claimant requires attention from another person in connection with their bodily functions 'for a significant portion of the day (whether during a single period or a number of periods)'.[168] This segment of time is undefined by the legislation, but is usually taken to mean about an hour a day.[169] In practice few awards are made expressly on this basis; the great majority of recipients of the lowest rate care component qualify on the ground that they 'cannot prepare a cooked main meal [for themselves if they have] the ingredients'.[170] This somewhat bizarre statutory formulation, echoing the former and much discredited household duties test for housewives' non-contributory invalidity pension, is a purely hypothetical test. It was designed to act as a proxy for the assessment of basic physical and mental functions (for example, physical dexterity and strength in terms of chopping vegetables, using taps, and handling pans and mental aptitude in planning and organising the cooking of a main meal for one person). The Disability Living Allowance Advisory Board has expressed the opinion that the main meal test 'has been liable to misinterpretation and abuse', and has recommended that any future test 'should be based on practical evaluations of what the person is able to do (not what they actually do) rather than on abstract legal concepts'.[171] In practice the four types of disability which are sig-

---

[166] SSCBA 1992, s. 72(1)(c)(ii). The statutory language originally reflected the day-time supervision requirement. In *Moran* (n. 163 above) the Court of Appeal held that continual supervision could be provided at night where the carer was asleep nearby, ready to be summoned if needs be. The effect of this decision was reversed, and the current formulation inserted, by SSA 1988, s. 1: see N. Wikeley, 'Training, Targeting and Tidying Up' [1988] *J.S.W.L.* 277–92, 289–91.

[167] Swales (1998), n. 144 above, 24.

[168] SSCBA 1992, s. 72(1)(a)(i).

[169] *CDLA/58/1993*; note that there is no requirement that the care be needed 'throughout the day', as with the day condition. It may be that many short periods of attention could constitute a 'significant portion of the day' even if in aggregate they amount to less than an hour: see *CSDLA/29/1994* (but, if so, would they not meet the higher threshold of being 'frequent . . . throughout the day'?; the DSS view is that this would be 'quite rare' in practice: see Swales (1998), n. 144 above, 31). Both Commissioners' decisions are discussed in M. Rowland, *Medical and Disability Appeal Tribunals: The Legislation* (London: Sweet & Maxwell, 1998), 24–5.

[170] SSCBA 1992, s. 72(1)(a)(ii). An internal DSS study estimated that 71 per cent of claimants of the lowest rate care component satisfied the main meal test alone, 14 per cent met both tests and 8 per cent the 'significant portion' test only; a further 7 per cent were identified as being erroneously in payment: Swales (1998), n. 144 above, 22–3.

[171] Social Security Committee (1998), n. 130 above, 5. This comment demonstrates a worrying misunderstanding on the part of an independent government advisory body as to how the test should be used in practice, where the focus is very much on whether specific functions can be (rather than are) performed.

nificantly associated with awards of the lowest rate care component are those connected with seeing, dexterity, personal care, and communication.[172] The number of awards of the lowest rate care component (as with the lower rate mobility component) has far exceeded the expectations of policy makers. It was originally anticipated that some 140,000 claimants would qualify;[173] by 1997 there were 379,000 current awards.[174]

(iii) The reach of disability living allowance

The most comprehensive study to date of the extent to which DLA has met its objectives in terms of targeting is the report by Sainsbury, Hirst, and Lawton.[175] This devoted particular attention to the workings of the new lower rates. The policy intention behind the introduction of these rates was to extend help to those less severely disabled people who did not formerly qualify for attendance allowance or mobility allowance. Further research, drawing on the OPCS data, confirmed that disabled people in the middle of the severity range[176] faced the most acute financial difficulties.[177] Yet about two-thirds of lower rate awards are combined with an award of the higher or middle rate of the other component; recipients of dual lower rate awards or of one lower rate alone constitute only about one in ten of all DLA recipients. Consequently the new lower rates have principally extended *additional* help to those who were previously covered by attendance allowance or mobility allowance.[178] Only about one in four recipients of the lower rate care component were found to fall within the target categories of 5–6 on the OPCS severity of disability range, with the majority being more severely disabled than anticipated. The targeting of lower rate care awards is therefore 'less than precise, at least in terms of overall severity'.[179] A similar picture emerges in relation to the mobility component: those in receipt of the lower rate are not invariably less severely disabled than higher rate recipients; 'indeed, the distribution of lower rate mobility recipients by overall severity closely mirrors that of higher rate recipients, and neither differs markedly from that of unsuccessful claimants'.[180]

These findings, however, do not necessarily mean that the eligibility criteria for the lower rate awards are inappropriate or that they are wrongly targeted. The reason for this is that overall severity as judged by the OPCS criteria encompasses more than those disabilities which give rise to care or mobility needs alone.[181]

---

[172] Sainsbury, Hirst, and Lawton (1995), n. 140 above, 48.
[173] DSS (1990), n. 129 above, 28.   [174] DSS (1997), n. 142 above, Table E2.06, 196.
[175] N. 140 above; see also M. Daly and M. Noble, 'The reach of disability benefits: an examination of disability living allowance' (1996) 18 *J.S.W.F.L.* 37–51.
[176] Using the standard OPCS scale of 1–10, with 1 representing the least severe and 10 the most severe disabilities. These are based on measurements of disability in 13 different functional areas (e.g. locomotion, dexterity, and behaviour); the separate scores are combined into a single index by taking a weighted sum of the three most serious disabilities, whilst ensuring an equal distribution across the final 10-point scale.
[177] R. Berthoud, J. Lakey, and S. McKay, *The Economic Problems of Disabled People* (London: PSI, 1993).
[178] Sainsbury, Hirst, and Lawton (1995), n. 140 above, 8.   [179] Ibid., 38.   [180] Ibid., 39.
[181] Ibid., 42.

Conversely eligibility for DLA is based on the effects of disability, rather than on either the nature or the severity of the disability.[182] This helps to explain why so many lower rate recipients fall above the target severity categories 5 and 6 on the OPCS scale. In part this is because claimants are often multiply (and hence severely) disabled. Moreover, many of the disabilities they have are unrelated to the DLA eligibility criteria, albeit that they contribute to an overall severity score.[183] The study none the less concluded that the new lower rate criteria succeed in identifying beneficiaries with distinct patterns of disability, and that by and large adjudication officers are in turn successful in consistently identifying those who are eligible for an award.[184] That said, it was also concluded that the boundary between lower rate recipients and unsuccessful claimants, especially on the care side, was 'somewhat blurred'.[185] In addition, unsuccessful claimants were often as poor as DLA recipients and, although somewhat less severely disabled than successful applicants, were just as likely to report extra disability-related costs.[186] This suggests that in practice 'the new lower rate awards are unlikely to have smoothed the so-called "cliff-edges" in provision between severely disabled people and less severely disabled people who would have failed to qualify for either of these former benefits'.[187]

Both the caseload and the expenditure on disability living allowance doubled between its introduction in 1992 and 1997–8.[188] Spending on DLA accounted for one-quarter of expenditure on disability benefits in 1993–4 and had risen to one-third by 1998–9, increasing on average by 11 per cent per annum in real terms.[189] Various reasons have been advanced for this growth, including take-up campaigns, demographic changes and the consequences of closures of long-stay institutions.[190] There have also been repeated concerns expressed about the standard of adjudication in DLA cases. The chaotic implementation of disability living allowance in 1992 resulted in rushed and inadequate adjudication.[191] In 1998 an internal DSS study concluded that almost a quarter of all awards lacked sufficient evidence upon which to

---

[182] Sainsbury, Hirst, and Lawton (1995), 53.　　　[183] Ibid., 54.

[184] Ibid., 59, 72. See further M. Hirst, 'Variations in the Administration of Disability Living Allowance' (1997) 31 *Social Policy & Administration* 136–56.

[185] Sainsbury, Hirst, and Lawton (1995), n. 140 above, 73. One of the reasons for this may be the failure of the DLA scheme to accommodate the needs of those with mental health problems; see further below in section 6. Hirst, n. 184 above, also identifies considerable variations in the interpretation of the criteria for the main meals test: 149.

[186] Sainsbury, Hirst, and Lawton (1995), n. 140 above, 35.

[187] Ibid., 41.

[188] Social Security Committee (1998), n. 130 above, vii.

[189] DSS, *Social Security Departmental Report: The Government's Expenditure Plans 1999/2000*, Cm 4214 (London: The Stationery Office, 1999), 86.

[190] N. 130 above; see also ibid., 2.

[191] In 1992 between 65 per cent and 70 per cent of awards were life awards; as one Minister has since conceded, 'many of those awards were somewhat flaky in the sense that they were not fully justified by the evidence'; Baroness Hollis of Heigham, Social Security Committee (1998), n. 130 above, 104; see also 111. Such concerns resulted in the highly controversial Benefit Integrity Project, intended to identify erroneous awards, and severely criticised by the Social Security Committee, ibid., xvii–xxv.

enable a decision to have been made.[192] The Disability Living Allowance Advisory Board adopted an even more critical stance, taking the view that the award was 'in conflict with the facts' in 63 per cent of cases in the sample,[193] and so concluding that the administration of DLA (and attendance allowance) 'is seriously flawed'.[194] In a review of these findings, Berthoud suggests that about one in ten payments of DLA 'are going to the wrong people'.[195] Yet at the same time take-up remains a significant problem: the most recent provisional statistics suggest that take-up for the care component is between 30 and 50 per cent and in the range of 50 to 70 per cent for the mobility component.[196] Even amongst the most severely disabled groups (OPCS categories 9 and 10), the estimated take-up is 50–70 per cent (care component) and 60–80 per cent (mobility component).[197]

These findings led the House of Commons Social Security Committee to conclude that the failings of disability living allowance are fundamental and can only be addressed by radical surgery:

> In its present form, DLA is an unstable benefit and its future, if unchanged, is almost impossible to predict. Its boundaries, which were far from clear to begin with, have been stretched in unforeseen and inconsistent ways by court decisions. The structure of the benefit and its administrative procedure fails in terms of simplicity and workability.[198]

The Government's initial response has been cautious.[199] The 1998 Green Paper on reform of disability benefits included notice of just one substantive change to the eligibility rules for disability living allowance, promising to extend entitlement to the higher rate mobility component to three and four year olds.[200] The other changes proposed were of a procedural nature, but were clearly designed in the long term to provide scope for limiting the further expansion of the benefit's boundaries.[201] It remains to be seen whether the Government seeks to institute a more radical reform in the eligibility rules for disability living allowance, such as developing a points-based 'all living test' analogous to the all work test for incapacity benefit (above).[202]

---

[192] Swales (1998), n. 144 above, 21 and 62–71. An accuracy rate of 71 per cent for all DLA adjudication has been reported by officials: House of Commons Social Security Committee, *Disability Living Allowance*, Third Report, Minutes of Evidence, H.C. 63, Session 1998–9 (London: The Stationery Office, 1999), 11.

[193] This might mean that the award was either too high or too low or for an inappropriate duration: see Social Security Committee (1998), n. 130 above, 24.

[194] Ibid., 2.

[195] R. Berthoud, *Disability Benefits: A review of the issues and options for reform* (York: Joseph Rowntree Foundation, 1998), 55.

[196] DSS, *First Findings from the Disability Follow-up to the Family Resources Survey*, Research Summary No. 5 (London: DSS, 1998), 13.

[197] Ibid., 13.   [198] Social Security Committee, n. 130 above, xxvii.

[199] Given the political sensitivities involved, this was to be expected: both the previous Conservative and the present Labour Government have experienced serious political difficulties over disability issues.

[200] DSS, *A New Contract for Welfare: Support for disabled people*, Cm 4103 (London: The Stationery Office, 1998), 11.

[201] Thus 'life' awards are replaced by 'indefinite' awards: ibid., 12.

[202] See also Social Security Committee (1998), n. 130 above, xiii and DSS, *A New Contract for Welfare: Support for disabled people*, Cm 4103 (London: The Stationery Office, 1998), 13.

The Government has certainly intimated that more radical change is on the agenda.[203]

B. Attendance Allowance

Attendance allowance (AA) survived the 1992 reforms but is now exclusively a benefit for people with care needs who make their first claim after attaining the age of sixty-five. Unlike the care component of DLA, it only comprises two rates: a higher rate (equivalent to the highest rate of the DLA care component) and a lower rate (confusingly equivalent to the middle rate of the DLA care component). The high levels of care needs amongst this group of people are reflected in the fact that amongst new claims there are approximately equal numbers of awards of each rate.[204] The most common disabling conditions are similar to those for DLA, although there tend to be more circulatory and eye- and ear-related conditions.[205] There is, however, a significant difference in terms of the factual bases of awards of middle rate DLA care component and the lower rate of AA. Amongst DLA claimants, numbers are nearly evenly split as between the 'attention' and 'supervision' heads of entitlement.[206] The picture is very different amongst the elderly, with nearly 90 per cent meeting the 'supervision' test, perhaps reflecting the higher risks associated with a propensity to fall in old age.[207]

The rules governing entitlement to AA are identical to those that apply to DLA in all bar two important respects. Thus a claimant who claims for the first time after reaching the age of sixty-five and who satisfies the day- and night-time tests qualifies for the higher rate of AA, while the day (or night) condition alone leads to an award of the lower rate of AA. The first and fundamental difference is that there is no parallel under the AA scheme to the lowest rate of the DLA care component. The second is that whereas the prior qualifying period for DLA is three months, it has remained at six months for AA claimants. It is difficult to perceive any justification for this continuing differentiation.

The only significant change to be made by the Welfare Reform and Pensions Act 1999 is to introduce a regulation-making power for attendance allowance which enables circumstances to be prescribed in which the day or night conditions are to

---

[203] 'In the short-term, the priority is to develop more effective legislative definitions of the key terms such as "attention" and "supervision". In the longer term, research is needed on alternative approaches to defining care and mobility needs': DSS, *Reply by the Government to the Fourth Report of the Select Committee on Disability Living Allowance*, Cm 4007 (London: The Stationery Office, 1998), 3.

[204] In 1996–7 there were 153,000 new awards (including awards on review or appeal) of the higher rate and 167,000 of the lower rate of AA: DSS (1997), n. 142 above, Table E1.01, 185. Overall, in 1997, there were 486,000 higher rate and 681,000 lower rate AA awards in payment: ibid., Table E1.05, 188.

[205] Swales (1998), n. 144 above, 11.

[206] Some 39 per cent of claimants meet the 'frequent attention' test, 34 per cent the requirement for 'continual supervision' and 27 per cent both: ibid., 24.

[207] Some 62 per cent qualified on the basis of 'continual supervision' alone, 8 per cent on 'frequent attention' alone, whilst 26 per cent were found to meet both criteria and 4 per cent were regarded as non-eligible: ibid., 27.

be taken as satisfied or not, as the case may be.[208] The rationale for this is unclear. It was presented at one level as merely a tidying up exercise, mirroring an existing provision for disability living allowance.[209] However, this latter provision has only been used to make special provision for claimants undergoing renal dialysis,[210] and an equivalent (if slightly different) regulation already applies also to attendance allowance in such cases.[211] It seems that the real underlying intention is to use the enabling power in future more widely to respond to developments in the case law.[212]

5. MEANS-TESTED BENEFITS

A. Income Support[213]

There is ample evidence of a strong correlation between disability and poverty, with disabled people being disproportionately represented amongst the ranks of recipients of means-tested benefits.[214] The prescribed groups of claimants who are eligible for income support, and hence are relieved of the need to 'sign on', include a wide variety of disabled people and carers.[215] Furthermore, the principal means-tested benefits (income support, housing benefit, and council tax benefit) make special provision for disabled claimants in two main ways. First, disability may be a ground for relaxing the rigour of the regulations in various respects. The most notable example is that DLA is disregarded in its entirety in assessing income for the purposes of means-tested benefits, whereas most other benefits count pound for pound against entitlement. The rationale for this is that DLA is assumed to be a contribution towards meeting the extra costs associated with disability, rather than everyday living expenses. Other forms of special consideration for disability tend to operate at the margins of eligibility. For example, the standard rules governing

---

[208] s. 66(1), inserting a new SSCBA 1992, s. 64(4).

[209] Ibid., s. 72(7).   [210] N. 132 above, reg. 7.

[211] Social Security (Attendance Allowance) Regulations 1991 (S.I. 1991 No. 2740), reg. 5, made under the specific authority of SSCBA 1992, s. 67(1).

[212] Thus the Explanatory Notes state that the power may be invoked 'when the conditions of entitlement to DLA need to be amended or clarified: for example, if a judicial decision departed significantly from the policy intention' (Notes on Bill, 98). But as the Social Security Committee has observed, 'allowing the rules to be changed more easily is no substitute for getting them right in the first place', n. 130 above, xii.

[213] The discussion here is confined to income support, but applies equally to housing benefit and council tax benefit. There is no special provision within the working families tax credit scheme for disabled people, but see further below on disability working allowance and now disabled person's tax credit. The structure of income support and its main provisions are outlined in Chapter 6.

[214] A. Walker and L. Walker, 'Disability and Financial Need—The Failure of the Social Security System' in Dalley (1991), n. 120 above, 20–56, remains a compelling analysis. See also Berthoud, Lakey, and McKay (1993), n. 177 above. In the study by Sainsbury, Hirst, and Lawton (1995), n. 140 above, 35 per cent of DLA claimants were in receipt of income support: 27.

[215] Income Support (General) Regulations 1987, Sched. 1B, paras 4–6 (carers), 7 (persons incapable of work), 8 (disabled workers), 10–11 (disabled students), 12 (deaf students), 13 (blind persons); note also paras 24–7 (persons appealing against a decision that they are not incapable of work).

income support housing costs preclude payment of the extra interest incurred where a claimant increases the size of their mortgage whilst on benefit. However, this rule does not apply where the mortgage is extended to buy a home which is better suited to the needs of a disabled person.[216]

Secondly, and more fundamentally, recognition of a person's status as being incapable of work or disabled leads to the award of one or more premiums in the context of these three main benefits. Four of the eight premiums in these schemes are directly related to disability: the disability premium, the severe disability premium, the disabled child premium, and the carer's premium. Moreover, three of these (with the notable exception of the disability premium) can be paid in addition to any other premium payable. But it is inherent in the very nature of premiums that they are a crude method of meeting individual need (see Chapter 5). As the SSAC commented when income support was introduced, 'to be soundly based any system of group rates ought to derive from research about the real differences in requirements between claimants, rather than simply institutionalize existing arbitrary distinctions or provide a sophisticated way of dividing the deserving and the undeserving poor'.[217] However, the major OPCS study of disability, which formed the backdrop to the introduction of DLA, did not report until after the Fowler Review had determined the structure of income support and the other means-tested benefits.

There are a number of different ways of qualifying for the disability premium. The usual way is a form of passporting: receipt of a 'qualifying benefit' automatically leads on to the award of the disability premium. The qualifying benefits include DLA, attendance allowance, and the long-term rate of incapacity benefit.[218] Other ways of qualifying for the disability premium include being registered blind or being granted an NHS invalid 'trike'. Couples receive the higher couple rate of the disability premium so long as at least one of the partners meets the qualifying condition.[219] The Labour Government's latest reforms include the introduction of a new higher rate of the disability premium,[220] to be paid to all income support claimants aged under sixty who are in receipt of the highest rate of the care component of DLA.[221]

---

[216] Similarly, the upper capital limit for disability working allowance was £16,000, unlike the £8,000 for family credit, in recognition of the possibility that disabled people may have savings to pay for adaptations to the home, special equipment, etc: see Ogus, Barendt, and Wikeley (1995), 531.

[217] SSAC, *Fourth Report* (London: HMSO, 1985), para. 3.5. As the SSAC has commented more recently, the logic behind the disability premium remains unclear: 'Either DLA is regarded as an adequate contribution to the extra costs of disability, to be paid regardless of need, or individual financial circumstances should dictate the level of payment. The present approach appears to back both horses at once': SSAC, *Social Security Provision for Disability: A Case for Change?* (London: The Stationery Office, 1997), 19.

[218] i.e. the claimant must have been incapable of work for at least 52 weeks; before 1995, this period was 26 weeks.

[219] If the claim is based on incapacity for work, it is the claimant who must meet the requirement.

[220] As part of the so-called Disability Income Guarantee.

[221] DSS (1998), n. 202 above, 10. This will help to bridge the gap between the ordinary disability premium and the severe disability premium. This effectively equalises the position for those aged under and over 60 respectively, as disabled people aged over 60 are already eligible for the higher pensioner premium, which is paid at a higher rate than the disability premium.

Receipt of the disability premium can already make a significant difference to the claimant's weekly income.[222] For this reason a substantial proportion of appeals against decisions under the all work test that a person is not incapable of work are in fact lodged by people in receipt of income support rather than incapacity benefit claimants.

The severe disability premium (SDP)[223] constitutes a significant cash enhancement on the ordinary disability premium[224] and the qualifying conditions are accordingly very tightly drawn. As a result eligibility for the severe disability premium is one of the most complex areas in the whole field of social security law. The enabling power in the primary legislation is extremely vague about premiums in general, merely stating that the applicable amount 'shall be such amount or aggregate of amounts as may be prescribed'.[225] There is, however, specific provision in the Act for the payment of a severe disability premium, as a result of concerted lobbying at the time of the passage of the original Social Security Act 1986.[226] The actual regulations governing entitlement to the SDP have been subject to amendment on several occasions, in large part prompted by the outcome of test cases.

There are three cumulative conditions which determine entitlement to the SDP. First, the claimant must receive a qualifying benefit; in this context this means the middle or highest rate of the DLA care component.[227] In the case of a couple, both partners must receive a qualifying benefit in order to receive the couple rate of the premium.[228] Secondly, there must be no non-dependant aged eighteen or over 'normally residing' with the claimant. Thirdly, there must be no-one who receives ICA for looking after the claimant. In *Chief Adjudication Officer v Foster*[229] the Social Security Commissioner held that the second and third qualifying conditions were *ultra vires*. In his view, in order to fall within the primary legislation, the prescribed conditions had to be specifically related to the extent of the claimant's disability. This decision was reversed in the Court of Appeal[230] and the House of Lords,[231] which held that the legislation granted the Secretary of State considerable discretion in defining severe disability for this purpose.[232] However, the second of the three qualifying conditions

---

[222] For example, in 1999–2000 the personal allowance for a single person aged 25 or over was £51.40; the disability premium of £21.90 represented an increase of more than 40 per cent on the basic level of income support.

[223] Not to be confused with the severe disablement allowance (SDA), a quite separate benefit in its own right which is abolished by the Welfare Reform and Pensions Act 1999 (see above at pp. 376–7).

[224] In 1999–2000, SDP was paid at £39.75 for single people and £79.50 for couples (the latter is almost as much again as the standard couple rate of the personal allowance). Moreover, this is paid on top of the standard disability premium.

[225] SSCBA 1992, s. 135(1). This has enabled both the introduction of new premiums (e.g. the carer's premium) and the withdrawal of existing ones (e.g. the lone-parent premium).

[226] SSCBA 1992, s. 135(5) and (6).

[227] Or the equivalent rates of attendance allowance.

[228] Or the claimant must receive the qualifying benefit and their partner be registered blind.

[229] [1993] AC 754.

[230] [1992] QB 31, Lord Donaldson MR strongly dissenting.   [231] See n. 229 above.

[232] See further the case notes by D. Feldman and N. Wikeley (1993) 109 *L.Q.R.* 544–6 and N. Harris (1993) 56 *M.L.R.* 710–21.

was redrafted in order to reverse the effect of the Court of Appeal's judgment in *Chief Adjudication Officer v Bate.*[233] Here the Court of Appeal had held that whereas a severely disabled young woman resided with her parents, her parents did not reside with her, as they were the householders and joint tenants. On this construction the parents did not fall within the definition of 'non-dependants' so as to exclude their daughter from receipt of the SDP. The House of Lords subsequently reversed the decision of the Court of Appeal, holding that the 'residing with' was entirely mutual in this type of situation.[234]

The other two premiums related to disability are more straightforward in terms of their eligibility criteria. The disabled child premium is paid where the claimant is responsible for a child in the household who either receives disability living allowance (at any rate) or is registered blind. It is paid at the same rate as the adult disability premium. As Mesher and Wood comment, the range of need within this broad category will be vast; under the former supplementary benefits regime, children with the most severe disabilities would have qualified for very substantial extra weekly payments by way of additional requirements.[235] The carer's premium, introduced as part of the package of reforms which led up to DLA, is paid where the claimant or their partner is receiving or treated[236] as receiving ICA.

B. Disability Working Allowance and Disabled Person's Tax Credit

Disability working allowance (DWA) was introduced in 1992 as a variant on family credit to assist disabled people in low-paid employment for at least sixteen hours a week.[237] It was originally envisaged that 50,000 people would benefit from DWA,[238] but by 1999 the claimant population was only 16,000.[239] Although the rejection rate on claims fell from 90 per cent at the outset to about 20 per cent by 1996,[240] the estimated rate of take-up was still just 21 per cent.[241] Awareness of disability working allowance was very low, and most recipients had only heard about the benefit *after*

---

[233] [1995] 3 F.C.R. 145; see G. Ashton, 'Case Analysis' (1995) 2 *J.S.S.L.* 155–9: 'An SSAT chairman dealing with SDP appeals during the past five years has been like a junior linesman in a football match in which the senior linesman keeps moving the goalposts; then, just before the final whistle, the referee declares that the game should have been rugby and awards extra time, and now the appeal committee is considering what game the players should have been playing.'

[234] [1996] 1 W.L.R. 814; see N. Harris, 'Case Analysis' (1996) 3 *J.S.S.L.* 130–4. This litigation also concerned the efficacy of the tortuous anti-test-case provisions, designed to limit the extent to which arrears could be awarded in 'look-alike' cases.

[235] J. Mesher and P. Wood, *Income-Related Benefits: The Legislation* (London: Sweet & Maxwell, 1998), 321.

[236] For example, where the carer would receive ICA but for the overlapping benefit rules.

[237] See Ogus, Barendt, and Wikeley (1995), 529–34.

[238] DSS, *The Way Ahead: Benefits for Disabled People*, Cm 917 (London: HMSO, 1990), 35.

[239] DSS, *Social Security Departmental Report: The Government's Expenditure Plans 1999/2000*, Cm 4214 (London: The Stationery Office, 1999), 122. See also Chapter 2, section 5.

[240] K. Rowlingson and R. Berthoud, *Disability, Benefits and Employment*, DSS Research Report No. 54 (London: HMSO, 1996), 174. The two main reasons for disallowances were either that the claimant was not in paid work at the relevant time or that they were not in receipt of one of the qualifying benefits.

[241] Ibid., 177.

they had actually started working.[242] Indeed, between 1992 and 1995 only 30,000 of the 1.5 million working-age recipients of one of the principal incapacity benefits[243] moved off benefits and into full-time work, nearly all of whom made this transition without the help of disability working allowance, the one benefit specifically designed for this purpose.[244]

The Labour Government's commitment to promote a greater integration between the tax and benefits systems necessarily meant that both family credit and disability working allowance, as in-work benefits, would be the first to be reformed. Disability working allowance was thus replaced by the disabled person's tax credit, with effect from October 1999.[245] The tax credit is more generous than its predecessor benefit in that the threshold, beyond which the tax credit is withdrawn, has been set at a higher level and the taper[246] itself has been reduced from 70 per cent to 55 per cent. In addition, the rules governing childcare costs and qualifying benefits have been relaxed somewhat.[247] A 'fast-track gateway' has also been promised for those who become long-term sick or disabled whilst in work, so enabling them to claim the new credit while still in work.[248]

The fundamental weakness of strategies such as disability working allowance and disabled person's tax credit is that they focus on the supply side. As Berthoud has noted, the failure of disability working allowance suggests that disabled people are not much affected by incentives.[249] The demand side of the equation is therefore equally if not more important. Disabled people themselves identify the main barriers to work to be the general lack of jobs, employers' perceptions of disabled people, and the limitations imposed by impairments (including the willingness or otherwise of employers to accommodate special needs).[250] Thus the ultimate success of the disabled person's tax credit will depend on the extent to which measures such as the Disability Discrimination Act 1995 and the Disability Rights Commission facilitate the employment of disabled people, as well as the state of the economy as a whole.

---

[242] Ibid., 146–7. Only about 200 of the 3,500 people claiming DWA in October 1993 had actually been encouraged into work by the benefit.

[243] i.e. during this period invalidity benefit, SDA, or income support with a disability premium in payment.

[244] K. Rowlingson and R. Berthoud (1996), n. 240 above, at 203.

[245] This is assessed and paid by the Inland Revenue, although it will not be available through the wage packet until April 2000. See generally Tax Credits Schemes (etc) Regulations 1999 (S.I. 1999 No. 2487)

[246] i.e. the rate at which the benefit/credit is withdrawn above a prescribed income threshold.

[247] For example, the qualifying period has been extended from 56 days to 182 days.

[248] Inland Revenue Press Release 99/99, issued 17 May 1999.

[249] R. Berthoud, *Disability Benefits: A review of the issues and options for reform* (York: Joseph Rowntree Foundation, 1998), 38. As Berthoud observes, the effect of incentives will vary according to the target group. Men tend to work, regardless of incentives, because they expect and are expected to do so; pensioners by and large do not do so, for precisely the opposite reasons.

[250] See generally K. Rowlingson and R. Berthoud (1996), n. 240 above, ch. 8. For an American study, see E. Schechter, 'Work While Receiving Disability Insurance Benefits: Additional Findings From the New Beneficiary Follow-up Survey' (1997) 60 *Social Security Bulletin*, 3–17.

6. MENTAL HEALTH, INCAPACITY, AND DISABILITY

Physical incapacity or disability has historically represented the paradigm case for support within the social security system, reflecting prevailing models of care and functional ability defined by the performance of tasks.[251] Yet those with mental health problems number amongst the most vulnerable in the community: research has demonstrated that those unemployed people with conditions relating to depression, mental illness, confusion, or communication problems were least likely amongst all people with disabilities to find work.[252] Social security law simplistically compartmentalises disabilities into being *either* physical *or* mental in origin, but the clinical reality is very different, as physical and psychological disorders often overlap in various complex ways.[253] The consequences of this somewhat arbitrary dichotomy of physical and mental disability pervades both the substantive and procedural aspects of establishing entitlement to benefit. This is evident in the case of both the major disability benefits—incapacity benefit and DLA.[254]

We have already seen in the case of incapacity benefit that there are entirely separate scoring systems under the all work test for physical and mental disabilities, with complex deeming provisions to deal with the claimant who suffers from both. The arbitrary demarcation line between the two categories of illness is reinforced by the regulations, which provide that physical disabilities can only be scored if they arise 'from a specific bodily disease or disablement' whereas mental health problems can only count if they arise 'from some specific mental illness or disablement'.[255] It is not uncommon to find a combination of depression and a relatively minor musculo-skeletal condition leading to serious mobility problems; yet this provision means that the disability as regards mobility must be deconstructed and account taken only of the (less significant) physical causative element. There is, however, as yet no published empirical research data to assist in forming a view as to whether it is more difficult for a claimant with a mental disability, as compared with one with a physical disability, to satisfy the all work test.[256]

---

[251] M. Hirst and R. Sainsbury, *Social Security and Mental Health,* Social Policy Report No. 6 (York: Social Policy Research Unit, 1996), 1, citing J. Twigg and K. Atkin, *Carers Perceived: Policy and Practice in Informal Care* (Buckingham: Open University Press, 1994).

[252] K. Rowlingson and R. Berthoud (1996), n. 240 above, 59.

[253] M. Hirst and R. Sainsbury, n. 251 above, 7, citing A. House, R. Mayou, and C. Mallinson (eds.), *Psychiatric Aspects of Physical Disease* (London: Royal College of Physicians and Royal College of Psychiatrists, 1995). See also K. Brown, J. Bird, and D. Bates, 'Assessing the psychosomatic component of disability' (1997) 4 *J.S.S.L.* 102–8.

[254] As has been recognised by Government: DSS (1998), n. 203 above, 5.

[255] Social Security (Incapacity for Work) (General) Regulations 1995 (S.I. 1995 No. 311), reg. 25(3) as amended by S.I. 1996 No. 3207. For a discussion of the position before the amendment, see J. M. Fotheringham, 'The "all work test" and physical disability caused by psychiatric illness' (1997) 4 *J.S.S.L.* 15–16.

[256] The writer's purely anecdotal impression is that claimants have to have very serious mental health problems before they reach 10 points under the all work test, whilst claimants with physical conditions, which may well rate lower on the OPCS scale in terms of their overall disability, may find it easier to reach the necessary 15 points. This impression is shared by advice workers: see House of Commons Social Security Committee, *Incapacity Benefit,* H.C. 80, Session 1996–7 (London: The Stationery Office, 1997), memorandum submitted by CPAG, 27.

The substantive constraints of eligibility rules are even more evident in the context of DLA.[257] The most common disabling conditions amongst recipients of DLA are musculo-skeletal, mental health, and nervous system problems.[258] Yet the distribution of awards for these different groups across the various rates is very uneven. Most notably, access to the higher rate mobility component is denied to those suffering from problems which are 'purely' mental in their origin.[259] Consequently recipients of the higher rate mobility component are more likely to have musculo-skeletal problems, while claimants with lower rate mobility awards are most likely to suffer from conditions associated with mental health or the nervous system: with the result that, judged by the OPCS criteria, they may in fact be *more* disabled.[260] Yet with the exception of the very narrowly defined group of severely mentally impaired people, those with severe learning difficulties or acute mental health problems are confined to the lower rate mobility component.[261]

The care component of DLA, on the other hand, is explicitly available to those who are 'severely physically *or* mentally disabled'.[262] The day and night conditions of entitlement can also be satisfied on the basis of either personal care or supervision needs. At first sight this suggests parity of treatment. On closer examination, however, there is an argument that this equality is largely formalistic in that effectively a higher threshold is required of those with mental disabilities. In the context of the day test, a claimant must have personal care needs which are '*frequent* . . . throughout the day', while the supervision requirement is met only if the need is '*continual* . . . throughout the day'.[263] As the authoritative annotated guide to the legislation observes, 'the fact that there are *lengthy* periods when no attention is required does not mean that attention is not required frequently throughout the day'.[264] The same commentator notes that although 'continual' is wider than 'continuous', this means only that 'the condition may be satisfied even though the claimant may safely be left alone for *short* periods'.[265]

These tests impact differently on those with physical and mental disabilities respectively as in practice there is a strong correlation between attention needs and musculo-skeletal problems on the one hand and mental health or nervous system disorders and supervision needs on the other.[266] It may also be that these distinctions mean that in terms of the practice of adjudication a more demanding standard is being applied by decision makers in relation to claimants with mental health

---

[257] For detailed proposals for a dedicated mental health test for entitlement to DLA, see the evidence of Elizabeth Bray in House of Commons Social Security Committee (1998), n. 130 above, 119–21.
[258] Swales (1998), n. 144 above, 11.
[259] With the very narrowly defined exception of the severe mental impairment rules: see n. 138 above.
[260] Swales (1998), n. 144 above, 12; see also Sainsbury, Hirst, and Lawton (1995), n. 140 above, 31.
[261] Unless they can establish that they are 'virtually unable to walk', a problematic test in this context: see N. Wikeley (1999), n. 138 above, 31.
[262] SSCBA 1992, s. 72(1).   [263] Ibid., s. 72(1)(b), emphasis added.
[264] Rowland (1998), n. 169 above, 25, emphasis added.   [265] Ibid., 27, emphasis added.
[266] Swales (1998), n. 144 above, 35.

problems than those with purely physical disabilities. A review of awards by the
Disability Living Allowance Advisory Board concluded that the level of consistency
between the main disabling condition and the stated care needs was 57 per cent in
the case of mental health problems and 49 per cent for nervous system disorders,
but only 28 per cent for musculo-skeletal conditions.[267]

An analogous point can be made with regard to both the night condition and the
test for the lowest rate DLA care component. We have already seen that it is
extremely difficult to satisfy the night-time supervision test.[268] So far as the lowest
rate care component is concerned, there is no specific provision for those with mental disabilities. The 'attention with bodily functions' test relates to a significant portion of the day, which may be as little as an hour a day.[269] There is no equivalent for
those with supervision needs.[270] Research has also demonstrated that one of the key
predictors associated with unsuccessful DLA applicants, as against recipients of the
lowest rate care component, is a tendency for the claimant to get so upset as to run
away, which clearly implies supervision needs.[271] It is true that the main meal test
encompasses mental health functions, such as planning and organising, but the prime
focus is again on physical functional limitations.

These substantive eligibility rules for DLA must be seen in the context of a
claiming and assessment process which at the best of times may appear complex
and bewildering; as Davis observes, 'the combination of managing mental illness
and claiming in a climate of benefit change can be daunting'.[272] The extensive DLA
questionnaire creates particular difficulties for those with mental health problems,
'partly because of the perceived imbalance between questions about physical
impairments and mental health but, more fundamentally, because the kinds of
questions involved fail to take sufficient account of the fluctuating and often
unpredictable nature of mental illness'.[273] A further problem is the emphasis on
self-assessment in the claiming process, which 'places a considerable burden on
people already coping with anxiety or depression, impaired perception and thinking, loss of motivation, mood swings including suicidal thoughts, or the side effects
of medication'.[274]

[267] Swales (1998), 44. [268] See above. [269] See n. 169 above.
[270] It is symptomatic of the confusion in this area that the SSAC itself has referred quite erroneously
to the test being that attention *or supervision* is required for a significant portion of the day: SSAC, *Social
Security Provision for Disability: A Case for Change?* (London: The Stationery Office, 1997), 14.
[271] Sainsbury, Hirst, and Lawton (1995), n. 140 above, 59–60.
[272] A. Davis, 'Users' Perspectives and Problems 2: What the research tells us' in G. Zarb (ed.), *Social
Security and Mental Health; Report on the SSAC Workshop*, SSAC Research Paper 7 (London: HMSO, 1996),
24–34, 31.
[273] G. Zarb, 'Social Security and Mental Health: Defining the Issues' in ibid., 3–10, 4.
[274] M. Hirst and R. Sainsbury (1996), n. 251 above, 18.

7. CONCLUSION

This chapter has demonstrated how the social security system as it relates to disability is 'piecemeal, poorly conceived and fails to achieve its purpose'[275]—assuming, that is, that there is indeed a discernible purpose. The Labour Government which was elected in 1997 came into office with no clear policy in respect of disability benefits.[276] However, since its election the Government has identified a series of key principles which, it is said, will underpin its programme of reconstructing the welfare state.[277] Three of those principles have direct relevance to the debate over the reform of disability benefits:

Principle One: The new welfare state should help and encourage people of working age to work where they are capable of doing so.

Principle Two: The public and private sectors should work in partnership to ensure that, wherever possible, people are insured against foreseeable risks and make provision for their retirement.

Principle Four: Those who are disabled should get the support they need to lead a fulfilling life with dignity.

The changes to incapacity benefit in the Welfare Reform and Pensions Act 1999 clearly reflect the first two principles in the Labour Government's reform strategy. The central philosophy, underlying the first principle, has been declared as being to encourage work for those who can and providing security for those who cannot.[278] The advent of the single gateway demonstrates, as Deacon has argued, that in effect 'the government is seeking to shift the dividing line between those who are expected to work and those who are not, with a greater proportion of lone parents and people with disabilities included within the labour force'.[279] In this context Diller's analysis of the basis for the award of disability benefits[280] in the United States is equally pertinent in the United Kingdom:

Public benefit programs use the concept of disability to create an economic and moral boundary that separates those who are required to work from those whose participation in the labor force is excused. Despite its appearance of medical objectivity, disability is a socially constructed status that can be defined in any number of ways. Definitions of disability both reflect and reinforce a series of normative values about the nature and extent of the social

---

[275] B. Massie, *Disabled People and Social Justice*, Commission on Social Justice, issue paper 12 (London: IPPR, 1994), 30.

[276] The Report of the Commission on Social Justice, an independent body set up by the late John Smith MP, concluded rather lamely that: 'The financial needs of disabled people must be addressed by any government committed to social justice, but further debate is needed about how best to do so': Commission on Social Justice, *Social Justice: Strategies for National Renewal* (London: Vintage, 1994), 245.

[277] See generally Green Paper (1998).

[278] DSS, *A New Contract for Welfare: Principles into practice*, Cm 4101 (London: The Stationery Office, 1998), Prime Minister's foreword, 1.

[279] A. Deacon, 'The Green Paper on Welfare Reform: A Case for Enlightened Self-interest?' (1998) 69 *Political Quarterly*, 306–11, 307.

[280] 'Disability' in the US context means 'incapacity' in the UK.

obligation to work. All disability benefit programs, like other public benefit programs, are created by a process of boundary drawing—a series of political, economic and moral decisions
that include some individuals in the category while excluding others.[281]

The emphasis on 'the centrality of paid work'[282] necessarily undermines the case
for incapacity benefit as available for an indefinite period. Indeed, there were initially
indications that the incoming Labour Government was contemplating replacing
incapacity benefit with a short-term allowance for thirteen weeks, followed thereafter
by reliance on a means-test.[283] The political furore associated with the Welfare
Reform and Pensions Act 1999 may have reduced the likelihood of such radical
change in the near future. However, further reform of incapacity benefit remains on
the agenda. One possibility is that the Government will seek to pursue its policy of
aligning JSA and incapacity benefit by reducing or abolishing the differential between
the weekly rates of the two benefits. The SSAC has explicitly recommended that
'there is a case for re-examining the balance between the levels paid to people who
are long-term unemployed and long term sick and disabled'.[284] The argument may
well be made that, in so far as the long-term sick and disabled have extra costs to
meet, these are met through DLA.[285]

The second of the Government's principles is primarily concerned with provision
for retirement, but is also reflected in the decision to means-test incapacity benefit by
reference to occupational and private pensions. In recent years governments of both
political persuasions have sought to encourage more private provision for welfare.
This trend has been particularly evident in the field of pensions but has also affected
the basic means-tested benefit of income support, at least so far as housing costs are
concerned.[286] The potential scope for the development of private insurance schemes
in the area of sickness and disability is much more limited.[287] Even within the enterprise culture of the United States, disability insurance is the least prevalent form of
private loss insurance.[288] Private insurance packages may appear to be a realistic
option for those in relatively low risk situations, but even in these cases the policy
terms may result in restricted coverage and questionable value for money.[289] The general effect of switching from a tax-funded base to risk-related premiums is bound to

---

[281] Diller (1996), n. 64 above, 363.   [282] Deacon (1998), n. 279 above, 306.

[283] Berthoud (1998), n. 249 above, 59.

[284] SSAC (1997), n. 270 above, 10; see further Berthoud (1998), n. 249 above, 26–7.

[285] The SSAC's caveat is significant: 'We are not advocating simply levelling down current benefit rates.
What we are suggesting is that the relative levels should be looked at, bearing in mind the need to provide
incentives and equity as well as an adequate income-replacement': SSAC, n. 270 above, 10.

[286] See N. Wikeley, 'Income Support and Mortgage Interest—The New Rules' (1995) 2 *J.S.S.L.* 168–78.

[287] See T. Burchardt and J. Hills, *Private Welfare Insurance and Social Security* (York: Joseph Rowntree
Foundation, 1997) and M. Howard and P. Thompson, *There May be Trouble Ahead* (London: Disability
Alliance and Disablement Income Group, 1995).

[288] K. S. Abraham and L. Liebman, 'Private Insurance, Social Insurance, and Tort Reform: Toward a
New Vision of Compensation for Illness and Injury' (1993) 93 *Columbia Law Rev.* 75–118, 81. Moreover,
'the prospect for the development of a more robust voluntary private market for disability insurance is
extremely weak': ibid., 105.

[289] Burchardt and Hills, n. 287 above, 61–4.

be regressive, with a redistributive effect to the disadvantage of women and those with health problems or disabilities.[290] There is, moreover, effectively no prospect of private cover for those disabled from birth or early childhood. The SSAC concluded that unless the insurance industry replicated the wide coverage of risks accepted by the state scheme, 'we see little prospect of a greater involvement of the private sector in provision for sickness, disability and unemployment in such a way that it could supplant state provision for the majority of the population and for high risk, vulnerable groups in particular'.[291]

The third principle which is relevant in this context is that disabled people should get the support they need to lead a fulfilling life with dignity. It is clear that this goal is seen as part of and subordinate to the first guiding principle; by definition the assumption is that the preferred route to dignity is through paid work. Official policy statements refer under this heading to the changes planned for incapacity benefit along with the disabled person's tax credit and the single gateway arrangements.[292] The logic behind this approach is that disability living allowance should be focused more tightly on the very severely disabled, with support for the less severely disabled being tied to labour market participation. At its most extreme, this approach would involve transferring the budget for DLA and attendance allowance to local authorities' social services departments, which would then use them to provide care in kind rather than assistance in cash.[293] However, such a radical change seems unlikely in the foreseeable future given the political controversy that such a policy would provoke. It seems more likely that attempts will be made within the existing framework to 'target' these extra costs benefits on a narrower group of the most severely disabled. Such a shift would be in keeping with the incremental approach to reform of disability benefits favoured by successive governments, thus steering away from any more fundamental review which would raise the issue of a comprehensive disability income. It would also be entirely consistent with the process of redrawing the boundaries of disability and incapacity which this chapter has sought to chart.

---

[290] Ibid., 64.

[291] SSAC, *State Benefits and Private Provision* (*The Review of Social Security*, Paper 2, 1994), 7. See also SSAC, *Social Security Provision for Disability: A Case for Change?* (London: The Stationery Office, 1997), 12–13.

[292] DSS, *Social Security Departmental Report: The Government's Expenditure Plans 1999/2000*, Cm 4214 (London: The Stationery Office, 1999), 17–18.

[293] This idea was floated in the early period of the Blair Government: Berthoud (1998), n. 249 above, 59. See also the suggestion that the funding for the income support residential allowance for those in long-term care be transferred to local authorities, discussed in Chapter 6.

13

Social Security and Housing

SIMON RAHILLY

1. INTRODUCTION

It has long been government housing policy to ensure that everyone has a decent home at a price that they can afford.[1] To this end, government expenditure has included subsidies to providers to help keep their costs down, and to consumers through tax relief (which has only been available to owners) and housing assistance paid within social security. The tremendous variation in housing costs between and within regions has meant that it has always been difficult to devise a national social security scheme that is both affordable to the nation and which also ensures that housing is affordable to individual households. The present arrangements include means-tested housing benefit to assist with rent charges (currently paid to some 4.5 million people), and means-tested council tax benefit for assistance with council tax (of which there are over 5 million recipients).[2] Both are administered by local authorities (though the financial and legal framework is determined by central government). By contrast, assistance with mortgage costs is via the means-tested benefits income support and JSA, which are administered by the Benefits Agency. This chapter examines the legal provisions for all three types of housing assistance, in the light of current policy issues and concerns.

Housing policy and social security policy are inescapably intertwined,[3] and their objectives have often clashed. Government housing policy in the 1980s was to reduce subsidy to local authority Housing Revenue Accounts, thus forcing rents up.[4] The Housing Act 1988 enabled housing associations to set their own assured rent levels. They were expected to finance an increasing part of their development costs by means of private loans as government grant was reduced. Private tenancies were also deregulated by the provisions of the 1988 Act, to help to revive the sector.[5] The higher rents which were an outcome of all these changes to housing policy,[6]

---

[1] See Department of the Environment and the Welsh Office, *Our Future Homes: Opportunity, Choice, Responsibility: The Government's Housing Policies for England and Wales*, Cm 2901 (London: HMSO, 1995), 11.

[2] DSS, *Social Security Statistics 1998* (Leeds: Corporate Document Services, 1998), 4. Council tax benefit, while not directly linked to housing, is included in this chapter because council tax in effect operates as a form of 'residence tax'.

[3] See SSAC, *Housing Benefit. The Review of Social Security*, Paper 3 (Leeds: BA Publishing Services Ltd., 1995), especially ch. 4.

[4] See P. Malpass, *Reshaping Housing Policy* (London: Routledge, 1990), ch. 7.

[5] See P. Malpass, 'The Unravelling of Housing Policy in Britain' (1996) 11(3) *Housing Studies*, 459–69.

[6] B. Randolph, 'The Re-privatisation of Housing Associations' in P. Malpass and R. Means (eds), *Implementing Housing Policy* (Buckingham: Open University Press, 1993), 39–58.

combined with a rise in the number of households and levels of unemployment, caused a significant increase in the demands made on the social security system to support rented housing. The fastest rate of growth in all benefits was in rent allowances in the private sector, which showed a growth of 15 per cent in real terms in the period from 1978–9 to 1992–3.[7] The impact of deregulation was clearly very significant as expenditure on rent allowances increased by 22 per cent per year between 1988–9 and 1993–4, whilst the increase for rent rebates in the council sector was 7.6 per cent.[8] This increase in public expenditure in fact ran counter to one of the Government's key objectives for social security, which was to ensure that its cost was consistent with its overall objectives for the economy.[9]

Concerns about cost have been central to recent government thinking about housing benefit and have resulted in a series of measures being introduced to attempt to keep housing costs affordable to the individual while containing the overall cost of housing assistance. These changes have added considerably to the complexity of housing benefit.[10] These additional complications have run counter to another of the Government's key aims for social security—that the system should be simple to understand and administer.[11] More recently, a further government preoccupation has emerged: the level of fraud. In 1985 the Government's review of housing benefit reported little hard information as to whether fraud and abuse were widespread problems, and only received evidence about individual cases.[12] By the 1990s fraud had come to occupy a major part of the Department of Social Security Annual Reports and was one of the few aspects of housing benefit to be considered in the 1998 Green Paper.[13] Housing benefit fraud has since become a key area in a major social security anti-fraud strategy (see section 9 below).

2. HOUSING BENEFIT AND COUNCIL TAX BENEFIT: AN OVERVIEW

Housing benefit was introduced in two stages in November 1982 and April 1983 following implementation of the Social Security and Housing Benefits Act 1982. The Government set up a review team, which published its report in 1985. This stated that there were 'inherent flaws in the structure and scope of the scheme which no amount of tinkering or fine tuning will put right'.[14] As a result the scheme was significantly revised by the provisions of the Social Security Act 1986 (see Chapter 5).

---

[7] DSS, *The Growth of Social Security* (London: HMSO, 1993).

[8] P. Malpass (1996), n. 6 above, 466.

[9] DSS, *Reform of Social Security*, Vol. 1, Cmnd. 9517 (London: HMSO, 1985), 2.

[10] The National Consumer Council said that 'the complexity of housing benefit is too great for us to attempt to explain it as we have attempted to explain other benefits': National Consumer Council, *Of Benefit to All. A Consumer Review of Social Security* (London: National Consumer Council, 1984).

[11] DSS, n. 9 above, 3.

[12] Housing Benefit Review Team, *Housing Benefit Review. Report of the Review Team*, Cmnd. 9520 (London: HMSO, 1985), para. 5.43.

[13] Green Paper (1998).   [14] N. 12 above.

The current legislative provisions are to be found within the SSCBA 1992 and associated regulations, principally the Housing Benefit (General) Regulations 1987[15] and the Council Tax Benefit (General) Regulations 1992,[16] whilst the administrative framework is found within the SSAA 1992.

Housing benefit and council tax benefit provide means-tested assistance towards the rent and council tax liability of a claimant for a property which is occupied as the home. Maximum assistance is available for incomes at or below income support levels and tapers off as income rises, but entitlement may be adjusted downwards if the rent is thought to be too high or the property too large. Some service charges may also be ineligible, and non-dependants may be expected to make a financial contribution towards housing and council tax costs. Claims must be made in writing to the local authority, and awards are made for a finite period, though subject to review when relevant circumstances change. Payments are made in arrears. There is the right of review, and of further review by a housing benefit review board. Local authorities receive subsidy towards the cost of benefit awards and administration.

The law provides for two alternative council tax benefits: main council tax benefit and 'alternative maximum council tax benefit'—commonly known as 'second adult rebate'. Claimants with adult non-dependants who do not pay them rent may be entitled to this second adult rebate. Entitlement is dependent upon the income of the non-dependant and is payable irrespective of any income and capital of the claimant. This alternative benefit was introduced because the presence of adult non-dependants may increase the council tax liability, yet their low income might mean that they are not able to contribute to its payment.[17]

3. THE MEANS-TEST

A Income and Capital: Alignment with Income Support

One of the aims of the Social Security Act 1986 was to align the means-tests for income support and housing benefit. Thus the applicable amount figure against which net income is compared for the calculation of benefit entitlement is based upon income support rates (see Chapter 6). Where net income does not exceed this figure, there is maximum entitlement. This means that those with an entitlement to income support (or income-based JSA) will also have a maximum entitlement to housing benefit and council tax benefit.

One area where the two benefits have not been aligned is the premium allowed for single parents within the applicable amount. This is higher than the premium within the income support calculation. Before the implementation of the Social Security

[15] HB(G) Regs 1987.

[16] S.I. 1992 No. 1814.

[17] For a fuller discussion of this, and other aspects of council tax benefit, see J. Zebedee and M. Ward, *Guide to Housing Benefit and Council Tax Benefit* (London: Shelter and Chartered Institute of Housing, 1999).

Act 1986, single parents received the same amount of housing benefit as claimants living with partners, for given levels of income. This was in line with recommendations that had been made by the Finer committee.[18] The higher premium within the housing benefit calculation can be seen as an attempt to mitigate the reduction in benefit entitlement brought about by alignment with income support which pays more to two people than to one. Recently governments have been attempting to reduce benefit entitlement to single parents as part of their family policy (see Chapter 9). The higher lone-parent premium has now been frozen for existing claimants, and is not available for new claimants. These changes increase the amount that single parents are expected to find for rent from given levels of income.

Another difference affects entitlement to council tax benefit for owner-occupiers with mortgages. Whilst the income support calculation includes mortgage interest payable, the council tax benefit calculation does not. The applicable amount is based solely upon the relevant personal allowances and premiums but does not include housing costs. This clearly reduces the cost of council tax benefit, but adds to the work disincentives for owners with mortgages.[19]

A further series of minor differences result from government attempts to increase work incentives by making housing benefit (in-work) slightly more generous, though recent research by the Department of Social Security suggests that these changes have had little influence.[20] The newly introduced full-time work premium for family credit is now disregarded, as is a small amount of income from child support. Claimants moving to work from income support or JSA can continue to receive their full housing benefit entitlement for the first four weeks in work. In addition a prescribed amount for childcare expenses can also be deducted from the net income figure.

Finally, there are differences to the rules for the treatment of capital and income. The capital limit for housing benefit is twice that set for income support: this concession was introduced to prevent significant numbers of pensioners with small amounts of savings becoming ineligible for assistance with their rates (and now their council tax). Moreover, for the calculation of net income, the earnings disregards for single parents within housing benefit are higher than for income support—providing an additional incentive to move from 'welfare to work'.

Alignment has produced some significant difficulties. For example, entitlement to the full rate of income support for single people is only achieved on reaching the age of twenty-five (see p. 129 above for criticism). This rule has been replicated within housing benefit, thus ensuring lower benefit for those under twenty-five for given levels of income and rent. Another consequence of alignment is that, after separation, only one parent will have allowances for the children built into their applicable

---

[18] M. Finer, *Report of the Committee on Lone Parent Families*, Cmnd. 5629 (London: HMSO, 1974).

[19] See P. Kemp, 'Housing Allowances and Fiscal Crisis for Welfare State' (1994) 9(4) *Housing Studies*, 531–42.

[20] DSS, *Moving into Work: bridging housing costs*, DSS Research Report No. 79 (London: The Stationery Office, 1998).

amount. The other may find it very hard to pay for accommodation which enables the children to stay.[21]

B. The Tapers

As net income rises above income support levels, so benefit entitlement tapers off. The steepness of the taper had been progressively increased during the 1980s. Before the Social Security Act 1986 there were six different rates of benefit withdrawal (or tapers). Simplifying the system meant reducing the number of tapers. There are now two tapers, with a less steep taper for council tax benefit (again to protect those pensioners who would otherwise have been made significantly worse off). High tapers reduce the cost of the system, but increase the marginal tax rate and thus the poverty trap for individual claimants; any increase in their income results in a significant loss of benefit so that overall they are left in more or less the same financial position. For claimants with rent and council tax to pay these tapers combine to result in the loss of 85 pence of benefits from each pound of additional gross earnings. In 1991 a couple with two children were only £14 better off in net income as their weekly earnings rose from £32 to £163.[22] This amounted to the equivalent of a 90 per cent rate of taxation. As rents rise, so the poverty trap applies across a larger range of income. There is also an affordability problem for those with incomes just above income support: their ratio of net rents to net income can increase above 30 per cent. The housing benefit tapers have combined with family credit tapers for families with children, so that there has been only 3 pence of additional disposable income for every additional pound of gross income.[23]

Various suggestions have been made to reduce the severity of a poverty trap which clearly runs counter to the Government's 'welfare to work' policy. Some centre around increasing the disregards.[24] This was the recommendation of the SSAC, which has made specific proposals such as disregarding contributions to private pension schemes[25] and introducing a disregard for owners to reflect their additional costs for house maintenance and mortgage payments.[26] Others have proposed the introduction of a dual taper scheme.[27] In addition to the present steep taper based upon full rent, there would be a second shallower taper based upon a proportion of the rent. At the lowest levels of income the existing arrangements would remain in place, thus ensuring full assistance for those with the lowest levels of income. As income rises the second taper will come into play when it results in a greater amount of

---

[21] See P. Kemp, 'HB: Some Peculiarities of the British' (1995) *Benefits*, No. 14, September, 1–5.

[22] J. Hills, *39 Steps to Housing Finance Reform* (York: Joseph Rowntree Foundation, 1991).

[23] S. Wilcox, *Unfinished Business: Housing Costs and the Reform of Welfare Benefits* (Coventry: Chartered Institute of Housing, 1998).

[24] See P. Kemp, *Housing Benefit: Time for Reform* (York: Joseph Rowntree Foundation, 1998).

[25] SSAC, *Fourth Report* (London: HMSO, 1985).   [26] Ibid.

[27] See for example J. Hills, n. 22 above and Commission on Social Justice, *Social Justice. Strategies for National Renewal* (London: Vintage, 1994).

benefit being payable. The lower taper will reduce the poverty trap and extend the range of income over which benefit would be payable. It will also reduce the rent affordability ratios. Whilst it is clear that there would be an additional cost to the Exchequer, this is reduced by the fact that the second taper is only based upon a proportion of rental costs being met. A final proposal is that the Government should modify its (now introduced) replacement for family credit, working families tax credit, and introduce an integrated work and housing tax credit scheme.[28] Whilst the taper on the work credit element would be steeper, it would not overlap with the tapers on the housing and council tax elements. The result would be that those who qualify for any amount of work credit would automatically qualify for the full housing credit.

A further concern with the present system is that it reduces the marginal cost of housing to zero; since the cost of extra housing is free, this leads to an 'upmarketing' effect.[29] This is because all those who are in receipt of benefit will have any additional costs met in full by increases to their benefit.[30] Although there is little hard evidence that benefits distort the housing market through upmarketing,[31] there are now various proponents of the view that benefit should be calculated on only a part of the rent, leaving all claimants with a minimum contribution and therefore a financial incentive to reduce housing costs.[32] This would entail increasing base benefits such as income support and JSA to enable those on benefit to be able to afford a minimum contribution to rent. One suggestion is that these benefits should include a notional contribution to a benchmark rent, but the extensive geographical variation of rent levels means that this would introduce a further level of complexity to the system. To prevent waste, the additions would need to be restricted to householders with housing costs, thus re-introducing the old, and administratively difficult, distinction between householders and non-householders.[33] It should be noted that there are already arrangements for dealing with high rents and rent increases within the private sector. This is considered below, in the section on rent restrictions.

4. ELIGIBILITY

Claimants can establish eligibility to housing benefit if they have a liability for housing costs for a dwelling which they occupy as their home.[34] Recent rules have removed eligibility from those who are treated as being persons from abroad (see below). 'Dwelling' is defined as residential accommodation.[35] This means that benefit is not available for commercial lettings—even where a landlord continues to

---

[28] S. Wilcox, n. 23 above.   [29] See J. Hills, n. 22 above, at 19.
[30] Benefit can be expressed as rent minus a proportion of excess income. If the rent increases (but income remains constant), then benefit will increase by the same amount.
[31] SSAC, n. 25 above, para. 3.1.   [32] See P. Kemp, n. 24 above.   [33] SSAC, n. 25 above, at 33.
[34] SSCBA 1992, s. 130.   [35] Ibid., s. 137(1).

accept rent in the knowledge that the tenant has taken up residence in a part of the premises and is sleeping there.[36]

A. Liability for Housing Costs

Housing costs which are eligible for benefit[37] include rent, licence fees, payments by way of mesne profits, site fees for mobile homes, and payments under rental purchase agreements (but exclude those associated with mortgages, costs for repairs and maintenance, and charges for water and sewerage). Excluded from the scheme are costs in respect of residential care and nursing homes for those on income support, payments for local authority homes where residents pay an inclusive charge for board and accommodation, and payments for arrears.[38] To be eligible for benefit, a person must have a legal liability for eligible housing costs, or be a partner, or former partner, of such a person. The courts have held that a church member living as a licensee of his church could have a legally binding relationship and an enforceable contract notwithstanding the fact that church members had more general (and unenforceable) obligations.[39] The authority may seek evidence to establish the existence of a legal liability.[40]

There are specified circumstances in which people are treated as not being liable for payments, and therefore ineligible for housing benefit.[41] People are ineligible if their payments are to a close relative with whom they live. The courts have confirmed that this does not apply where the accommodation is separate and self-contained.[42] Claimants are also ineligible if their arrangement is not commercial or if the local authority considers that it has been created to take advantage of the housing benefit scheme. This regulation is designed to prevent 'contrived tenancies' and the courts have held that since its intent is to prevent abuse of the system there needs to be conduct which appears improper to the beholder.[43] In considering this issue, the Court of Appeal looked at arrangements that had existed before housing benefit was introduced and at whether either the tenant or landlord 'had been motivated by dubious

---

[36] *R v Warrington Borough Council, ex p Williams* (1997) 29 H.L.R. 827.

[37] HB(G) Regs 1987, reg. 10.

[38] HB(G) Regs 1987, reg. 8. On income support in residential homes, see Chapter 6.

[39] *R v Stratford-on-Avon District Council Housing Benefit Review Board and Secretary of State for Social Security, ex p White* (1998) *The Times*, 23 April (CA).

[40] *R v Sefton MBC ex p Read* (1998), 6 March (unreported) (CA).

[41] HB(G) Regs 1987, reg. 7. The provisions within this regulation were extended in January 1999 by the Housing Benefit (General) Amendment (No. 2) Regulations 1998 (S.I. 1998 No. 3257) to include payments: (i) to former partners; (ii) to companies or trusts in which the claimant is a director or a beneficiary; (iii) to landlords where the claimant is responsible for their child; (iv) where the landlord requires the claimant to live in the accommodation as a condition of employment.

[42] *R v Kingswood District Council, ex p Dadds* (1997) 29 H.L.R. 700. See S. Rahilly, 'Case Analysis' (1997) 4 *J.S.S.L.* 177–81.

[43] *Per* Sedley J in *Solihull Metropolitan Borough Council Housing Department Review Board v Simpson* (1994) 26 H.L.R. 370, as approved by the Court of Appeal (1995) 27 H.L.R. 41.

ingenuity to create the liability'.[44] There should be no presumption against the claimant, and it is therefore for the authority to show grounds that abuse exists.

The 'contrived tenancy' rule has led to a number of actions for judicial review. In many of these cases it is clear that the authority had considered the contractual rent to be considerably higher than that assessed by the rent officer as representing a 'market rent'. However, the mere fact that the applicant has entered into an agreement which is beyond her means, without assistance from benefit, is not by itself sufficient to establish a contrived tenancy.[45] Whilst authorities should not attach a wholly disproportionate weight to the claimant's ability to pay the rent charged, it is a factor that can be taken into account.[46] Similarly the means, circumstances, and intent of the landlord may be relevant factors. In one case a landlord had deliberately advertised for elderly tenants in order to charge them high rents knowing that (at that time) the authority could not easily restrict benefit payments on high rents if the tenants were elderly. It was held to be lawful for the authority to conclude that the tenancy had been created to take advantage of the benefit system.[47] In some of the cases coming before the courts the denial of benefit has been partly influenced by the fact that landlord and tenant have been related.[48] In deciding whether or not the tenancy is contrived authorities should ask what would be the consequence of non-payment of benefit: would the claimant be asked to leave?[49]

It should be noted that no benefit at all is payable if the authority decides that the applicant should not be treated as liable for housing payments. Alternatively, where the authority is satisfied that there is a liability but that the rent is high, it may decide to restrict the eligible rent for benefit purposes. This is discussed later in the chapter.

B. Occupy the Dwelling as their Home

The general rule is that a person can only be entitled to benefit for one home—the one that they normally occupy.[50] Authorities must have regard to all dwellings that a person occupies in deciding which one they normally occupy as their home.[51] Where claimants are forced to move into temporary accommodation because of essential repair work to their normal home and are liable for housing payments for one (but not both) of the properties, they are treated as normally occupying that dwelling.[52] There are limited exceptions to the general rule.

Benefit is payable on two homes for up to fifty-two weeks where it would be reasonable to do so, and where the claimant has left because of fear of violence in that

---

[44] *R v Stratford-on-Avon District Council Housing Benefit Review Board and Secretary of State for Social Security, ex p White* (1998) *The Times*, 23 April (CA).

[45] *R v Housing Benefit Review Board of Sutton London Borough, ex p Keegan* (1995) 27 H.L.R. 92.

[46] *R v Kingswood District Council, ex p Dadds* (1997) 29 H.L.R. 700

[47] *R v Manchester City Council, ex p Baragrove Properties Limited* (1991) 23 H.L.R. 337.

[48] For example, *ex p Dadds* (1997), n. 46 above.

[49] *Solihull Metropolitan Borough Council Housing Department Review Board v Simpson* (1994) 26 H.L.R. 370.

[50] SSCBA, s. 130, and HB(G) Regs 1987, reg. 5.   [51] HB(G) Regs 1987, reg. 5(2).

[52] Ibid., reg. 5(4).

home or from a former member of the family, provided the claimant intends to return to the former home.[53] Secondly, where claimants have been housed by a housing authority in two dwelling houses because of their family size, then they are eligible for benefit on both houses.[54] Thirdly, benefit is payable for up to four weeks on two homes when a claimant has moved to a new home, and has an unavoidable liability to make payments for both.[55]

Benefit is not normally payable until the dwelling house is actually occupied. Only then does it become a home. However, where someone has moved in, but was liable for payments before they moved, and where the delay was reasonable, benefit can be paid for a period of up to four weeks before the move in the following situations: first, where the delay was to allow for adaptations to meet disablement needs; secondly, to await the outcome of an application to the social fund from a household that includes a pensioner, a child, or someone incapable of work for more than a year; and thirdly, where the claimant was moving from hospital or residential accommodation. In all these cases there is an additional requirement that the claim for benefit was made before the move.[56]

Temporary absences used to be allowed for up to fifty-two weeks provided the property had not been sublet, the absence was unlikely to exceed (or in exceptional circumstances substantially exceed) fifty-two weeks, and the claimant intended to return. However, in 1995 the Government restricted this provision to certain specified situations (such as hospitalisation, receiving medical tretament in residential home for care, or being on remand). For other cases (such as imprisonment) the period was reduced to thirteen weeks.[57] Where a claimant moves backwards and forwards the temporary absence begins on each occasion; it is not aggregated.[58] Physical ties such as personal belongings may be relevant in deciding whether there is the required intention to return.[59] There is separate provision within the regulations to enable benefit to continue for up to thirteen weeks to enable a claimant to have a trial period in residential accommodation.[60]

C. People from Abroad

Housing benefit counts as 'public funds' for immigration purposes. This means that a claim for housing benefit is contrary to the immigration conditions imposed on those granted limited leave to enter the country. The Asylum and Immigration Act 1996 made certain 'persons from abroad' ineligible for benefit. These include those with limited leave to enter the country, those whose claim for asylum was not made immediately they arrived, and those who have not established habitual residence. The rules for eligibility for housing benefit are the same as those for income support (and

---

[53] Ibid., reg. 5(5)(a).   [54] Ibid., reg. 5(5)(c).   [55] Ibid., reg. 5(5)(d).   [56] Ibid., reg. 5(6).
[57] Ibid., reg. 5(8).
[58] *R v Penwith District Council Housing Benefit Review Board, ex p Burt* (1992) 22 H.L.R. 292.
[59] *R v Housing Benefit Review Board, ex p Robertson* (1988) *The Independent*, 5 March.
[60] HB(G) Regs 1987, reg. 5(7B) and (7C).

for eligibility for assistance as a homeless person under the provisions of the Housing Act 1996). They are complex, and there is some evidence that housing authorities are approaching decision making in different ways.[61]

5. RESTRICTIONS

The housing benefit scheme has always allowed authorities to reduce the amount of rent that is eligible for benefit where it was considered that the rent was too high or the property too large, and to restrict any increase of rent during a benefit period. Recent concerns about the rising cost of the scheme (fuelled largely by increases in rent levels) have converged with concerns about abuse of the system, to focus on new methods of restricting the amount of rent that is eligible for benefit. In effect there are now two sets of rules: transitional arrangements for existing tenants who were entitled to benefit on 1 January 1996[62] and new rules for claimants after that date.[63] Note that all claimants are protected from the impact of any rent restrictions for a period of thirteen weeks, provided that they were able to afford their rent prior to their claim for housing benefit.[64]

A. Rent Restrictions Prior to 2 January 1996

These restrictions still apply to those claimants who have been continuously in receipt of benefit for the same home since before 2 January 1996. A break in a claim (unless for a period of less than four weeks), or a move to a new home (unless made necessary because the previous home became uninhabitable), will result in the new rules applying. There is protection when the former claimant dies, or where the new claim arises because a former partner leaves. These restrictions continue to apply to accommodation funded by the Resettlement Agency or provided by the voluntary sector with care, support, or supervision.

The old regulation 11 gave an authority the power to restrict rents when it considered the rent to be too high, or the property too large. It also had the power to refer rents to the rent officer for the registration of a fair rent, and this was often a very successful way to reduce the rent liability and therefore the amount of benefit that needed to be paid. The Housing Benefit Review Team had recommended that authorities should be encouraged to prevent abuse[65] and called for subsidy arrangements that provided authorities with incentives to do so.[66] This was taken up by the

---

[61] See S. Rahilly, 'Housing for the Homeless and Immigration Control: the Provisions of the Housing Act 1996 and the Asylum and Immigration Act 1996' (1998) 20(3) *J.S.W.F.L.* 237–50. The income support rules affecting asylum seekers are discussed by Neville Harris in Chapter 6 at pp. 197ff.

[62] Housing Benefit (General) Amendment Regulations 1995 (S.I. 1995 No. 1644).

[63] HB(G) Regs 1987, reg. 11.   [64] Ibid., reg. 11(9).

[65] Housing Benefit Review Team, *Housing Benefit Review. Report of the Review Team*, Cmnd. 9520 (London: HMSO, 1985), para. 5.21.

[66] Ibid., para. 5.9.

Government in its Green Paper with a proposal to change the subsidy arrangements to ensure that authorities had incentives to control costs.[67] Subsequently subsidy was paid in full up to the registered rent, but was reduced to 25 per cent for any part of a rent above a local average, where there was no fair rent registered.

The Housing Act 1988 ended rent regulation for tenancies created after January 1989. Rent officers were given a new role to determine market rents in respect of individual properties of appropriate size, for subsidy purposes. Whilst central government reimburses authorities for most of the benefit costs up to the determination made by the rent officer, only 60 per cent of costs are subsidised above that level, and then only for specified vulnerable groups. Regulation 11 was amended to require an authority to consider whether the claimant occupies a property which is larger than is reasonably required, or whether the rent payable is unreasonably high compared with suitable alternative accommodation elsewhere. When an authority considers that this is the case, it must reduce the maximum rent that is eligible for benefit to 'such amount as it considers appropriate'.[68] In looking at the question of size, the authority should consider the needs of all those in occupation, and must have regard to any suitable alternative accommodation occupied by households of the same size. As far as cost is concerned, the regulation requires not merely that the rent is high, but that it is unreasonably high compared to suitable alternative accommodation. This should include consideration of any relevant characteristics of the property together with the circumstances of the household. The comparable property should be reasonably equivalent, for example in terms of security of tenure. Where a tenant had a shorthold tenancy for a term of five years, then it was for the authority to show that its security was reasonably equivalent to shorthold tenancies with terms of only six months before they could be used as comparables.[69] With regard to where the alternative accommodation used for comparison should be located, the Code of Guidance Manual advises that it can be outside the authority's own area, provided that it would be suitable for the claimant's needs.[70] The courts have held that it is reasonable for an authority to make comparisons with similar properties outside its own area, where more local comparators are not possible.[71]

In making its decisions, an authority may have regard to the rent officer determinations (which impact upon the subsidy payable). The Audit Commission reported that some authorities always used rent officer determinations to decide whether rents should be restricted.[72] This was consistent with other research which had shown that

---

[67] DSS, *Reform of Social Security*, Vol. 1, Cmnd. 9517 (London: HMSO, 1985), para. 13.7.

[68] HB(G) Regs 1987, reg. 11(2).

[69] *R v Sefton Housing Benefit Review Board, ex p Brennan* (1996) 29 H.L.R. 735.

[70] DSS, *Housing Benefit and Council Tax Benefit Guidance Manual* (London: The Stationery Office, regularly updated), para. A4.106.

[71] *R v City of Westminster, ex p Hamandi* (1998) (unreported) Case No. CO/2265/97.

[72] Audit Commission, *Remote Control: The National Administration of Housing Benefit* (London: HMSO, 1993).

in 86 per cent of cases authorities had followed rent officer determinations, whilst in Inner London the figure was 92 per cent.[73]

The regulation provides some protection for 'vulnerable groups'. These are households which include someone who is aged over sixty, or is incapable of work, or a child. Rents for these households cannot be restricted unless there is suitable alternative accommodation available and the authority considers that it is reasonable to expect the claimant to move.[74] For these vulnerable groups, an unreasonably high rent is not by itself sufficient for it to be restricted; the authority must show that there is suitable alternative accommodation available, and that it would be reasonable to expect the claimant to move.[75] The Court of Appeal has held that it is not necessary for an authority to identify a specific property to which the household could move,[76] although in Scotland it has been held that the authority needs to do more than merely identify an active market.[77] Whilst the authority needs to be satisfied that there is an active market for properties of the relevant type, it need not concern itself with financial considerations that may make that market inaccessible (for example because of the need for a deposit).[78]

The Government's view was that housing benefit should be based more on average rents for suitable accommodation in the area, rather than on appropriate rents for particular properties. This would not only help to contain the overall cost of housing benefit but might also provide tenants with an incentive to find cheaper accommodation. It therefore introduced new regulations to increase the extent to which rents would be restricted.[79]

B. Restrictions from 2 January 1996

Under the old arrangements, rent officer determinations are simply factors that authorities can take into account. Under the new arrangements they establish what is to be the eligible rent for benefit purposes. Rent officers set 'local reference rents' for each type of property. These represent the mid point between the highest and lowest rents for properties of that size in the locality, disregarding exceptionally high or low rents. Authorities must refer all private sector claims to rent officers,[80] together with those where the landlord is a registered housing association, if the authority considers the property to be too large or the rent unreasonably high.[81] Rent officers

---

[73] P. Kemp, and P. McLaverty, *Unreasonable rents and Housing benefit*, Housing Research Finding No. 70 (York: Joseph Rowntree Foundation, 1992).
[74] HB(G) Regs 1987, reg. 11(3).
[75] *R v Sefton Borough Council, ex p Cunningham* (1991) 23 H.L.R. 534.
[76] *R v East Devon District Council, ex p Gibson* (1993) 25 H.L.R. 487.
[77] *McLeod v Housing Benefit Review Board for Banff and Buchan District* [1988] SCLR 165, Court of Session. For a discussion on this point see Findlay's note to Regulation 11 of the HB(G) Regs 1987 in L. Findlay, R. Poynter, and M. Ward, *CPAG's Housing Benefit and Council Tax Benefit Legislation* (London: CPAG, 1998).
[78] *R v Waltham Forest LBC ex p Holder* (1996) 29 H.L.R. 71.
[79] Housing Benefit (General) Amendment Regulations 1995 (S.I. 1995 No. 1644).
[80] HB(G) Regs 1987, reg. 12A.   [81] HB(G) Regs 1987, reg. 12A and Sched. 1A para. 3.

determine a 'property specific rent', which is based on their assessment of a market rent for that property, and a 'relevant rent', which is the lower of either the property specific rent or a notional market rent for a property of an appropriate size. Where the relevant rent is less than the local reference rent, the maximum eligible rent is the relevant rent. In this case there will only be a rent restriction if it is less than the contractual rent. Otherwise, the maximum eligible rent is restricted to the local reference rent plus up to half of the difference between it and the relevant rent.

The Government was concerned that these restrictions did not go far enough in respect of young people because, it argued, housing benefit enabled them to rent accommodation that those not on benefit would not be able to afford. This in turn produced work disincentives (given the relatively low earnings levels of young people). The rules were therefore further extended from 7 October 1996 so that the maximum rent for single claimants aged under twenty-five cannot exceed a local reference rent for single-roomed accommodation.[82] These restrictions apply both to new claims and to existing claims when they are renewed. Tenants of registered housing associations are exempt, as are single claimants aged under twenty-two who have recently left the care of a local authority.

Before the ink had dried on these new measures to restrict rents, the Government proposed yet further restrictions.[83] The proposal was to limit the rent for all single claimants to an average single-roomed rent for the locality, and to remove the 50 per cent top-up above reference rents that was available to some claimants. In the event the incoming Labour Government decided not to proceed with the proposal for single people, but from 6 October 1997 rents for all new claimants are restricted to the appropriate local reference rent.

There is now no specific protection for vulnerable groups. Instead, an authority has a discretionary power to increase the benefit payable to claimants whose rents have been restricted, if it is satisfied that the claimant, or a member of the family, would suffer exceptional hardship because of the restriction.[84] However, this is not only discretionary, it is also cash-limited. Each authority has an overall amount of annual expenditure which it is permitted to spend for this purpose.

Prospective tenants can apply for a pre-tenancy determination, which will enable them to find out the extent of any rent restriction before they accept a tenancy. Authorities must refer such requests to the rent officer.[85] There is no charge and the determination made by the rent officer is binding in the event of a subsequent claim for benefit.

These changes have all been introduced with little research, driven by a policy imperative to attempt to cut costs. Many of the changes have added considerably to the complexity of the benefit, although the most recent changes are a good example of negative simplification, at the expense of individual claimants who will now be

[82] Housing Benefit (General) Amendment Regulations 1996 (S.I. 1996 No. 965).
[83] Housing Benefit (General) Amendment Regulations 1997 (S.I. 1997 No. 852).
[84] HB(G) Regs 1987, reg. 61(3).   [85] Ibid., reg. 12A.

experiencing difficulties in paying their contractual rent. The Housing Benefit Review Team had commented that tenants had little control over their costs—and this was at a time when many in the private sector could apply for a 'fair rent'.[86] Research in 1995 showed that rent restrictions were affecting about one in three private sector tenants.[87] Whilst half of these had asked their landlord to reduce their rent, their likelihood of success was no more than 50 per cent. The likely result of rent restrictions was rent arrears, with one in six tenants moving on. Clearly, tenants who have had their rents restricted are already having to pay for a part of their rent from other income. They already have the 'incentives to shop around' that some critics are suggesting should be introduced by making maximum benefit less than the full rent payable.[88]

C. Council Tax

In its 1985 Green Paper the Government argued that, on the ground of political accountability, maximum benefit should be less than 100 per cent, leaving every household to pay a contribution to their local authority charge. This undoubtedly contributed to the subsequent unpopularity of the 'poll tax' (community charge) and to the considerable collection difficulties faced by local authorities. When the poll tax was replaced by council tax, the maximum entitlement to the new council tax benefit became the full tax liability. Until recently there has been no provision for restrictions of benefit on the grounds of high council tax liability: the actual tax payable has been the maximum benefit. However, in April 1998 restrictions were introduced for claimants in properties in the highest tax bands—F, G, and H. At the last moment the Government agreed that existing claimants would not be affected by these restrictions, provided they continue to occupy the same property.

6. SERVICE CHARGES

Service charges, except those that are excessive, may be covered by housing benefit to the extent that their payment is a condition of occupation.[89] However, the regulations specify that certain service charges are ineligible.[90] When ineligible service charges are not separately identifiable within the rent, it is up to the authority to apportion a fair charge for that service. The burden is on the applicant to satisfy the authority that costs are eligible,[91] and there would appear to be considerable scope

---

[86] Housing Benefit Review Team, *Housing Benefit Review. Report of the Review Team*, Cmnd. 9520 (London: HMSO, 1985), para. 2.17.

[87] P. Kemp, and P. McLaverty, *Unreasonable rents and Housing benefit*, Housing Research Finding No. 70 (York: Joseph Rowntree Foundation, 1992).

[88] P. Kemp, *Housing Benefit: Time for Reform* (York: Joseph Rowntree Foundation, 1998).

[89] HB(G) Regs 1987, reg. 10(1)(e).

[90] Ibid., reg. 10(3) and Sched. 1.

[91] *R v Stoke-on-Trent City Council, ex p Highgate Projects* (1996) 29 H.L.R. 271.

for a knowledgeable tenant and landlord to maximise the extent to which service charges are eligible for housing benefit. Ineligible services or related charges include meals, laundry (but not the costs of the provision of equipment), leisure items including TV fees, cleaning (except for communal areas or where the claimant is unable to clean), transport, charges which enable the claimant to acquire furniture, alarms (except for those in specialist accommodation because of age, sickness, or disability), medical expenses, charges for nursing or personal care, and fuel charges (where these charges are not identifiable then fixed amounts are specified within the regulations).

A final area of ineligibility relates to the costs of general counselling and support services.[92] This provision has been subject to litigation, amendment, and government review.[93] These service charges are ineligible except those which 'relate to the provision of adequate accommodation', or are provided by either the landlord or an employee who spends the majority of their time, during which they provide services, providing services which are otherwise eligible. This provision has been extremely important for supported housing schemes, but where the '50 per cent test' cannot be passed the counselling and support must relate to the provision of adequate accommodation. This was considered by the High Court which held that this should be interpreted to mean that the services must help preserve the fabric of the building.[94] This decision has since been upheld by the Court of Appeal.[95] Both tenants who appealed had learning difficulties and claimed that support was essential to enable them to be able to continue to live in the accommodation. In this sense the support 'related to the provision of adequate accommodation'. The Court rejected this argument in favour of a narrower interpretation that the services needed to relate to the provision of physically suitable, and therefore adequate, accommodation. Back in 1985 the SSAC had argued that housing benefit should be seen as an integral part of any care in the community policy, and that the question of eligible service charges should be seen in this light.[96] After the High Court ruling, the Government introduced interim regulations to protect existing supported accommodation projects, but deferred a decision about the long-term future of this difficult question until the outcome of an inter-departmental review which had been considering the matter for over two years. Whilst the importance of these services was never denied, the issue seemed to be whether they should be funded through social security or through social services. The review recommended that responsibility for the funding of the costs of support should be transferred to social services, and the Government is now proposing to create a new cash-limited single budget for local authorities to allocate according to individual need.[97] In the meantime transitional housing benefit will be

---

[92] HB(G) Regs 1987, Sched. 1 para. 1(e).
[93] *R v North Cornwall District Council, ex p Singer, Barrett and Bateman*, (1993) 26 H.L.R. 360, and Housing Benefit (General) Amendment Regulations 1994 (S.I. 1994 No. 1003).
[94] *R v Sutton London Borough Council Housing Benefit Review Board, ex p Harrison* (1997) 23 July (QBD).
[95] *R v Swansea City and County Council, ex p Littler* (1998) *The Times*, 9 September.
[96] SSAC, *Fourth Report* (London: HMSO, 1985).
[97] DSS, *Supporting People* (London: The Stationery Office, 1998).

available to pay for support services,[98] but this funding will be transferred into the local authorities' single budget in 2003. This proposal seems very similar to the arrangements introduced for residential care and nursing homes (see section 12.A below); assistance with the cost is dependent upon assessment of need by social services—and upon the size of the budget.

7. NON-DEPENDANTS

In most cases the presence of a non-dependant aged eighteen or over will result in a reduction in the maximum amount of housing benefit.[99] The amount of the reduction is determined by whether the non-dependant is working, and if so by their gross weekly income. The amounts that have been deducted for non-dependants have risen considerably and this has been one of the easiest ways in which the Government has been able to cut the cost of housing benefit. The maximum deductions have been increased from £4.70 per week in 1984–5 to £46.35 per week in 1999/2000. These increases have continued apace despite criticism that they were already unreasonably high in relation to housing costs and income.[100] The Housing Benefit Review Team[101] had highlighted this as an area in need of simplification and called for a flat-rate structure, with non-dependants expected to make either a full, or a reduced, or a nil contribution according to income. Alternatively, it suggested a rent share system. The arrangements were made more complex in 1998 with an increase in the number of rates of deduction for housing benefit from four to six, and for council tax benefit from two to four. The Government's justification for this change was that this helped 'ensure that help is more clearly focused on those households that need it most'.[102]

There are a limited number of situations in which there are no deductions for non-dependants. First, where the claimant or partner is blind, or receiving attendance allowance, or the care component of disability living allowance. Secondly, where the non-dependant is considered to have their normal home elsewhere, is a YTS trainee, a full-time student who is not working, has been in prison or hospital for more than six weeks, or is aged less than twenty-five and is in receipt of income support or JSA.[103]

The definition of 'non-dependant' has been subject to frequent attention by the

[98] Draft Housing Benefit (General) Amendment Regulations 1999 were referred to the SSAC in May/June 1999.
[99] HB(G) Regs 1987, reg. 63.　　[100] SSAC (1985), op. cit., n. 96 above.
[101] Housing Benefit Review Team, *Housing Benefit Review. Report of the Review Team*, Cmnd. 9520 (London: HMSO, 1985). See further Chapter 5.
[102] DSS, *Social Security Departmental Report*, Cmnd. 3613 (London: The Stationery Office, 1997), para. 372. (In the next paragraph the report calls for the increase in all deductions by an across-the-board £1 per week; for non-dependants with the lowest levels of income this represented an increase of 17 per cent, from £6 to £7.)
[103] HB(G) Regs 1987, reg. 63(6).

courts and amendment by ensuing regulations, although this has usually been because of its significance in determining entitlement to the severe disability premium (see Chapter 12). A non-dependant is any adult who normally resides with the claimant and is not a member of their family.[104] 'Resides with' means shares any accommodation except bathroom, toilet or communal area, without having a separate liability to pay for housing costs. Excluded as a non-dependant are those to whom rent is paid, those who are in joint occupation with a joint liability for housing costs, and those with a liability to pay rent to the claimant. But these three exceptions will not apply to close relatives, if the rent payments are not on a commercial basis, or if they have been set up to take advantage of the benefit scheme.[105] Where people who are not related have a joint liability, then each can make a separate claim for benefit and the authority will have to assess their share of the rent and any service charges. Non-dependants, by contrast, are not eligible for benefit.

Whilst increases to the non-dependant deduction have represented an easy way for governments to try to contain housing benefit spending, they present considerable difficulties for claimants and landlords. The claimant may not know the income of the non-dependant, and the deduction may bear no relation to the actual contribution made towards housing costs (if any). Arguably they have discouraged sharing and thus added to housing demand and homelessness. They are undoubtedly a source of rent arrears, and pursuance of the non-dependant deduction is notoriously difficult, especially as it does not count towards the arrears that are required before direct payments from other benefits (such as income support) can be made.

8. AWARDS AND PAYMENTS

Claims must be in writing on forms which are provided by the authority free of charge.[106] Whilst housing benefit and council tax benefit can usually be claimed together, the claims need to be made separately from other benefits such as income support. The date of claim is normally the date at which the form is received by the authority; claimants of income support or JSA may submit housing benefit claims to the authority or to the Benefits Agency, and if they do so within four weeks the date of claim is the same as for the other benefit. The overlap in entitlement to different benefits is considerable, and the DSS has now set up pilot projects in which the Benefits Agency and two London boroughs are using a single point of contact for assessment of entitlement to more than one benefit.[107] Claimants must 'furnish such certificates, documents, information and evidence in connection with the claim . . . as may reasonably be required by the appropriate authority'.[108] Otherwise the authority is under no duty to determine the claim.[109] The courts have held that it was

---

[104] Ibid., reg. 3.   [105] Ibid., regs 3 and 7.
[106] Ibid., reg. 72.
[107] C. Lipman, 'Benefits Set for Radical Overhaul' (1998) *Inside Housing*, 3 July, 6.
[108] HB(G) Regs 1987, reg. 73.   [109] Ibid., reg. 76(2)(b).

reasonable for an authority to require evidence of rent payments, in addition to a tenancy agreement, when a claimant sought to renew a benefit claim.[110]

Authorities should determine applications for benefit within fourteen days or 'as soon as reasonably practicable thereafter', and should notify any person affected in writing; they in turn may write to ask for a written statement setting out the reasons for that determination.[111] In practice one of the main criticisms of housing benefit has been the delays in decisions; the Court of Appeal was not prepared to state that similar wording in the regulations for income support required the appointment of sufficient staff to ensure that all claims are determined within fourteen days.[112] Unreasonable delays may well amount to maladministration which can be referred to the local government ombudsman. When, through no fault of the claimant, the authority is unable to make a decision within fourteen days, it must make a payment on account 'of such amount as it considers reasonable'.[113] Benefit can be adjusted for any underpayment or overpayment when the determination is subsequently made.

In most cases the benefit period begins in the week following the date of claim (though it will begin in the week of the date of claim for those whose rent liability only commenced in that week).[114] Unlike many other benefits the award is not indefinite, but runs for a specified period as thought reasonable by the authority, but not exceeding sixty weeks.[115] This means that benefit will expire, even when there has been no change of circumstances and the onus is on the claimant to reapply. During the benefit period the claimant is under a duty to notify the authority of any change in circumstances which they may reasonably expect to know to be relevant to the claim.[116]

A. Direct Payments

From October 1996 the initial payment of a rent allowance for tenants in the privately rented sector can be made payable to the landlord; otherwise benefit is normally paid to the tenant. The prospect of direct payments for all its tenants was undoubtedly one of the attractions of housing benefit for authorities, and the hope was that automatic direct payments would help bring down the level of rent arrears by a third.[117] The Housing Benefit Review Team thought that it made no sense for authorities to pay out benefit and then to have to collect it. By contrast it concluded that direct payments in the private sector would represent too much of an interference in an individual's private affairs.[118] Others have suggested that mandatory rent

---

[110] *R v Sefton MBC, ex p Read* (1998) 6 March (unreported) (CA) Case No. FC3 97/6363 CMS4.
[111] HB(G) Regs 1987, regs 76(3) and 77.
[112] *R v Secretary of State for Social Services and the Chief Adjudication Officer, ex p CPAG and others* [1990] 2 QB 540.
[113] HB(G) Regs 1987, regs 91 and 91A.   [114] Ibid., reg. 65.   [115] Ibid., reg. 66.
[116] Ibid., reg. 75.
[117] Audit Commission, *Bringing Council Tenants Arrears Under Control: A Review* (London: The Audit Commission, 1984).
[118] Housing Benefit Review Team, *Housing Benefit Review: Report of the Review Team*, Cmnd. 9520 (London: HMSO, 1985).

direct reduces the ability to budget flexibly, and merely transfers debts to other areas.[119]

In the private sector, payments will be made direct to the landlord if either the claimant has a direct payment from income support because of rent arrears, or has more than eight weeks' arrears[120] (unless it is in the claimant's overriding interest not to do so; in this case the authority can withhold payment).[121] In addition, direct payments may be made at the request of the claimant, or where they are thought by the authority to be in the claimant's interest.[122] About 60 per cent of claimants in the private sector have their rent paid direct to their landlord.[123] Benefit can be withheld if the authority is satisfied that the claimant is not paying rent regularly, or where there are doubts about the claimant's entitlement.[124]

B. Backdating

An authority must backdate a claim for a past period back to the first day from which a claimant can show continuous good cause for their failure to claim. This is subject to an overall limit of fifty-two weeks from the date of claim for backdating.[125] This limit clearly makes it important to claim for the backdated period as soon as possible. 'Good cause' has been described as a 'work of art',[126] and is the phrase that formerly governed backdating for other benefits such as income support. It has been held to mean some fact which, given all the circumstances including the claimant's age, experience, health, and knowledge, would probably have caused a reasonable person to act in the same way.[127] The Social Security Bill 1998 sought to restrict backdating for housing benefit to a maximum of four weeks, but amendments made by the House of Lords resulted in the provisions being left unaltered.

C. Overpayments

Overpayments can arise for a variety of reasons: claimant error, change of circumstances, or error by either the authority or the Benefits Agency. It has been estimated that the cost of errors which result in housing benefit overpayments is about £200m per year. This contrasts with an estimated £100m per year of underpayments,[128] in

---

[119] National Consumer Council, *Of Benefit to All* (London: National Consumer Council, 1984), para. 13.33.
[120] HB(G) Regs 1987, reg. 93. [121] Ibid., reg. 95(1). [122] Ibid., reg. 94.
[123] DSS, *Social Security Departmental Report*, Cmnd. 3613 (London: The Stationery Office, 1997), para. 221.
[124] HB(G) Regs 1987, reg. 95.
[125] Ibid., reg. 72(15). These provisions were introduced with effect from 1 April 1996, and reversed the effect of the decision by the Court of Appeal in *R v Aylesbury Vale District Council Housing Benefit Review Board, ex p England* (1996) 29 H.L.R. 303.
[126] L. Findlay, R. Poynter, and M. Ward, *CPAG's Housing Benefit and Council Tax Benefit Legislation* (London: CPAG, 1998), notes to reg. 72.
[127] *R(S) 2/63*. For a fuller discussion of 'good cause' see M. Partington, *Claim in Time: Time Limits for Social Security Law*, 3rd edn. (Legal Action Group, 1994), ch. 2.
[128] E. Humphrey, 'Money to Burn' (1997) *Inside Housing*, 8 August, 14–15.

addition to unclaimed benefit which is estimated by the Government to be in the range from £780m to £1,380m.[129] Overpayments are amounts of benefit paid to which there was no entitlement.[130] The decision that there has been an overpayment will be made by reviewing the amount of benefit paid. Whilst most other benefit overpayments are recoverable if caused by misrepresentation or failure to disclose, housing benefit overpayments are all recoverable, except those caused by errors of the authority or the Benefits Agency, where the claimant did not contribute to the error and could not have been expected to realise that they had been overpaid.[131] Unlike backdating, there is no time limit for recovery of overpayments.

The decision as to whether the overpayment should be recovered is left to the discretion of the authority.[132] Recovery may be sought from the claimant, or the person to whom the overpayment was made (this may be the landlord where there are direct payments), or from any person whose misrepresentation or failure to disclose a material fact caused the overpayment.[133] The authority can also seek recovery by deduction from any ongoing housing benefit entitlement. Where this is not possible the authority can request that the Secretary of State recovers the money from other social security benefits in payment.[134] This means that the authority may well have a choice as to the person from whom it seeks to recover the money. One area of difficulty was where benefit had been paid direct to a landlord from whom an overpayment was recovered. The housing benefit regulations have been amended so that the tenant now becomes liable for any rent arrears that may have accrued because of the overpayment.

9. FRAUD

Whilst regulations on high rents and contrived tenancies have been concerned with ensuring that the benefit system is not abused, governments have more recently focused their concern upon fraudulent abuse of the system—by individual claimants and their landlords as well as large-scale organised fraud. Estimates of the degree of benefit fraud vary widely. The Government's recent Green Paper[135] suggests a conservative figure of £2 billion per year for social security as a whole, rising to a possible £7 billion. These figures are based on departmental benefit reviews which investigated samples of claims. The benefit review into housing benefit in 1996 suspected fraud in 8 per cent of claims, with a total estimated loss of about £1 billion. per year.[136] These figures are subject to considerable dispute: they are merely estimates based on samples containing judgments about suspicious claims and include overpayments resulting from errors and misunderstandings. However, they have

---

[129] DSS Press Release, 10 October 1997. [130] HB(G) Regs 1987, reg. 98. [131] Ibid., reg. 99.
[132] Ibid., reg. 100. [133] Ibid., reg. 101. [134] Ibid., regs 102 and 105.
[135] DSS, *Beating Fraud is Everyone's Business*, Cm 4012 (London: The Stationery Office, 1998).
[136] Ibid., 56.

been seized upon by the Government to justify its considerable concern with fraud, particularly in the context of housing benefit.

The 1997 Social Security Departmental Report[137] highlights 'bearing down on fraud and abuse' as one of the Government's main priorities. Many of the proposals apply specifically to housing benefit and are repeated in the subsequent social security Green Paper.[138] They are grouped under three headings: detection, deterrence, and prevention. The Audit Commission had pointed to a significant variation in practice between authorities, and to the fact that authorities had little incentive to investigate fraud when they bore the cost and government received the savings.[139] Since then there have been significant changes to the subsidy arrangements to attempt to provide financial incentives to authorities to detect fraud (see below). The Government has established a Benefit Fraud Inspectorate, which is to inspect and report on benefits administration in each authority. It has also provided challenge funding to enable authorities to bid for financial support for new initiatives such as home visiting, with the requirement that they deliver a weekly benefit saving of £3.50 for every £1 of challenge funding. More recently there has been the suggestion of developing a 'highly-skilled anti-fraud profession',[140] complete with its own specific training. Whilst fraud investigations by authorities have been rare, prosecutions have been even rarer. The Social Security Administration Fraud Act 1997 enables authorities to impose a financial penalty (30 per cent of the overpayment) as an alternative to prosecution. It also creates a new criminal offence of dishonest misrepresentation.

Initiatives to improve prevention have included the sharing of information via computer links with the Benefits Agency, and more rigorous checks at the outset of a claim. Here again the Audit Commission had noted considerable variation in practice, and the Government is now attempting to introduce rigour and consistency by producing a 'Verification Framework' for all claims.[141] This will include identification checks and standards required for evidence to support a claim. It is clear that the Government is intent upon changing the climate and culture of benefit administration to one where claims are viewed suspiciously, and the emphasis is on looking to refuse rather than to accept claims. No longer is the concern with lack of take-up, even though the Government estimates that the average amount unclaimed is over £25.00 per week, and that this is especially a problem in the private sector and for older people.[142]

---

[137] N. 123 above.   [138] Green Paper (1998) ch. 9.
[139] Audit Commission, *Remote Control: The National Administration of Housing Benefit* (London: HMSO, 1993), para. 58.
[140] DSS, *Beating Fraud is Everyone's Business*, Cmnd. 4012 (London: The Stationery Office, 1998), ch. 7.
[141] Green Paper (1998), 69.
[142] Department of Social Security, Press Release, 'Income related benefits. Estimates of Take-up in 1995/96', 10 October 1997.

10. SUBSIDIES

Central government has been concerned that local authorities who administer the scheme should do so efficiently and effectively. Government subsidies paid to authorities towards the cost of benefits and their administration have been used to 'reinforce local authority interest in prudent administration'.[143] Subsidies are determined by an annual housing benefit and council tax benefit subsidy order. Reduced subsidy has been used to discourage benefit expenditure—and more recently additional payments have sought to encourage successful fraud detection. Local authority decision making is influenced not only by the law (which gives it a considerable degree of discretion) but also by the financial implications.

When housing benefit was introduced, authorities needed to employ staff for its administration. The initial subsidy for administration was based upon actual costs; the variation in costs between authorities may have reflected the differential extent to which they promoted the new scheme, but the Government's concern was that it also reflected variations in efficiency. It therefore moved towards a subsidy based upon workload. This arrangement may well encourage authorities to save on the cost of administration, but there must be concern that it may be at the expense of the quality of service.

Central government meets the cost of 95 per cent of benefit payments. However, reduced subsidy is payable for high rents and backdating, with none for additional payments. These reduced subsidies are intended to ensure that authorities have a financial incentive to control benefit expenditure in these areas. The worry is that authorities will fail to give proper consideration to the considerable discretionary powers that they have, and that decisons will be driven by considerations of subsidy rather than the merits and circumstances of individual claims.[144] Martin Partington asks what should happen when there is a conflict between the housing benefit rules and the subsidy rules.[145] Whilst this was at issue in the case of *R v Housing Benefit Review Board of the London Borough of Brent, ex parte Connery*,[146] Partington considers that 'the really crucial issue—about the relative priorities of the scheme rules and the subsidy rules—has been ducked'.[147]

The case of overpayments and fraud is particularly interesting. Subsidy is determined by the cause of the overpayment. There is no subsidy where it has been caused by an error of the authority, whereas the overpayment qualifies for full subsidy when the error was made by the DSS, and 25 per cent where it is claimant error. As the Audit Commission noted, these arrangements gave authorities an incentive to

---

[143] Housing Benefit Review Team, *Housing Benefit Review: Report of the Review Team*, Cmnd. 9520 (London: HMSO, 1985), para. 5.21.
[144] For a fuller discussion see S. Rahilly, 'Housing Benefit: the Impact of Subsidies on Decision-making' (1995) 2 *J.S.S.L.* 198–209.
[145] M. Partington, 'Judicial Review and Housing Benefit' in T. Buck (ed.), *Judicial Review and Social Welfare* (London: Pinter, 1998), 182–201.
[146] (1990) 20 H.L.R. 40.   [147] M. Partington (1998), op. cit., 197.

ignore overpayments—particularly where they would be unlikely to recover the money.[148] Where they did decide that there had been an overpayment, recovery was often routine, although in law this should be a matter of discretion.[149] The arrangements were changed in August 1993, and those overpayments which are attributed to fraud now attract full subsidy. The intention is to encourage authorities to detect claimant fraud. To this end the Government has also set targets for fraud detection, with penalties and bonuses attached. The Labour Government has recognised that these arrangements might encourage authorities to detect rather than prevent fraud, to 'let in fraud' so that it can then be detected and to overstate their achievements.[150]

Subsidy arrangements for the rent rebates paid to council tenants are slightly different. Part VI of the Local Government and Housing Act 1989 provided that these subsidies should be paid into the authority's ring-fenced Housing Revenue Account (HRA) and combined with any other 'subsidies' received by that account, such as general subsidy towards debt repayment charges, and income from the council's general fund. The annual subsidy payment is now calculated on the basis of the notional deficit that the Government assumes that authority to have. This calculation is derived from notional income and expenditure, based upon government assumptions about appropriate figures for rental income, management and maintenance expenditure, and so on. In this calculation most rebate expenditure will fully qualify, but expenditure on backdating and overpayments (except those due to fraud or DSS error) does not. Government has been able to reduce the subsidy required to make up the notional deficit on the assumption that rental income will increase, and since the HRA is not allowed to show a loss, authorities have had little option but to put up their rents in line with Government guidelines. Recently the Government has become concerned that authorities have put up their rents above the guidelines, and from 1996–7 qualifying expenditure for subsidy has been restricted to the guideline rents. Thus the Government has begun to use housing benefit to control rent levels in the public sector.

It is not just those elements of rent rebate expenditure that do not qualify for subsidy which have to be met by the rents of council tenants. As rents have risen, so the amount of subsidy required to balance the HRA has declined. The present position is that for many councils the total amount of subsidy paid is significantly less than the cost of rebate expenditure. Nationally the figure is about £1.3 billion. This has been described as a 'double tax' for council tenants.[151] Not only do they contribute as taxpayers to the cost of rebates, they also have to contribute through their rents to the shortfall to rebate subsidy.

---

[148] Audit Commission, n. 139 above, para. 56.
[149] L. Burrows, L. Phelps, and P. Walentowicz, *For Whose Benefit? The Housing Benefit Scheme Reviewed* (London: NACAB and Shelter, 1993).
[150] DSS, *Beating Fraud is Everyone's Business*, Cmnd. 4012 (London: The Stationery Office, 1998), para. 6.4.
[151] A. Mitchell, 'Time to Bring Back Real Social Housing' (1998) *Housing Today*, No. 75, 19 March, 13.

11. HOUSING BENEFIT REVIEWS

The provisions for housing benefit do not contain a right of appeal, but rather a two-stage review. This arrangement was a compromise introduced via an amendement to the Social Security and Housing Benefits Bill in 1982.[152] The review boards, which are not required to have a lawyer chair, have been described as the new slums of the tribunal system and they have been criticised for their lack of independence and expertise[153] and for the inadequacy of the official information and guidance concerning their operation.[154] The Government review in 1985 concluded that there was no evidence to justify any change, because so few reviews had taken place. It also noted that authorities would be reluctant to see them transferred to a separate body since they were responsible for meeting the cost of decisions.[155] Whilst the Social Security Act 1986 attempted to align the means-tested benefits, it made no changes to the very different arrangements available to challenge decisions.

A review of a determination can be carried out at any time where there has been a change of circumstances, where the determination was made in ignorance of, or mistake about, a material fact, or where there was a mistake as to the law.[156] In addition, a determination made by the authority must be reviewed by that authority if it receives written representations, from a person affected, within six weeks of the determination (or from receipt of a statement of reasons for the determination).[157] This has been referred to as a mandatory internal review by Eardley and Sainsbury, who suggest that this first tier acts as an effective filter for the second stage.[158] In their two-year research funded by the DSS they noted significant variations in the ways in which representations were accepted as formal requests for review. Formal reviews were often seen as evidence of administrative failure, and requests were often dealt with informally by sending out further particulars. Dealing with the request informally obviated the duty to issue a further notice of determination, with details of the right to request a further review within four weeks of its receipt.[159]

The second tier of review requires a further request in writing. This must be signed by the person who made the original representations, and must set out the grounds for the request of a further review. This is conducted by a review board,[160] which is comprised of three councillors from the authority whose decision is being

---

[152] See p. 214 above.
[153] N. Wikeley, 'Housing Benefit Review Boards; the New Slum?' (1986) 5 *Civil Justice Quarterly*, 18–23. See also Chapter 5, section 2.F. As noted by Roy Sainsbury in Chapter 7, review boards have remained outside the jurisdiction of the Council on Tribunals.
[154] SSAC, *Fourth Report* (London: HMSO, 1985).
[155] Housing Benefit Review Team, *Housing Benefit Review. Report of the Review Team*, Cmnd. 9520 (London: HMSO, 1985).
[156] HB(G) Regs 1987, reg. 79(1).
[157] Ibid., reg. 79(2) and (4). Time periods can be extended if there is a special reason.
[158] T. Eardley and R. Sainsbury, 'Managing Appeals: Control of Housing Benefit Internal Reviews by Local Authority Officers' (1993) 22(4) *J. of Social Policy*, 461–85.
[159] HB(G) Regs 1987, reg. 77 and Sched. 6.   [160] Ibid., reg. 81.

contested; although the Board is appointed by the authority it has an independent status.[161] The board must conduct an oral hearing, giving the complainant the right to be heard and represented, but there is no requirement for the hearing to be public, nor for the chairs to be legally qualified. Wikeley suggests that board members may be reliant on the clerk (usually a solicitor from the authority's legal department).[162] Sainsbury and Eardley highlighted the board members' lack of training.[163] Perhaps their most interesting finding was that very few boards had been convened. Of the thirty-nine local authorities which they studied, six had never convened a review board up to 1990. In the three years after 1988 a quarter had not had a review board, and of the remainder over a half had only five or fewer. Sainsbury and Eardley concluded that the arrangements gave authorities significant control over the flow of reviews; over 95 per cent did not proceed beyond the initial stage.

A final major difference from social security appeal tribunals is that there is no right of further appeal to a Social Security Commissioner. The only options that may be available are challenge by judicial review, or complaint to the Local Government Ombudsman. The courts have held that the former is only possible if all alternative remedies available have been exercised.[164] However, the court retains an overriding discretion, and whilst it might be appropriate to expect a complaint to the ombudsman about maladministration, this would not be appropriate for judicial review grounds such as 'illegality, [dis]proportionality and irrationality'.[165] Complaints to the local ombudsman indicate continuing concerns about the quality of administration. In one year 211 complaints about Lambeth Council were considered by the ombudsman who concluded that they showed a litany of faults, errors, delays, and misleading information.[166]

12. INCOME SUPPORT AND HOUSING COSTS

A. Boarders and Persons in Residential Care and Nursing Homes

When housing benefit was introduced, assistance with housing costs for boarders remained with supplementary benefit. 'Boarders' included those in board and

---

[161] *R v Birmingham City Council Housing Benefit Review Board, ex p Birmingham City Council* (1991) 31 October (unreported) QBD, cited in L. Findlay, R. Poynter, and M. Ward, *CPAG's Housing Benefit and Council Tax Benefit Legislation* (London: CPAG, 1998), 245.

[162] N. Wikeley, n. 153 above.

[163] R. Sainsbury and T. Eardley, 'Housing Benefit Review Boards: a Case for Slum Clearance?' [1992] *P. L.* 551–9. In their study, three-quarters of the councillors sitting on review boards had received no training, and only 9 per cent had received any training since the introduction of the significant changes in 1988.

[164] See e.g. *R v Lambeth London Borough Council, ex p Ogunmuyiwa* (1997) 29 H.L.R. 950.

[165] *Per* Sir Louis Blom-Cooper QC in *R v Lambeth London Borough Council, ex p Crookes* (1995) 29 H.L.R. 28. See generally M. Partington, 'Judicial Review and Housing Benefit' in T. Buck (ed.), *Judicial Review and Social Welfare* (London: Pinter, 1998), 182–201.

[166] (1997) *Inside Housing*, 8 August.

lodgings, hostels, and those in residential care and nursing homes. The Government became increasingly concerned about alleged abuse: the suggestion was that young people in particular were deliberately leaving home to move to board and lodgings at seaside resorts (the 'Costa del Dole'), knowing that the costs would be met by benefit. The 1980s saw a series of attempts by the Government to restrict benefit entitlement, and various legal challenges to the *vires* of the new regulations.[167] From April 1989, housing costs for those living in hostels and board and lodgings were incorporated within housing benefit, leaving costs for residential care and nursing homes to be met up to specified limits by income support.

The National Health Service and Community Care Act 1990 led to the introduction of new funding arrangements for 'care in the community'. Those entering residential care after April 1993 remain eligible for income support, which includes a fixed residential allowance,[168] but this is unlikely to enable the cost of the accommodation to be met. Additional funding is dependent upon an assessment of needs and resources by the local social services authority. The effect of this change is to end the system whereby the social security budget has an open-ended commitment to meet the residential care costs of those on benefit. In its place there is provision for much more limited assistance from social security; additional funding is dependent upon the resources of the local authority as well as its assessment of needs. See further the discussion by Neville Harris in Chapter 6 (at pp. 195–7 above).

B. Mortgage Interest

A further area of housing costs that has remained outside the parameters of housing benefit is assistance with mortgage payments. Whilst this has led to continuing inequity on the basis of tenure, the main concern of the Government has not been to create a common benefit, but rather to maintain an incentive to work by reducing the assistance available for mortgages within income support. Assistance with mortgages has always been restricted to the interest on any loans taken out either for the purchase of a dwelling occupied as the home, or for repairs or improvements to maintain it in a habitable condition. Capital repayments, water rates, and house insurance are all ineligible for assistance. Further safeguards require that the loan to purchase the home was not taken out during the benefit period.

Non-dependants are expected to make a contribution towards housing costs (and deductions are made in exactly the same way as for housing benefit). Housing costs can be restricted if they are thought to be excessive (either because of the size of the property or because of its cost), provided it is reasonable to expect the claimant to move to suitable alternative accommodation. This echoes the original safeguard within housing benefit. It has more recently been extended to include an upper limit.

---

[167] For a full discussion see N. Harris, 'Board and Lodging Payments for Young People' [1987] *J.S.W.L.* 150–74.

[168] See pp. 195–7 above for the rules in detail.

Additional restrictions have been introduced to help maintain the incentive to work. Unlike housing benefit there is no taper as income rises. When entitlement to income support (or JSA) ends, there is no assistance available with mortgage interest. The Government was of the view that unemployed people were most likely to return to work in the first six months of unemployment, and that benefit payments should not act to dissuade people from returning to work because they were inflated by the inclusion of mortgage interest. It therefore decided that benefit should not include assistance with mortgage costs for the first eight weeks, and then only 50 per cent for the following eighteen weeks. Those still entitled to benefit after this six-month period are entitled to full mortgage interest. In line with its emphasis on personal responsibility the Government advocated that all new borrowers should take out insurance cover against future loss of income. Accordingly, those whose mortgages began after October 1995 are not able to receive any assistance with mortgage costs for the first thirty-nine weeks of their benefit claim. Yet research has shown that borrowers have little knowledge of these changes and that only one in five have private insurance. Furthermore, three-quarters of those at greatest risk are not insured. The position could become particularly serious if interest rates start to rise again.[169]

Mortgage interest is in fact another area where there has been significant tension between the Government's housing policy and its social security policy. Housing policy throughout the 1980s was dominated by the promotion of owner occupation. But by promoting owner occupation down the income scale and to people whose employment was insecure it contributed to the growing level of mortgage arrears and repossessions. Cuts to mortgage interest within social security benefits further added to the problem. The Government's response was to forsake its commitment to freedom and choice and pay all mortgage costs included within benefit direct to the lenders in an attempt to encourage them to reduce the number of repossessions.

Whilst recent changes have been driven by a desire to maintain the work incentive, they have added to the housing debts of those on benefit. At the same time they have failed to remove the 'unemployment trap', since there is still no assistance available for those who work for more than sixteen hours, no matter how low their income.[170] In 1985 both the SSAC and the Inquiry into British Housing called for a unified housing benefit for all tenures.[171] This has been repeated by the SSAC on several occasions since.[172] The universal housing allowance proposed by the Inquiry into British Housing would be determined by household size and could rise where there were additional costs associated with age, special needs, and regional location. The proposal was that this maximum allowance would be payable irrespective of tenure, and would reduce as income rises, and that its cost would be met by ending

---

[169] J. Ford and E. Kempson, *Bridging the Gap? Safety Nets for Mortgage Borrowers* (York: York Publishing Services, 1997).

[170] Family credit has taken no account of mortgage costs.

[171] SSAC, *Fourth Report* (London: HMSO; 1985) and National Federation of Housing Associations, *Inquiry into British Housing* (London: National Federation of Housing Associations, 1985).

[172] See for example SSAC (ibid.), 23.

mortgage interest tax relief. Whilst this proposal may have been in tune with the social security principle of targeting, there was concern that the impact of the abolition of tax relief might have conflicted with the housing imperative of support for owner-occupation. Whilst subsequent reductions in the value of tax relief eased the path towards its eventual abolition, they also removed the possibility that it could be used to fund a universal housing allowance.

13. CONCLUSION

The high profile that government has given to the need to eradicate fraud may have served to obscure its uncertainty as to the best way forward. Whilst it is clear that fundamental decisions about housing benefit reform need to be made, difficulties arise because of the way that it impacts upon other policy areas—such as housing and social services. It is the reductions in subsidy to the providers and the associated growth in rent levels which have exacerbated the difficulties within housing benefit. The growth in owner-occupation, in line with housing policy, has led to increased numbers of owners on low incomes with mortgage difficulties, and the need for the benefit system to become tenure-neutral. Emphasis on care in the community has highlighted the need for supported housing, with the necessary provision of services to meet personal needs so that the accommodation is sustainable. As a result, the scope of the benefit is in need of urgent review to clarify the boundaries between housing benefit and social services.

Housing benefit has been the subject of considerable scrutiny. With its cost now in the region of £12 billion per year, and its considerable contribution to work disincentives which make the 'welfare to work' policy even more difficult to achieve, it is no wonder that reform has been high on the Government agenda. A Green Paper is being prepared jointly by the DSS and the DETR.[173] It will consider the restructuring of rents as well as reforms to housing benefit.[174] What is needed has been described as a difficult three-card trick:[175] the need to contain costs, and increase incentives,[176] at the same time as preventing hardship. Incremental changes to the level of disregards and tapers could ease the poverty trap; the cost of these changes could be alleviated by reducing the extent to which maximum benefit meets full housing costs. But the danger is not just that this will be seen by households as a new poll tax, but also that it will significantly add to rent arrears, and in turn impact upon lender confidence. Recent housing policy has been predicated upon a public/private sector mix of capital investment, safeguarded by housing benefit. The Government has to be careful that reform of housing benefit does not destabilise the housing market.

[173] This was announced by the Chancellor of the Exchequer during the budget speech on 9 March 1999. At the time of going to press, publication was considered to be imminent.
[174] See DETR press release on 9 March 1999.
[175] S. Wilcox, 'More Tough Choices' (1998) *ROOF*, September/October, 12.
[176] Note that s. 79 of the Welfare Reform and Pensions Act 1999 makes provision for a scheme under which a payment might be made as a financial incentive to tenants in the public or social sector to reduce their housing costs (and therefore the cost of housing benefit) by moving to smaller accommodation.

Radical changes have been proposed. One is to combine housing benefit with the new tax credit scheme to provide an integrated 'work credit'.[177] Another is to replace the system of *ex post* allowances based on actual cost with *ex ante* assistance which provides low-income households with a subsidy to help them bid for housing of their choice.[178] The key importance of housing benefit to a range of social policy agendas means that radical change will have substantial repercussions; the alternative is continuing incremental changes which will no doubt continue to add to the complexity of the benefit.

---

[177] S. Wilcox, above n. 175.
[178] K. Gibb, 'A Housing Allowance for the UK? Preconditions for an Income-related Housing Subsidy' (1995) 10(4) *Housing Studies*, 517– 32.

14

Social Security, Money Management, and Debt

SIMON RAHILLY

1. INTRODUCTION

Successive governments have sought to contain spending on social security and maintain the poor-law principle of lesser eligibility—which is closely related to the current Government's policy agenda of 'welfare to work'. The imperative has been to ensure that benefit claimants remain at the lowest end of the range of incomes. Social security not only serves to relieve poverty, it also perpetuates it with low rates of benefit compared with other incomes (see Chapter 2). The promotion of self-reliance means that there will be strict limits on the provision of any extra assistance to help with particular financial difficulties.

Supplementary benefit had been very specific as to what claimants should be able to buy with their benefit:

. . . all items of normal expenditure on day-to-day living, other than housing benefit expenditure (. . .) including in particular food, household fuel, the purchase, cleaning, repair and replacement of clothing and footwear, normal travel costs, weekly laundry costs, miscellaneous household expenses such as toilet articles, cleaning materials, window cleaning and the replacement of small household goods (for example crockery, cooking utensils, light bulbs) and leisure and amenity items such as television licence and rental, newspapers, confectionery and tobacco.[1]

Other items which were not 'normal expenditure on day-to-day living' could be met by weekly additions which took into account the detailed costs associated with individual circumstances, or by single payments to meet the costs of specified one-off items (see pp. 129–132 above). For income support there are no equivalent regulations specifying what the benefit is intended to cover. The implication must be that it is intended to cover everything. Any additional assistance is now contained within a social fund which is largely discretionary and loans based. Yet recent decades have been characterised by growing expectations as well as growing income inequalities. Being on benefit, being on the lowest levels of income, means fewer available options to realise expectations and requires greater skill in the management of scarce resources. Debts will inevitably loom large in the attempt to survive on low levels of income, but whilst direct deductions from benefit may represent a useful strategy in the management of debt they are not available 'on demand'.

The Government's desire to promote individual responsibility and independence (and to reduce dependency) requires that claimants retain control over their benefit

---

[1] Supplementary Benefit (Requirements) Regulations 1983 (S.I. 1983 No. 1399), reg. 4(1).

income. Yet there remain significant provisions for reducing that freedom and independence when it is decided that claimants have not acted responsibly: measures include the imposition of direct deductions, the withholding of all or part of benefit, and the operation of sanctions and benefit penalties. This chapter seeks to explore the interconnections between debt and social security, by considering both the ways in which social security might be said to contribute to the debts and hardship faced by claimants as well as the ways in which it might be said to provide assistance through direct payments and grants and loans from the social fund.

2. CREDIT AND DEBT

The words 'credit' and 'debt' are often used interchangeably with reference to loans. But whilst loans may initially be described as forms of credit, they obviously become debts when due payments are not made.[2] Consumer credit doubled in the 1980s,[3] and by 1989 75 per cent of households had access to some form of credit (excluding mortgages).[4] The use of loans to assist with household budgeting became the norm. Berthoud, reporting that age and family structure are closely related to the use of credit, notes that unemployed couples with children make significantly more use of credit than pensioners. However, their level of credit is less than the population as a whole. Low-income households are unable to access many forms of credit, and are more likely to have to use high-cost credit such as mail order and money lending.[5] People on means-tested benefits are most likely to be excluded from financial services, with the consequence that they have to rely entirely upon cash transactions. Huby and Dix carried out a quantitative survey of 1,724 respondents with low incomes. Two-thirds reported that they were repaying a loan; the most common source of the loan was a catalogue, followed by family and friends. An additional 50 per cent were repaying social fund loans.[6] The researchers' estimate was that on average 22 per cent of income was spent on the repayment of loans. Borrowing from family and friends was more often an adopted strategy than a preferred one; the amounts tended to be small, and were often constrained by the low income of family and friend. The preferred option was to seek assistance from the DSS, though not all who preferred this option actually tried it, especially when their need was for a 'regular' as opposed to a 'one-off' item.[7] Other strategies included avoiding or delaying payment (especially when there was not thought to be a threat of retribution), and deciding to go without.[8] Past experience and the perceived likelihood of success would help to determine the strategy that is actually used.

---

[2] J. Ford, *Consuming Credit: Debt and Poverty in the UK* (London: CPAG, 1991).
[3] R. Berthoud, *Credit, Debt and Poverty*, SSAC Research Paper 1 (London: HMSO, 1989), 1.
[4] J. Ford, op. cit., 15.   [5] Ibid., ch. 2.
[6] M. Huby and G. Dix, *Evaluating the Social Fund* (London: HMSO, 1992), Tables 3.6 and 3.7.
[7] Ibid., Tables 3.1 and 3.2.
[8] Ibid., ch. 2. The introduction of fuel meters and cards will have significantly increased the level of self-disconnections because of insufficient income.

An analysis of enquiries to citizens' advice bureaux shows that enquiries about consumer and debt problems have grown significantly and now represent the largest enquiry category: 50 per cent of their clients in debt were not in full-time work.[9] A survey carried out by the National Association of Citizens' Advice Bureaux in 1990 showed that 69 per cent of those with debts were attempting to cope with three or more debts, and that severe debts were particularly common amongst unemployed people, disabled people, and carers.[10] Berthoud concludes that more than half of unemployed families with children are in debt.[11] It is clear that being in debt is a fact of life for many who are poor.

Households with low incomes tend to spend a greater proportion of their income on 'essentials'. Berthoud's research showed that benefit claimants incurred on average 2.5 'special expenses' (such as clothing, redecoration, fuel bills) every six months and were particularly anxious about fuel bills and children's clothes.[12] This finding was mirrored by Huby and Dix's quantitative survey.[13] Saving out of benefit income is rare: 60 per cent of Huby and Dix's respondents never managed to save, and an additional 18 per cent said that they hardly ever saved.[14] Howells argues that there is a clear need for the state to provide credit to assist claimants with the essentials which they cannot afford out of their weekly benefit, and that this power could be used creatively as a 'positive social service'.[15] However, he recognises that this will not be a positive service if it becomes a 'surrogate for the under-resourced basic income support system'.[16]

The adequacy of benefits (like the definition of poverty) is a much-contested issue in academic and political circles. The notion that social security provides a 'safety net' must remain open to question when the Government has not attempted to measure the adequacy of the net. In setting the initial scale rates for income support the Conservative Government specifically rejected an examination of need and poverty, on the basis that they could not be objectively measured.[17] Instead it aimed to determine priorities for spending by the identification of those with the greatest need.[18] A second objective of ensuring that social security was consistent with the Government's objectives for the economy required that benefits had to be set at levels which provided a clear incentive to work. Many people fall through the safety net because they are ineligible for assistance. Examples include 'people from abroad' (see Chapter 6) and students (see Chapter 11). Others may be eligible for benefit, but only for a particularly restricted amount—for example because they are under twenty-five years old. Certain expenses are not taken into account by the safety net: for example

[9] NACAB, *The Cost of Living* (London: NACAB, 1992). [10] Ibid., paras 10.1 and 10.2.
[11] R. Berthoud n. 3 above. [12] Ibid., para. 1.13
[13] M. Huby and G. Dix, n. 6 above, Table 2.1 [14] Ibid., Table 3.5.
[15] G. Howells, 'Social Fund Budgeting Loans—Social and Civil Justice?' (1990) 9 *Civil Justice Quarterly*, 118–38.
[16] Ibid., 123.
[17] Green Paper (1985) Vol. 2, paras 2.50 and 2.51. For a discussion on the adequacy of benefits see C. Walker, *Managing Poverty* (London: Routledge, 1993). See generally Chapter 2 above.
[18] Green Paper (1985) Vol. 1, para. 4.6.

there is no allowance for water rates, house insurance, or mortgage capital repayments, and there are now considerable restrictions as regards allowable rent and mortgage interest costs as well as significant deductions where there are non-dependants living with the claimant.[19]

Means-tested benefits serve many functions; in addition to providing a safety net, they are also reinforcing immigration controls, work incentives, labour discipline, and family values.[20] Conditions are attached to benefits and are often enforced by sanctions which operate to reduce benefit entitlement. For example, benefit sanctions apply to jobseekers who are not actively seeking work, who have failed to go for a job or an interview, or who have been dismissed for misconduct or left work voluntarily without just cause. Penalties are applied when a claimant or partner are involved in an industrial dispute, or when a lone parent fails to co-operate with the Child Support Agency. The result is that many claimants receive benefits below an already inadequate safety net.[21]

In addition, means-tested benefits, in particular, are fraught with problems of take-up and administrative error. Recent additional restrictions in the backdating of benefit entitlement have made take-up an even more serious issue.[22] Whilst Government figures show improvements in levels of take-up since 1988 when these benefits were introduced, there remain a substantial number of people eligible for benefits who are not receiving them (see Chapter 2). Piachaud has suggested that the actual number of eligible non-claimants may have risen.[23] The Government's focus has been on the elimination of fraud rather than the promotion of take-up, but this emphasis on fraud may well deter genuine claims.[24] Fraud itself may be a response to the difficulties of managing on a low income and the growing number of conditions attached to benefit entitlement. Rowlingson suggests that the rules which only allow a very small amount of income to be disregarded for income support and income-

---

[19] See Chapter 13. For a fuller discussion of the impact of the inability to pay for water charges see M. Huby, 'Water Poverty and Social Policy: a Review of Issues for Research' (1995) 24(2) *J. of Social Policy*, 219–36.

[20] See L. Dominelli, 'Thatcher's attack on social security: restructuring social control' (1988) *Critical Social Policy*, No. 23, 46–61.

[21] See L. Rhodes, 'Living Below Benefit Level' (1991) *Poverty*, No. 79, 15–17. See further Chapter 2.

[22] Social Security (Claims and Payments) Regulations 1987 (S.I. 1987 No. 1968), reg. 19. The prescribed time for claiming the means-tested benefits is the first day of the period for which the claim is made. There is no longer the possibility of a 12-month backdated claim based on establishing 'good cause'. Regulation 19(4) and (5) provides for a limit of 3 months provided that one of a limited list of circumstances exists (e.g. illness or disability and it was not reasonably practicable to obtain assistance from another person; information from the DSS or Department for Education and Employment which led the claimant to believe that the claim would not succeed). In addition, regulation 19(6) and (7) gives the Secretary of State the power to backdate for up to one month where this would be consistent with the proper administration of the benefit and one of a list of prescribed circumstances exists (e.g. transport or postal difficulties).

[23] D. Piachaud, 'The Growth of Means-Testing', in A. Walker and C. Walker (eds), *Britain Divided* (London: CPAG, 1997), 75–83.

[24] K. Rowlingson and C. Whyley, 'The Right Amount to the Right People? Reducing Fraud, Error and Non-Take-Up of Benefit', *Benefits*, January 1998, 7–10.

based JSA may provide a 'perverse incentive to commit fraud'.[25] Cook describes the combined demands of a flexible labour market and a stricter benefit system as acting like a 'pincer movement'. This may contribute to a growth in 'illegitimate' work at lower rates of pay, but in addition to benefit.[26]

In addition to those who have an entitlement but who are not claiming benefits to which they are entitled are those who are underpaid benefit due to errors in adjudication, as Roy Sainsbury notes in Chapter 7. Errors associated with the means-tested benefits are particularly prevalent. In 1996–7 the Chief Adjudication Officer commented that adjudication was incorrect in 45 per cent of income support decisions that were examined.[27] In 40 per cent of decisions examined the conclusion was that incorrect adjudication had either resulted in an incorrect payment or one of doubtful accuracy. Rowlingson's analysis of a Benefit Review conducted by the Benefits Agency in 1994 indicated that underpayments amounted to £120 million, compared to overpayments of £380 million.[28] While there are specific time-limits on the backdating of underpaid benefit following a review (although not where the review results from an official error or from newly discovered evidence),[29] overpayments may all be recovered if they are the result of the claimant's 'misrepresentation or failure to disclose'.[30] By 1998 there were 119,000 income support recipients with overpayments being recovered at an average of nearly £5 per week (see table Table 14.1, below).

In conclusion, it can be said that whilst credit has become commonplace throughout society it is debt that is of particular concern to those on benefit. In part this is an inevitable consequence of Government policy to ensure that benefit incomes are at the lowest end of an ever-widening income range. The result is that benefit levels often provide an inadequate income to meet the basic essentials. The position is worse for those with incomes below benefit level either because they are not receiving benefits to which they are entitled or because their failure to comply with conditions of entitlement has resulted in sanctions and reductions to benefit. Low income translates into reduced room for manoeuvre, and whilst claimants use a range of

---

[25] Ibid.

[26] D. Cook, 'Between a Rock and a Hard Place: The Realities of Working "On the Side"', *Benefits*, January 1998, 11–15. For a fuller discussion of the issue of fraud from the perspective of a benefit claimant see H. Dean and M. Melrose, 'Unravelling citizenship: the significance of social security fraud' (1996) 16(3) *Critical Social Policy*, 3–31 and idem, 'Manageable discord: fraud and resistance in the social security system' (1997) 31(2) *Social Policy and Administration*, 103–18 and D. Cook, *Poverty, Crime and Punishment* (London: CPAG, 1997).

[27] Central Adjudication Services, *Annual Report of the Chief Adjudication Officer 1996–97* (London: HMSO, 1997), 15.

[28] K. Rowlingson and C. Whyley, n. 24 above.

[29] Previously governed by the Social Security (Adjudication) Regulations 1995 (S.I. 1995 No. 1801), regs 57 and 63 but now being replaced by the Social Security and Child Support (Decisions and Appeals) Regulations 1999 (S.I. 1999 No. 991) (see Part II thereof).

[30] SSAA 1992, s. 71 For a full discussion of overpayments see P. Stagg, *Overpayments and Recovery of Social Security Benefits* (London: LAG, 1996) and P. Stagg, 'The Social Security (Overpayments) Act 1996' (1997) 4 *J.S.S.L.* 155–71. Section 36 of the SSA 1998 provides that overpayments of social fund grants are now also recoverable where the applicant had misrepresented or failed to disclose a material fact.

financial strategies it is clear that for many the preferred option is to seek assistance from the DSS.

3. DIRECT PAYMENTS

Benefits are usually paid to claimants themselves, whether by giro, order book, or credit transfer to a bank account, leaving them free to spend the money as they think fit. Payments from the social fund may be made to the applicant or direct to a third party (such as a supplier)[31] whilst social services authorities providing assistance under the National Assistance Act 1948 must use vouchers and payments in kind.[32] Whilst cash payments direct to claimants and vouchers may represent the two ends of the spectrum, the Social Security (Claims and Payments) Regulations 1987 provide for a range of situations in which an element of control can be exerted over a claimant's benefit. These include payment to an appointee when the claimant is unable to act,[33] payment to another person to 'protect the interest of the beneficiary',[34] and the withholding or suspension of benefit.[35] In addition, deductions can be made from benefit and paid direct to third parties.[36] Table 14.1 shows that just under a third of the 5 million income support claimants have an amount deducted at source for a direct payment.

It can be seen that direct deductions include payments to third parties for fuel, mortgage, fines, and so on, which may may well serve to prevent sanctions such as eviction, disconnection, or imprisonment, as well as repayments to the Secretary of State for social fund loans and overpayments. Some deductions include amounts for arrears (where the average deduction in August 1998 was £5.44), whilst others are for current costs (the average amount for these was £16.15). The overall caseload now seems to be fairly stable, but it trebled in the period 1991 to 1993.[37] The largest number of direct deductions (586,000) was for the repayment of social fund loans. This number has been steadily increasing, as has the number of deductions for council tax arrears.

There are some direct deductions over which claimants have no control. Deductions for mortgage interest are automatic provided that the lender is covered by the mortgage payments scheme. These arrangements were introduced in 1992 in an attempt to stem the escalating number of mortgage repossessions. Deductions

[31] SSCBA 1992, s. 138(3).
[32] For example to people who are ineligible for benefit because they are a 'person from abroad'. Under the terms of the 1999 Asylum and Immigration Bill these limited responsibilities will be transferred to the Home Office: see Chapter 6.
[33] S.I. 1987 No. 1968, above n. 22, reg. 33. [34] Ibid., reg. 34. [35] Ibid., regs 37AA and 37.
[36] Ibid., reg. 35 and Sched. 9. Direct deductions for community tax, council tax, and fines are governed by specific provisions such as the Council Tax (Deductions from Income Support) Regulations 1993 (S.I. 1993 No. 494).
[37] R. Mannion, S. Hutton, and R. Sainsbury, *Direct Payments from Income Support* (London: HMSO, 1994), Table 2.3.

Table 14.1. Direct deductions from income support, 1994 and 1998[38]

Type of deduction	Aug 1994 000s	Aug 1998 000s	Average amount Aug 1998, £pw
All types	1,604	1,530	12.56
Electricity	56	32	10.78
Gas	178	79	10.88
Water and sewerage	165	127	6.49
Mortgage interest	275	263	37.34
Other housing costs	114	103	11.86
Community charge	293	83	2.58
Council tax	11	125	2.57
Fines recovery	4	12	2.54
Social fund loan recovery	432	586	8.51
Overpayment recovery	72	119	4.99
Child support maintenance	4	1	4.66
Number of claimants with one or more deductions	1,048	1,115	
% of all claimants	27.9	29.0	

for social fund loans are also automatic (see below), and overpayments of benefit will be recovered by direct deduction when they have resulted from the claimant's misrepresentation or failure to disclose a material fact.[39] In other situations direct deductions might not be possible even if the claimant wants them. This is because they are subject to conditions prescribed in the regulations. For fuel the debt must have reached a prescribed level,[40] the fuel supply must continue to be needed, and it must be in the interests of the claimant that deductions should be made. The prescription of a maximum amount that may be deducted for arrears may well provide the claimant with the most reasonable financial arrangement to prevent disconnection, but there is a concern about the unlimited amount that can be deducted for current consumption. Once any arrears have been cleared it remains possible for the regular deductions to continue. For direct deductions for water charges there is also a requirement that it should be in the claimant's interest, as with fuel charges (above). In addition the claimant must have failed to budget for these costs.[41] Deductions for council tax and community charge arrears can be made if the local authority has obtained a liability order from the magistrates' court (or equivalent from a sherriff's

[38] DSS, *Income Support Quarterly Statistical Enquiry*, August 1998, Tables 12.1 and 12.2.
[39] SSAA 1992, s. 71.
[40] £51.40 in 1999–2000: Social Security (Claims and Payments) Regulations 1987, op. cit., Sched. 9 para. 6.
[41] Ibid., para. 7.

court in Scotland) and the magistrates' court (or any court in Scotland) can apply to the Benefits Agency for direct payments for a fine.

Assistance with rent is via housing benefit (see Chapter 13); this is automatically paid direct for council tenants, and can be paid direct for tenants in the private sector. Direct deductions for rent arrears (including any inclusive charges) can be made, provided the arrears amount to at least four times the weekly rent. If the arrears have accrued over an eight-week period the landlord may request direct payments. Where the period is shorter, direct deductions are only possible if they would be in the 'overriding interest' of the claimant.[42]

The various deductions above can be made from income support or income-based JSA, together with any incapacity benefit, retirement pension, or severe disablement allowance which are paid with them. However, regulations limit the amount that can be paid in respect of arrears[43] and place an overall ceiling where there are deductions for more than one debt.[44] Where this amount might be exceeded there is a statutory order of priority, which places child maintenance and fines at the bottom of the list.[45] These ceilings only apply to direct payments for arrears and not to deductions for current liabilities, but the claimant's consent is required when the combined deduction for arrears and current consumption of fuel, rent arrears, water charges, and housing costs arrears would amount to more than 25 per cent of their benefit entitlement for personal allowances and premiums.

Direct deductions from benefit can be compared with deductions from wages. They assist claimants with budgeting and provide security to creditors. They can also provide a degree of choice, but this choice is not absolute; as has already been discussed, some direct payments are automatic, whilst others are dependent upon the prescription within the regulations. Mannion, Hutton, and Sainsbury found that direct payments attracted positive all-round support.[46] Most of the direct deductions taken from their sample of claimants had been levied rather than requested,[47] although this figure would have been affected by mortgage deductions which are all automatic. Nevertheless, the increased number of deductions had been matched by an increased number of requests, about a quarter of which were refused—mainly because the person was not in receipt of income support or income-based JSA. On the positive side, claimants reported that direct payments prevented sanctions, prioritised budgeting and were cheaper than the alternatives. Criticisms included a lack of information (such as statements of account), some administrative errors and delays, a reduction in cash flow, and the high levels set by the fuel companies to represent current fuel consumption.[48] One measure of the success of direct payments was that there was no evidence of appeals (even when the deductions had been levied rather than requested). Another

---

[42] Social Security (Claims and Payments) Regulations 1987, above n. 22, Sched. 9, para. 5.
[43] To 5 per cent of the income support personal allowance for a single person aged over 25 (£2.57 in 1999–2000).
[44] In 1999–2000 this is usually £7.80.
[45] Social Security (Claims and Payments) Regulations 1987, above n. 22, Sched. 9 para. 9.
[46] R. Mannion, S. Hutton, and R. Sainsbury, n. 37 above, 88.   [47] Ibid., 29.   [48] Ibid., ch. 4.

was that there was some concern about the consequences of coming off direct payments (for example when benefit entitlement ended). This may act as a disincentive to leave benefits for work and may be viewed with some concern by a Government committed to the promotion of 'welfare to work' policies.

4. THE SOCIAL FUND

A. Introduction

The other main ways in which the social security system has provided help for those facing potential hardship and debt is by the provision of advice and additional financial assistance. This is the brief of the social fund. The background to its introduction and the rationale behind it are discussed by Neville Harris in Chapter 5. The fund has been described as an 'umbrella with four distinct schemes'.[49] These comprise, first, regulated grants for maternity, funerals, cold weather and winter fuel payments: whilst limited in their scope, these provide some official recognition that benefits are insufficient to cover every essential need. The other three 'schemes' are all discretion-based: community care grants; budgeting loans; and crisis loans, which unlike the other two are not restricted to those with an entitlement to benefit. Social fund officers (now referred to as 'appropriate officers') are appointed by the Secretary of State to make decisions and administer the fund.[50] Thus the scheme is administered separately from other benefits, although it requires considerable liaison with other sections. It should be noted that Walker, Dix, and Huby's research points to the work of social fund officers in fact being accorded low priority by other sections, and to feelings of antipathy from outside organisations.[51]

Maternity and funeral payments from the social fund replaced the universal maternity grant and death grant. Additional single payments had been available to those on supplementary benefit. Under the provisions of the Social Security Bill 1986 it was originally proposed that payments would be made in accordance with directions and guidance issued by the Secretary of State, in the same way as for other payments from the social fund. However, the Government accepted that they should be governed by regulation and subject to the same adjudication procedures as the remainder of the social security system.[52] As noted in Chapter 5, the Social

---

[49] G. Howells, 'Social Fund Budgeting Loans—Social and Civil Justice?' (1990) 9 *Civil Justice Quarterly*, 118–38, 119.

[50] SSAA 1992, s. 64. Section 36 of the SSA 1998 renames Social Fund Officers as 'appropriate officers', but the term social fund officer will be used for this chapter.

[51] R. Walker, G. Dix, and M. Huby, *Working the Fund* (London: HMSO, 1992), 13.

[52] Trevor Buck suggests that this is because these expenses were thought to be more 'predictable and certain': T. Buck, *The Social Fund: Law and Practice* (London: Sweet and Maxwell, 1996), 37. Mark Drakeford points to the 'continuing force which the twin poles of cradle and grave continued to exercise over policy makers': M. Drakeford, 'Last Rights? Funerals, Poverty and Social Exclusion' (1998) 27(4) *J. of Social Policy*, 507–24.

Fund (Maternity and Funeral Expenses) Act 1987[53] enabled the Secretary of State to make the necessary regulations for maternity and funeral expenses[54] and these were introduced ahead of the discretionary social fund (covered by the Social Security Act 1986) in April 1987. Cold weather payments were added to the regulated social fund by the Social Security Act 1988[55] with effect from November 1988, and the same statutory provision was used to introduce winter fuel payment in January 1998.[56]

It is the discretionary social fund that has attracted the greatest amount of attention and controversy[57]—because of the significance of discretion in decision making, the absence of a right of appeal to an independent tribunal, the fact that it is largely comprised of repayable loans, and the way that it operates within a fixed predetermined budget. It was clearly seen as a safety net for the safety net: 'to provide for exceptional circumstances and emergencies faced by a minority of claimants and to help those who find difficulty in managing their resources and budgeting'.[58] The discretionary nature of the fund was thought to be necessary to ensure that 'appropriate and flexible help can be given to those in genuine need'.[59] It has converted 'claimants' into 'applicants',[60] whilst the fixed budget has determined that the fund is supply-led rather than demand-led. It is as an instrument of financial control that it has been pronounced a success,[61] although the use of discretion in decision making has resulted in the administration costs for the social fund being by far the highest among all social security benefits. In 1994–5, 46 per cent of benefit expenditure on the social fund was spent on its administration.[62]

[53] See now SSCBA 1992, s. 138(1)(a). This provides for 'prescribed amounts . . . in prescribed circumstances (for) maternity expenses and funeral expenses', and should be contrasted with s. 138(1)(b) which allows other needs to be met 'in accordance with directions given or guidance issued'. The demarcation between the regulatory scheme (as provided by subs. (1)(a)) and the discretionary scheme (as in subs. (1)(b)) was reinforced by Harrison J in *R v Social Fund Inspector, ex p Harper* (1997) 7 February (unreported) Case No. CO/1904/96, QBD, in which he held that 'other needs' means needs exclusive of maternity and funeral expenses. For a discussion of this case see T. Buck, 'Case Analysis' (1997) 4(3) *J.S.S.L.* 134–8.

[54] Social Fund Maternity and Funeral Expenses (General) Regulations 1987 (S.I. 1987 No. 481).

[55] See now SSCBA 1992, s. 138(2) and Social Fund Cold Weather Payments (General) Regulations 1988 (S.I. 1988 No. 1724).

[56] Social Fund Winter Fuel Payment Regulations 1998 (S.I. 1998 No. 19).

[57] Published research into the operation of the social fund in its early years includes Social Security Research Consortium, *Cash Limited, Limited Cash* (London: AMA, 1992) and S. Becker and R. Silburn, *The New Poor Clients* (Wallington: Community Care and Benefits Research Unit, 1990).

[58] Green Paper (1985) Vol. 1, para. 9.8.   [59] Ibid.   [60] S. Becker, and R. Silburn, n. 57 above.

[61] See for example G. Craig, 'It Won't Be You: Britain's Forgotten Lottery', (1998) *Benefits*, September, 50–2.

[62] *Secretary of State for Social Security and Chief Secretary to the Treasury Social Security Department Report (1996)*, Figure 28. When expressed as a proportion of net costs the figure is 60 per cent. The Government has subsequently revised the way that these figures are presented to express administration costs as a proportion of expenditure plus loans recovered. This reduced the proportion to 21.5 per cent in 1996/97: HM Treasury, *The Government's Expenditure Plans 1998–99* (London: HMSO, 1998), Figure 19.

B. The Regulated Social Fund

(i) Maternity Expenses Payments

Entitlement to a maternity payment is confined to those in receipt of a means-tested benefit: income support, income-based JSA, working families tax credit, and disabled person's tax credit. The claim must be made in the period from eleven weeks before the expected week of confinement until three months after the actual date. There is also an entitlement to those who claim within three months of the date of an adoption and to those granted a parental order under the Human Embryology and Fertilisation Act 1990 enabling them to have a child by a surrogate mother. In the case of adoptions the child must be less than twelve months old when the claim is made. Any capital in excess of £500 must be deducted from the payment, and involvement in a trade dispute can result in disqualification.

Maternity expenses payments have remained at £100 since 1990 when they were increased from their original £85. Whilst this is more than the £25 that was paid as the universal maternity grant that these payments replaced, it still falls far short of the amount required to meet the needs of a new child. Payment is not for 'prescribed items' with a requirement to establish need but simply takes the form of a lump sum towards costs. 'Maternity expenses' has been narrowly interpreted as meaning the needs of a newly born baby.[63] Claimants on income support or income-based JSA may be able to request assistance for items such as fire-guards, safety gates, and buggies (which do not fall within the narrow definition of 'maternity expenses') from the discretionary social fund.

(ii) Funeral Payments

Beveridge's universal death grant had been set at £20. By 1982 it had only risen to £35 (but in that year 13,000 supplementary benefit claimants were awarded additional single payments towards funeral costs.)[64] The introduction of the social fund widened the numbers eligible for assistance to those in receipt of any of the means-tested benefits (as for maternity expenses above). Ten years later, 72,000 awards were made for the reasonable costs of a funeral. These averaged £924 each,[65] and in 1995 the Government introduced a limit of £500 on the amount that was payable to funeral directors for their fees. This was despite criticism from the SSAC that this sum would be insufficient to cover the actual charges.[66] The limit was increased in 1997, but only to £600.[67]

In addition, a new test became applicable where there is no surviving partner. This considers the ability of other close relatives to pay for the funeral.[68] The previous

---

[63] See T. Buck, 'Judicial Review and the Discretionary Social Fund: the Impact on a Respondent Organisation' in T. Buck (ed.), *Judicial Review and Social Welfare* (London: Pinter, 1998), 114–41, 126.
[64] M. Drakeford, n. 52 above, 513.   [65] Ibid.   [66] T. Buck (1996), n. 52 above, 291.
[67] Social Fund Maternity and Funeral Expenses Regulations 1987 (S.I. 1987 No. 481), reg. 7A, as amended by the Social Fund Maternity and Funeral Expenses (General) Amendment Regulations 1997 (S.I. 1997 No. 2538).
[68] Social Fund Maternity and Funeral Expenses Regulations 1987 (S.I. 1987 No. 481), reg. 7, as amended by S.I. 1997 No. 2538, n. 67 above.

rule was simply that before a payment could be made to the claimant it was necessary that there was not another close relative who had been equally or more closely
related to the deceased, who might reasonably meet the funeral costs, having regard
to their financial position, unless it was reasonable for the claimant to accept responsibility for the cost in view of the extent of their acquaintanceship with the deceased.
The position now is that provided they have accepted responsibility for the funeral,
partners (but not same-sex) of the deceased are eligible, as are parents (provided
there is not an absent parent who is not on benefit). Otherwise close relatives and
close friends who have accepted responsibility for a funeral will be eligible, but only
where it is considered reasonable for them to have accepted this responsibility.[69]
However, in addition, there must be no other 'immediate family member' (parent,
son, or daughter) who is not on benefit and was not estranged from the deceased,[70]
and no other close relative (which includes relatives by marriage) who was in closer
contact with the deceased, or was not on benefit and who was in equally close contact with the deceased. In other words, where there are other close relatives, the
nature and extent of their contact with the deceased is compared with that of the
claimant. This requires consideration of both the quantity and the quality of any
contact[71] and in effect requires the family to take responsibility for the funeral
before a payment will be made from the social fund. These rules may well deny
assistance to single parents, homosexual partners, and other carers. Refusal of a payment is not dependent upon there being some other person who will, in fact, pay for
the funeral, and Mark Drakeford's research in Wales suggests that these arrangements have resulted in both an increased indebtedness and a rise in the number of
requests being made to the local authority for assistance with a funeral.[72] The changes
to the rules governing funeral expenses payments resulted in 9,000 fewer awards
being made in 1997–8 compared with the previous year.[73]

A requirement of the original provisions was that the funeral took place in the
UK. This was considered by the European Court of Justice in *O'Flynn v Adjudication
Officer*.[74] Here an Irish national was resident in the UK where his son died. However,
the funeral took place in Ireland and the ECJ held that the rule discriminated against
nationals of other Member States who were more likely to have to arrange funerals
in their country of origin. As a result the rules have now been revised to include
funerals in an EEA state where either the deceased or the applicant are workers for
the purposes of EC Regulations.

---

[69] *CIS 12783/1996* (to be reported as *R(IS) 3/98*) has held that this should be decided with regard to
the entire relationship with the deceased, not just over the period preceding the death.

[70] Some other immediate family members are excluded; for example, those who are students: n. 68
above.

[71] See *CIS 8485/1995*.

[72] The increase in burials being carried out by authorities warns of the possible re-emergence of the
pauper's grave, which Beveridge had been keen to eradicate.

[73] Secretary of State for Social Security, *Annual Report by Secretary of State for Social Security on the Social
Fund*, Cm 4003 (London: The Stationery Office, 1998), para. 2.4.

[74] *Case C-237/94*, [1996] All ER (EC) 541.

(iii) Cold Weather Payments

In 1997–8 a total of £0.5 million was awarded in cold weather payments. Entitlement[75] is automatic (and no separate claim need be made for a payment) for those in receipt of income support or income-based JSA with a relevant pensioner or disability premium or with a child under the age of five in the household. It arises in respect of a 'period' or 'forecasted period' of 'cold weather', that is a period of seven consecutive days during which the average of the mean daily temperatures is, or is forecast to be, equal to or less than freezing, as determined by the appropriate weather stations. The Government has refused to take into account the wind-chill factor, but has recently increased the number of weather stations from seventy to seventy-two. No additional weekly payments were, however, made in 1997–8.[76] The payments have been criticized because of the stringent conditions which are required before payments are triggered and for the relatively small amounts involved. These have remained at a flat rate of £8.50 per week since 1996.

(iv) Winter Fuel Payments

Winter fuel payment (which takes the form of a one-off payment) is also automatically made to pensioners receiving income support.[77] A reduced amount has been payable to others over pensionable age. The Government committed £400 million to this payment for the two years 1997–8 and 1998–9 (with £20 million required for administration costs); one and a half million pensioners on income support received a £50 payment in November 1998 and a further eight and a half million pensioners received a £20 or £10 payment in January 1999.[78] The amount has been raised to £100 per pensioner household in the winter 1999–2000,[79] representing a substantial increase for a social security payment.

C. The Discretionary Social Fund

(i) Discretion

The discretionary social fund comprises community care grants, budgeting loans, and crisis loans. Whilst all are discretionary, social fund officers are required by statute to have regard to all the circumstances of the case, and in particular to:

(a) the nature, extent and urgency of the need;
(b) the existence of resources from which the need may be met;
(c) the possibility that some other person or body may wholly or partly meet it;

---

[75] SSCBA 1992, s. 138(2); Social Fund Cold Weather Payments (General) Regulations 1988 (S.I. 1988 No. 1724).

[76] Cm 4003, n. 73 above.

[77] Social Fund Winter Fuel Payment Regulations 1998 (S.I. 1998 No. 1724). See p. 182 above

[78] N. 73 above, and Secretary of State for Social Security, *Annual Report by the Secretary of State for Social Security on the Social Fund 1998/99*, Cm 4351 (London: The Stationery Office, 1999), para 2.7.

[79] Social Fund Winter Fuel Payment Amendment Regulations 1999 (S.I. 1999 No. 1880).

(d) where the payment is repayable, the likelihood of repayment and the time within which repayment is likely;
(e) any relevant allocation under section 168(1) to (4) of the [SSAA].[80]

The law does not indicate any priority or weighting between these five areas of consideration; nor does it define 'need'. The individual application must be considered, together with any supporting evidence, so that a view can be reached as to the 'nature, extent and urgency' of its particular need. Given that 'other persons' are considered in subsection (1)(c), Ogus, Barendt, and Wikeley suggest that the resources in (1)(b) must refer to those of the applicant together with any partner and dependent child.[81] Resources such as attendance allowance, the care component of DLA,[82] and arrears of benefits which are disregarded for the purposes of means-tested benefits such as income support, may well be taken into account for applications to the social fund. Subsection (1)(c) suggests a significant extension of the usual aggregation rules for means-tested benefits and even of the 'family' test of reponsibility introduced for funeral payments; the social fund officer has to decide whether there is a possibility of a third party (which could be a relative or friend, agency, or charity) meeting the need. The social fund is a fund of very last resort. The ability to repay is of relevance to budgeting and crisis loans, whilst the budgets are central to decision making for all of the discretionary fund.

The discretion of social fund officers is subject to directions and guidance issued by the Secretary of State.[83] Directions do not have to be approved by Parliament, nor presented in draft form to a body such as the SSAC for consultation. The nature and scope of the power to issue directions and guidance was considered by the court in *R v Secretary of State for Social Services and the Social Fund Inspectors, ex parte Stitt, Sherwin and Roberts*. Woolf LJ had expressed surprise in the Divisional Court that the statute gave such sweeping powers to the Secretary of State.[84] But the Court of Appeal agreed that the Secretary of State did have the power to issue directions which defined which needs might be met (and which would not).[85] The directions also determine which applicants are eligible for assistance. Additional provisions were introduced from July 1990[86] to give the Secretary of State an explicit power to order social fund officers to keep within their office budgets.[87] Other explicit powers include those to set upper and lower limits on payments, to prevent repeat applications (unless there has been a relevant change of circumstances) within a set period of time (currently twenty-six weeks),[88] and to make eligibility for some parts of the fund conditional on being in receipt of qualifying benefits.[89]

In *Stitt, Sherwin and Roberts*, Woolf LJ distinguished between directions, which must

---

[80] SSCBA 1992, s. 140(1). The SSA 1998 has made changes to the statutory criteria in respect of budgeting loans only: see section (iv) below.
[81] Ogus, Barendt, and Wikeley (1995), 514.
[82] But not the mobility component: see SSCBA 1992, s. 73(14).
[83] SSCBA 1992, ss 138(1)(b) and 140(2).   [84] (1990) *The Times*, 23 February (QBD).
[85] (1990) *The Times*, 5 July (CA).   [86] SSA 1990, s. 10.   [87] SSCBA 1992, s. 140(3).
[88] Social Fund Direction 7.   [89] SSCBA 1992, s. 140(4).

be followed, and guidance, which must be taken into account but is not binding.[90] The guidance issued by the Secretary of State is contained in the *Social Fund Guide*. The courts have pointed to its importance in ensuring that there is some consistency and fairness in decision making and have commented that the way that the guidance is taken into account must be transparent.[91] In addition to this central guidance, social fund officers must also take into account local guidance issued by the nominated social fund officer for the area.[92] Walker, Dix, and Huby report that the intention to tailor local spending to reflect local needs has failed to materialise and that local priorities are dominated by central directions and guidance.[93] In any event, although social fund officers surveyed stated that they attempted to give priority to consistency in decision making, individual discretion was evident throughout the processing of applications (for example, in deciding whether to interview). Moreover, decisions relied upon judgments which were often intuitive and peer aided and there was a substantial variation between offices as to which needs were considered eligible to be met.[94]

In summary, therefore, the general framework within which discretion is to be exercised is set out in the statute. This is subject to decisions being in accordance with any directions issued by the Secretary of State, one of which is that budgets must not be exceeded. In addition, social fund officers must have regard to guidance issued by the Secretary of State, as well as any by the local office. The outcome is what has been termed 'structured discretion',[95] a form of discretion with rules, which attempts to ensure consistency and flexibility. The danger is that it does neither, but introduces considerable uncertainty and reinforces the powerlessness of the applicant.

(ii) Budgets

In deciding whether to make a social fund award from the discretionary social fund, regard must be had to the local office budgets, which cannot be overspent.[96] This results in obvious limitations to the fund's ability to assist all those facing financial hardship. Whilst the determination of a fixed budget at the outset represented a new approach, it would be a mistake to think that the Government does not attempt to control spending in other areas of social security. The usual method is by adjusting the rules of entitlement, although this requires new regulations or statutes. Howells argues that the social fund represents a more honest approach, and one which makes more evident the extent of the Government's political commitment.[97] What is important is the size of the budget.

---

[90] N. 84 above. One of the central issues in these cases was whether guidance could make it mandatory to keep within budgets.

[91] *R v Independent Review Service, ex p Connell* (1994) 3 November (unreported) (QBD) (CO/1811/94). See T. Buck, 'Case Analysis' (1995) 2(2) *J.S.S.L.*, 113–16.

[92] SSCBA 1992, s. 140(5).

[93] R. Walker, G. Dix, and M. Huby, *Working the Fund* (London: HMSO, 1992), 15.

[94] Ibid., 28.

[95] G. Howells, 'Social Fund Budgeting Loans—Social and Civil Justice?' (1990) 9 *Civil Justice Quarterly*, 118–38, 126.

[96] Social Fund Direction 42.   [97] G. Howells, op. cit., 124–5.

Allocations to districts are made by the Secretary of State.[98] They can include amounts to be received by the repayment of loans,[99] and can specify 'different amounts for different purposes'.[100] In other words there is an allocation for community care grants and separate budgets for crisis and budgeting loans. Whilst allocations are usually made once a year, they can be made at any time that the Secretary of State considers appropriate.[101] The initial division between grants and loans was based upon research carried out by the Social Policy Research Unit at York University, which analysed single payments expenditure using draft social fund guidance.[102] Initial allocations to individual offices were made largely in relation to their proportion of total supplementary benefit single payments expenditure, but also with regard to the size of the claimant caseload, with weighting accorded to particular claimant groups. Subsequent allocations have been based upon the previous year's allocation, but have come to include a measure of demand as expressed by numbers of refusals because of the budget or lack of priority. Buck suggests that there has been an 'increased sophistication in the construction of the formula'.[103]

The initial allocation (in 1988–9) was for gross expenditure of £203 million (see Table 14.2). Since nearly three quarters of that amount was for repayable loans, this represented a considerable reduction on previous expenditure incurred on single payments (see Chapter 5, at pp. 133–4). In the first year there was a significant underspend of the budget,[104] but this was not to be repeated. Table 14.2 shows that the growth in the loans budget has been much greater than the growth in the grants budget. In net figures the overall budget has remained relatively constant, and the 'growth' in gross spending has been financed by recycling the increasing amount which is recovered from loan repayments. The Government describes this feature of the fund as one which combines effectiveness with value for money for the taxpayer; between 1988 and the end of 1995 £1.6 billion worth of loans had been made at a net cost of £334 million.[105]

Directions reinforce the fact that the budgets for grants and for loans are separate, and that neither budget can be overspent.[106] The amounts allocated must be controlled and managed by means of prioritising particular needs,[107] and area social fund officers have both to make a plan for expenditure throughout the year[108] and issue guidance

---

[98] SSAA 1992, s. 168.   [99] Ibid., s. 168(2).   [100] Ibid., s. 168(3)(b).
[101] Ibid., s. 168(3)(c). A small contingency reserve has been used to enable additional allocations to be made during the year to particular districts where unexpected needs arise. Whilst this has been used predominantly to provide increased funds for loans, a recent example has been for community care grants to help rehouse evacuees from Monserrat: see Secretary of State for Social Security, *Annual Report by Secretary of State for Social Security on the Social Fund 1997–98*, Cm 4003 (London: The Stationery Office, 1998), 15.
[102] National Audit Office, *The Social Fund* (London: HMSO, 1991), para. 2.2.
[103] T. Buck, *The Social Fund: Law and Practice* (London: Sweet and Maxwell, 1996), 49.
[104] This may have been due to large-scale take-up campaigns being given to single payments, or to initial antipathy to the fund, or merely lack of information and 'bedding down' commonly associated with the introduction of new benefits.
[105] HM Treasury, *The Government's Expenditure Plans 1997* (London: The Stationery Office, 1997), para. 84.
[106] Social Fund Direction 42.   [107] Social Fund Direction 40.
[108] Social Fund Direction 41(a).

Table 14.2. Gross and net expenditure on discretionary social fund (£millions)[109]

	Gross	Grants	Loans	Repayments	Net
1988–89	203	60	143	48	155
1989–90	203	60	141	108	95
1990–91	215	63	150	125	90
1991–92	228	68	160	148	80
1992–93	302	91	211	188	114
1993–94	346	95	250	210	136
1994–95	368	94	274	233	135
1995–96	401	96	305	263	138
1996–97	433	97	336	299	134
1997–98	467	97	370	333	134
1998–99	501	98	403	361	140

specifying both the relative priorities of particular needs (high, medium, and low) as well as the levels of priority that can be met.[110] Priorities and guidance can be varied during the course of the year, to ensure that spending keeps within allocations, and the area social fund officers are required to monitor and review their plan for expenditure at least once per month and make changes where necessary.[111] Whilst Walker, Dix, and Huby's research suggested that local offices tended to adopt national budget profiles, there was considerable diversity of decisions reflecting different budgets as well as different approaches to the management of the budgets. As a result there was both 'territorial inequity', with identical applications receiving variable outcomes in different offices, and 'temporal inequity', with variable chances of success depending upon the time at which the application was made.[112] It is this variation between offices and over time that has resulted in the social fund being described as a 'lottery'.[113]

(iii) Community Care Grants

Community care grants may only be awarded in the four situations which are set out in Direction 4. The first concerns the need to help applicants, members of their family and those for whom they are caring, to re-establish themselves within the community after a stay in institutional or residential care, or to help them set up home as part of a planned resettlement programme after being without a settled way of life, or to help them remain in the community.[114] Whilst 'family' will include married and

---

[109] HM Treasury, *The Government's Expenditure Plans, 1988–1998* (London: The Stationery Office, 1998); Secretary of State for Social Security, *Annual Report by Secretary of State for Social Security on the Social Fund 1997/98*, Cm 4003 (London: The Stationery Office, 1998), 15 and (same) *1998/99*, Cm 4351 (London: The Stationery Office, 1999), Annexe 1.

[110] Social Fund Direction 41(b).   [111] Social Fund Direction 41(c) and (d).

[112] R. Walker, G. Dix, and M. Huby, *Working the Fund* (London: HMSO, 1992).

[113] See for example G. Craig, 'It Won't Be You: Britain's Forgotten Lottery' (1998) *Benefits*, September, 50–2.

[114] Social Fund Direction 4(a)(i) and (ii).

unmarried couples, with or without children, and lone parents, the *Social Fund Guide* suggests that 'family' should be flexibly interpreted and can also include, for example, women who are least twenty-four weeks pregnant.[115] It has been suggested that 'family' for these purposes might also cover other groupings such as siblings and gay and lesbian couples, although a close relationship in terms of financial and mutual dependency is likely to be required.[116] The word 're-establish' has been interpreted literally to require the person to have previously lived in the community in the UK.[117] The *Social Fund Guide* states that 'institutional or residential care' means accommodation in which the applicant was resident because they were unable to live independently and which provides a substantial amount of care or supervision.[118] When considering a women's hostel the court has held that the key issue is not so much whether the applicant in fact received care or supervision there, but whether it was the rationale or objective of the institution to provide it.[119] Whilst the *Social Fund Guide* suggests that 'stay' should mean a period of at least three months,[120] Woolf LJ has stated that social fund officers should not give undue importance to this suggested period;[121] applicants should not be disqualified from eligibility for a grant to help them stay in the community because of a short period in residential care; a common-sense approach should be adopted.[122] Directions and guidance were revised in April 1997 to provide assistance to homeless people setting up home as part of a planned programme of rehabilitation.[123]

Secondly, community care grants may be awarded to relieve exceptional pressure on applicants and their families.[124] In one case it was held that the lack of a fridge, which would in turn require daily shopping, could in certain circumstances (e.g. illness) result in exceptional pressure on a family with five children (three of whom were under five, and all of whom were in poor health).[125] The individual facts of each case will be all important; in another case it was held that the pressures placed upon a lone parent with a young child to move out of her mother's house, following her mother's widowhood, were not exceptional.[126]

Thirdly, community care grants may be awarded to allow the applicant to care for a prisoner or young offender on temporary release.[127] The *Social Fund Guide* suggests that it would normally be reasonable to base the award on one seventh of the weekly rate of income support for each day.[128] Finally, community care grants may be awarded

---

[115] *Social Fund Guide*, para. 3503.
[116] T. Buck, *The Social Fund: Law and Practice* (London: Sweet and Maxwell, 1996), 322.
[117] *R v Social Fund Inspector, ex p Ali, Broadhurst, Rampling, Mohammed* (1992) *The Times,* 25 November (QBD).
[118] *Social Fund Guide*, para. 3201.   [119] *R v Social Fund Inspector, ex p Ibrahim* [1994] C.O.D. 260.
[120] Para. 3203.
[121] *R v Secretary of State for Social Services and the Social Fund Inspectors ex parte Stitt, Sherwin and Roberts* (1990) *The Times,* 23 February.
[122] In *Sherwin,* as above.   [123] Social Fund Direction 4(a)(v).
[124] Social Fund Direction 4(a)(iii).
[125] *R v Social Fund Inspector, ex p Ali* (1992) *The Times,* 25 November.
[126] *R v Social Fund Inspector, ex p Broadhurst,* decided with *Ali* (above).
[127] Social Fund Direction 4(a)(iv).   [128] Para. 3622.

to assist with travel expenses in the UK (and any overnight charges) to: 'visit some-one who is ill'; 'attend a relative's funeral'; 'ease a domestic crisis'; facilitate a visit to 'a child who is with another parent pending a court decision'; or to enable a 'move to suitable accommodation'.[129]

The directions specify a list of excluded items.[130] These include costs associated with telephones, fuel costs, housing costs (apart from minor repairs and improve-ments), council tax and water charges, most daily living expenses, and funeral expenses. Also excluded are 'expenses which the local authority has a statutory duty to meet'. It is suggested that this exclusion should only apply when the authority has accepted and is shortly to act upon a duty.[131] Eligibility for a community care grant is restricted to those who are in receipt of income support or income-based JSA at the time the application is received in a local office.[132] Applicants are also eligible for grants to help re-establish themselves within the community if they are likely to be discharged within six weeks of the application and are likely to be in receipt of income support or income-based JSA on discharge.[133] Applicants will be ineligible if they (or their partner) are involved in a trade dispute—except for assistance with travel expenses required for some visits to people who are ill.[134] Capital resources of more than £1,000 for applicants over sixty and £500 for others will result in any awards being reduced by the amount of capital over the relevant figure; only pay-ments from the Family Fund are disregarded.[135] Whilst there is no maximum amount for a grant, the minimum amount for any award (apart from living expenses for prisoners on temporary release and travel expenses) is £30.[136] The average amount of community care grant awarded in 1997–8 was £436.[137]

Guidance is intended to help social fund officers to assess the level of priority to accord to particular applications. High priority should be given if a grant 'will have a significant and substantial impact in resolving or improving the circumstances of an applicant and be very important in fulfilling the purpose of community care grants'.[138] Circumstances such as disability and illness may affect priority, and certain items may receive greater priority than others. Table 14.3 details expenditure on com-munity care grants and budgeting loans for 1997–8 and shows that pensioners and disabled applicants are more likely than the unemployed or lone parents to receive grants rather than loans. This leads to the conclusion that the distinction between the 'deserving' and 'undeserving' is perpetuated within the social fund, with the former more likely to get grants and the latter more likely to receive loans.

Table 14.4 shows that the largest proportion of expenditure is on furniture and household items. When spending on washing machines is included this accounts for

---

[129] Social Fund Direction 4(b).   [130] Social Fund Direction 29.
[131] T. Buck, *The Social Fund: Law and Practice* (London: Sweet and Maxwell, 1996), 390.
[132] Social Fund Direction 25(a).   [133] Social Fund Direction 25(b).
[134] Social Fund Direction 26.   [135] Social Fund Direction 27.   [136] Social Fund Direction 28.
[137] Secretary of State for Social Security, *Annual Report by Secretary of State for Social Security on the Social Fund 1998–99*, Cm 4351 (London: The Stationery Office, 1999), Annex 1.
[138] *Social Fund Guide*, para. 3709.

Table 14.3. Community care grants and budgeting loans:
expenditure by client group 1998–9[139]

| | Community care grants | | Budgeting loans | |
	Amount £m	%	Amount £m	%
Pensioners	11.5	11.8	13.5	3.9
Unemployed	10.6	10.8	52.9	15.4
Disabled	27.8	28.4	68.0	19.8
Lone parent	32.4	33.1	170.2	49.4
Others	15.6	15.9	39.6	11.5
TOTAL	97.9	100.0	344.2	100.0

over 70 per cent of all spending. This figure has remained fairly consistent since the inception of the social fund,[140] although the proportion of community care grant expenditure on washing machines has grown from 3 per cent in 1988–9 to 10 per cent in 1998–9. By contrast the amount spent on clothing and footwear remains small and has declined in proportionate terms over the same period from 6.6 per cent to 4.8 per cent of the total.

Table 14.4. Discretionary social fund:
proportionate gross expenditure by item 1998–9[141]

Itemp		Community care grants (%)	Budgeting loans (%)	Crisis loans (%)
Furniture &	Cookers	15.0	18.6	12.4
household	Beds	14.7	19.1	9.1
items	Floor covering	12.1	10.3	1.3
	Misc.	20.4	20.2	5.8
	(Total	62.2	68.2	28.6)
Washing machines		9.9	11.2	
Bedding		7.6	9.0	4.0
Home improvement and repair		0.0		
Removal expenses		4.8		
Travelling expenses		3.8		
Clothing & footwear		4.8	2.8	1.2
Living expenses (general)				27.3
Living expenses (alignment)				33.2
Others		6.8	8.9	4.4

---

[139] N. 137 above, Annex 3.   [140] T. Buck, above n. 131, at 66.
[141] N. 137 above, Annexes 4, 6, and 8. The figures show the percentage of total gross expenditure for each type of payment on an itemised basis.

Expenditure on community care grants rose from £60 million (if we discount the first year when there was a noticeable 'underspend') to £96 million by the middle of the 1990s. This increase did not keep up with the increase in the number of applicants over the same period—from 300,000 to 1,200,000.[142] As a result there has been a growth in the number of refusals (now about 1 million per year), and in the refusal rate (from 48 per cent to 80 per cent). The reasons for refusal are detailed in Table 14.5, which shows that 79 per cent of community care grant refusals (approximately 750,000 in number) are on the ground that Direction 4 is not met. This leads Buck to suggest that this is effectively 'another form of regulated scheme'.[143] A total of 90,000 claimants met the criteria outlined in Direction 4 as well as other requirements, but were refused because they had 'insufficient priority'. Essentially this means that although they fitted the criteria for a grant, the budget was insufficient to enable any payment to be made. The total number refused for this reason since the scheme was introduced stands at over 600,000.[144] Huby and Dix could not clearly distinguish between the needs and circumstances of those who were successful and those who were not. They concluded that the social fund was only meeting its community care objectives 'to a limited extent'.[145]

Table 14.5. Community care grants: reasons for refusal 1998–9[146]

Reason for refusal	Number	%
Savings	1,780	0.2
Not in receipt of income support and unlikely to be	76,688	8.1
Excluded items	9,059	1.0
Direction 4 not satisfied	746,667	79.2
Amount less than £30, not travelling expenses	413	0.0
Previous application	11,845	1.3
Insufficient priority	91,251	9.7
Other	4,554	0.5
Total	942,257	100

[142] See for example G. Craig, 'It Won't Be You: Britain's Forgotten Lottery', (1998) *Benefits*, September, 50–2.
[143] T. Buck, (1996), n. 131 above, at 66.
[144] G. Craig, op. cit., n. 142 above. This excludes the total for 1998–9.
[145] M. Huby and G. Dix, *Evaluating the Social Fund* (London: HMSO, 1992), paras 8.7 and 8.8.
[146] Secretary of State for Social Security, *Annual Report by Secretary of State for Social Security on the Social Fund 1998–99*, Cm 4351 (London: The Stationery Office, 1999), Annex 5.

(iv) Budgeting Loans

A total of over £340 million in budgeting loans was paid out in 1998–9 (see Table 14.3), with the result that this area of the fund involved by far the greatest level of expenditure. Budgeting loans constitute what Craig has called the 'ideological heart and soul of the social fund'.[147] They may be paid to 'assist an applicant to meet important intermittent expenses . . . for which it may be difficult to budget'.[148] These discretionary payments can meet the cost (or part of the cost) of what are sometimes referred to as 'one-off expenses'. Table 14.4 shows the areas covered and the relative expenditure on each. It can be seen that furniture and household items, especially beds and cookers, are the largest areas of expenditure. Payments to successful applicants take the form of repayable loans.[149] To be eligible, applicants must be in receipt of income support or income-based JSA and they (or their partner) must have been on benefit for at least twenty-six weeks prior to the decision.[150] The minimum amount is £30 whilst the maximum amount that an applicant and their partner can have outstanding on social fund loans is £1,000.[151] A further restriction is that the applicant cannot be awarded more than they are 'likely to be able to repay'.[152]

Table 14.6 shows that an inability to repay resulted in 11,102 refusals (2.5 per cent of the total) in 1998–9 (more than double that in the previous year) whilst just over 3 per cent of refusals were because the items were excluded.[153] The most common reason was that the applicant had not been in receipt of the required benefit for twenty-six weeks. This accounted for over 40 per cent of the refusals and suggests

Table 14.6. Budgeting loans: reasons for refusal 1998–9[154]

Reason for refusal	Number	%
Not on income support	83,143	18.9
Not on income support for 26 weeks	190,847	43.3
Excluded items	13,443	3.1
Inability to repay	11,102	2.5
Community care grant awarded	37,064	8.4
Previous application	23,987	5.4
Insufficient priority	67,714	15.4
Other	13,238	3.0
Total	440,538	100.0

[147] G. Craig, op. cit., n. 142 above.   [148] Social Fund Direction 2.
[149] Social Fund Direction 5.
[150] Social Fund Direction 8. The critical date is the date of decision (as opposed to the date of application).
[151] Social Fund Direction 10.   [152] Social Fund Direction 11.
[153] Social Fund Direction 12; for a full discussion of these exclusions see T. Buck, *The Social Fund: Law and Practice* (London: Sweet and Maxwell, 1996), 346–62.
[154] Above n. 146, Annex 7.

that it is not only those who have been on benefit for a longer term that find themselves in need of additional financial assistance. 'Insufficient priority' accounted for 15 per cent of refusals; this is much more significant as a reason for refusal than for community care grants (see Table 14.5), and suggests that the budget is in relative terms more likely to be the reason for refusal for a loan than a grant—even though the former is repayable. However, the overall refusal rate for budgeting loans continues to be below that for grants, and has fallen to 36 per cent from an initial 41 per cent.[155]

Social fund officers not only have a duty to determine budgeting loans, they are also expected to be able to give advice on budgeting. In fulfilling this function they act as 'money advisers'. Advice might be given following a request to reschedule loan repayments, or when claimants appear to be experiencing extreme difficulties in budgeting. Requests for assistance might be made by social fund applicants, or on their behalf by an outside agency. Walker, Dix, and Huby could find no evidence of referrals from agencies, who often thought that there was an incompatibility between social fund adjudication and the provision of money advice.[156] Furthermore, they found little interest on the part of applicants, and little training and time given to social fund officers for this work.[157]

The Social Security Act 1998 has heralded changes for budgeting loans, with the aim of introducing a 'fact based approach' from April 1999.[158] Discretion is replaced by automated decision making: decisions will no longer be based upon an assessment of the 'nature, extent and urgency of the need'. Items will not be prioritised, and applicants will merely have to indicate a broad category under which they are applying. Whilst applications for assistance for items that are outside the scope of these broad categories may be refused, there will no longer be a list of specific exclusions,[159] nor will there be restrictions on repeat applications. The maximum amount that may be paid as a budgeting loan to any individual applicant will in future be determined by the local budget, by whether the applicant has any existing loans, by the length of time on benefit, and by family size.[160] The existing overriding maximum

---

[155] Above n. 146, Annex 1 and G. Craig, 'It Won't Be You: Britain's Forgotten Lottery' (1998) *Benefits*, September, 50–2.

[156] NACAB, *The Cost of Living* (London: NACAB, 1992), for example, argued that social fund officers would be in a compromised position if they combined their role as creditor with that of adviser.

[157] R. Walker, G. Dix, and M. Huby, *Working the Fund* (London: HMSO, 1992), ch. 6.

[158] SSA 1998, s. 71, and Secretary of State for Social Security, *Annual Report by Secretary of State for Social Security on the Social Fund 1997–98*, Cm 4003 (London: The Stationery Office, 1998), 12.

[159] Previously in Social Fund Direction 12. For example, Direction 12(j) excluded various medical and related needs. In *R v Social Fund Inspector, ex p Connick* [1994] C.O.D. 74, Hidden J rejected the social fund inspector's argument that a need for incontinence pads should not be met under the social fund simply because such a need suggested that there was a medical problem. The question was whether the item sought was a 'medical item'. (This was the approach taken in Commissioner's decision *CSB/1360/86(T)*, which Hidden J followed.) The fact that a need for an everyday item arose because of a medical condition was considered not to preclude a payment.

[160] Thus arrangements for prioritisation will no longer be determined locally, and will become consistent in the sense that they will be determined by a universal system for weighting. Factors of between 1 (for 6 months) and 1.5 (for 3 or more years) will be applied according to the length of time on benefit. Additional weighting of one-third will be applied when the applicant has a partner, with two-thirds for the first child and one-third for each additional child.

of £1,000 will be retained, but awards will also take into account existing loans.[161] Section 71 of the Social Security Act 1998 enables the common, and cumbersome, application form which had permitted an application for a loan to be considered for a grant (and vice versa) to be replaced by three separate application forms for grants and loans. Table 14.6 (above) shows that over 37,000 applicants were refused a budgeting loan in 1998–9 because they were awarded a community care grant. Whilst it is argued that the new application forms will result in considerable simplification for applicants, there must be a danger that some people will not receive grants because they make the wrong application.

(v) Crisis Loans

Crisis loans may be awarded 'in an emergency, or as a consequence of a disaster, provided that the provision of such assistance is the only means by which serious damage or serious risk to the health or safety of that person, or to a member of his family, may be prevented'.[162] Where a community care grant is being paid to enable an applicant to re-establish themselves within the community, a crisis loan can also be paid for rent in advance to a private sector landlord.[163] Applicants for crisis loans do not have to be in receipt of a qualifying benefit; they merely need to have insufficient resources to meet their immediate short-term needs.[164] However, certain people are excluded (for example those in residential accommodation, in prison, or in accommodation provided by a religious order).[165] Full-time students not in receipt of income support and 'people from abroad' can only be awarded a crisis loan after a disaster.[166] The same restriction applies to those involved in trade disputes (who can additionally be considered for items for cooking and space heating).[167] Crisis loans are more likely to be awarded for living expenses than for particular items. Table 14.4 (above) shows that a third of crisis loans are awarded for living expenses 'alignment' (i.e. to cover the period before another benefit becomes payable). A further quarter of all expenditure on crisis loans is for general living expenses: the amount awarded here is based upon 75 per cent of the adult personal allowance for income support together with amounts for children at the under-eleven rate,[168] with further possible reductions for those who have been held to be 'voluntarily unemployed'.[169]

The maximum amount allowed in crisis loan for an item is the cost of repair, or the reasonable costs of replacement or purchase, subject to a requirement that the total amount outstanding to the social fund does not exceed £1,000.[170] Once again there is a list of excluded items.[171]

---

[161] The formula that is proposed will limit a loan when an applicant already has an existing SF debt in the following way: Loan = Maximum Amount − (Debt + Loan).

[162] Social Fund Direction 3(a). Neither 'emergency' nor 'disaster' is defined in the directions.

[163] Social Fund Direction 3(b).   [164] Social Fund Direction 14.

[165] Social Fund Direction 15.   [166] Social Fund Direction 16.   [167] Social Fund Direction 17.

[168] Social Fund Direction 18.   [169] Social Fund Direction 20.   [170] Social Fund Direction 21.

[171] Social Fund Direction 23.

(vi) Repayments

The likelihood of repayment and the length of time required to repay are two of the factors that are required to be considered in making decisions about budgeting and crisis loans.[172] This statutory requirement is repeated in Directions 11 and 22, which confirm that loans may not 'be awarded in excess of amounts that the applicant is likely to be able to afford to repay'. This leads to the ironic possibility that those with the greatest financial difficulties are the least able to receive assistance. Guidance suggests that loans need to be repaid within seventy-eight weeks, or in exceptional circumstances 104 weeks.[173] The Secretary of State has the power to recover all social fund loans,[174] and guidance suggests that this will be at the rate of 15 per cent of the income support applicable amount (excluding any housing costs).[175] This rate can be reduced to 10 per cent or 5 per cent where the applicant has existing commitments. Loan repayments can be rescheduled if the loan could be repaid more quickly, or if hardship would result from continuing the repayments at the current rate.[176] Recovery can be from the applicant, their partner, and in some cases from a liable relative or a sponsor[177] and will usually be by direct deduction from benefits apart from child benefit, disability living allowance, and attendance allowance.[178]

Whilst the numbers applying for loans must indicate the fact that to claimants and others needing support they represent a welcome feature of the social security system, it is hard to escape the conclusion that the award of a loan contributes to future hardship. Their attraction may be that they have the potential to provide for some flexibility to enable immediate needs to be met. But applicants have little control over the rates of repayment, which are in general set at relatively high rates given the level of claimants' total income. Table 14.1 (above) shows that, in August 1998, 586,000 income support recipients were having a social fund loan recovered and that the average weekly amount being recovered was £8.51. This figure can be contrasted with the maximum deduction for fuel arrears of £2.55. During the repayment period applicants will receive an income that is significantly below standard benefit levels which are themselves already inadequate. Howells has contrasted these arrangements with those in the Netherlands, where the scale rates of benefits have included a notional allowance of 12 per cent to cover one-off expenses and where repayments of loans were on easier terms.[179]

(vii) Reviews

Decisions on the discretionary social fund cannot be appealed to an independent tribunal, but there is a right to an internal office review and then to an external review by a Social Fund Inspector (SFI). Requests for review must be made in writing within

---

[172] SSCBA 1992, s. 140(1)(d). [173] *Social Fund Decision and Review Guide*, paras 4003 and 4004.
[174] SSAA 1992, s. 78(2). [175] *Social Fund Decision and Review Guide*, para. 4013.
[176] Ibid., para. 4040. [177] SSAA 1992, s.78(3).
[178] Social Fund (Recovery by Deductions from Benefits) Regulations 1988 (S.I. 1988 No. 35).
[179] G. Howells, 'Social Fund Budgeting Loans—Social and Civil Justice?' (1990) 9 *Civil Justice Quarterly*, 118–38, at 135–7.

twenty-eight days of the determination;[180] the request must set out the particulars of
the grounds for review. The review will be carried out by a social fund officer acting
as a reviewing officer. If the social fund officer is unable to revise the decision wholly
in the applicant's favour, the applicant is to be given the opportunity to attend an
office interview, before the review determination is made.[181] The office interview
should enable the social fund officer to explain the reasons for the decision, and the
applicant to make representations and present any new evidence.[182] This is the only
point at which the applicant has the opportunity to make oral representations. The
actual review consists of two stages: firstly the reviewing officer must consider
whether the decision was procedurally correct.[183] This has been likened by Woolf LJ
to judicial review.[184] The second stage is to consider the merits of the case.[185] The
decision must be given in writing and must contain information as to the applicant's
right to request a further review by a SFI. About 10 per cent of decisions result in
applications for review. Of these, just over one-third are revised by social fund officers at the internal review.[186]

As Neville Harris notes in Chapter 5, SFIs were introduced via a Government
amendment to the Social Security Bill 1986 in response to pressure that there should
be some external review of social fund officer decisions. They are appointed by the
Social Fund Commissioner (who is in turn appointed by the Secretary of State) and
work for what is now called the Independent Review Service (IRS) based in
Birmingham.[187] Their powers are to confirm, substitute, or refer back decisions made
by social fund officers.[188] The post of Social Fund Commissioner was created via an
amendment in the House of Lords, to ensure the independence of SFIs.[189] Unlike
the Social Security Commissioners, the Social Fund Commissioner does not consider
appeals on individual cases but is responsible for the appointment of SFIs, monitoring the quality of decision making, and presenting an annual report to the
Secretary of State.

Applications for review by the SFI must be made in writing, setting out the
grounds, to the local Benefits Agency office. Again there is a twenty-eight-day time-
limit. Copies of all relevant documentation are then forwarded to the IRS which in

---

[180] This time-period can be extended where there are 'special reasons': Social Fund (Application for
Review) Regulations 1988 (S.I. 1988 No. 34), reg. 2(3).
[181] Social Fund Direction 33.   [182] Social Fund Direction 34.   [183] Social Fund Direction 39.
[184] In *R v Secretary of State for Social Services and the Social Fund Inspectors, ex p Stitt, Sherwin and Roberts* (1990)
The Times, 23 February.
[185] Social Fund Direction 32.
[186] Secretary of State for Social Security, *Annual Report by Secretary of State for Social Security on the Social
Fund 1998–99*, Cm 4351 (London: The Stationery Office, 1999), Annex 10.
[187] Trevor Buck notes that about 25 per cent of SFI appointments are 'external' to the civil service and
that these tend to be on fixed term contracts: T. Buck, 'Judicial Review and the Discretionary Social Fund:
the Impact on a Respondent Organisation' in T. Buck (ed.), *Judicial Review and Social Security* (London: Pinter,
1998), 114–41, 118.
[188] SSAA 1992, s. 66.
[189] Note that whilst legal advice is received from the DSS solicitors, the IRS also commissions independent legal advice. See T. Buck, (1998), op. cit., 123.

turn provides copies for the applicant. The openness of the procedure has been commended (perhaps by contrast with that of the social fund officer), as has the thoroughness of the examination provided by the SFI and their independence from the social fund officers.[190] In providing a second review the IRS might be said to be providing some external inspection and supervision of initial decision making. Whilst the role of the SFI is inquisitorial,[191] this is hampered by the fact that the applicant has no right to an oral hearing. SFIs are essentially carrying out paper reviews, and the onus is therefore on the applicant to provide any new evidence. If the applicant presents expert evidence (e.g. a consultant's report), then that should, prima facie, be accepted in the absence of conflicting expert evidence. If the inspector is unhappy with any evidence then the applicant should be given the opportunity to comment.[192]

Of the decisions reviewed by SFIs in 1998–9, 60 per cent were confirmed and 38 per cent resulted in a substituted decision. Only 1 per cent were referred back for redetermination.[193] In addition there were over 500 reviews carried out by SFIs under section 66(5) of the Social Security Administration Act 1992. This provision gives SFIs a general discretionary power to review their own decisions and to make corrections where there have been accidental errors, procedural irregularities, mistakes or omissions of material fact, or errors of law, and may thus obviate the need to seek judicial review.[194]

Whilst the social fund may be discretionary, applicants still have the right to have their applications dealt with fairly, and with proper regard to both their personal circumstances as well as the provisions of statute, directions, and guidance. Unlike other areas of social security adjudication decisions must also have regard to other competing applications. For this reason (and perhaps because of the relatively small amount of money that is often involved) the Government did not think that the traditional independent appeal tribunal was appropriate. The addition of a second review by a SFI (independent of the local office social fund officer and appointed by the Social Fund Commissioner) clearly represented a step towards ensuring that decisions are seen to be fair, but there remains the problem that the absence of a right to an oral hearing means that applicants may well feel denied an opportunity to put their case. Furthermore, in 1998–9 less than 10 per cent of those applicants who

---

[190] G. Dalley and R. Berthoud, *Challenging Discretion: the Social Fund Review Procedure* (London: PSI, 1992).

[191] T. Buck, *The Social Fund: Law and Practice* (London: Sweet and Maxwell, 1996), 105 whose discussion on this was approved by Dyson J in R v *Social Fund Inspector, ex p Taylor (1998) The Times*, 20 January (QBD). This case is discussed in T. Buck, 'Case Analysis' (1998) 5(2) *J.S.S.L.* 89–94.

[192] R v *Social Fund Inspector, ex p Taylor*, op. cit.

[193] Over the years the proportion of social fund officer decisions which have been confirmed has risen from 52 per cent to 63 per cent. However more significant has been the changes in the proportion which result in a substituted decision (4 per cent in 1988/89 and 38 per cent in 1998/99) and those which are referred back (down from 44 per cent in 1988/89 to 1 per cent in 1998/99).

[194] For a full discussion of this point and of the use of judicial review in the context of the social fund see T. Buck, 'Judicial Review and the Discretionary Social Fund: the Impact on a Respondent Organisation' in T. Buck (ed.), *Judicial Review and Social Welfare* (London: Pinter, 1998), 114–41.

had failed in their request for review at the initial stage proceeded to apply to the SFI,[195] suggesting the procedure is problematic in relation to accessibility.

5. CONCLUSION

The means-tested benefits represent the safety net of the social security system, yet are not based upon an agreed determination of levels of income which are adequate to meet needs (see Chapter 2). Nevertheless, the implicit official assumption is that benefit levels are, in fact, adequate to meet all essential needs. This is accompanied by the view that if additional assistance is required by some claimants, it is because of their inability to budget. Yet all the evidence points to the fact that budgeting on benefit income is not possible without hardship; coping strategies include borrowing and 'going without'. Debts are the norm. Direct payments from benefit provide a welcome method of guaranteeing future fuel, water, and shelter, but further reduce disposable income. This in turn reduces the ability to meet occasional needs by making flexible adjustments to weekly expenditure.

Grants provided by the regulated social fund are limited in their scope and extent. The discretionary social fund is constrained by a fixed budget, and provides for limited grants associated with care in the community, together with repayable loans, which in turn lead to a greater indebtedness. It is associated with temporal and geographical inconsistencies. Whilst decisions may be reviewed, there is a lack of independence in the initial review and no means of establishing case law (except through judicial review).

With a realisation that the social fund is here to stay, initial calls for its abolition have given way to suggestions for reform. Some have argued that the provision of mandatory grants in the regulated system should be expanded. The Social Security Advisory Committee has proposed that mandatory grants should be paid in defined circumstances such as setting up a new home, moving out of care, and in domestic emergencies. Otherwise loans should be available, but there should be an easing of the repayment terms. In order to prevent increased indebtedness it proposed that no further loan should be made until a significant proportion of the first has been repaid.[196] Others have proposed 'bonuses' to be paid at regular intervals. Regular grants, in the light of ongoing needs, had been proposed by the SSAC in 1985.[197] The Commission on Social Justice (which was established by the Labour Party when it was in opposition) called for regular additional payments, together with special payments for defined crises, and discretion to meet other needs.[198] Craig had proposed a similar arrangement.[199] In extending the annual winter fuel bonuses to pensioners

---

[195] N. 186 above, Appendix 10.
[196] SSAC, *The Social Fund—A New Structure* (London: HMSO, 1992).
[197] SSAC, *Fourth Report* (London: HMSO, 1985).
[198] Commission on Social Justice, *Social Justice* (London: Vintage, 1994).
[199] G. Craig, *Replacing the Social Fund: a Strategy for Change* (York: Joseph Rowntree Foundation, 1992).

and in making length of time on benefit a criterion to determine priorities for budgeting loans, the Government might argue that it has drawn from some of these proposals. Ultimately, it is a matter of resources—of whether more resources should be put into increasing benefit levels, at a cost to government spending, or whether government should seek to continue to contain resources, at a cost to claimants. Repayable loans may well represent an important option to help claimants meet a financial crisis, but the framework of discretion and fixed budgets results in unfairness to those who are denied the option, whilst the inadequacy of benefits merely extends the indebtedness of those who are successful.

15

Social Security and Industrial Injury

STEPHEN JONES

1. INTRODUCTION[1]

Disablement caused by accidents or disease arising out of and in the course of employed earner's employment has, by virtue of the social security industrial injuries support it attracts, enjoyed an historical preference and a unique position in the system of social security which has developed over the past one hundred years. There are currently four benefits which reflect that preference. The first and most important is disablement benefit.[2] This provides compensation by means of a weekly pension related to the percentage degree of disablement suffered by the claimant. The next two, which take the form of additions to disablement benefit, are the increases in respect of constant attendance[3] and exceptionally severe disablement[4] which are payable only to those claimants who are 100 per cent disabled and have significant care needs. Finally, there is reduced earnings allowance (or, for those over retirement age, retirement allowance), which compensates to a limited extent for loss of earnings caused by disablement. This is now only available in respect of accidents or diseases which first occurred before 1 October 1990. This chapter looks at some of the more important elements of the industrial preference and considers whether the preference is still justified. The Government has announced its intention to produce a consultation paper for reform of the scheme by transferring the cost of the relevant benefits to employers who will take out insurance.[5] There is no suggestion that the preferential treatment itself will be removed, but the cost will be shifted from general taxation to the employer.

To the question why a separate chapter should be devoted to industrial injury in the social security system there are a number of possible answers. The first is that the preferential treatment given to those suffering from the effects of industrial injury is celebrating a double anniversary. Just over one hundred years ago the Workmen's

---

[1] On this subject generally see R. Lewis, *Compensation for Industrial Injury* (Abingdon: Professional Books, 1987); Ogus, Barendt, and Wikeley (1995) chs. 7 (industrial injury) and 8 (war pensions); N. Wikeley, *Compensation for Industrial Disease* (Aldershot: Dartmouth, 1993); and P. Cane, *Atiyah's Accidents, Compensation and the Law*, 5th edn. (London: Butterworths, 1993). For the annotated legislation see M. Rowland, *Medical and Disability Appeal Tribunals: the Legislation* (London: Sweet and Maxwell, 1998) and D. Bonner, I. Hooker, and R. White, *Non-Means Tested Benefits: the Legislation* (London: Sweet and Maxwell, 1998). These last two volumes are updated regularly with new editions.

[2] SSCBA 1992, ss 94 and 103.　　[3] Ibid., s. 104.　　[4] Ibid., s. 105.

[5] *The Independent,* 3 March 1999, 2. See also the concluding comments in N. Wikeley, 'The New Prescribed Disease: Coal Miners' Chronic Bronchitis and Emphysema' (1994) 1 *J.S.S.L.* 23–36 at 36.

Compensation Act 1897 came into force and introduced for the first time the principle of compensation without proof of fault for injuries caused by accidents arising out of and in the course of an employed earner's employment. In 1906 this principle was extended to cover six prescribed diseases. Just over fifty years ago the National Insurance (Industrial Injuries) Act 1946 brought into effect the post-war system which transferred responsibility for compensation for industrial injuries from the employer to the state within the national social security system.

The second reason for dealing with this topic in isolation is that the treatment of those suffering from industrial injury is almost unique in the social security system. The major benefit payable—disablement benefit—is based on the system of compensation for disablement introduced for war pensioners in 1917, as modified by the Personal Injuries (Civilians) Scheme.[6] Disablement benefit is awarded for a loss of faculty unrelated to any effect this may have on the earning power of the disabled person. Unlike incapacity benefit or JSA and their respective predecessors—sickness and invalidity benefit and unemployment benefit, for example—disablement benefit is not an income replacement benefit nor is it dependent on contributions. Unlike DLA or attendance allowance,[7] disablement benefit does not seek to provide for the extra costs of disablement such as mobility and care needs. Unlike income support, family credit (being replaced by working families tax credit), or DWA (or now disabled person's tax credit), disablement benefit does not take into account the means of the disabled person or her or his dependants, although it is itself taken into account as a resource for the purposes of all means-tested benefits. An employed earner who, for example, loses an eye as a result of an injury caused by an accident arising out of and in the course of her or his employment will receive compensation in the form of a weekly, tax-free, non-contributory pension for life. The loss of an eye may have no effect on that person's ability to remain as an employed earner and compensation will continue beyond that earner's retirement if the degree of disablement is assessed for life. For the loss of an eye, disablement would be assessed most probably at 40 per cent.[8] This degree of disablement would entitle the disabled person to a pension (at today's benefit levels) of £41.88 per week. This would be payable for life (in the event of a permanent disability) with annual upratings in the level of benefit. This is almost unique—only under the war disablement scheme is there similar preferential treatment. As disablement benefit is not based on a contribution record it means that an employed earner is covered from their first day of work. Most other social security benefits have either a qualifying period or a contribution require-

---

[6] H. Bolderson, *Social Security, Disability and Rehabilitation* (London: Jessica Kingsley, 1991). See in particular ch. 13 on the political pressures which changed the original Beveridge proposal to those contained first in the White Paper, *Social Insurance Part II: Workmen's Compensation, Proposals for an Industrial Injury Insurance Scheme*, Cmd 6551 (London: HMSO, 1944) and finally in the National Insurance (Industrial Injuries) Act 1946.

[7] See Chapter 12.

[8] See paragraph 32 of Schedule 2 to the Social Security (General Benefit) Regulations 1982 (S.I. 1982 No. 1408).

ment. DLA, for example, has a qualifying period in most cases of three months with a prospective period of a further six months.[9] Moreover, incapacity benefit, for example, has a contribution requirement which, although not particularly stringent, is being strengthened.[10]

A third reason for giving discrete attention to this field is that by isolating this topic because of its preferential and unique treatment of those suffering from industrial injury it is perhaps easier to focus attention on the question whether there is any justification for continuing the preference either in its present form or at all.

Despite the case for a discrete focus on this topic, there is a counter-argument relating to its relative lack of importance alongside the remainder of the social security system and the fact that its main justification could be described as historic. In a total annual social security budget of approaching £100 billion, expenditure on industrial injuries benefit is approximately £750 million. This can be compared with the figure of £24 billion on benefits for those with a long-term illness or disability. It is arguable that a blueprint for a social security system today would not include separate provision for an industrial preference: such a system would look at the needs of all people who are disabled and address the functional effects of that disability regardless of the cause. A modern system, it could be argued, would not reward those who are injured simply on the basis of causation.[11] That of course ignores a hundred years of history. It will be seen that the reasons for maintaining a preference are difficult to justify: there are many anomalies and exclusions from benefit and many commentators have argued that the preference is indefensible.[12] Nevertheless, the preference still exists both in this country and in many other countries and it is probably politically impossible to remove the preference and financially impossible to improve the position of those excluded by extending the principle of disablement benefit to all disablement from whatever cause. This chapter will therefore look at key features of the scheme as it exists today and consider the changes which have occurred since 1980 in reducing the extent of the preference. It will also compare the provision within the social security system with damages in the tort scheme and conclude by considering whether there are any signs that the preference is being actively considered for abolition.

2. THE HISTORY OF INDUSTRIAL INJURIES LEGISLATION

The Workmen's Compensation Act 1897 was described by Beveridge as the pioneer system of social security in Britain.[13] The recognition that in an industrialised society

---

[9] See SSCBA 1992, s. 72(2).   [10] See Chapter 12.

[11] Another example of a benefit introduced for a particular cause is the vaccine damage payments scheme under the Vaccine Damage Payments Act 1979. See R. Goldberg, 'Vaccine Damage and Causation—Social and Legal Implications' (1996) 3 *J.S.S.L.* 100–20.

[12] P. Cane, *Atiyah's Accidents, Compensation and the Law*, 5th edn. (London: Butterworths, 1993), 296.

[13] Beveridge Report (1942), para. 80.

workers who are vulnerable to accidents and work-related illnesses and diseases, and whose value as labour in the market-place may, if they succumb to illness or disability, be reduced, was an important step in the development of the welfare state. By the end of the nineteenth century there was in place not only factory and mines legislation which regulated child labour and working hours and conditions, but also a workmen's compensation scheme which enabled workmen to claim from their employers a sum related to (but well below) their average earnings without the need to prove that the injury was the result of negligence. The scheme was later extended to cover all manual and lower-paid non-manual occupations and to give employees rights to compensation in respect of occupational diseases.

Beveridge weighed up the advantages and disadvantages of the workmen's compensation scheme. On the positive side, it had made it relatively easy for workers to claim compensation and, by preserving the connection between the employer and employee, had in some cases facilitated the return of the employee to work; it had given employers freedom to make their own insurance arrangements, which could cover their common law liability as well; and it had a wider social benefit, in providing a 'financial incentive towards prevention of accidents, to the benefit of employers and employees alike'.[14] Beveridge also noted a number of disadvantages. The scheme rested in the last resort on the threat of litigation, with disputes having to be settled in the courts at some expense. It failed to offer the employee complete security that he or she would be paid, because insurance was not compulsory; furthermore, employers and employees could generally negotiate lump sum settlements which could prove attractive to an employee but would leave him or her without a permanent source of income. The fact that employers bore the cost of compensation caused problems where an industrial disease arose after an employee had worked for a series of employers in succession. The scheme was also expensive to administer.[15]

Beveridge recommended that industrial injury and disease should be brought within the scope of his unified scheme for social security, but treated differently and separately from other cases of disability and illness. He proposed a cash disability benefit paid at a flat rate for the first thirteen weeks of disablement. After thirteen weeks compensation would be earnings-related and there would be industrial pensions for prolonged incapacity due to accidents or disease arising out of and in the course of employment. The cost of the benefit would be met through normal insurance contributions plus a special levy on employers in industries where the risk of injury and disease was materially greater than the norm.

The National Insurance (Industrial Injuries) Act 1946 introduced the new scheme. Beveridge's plans had been modified following the Government's rejection of certain elements of it. The Act set in place injury benefit which was paid for the first six months of incapacity, before disablement benefit became available, depending on the extent of the disability. There was a special hardship allowance, based on need,

---

[14] Beveridge Report (1942), para. 78.   [15] Ibid., para. 79.

available to supplement income in cases where the injury sustained had reduced the employee's future earnings capacity by preventing him or her from following his or her regular occupation or one offering similar remuneration. Finally, the Act made provision for death benefits for the dependants of the worker who died as a result of his injury or disease; this was paid at a flat rate for six months and thereafter at a lower rate.

The industrial injuries scheme was reformed in 1982 following a series of reviews and a Government White Paper.[16] Among the problems which had been highlighted were the high cost of administration as against the relatively minor additional benefits the scheme provided over and above other benefits. The Government's rationalisation of the industrial injuries scheme involved the abolition of injury benefit in 1982 and industrial death benefit in 1986. Both these benefits had seen the extent of their industrial preference eroded so that in 1981 their value was, respectively, only 12 per cent and 2 per cent greater than their non-industrial counterparts. Moreover, the average duration of injury benefit was three weeks and the administrative cost involved in adjudicating claims was considered too high.[17] Industrial death benefit was withdrawn from April 1988 and at that time represented only an industrial preference of 2 per cent above the pensions available for widows in the general social security scheme.[18] Another casualty of the 1980s was hospital treatment allowance. This had increased the amount of disablement pension to 100 per cent while a claimant was receiving in-patient treatment in hospital. The rationale had been to encourage such beneficiaries to receive hospital treatment. It was abolished from 6 April 1987 as it was felt to be unnecessary given the rise in occupational sickness schemes. At the time of its abolition it was costing about £200,000 a year.[19]

As noted above, there is no contribution condition for disablement benefit. There was no contribution requirement for injury benefit either and, when this was abolished in 1982, those who were incapable of work by reason of an accident arising out of and in the course of their employment or by reason of a prescribed disease were treated as though the contribution requirements for sickness and invalidity benefit were satisfied—in effect an employed earner was covered from the first day of employment against the effect of disablement and also was treated as potentially entitled to sickness benefit and, for longer-term sickness, invalidity benefit. As a consequence, unemployability supplement was also withdrawn by the Social Security Act 1986. This benefit had been available to those incapable of work and likely to remain permanently incapable but who lacked sufficient national insurance contributions to qualify for the long-term sickness or invalidity benefits. When it was abolished there were about 300 people receiving the benefit and their position was protected.[20] This

---

[16] Secretary of State for Social Services, *Reform of the Industrial Injuries Scheme*, Cm 8402 (London: HMSO, 1981).

[17] Ibid., discussed by D. Carson, 'Recent Legislation and Reports' [1982] *J.S.W.L.* 96–8.

[18] Ogus, Barendt, and Wikeley (1995), 347.

[19] Ibid., 348. In the 1981 White Paper (n. 16 above, at paras 45 and 46) it was considered anomalous.

[20] See R. Lewis, *Compensation for Industrial Injury* (Abingdon: Professional Books, 1987), 162.

preferential treatment for contribution purposes was itself abolished by the Social Security (Incapacity for Work) Act 1994 and was not applied to entitlement for incapacity benefit. This example of the preference was considered to be anachronistic and an unnecessary complication in a new benefit. Only about 1 per cent of sickness benefit claimants had needed to use the concession and the Government saw income support, housing benefit, and severe disablement allowance as providing sufficient coverage.[21] Reduced earnings allowance and retirement allowance were introduced in 1986 to replace special hardship allowance but were later abolished for new claims for accidents which occurred, or diseases where the onset was, after September 1990. Disablement benefit and its two additions of constant attendance allowance[22] and exceptionally severe disablement allowance are now all that remain of the post-1946 provisions. To those entitled, however, they still represent considerable preferential treatment.

3. THE INDUSTRIAL PREFERENCE TODAY

The industrial preference has been described as 'the more favourable treatment given to the victims of industrial accidents and diseases over those disabled by other causes ...'[23] This is now represented mainly by disablement benefit. Reduced earnings allowance which is considered below has been abolished for accidents arising after September 1990 but is still being paid to around 150,000 claimants. Increases to disablement benefit for constant attendance and exceptionally severe disablement are paid to a very small number of beneficiaries (see below). The preference can be considered under two separate heads: administrative and financial.

A. Administrative Preference

In three respects the administration of claims relating to industrial injury or disease disclose preferential treatment. The first involves the presumption that an accident which arises in the course of an employed earner's employment is also deemed to arise out of that employment.[24] The presumption can be rebutted and has no application where all the facts are known: it will assist a claimant where there is some doubt over the circumstances of the accident. The second area of administrative preference is apparent in the ease of exportability of disablement benefit. Generally

---

[21] D. Bonner, 'Incapacity for work: a new benefit and new tests' (1995) 2 *J.S.S.L.* 86–112 at 93–4.

[22] The Government has retained the power to abolish constant attendance allowance but has not yet exercised that power: SSCBA 1992, s. 104(3).

[23] Ogus, Barendt, and Wikeley (1985), 297. See also R. Lewis, *Compensation for Industrial Injury* (Abingdon: Professional Books, 1987); R. Lewis, 'Tort and Social Security: the importance attached to the cause of disability with special reference to the industrial injuries scheme' (1980) 43 *M.L.R.* 514–31.

[24] SSCBA 1992, s. 94(3). See *R v N.I. (Industrial Injuries) Commissioner, ex p Richardson* [1958] 1 W.L.R. 851 and the other authorities referred to in D. Bonner, I. Hooker, and R. White, *Non-Means Tested Benefits: The Legislation* (London: Sweet and Maxwell, 1998), 184.

incapacity benefit is only payable within the United Kingdom except for temporary absences abroad and in well-defined circumstances. The same applies for most other contributory benefits where the claimant is demonstrating some link with employment—for example, contribution-based JSA. Most means-tested benefits are restricted to the United Kingdom, as are non-means-tested benefits such as DLA and attendance allowance.[25] Disablement benefit is not so confined and, like retirement pension and widow's benefits, is payable abroad.[26] This is illustrated by the case of a national of the Czech Republic who was employed on a farm in the United Kingdom from 31 July to 30 August 1991. A tractor went over his foot and he became incapable of work. He returned to the Czech Republic and claimed sickness benefit,[27] but this was refused on the basis that his absence from Great Britain was not temporary. He had, however, also claimed disablement benefit as a result of the injury to his foot and was assessed as 20 per cent disabled. The disablement pension could be paid to him in the Czech Republic.[28]

The Department of Social Security has funded research into the exportability of benefits paid for old age, disability, and widowhood in twelve countries of the Organisation for Economic Co-operation and Development.[29] The report was produced in 1993 and the authors had this to say about the position in the United Kingdom:

In the UK, whereas comparatively severe restrictions are placed on the exportability of the incapacity benefits, Disablement Benefit under the Industrial Injury Scheme is fully retainable abroad and can be claimed from abroad if the accident or disease was contracted in the UK. It may be worth noting that this benefit is paid for loss of faculty rather than work incapacity, and is therefore paid regardless of whether a person is working/earning. The benefit is compensatory and the concern about monitoring and a possible change in the condition of the person leading to a need to reduce benefit does not apply. There are, however, restrictions on taking abroad the additional allowance which may be paid with disablement benefit if a person requires attendance or is exceptionally severely disabled and these cannot be claimed from abroad.[30]

---

[25] See for example, *Snares v Chief Adjudication Officer* (1997) *The Times,* 2 December; *Partridge v Adjudication Officer* (1998) *The Times,* 2 July; *Perry v Chief Adjudication Officer* (1998) *The Times,* 20 October; and *Swaddling v Chief Adjudication Officer* Case C-90/97 (ECJ), 25 February 1999, discussed by Tamara Hervey in Chapter 8.

[26] Constant attendance allowance and reduced earnings allowance are, however, subject to restrictions: see the Social Security Benefit (Persons Abroad) Regulations 1975 (S.I. 1975 No. 563), reg. 9.

[27] Sickness benefit was then available, in the absence of any entitlement to statutory sick pay, for those incapable of work for a period of up to 6 months. The contemporary parallel benefit is short-term incapacity benefit at the lower rate. The claimant would presumably have been entitled to sickness benefit on contribution grounds because of the concession, now removed, granted to those who became incapable of work because of an industrial accident or disease.

[28] *CS/310/1993* (noted at (1997) 4 *J.S.S.L.* D 186). See also the Social Security (Persons from Abroad) Regulations 1975 (S.I. 1975 No. 563).

[29] H. Bolderson and F. Gains, *Crossing National Frontiers,* DSS Research Report No. 23 (London: HMSO, 1993).

[30] Ibid., 94.

It should be noted that, of all the benefits studied in the research, disablement benefit was the only one, retirement pension included, where there was no restriction on annual uprating where the beneficiary was abroad.[31]

The third example of the preferential treatment which used to apply to disablement benefit was the time-limit for claiming the benefit. From April 1997 this has been restricted to the period of three months after the expiry of fifteen weeks from the time of the injury or onset of the disease and there is no provision to extend this period further—that is, the maximum backdating allowed is now three months.[32] Previously, disablement benefit had been unique in that it could be backdated indefinitely if good cause could be shown. For most other benefits there had been an absolute bar of twelve months.[33] For disablement benefit and reduced earnings allowance there was no absolute time limit.[34] The potential advantage of this for a claimant is dramatically illustrated in the case of a person who at the age of seventeen lost an eye in an accident.[35] The accident occurred in 1959. Her claim for disablement benefit was made in March 1993—over thirty-three years later. On the particular facts of the case the Commissioner decided that she had shown continuous good cause for the delay in claiming from the date of the injury to the date of her actual claim. On the assumption that a loss of an eye would be assessed at 40 per cent,[36] this claimant would, therefore, be entitled to receive compensation based on an award of 40 per cent for the rest of her life payable by means of a pension. This would, of course, be unrelated to her other circumstances. In addition, she would receive arrears representing the pension she had foregone for the previous thirty-three years. The Commissioner's decision only deals with the issue of good cause for the late claim but the sums involved for this claimant would be considerable and significantly larger than any claim for damages under the tort scheme. It is also apparent from this example that the limitation period for any damages claim would have expired long ago. This preferential treatment of claims for disablement benefit has now been brought into line with most other benefits: as noted above, the maximum backdating will henceforth be three months.[37]

B. Financial Preference

The financial value to an individual of the industrial preference can be simply illustrated. In 1987 Lewis compared the financial position of two claimants with similar

[31] H. Bolderson and F. Gains, *Crossing National Frontiers*, above n. 29, 81.

[32] See the Social Security (Claims and Payments) Regulations 1987 (S.I. 1987 No. 1968), reg. 19 and Sched. 4, as amended with effect from 14 March 1997 by the Social Security (Miscellaneous Amendments) Regulations 1997 (S.I. 1997 No. 793). The SSAC reported on the changes in Cm 3586.

[33] SSAA 1992, s. 1.

[34] M. Partington, *Claim in Time*, 3rd edn. (London: L.A.G. Books, 1994), 144.

[35] *CI/1037/1995* noted at (1997) 4 *J.S.S.L.* D 87. In similar vein, see M. Partington, n. 34 above, 160, where he refers to an Ombudsman enquiry about a claim backdated for almost 10 years.

[36] See list of injuries in Schedule 2 to the Social Security (General Benefit) Regulations 1982 (S.I. 1982 No. 1408): injury No. 32, 'Loss of one eye, without complications, the other being normal'.

[37] See n. 32 above.

disabilities. The one whose injuries were caused by an industrial accident was entitled to disablement pension at the rate of 100 per cent, constant attendance allowance at the higher rate, and also exceptionally severe disablement allowance. The other, whose disabilities were not caused by an industrial accident, was entitled to attendance allowance and mobility allowance. The difference in the amount of benefit in 1987 was over £100 per week. The capitalised value of the preference was calculated at £144,300 for a 39-year-old claimant and £197,200 for a 21-year-old. Likewise, a claimant who was entitled to reduced earnings allowance could find himself better off after the accident than before[38] and almost £60 per week better off than a comparable claimant who could not receive disablement benefit and reduced earnings allowance. The capitalised values of the preference for a 39-year-old and 21-year-old were respectively calculated to be £76,000 and £104,700. The only difference between the two hypothetical claimants was that one was within the industrial injuries scheme and the other was not.[39] The first example is an extreme one as there are few claimants entitled to constant attendance allowance and exceptionally severe disablement allowance; but the principle holds true.

4. RATIONALE FOR A SEPARATE INDUSTRIAL INJURIES SCHEME

The rationale for a separate scheme for those injured as a result of an accident arising out of and in the course of employment has been regularly questioned. Beveridge justified separate treatment on three main grounds.[40] In the first place, certain industries were particularly dangerous but essential and it was right that people should enter them with the assurance of special provision against their risks. Secondly, a person disabled at work was disabled in the course of employment while working under orders: that was not generally true of other accidents. Finally, Beveridge considered that if special provision was made for accidents and diseases under the social security system it would limit actions in tort and negligence. These principles he considered justified preferential treatment. In 1978 the Pearson Report[41] recommended that the scheme should be extended to the self-employed and also that it should be extended to cover commuting accidents, as well as being used as a model for injuries arising from road accidents. More recently the Industrial Injuries Advisory Council[42] (IIAC) has again questioned whether a separate scheme

---

[38] Because neither disablement pension nor reduced earnings allowance are taxable.

[39] R. Lewis, *Compensation for Industrial Injury* (Abingdon: Professional Books, 1987), 15–16.

[40] Beveridge Report (1942), para. 81.

[41] Pearson Committee, *Report of the Royal Commission on Civil Liability and Compensation for Personal Injury*, Cmnd 7054 (London: HMSO, 1978).

[42] The Industrial Injuries Advisory Committee was established under the National Insurance (Industrial Injuries) Act 1946. The statutory provision for the Council is currently contained in s. 171 of the SSAA 1992. Its remit is to provide independent advice to the Secretary of State on matters concerning the industrial injuries scheme. The Council is concerned exclusively with occupational injuries whether arising from accident or disease. It has three roles: to advise on the prescription of industrial diseases, to

can be justified and, perhaps not surprisingly, has decided that it can. In the opinion of the IIAC the case for maintaining a scheme[43] begins from the proposition that work is necessary to society and that individuals who are capable of work and have no other responsibilities have no right not to seek work and still receive social security benefits. All work carries some risks of accident and although there has been a move away from the more dangerous heavy industries to service industries these nevertheless carry risks. Moreover, the growth in small companies and sub-contractors working under pressure is creating new risks of injury. The IIAC concluded that society should have in place a system for dealing with the consequence of occupational injury, including compensation for the injury itself and provision to meet the financial consequence of the injury for the individual and her/his dependants. Only a separate scheme alongside tort and general social security provision would do this. The IIAC further argues that the existence of a special scheme would assist in the prevention of occupational injury through the identification of the consequences of injury and through research into occupational disease.

5. CURRENT PROVISION FOR INDUSTRIAL INJURIES

A. Background: Principles

The scheme as established in 1948 was based on the principle contained in the Workmen's Compensation Act 1897 (above)—that compensation should be payable for injury caused by an accident arising out of and in the course of employed earner's employment without the need to prove fault. Causation remains crucial to entitlement but fault is irrelevant unless the activity engaged in takes the employee outside the scope of the scheme, for example, so that the accident does not arise out of or in the course of employment. The financial benefits, however, were based on those of the Personal Injuries (Civilian) Scheme. There would be a short-term injury benefit for up to twenty-six weeks and an allowance thereafter for any disablement resulting from loss of faculty. In addition, the civilian scheme did not distinguish between citizens according to rank and this principle continued in the assessment of loss of faculty. The problem of the effect of an injury on earning capacity was addressed partially by the special hardship allowance. The origins of the Personal

advise on regulations under the SSCBA 1992, and to advise on the industrial injuries scheme itself. See further J. M. Harrington et al., 'Industrial Injuries Compensation', (1991) *British J. of Industrial Medicine*, 577–8 and idem 'The Industrial Injuries Advisory Council' (1994) 1 *J.S.S.L.* 70. See also N. Wikeley, *Compensation for Industrial Disease* (Dartmouth Publishing Co, 1993), 85–90 and R. Lewis, *Compensation for Industrial Injury* (Abingdon: Professional Books, 1987), 95–7. The IIAC has been criticised for its low profile (Wikeley, op cit., 200) and this is a point acknowledged by the Council itself—see IIAC, *Periodic Report 1993* (London: HMSO, 1993), 3–4. A further Periodic Report is proposed following completion of the current review of the schedule of Prescribed Diseases (information provided to the author by the IIAC).

[43] Ibid., 5–6.

Injuries (Civilian) Scheme had nothing to do with either war pensions or workmen's compensation but the scheme contained elements of both.[44]

The principle that employed earners might recover from their employers for injury caused by accident arising out of and in the course of their employment was reflected in the 1897 Act. (Compensation was related to their own earnings and usually paid by way of a lump sum.) In 1906 the scheme was extended to cover six prescribed diseases;[45] this list of prescribed diseases was extended over time. This provision of compensation for injury by accident and for prescribed diseases has been continued (see below). Compensation comprised a number of different elements in the 1946 Act. Disablement Benefit was a non-contributory tax-free award for the loss of faculty suffered by the employee. It was assessed as a percentage from 1–100 per cent. An award of between 1–19 per cent was paid by way of a lump sum or gratuity and 20 per cent and above by way of a weekly pension. It was payable regardless of the effect of the injury on earning power. This was intended to ensure that the injury would not act as a disincentive to the employed person to return to work. If there was, incidentally, loss of earning power a special hardship allowance was payable, subject to an overall maximum figure, to compensate the employee for his particular loss: again this was not means-tested nor taxed and was non-contributory. This was in response to concern over the 'engine driver's eye' and the 'compositor's finger', that is, where the disablement has a particularly adverse effect on an employed person's career although the disablement itself does not, standing alone, amount to a severe disablement. The loss of a little finger, for example, is assessed at 7 per cent. This would, however, probably prevent a compositor from continuing his employment.

If an employee was severely disabled with an assessment of 100 per cent, a constant attendance allowance could be paid. This had been part of the war pensions scheme since 1917 and had subsequently been introduced into the Civilian Injuries Scheme.[46] From 1966, following a recommendation of the McCorquodale Committee on the Assessment of Disablement, an exceptionally severe disablement allowance was added for those claimants receiving constant attendance allowance which was paid to those with the higher or intermediate rates of constant attendance allowance and who were exceptionally severely disabled. None of these benefits were

---

[44] H. Bolderson, *Social Security, Disability and Rehabilitation* (Jessica Kingsley Publishers, 1991), 137–8. The state scheme applies only to accidents or diseases occuring after 5 July 1948. Provision was therefore made to continue entitlement in respect of accidents occurring before that date and for particular diseases which first arose before that date. See Workmen's Compensation (Supplementation) Scheme 1982 (S.I. 1982 No. 1489) and the Pneumoconiosis, Byssinosis and Miscellaneous Diseases Scheme 1983 (S.I. 1983 No. 136). The number of beneficiaries is small: for example, in 1997 there were 645 entitled under the accident provisions and 269 under the diseases scheme: DSS, *Social Security Statistics* (London: Stationery Office, 1997), Tables F4.01 and F4.05. See R. Lewis, *Compensation for Industrial Injury* (Abingdon: Professional Books, 1987), ch. 11.

[45] Section 8 of and Schedule 3 to the Workmen's Compensation Act 1906.

[46] H. Bolderson, n. 44 above, 140–1. The debate reflects the tension between war pensioners, on the one hand, whose compensation was granted for a condition arising from a specific cause, and those incapable of work for whatever cause.

means-tested, taxed or depended on contributions. Injury benefit was payable at a higher rate than ordinary sickness benefit and the contribution condition was deemed to be satisfied if the cause of the incapacity for work was industrial.

The preference given to those suffering injury by accident and by reason of a prescribed disease was simply not available to anyone else: unless the disablement came within the scheme there was no entitlement. Excluded automatically were the self-employed,[47] those injured by a process which was neither an accident nor recognised as a prescribed disease, and those whose disablement was not work-related. To give a very simple example in relation to the first of these exclusions: two men working side by side on a construction site are involved in an accident which causes each to lose the sight in one eye. The man who is an employed earner will receive a pension based on an assessment of 30 per cent for the remainder of his life.[48] His colleague who is self-employed will receive nothing under the scheme. This disparity of treatment was well recognised by Beveridge when he said that '[i]f a workman loses his leg in an accident, his needs are the same whether the accident occurred in a factory or in the street'[49]; but only in the former case is he likely to come within the scheme. The Pearson Committee recommended extension of the scheme to cover the self-employed and this has been echoed by the IIAC at least in relation to those involved in construction and agriculture.[50] The self-employed were covered by the national insurance scheme for sickness benefits but their reason for exclusion from the industrial injuries scheme has been described as based on a frail theoretical foundation.[51] There are three main arguments against reform: first, that there has been insufficient demand from the self-employed themselves. Secondly, that coverage would create difficulties in determining the scope of employment and, thirdly, that it would amount to a significant extension of the scheme.[52]

The scheme has since 1897 distinguished between accidents and diseases and that distinction has been maintained into the present scheme (see sections B and C below). Accidents continue to provide the majority of the situations in which claims for disablement benefit arise. In 1997, accidents accounted for 81 per cent of the

---

[47] The self-employed are the largest group excluded from potential benefit. As they may be working alongside others who are employed earners and therefore run the same risks of injury this exclusion is difficult to support, especially in the construction industry and in farming. See IIAC, Consultation Papers, *Inclusion of the self-employed in construction and agriculture* (London: IIAC, 1991); J. C. Brown, *A Policy Vacuum: social security for the self-employed* (York: Joseph Rowntree Foundation, 1992); IIAC, *Periodic Report 1993: A review of recent activity of the Industrial Injuries Advisory Council concerning work related ill health* (London: HMSO, 1993).

[48] Social Security (General Benefit) Regulations 1982 (S.I. 1982 No. 1408), Sched. 2. Injury No. 33 refers to 'loss of vision of one eye, without complication or disfigurement of the eyeball, the other being normal'.

[49] Beveridge Report (1942), para. 80.

[50] IIAC, *The Industrial Injuries Scheme and the self-employed in construction and agriculture* (London: HMSO, 1991).

[51] J. C. Brown, *A Policy Vacuum: social security for the self-employed* (York: Joseph Rowntree Foundation, 1992), 23 and 171–9.

[52] Ogus, Barendt, and Wikeley (1995), 301. See also IIAC *Periodic Report* 1993, op. cit., 16–18.

total 262,000 awards of disablement pension[53] and, of the assessments actually made in that year, 20,000 related to accidents with 5,000 for prescribed diseases.[54]

B. Entitlement for Injury Caused by Accident

(i) 'Arising out of and in the course of employment'

To qualify under the scheme an employed earner must suffer personal injury caused either by a prescribed disease[55] or 'by accident arising out of and in the course of employment'.[56] These last words have given rise to difficulty in application to individual facts. The Workmen's Compensation Act 1897, the National Insurance (Industrial Injuries) Act 1946, and its successors all left room for considerable doubt whether the formula is satisfied in individual cases. It has been suggested that the words 'in the course of' delimit the time, place, and activity of the work and that the 'out of' criterion concerns itself with the cause or connection between the accident and the work.[57] In the view of a former Chief Commissioner: [58]

'[a]rising out of' now causes comparatively little difficulty, because Parliament in 1961 successfully identified most of the hard cases under this head and simply enacted that in those cases the accident should be deemed to arise out of the employment.[59] I think that this was one of the most satisfactory pieces of legislation ever enacted in this field. It is based on an idea which is so good that it could be used elsewhere . . . Unfortunately Parliament has never succeeded in giving the same treatment to 'in the course of'.[60]

The words 'arising out of' do, nevertheless, give some difficulty. For example, a Commissioner had to give a ruling on a lorry driver who suffered post-traumatic stress syndrome after hearing of the Zeebrugge ferry disaster on his cab radio the day after himself travelling as a passenger on the ship. He had known many of the crew and passengers on board. It was accepted that this was an accident and that it

---

[53] DSS, *Social Security Statistics 1998* (Leeds: Corporate Document Services, 1998), Table F2.05.

[54] Ibid., Table F2.06.   [55] SSCBA 1992, s. 108(1)(a).

[56] Ibid., s. 94(1). There is an exhaustive review of the cases in the notes to this section in D. Bonner, I. Hooker, and R. White, *Non-Means Tested Benefits: the Legislation* (London: Sweet and Maxwell, 1998).

[57] Ogus, Barendt, and Wikeley (1995), 307. The example given is where a workman at a bench sits on a pin which he placed earlier in his pocket: the accident occurs in the course of the employment but does not arise out of it. See generally R. Lewis, *Compensation for Industrial Injury* (Abingdon: Professional Books, 1987), ch. 3. See also P. Cane, *Atiyah's Accidents Compensation and the Law*, 5th edn. (London: Butterworths, 1993), 279–80. Cane uses the analogy of a workman at a bench who is injured by an escaped prisoner: the accident would arise in the course of the employment but not out of the employment, unless the workplace happened to be in a prison.

[58] Sir R. Micklethwait, *The National Insurance Commissioners* (London: Stevens and Sons, 1976), 82–3.

[59] Social Security Act 1975, s. 55, now SSCBA 1992, ss 97–101. The types of situations covered include accidents in the course of illegal employments (s. 97), acting in breach of regulations (s. 98), travelling in employer's transport (s. 99), accidents happening while meeting an emergency (s. 100), and accidents caused by another's misconduct or caused by insects, animals, lightning, etc (s. 101). For detailed consideration of decisions arising from these sections see the notes to them in D. Bonner, I. Hooker, and R. White, *Non-Means Tested Benefits: The Legislation* (Sweet and Maxwell, 1998), 201–6.

[60] Sir R. Micklethwait, *The National Insurance Commissioners* (London: Stevens and Sons, 1976), 82–3.

had occurred in the course of the employment. The Commissioner did not accept, however, that the accident arose out of the employment.[61]

The chief problem of making an appropriate connection between the accident and work relates to the need for the accident to have occurred 'in the course of employment',[62] which Bonner describes as a 'troublesome rubric'.[63] In *Chief Adjudication Officer and another v Rhodes*[64] the Court of Appeal held that the test was whether the employed person was at the time doing something he or she was employed to do or something 'reasonably incidental' to it. The case involved an employee of the DSS, Rhodes, who, while on sick leave from work, was assaulted by her next door neighbour while on her driveway. The neighbour suspected, correctly as it turned out, that Rhodes had informed the DSS that he was working while at the same time claiming benefit. The Court of Appeal by a majority decision reversed the decision of the Social Security Commissioner[65] and held that the accident had not arisen 'in the course of employment'. It is interesting that in his dissenting judgment Swinton Thomas LJ decided that the context in which the claimant had been assaulted was important and not the place. The majority followed the decision in *Faulkner v Chief Adjudication Officer*,[66] which concerned a police officer injured while playing football for a police team. The claimant argued that good community policing was enhanced by police officers being seen to be involved in community activities. The Court of Appeal disagreed. The question was 'what was he employed to do?' He was in the drugs squad. Playing football was not reasonably incidental to his activities in the drugs squad.[67] These cases can be contrasted with others concerning a fire officer injured while playing volleyball[68] and a nurse at a mental hospital injured while playing football against some of the patients;[69] in both cases they were held to have suffered accidents arising in the course of their employment.

Issues arise where employees are injured while travelling—the test is described simply as whether someone is travelling 'to' work, in which case he or she will not be covered, or travelling while 'in' work, in which case s/he will succeed. To apply the test is far from simple. Both the House of Lords[70] and Court of Appeal[71] have

---

[61] *CI/289/1994* (1997) 4 J.S.S.L. D 44.

[62] See generally, R. Lewis, *Compensation for Industrial Injury* (Abingdon: Professional Books, 1987), ch. 3; Ogus, Barendt, and Wikeley (1995), 317–23.

[63] D. Bonner, 'Compensation for assault: an unusual dimension to the industrial injuries system' (1998) 5 *J.S.S.L.* 72–82, 72.

[64] (1998) *The Times*, 25 August. See D. Bonner, 'Case Analysis' (1999) 6 *J.S.S.L.* 33–9.

[65] See Bonner, n. 63 above.

[66] (1994) *The Times*, 8 April. See S. Jones, 'Case Analysis' (1995) 2 *J.S.S.L.* 45–8.

[67] Ibid. The Court of Appeal endorsed the approach taken in *R v National Insurance Commissioner, ex p Michael* [1977] 2 All ER 420. See also Sir R. Micklethwait, n. 60 above, at 83–4, where the author considers that the law is unsatisfactory.

[68] *R(I) 68/51.*   [69] *R(I) 13/51.*

[70] *Smith v Stages* [1989] AC 928, a case concerned with an action for damages by an employee following a road accident. At issue was whether the injured employee was in the course of his employment at the time.

[71] *Nancollas v Insurance Officer* [1985] 1 All ER 833.

attempted to deal with the issue. Proposals to extend the scheme to cover commuting accidents (see above) have not been taken up and there is a very limited statutory exception for accidents which occur while an employed earner is being carried in a vehicle operated or provided by his employer.[72]

(ii) *Accident or Process?*[73]

Even whether an accident has occurred or not can still be far from clear. 'Accident' is not defined in the legislation but the decisions point to two essential features: there must be an identifiable event which must be limited in duration. The starting point must be the dictum of Lord MacNaghten that an accident 'is an unlooked-for mishap or an untoward event which is not expected or designed'.[74] This can include the injury itself where there is an internal physiological change for the worse which has these two features.[75] A claimant suspended from work pending a security investigation claimed that he suffered anxiety, depression, and loss of confidence amounting to a nervous breakdown. The Commissioner refused the appeal holding that: '[t]he employers' action might have been unexpected by the claimant, although whether it was or was not was unknown, but that did not make it an accident. The word "accident" carried with it the concept of an unwelcome and unexpected mishap arising in the course of events.'[76] A line has been drawn between injury by a series of accidents and injury by any other multiple events or continuous hazards caused by a process which is outside the scheme. In *Roberts v Dorothea Slate Quarries Co*[77] Lord Porter made the following distinction:

. . . two types of cases have not been sufficiently differentiated. In one type there is found to be a simple accident followed by a resultant injury . . . or a series of specific and ascertainable accidents followed by an injury which may be the consequence of any or all of them . . . In

---

[72] SSCBA, s. 99.

[73] See J. Stapleton, *Disease and the Compensation Debate* (Oxford, Clarendon Press, 1986), ch. 3 and particularly at 49–59.

[74] *Fenton v Thorley* [1903] AC 442 at 448. See also *Trim Joint District School Board v Kelly* [1914] AC 667, where an attack on a schoolmaster which was clearly planned by his assailants was nevertheless unforeseen by the victim.

[75] W. R. Lee, 'An Accidental Heart Attack?' (1995) 2 *J.S.S.L.* 9–23; *Jones v Secretary of State for Social Services* [1972] 1 All ER 145.

[76] *CI/5249/95* (noted at (1997) 4 *J.S.S.L.* D46) and upheld on appeal in *Oakley v Chief Adjudication Officer* (1997) 6 March, unreported but noted at (1998) 5 *J.S.S.L.* D12. See also *CI/15589/1996* noted at (1998) 5 *J.S.S.L.* 139–45 where the Commissioner suggested that in some occupations—e.g. the police and other emergency services—where there was a greater risk of violence, an incident might not be classified as an accident. The case concerned an altercation between a known violent prisoner and a prison officer as a result of which the officer suffered mental stress and had to retire. This approach has been doubted by the Court of Session in *Chief Adjudication Officer v Faulds* (1998) SCLR 718. This considered the case of a fire officer who suffered post-traumatic-stress syndrome as a result of witnessing the victims of particularly horrific fires and motor accidents. The court confirmed the accident declaration and stressed that it was not the foreseeability of the occurrence or commonness of the hazard that matters so much as the absence of any intention or plan or design that such an event should occur. Traumatic events were foreseeable in employment as a fire officer: if an employee suffered a reaction that could be injury caused by accident where the injury itself would be the accident.

[77] [1948] 2 All ER 201.

either case it is immaterial that the time at which the accident occurred cannot be located. In the other type, there is a continuous process going on substantially from day to day, though not necessarily from minute to minute or even from hour to hour, which gradually and over a period of years produces incapacity. In the first of these types the resulting incapacity is held to be injury by accident. In the second it is not . . . There must . . . come a time when the indefinite number of so-called accidents and the length of time over which they occur take away the element of accident and substitute that of process.[78]

The IIAC has reported on whether or not the gap in coverage in the scheme between injury caused by accident, on the one hand, and injury caused by a prescribed disease, on the other, should be filled.[79] It notes that there is little evidence of the extent of the scale of the problem. One option would be to introduce a statutory definition of 'accident' which would embrace injury by process. The suggested definition would extend to any series of impacts or exposures at work which result in injury, even if repeated continually and/or over a very long period of time.[80] Another option would be to remove the requirement of injury by 'accident' and to compensate for injury arising out of and in the course of employment—an approach which has been adopted elsewhere:

This approach would be similar to the position under the current provisions whereby certain physiological changes for the worse are held to be injury by accident, providing there is evidence of occupational causation, by virtue of the injury itself. However, removal of the need for an accident would remove the limitations which this phrase conveys and open entitlement to any kind of injury, however manifesting itself, providing there was satisfactory evidence of occupational causation.[81]

The third option would be to introduce a system of individual proof to allow employed earners to recover benefit if they could prove that the injury was occupational in origin. Such an approach has been recommended by the European Commission[82] and had also been considered and recommended by the IIAC in 1981 but excluding claims for specified common diseases.[83] That recommendation was not accepted by the Government at the time. On balance the IIAC does not now feel there are grounds for recommending any of these three options because the extent of the gap in coverage for injury by process is unclear. Its recommendations for prescribed diseases will be considered below.

[78] [1948] 2 All ER, at 205–6.
[79] IIAC, *Coverage under the industrial injuries scheme for injury by 'process'*, Position Paper 9 (London: IIAC, 1995), paras 19–24.
[80] Cf. the oboist in *CI/72/1987* who was entitled to a declaration that he had suffered injury by accident when he developed a hernia of the throat. *CWI/29/1974* (referred to in the IIAC report (ibid.)) concerned a claimant who contracted traumatic oedema of the right index finger which she attributed to her work as a trimmer in a garment factory, involving the constant use of a pair of scissors. In view of the length of time and the course of development it would have to be regarded as having developed by process and not by accident.
[81] IIAC Position Paper 9, op. cit., para. 20.3.
[82] Recommendation 90/326/EEC, 22 May 1990 and COM(96) 454 final of 20 September 1996.
[83] IIAC, *Industrial Diseases: A Review of the Schedule and the Question of Individual Proof*, Cm 8393 (London: HMSO, 1981).

C. Entitlement in Respect of Prescribed Diseases

(i) Prescription

The Workmen's Compensation Act 1906 provided the first cover for injury caused by disease. This followed the decision of the House of Lords *Brintons v Turvey*[84] that an employed earner had suffered injury by accident when being infected by anthrax. The original list consisted of the following: anthrax, lead poisoning or its sequelae, mercury poisoning or its sequelae, phosphorous poisoning or its sequelae, arsenic poisoning or its sequelae, and ankylostomiasis.[85] The list was gradually extended until 1946. Prescription is now covered by section 108 of the Social Security Contributions and Benefits Act 1992. This allows for a disease to be prescribed when the Secretary of State is satisfied that it is one that ought to be treated as a risk of occupation and not a risk common to all and that the attribution of particular cases to the nature of the employment can be established or presumed with reasonable certainty: 'In other words a disease can only be prescribed if there is a recognised risk to workers in a certain occupation and a link between the disease and occupation can be reasonably presumed or established in individual cases.'[86]

In deciding whether or not to recommend prescription the IIAC considers published research into the incidence of particular illnesses in specific industries. The IIAC must be satisfied either that a link between a disease and a particular employed earner's employment can be established in an individual case or that epidemiological evidence shows a risk of contracting that disease which is at least double for a particular occupational group which must be capable of being defined by reference to job titles, or tools or substances used:

This criterion is easily satisfied by diseases which are specific to an occupational exposure, such as heavy metal poisoning, and where the association between occupational exposure and disease is very strong, as is that between exposure to asbestos and mesothelioma, a disease which, in the absence of asbestos exposure has a very low incidence.[87]

Thus in its report on occupational lung cancer[88] the IIAC was unable to recommend prescription in relation to gas retort workers despite the strong evidence that they are at an increased risk of disease: the relative risk was not sufficiently high.[89] The IIAC also considered the incidence of lung cancer in painters and chrome platers. In the former the IIAC concluded that the published evidence pointed strongly to a hazard:

However [the evidence does] not indicate the carcinogen(s) responsible, and it is not possible at present to distinguish a subset of painters at particularly high risk. Overall, the data suggest

---

[84] [1905] AC 230.   [85] Workmen's Compensation Act 1906, Sched. 3.

[86] IIAC, *Work Related Upper Limb Disorders*, Cm 1936 (London, HMSO, 1992), para. 5.

[87] IIAC, *Periodic Report 1993* (London: HMSO, 1993), 23.

[88] IIAC, *Occupational Lung Cancer*, Cm 37 (London: HMSO, 1986).

[89] J. M. Harrington, A. J. Newman Taylor, and D. Coggan, 'Industrial Injuries Compensation' (1991) *British J. of Industrial Medicine*, 577–8.

a relative risk of less than two. At this level of risk it is not possible when a painter develops lung cancer to conclude that on the balance of probabilities his tumour was caused by work.[90]

In the case of chrome platers the IIAC concluded that the risk of lung cancer was elevated but not to the point where the disease could be attributed to such work with any certainty.[91] In its recommendations on *Diseases Induced by Ionising and Non-Ionising Radiation*[92] the IIAC includes as the prescribed occupation 'Exposure to electromagnetic radiations (other than radiant heat) or to ionising particles where the dose is sufficient to double the risk of [the cancer's] occurrence'. This appears to be the first statutory recognition of the test applied by the IIAC in recommending the prescription of diseases.

Non-industrial factors, such as smoking, pose potential difficulties. Where an occupational disease also has a non-occupational cause the disease can still be prescribed provided that the risk is doubled by the occupational hazard: 'In theory a problem might arise if the non-occupational cause functioned as an effect modifier—for example, if the risk of lung cancer were doubled in non-smokers but not in smokers. In practice, this has not been an issue to date.'[93]

The current list is divided into four sections.[94] Section A lists conditions due to physical agents; Section B, conditions due to biological agents; Section C, conditions due to chemical agents; and Section D, miscellaneous conditions. There are sixty-seven conditions listed and the schedule is in two parts. The first part mentions the particular disease, for example, carpal tunnel syndrome (disease A12), and the second part the prescribed occupation, for example, for carpal tunnel syndrome '[t]he use of hand-held powered tools whose internal parts vibrate so as to transmit that vibration to the hand, but excluding those which are solely powered by hand'.[95] As can be seen from this example, the prescribed tool has been defined quite narrowly: an employed earner who is suffering from carpal tunnel syndrome must, in addition, prove that she has used the prescribed machinery.

In January 1997 the IIAC announced a general review[96] of the current list to examine the present details of prescription, make changes where necessary, and also

[90] IIAC, *Lung Cancer in Painters*, Position Paper No. 6 (London: IIAC, 1991).

[91] IIAC, *Lung Cancer in Chrome Platers*, Position Paper No. 7 (London: IIAC, 1991).

[92] Cm 4280 (London: The Stationery Office, 1999).

[93] J. M. Harrington, A. J. Newman Taylor, and D. Coggan, n. 89 above. See also N. Wikeley, 'The New Prescribed Disease: Coal Miners' Chronic Bronchitis and Emphysema' (1994) 1 *J.S.S.L.* 23–36.

[94] The Social Security (Industrial Injuries) (Prescribed Diseases) Regulations 1985 (S.I. 1985 No. 967), as amended. The details with commentary are contained in D. Bonner, I. Hooker, and R. White, *Non-Means Tested Benefits: The Legislation* (London: Sweet and Maxwell, 1998).

[95] Part I of Schedule 1 to the Social Security (Industrial Injuries) (Prescribed Diseases) Regulations 1985, op. cit. The terms of prescription for this disease were changed to the present form of words on 24 March 1996 following a number of decisions of Commissioners on the correct meaning of the original formula 'hand-held vibrating tools'. See Bonner, Hooker, and White, n. 94 above.

[96] IIAC, *Review of the Schedule of Prescribed Diseases*, Position Paper No. 10 (London: IIAC, 1997); Press Release 97/041, 27 February 1997. The first report issued since the review process is IIAC, *Diseases Induced by Ionising and Non-Ionising Radiation*, Cm 4280 (London: The Stationery Office, 1999). The Government has accepted the recommendations in the report: Press Release 99/045, 2 March 1999.

to consider the extent to which the list complies with the European Commission's recommended Schedule of Occupational Diseases. In a previous report[97] the IIAC had noted that the UK industrial injuries scheme covered approximately 80 per cent of the EC annex with 5 per cent under review and 10 per cent rejected because of a lack of evidence. The remaining 5 per cent of conditions on the EC list were either benign conditions or irrelevant to the UK. The EC Recommendation contains, for example, the condition *506.30 Meniscus lesions following extended periods of working in a kneeling or squatting position*. In its review the IIAC agreed that the evidence 'on knee osteoarthritis points strongly to an occupational hazard in jobs that entail frequent or prolonged kneeling or squatting. However, it does not identify any occupations or occupational activities that clearly carry a doubling of risk.'[98] The IIAC could not therefore recommend that this condition be prescribed in relation to any particular occupation. Any damage to the knee following an accident might be eligible for compensation under the scheme in any event.

(ii) Individual Proof

The EC Recommendation proposes that each member country should have in place an individual proof system in addition to a scheduled list. This had been recommended by the IIAC in its review of the Schedule in 1981.[99] That approach was not accepted by the Government and since then the IIAC has adopted a slightly different position on the question of individual proof.

The IIAC's report on occupational asthma[100] proposed that additional specific workplace agents should be added to the list of exposures which were deemed to cause asthma. In addition a further category of 'any other sensitising agent inhaled at work' was suggested and accepted.[101] A similar stance was proposed for carpal tunnel syndrome in the Council's report on work-related upper limb disorders[102] which recommended that the condition of carpal tunnel syndrome be prescribed on an individual case basis where temporally-related and relevant workplace exposure could be demonstrated. This recommendation was not followed. The IIAC noted that in effect individual proof operates for occupational dermatitis since the terms of prescription do not specify any particular sensitising agents.[103] The IIAC has stated that: '[a]t present, it is the Council's view that the concept of individual proof is best

---

[97] IIAC, *European Commission Recommendation—Occupational Diseases*, Position Paper No. 8 (London: IIAC, 1995), para. 9.

[98] IIAC, *Disorders of the Knee*, Cm 2842 (London: HMSO, 1995).   [99] N. 83 above .

[100] IIAC, *Occupational Asthma*, Cm 1244 (London: HMSO, 1990).

[101] Prescribed Disease D7 Category (x) 'any other sensitising agent': Schedule 1 to the Social Security (Industrial Injuries) (Prescribed Diseases) Regulations 1985, op. cit.

[102] IIAC, *Work Related Upper Limb Disorders* (London: HMSO, 1992). See also IIAC, *Periodic Report 1993* (London: HMSO, 1993), 21.

[103] Prescribed Disease D5—the prescribed occupation is 'exposure to dust, liquid or vapour or any other external agents except chromic acid, chromates or bi-chromates, capable of irritating the skin (including friction or heat but excluding ionising particles or electromagnetic radiations other than radiant heat)'.

considered on a case by case basis as the Council reviews its work. Blanket adoption of the concept would not alter to any great extent the valid extension of the prescribed disease system to those who have a justifiable claim.' In its report on the prescribed disease allergic rhinitis,[104] for example, the IIAC did consider whether to extend the range of substances exposure to which would cause the condition to include the category of 'any other sensitising agent', but did not recommend this.[105] In other cases it is acknowledged that the terms of prescription can be too narrow because less attention is paid to the activity or tools involved and rather more to the particular industry in which the claimant is employed. In its review of vibration white finger (VWF), the IIAC recommended that the prescribed occupational exposures[106] should be replaced by the tools commonly used and the materials held against such tools. This recommendation also has not been implemented. The effect of the limited prescription in cases of VWF can be seen, for example, in the case of a claimant employed as an arborist/tree surgeon by a local authority who used a chain saw and who claimed he suffered from VWF. The Commissioner rejected his claim on appeal on the grounds that his work did not amount to 'forestry' and only use of a chain saw in forestry was prescribed.[107] Again a claimant who had been exposed to paper dust argued that this was the cause of his occupational asthma. The Commissioner rejected his appeal on the grounds that paper dust was not 'wood dust' within the prescribed occupations.[108]

These cases are merely examples of the very fine questions of fact and law which the adjudicating authorities are called on to decide in relation to the conditions of prescription. If anything, this jurisprudence gives support to the view that cases should be decided on the basis of individual proof and not depend on fine points of construction.[109] Any general system of individual proof would have cost and administrative implications and there is no sign that the system will be adopted in this country despite having support from the European Commission.[110]

[104] Prescribed Disease D4, in Schedule 1 to the Social Security (Industrial Injuries) (Prescribed Diseases) Regulations 1985 (S.I. 1985 No. 967) as amended.
[105] IIAC, *Inflammation or Ulceration of the Mucous Membrane of the Upper Respiratory Passages or Mouth produced by Dust, Liquid or Vapour*, Cm 2845 (London: HMSO, 1995).
[106] Contained in Schedule 1 to the Social Security (Industrial Injuries) (Prescribed Diseases) Regulations 1985, op. cit.
[107] Ibid., Schedule 1, P.D. A.11 occupation (a), Social Security (Industrial Injuries) (Prescribed Diseases) Regulations 1985, op. cit., as amended. *CI/3924/1997* (starred 24/98) (1998) 5 *J.S.S.L.* D185.
[108] *CI/6819/95* noted at (1996) 3 *J.S.S.L.* D187. Also compare the decisions in *CI/073/1994* ibid. D41 and *CI/4987/1995* ibid. D186, where there is disagreement between Commissioners on the meaning of 'any other sensitising agent'. In the first case the Commissioner had to consider a claimant subject to passive smoking and in the latter to human and animal faeces, household dust, and lice.
[109] See for example *CI/12678/1996* (1997) 4 *J.S.S.L.* D92. It was accepted that the claimant had contracted nasal cancer. The Commissioner decided, however, that he did not come within Prescribed Disease D6 because although he had worked as a painter on wooden goods he had not worked *in or about a building* where 'wooden goods . . . are repaired'. The Commissioner reached his decision as to the extent of the prescribed occupation in this case after referring to para. 60 of the report of the IIAC, *Industrial Diseases: A Review of the Schedule and the Question of Individual Proof*, Cmnd 8393 (London: HMSO, 1981).
[110] In COM(96) 454, Brussels 20.09.96, the Commission considers that 'the mixed system of compensation could be introduced on a wider scale in the Member States, allowing, in certain cases, for compensation in respect of diseases which are occupational in origin but are not included in a national schedule,

D. Disablement Benefit[111]

The primary method of compensation for those who suffer personal injury as a result of either an accident arising out of and in the course of their employment or a prescribed disease is disablement benefit. It is designed to compensate for the injury suffered without any further consideration of the effect this might have on the ability to work. The beneficiary must suffer a loss of physical or mental faculty. That has been described as 'an impairment of the proper functioning of part of the body or mind'.[112] It can include disfigurement whether or not accompanied by any loss of physical faculty.[113]

The degree of loss of faculty in any given case is a decision made by the medical adjudicating authorities. To achieve some degree of consistency, however, there is a schedule of prescribed degrees of disablement for particular types of injury, for example, amputations, loss of sight.[114] Outside this schedule the general principles for assessing the extent of disablement are that that they should be by reference to the disabilities incurred as a result of the relevant loss of faculty compared with a person of the same age and sex whose physical and mental condition is normal.[115] Regulations also set down the principles for assessment where there are successive industrial accidents or industrial injuries which are preceded or succeeded by non-industrial injuries.[116] The assessments can be provisional or final and also subject to review on the grounds of unforeseen aggravation. This can be seen as an advantage enjoyed over the common law system of assessment, where awards tend to be final and interim awards are the exception rather than the rule.

In 1946 a claimant had to show that the loss of faculty resulting from the relevant injury was both permanent or substantial—meaning that it would be assessed as at least 20 per cent.[117] Disablement benefit was payable from a date twenty-six weeks after the injury was sustained, that is, at the end of the period during which the separate industrial injuries benefit was payable. In 1953, following pressure to extend the scheme to those with less serious injuries, entitlement was introduced for a gratuity or lump sum for assessments of between 1–19 per cent with a pension payable for those with an assessment of 20 per cent and above. Perhaps not surprisingly, the bulk of the assessments from that time onwards were in the 1–19 per cent range and it is estimated that in 1983 90 per cent of all assessments came within that lower range.

---

where the worker concerned provides evidence that the ailment is occupational in origin; this could be a very positive development, making it possible in the medium or long term to move away from the current approach involving a specific list of occupational diseases for which compensation is available.'

[111] See generally R. Lewis, *Compensation for Industrial Injury* (Abingdon: Professional Books, 1987), chs 5–7 and M. Rowland, *Medical and Disability Appeal Tribunals: The Legislation* (Sweet and Maxwell, 1998).

[112] *Jones v Secretary of State for Social Services* [1972] AC 944 at 1009.

[113] SSCBA 1992, s. 122(1).

[114] The Social Security (General Benefit) Regulations 1982 (S.I. 1982 No. 1408), reg. 11 and Sched. 2.

[115] SSCBA 1992, Sched. 6.

[116] N. 114 above, reg. 11. See for example, the discussion of the 'connection factor' in *R(I)1/95* and the notes to reg. 11 in M. Rowland, op. cit., n. 111 above.

[117] Ogus, Barendt, and Wikeley (1995), 332.

The Social Security Act 1986 abolished the payment of benefit where the assessment was less than 14 per cent except in the case of three lung diseases: pneumoconiosis, byssinosis, or diffuse mesothelioma.[118] For these three diseases an assessment of 1–10 per cent is paid at 10 per cent and between 11–24 per cent at 20 per cent. Between 14–24 per cent, it became payable at the rate of 20 per cent, between 25–34 per cent at 30 per cent, and so on.[119] This amendment thus excluded a considerable number of claims for compensation at a stroke with effect from 1 October 1986 but was also consistent with the stated policy aim of concentrating resources on the more serious disabilities (see below). The scheme was at the same time improved for those with an assessment of between 14–19 per cent as these were treated as assessments of 20 per cent with an entitlement to a weekly pension (which is uprated annually) instead of a lump sum gratuity. If a disablement was permanent this pension would continue for the lifetime of the employee: entitlement did not stop on retirement from work nor was entitlement affected by the receipt of any other benefit.

While the Social Security Act 1986 excluded those with lesser degrees of disablement completely, it is estimated that it improved the position of about 3,400 people a year who would henceforth receive a pension instead of a gratuity.[120] These changes followed on from the abolition of the separate industrial injury benefit. Originally this had represented a considerable preference over ordinary sickness benefit but by the time of its abolition the preference was marginal and not justifiable in expense.[121] One result of abolishing the separate injuries benefit was to make disablement benefit payable from fifteen weeks after the initial accident/prescribed disease instead of twenty-six weeks as previously. The abolition of industrial injury benefit and reduced availability of disablement benefit combined to cause a significant reduction in the number of claims. In 1986 there were, for example, 61,740 initial assessments for disablement benefit, but in 1988 only 12,980. The changes have had a significant effect on entitlement arising out of certain prescribed diseases. For example, assessments for those suffering from occupational asthma or vibration white finger (VWF) tend to fall below the 14 per cent threshold: DSS figures for 1992–3 and 1993–4 show that less than 15 per cent of claims relating to VWF reached it.[122] As Lewis comments:

[N]ow these workers cannot obtain industrial injuries compensation for the loss in quality of their lives. Much of the effort to ensure that such diseases became listed as associated with certain occupations, in order for them to be recognised for compensation purposes has been wasted.[123]

---

[118] Social Security (Industrial Injuries) (Prescribed Diseases) Regulations 1985 (S.I. 1985 No. 967), reg. 20(1).

[119] SSCBA 1992, s. 103.

[120] R. Lewis, 'The Government's Philosophy Towards Reform of Social Security: The Case of Industrial Injuries Benefit' (1986) 15 *I.L.J.* 256–65 at 260.

[121] R. Lewis, 'Consultation and Cuts: the Review of Industrial Injuries Benefit' [1980] *J.S.W.L.* 331–40 at 334.

[122] Health and Safety Commission, *Health and Safety Statistics 1994/5* (London: HMSO, 1995), Table 26.

[123] R. Lewis, n. 120 above, at 259.

Overall numbers for whom disablement benefit is in payment have not declined, however, and indeed there has been a slow but steady increase over the past ten years in the number of claims and expenditure on the scheme,[124] which has precipitated the proposed review of the scheme and the possibility of transferring the cost to the employer and the insurance company.[125] The gradual increase is largely due to the continuing nature of most assessments for disablement benefit: a life assessment means exactly that—it continues for the life of the claimant.

As at April 1997, accidents accounted for 81 per cent of the awards of disablement benefit, pneumoconiosis for 4.5 per cent, occupational deafness 5.5 per cent, with the other prescribed diseases making up the remaining 8 per cent.[126] There were in total 262,000 disablement pensions current, broken down as shown in Table 15.1.

Of these claimants, 216,000 were men: 23 per cent were over the age of 70 with a further 12 per cent also of pensionable age.[127] Of the 7,000 female claimants, 32 per cent were of pensionable age,[128] which illustrates the fact that disablement pension is designed to compensate for the loss of faculty suffered by a claimant regardless of any continuing connection with the workplace.

E. Constant Attendance Allowance and Exceptionally Severe Disablement Allowance

When the industrial injuries scheme was brought into the social security fold after the Second World War it was felt that those claimants whose severe disablement required constant attendance should receive an additional weekly benefit. Constant attendance allowance is payable to claimants who have a 100 per cent assessment of dis-

Table 15.1. Disablement pensions in payment as at 5 April 1997[129]

Rate	Numbers
Less than 20 %	74,000
20–24 %	71,000
25–34 %	56,000
35–44%	26,000
45–54 %	13,000
55–64 %	8,000
65–84 %	8,000
85–100 %	6,000

---

[124] From 1983 to 1997 there was a gradual increase from 188,000 to 262,000 recipients of disablement benefit. See DSS, *Social Security Statistics 1998* (Leeds: Corporate Document Services, 1998), 4.

[125] As reported in *The Independent*, 3 March 1999. On the potential role of insurance in the field of disability, see further the Conclusion to Chapter 12 by Nick Wikeley.

[126] DSS, *Social Security Statistics 1998* (Leeds: Corporate Document Services, 1998), Table F2.05.

[127] Ibid., Table F.2.04.   [128] Ibid.   [129] Ibid.

ablement and require constant attendance. This addition was based on a similar addition in the war pension scheme[130] and is now payable at two different rates dependent on the degree of attendance required.[131] In addition, following the report of the McCorquordale Committee on the Assessment of Disablement in 1966,[132] an exceptionally severe disablement allowance is payable to those claimants who receive the constant attendance allowance and whose entitlement to constant attendance allowance is likely to be permanent.[133] The number receiving these additions is small. In 1996, approximately 2,000 people were receiving the constant attendance allowance and 1,000 the exceptionally severe disablement allowance.[134] These compare with the figures for 1983 when there were 3,600 people assessed at 100 per cent disabled and of these 2,170 received the constant attendance allowance; and a further 90 per cent of those receiving the higher rate of constant attendance allowance received the exceptionally severe disablement allowance.[135] The current numbers are small compared with those receiving attendance allowance or DLA. Under the general social security scheme in 1998 there were over one million recipients of attendance allowance and nearly two million in receipt of DLA.[136]

Constant attendance allowance is an overlapping benefit for the purposes of DLA and attendance allowance, but it still retains a preferential characteristic. The higher rate of constant attendance allowance is currently £86.60. This compares with a higher rate of attendance allowance or disability living allowance care component of £52.95 (from April 1999–2000). Exceptionally severe disablement allowance[137] entitles a recipient to an additional £40.50 per week (at 1999–2000 rates) where the claimant is receiving constant attendance allowance at the higher rate and the need for that attendance is likely to be permanent. To receive either of these additions a claimant must be in receipt of a 100 per cent award of disablement benefit which is currently payable at a rate of £108.10. In a very extreme case, therefore, two people with identical disabilities and needs could have a differential income of £185.25 per week, representing the 100 per cent disablement pension and the combined constant attendance allowance and exceptionally severe disablement allowance when compared with the highest care component of DLA or attendance allowance. (Of course, the mobility component of disability living allowance would still be available to the industrially injured if she or he satisfied the test.) The Government has reserved the power to withdraw entitlement to constant attendance allowance[138] but this has not been exercised to date. Note that entitlement to constant attendance allowance and exceptionally severe disablement allowance is determined by the

[130] See Ogus, Barendt, and Wikeley (1995), ch. 8.
[131] SSCBA 1992, s. 104 and Sched. 4 para. 2.   [132] Cmnd 2847 (London: HMSO, 1966).
[133] SSCBA 1992, s. 105 and Sched. 4 para. 3.
[134] DSS, *Social Security Statistics 1997* (London: The Stationery Office, 1997), Fig. F2.10. This is the most recent year for which figures on these payments are currently available.
[135] Cited in R. Lewis, *Compensation for Industrial Injury* (Abingdon: Professional Books, 1987), 159.
[136] DSS, *Social Security Statistics 1998* (London: Stationery Office, 1998), 4. See further Chapter 12.
[137] Under s. 105 of the SSCBA 1992.   [138] See ibid., s. 104(3).

Secretary of State and falls outside the normal adjudication process for disability living allowance.[139]

For those who are severely disabled the industrial preference can clearly mean a significant financial benefit compared with the general social security scheme. At the other end of the scale, however, the industrial preference has been gradually withdrawn. As noted above, in 1986 the Government withdrew entitlement to benefit from those whose assessments were less than 14 per cent. This move was explained in terms of targeting benefit on those who had more serious disabilities and by the fact that special hardship allowance was not to be abolished but would be replaced by reduced earnings allowance (below).

F. Reduced Earnings Allowance and Retirement Allowance

This was payable to a claimant with at least 1 per cent assessment who had lost earning capacity as a result of the relevant disablement caused by accident or disease up to 30 September 1990. The benefit, for which there is continuing entitlement for those in receipt of it up to that date, was designed to reflect the loss of wages concerned and to this extent was a reflection of the system of compensation under the Workmen's Compensation Act 1897 which was to compensate for the lost earnings of the workman who had been injured. Special hardship allowance had been a feature of the scheme from 1946 and enabled a claimant to receive an additional benefit to reflect the loss of earnings involved subject to a maximum. Special hardship allowance itself could not exceed the figure for a 40 per cent disablement pension and, when combined with disablement pension, the total could not exceed the amount for a 100 per cent pension. In 1986 this principle was continued but with three main changes: the benefit was renamed reduced earnings allowance (REA); the maximum that could be paid to a claimant was raised to 140 per cent when combined with disablement benefit; and the rate payable after reaching retirement was reduced and renamed retirement allowance. As Lewis comments,[140] however, the increase to a maximum of 140 per cent would only benefit the 3,700 disablement pensioners with assessments of 70 per cent and above—a small number of claimants who represented only 2 per cent of the whole. The changes did not increase the maximum amount of the reduced earnings allowance from 40 per cent (of the amount of disablement benefit) to 150 per cent as the 1981 White Paper had recommended.[141] Had that proposal been adopted then, it would have substantially improved the position of the 90 per cent of beneficiaries who failed to receive their full compensation for

[139] See the Social Security and Child Support (Decisions and Appeals) Regulations 1999 (S.I. 1999 No. 991), replacing the Social Security (Adjudication) Regulations 1995 (S.I. 1995 No. 1801). See further Chapter 7.

[140] R. Lewis, 'The Government's Philosophy Towards Reform of Social Security: The Case of Industrial Injuries Benefit' (1986) 15 *I.L.J.* 256–65 at 261.

[141] Secretary of State for Social Services, *Reform of the Industrial Injuries Scheme*, Cm 8402 (London, HMSO, 1981).

their loss of earnings. It had always been anomalous that beneficiaries continued to receive REA to reflect their loss of earnings even long after they would have retired or, even, been incapable by reason of age from carrying on their previous employment.[142] The change to a retirement allowance was, therefore, designed to remove this anomaly. Retirement allowance converted an award of REA where the recipients were over pensionable age and had given up regular employment and were receiving awards of REA of at least £2.00 per week. The amount of the allowance is the lesser of 10 per cent of the current award of disablement benefit or 25 per cent of the amount of REA in payment before the claimant retired. The maximum award of REA is in fact equivalent to 40 per cent disablement benefit.

These provisions are not without their difficulty. For example, the different age limits for men and women have been challenged on the grounds that they are in breach of EC Council Directive 79/7/EEC on equal treatment.[143] There have also been difficulties surrounding the question whether claimants have or have not given up regular employment: if they had before 10 April 1989 their entitlement to REA was frozen at the rate then in payment.[144] In its report in 1990 the IIAC commented on the value of the reduced earnings allowance as it

enabled employees in the early stages of a potentially crippling or even fatal occupational illness to move to a safer job. It is vital to retain such a measure which acts to protect the individual from further harm. Indeed it would be desirable to encourage greater use of this benefit, and if necessary to increase its rate, to strengthen its preventive role.[145]

In its White Paper on benefits for disabled people,[146] which appeared in the same month, the Government indicated its intention to abolish REA in its entirety. The reason given was largely that 'the majority of REA recipients who are not working are also receiving IVB [invalidity benefit], the contributory benefit which is payable regardless of the cause of incapacity'.[147] Linked to this reason was the proposal of the Government to introduce a disability employment credit 'targeted specifically on

---

[142] This would clearly apply to those injured playing e.g. professional football or rugby league: participation in the professions can in any event only be continued for a limited period.

[143] See *CI/094/1994*; *CI/600/1994*; and *CI/7308/1995*, noted at (1998) 5 *J.S.S.L.* D 40–1, holding that the conditions linked to pensionable age had no discriminatory effect for the purposes of the Directive. The claimants appealed to the Court of Appeal which upheld the decision of the Commissioner: *Plummer and Another v Chief Adjudication Officer* (1998) 8 December, noted at (1999) 6 *J.S.S.L.* D 64. See also the directions given by Commissioner Howell in *CI/16608/1996*. There has now been a reference to the European Court of Justice seeking a preliminary ruling whether the different cut-off ages for male and female REA claimants infringe the Equal Treatment Directive and, if so, what the consequences are: ECJ reference *C-196/98 Hepple and others v CAO*, registered 22 May 1998.

[144] See SSCBA 1992, Sched. 7 Part IV, and the detailed commentary on these provisions in D. Bonner, I. Hooker, and R. White, *Non-Means Tested Benefit: the Legislation* (London: Sweet and Maxwell, 1998), 246–55.

[145] IIAC, *The Industrial Injuries Scheme and the Reform of Disability Income*, Position Paper No. 5. (London: IIAC, 1990). See also IIAC, *Periodic Report 1993* (London: HMSO, 1993), 10, where the IIAC expresses concern that extension of benefits for disabled people generally was being financed at the expense of the scheme for occupational injury.

[146] DSS, *The Way Ahead: Benefits for Disabled People*, Cm 917 (London: HMSO, 1990).

[147] Ibid., para. 6.12.

people who are only partially rather than wholly incapable of work'.[148] In January 1990 a delegation from the IIAC met the Secretary of State for Social Security to discuss the proposed abolition of REA; but there was no change of policy.[149] Notwithstanding the comments of the IIAC concerning the validity of REA and the expectations raised in 1986 that this benefit would remain for the compositor who had lost his or her finger, REA was abolished by the Social Security Act 1990 in respect of any accident or diseases first occurring after 1 October 1990. REA remains, therefore, only for those who either had a previous entitlement at the date of change or whose claim can be related back to an accident or disease occurring before this cut-off date.

REA and its predecessor special hardship allowance had not been without their critics on the grounds of the complexity of the system,[150] but the expectation of the Government in 1990 that a disability employment credit would take the place of REA (above) has not been borne out. Disability working allowance—which is the benefit which fulfilled the purpose of the proposed credit—was a means-tested benefit which was introduced with effect from April 1992, modelled on family credit. It aimed to top up the earnings of those who had been in receipt of specific benefits related to disability.[151] The take-up was very disappointing but there are hopes of improvement under the benefit's sucessor, disabled person's tax credit, introduced under the Tax Credits Act 1999.[152] Government estimates of 50,000[153] eligible claimants of DWA can be compared with figures for October 1996 of only 11,350 actual recipients.[154] By comparison, REA was still in 1996 being received by 151,000 people. If it was the case that the majority of those receiving reduced earnings allowance were also receiving invalidity benefit—and no figures were given in the White Paper to support this view[155]—the problem could have been cured by providing that the two benefits could not be received at the same time.[156]

6. ADMINISTRATION AND ADJUDICATION

The separate entitlement to benefits in respect of industrial injury has been criticised on account of administrative cost. The major benefit—disablement pension[157]—involves two types of decision. The decision whether the relevant

---

[148] Ibid., para. 5.11. This was later introduced as disability working allowance: see Chapter 12 above.
[149] IIAC, *Periodic Report* (1993), op. cit., 10. See also N. Wikeley, *Compensation for Industrial Disease* (Aldershot: Dartmouth, 1993), 200.
[150] And this complexity continues, see e.g. *CI/094/1994* and *CI/600/94* (1998) 5 *J.S.S.L.* D 40.
[151] See Chapter 12 at pp. 392–3.   [152] Ibid.
[153] DSS, *The Way Ahead: Benefits for Disabled People*, Cm 917 (London: HMSO, 1990), para. 5.17.
[154] P. Larkin, 'Social Security provision for disability: a case for change?' (1998) 5 *J.S.S.L.* 9–17 at 14. More recent take-up figures for DWA are cited in Chapter 12 above.
[155] N. 153 above, para. 6.12.
[156] See further S. R. Jones, 'Industrial preference: in decline?' (1991) XIV *Liverpool Law Rev.*, 63–74.
[157] SSCBA 1992, s. 103.

accident had resulted in a loss of faculty and the degree of disablement resulting from that loss of faculty are the disablement questions.[158] Until the Social Security Act 1998 changes, these were referred to an adjudicating medical practitioner or practitioners and thence, on appeal, to a medical appeal tribunal.[159] On the other hand, decisions whether an accident arose out of and in the course of employment, or whether an employed earner worked in a prescribed occupation, were matters for the adjudication officer and thence on appeal to a social security appeal tribunal. The Social Security Act 1998 made some significant changes to this adjudication structure which were implemented throughout 1999. The same distinction will be made between disablement questions and others, but, for example, there will be unified appeal tribunals in place of the social security appeal tribunal, the medical appeal tribunal, and other tribunals. Issues relating to disablement and disease will be referred by the Secretary of State to a medical practitioner, and the Secretary of State shall have regard to the practitioner's report (among other factors) in making a decision.[160] Adjudication officers are to disappear as separate legal entities, although their functions will remain and will in effect be exercised on behalf of the Secretary of State.[161] Overall, adjudication is being streamlined but will remain fairly complex, with continuing attendant rights of appeal to the Social Security Commissioner and beyond.

In addition, the collection of evidence about the work history of a claimant, particularly in cases of occupational deafness, where a claimant has to have worked for at least ten years in a prescribed occupation, continues to make the scheme expensive to administer. It was estimated that the proportion of administrative costs to benefit expenditure for the industrial injuries scheme was 13.3 per cent compared with 4.4 per cent for the social security system as a whole.[162] It must be said that this nevertheless compares very favourably with the cost of actions in tort: it costs 85 pence to put each £1 of tort damages into an accident victim's pocket.[163]

---

[158] SSCBA 1992, s. 45.

[159] On medical appeal tribunals, see R. Sainsbury, *Survey and Report into the Working of the Medical Appeal Tribunals* (HMSO, London 1992) and Chapter 7 above.

[160] Social Security and Child Support (Decisions and Appeals) Regulations 1999 (S.I. 1999 No. 991), reg. 12, which applies to decisions concerning: (i) the extent of a personal injury for the purposes of the right to industrial injuries benefit (under SSCBA 1992, s. 94); (ii) whether the claimant has a prescribed disease (see above); and (iii) whether the claimant has a disablement for the purposes of disablement pension (under SSCBA 1992, s. 103) or the extent of any such disablement. Under reg. 12(3)(b), regard shall be had to the experience of the reporting practitioner in those matters, and of any other reporting medical practitioner who has carried out an examination of the claimant under s. 19 of the Social Security Act 1998.

[161] Social Security Act 1998, s. 1. See N. Wikeley, 'Decision making and appeals under the Social Security Act 1998' (1998) 5 *J.S.S.L.* 104–17. The Green Paper of the Conservative Government which preceded these changes in the appeals system is DSS, *Improving Decision Making and Appeals in Social Security*, Cm 3328 (London: HMSO, 1996). See further Chapter 7.

[162] Figures taken from R. Lewis, *Compensation for Industrial Injury* (Aldershot: Professional Books, 1987), 11.

[163] Ibid. See also the critique of the cost of tort actions in P. Cane, *Atiyah's Accidents, Compensation and the Law*, 5th edn. (London: Butterworths, 1993). P. S. Atiyah, *The Damages Lottery* (Oxford: Hart Publishing, 1997), 179, reckons that the amount paid out annually in damages is £1 billion at an administrative cost of about £800 million.

7. RELATIONSHIP TO AND COMPARISON WITH TORT[164]

What has remained from the Workmen's Compensation Act 1897 is the concept that an employed earner should receive compensation without having to prove fault. Beveridge advocated a change from compensation being paid by an employer to being shared by society as a whole. As we have seen, one of the three reasons by which Beveridge justified the continuance of an industrial preference was that this would result in a decline in the number of actions for damages arising from work accidents. The approach in fact adopted was to permit tort actions but to reduce the damages awarded for loss of earnings by one half of the social security benefits received or likely to be received in a five-year period from the date of the injury.[165] It was considered important to retain social security benefits to provide immediate protection for injured employees, and it was felt that as employees contributed to social security benefit through the payment of national insurance contributions they should receive half those benefits without affecting a tort claim. The compensator could therefore deduct from the damages for loss of earnings payable one half of the value of certain social security benefits received during the five-year period. This only applied to court awards, not to settlements reached between the parties. The reason behind this was to prevent the victim from recovering twice over. The value of the benefits was not paid to the Secretary of State: the relevant amounts were retained by the compensator in reduction of the damages payable.

These principles were amended in 1989[166] when it was enacted that all social security benefits received in the five years after the accident/injury or the date of settlement, whichever came first, should be deducted from all tort damages—including damages for pain and suffering as well as loss of earnings—but paid over to the Secretary of State. In addition, there was no longer any discretion as to whether or not the benefits would be deducted and neither were the provisions confined to court awards. The 1948 Act had allowed the parties to ignore its provisions in reaching settlements. This could no longer apply. Settlements of £2,500 and below were exempt, but no account was to be taken of reductions in damages because of the contributory negligence of the employee.

There was subsequent pressure to amend the legislation because of the perceived injustice of not exempting damages for pain and suffering from the recoupment provision. The Social Security (Recovery of Benefits) Act 1997 retained the broad principles of the 1989 reform but with some significant amendments. For court orders or agreements reached on or after 6 October 1997 the new provisions will apply. For accidents or diseases occurring before that date and after 1 January 1989, the 1989

---

[164] See P. Cane, *Atiyah's Accidents, Compensation and the Law*, 5th edn. (London Butterworths, 1993), 326–30; R. Lewis, *Compensation for Industrial Injury*, op. cit., 11–15; idem, 'Deducting collateral benefits from damages: principle and policy' (1998) 18 *L.S.* 15–40.

[165] Law Reform (Personal Injuries) Act 1948.

[166] Social Security Act 1989, s. 22 and Sched. 4. See N. Wikeley, 'Tort and the Clawback of Social Security Benefits' (1991) 10 *C.J.Q.* 10–15.

scheme will continue; and for accidents or diseases before 1989, there will be no right for the Secretary of State to recover benefit from the compensator. The major change in the new scheme is to limit the recoverability to three heads of compensation: compensation for earnings lost during the relevant period; compensation for the cost of care incurred during the relevant period; and, lastly, compensation for loss of mobility during the relevant period. Compensation paid in respect of pain and suffering is to be discounted. As Rowland explains:

Under this new provision, the extent to which the compensation payment may be reduced is limited by the extent to which compensation is attributable to a relevant head (i.e. compensation for loss of earnings, compensation for the cost of care or compensation for loss of mobility).[167] This is likely to encourage parties to pay even closer attention to benefits than they have hitherto and will often require them to agree the proportion of the compensation attributable to each head before a claim is settled. One effect may be to encourage compensators to join with victims in challenging certificates of recoverable benefits on the ground that some of the listed benefits have not been payable 'in respect of' the relevant accident, injury, or disease.[168]

Atiyah has compared the social security system with the system of payment for damages and concludes that social security has a number of advantages. First, the decision-making process is faster and is designed to determine the claimant's entitlement to benefit rather than to negotiate a settlement dependent on the relevant strengths of the two parties. There can be no negotiation under the state scheme: there is a statutory entitlement or there is not; the parties cannot themselves agree a compromise of a disputed point. Secondly, all social security benefits (with the exception of widow's initial lump sum and vaccine damage payments) are paid periodically. Most awards of tort damages, on the other hand, are paid in a lump sum which is available to be spent at will by the victim.[169] Thirdly, the requirement of employers to investigate and report on industrial accidents benefits employees who have to prove their case, and the ability to apply for an accident declaration allows the issue whether an accident arose out of and in the course of employment to be determined at an early stage. Moreover, the system of determining medical questions under the social security system is better. Fourthly, the social security system provides scope for reassessment of the disablement. Many awards of disablement benefit are provisional and are uprated annually. Even final awards can be reviewed on the grounds of unforeseen aggravation. Tort claims tend to be settled by once-and-for-all payments based on speculation as to the future.

Atiyah considers that in some respects the tort system is superior: the commitment to full compensation and to earnings-related compensation makes it in prin-

[167] Social Security (Recovery of Benefits) Act 1997, s. 8 and Sched. 2.
[168] M. Rowland, *Medical and Disability Appeal Tribunals: the Legislation* (London: Sweet and Maxwell, 1998), 190.
[169] Larger sums may be subject to the terms of a structured settlement designed to produce an income over a longer period of time. See R. Lewis, 'Legal limits on the structured settlement of damages' [1993] *C.L.J.* 470–86.

ciple more generous than the social security system, which aims only to meet certain minimum needs. The tort system also deals more satisfactorily with partial incapacity and is also less sexually discriminatory. Atiyah also considers that the benefits for the long-term disabled within the social security system display a 'laudable' preference over the short-term benefit. Tort claims, however, tend to favour those with short-term injuries.[170] He concludes that the preference within the social security system in favour of the industrially injured is simply 'indefensible'.[171]

Atiyah's main criticisms of the tort system are that it is expensive to administer and benefits only a small number of accident victims who must show someone else was at fault before recovery can take place. Excluded, for example, are those born with disabilities, who become disabled through illness or natural causes, or who are victims of simple accidents where no-one is to blame. Moreover, for those who do recover through the tort system it is really society as a whole which pays the compensation through increased costs passed on by insurance companies and their insured, so that there is little deterrence effect.

More recently, Atiyah has challenged the whole idea of tort claims for personal injury and recommends that they should be abolished and replaced by first-party insurance.[172] Increasingly, he sees the system of compensation for personal injury as a lottery which is very wasteful in its operation and benefits a very small number of people. First-party insurance could be made compulsory for motoring accidents where there is already compulsory third-party insurance and it would not take much to extend the cover to include injury to the insured victim. For other accidents and injuries the idea of insurance is more alien and instead of a compulsory system Atiyah recommends the abolition of the action for personal injury and leaving it to the market-place to encourage and develop the role of insurance, with some residual state scheme for those who either cannot afford to take out insurance or for some other reason do not do so. The advantages Atiyah sees are many.[173] First, the wasteful legal and administrative costs involved in the present tort scheme would be eliminated. Secondly, there would be improved cover against a large variety of risks. Thirdly, the artificial distinction which the law creates between accidental injuries and disabilities from other causes would be eliminated. Fourthly, a shift to insurance would enhance consumer choice and allow people to choose the level of cover they need. The retired and unemployed would not, for example, wish or need to insure against loss of earnings. Finally, the replacement of the action for personal injury by first-party insurance would reduce the adversarial process. He argues that in the long run the actual cost to society would be less, as society would no longer bear the cost of expensive damages claims.

The feature of these proposals which is particularly interesting is that they mirror

---

[170] P. Cane, n. 164 above, at 298.   [171] Ibid., 296.

[172] P. S. Atiyah, *The Damages Lottery* (Oxford: Hart Publishing Limited, 1997).

[173] Ibid., 185–93. For critiques of these views, see T. Weir, [1998] *C.L.J.* 204–6 and J. Conaghan and W. Mansell, 'From the Permissive to the Dismissive Society: Patrick Atiyah's Accidents, Compensation and the Market' (1998) 25 *J. of Law and Society*, 284–93.

the suggestion that compensation for industrial injury under the state scheme should no longer be funded by the state but transferred to the insurance companies. Where the proposals would mark a difference from the present industrial injuries scheme, however, is that they would make no distinction between the cause of the injury or, presumably, with whether a claimant was employed or self-employed. If, however, insurance companies themselves became involved in expensive disputes as to their liability under first-party insurance claims there is obviously a danger of a return to the litigation-driven situation which Beveridge recognised in the Workmen's Compensation Scheme and sought to avoid. A more fundamental problem with Atiyah's scheme would appear to be the lack of compulsion to take out first-party insurance. Any proposal to move the funding of industrial injuries benefits to the employer's insurance company would, presumably, be compulsory.

8. CONCLUSION

There is still an industrial preference. Most obviously this is represented by disablement benefit and its two additions—constant attendance allowance and exceptionally severe disablement allowance. Virtually every other preferential feature has disappeared since 1980, except that beneficiaries of disablement benefit do continue to receive favourable treatment if they live abroad. For those who receive disablement benefit, the financial advantages can compare favourably with those available under the tort system, particularly in the case of those who are quite severely disabled at a young age—the value of the social security benefits over their lifetime is likely to exceed any tort award for damages. To succeed in tort, moreover, depends on a finding of fault. However, it has been argued that the erosion of the industrial preference and the narrowing of the gap in benefits payable to those injured at work and those incapacitated from other causes means that, as Atiyah says:

the unions probably regret that workers' compensation laws were ever taken over by the state. Had they remained a responsibility of industry and private insurers, the government could have constantly increased the level of benefits payable, while leaving industry to pay the bill.[174]

Of immediate interest is whether there is any future for such preference as continues to exist. There appears to be little argument outside the IIAC in favour of maintaining, let alone extending, a separate system which Lewis has referred to as a caste system.[175] In the recent Green Paper on welfare, however, there is little mention of the industrial injuries scheme. It is noted, certainly, but as an example of private–public partnerships and there is no mention of whether this should change:

---

[174] P. S. Atiyah, *The Damages Lottery*, op. cit., 106.

[175] R. Lewis, 'Tort and Social Security: the importance attached to the cause of disability with special reference to the Industrial Injuries Scheme' (1980) 43 *M.L.R.* 514–31 at 526.

Employers are required to insure against the risk of work injuries for which they are at fault. In 1995 they paid out £738 million in compensation and costs. The Government compensates workers—through Industrial Injuries Benefits—for injuries and for certain industrial diseases. Last year these benefits amounted to £730 million.[176]

This is all the Green Paper says on this subject. In its last periodic report the IIAC was in no doubt that there was a special place for industrial injuries benefits and nothing published by the IIAC since that date suggests any change in their attitude. The gaps in provision identified in that report still remain, and particularly for those who are self-employed. In its recent report on disability benefits generally the SSAC was unable to discuss the war disablement scheme and the industrial injuries scheme because of its restricted remit.[177]

In another recent Green Paper, on benefits for disabled people,[178] the position of those receiving disablement benefit and its additions is again referred to, but without any indication of changes.[179] The areas identified in the Green Paper for consultation and change are incapacity benefit, severe disablement allowance, and disability living allowance. There is no statement as to possible reforms this Government would seek to make to the industrial injuries preference except to transfer the cost of payment from the state to the employer, the employer's insurance company, and thence to the consumer. A comparable transfer of administrative responsibility for the payment of benefit was achieved when statutory sick pay replaced sickness benefit for those who had an employer.[180] The major difference between statutory sick pay and entitlement to benefit for industrial injuries is that the latter undoubtedly generates a far larger number of appeals. If responsibility for payment is to be transferred to the employers and the insurance industry, serious thought will have to be given as to how disputes will be dealt with and paid for.

For political and historical reasons, however, it is perhaps unlikely that disablement benefit will be removed, although there is already provision to repeal entitlement to constant attendance allowance and exceptionally severe disablement allowance. REA is withering on the vine, but for the foreseeable future there is no evidence of an immediate intention to abolish or modify what is left. The profile of the industrial preference since 1980 has been one of a decline in importance and the removal of a number of small preferences which, with the exception of REA, had become anomalous or simply too expensive to administer for the little benefit provided. It can be argued that what remains of the preference duplicates provision elsewhere or is simply too complicated. Recent cases show that there is still considerable legal mileage in trying to unravel the complexities of the system. This provides an unfavourable comparison with other aspects of the social security system given the relatively small

---

[176] Green Paper (1998), ch. 4, para. 2.

[177] P. Larkin, 'Social security provision for disability: a case for change?' (1998) 5 *J.S.S.L.* 9–17.

[178] Secretary of State for Social Security, *A New Contract for Welfare: Support for Disabled People*, Cm 4103 (London: Stationery Office, 1998).

[179] Ibid., Annexe One, para. 10.   [180] See Ogus, Barendt, and Wikeley (1995), 160.

amount of money devoted to the scheme compared with the social security budget as a whole. There is no move to duplicate disablement benefit or use it as a model in other parts of the social security system. In fact the reverse is the case. There is, however, no current government proposal to remove disablement benefit in its present form and this part of the industrial preference must now have some kind of entrenched status which for political reasons it would be difficult to remove.

Bibliography

Abberley, P., 'Counting Us Out: a discussion of the OPCS disability surveys' (1992) 7 *Disability, Handicap and Society*, 139–55.

Abel-Smith, B., and Townsend, P., *The Poor and the Poorest* (London: Bell, 1965).

Abraham, K. S., and Liebman, L., 'Private Insurance, Social Insurance, and Tort Reform: Toward a New Vision of Compensation for Illness and Injury' (1993) 93 *Columbia Law Rev.* 75–118.

Adler, M., et al., 'The conduct of tribunal hearings', in Adler, M., and Bradley, A., *Justice, Discretion and Poverty* (Abingdon: Professional Books, 1976), 109–29.

Adler, M., and Asquith, S., *Discretion and Welfare* (London: Heinemann, 1981).

Adler, M., 'Towards a sociology of social security' in Adler, M., Bell, C., Clasen, J., and Sinfield, A., *The Sociology of Social Security* (Edinburgh: Edinburgh University Press, 1991), 1–15.

Adler, M., 'The habitual residence test: a critical analysis' (1995) 2 *J.S.S.L.* 179–95.

Adler, M., 'The Underclass: Rhetoric or Reality?', in Lundy, L., et al. (eds), *In Search of the 'Underclass': Working Papers from the SLSA One Day Conference in Queen's University Belfast* (Belfast: Queen's University Faculty of Law, 1997), 108–16.

Adler, M., and Bradley, A. W. (eds), *Justice, Discretion and Poverty: Supplementary Benefit Appeal Tibunals in Britain* (Abingdon: Professional Books, 1976).

Alcock, P., *Poverty and State Support* (London: Longman, 1987).

Alcock, P., 'Why citizenship and welfare rights offer new hope for new welfare in Britain' 9(2) (1989) *Critical Social Policy*, 32–43.

Alcock, P., 'Social Insurance in Crisis?' (1992) *Benefits*, 6.

Alcock, P., *Social Policy in Britain: Themes and Issues* (London: Macmillan, 1996).

Alcock, P., 'The advantages and disadvantages of the contribution base in targeting benefits: A social analysis of the insurance scheme in the United Kingdom', (1996) 49(1) *International Social Security Review*, 31–49.

Alcock, P., 'Welfare and Self-Interest', in Field, F., *Stakeholder Welfare* (London: IEA, 1996), 52–3.

Alcock, P., 'Making Welfare Work—Frank Field and New Labour's Social Policy Agenda' (1997) *Benefits* (September/October), 34–8.

Alcock, P., *Understanding Poverty*, 2nd edn. (Basingstoke: Macmillan, 1997).

Allbeson, J., 'Seen but not heard: young people', in Ward, S. (ed.), *DHSS in Crisis* (London: CPAG, 1985), 97.

Allbeson, J., and Smith, R., *We Don't Give Clothing Grants Anymore* (London: CPAG, 1984).

Allen, D., 'Cohesion and Structural Adjustment', in Wallace, H., and Wallace, W. (eds), *Policy-making in the European Union* (Oxford: OUP, 1996), 157–84.

Anon, 'Dethroning the Welfare Queen: The Rhetoric of Reform' (1994) 107(8) *Harvard Law Review*, 2013–30.

Armstrong, H., 'Community Regional Policy', in Lodge, J. (ed.), *The European Community and the Challenge of the Future* (London: Pinter, 1993), 131–51.

Ashton, G., 'Case Analysis' (1995) 2 *J.S.S.L.* 155–9.

Atiyah, P. S., *The Damages Lottery* (Oxford: Hart Publishing, 1997).

Atkinson, A. B., *Poverty and Social Security* (Hemel Hempstead: Harvester Wheatsheaf, 1989).

Atkinson, T., and Micklewright, J., 'Turning the Screw: Benefits for the Unemployed 1979–88', in Dilnot, A., and Walker, I. (eds), *The Economics of Social Security* (Oxford: Oxford University Press, 1989), 17–51.

Audit Commission, The, *Bringing Council Tenants Arrears Under Control: A Review* (London: The Audit Commission, 1984).

Audit Commission, The, *The National Administration of Housing Benefit* (London: HMSO, 1993).

Baldock, J., 'Patterns of change in the delivery of welfare in Europe', in Taylor-Gooby, P., and Lawson, R., *Markets and Managers: New Issues in the Delivery of Welfare* (Milton Keynes: Open University Press, 1993), 24–37.

Baldwin, J., Wikeley, N., and Young, R., *Judging Social Security: the adjudication of claims for benefit in Britain* (Oxford: Clarendon Press, 1992).

Baldwin, P., 'Beveridge in the Longue Duree', in Hills, J., Ditch, J., and Glennester, H. (eds), *Beveridge and Social Security: An International Perspective* (Oxford: Clarendon Press, 1994), 37–55.

Baldwin, S., and Parker, G., 'Support for Informal Carers—the Role of Social Security', in Dalley, G. (ed.), *Disability and Social Policy* (London: PSI, 1991), 163–98.

Banks, M. H., and Ullah, P., *Youth Unemployment. Social and Psychological Perspectives*, Research Paper No. 61 (London: Department of Employment, 1987).

Barnard, C., *EC Employment Law* (Chichester: Wiley, 1996).

Barnes, C., and Mercer, G. (eds.), *Exploring the Divide: Illness and Disability* (Leeds: Disability Press, 1996).

Barnes, M., 'Comment' (1999) *Poverty* No. 103, 1.

Barr, N., *The Economics of the Welfare State*, 2nd edn. (London: Weidenfeld and Nicolson, 1993).

Barry, N., *Welfare* (Milton Keynes: Open University Press, 1990).

Bartrip, P. W. J., and Burman, S. J., *The Wounded Soldiers of Industry* (Oxford: Clarendon Press, 1983).

Bates, F., 'Social Security Law and Children with Disabilities: Change and Decay in Australian Statute Law' (1998) 18(3) *Statute Law Rev.* 215–34

Becker, S., and Silburn, R., *The New Poor Clients* (Wallington: Community Care and Benefits Research Unit, 1990).

Bell, J., 'Discretionary Decision-making: A Jurisprudential View', in Hawkins, K. (ed.), *The Uses of Discretion* (Oxford: Oxford University Press, 1992), 47–88.

Bell, K., Collinson, P., Turner, S., and Webber, S., 'National Insurance Local Tribunals' (1974) 3(4) *J. of Social Policy*, 289–315.

Bell, K., *Research Study on Supplementary Benefit Appeal Tribunals: Review of Main Findings; Conclusions; Recommendations* (London: HMSO, 1975).

Bellamy, C., 'Transforming Social Security Benefits' (1996) 74 *Public Administration*, 159–79.

Benefits Agency, The, *Benefit Review (Income Support and Unemployment Benefit)* (Leeds: The Benefits Agency, 1995).

Berthoud, R., *Reform of Social Security. Working Papers* (London: Policy Studies Institute, 1984).

Berthoud, R., *The Examination of Social Security* (London: PSI, 1985).

Berthoud, R., *Selective Social Security. An Examination of the Government's Plan* (London: PSI, 1986).

Berthoud, R., *Credit, Debt and Poverty: Social Security Advisory Committee Research Paper 1* (London: HMSO, 1989).

Berthoud, R., 'The medical assessment of incapacity: a case study of research and policy' (1995) 2 *J.S.S.L.* 61–85.

Berthoud, R., *Disability Benefits: A Review of the Issues and Options for Reform* (York: Joseph Rowntree Foundation, 1998).

Berthoud, R., Lakey, J., and McKay, S., *The Economic Problems of Disabled People* (London: PSI, 1993).

Bett, M., 'The role of the Social Security Advisory Committee' (1994) 1 *J.S.S.L.* 105–9.

Beveridge, W. H., *Unemployment. A Problem of Industry* (London: Longman, 1930).

Beveridge, W. H., *Social Insurance and Allied Services: Report by Sir William Beveridge*, Cmnd. 217 (London: HMSO, 1942).

Billings, P., 'Case Analysis' (1999) 6 *J.S.S.L.* 137–44.

Bloch, A., 'Ethnic inequality and social security policy', in Walker, A., and Walker, C. (eds), *Britain Divided* (London: CPAG, 1997), 111–22.

Bolderson, H., 'Compensation for Disability' (1974) 3 *J. of Social Policy*, 193–211.

Bolderson, H., 'The Right to Appeal and the Social Fund' (1988) *J.L.S.* 279–92.

Bolderson, H., *Social Security, Disability and Rehabilitation: Conflicts in the Development of Social Policy 1914–1946* (London: Jessica Kingsley Publishers, 1991).

Bolderson, H., and Gains, F., *Crossing National Frontiers* (London: HMSO, 1993).

Bolderson, H., and Mabbett, D., 'Mongrels or thoroughbreds: A cross-national look at social security systems' (1995) *European Journal of Political Research*, No. 28, 19–39.

Bonner, D., 'Incapacity for work: a new benefit and new tests' (1995) 2 *J.S.S.L.* 86–112.

Bonner, D., 'Compensation for assault: an unusual dimension to the industrial injuries system' (1998) 5 *J.S.S.L.* 72–82.

Bonner, D., 'Case Analysis' (1999) 6 *J.S.S.L.* 33–9.

Bonner, D., Hooker, I., and Smith, R., *Non-Means Tested Benefits: the Legislation* (London: Sweet and Maxwell, 1998).

Bottomley, D., McKay, S., and Walker, R., *Unemployment and Jobseeking,* DSS Research Report No. 62 (London: The Stationery Office, 1997).

Bradley, A. W., 'Recent Reform of Social Security Adjudication in Great Britain' (1985) 26 *Les Cahiers de Droit*, 403–49.

Bradshaw, J., 'A defence of social security', in Bean, P., Ferris, J., and Whynes, D. (eds), *In Defence of Welfare* (London: Tavistock, 1985), 227–56.

Bradshaw, J., 'Implementing Thatcherite Policies: Audit of an Era', in Marsh, D., and Rhodes, R. A. W., *Implementing Thatcherite Policies: Audit of an Era* (Milton Keynes: Open University Press, 1992), 81–93.

Bradshaw, J. (ed.), *Budget Standards for the UK* (Aldershot: Avebury, 1993).

Bradshaw, J., 'Developments in social security policy', in Jones, C. (ed.), *New Perspectives on the Welfare State in Europe* (London: Routledge, 1993), 44–63.

Bradshaw, J., *Household Budgets and Living Standards* (York: Joseph Rowntree Foundation, 1993).

Bradshaw, J., and Lynes, T., *Benefit Uprating Policy and Living Standards*, Social Policy Report 1 (York: Social Policy Research Unit, 1995).

Bradshaw, J., and Millar, J., *Lone Parent Families in the U.K.*, Department of Social Security Research Report No. 6 (London: HMSO, 1991).

Briggs, A., 'The welfare state in historical perspective' (1961) 2(2) *European Journal of Sociology*, 221–58.

Brown, J. C., *Family Income Support—Part II: Children in Social Security* (London: Policy Studies Institute, 1984).

Brown, J. C., *A Policy Vacuum: Social Security for the Self-employed* (York, Joseph Rowntree Foundation, 1992).

Brown, J., *Escaping From Dependence, Part-time Workers and The Self-Employed: The Role of Social Security* (London: Institute for Public Policy Research, 1994).

Brown, K., Bird, J., and Bates, D., 'Assessing the psychosomatic component of disability' (1997) 4 *J.S.S.L.* 102–8.

Bruce, M., *The Coming of the Welfare State*, 2nd edn. (London: B.T. Batsford, 1965), 240.

Bryson, A., Ford, R., and White, M., *Making Work Pay: Lone Mothers, Employment and Well-being* (Layerthorpe: Joseph Rowntree Foundation, York Publishing Services Ltd, 1997).

Bryson, L., *Welfare and the State* (London: Macmillan, 1992).

Buck, T., 'Actively seeking work' (1989) 18 *I.L.J.* 258–65.

Buck, T., 'The Way Ahead: Benefits for the Disabled' (1990) 19 *I.L.J.* 125–32.

Buck, T., 'The Disabled Citizen', in Blackburn, R. (ed.), *Rights of Citizenship* (Oxford: Mansell, 1993), 179–200.

Buck, T., 'Case Analysis' (1995) 2 *J.S.S.L.* 113–16.

Buck, T., *The Social Fund: Law and Practice* (London: Sweet and Maxwell, 1996).

Buck, T., 'Jobseeker's allowance: policy perspectives' (1996) 3 *J.S.S.L.* 149–64.

Buck, T., 'R. v. Social Fund Inspector, ex p. Harper' (1997) 4 *J.S.S.L.* 134–8.

Buck, T., 'Judicial Review and the Discretionary Social Fund: the Impact on a Respondent Organisation', in Buck, T. (ed.), *Judicial Review and Social Welfare* (London: Pinter, 1998), 114–41.

Buck, T., 'R. v. Social Fund Inspector, ex p. Taylor' (1998) 5 *J.S.S.L.* 89–94.

Bull, D., 'The Anti-Discretion Movement in Britain: Fact or Phantom?' (1980) *Journal of Social Welfare Law*, 65–83.

Burchardt, T., and Hills, J., *Private Welfare Insurance and Social Security* (York: Joseph Rowntree Foundation, 1997).

Burghes, L., and Stegles, R., *No Choice at 16: a study of educational maintenance allowances*, Poverty Pamphlet No. 57 (London: CPAG, 1983).

Burrows, L., Phelps, L., and Walentowicz, P., *For Whose Benefit? The Housing Benefit Scheme Reviewed* (London: NACAB and Shelter, 1993).

Burrows, N., and Mair, J., *European Social Law* (Chichester: Wiley, 1996).

Byrne, D., and Jacobs, J., *Disqualified from Benefit: the operation of benefit penalties* (London: Low Pay Unit, 1988).

Callender, C., and Kempson, E., *Student Finances: Income Expenditure and Take-up of Student Loans* (London: Policy Studies Institute, 1996).

Calvert, H., 'Appeal Structures of the Future', in Adler, M., and Bradley, A. (eds), *Justice, Discretion and Poverty* (Abingdon: Professional Books, 1976), 183–207.

Cane, P., *Atiyah's Accidents, Compensation and the Law*, 5th edn. (London: Butterworths, 1993).

Carney, T., 'Merits review of contractual social security payments' (1998) 5 *J.S.S.L.* 18–43.

Carney, T., and Hanks, P., *Social Security in Australia* (Melbourne: Oxford University Press, 1994).

Carson, D., 'Recent Legislation' (1982) *J.S.S.L.* 96–8.

Carter, M., 'The squeeze on asylum seekers' (1996) *Poverty*, No. 94, 9–11.

Casson, M., *Youth Unemployment* (London: Macmillan, 1979).

Castles, F. G., 'The institutional design of the Australian Welfare State' (1997) 50(2) *I.S.S.R.* 25–41.

Central Adjudication Services, *Annual Report of the Chief Adjudication Officer 1996–97* (London: Stationery Office, 1997).

Central Adjudication Services, *Annual Report of the Chief Adjudication Officer, 1997–1998* (London: Stationery Office, 1998).

Chalmers, D., and Szyszczak, E., *European Union Law volume 2: Towards a European Polity* (Aldershot: Dartmouth, 1998).

Charlesworth, L., 'The Poor Law: A Modern Legal Analysis' (1999) 6 *J.S.S.L.* 79–92.

Chief Supplementary Benefit Officer, *CSBO Memo No. 15* (London: SBC, 1982).

Child Poverty Action Group, *Child Support Handbook*, 6th edn. (London: Child Poverty Action Group, 1998).

Children's Society, The, *Children in Focus, Young People and Citizenship—A Public Debate, 29 January 1992* (London: The Children's Society, 1992).

Chiozza Money, L. G., *Insurance Versus Poverty* (London: Methuen, 1912).

Chislom, L., and Bergeret, J. M., *Young People in the European Community* (Luxembourg: Commission of the European Communities, 1991).

Clark, J., and Langan, M., 'Restructuring Welfare: The British Welfare Regime in the 1980s', in Cochrane, A., and Clarke, J. (eds), *Comparing Welfare States: Britain in International Context* (London: Sage, 1993), 69–74.

Clarke, J., 'The problem of the state after the welfare state' (1996) *Social Policy Review*, No. 8, 13–39.

Clasen, J., *Paying the Jobless* (Aldershot: Avebury, 1994).

Cochrane, A., 'Comparative Approaches to Social Policy' and 'Looking for a European Welfare State', in Cochrane, A., and Clarke, J. (eds), *Comparing Welfare States: Britain in International Context* (London: Open University Press, 1993), 239–68.

Coffield, F., Borrill, C., and Marshall, S., *Growing Up at the Margins* (Milton Keynes: Open University Press, 1986).

Cohen, R., Coxall, J., and Sadiq-Sangster, A., *Hardship in Britain. Being Poor in the 1990s* (London: Child Poverty Action Group, 1992).

Commission of the European Communities, *Social Protection in Europe 1993* (Luxembourg: Office for Publications of the European Communities, 1994).

Commission of the European Communities, *Modernising and Improving Protection in the European Union,* COM(97)102 Final (Brussels: Office for Official Publications of the European Communities, 1997).

Commission on Citizenship, *Report of the Commission on Citizenship* (London: HMSO, 1990).

Commission on Social Justice, *Making Sense of Benefits* (London: IPPR, 1993).

Commission on Social Justice, *The Justice Gap* (London: IPPR, 1993).

Commission on Social Justice, *Social Justice in a Changing World* (London: IPPR, 1993).

Commission on Social Justice, *Social Justice: Strategies for National Renewal: The Report of the Commission on Social Justice* (London: Vintage, 1994).

Conaghan, J., and Mansell, W., 'From the Permissive to the Dismissive Society: Patrick Atiyah's Accidents, Compensation and the Market' (1998) 25 *J.L.S.* 284–93.

Cook, D., *Poverty, Crime and Punishment* (London: CPAG, 1997).

Cook, D., 'Between a Rock and a Hard Place: The Realities of Working "On the Side"', *Benefits,* January 1998, 11–15.

Cooper, J., and Vernon, S., *Disability and the Law* (London: Jessica Kingsley, 1996).

Cooper, S., *Family Income Support Part 2: the education and training benefits* (London: PSI, 1985), 108–10.

Corden, A., *Taking Up a Means Tested Benefit. The Process of Claiming F.I.S.* (London: HMSO, 1983).

Corden, A., *Changing Perspectives on Benefit Take-up* (London: HMSO, 1995).

Corden, A., Self-employed people in the United Kingdom: Included or excluded?' (1999) 52(1) *I.S.S.R.*

Council on Tribunals, *Social Security—Abolition of independent appeals under the proposed Social Fund*, Cmnd. 9722 (London: HMSO, 1986).

Cowling, K., *Out of Work. Perspectives of Mass Unemployment* (Coventry: University of Warwick, 1983).

Cox, R. H., 'The Consequences of Welfare Reform: How Conceptions of Social Rights are Changing' (1998) 27(1) *J. of Social Policy*, 1–16.

Cox, S., *Migration and Social Security Handbook* (London: CPAG, 1997).

CPAG, *CPAG's Evidence to the Social Security Reviews 1984. Changed Priorities Ahead?* (London: CPAG, 1984).

Craig, G., *Replacing the Social Fund: a Strategy for Change* (York: Joseph Rowntree Foundation, 1992).

Craig, G., 'It Won't Be You: Britain's Forgotten Lottery' (1998) *Benefits*, September, 50–2.

Craig, P., and de Búrca, G., *EU Law: Text, Cases and Materials* (Oxford: Oxford University Press, 1998).

Cranston, R., *Legal Foundations of the Welfare State* (London: Weidenfeld and Nicolson, 1985).

Creedy, J., and Disney, R., *Social Insurance in Transition. An Economic Analysis* (Oxford: Clarendon Press, 1985).

Creedy, J., and Disney, R., 'The New Pension Scheme in Britain', in Dilnot, A., and Walker, I. (eds), *The Economics of Social Security* (Oxford: Oxford University Press, 1989), 224–38.

Cullen, J., and O'Kelly, R., 'The cost of pensions and the myth of funding', in Silburn, R., *The Future of Social Security* (London: The Fabian Society, 1985).

Curtin, D., 'Occupational Pension Schemes and Article 119: beyond the fringe?' (1987) 24 *C.M.L.Rev.,* 215–57.

Curtin, D., 'Scalping the Community Legislator: Occupational Pensions and *Barber*' (1990) 27 *C.M.L.Rev.,* 475–506.

Cusack, R., and Roll, J., *Families Rent Apart* (London: CPAG, 1985).

CVCP, *CVCP Survey of Student Financial Support 1995* (London: CVCP, 1996).

Dalley, G. (ed.), *Disability and Social Policy* (London: PSI, 1991).

Dalley, G., and Berthoud, R., *Challenging Discretion: The Social Fund Review Procedure* (London: Policy Studies Institute, 1992).

Daly, M., and Noble, M., 'The reach of disability benefits: an examination of disability living allowance' (1996) 18 *J.S.W.F.L.* 37–51.

Davis, A., 'Users' Perspectives and Problems 2: What the research tells us', in Zarb, G. (ed.), *Social Security and Mental Health; Report on the SSAC Workshop*, SSAC Research Paper 7 (London: HMSO, 1996), 24–34.

Davis, G., Cretney, S., Bader, K., and Collins, J., 'The Relationship between Public and Private Financial Support following Divorce in England and Wales', in Weitzman, L., and Maclean, M. (eds.), *Economic Consequences of Divorce: The International Perspective* (Oxford: Clarendon Press, 1992), 311–41.

Davison, R. C., *British Unemployment Policy. The Modern Phase since 1930* (London: Longmans, 1938).

Deacon, A., *In Search of the Scrounger* (London: Bell, 1976).

Deacon, A., 'Welfare and Character', in Field, F., *Stakeholder Welfare* (London: IEA, 1996), 60–74.

Deacon, A., *Benefit Sanctions for the Jobless: Tough Love or Rough Treatment?* (London: Employment Policy Institute, 1997).

Deacon, A., 'The Green Paper on Welfare Reform: A Case for Enlightened Self-interest?' (1998) 69 *Political Quarterly*, 306–11.

Deacon, A., and Bradshaw, J., *Reserved for the Poor—The Means Test in British Social Policy* (Oxford: Martin Roberton, 1983).

Deacon, A., and Mann, K., 'Moralism and Modernity: The Paradox of New Labour Thinking on Welfare' (1997) *Benefits*, September/October, 2–6.

Deakin, S., 'Labour Law as Market Regulation', in Davies, P., et al. (eds), *European Community Labour Law: Principles and Perspectives* (London: Clarendon, 1996), 63–94.

Dean, H., *Social Security and Social Control* (London: Routledge, 1991).

Dean, H., 'Social Security: The income maintenance business', in Taylor-Gooby, P., and Lawson, R., *Markets and Managers: New Issues in the Delivery of Welfare* (Milton Keynes: Open University Press, 1993), 85–105.

Dean, H., 'Underclass or undermined? Young people and social citizenship', in Macdonald, R. (ed.), *Youth, the 'Underclass' and Social Exclusion* (London: Routledge, 1997), 55–69.

Dean, H., and Melrose, M., 'Unravelling citizenship: the significance of social security fraud' (1996) 16(3) *Critical Social Policy*, Issue 48, 3–31.

Dean, H., and Melrose, M., 'Manageable discord: fraud and resistance in the social security system' (1997) 31(2) *Social Policy and Administration*, 103–18.

Dean, H., and Taylor-Gooby, P., 'Statutory Sick Pay and the Control of Sickness Absence' (1990) 19 *J. of Social Policy*, 47–67.

De Noble, B. D., 'Reduction of Welfare Dependency Via Incentives To Recipients—Commendable Goal, But At What Cost?' (1993–4) 32(4) *University of Louisville Journal of Family Law*, 885–900.

Department for Education and Employment, *Employment for the 1990s*, Cm 540 (London, HMSO, 1988).

Department for Education and Employment, *Training for Employment*, Cm 316 (London: HMSO, 1988).

Department for Education and Employment, *Higher Education in the 21st Century* (London: DfEE, 1997).

Department for Education and Employment, *Investing in the Future: Supporting Students in Higher Education* (London: DfEE, 1997).

Department for Education and Employment and Department of Social Security, *A New Contract for Welfare: The Gateway to Work*, Cmnd 4102 (London: The Stationery Office, 1998).

Department of Education and Employment, *DfEE Departmental Report*, Cm 3910 (London: The Stationery Office, 1998).

Department for Education and Employment, *The Learning Age: A New Renaissance for a New Britain*, Cm 3790 (London: The Stationery Office, 1998).

Department for Education and Employment, Press Notice 431/98, 17 September 1998.

Department for Education and Employment, Press Notice 555/98, 30 November 1998.

Department for Education and Employment, *Statistics of Education: Student Support England and Wales 1996/97* (London: The Stationery Office, 1998).

Department for Education and Employment, *Learning to Succeed: A new framework for post-16 learning*, Cm 4392 (London: The Stationery Office, 1999).

Department of Education and Science, Administrative Memorandum 3/1984 (London: DES, 1984).

Department of Education and Science, *Top-Up Loans for Students*, Cm 520 (London: HMSO, 1988).

Department of Employment, *In Working Order: A Study of Industrial Discipline* (London: HMSO, 1973).

Department of Employment/Department of Social Security, *Jobseeker's Allowance*, Cm 2687 (London: HMSO, 1995).

Department of the Environment, *Housing Benefit Review (Request for Evidence)* (London: Department of the Environment, 1984).

Department of the Environment and the Welsh Office, *Our Future Homes: Opportunity, Choice, Responsibility: The Government's Housing Policies for England and Wales*, Cmnd 2901 (London: HMSO, 1995).

Department of Health, *Caring about Carers: National Strategy for Carers* (London: The Stationery Office, 1999).

Department of Health and Social Security, *National Superannuation and Social Insurance: Proposals for Earnings-Related Social Security*, Cmnd 3883 (London: HMSO, 1969).

Department of Health and Social Security, *Strategy for Pensions*, Cmnd 4755 (London: HMSO, 1971).

Department of Health and Social Security, *Supplementary Benefits Handbook* (London: DHSS, 1972).

Department of Health and Social Security, *Better Pensions*, Cmnd 5713 (London: HMSO, 1974).

Department of Health and Social Security and Finer, M., *Report of the Committee on One Parent Families*, Cmnd 5629 (London: HMSO, 1974).

Department of Health and Social Security, *Social Security Bill 1975, Report by the Government Actuary on the Financial Provisions of the Bill*, Cmnd 5928 (London: HMSO, 1975).

Department of Health and Social Security, *Social Assistance: A Review of the Supplementary Benefit Scheme in Great Britain* (London: DHSS, 1978).

Department of Health and Social Security, *Reform of the Supplementary Benefit Scheme*, Cmnd 7773 (London: HMSO, 1979).

Department of Health and Social Security, *Response to the House of Commons Education, Science and the Arts Committee, Minutes of Evidence*, 20 April 1983, Q.730.

Department of Health and Social Security, *Housing Benefit Review. Report of the Review Team*, Cmnd 9520 (London: HMSO, 1985).

Department of Social Security, *Children Come First*, Cm 1264, I (London: HMSO, 1990).

Department of Social Security, *The Way Ahead—Benefits for disabled people*, Cm 917 (London: HMSO, 1990).

Department of Social Security, *The Growth of Social Security* (London: HMSO, 1993).

Department of Social Security, *The Income-Related Benefits Schemes (Miscellaneous Amendments) (No. 2) Regulations 1994, Note for the Social Security Advisory Committee* (London: DSS, 1994).

Department of Social Security, *Households Below Average Income—A Statistical Analysis 1979–1992/93* (London: HMSO, 1995).

Department of Social Security, *The Reform of Social Security*, Cmnds 9517–9519 (London: HMSO, 1995).

Department of Social Security, *Households Below Average Income—A Statistical Analysis 1979–1993/94* (London: HMSO, 1996).

Department of Social Security, *Improving Decision Making and Appeals in Social Security*, Cm 3328 (London: HMSO, 1996).

Department of Social Security, *Restructuring Benefits for Lone Parents, Note to the Social Security Advisory Committee* (London: DSS, 1996).

Department of Social Security, Press Release, 'Income related benefits. Estimates of Take-up in 1995/96', 10 October 1997.

Department of Social Security, *Social Security Departmental Report: 1997*, Cm 3613 (London: The Stationery Office, 1997).

Department of Social Security, *Social Security Statistics 1997* (London: The Stationery Office, 1997).

Department of Social Security, *Beating Fraud is Everyone's Business*, Cm 4012 (London: The Stationery Office, 1998).

Department of Social Security, *Children First: a new approach to child support*, Cm 3992 (London: The Stationery Office, 1998).

Department of Social Security, *Explanatory Memorandum to the Social Security Advisory Committee* (London: DSS, 1998).

Department of Social Security, *First Findings from the Disability Follow-up to the Family Resources Survey*, Research Summary No. 5 (London: DSS, 1998).

Department of Social Security, *Income Support Quarterly Statistical Enquiry* (London: DSS 1998 (August)).

Department of Social Security, *Moving into Work: Bridging Housing Costs,* DSS Research Report No. 79 (Leeds: Corporate Document Services, 1998).

Department of Social Security, *New Ambitions for our Country: A New Contract for Welfare*, Cm 3805 (London: The Stationery Office, 1998).

Department of Social Security, *A New Contract for Welfare: The Gateway to Work*, Cm 4102 (London: The Stationery Office, 1998).

Department of Social Security, *A New Contract for Welfare: Partnership in Pensions*, Cm 4179 (London: The Stationery Office, 1998).

Department of Social Security, *A New Contract for Welfare: Principles into Practice*, Cm 4101 (London: The Stationery Office, 1998).

Department of Social Security, *A New Contract for Welfare: Support for Disabled People*, Cm 4103 (London: The Stationery Office, 1998).

Department of Social Security, *A New Contract for Welfare: Support in Bereavement*, Cm 4101 (London: The Stationery Office, 1998).

Department of Social Security Press Notice 98/044, 2 March 1998.

Department of Social Security, *Reply by the Government to the Fourth Report of the Select Committee on Disability Living Allowance*, Cm 4007 (London: The Stationery Office, 1998).

Department of Social Security, *Social Security Statistics 1998* (Leeds: Corporate Document Services, 1998).

Department of Social Security, *Supporting People* (London: The Stationery Office, 1998).

Department of Social Security, *A New Contract for Welfare: Children's Rights and Parents' Responsibilities*, Cm 4349 (London: The Stationery Office, 1999).

Department of Social Security, *Social Security Departmental Report: The Government's Expenditure Plans 1999/2000*, Cm 4214 (London: The Stationery Office, 1999).

Department of Social Security, *Housing Benefit and Council Tax Benefit Guidance Manual* (London: DSS: updated regularly).

Department of Trade and Industry, *Fairness at Work*, Cm 3968 (London: The Stationery Office, 1998).

Dewar, J., 'Reducing Discretion in Family Law', in Eekelaar, J., and Nhlapo, T. (eds), *The Changing Family: Family Forms and Family Law* (Oxford: Hart, 1998), 233–50.

Diamond, P., 'The end of discretionary awards' (1996) 8(1) *Education and the Law*, 61–8.

DIG, *'A New Contract for Welfare: Support for Disabled People'; Response from Disablement Income Group* (London: DIG, 1999).

Diller, M., 'Entitlement and Exclusion: The Role of Disability in the Social Welfare System' (1996) 44 *U.C.L.A. Law Review*, 361–465.

Dilnot, A., Kay, J., and Morris, N., *The Reform of Social Security* (Oxford: Clarendon Press, 1984).

Dilnot, A., and Stark, G., 'The Poverty Trap, Tax Cuts and the Reform of Social Security', in Dilnot, A., and Walker, I., *The Economics of Social Security* (Oxford: Oxford University Press, 1989), 169–78.

Dilnot, A., and Webb, S., 'The 1988 Social Security Reforms', in Dilnot, A., and Walker, I., *The Economics of Social Security* (Oxford: Oxford University Press, 1989), 239–67.

Disney, R., Emmerson, C., and Tanner, S., *Partnership in Pensions: An Assessment* (London: Institute for Fiscal Studies, 1999).

Disney, R., Grundy, E., and Johnson, P., *The Dynamics of Retirement*, DSS Research Report No. 72 (London: The Stationery Office, 1997).

Disney, R., and Webb, S., 'Why are there so many long term sick in Britain?' (1991) 101 *Economic Journal*, 252–62.

Ditch, J., and Spicker, P., 'The impact of European law on the development of social security policies in the United Kingdom' (1999) 52 *I.S.S.R.* 75–90.

D.L.A.A.B., *Child Mobility and Disability Living Allowance* (London: D.L.A.A.B., 1998).

Dominelli, L., 'Thatcher's attack on social security: restructuring social control' (1988) *Critical Social Policy,* Issue 23, 46–61.

Dominelli, L., *Welfare Across Continents—Feminist Comparative Social Policy* (Hemel Hempstead: Harvester Wheatsheaf, 1991).

Donnison, D., 'Supplementary Benefits: Dilemmas and Priorities' (1976) 5 *J. of Social Policy,* 337–59.

Donnison, D., 'Dear David Bull, Frank Field, Michael Hill and Ruth Lister' (1976) 6 *Social Work Today*, No. 20, 8 January.

Donnison, D., 'Against Discretion' (1977) 41/780 *New Society*, 534–6.

Doyle, B., 'Disabled Workers' Rights, the Disability Discrimination Act and the UN Standard Rules' (1996) 25 *I.L.J.* 1–14.

Drabble, R., and Lynes, T., 'The Social Fund—Discretion or Control?' [1989] *P. L.* 297–322.

Drakeford, M., 'Last Rights? Funerals, Poverty and Social Exclusion' (1988) 27 *J. of Social Policy*, 507–24.

Duffy, K., 'Combating social exclusion and promoting social integration in the European Union', in Oppenheim, C. (ed.), *An Inclusive Society: Strategies for Tackling Poverty* (London: IPPR, 1998), 227–51.

Durcan, J. W., and McCarthy, W. E. J., 'The State Subsidy Theory of Strikes: An Examination of the Statistical Data for the period 1956–1970' (1974) 12 *British Journal of Industrial Relations*, 26–47.

Dworkin, R., *Taking Rights Seriously* (London: Duckworth, 1978).

Eardley, T., and Sainsbury, R., 'Managing Appeals: Control of Housing Benefit Internal Reviews by Local Authority Officers' (1993) 22(4) *J. of Social Policy*, 461–85.

Eekelaar, J., and Maclean, M., *Maintenance after Divorce* (Oxford: Clarendon Press, 1986).

Eichenhofer, E., 'A European Perspective on the Bill', in Adler, M., and Sainsbury, R. (eds), *Adjudication Matters: Reforming Decision Making and Appeals in Social Security* (Edinburgh: Department of Social Policy, University of Edinburgh, 1998), 39–44.

Employment Committee, The, Second Report, *The Right to Work/Workfare,* HC 82 Session 1995–6 (London: HMSO, 1996).

Esping-Andersen, G., *The Three Worlds of Welfare Capitalism* (Cambridge: Polity, 1990).

Esping-Andersen, G., *Welfare States in Transition: National Adaptations in Global Economies* (London: Sage, 1996).

European Foundation for the Improvement of Living and Working Conditions, *Growing Up and Leaving Home: Recommendations of a European Seminar* (Luxembourg: Commission of the European Communities, 1990).

Euzéby, C., 'Social security for the twenty-first century' (1998) 51(2) *I.S.S.R.*, 3–16.

Evans, M., Piachaud, D., and Sutherland, H., *Designed for the Poor—Poorer by Design? The Effects of the 1986 Social Security Act on Family Incomes,* Discussion Paper WSP/105 (London: Suntory-Toyota International Centre for Economics and Related Disciplines, 1994).

Ewing, K. D., *The Right to Strike* (Oxford: Clarendon Press, 1991).

Farmer, J. A., *Tribunals and Government* (London: Weidenfeld and Nicolson, 1974).

Feldman, D., and Wikeley, N., '*Challenging the Vires of Regulation*' (1993) 109 *L.Q.R.* 544–6.

Fenton, N., 'Higher Education—the writing is on the wall' (1998) *Poverty*, No. 101, 12–14.

Fenn, P., 'Sources of Disqualification for Unemployment Benefit, 1960–76' (1980) XVIII *British Journal of Industrial Relations*, 240–53.

Ferri, E., and Smith, K., *Parenting in the 1990s* (London: Family Policy Studies Centre, 1996).

Ferrera, M., 'The Four Social Europes: Between Universalism and Selectivity', in Rhodes, M., and Mény, Y. (eds), *The Future of European Welfare: a new social contract* (Basingstoke: Macmillan, 1998), 81–96.

Field, F., *Making Welfare Work* (London: IEA, 1995).

Field, F., 'Britain's Underclass: Countering the Growth', in Murray, C., et al., *Charles Murray and the Underclass—The Developing Debate* (London: IEA, 1996), 57–60.

Field, F., *How to Pay for the Future: Building a Stakeholders' Welfare* (London: IEA, 1996).

Field, F., *Stakeholder Welfare* (London: IEA, 1996).

Fierst, H., and Spector, F., 'Unemployment Compensation in Labor Disputes', (1940) 49 *Yale Law Journal*, 461–80.

Finch, H., and Elam, G., *Managing Money in Later Life*, DSS Research Report No. 38 (London: HMSO, 1995).

Finch, J., *Family Obligations and Social Change* (London: Polity Press, 1989).

Finch, J., and Mason, J., *Negotiating Family Responsibilities* (London: Tavistock/Routledge, 1993).

Finch, J., Mason, J., Masson, J., Wallis, L., and Hayes, L., *Wills, Inheritance and Families* (Oxford: Clarendon Press, 1996).

Findlay, L., Poynter, R., and Ward, M., *Child Poverty Action Group's Housing Benefit and Council Tax Benefit Legislation* (Sweet and Maxwell, 1998).

Finer, M., and Department of Health and Social Security, *Report of the Committee on One Parent Families*, Cmnd 5629 (London: HMSO, 1974).

Finer, M., and McGregor, O., 'The History of the Obligation to Maintain', Appendix 5, in Finer, M., *Report of the Committee on One Parent Families*, Cmnd 5629 (London: HMSO, 1974).

Ford, J., *Consuming Credit. Debt and Poverty in the UK* (London: CPAG, 1991).

Ford J., and Kempson, E., *Bridging the Gap? Safety nets for mortgage borrowers* (York Publishing Services, 1997).

Ford, R., Marsh, A., and Range, M., *What Happens to Lone Parents*, Department of Social Security Research Report No. 77 (London: The Stationery Office, 1998).

Fotheringham, J. M., 'The "all work test" and physical disability caused by psychiatric illness' (1997) 4 *J.S.S.L.* 15–16.

Fragnière, G., *Strategies for Solving the Malaise*, Paper for the Public Parliamentary Hearing on Youth Unemployment, The Hague, 3–4 September 1985 (The Hague: Council of Europe, 1985).

Fraser, D., *The Evolution of the British Welfare State*, 2nd edn. (London: Macmillan, 1984).

Friedman, M., and Friedman, R., *Free to Choose* (London: Penguin, 1980).

Fry, D., and Stark, G., 'The Take-Up of Supplementary Benefit: Gaps in the "Safety Net"?', in Dilnot, A., and Walker, I., *The Economics of Social Security* (Oxford: Oxford University Press, 1989), 179–91.

Fulbrook, J., *Administrative Justice and the Unemployed* (London: Mansell, 1978).

Fulbrook, J., 'The Jobseekers Act 1995: Consolidation with a Sting of Contractual Compliance' (1995) 24 *I.L.J.* 395–401.

Further Education Unit, *FEU Guidance Note No. 3, Curriculum Implications of the 12/21 hour rules* (London: FEU, 1984).

Further Education Student Support Advisory Group, *New Arrangements for Effective Student Support: I Further Education* (London, DfEE, 1998).

Galbraith, J. K., 'The Good Society Considered: The Economic Dimension' Address at St David's Hall, Cardiff, Wales, 26 January 1994 (published as a pamphlet insert in the *Journal of Law and Society*, 1994).

Galligan, D. J., *Discretionary Powers: A Legal Study of Official Discretion* (Oxford: Clarendon Press, 1986).

Garnham, A., and Knights, E., *Putting the Treasury First—The Truth about Child Support* (London: Child Poverty Action Group, 1994).

Garside, W. R., 'Juvenile Unemployment and Public Policy Between the Wars' (1977) 30 *Econ. History Review*, 322–99.

Genn, H., and Genn, Y., *The Effectiveness of Representation at Tribunals: Report to the Lord Chancellor* (London: Lord Chancellor's Department, 1989).

Gennard, J., *Financing Strikes* (London: Macmillan, 1977).

Gennard, J., and Lasko, R., 'Supplementary Benefits and Strikers' (1974) 12 *British Journal of Industrial Relations*, 1–25.

George, C., et al., *National Welfare Benefits Handbook*, 27th edn. (London: CPAG, 1998).

George, C., et al., *Welfare Benefits Handbook, Vols 1 and 2* (London: CPAG, 1999).

George, V., *Social Security and Society* (London: Routledge and Kegan Paul, 1973).

George, V., 'The Future of the Welfare State', in George, V., and Taylor-Gooby, P. (eds), *European Welfare Policy: Squaring the Welfare Circle* (Basingstoke: Macmillan, 1996), 1–30.

George, V., 'Political Ideology, Globalisation and Welfare Futures in Europe' (1998) 27 *J. of Social Policy*, 17–36.

George, V., and Wilding, P., *Ideology and Social Welfare* (London: Routledge, 1985).

Gibb, K., 'A Housing Allowance for the UK? Preconditions for an Income-related Housing Subsidy' (1995) 10(4) *Housing Studies*, 517–32.

Gilbert, B. B., *The Origins of National Insurance in Great Britain* (London: Michael Joseph, 1966).

Gilbert, B. B., *British Social Policy 1914–1939* (London: B.T. Batsford, 1970).

Ginsburg, N., *Divisions of Welfare* (London: Sage, 1992).

Glendinning, C., 'Dependency and Interdependency: the Incomes of Informal Carers and the Impact of Social Security' (1990) 19 *J. of Social Policy*, 469–97.

Glendinning, C., and Millar, J. (eds.), *Women and Poverty in Britain* (Brighton: Wheatsheaf, 1987).

Glennester, H., and Evans, M., 'Beveridge and his Assumptive Worlds: The Incompatibilities of a Flawed Design', in Hills, J., Ditch, J., and Glennester, H. (eds), *Beveridge and Social Security: An International Retrospective* (Oxford: Clarendon Press, 1994), 56–72.

GMB/NUS, *Students at Work* (London: NUS, 1996).

Goldberg, R., 'Vaccine Damage and Causation: Social and Legal Implications' (1996) 3 *J.S.S.L.* 100–20.

Golding, P. (ed.), *Excluding the Poor* (London: Child Poverty Action Group, 1986).

Gomà, R., 'The social dimension of the European Union: a new type of welfare system?' (1996) 3 *Journal of European Public Policy*, 209–30.

Goode, J., Callender, C., and Lister, R., *Purse or Wallet? Inequalities and Income Distribution within Families on Benefits* (London: Policy Studies Institute, 1998).

Goode, R., *Pension Law Reform—The Report of the Pension Law Review Committee* (London: HMSO, 1993).

Goodman, A., Johnson, P., and Webb, S., *Inequality in the UK* (Oxford: Oxford University Press, 1997).

Gordon, D., and Pantazis, C. (eds), *Breadline Britain in the 1990s* (Aldershot: Ashgate, 1997).

Goriely, T., 'Rushcliffe Fifty Years On: The Changing Role of Civil Legal Aid Within the Welfare State' (1994) 21(4) *J.L.S.* 545–66.

Gough, I., *The Political Economy of the Welfare State* (London: Macmillan, 1979).

Gould, A., 'The end of the middle way? The Swedish welfare state in crisis', in Jones, C. (ed.), *New Perspectives on the Welfare State in Europe* (London: Routledge, 1993), 157–76.

Government Actuary's Department, *Report by the Government Actuary on the drafts of the Social Security Benefits Up-rating Order 1999 and the Social Security (Contributions) (Re-rating and National Insurance Fund Payments) Order 1999*, Cm 4199 (London: The Stationery Office, 1999).

Government Statistical Service/Department of Social Security, *Income Related Benefits: Estimates of Take Up in 1992* (London: Government Statistical Service/Department of Social Security, 1995).

Green, D., 'Welfare and Civil Society', in Field, F., *Stakeholder Welfare* (London: IEA, 1996), 75–91.

Gregg, P., Harkness, S., and Machin, S., 'Poor Kids: Trends in Child Poverty in Britain, 1968–96' (1999) 20(2) *Fiscal Studies,* 163–87.

Gueron, J. M., and Pauley, E., *From Welfare to Work* (New York: Russell Sage Foundation, 1991).

Hakim, C., 'Unemployment and Marginal Work in the Black Economy', in McLaughlin, E. (ed.), *Understanding Unemployment* (London: Routledge, 1992), 154–9.

Handler, J. F., '"Constructing the Political Spectacle": The Interpretation of Entitlements, Legalization, and Obligations in Social Welfare History' (1990) 56 *Brooklyn L.R.* 897–974.

Hargreaves, S., 'Social Europe after Maastricht: is the United Kingdom really opted out?' (1997) 19(1) *J.S.W.F.L.* 1–15.

Harlow, C., and Rawlings, R., *Pressure through Law* (London: Routledge, 1993).

Harrington, J. M., 'The Industrial Injuries Advisory Council' (1994) 1 *J.S.S.L.* 70–5.

Harrington, J. M., Newman Taylor, A. J., and Coggan, D., 'Industrial Injuries Compensation' (1991) *British Journal of Industrial Medicine*, 577–8.

Harris, D., *Justifying State Welfare* (Oxford: Basil Blackwell, 1987).

Harris, J., *Unemployment and Politics* (Oxford: Clarendon Press, 1972).

Harris, J., *William Beveridge: A Biography* (Oxford: Oxford University Press, 1977).

Harris, N., 'Reform of the Supplementary Benefit Appeal System' [1983] *J.S.W.L.* 212–27.

508 *Bibliography*

Harris, N., 'Board and Lodging Payments for Young People' [1987] *J.S.W.L.* 150–74.

Harris, N., 'Raising the Minimum Age of Entitlement to Income Support: Social Security Act 1988' (1988) 15 *J.L.S.* 201–15.

Harris, N., *Social Security for Young People* (Aldershot: Avebury, 1989).

Harris, N., 'Social Security, Student Loans and Access to Education' (1991) 54 *M.L.R.* 258–70.

Harris, N., 'Challenging the *Vires* of Social Security Regulations: The Implications of *Foster v Chief Adjudication Officer*' (1993) 56 *M.L.R.* 710–21.

Harris, N., 'The Social Security Commissioners' (1993) *I.L.J.* 222–6.

Harris, N., 'Workfare schemes' (1994) *J.S.S.L.* 50–1.

Harris, N., 'Case Analysis' (1996) 3 *J.S.S.L.* 130–4.

Harris, N., 'Unmarried cohabiting couples and social security in Britain' (1996) 18(2) *J.S W.F.L.* 123–46.

Harris, N., 'Research reveals problems with HB and CTB extended payments scheme' (1998) 5(4) *J.S.S.L.* 154–5.

Harris, N., and Wikeley, N., 'The strange death of national insurance?', editorial in (1998) 5(4) *J.S.S.L.* 147–8.

Harris, N., and Wikeley, N., 'Editorial' (1999) 6 *J.S.S.L.* 1–3.

Hasson, R., 'Discipline and Punishment in the Law of Unemployment Insurance—a Critical View of Disqualifications and Disentitlement' (1987) 25(3) *Osgoode Hall Law Journal*, 615–37.

Harris, R., *Beyond the Welfare State* (London: IEA, 1988).

Hayek, F. A., *The Road to Serfdom* (London: Routledge and Kegan Paul, 1944).

Hayek, F. A., *Individualism and the Economic Order* (London: Routledge and Kegan Paul, 1949).

Hayck, F. A., *Law, Legislation and Liberty Vol. 2* (London: Routledge and Kegan Paul, 1976).

Health and Safety Commission, *Health and Safety Statistics 1994/5* (London: HMSO, 1995).

Heater, D., 'Citizenship: A Remarkable Case of Sudden Interest' (1991) 44(2) *Journal of Parliamentary Affairs*, 140–56.

Hedges, A., and Thomas, A., *Making a Claim for Disability Benefits*, DSS Research Report No. 27 (London: HMSO, 1994).

Hemming, R., 'Should pensions be funded?' (1999) 52(2) *I.S.S.R.* 3–29.

Herbert, A., and Callender, C., *The Funding Lottery: Student support in further education* (London: Policy Studies Institute, 1997).

Herman, M., *Administrative Justice and Supplementary Benefits* (London: Bell, 1972).

Hervey, T., 'Buy Baby: The European Union and the Regulation of Human Reproduction' (1998) 18 *O.J.L.S.* 207–33.

Hervey, T., *European Social Law and Policy* (Harlow: Longman, 1998).

Hervey, T., 'Welfare Rights as Social Citizenship: Can the EU Deliver?' Paper at the Jean Monnet Conference on EU Citizenship and Human Rights, University of Liverpool, 4 July 1998.

Hervey, T., and O'Keeffe, D. (eds), *Sex Equality Law in the European Union* (Chichester: Wiley, 1996).

Hervey, T., and Shaw, J., 'Women, Work and Care: Women's Dual Role and Double Burden in EC Sex Equality Law' (1998) 8 *Journal of European Social Policy*, 43–63.

Hewitt, M., *Welfare, Ideology and Need: Developing Perspectives on the Welfare State* (Hemel Hempstead: Harvester Wheatsheaf, 1992).

Hill, M., *Social Security Policy in Britain* (Aldershot: Edward Elgar, 1990).

Hill, M., 'The 1986 Social Security Act: Ten Years On' (1996) *Benefits* No. 15, 2–4.

Hills, J. (ed.), *The State of Welfare: The Welfare State in Britain since 1984* (Oxford: Clarendon Press, 1991).

Hills, J., *39 Steps to Housing Finance Reform* (York: Joseph Rowntree Foundation, 1991).

Hills, J., Ditch, J., and Glennester, H. (eds), *Beveridge and Social Security: An International Retrospective* (Oxford: Clarendon Press, 1994).

Himmelfarb, G., *The Idea of Poverty* (London: Faber and Faber, 1985).

Hirst, M., and Sainsbury, R., *Social Security and Mental Health*, Social Policy Report No. 6 (York: Social Policy Research Unit, 1996).

Hirst, M., 'Variations in the Administration of Disability Living Allowance' (1997) 31 *Social Policy & Administration*, 136–56.

HM Treasury, *The Government's Green Paper, 'Reform of Social Security'* (London: HMSO, 1985).

HM Treasury, *The Government's Expenditure Plans 1997* (London: The Stationery Office, 1997).

HM Treasury, *The Government's Expenditure Plans 1988–98* (London: The Stationery Office, 1998).

HM Treasury, *The Modernisation of Britain's Tax and Benefit System: No. 3, The Working Families Tax Credit and Work Incentives* (London: The Stationery Office, 1998).

HM Treasury, *Work Incentives* (London: The Stationery Office, 1998).

Holmes, P., Lynch, M., and Mohlo, I., 'An Econometric Analysis of the Growth of Numbers Claiming Invalidity Benefit: An Overview' (1991) 20 *J. of Social Policy*, 87–105.

Home Office, *Fairer, Faster and Firmer: a modern approach to immigration and asylum*, Cm 4018 (London: The Stationery Office, 1998).

Horton, C., *Nothing Like a Job* (London: Youthaid, 1985).

Hoskyns, C., *Integrating Gender* (London: Verso, 1996).

Hoskyns, C., and Luckhaus, L., 'The European Community Directive on Equal Treatment in Social Security' (1989) 17 *Policy and Politics*, 321–55.

House, A., Mayou, R., and Mallinson, C. (eds), *Psychiatric Aspects of Physical Disease* (London: Royal College of Physicians and Royal College of Psychiatrists, 1995).

House of Commons Select Committee on Education and Employment, *Sixth Report, 1997–98, Further Education* (London: The Stationery Office, 1998).

House of Commons Select Committee on Public Accounts, *21st Report: Child Support Agency, Client Funds Account 1996/97* (London: House of Commons, 1998).

House of Commons Social Services Committee, *Third Report 1981–82*, HC 26–I (London: HMSO, 1982).

House of Commons Social Services Committee, *First Report, Session 1985/86, Reform of Social Security*, HC 180 (London: HMSO, 1986).

House of Commons Social Services Committee, *Seventh Report, Session 1984/85, The Goverment's Green Paper 'Reform of Social Security'* (London: HMSO, 1985).

House of Commons Social Security Committee, *Incapacity Benefit*, Minutes of Evidence, HC 80, Session 1996–97 (London: The Stationery Office, 1997).

House of Commons Social Security Committee, *Disability Living Allowance*, Fourth Report, Minutes of Evidence, HC 641, Session 1997/98 (London: The Stationery Office, 1998).

House of Commons Social Security Committee, *Disability Living Allowance*, Third Report, Minutes of Evidence, HC 63, Session 1998/99 (London: The Stationery Office, 1999).

House of Lords Select Committee on the European Communities, Session 1990–91, 14th report, *Young People in the European Community*, with Evidence, HL Paper 63–II (London: HMSO, 1991).

Housing Benefit Review Team, *Housing Benefit Review: Report of the Review Team*, Cmnd 9520 (London: HMSO, 1985).

Howard, M., *Too Young to Count* (London: Disability Alliance, 1994).

Howard, M., and Thompson, P., *There May be Trouble Ahead* (London: Disability Alliance and Disablement Income Group, 1995).

Howarth, C., *Monitoring Poverty and Social Exclusion: Labour's inheritance* (York: Joseph Rowntree Foundation, 1998).

Howells, G. G., 'Social Fund Budgeting Loans—Social and Civil Justice?' (1990) 9 *C.J.Q.* 118–38.

Huby, M., 'Water Poverty and Social Policy: a Review of Issues for Research' (1995) 24 *Journal of Social Policy*, 219–36.

Huby, M., and Dix, G., *Evaluating the Social Fund* (London: HMSO, 1992).

Huby, M., and Walker, R., 'Adapting to the social fund' (1991) 25(4) *Social Policy and Administration* 329–49.

Humphrey, E., 'Money to Burn' (1997) *Inside Housing*, 8 August, 14–15.

Hunter, C., 'Asylum seekers' rights to housing: New recipients of the Old Poor Law', in Nicholson, F., and Twomey, P. (eds) (1998) (below), 329–49.

Hutton, W., *The State We're In*, rev. edn. (London: Vintage, 1996).

Hutton, W., *The State to Come* (London: Vintage, 1997).

Industrial Injuries Advisory Council, *Report of the Sub-Committee of the Industrial Injuries Advisory Council appointed to consider a response to the Government's White Paper entitled 'Reform of the Industrial Injuries Scheme' (Cmnd 8402)*, Position Paper No. 1 (London: HMSO, 1981).

Industrial Injuries Advisory Council, *Vibration White Finger*, Cmnd 8350 (London: HMSO, 1981).

Industrial Injuries Advisory Council, *Occupational Lung Cancer*, Cm 37 (London: HMSO 1986).

Industrial Injuries Advisory Council, *Repetitive Strain Injuries*, Position Paper No. 2 (London: HMSO, 1986).

Industrial Injuries Advisory Council, *Acquired Immune Deficiency Syndrome (AIDS)*, Position Paper No. 4 (London: I.I.A.C., 1988).

Industrial Injuries Advisory Council, *Recovery of Benefits from Awards of Damages in Tort*, Position Paper No. 3 (London: 1988).

Industrial Injuries Advisory Council, *The Industrial Injuries Scheme and the Reform of Disability Income*, Position Paper No. 5 (London: I.I.A.C., 1990).

Industrial Injuries Advisory Council, *Lung Cancer in Painters*, Position Paper No. 6 (London: I.I.A.C., 1991).

Industrial Injuries Advisory Council, *Lung Cancer in Chrome Platers*, Position Paper No. 7 (London: I.I.A.C., 1991).

Industrial Injuries Advisory Council, *Work Related Upper Limb Disorders*, Cm 1936 (London: HMSO, 1992).

Industrial Injuries Advisory Council, *Periodic Report 1993* (London: HMSO, 1993).

Industrial Injuries Advisory Council, *Coverage under the Industrial Injury Scheme for injury by 'process'*, Position Paper No. 9 (London: I.I.A.C., 1995).

Industrial Injuries Advisory Council, *European Commission Recommendation—Occupational Diseases*, Position Paper No. 8 (London: I.I.A.C., 1995).

Industrial Injuries Advisory Council, *Inflammation or Ulceration of the Mucous Membrane of the Upper Respiratory Passages or Mouth produced by Dust, Liquid or Vapour*, Cm 2845 (London: HMSO, 1995).

Industrial Injuries Advisory Council, *Review of the Schedule of Prescribed Diseases*, Position Paper No. 10 (London: I.I.A.C., 1997).

Inland Revenue Press Release 99/99, issued 17 May 1999.

Institute for Fiscal Studies, *1985 Benefit Reviews: The Effects of the Proposals* (London: IFS, 1985).

Institute for Fiscal Studies, *Income Support and Staying in School: What can we learn from Australia's AUSTUDY Experiment?* (London: I.F.S., 1995).

Jacobs, E., and Douglas, G., *Child Support: The Legislation*, 3rd edn. (London: Sweet & Maxwell, 1997).

Jacobs, J., *Benefit of the Doubt* (London: NACAB, 1994).

Jennings, W. I., 'Poor Relief in Industrial Disputes' (1930) 46 *L.Q.R.* 225–34.

Johnson, P., *The Pensions Dilemma* (London: Institute for Public Policy Research, 1994).

Jones, C. (ed.), *New Perspectives on the Welfare State in Europe* (London: Routledge, 1993).

Jones, G., and Wallace, C., *Youth, Family and Citizenship* (Milton Keynes: Open University Press, 1992).

Jones, S. R., 'Industrial Preference: in Decline?' [1991] XXX(1) *L.L.R.* 63–74.

Jordan, B., 'Want' (1991) 25/1 *Social Policy and Administration*, 14–26.

Jordan, B., *A Theory of Poverty and Social Exclusion* (Cambridge: Polity, 1996).

Jordan, B., *The New Politics of Welfare* (London: Sage, 1998).

Joshi, H., and Davies, H., 'The Paid and Unpaid Roles of Women: How should social security adapt?', in Baldwin, S., and Falkingham, J. (eds), *Social Security and Social Change* (Hemel Hempstead: Harvester Wheatsheaf, 1994), 235–54.

Joshi, H., Davies, H., and Land, H., *The Tale of Mrs Typical* (London: Family Policy Studies Centre, 1996).

Keeler, J. F., 'Social Insurance, Disability and Personal Injury' (1994) 44 *Univ. Toronto L.J.* 275–352.

Kemp, P. A., 'The reform of housing benefit' (1987) 21(2) *Social Policy and Administration*, 171–86.

Kemp, P. A., 'Housing Allowances and Fiscal Crisis for Welfare State' (1994) 9(4) *Housing Studies*, 531–42.

Kemp, P. A., 'HB Some Peculiarities of the British' (1995) *Benefits*, No. 14, 1–5.

Kemp, P. A., *Housing Benefit: Time for Reform* (York: Joseph Rowntree Foundation, 1998).

Kemp, P. A., and McLaverty, P., *Unreasonable Rents and Housing Benefit*, Housing Research Finding No. 70 (York: Joseph Rowntree Foundation, 1992).

Kemp, P. A., and Raynsford, N. (eds), *Housing Benefit: The Evidence* (London: Housing Centre Trust, 1984).

Kempfer, K., 'Disqualifications for Voluntary Leaving and Misconduct', (1945) 55/134 *Yale Law Journal* 147–66.

Kempson, E., *Life on a Low Income* (York: York Publishing Services Ltd, 1996).

Kennedy, H. (QC) (Chair), *Learning Works: Widening Participation in Further Education* (London: FEFC, June 1997).

Kenner, J., 'Economic and Social Cohesion: The Rocky Road Ahead' (1994) *Legal Issues in European Integration*, 1–37.

Kestenbaum, A., and Cava, H., *Work, Rest and Pay: The deal for personal assistance users* (York: Joseph Rowntree Foundation, 1998).

Kiernan, K., Land, H., and Lewis, J., *Lone Motherhood in Twentieth-Century Britain* (Oxford: Oxford University Press, 1998).

Kleinman, M., and Piachaud, D., 'European Social Policy: Conceptions and Choices' (1993) 3 *Journal of European Social Policy,* 1–19.

Knights, E., 'Child Support Update' (1997) 27 *Family Law,* 559–63.

Kohler., P. A., Zacker, H. F., and Partington, M. (ed.), *The Evolution of Social Insurance 1881–1981* (London: Frances Pinter, 1982).

Kuper, B. O., 'The Green and White Papers of the European Union: The Apparent Goal of Reduced Social Benefits' (1994) 4(2) *Journal of European Social Policy,* 129–37.

Labour Party, The, *New Labour: Because Britain deserves better* (London: Labour Party, 1997).

Lakhani, B., 'Asylum seekers on the streets' (1996) *Poverty,* No. 93, 7–9.

Land, H., 'The Introduction of Family Allowances', in Hall, P., et al. (eds), *Change, Choice and Conflict in Social Policy* (London: Heinemann, 1975).

Land, H., 'Social Policy and the Family: The Social Construction of Dependency', Paper presented at conference on 'The goals of social policy: past and future', University of London, 17–18 December 1987.

Land, H., 'The Demise of the Male Breadwinner—In Practice but not in Theory: A challenge for social security systems', in Baldwin, S., and Falkingham, J. (eds), *Social Security and Social Change* (Hemel Hempstead: Harvester Wheatsheaf, 1994), 100–15.

Land, H., and Lewis, J., *The Emergence of Lone Motherhood as a Problem in Late Twentieth Century Britain,* Discussion Paper WSP/134 (London: Toyota Centre, LSE, 1997).

Larkin, P., 'Social security provision for disability: a case for change?' (1998) 5 *J.S.S.L.* 10–17.

Lawrence, R., *Tribunal Representation—The Role of Advice and Advocacy Services* (London: Bedford Square Press, 1980).

Layard, R., *How to Beat Unemployment* (Oxford: Oxford University Press, 1986).

Layard, R., Nickell, S., and Jackman, R., *The Unemployment Crisis* (Oxford: Oxford University Press, 1994).

Lazar, H., and Stoyko, P., 'The future of the Welfare State', (1998) 51(3) *I.S.S.R.* 3–36.

Lee, W. R., 'An Accidental Heart Attack?' (1995) 2 *J.S.S.L.* 9–23.

Le Grand, J., 'The State of Welfare', in Hills, J. (ed.), *The State of Welfare: The Welfare State in Britain since 1984* (Oxford: Clarendon Press, 1991), 358–60.

Leibfried, S., and Pierson, P., *European Social Policy: Between Fragmentation and Implementation* (Washington DC: Brookings, 1995).

Lesser, L., 'Labor Disputes and Unemployment Compensation' (1945) 55 *Yale Law Journal,* 167–201.

Lewis, D., 'Losing Benefits Through Misconduct: Time to Stop Punishing the Unemployed?' (1985) *J.S.W.L.* 145–50.

Lewis, N., 'Supplementary Benefit Appeal Tribunals' [1973] *P.L.* 257–84.

Lewis, N., 'Discretionary Justice and the Supplementary Benefits System', in Adler, M., and Bradley, A. (eds), *Justice, Discretion and Poverty* (Abingdon: Professional Books Ltd, 1976), 77–89.

Lewis, N., and Seneviratne, M., 'A Social Charter for Britain', in Coote, A. (ed.), *The Welfare of Citizens* (London: Institute for Public Policy Research/Rivers Oram Press, 1992), 31–54.

Lewis, P., 'Less Work, Less Money, Less Hope', *Poverty,* No. 62, Winter 1985/86, 18.

Lewis, P., and Willmore, I., *The Fowler Review. Effect on Young People* (London: Youthaid, 1985).

Lewis, R., 'Consultation and Cuts: The Review of Industrial Injuries Benefit' (1980) *J.S.W.L.* 330–40.

Lewis, R., 'Tort and Social Security: the importance attached to the cause of disability with special reference to the Industrial Injuries Scheme' (1980) 43 *M.L.R.* 514–31.

Lewis, R., 'The Privatisation of Sickness Benefit' (1982) 11 *I.L.J.* 245–54.

Lewis, R., 'The Government's Philosophy Towards Reform of Social Security: The Case of Industrial Injuries Benefit' (1986) 15 *I.L.J.* 256–65.

Lewis, R., *Compensation for Industrial Injury* (Abingdon: Professional Books Ltd, 1987).

Lewis, R., 'Legal limits on the structured settlement of damages' [1993] *C.L.J.* 470–86.

Lewis, R., 'Deducting collateral benefits from damages: principle and policy' (1998) *L.S.* 15–40.

Lilley, P., *Providing for Pensions* (London: Politeia, 1996).

Lipman, C., 'Benefits Set for Radical Overhaul' (1998) *Inside Housing*, 3 July, 6.

Lister, R., *Moving Back to the Means-test* (London: Child Poverty Action Group, 1980).

Lister, R., 'The New Supplementary Benefit Regulations: Comment' [1980] *J.S.W.L.* 341–3.

Lister, R., 'The Politics of Social Security: An Assessment of the Fowler Review', in Dilnot, A., and Walker, I., *The Economics of Social Security* (Oxford: Oxford University Press, 1989), 200–23.

Lister, R., 'Social Security', in McCarthy, M. (ed.), *The New Politics of Welfare* (Basingstoke: Macmillan, 1989), 104–31.

Lister, R., *The Female Citizen* (Liverpool: Liverpool University Press, 1989).

Lister, R., *The Exclusive Society. Citizenship and the Poor* (London: Child Poverty Action Group, 1990).

Lister, R., 'Citizenship Engendered' (1991) 11(2) *Critical Social Policy,* 65–71.

Lister, R., 'Social Security in the 1980s' (1991) 25(2) *Social Policy and Administration,* 91–107.

Lister, R., *Women's Economic Dependency and Social Security* (Manchester: Equal Opportunities Commission, 1992).

Lister, R., '"She has other duties"—Women, citizenship and social security', in Baldwin, S., and Falkingham, J. (eds), *Social Security and Social Change* (Hemel Hempstead: Harvester Wheatsheaf, 1994), 31–44.

Lister, R., 'In search of the "underclass"', in Lundy, L., et al (eds), *In Search of the 'Underclass': Working Papers from the SLSA One Day Conference in Queen's University Belfast* (Belfast: Queen's University Faculty of Law, 1997), 1–16.

Lister, R., 'From equality to social inclusion: New Labour and the welfare state' (1998) 18(2) *Critical Social Policy*, 215–25.

Lister, R., and Oppenheim, C., 'Ten years after the 1986 Social Security Act', *Social Policy Review,* 8 (1996), 84–105.

Loosemore, J., 'Policy and discretion in supplementary benefit decisions' (1980) 130 *N.L.J.* 495.

Lord Chancellor, The, *Rights Brought Home: The Human Rights Bill* (London: The Stationery Office, 1997).

Lowe, N. V., and Douglas, G., *Bromley's Family Law,* 9th edn. (London: Butterworths, 1998).

Lowe, R., 'A Prophet Dishonoured in his Own Country? The Rejection of Beveridge in Britain, 1945–1970', in Hills, J., Ditch, J., and Glennester, H. (eds), *Beveridge and Social Security: An International Retrospective* (Oxford: Oxford University Press, 1994), 118–33.

Luckhaus, L., 'Severe Disablement Allowance: The Old Dressed up as New' [1986] *J.S.W.L.* 153–69.

Luckhaus, L., 'New Disability Benefits: Beveridge Turned Upside Down' (1992) 21 *I.L.J.* 237–44.

Lundy, L., 'Unemployment Benefit after a withdrawal of labour' (1994) *I.L.J.* 127–40.

Lundy, L., 'Income Support and Strikers' (1995) 2 *J.S.S.L.* 129–41.

Lundy, L., 'Case Analysis' (1997) 4 *J.S.S.L.* 129–33.

Lundy, L., 'State Assistance with House Purchases—Mortgage Interest and Social Security' (1997) *Conveyancer and Property Lawyer*, 36–46.

Lush, A. J., *The Young Adult* (Cardiff: University of Wales Press Board, 1941).

Lustgarten, L., 'The New Legislation II: Reorganising Supplementary Benefit' (1981) 131 *N.L.J.* 96.

Lynes, T., *National Assistance and National Prosperity* (Welwyn: The Codicote Press, 1962).

Lynes, T., 'Unemployment Assistance Tribunals in the 1930s', in Adler, M., and Bradley, A. (eds), *Justice, Discretion and Poverty: Supplementary Benefit Appeal Tribunals in Britain* (Abingdon: Professional Books Ltd, 1976), 5–31.

Lynes, T., 'Not seen and not heard' (1998) *The Guardian*, 7 January.

Lynes, T., 'The end of Independent Adjudication?', in Adler, M., and Sainsbury, R. (eds), *Adjudication Matters: Reforming Decision Making and Appeals in Social Security*, New Waverley Papers SP14 (Edinburgh: University of Edinburgh Department of Social Policy, 1998), 30–3.

Macdermott, T., Garnham, A., and Holterman, S., *Real Choices—for lone parents and their children* (London: Child Poverty Action Group, 1998).

Macdonald, R., 'Youth, social exclusion and the millennium' in Macdonald, R. (below), 167–97

Macdonald, R. (ed.), *Youth, the Underclass and Social Exclusion* (Routledge: London, 1997).

Mack, J., and Lansley, S., *Poor Britain* (London: Allen and Unwin, 1985).

Macnicol, J., 'Family Allowances and Less Eligibility', in Thane, P. (ed.), *The Origins of British Social Policy* (London: Croom Helm, 1978), 176–98.

Macnicol, J., *The Movement for Family Allowances 1918–1945* (London: Heinemann, 1980).

Macnicol, J., 'Beveridge and Old Age', in Hills, J., Ditch, J., and Glennester, H., *Beveridge and Social Security: An International Retrospective* (Oxford: Oxford University Press, 1994), 73–96.

Maduro, M. P., *We the Court: The European Court of Justice and the European Economic Constitution* (Oxford: Hart, 1998).

Malpass, P., *Reshaping Housing Policy* (Routledge, 1990).

Malpass, P., 'The Unravelling of Housing Policy in Britain' (1996) 11(3) *Housing Studies,* 459–70.

Mandelstam, M., *Equipment for Older or Disabled People and the Law* (London: Jessica Kingsley, 1997).

Mandelstam, M., *Community Care Practice and the Law*, 2nd ed. (London: Jessica Kingsley, 1999).

Mannion, R., Hutton, S., and Sainsbury, R., *Direct Payments from Income Support* (London: HMSO, 1994).

Marks, G., 'Structural Policy in the EC', in Sbragia, A. (ed.), *Euro-Politics* (Washington DC: Brookings, 1992), 191–224.

Marshall, T. H., 'The Right to Welfare', in Timms, N., and Watson, D. (eds), *Talking About Welfare* (London: Routledge, 1976), 51–63.

Marshall, T. H., 'Citizenship and Social Class', in Marshall, T. H., and Bottomore, T., *Citizenship and Social Class* (London: Pluto, 1992), 3–51.

Mashaw, J., *Bureaucratic Justice* (Boston: Yale University Press, 1983).

Massie, B., *Disabled People and Social Justice*, Commission on Social Justice issue paper 12 (London: IPPR, 1994).

McCarthy, M. (ed.), *The New Politics of Welfare* (London: Macmillan, 1989).

McCormick, J., 'Prospects for Pensions Reform', in McCormick, J., and Oppenheim, C. (eds), *Welfare in Working Order* (London: IPPR, 1998), 175–251.

McCrae, J., and Taylor, J., 'The working families tax credit', *Poverty*, No. 100 (1998), 7–9.

McGlynn, C., 'Equality, Maternity and Questions of Pay' (1996) 21 *E.L.Rev.*, 327–32.

McLaughlin, E., *Social Security and Community Care*, DSS Research Report No. 4 (London: HMSO, 1991).

McLaughlin, E., *Flexibility in Work and Benefits* (London: Institute for Public Policy Research, 1994).

McLaughlin, E., 'Researching the Behavioural Effects of Welfare Systems', in Millar, J., and Bradshaw, J. (eds), *Social Welfare Systems: Towards a New Research Agenda* (Bath: University of Bath, 1996).

McLaughlin, E., 'Taxes, benefits and paid work', in Oppenheim, C. (ed.), *An Inclusive Society. Strategies for Tackling Poverty* (London: Institute for Public Policy Research, 1998), 95–111.

McLaughlin, E., Millar, J., and Cooke, K., *Work and Welfare Benefits* (Aldershot: Avebury, 1989).

Mead, L., *The Politics of Poverty* (New York: Basic Books, 1992).

Mesher, J., *Supplementary Benefit and Family Income Supplement: the Legislation* (London: Sweet and Maxwell, 1984).

Mesher, J., 'The Poor Law Strikes Back: 1909–1948–1984', in Hoath, D. (ed.), *75 Years of Law at Sheffield, 1909–1984. The Edward Bramley Jubilee Lectures* (Sheffield: Faculty of Law, University of Sheffield, 1985).

Mesher, J., *CPAG's Supplementary Benefit and Family Income Supplement: the Legislation* (London: Sweet and Maxwell, 1987).

Mesher, J., 'The Legal Structure of the Social Fund', in Freeman, M. D. A. (ed.), *Critical Issues in Welfare Law* (London: Stevens, 1990), 35–57.

Mesher, J., and Wood, P., *Income Related Benefits: The Legislation* (London: Sweet and Maxwell, 1997).

Mesher, J., and Wood, P., *Income Related Benefits: The Legislation* (London: Sweet and Maxwell, 1998).

Micklethwait, Sir R., *The National Insurance Commissioners* (London: Stevens & Sons, 1976).

Middleton, S., *Statutory Sick Pay: The response of employers to the 1991 changes*, DSS Research Report No. 24 (London: HMSO, 1994).

Middleton, S., Ashworth, K., and Walker, R., *Family Fortunes* (London: Child Poverty Action Group, 1994).

Middleton, S., Ashworth, K., and Braithwaite, I., *Small Fortunes: spending on children, childhood poverty and parental sacrifice* (York: Joseph Rowntree Foundation, 1997).

Midgeley, J., 'Has social security become irrelevant?' (1999) 52(2) *I.S.S.R.* 91–9.

Millar, J., 'Quarter of Britons "are below the poverty line"' (1993) *The Independent*, 1 September.

Millar, J., 'Women', in Walker, A., and Walker, C. (eds), *Britain Divided* (London: Child Poverty Action Group, 1997), 99–110.

Millar, J., and Glendinning, C., 'Gender and Poverty' (1989) 18(3) *Journal of Social Policy* 363–81.

Millar, J., and Glendinning, C. (eds), *Women and Poverty in Britain* (Hemel Hempstead: Harvester Wheatsheaf, 1992).

Millar, J., Webb, S., and Kemp, M., *Combining Work and Welfare* (Layerthorpe: York, 1997).

Miller, F., 'The British Unemployment Assistance Crisis of 1935' (1979) 14 *Journal of Contemporary History* 329–51.

Minford, P., and Ashton, P., *Unemployment: Cause and Cure* (Oxford: Basil Blackwell, 1985).

Mingione, E., *Urban Poverty and the Underclass—A Reader* (Oxford: Blackwell, 1996).

Minister of Reconstruction, *Social Insurance, Part I*, Cmd 6550 (London: HMSO).

Ministry of Social Security, *Annual Report 1966* (London: HMSO, 1967).

Ministry of Social Security, *Submitted Memorandum to the Royal Commission on Trade Unions and Employers' Associations 1965–1968*, Cmnd 3623 (London: HMSO, 1968).

Mishra, R., *The Welfare State in Crisis* (Brighton: Wheatsheaf, 1984).

Mishra, R., 'Social policy in the postmodern world', in Jones, C. (ed.), *New Perspectives on the Welfare State in Europe* (London: Routledge, 1993), 18–40.

Mitchell, A., 'Time to Bring Back Real Social Housing' (1998) *Housing Today*, Issue 75, 19 March, 13.

Mnookin, R. H., *Child, Family and State. Problems and Materials on Children and the Law* (Boston: Little, Brown and Co, 1978).

Moroney, R. M., *The Family and the State* (London: Longmans, 1976).

Morris, L., and Llewelyn, T., *Social Security Provision for the Unemployed. A Report for the Social Security Advisory Committee*, Social Security Advisory Committee Research Paper 3 (London: HMSO, 1991).

Mosley, H., 'The social dimension of European integration' (1990) 129 *International Labour Review*, 147–63.

Mullan, K., and McKeown, G., 'Supporting full-time students in higher education—the role of social security benefits' (1999) 6 *J.S.S.L.* 56–78.

Mullen, T., 'The Social Fund—Cash-Limiting Social Security' (1989) 52 *M.L.R.* 64–92.

Murdoch, J. L., 'Encouraging Citizenship: Report of the Commission on Citizenship' (1991) 54(3) *M.L.R.*, 439–41.

Murphy, M., and Sullivan, O., 'Unemployment, Housing and Household Structure Among Young Adults' (1986) 15(2) *Journal of Social Policy*, 205–22.

Murray, C., 'The Emerging British Underclass', in Murray, C., and Lister, R., *Charles Murray and the Underclass—The Developing Debate* (London: IEA Health and Welfare Unit in association with *Sunday Times*, 1996), 23–53.

Murray, C., 'Underclass: the Crisis Deepens', in Murray, C., and Lister, R., *Charles Murray and the Underclass—The Developing Debate* (London: IEA Health and Welfare Unit in association with Sunday Times, 1996), 99–135.

Murray, C., 'All locked up in the American dream' (1999) *The Sunday Times*, 7 February.

National Assistance Board *Annual Report 1951* (London: HMSO, 1951).

National Audit Office, *The Social Fund* (London: HMSO, 1991).

National Audit Office, *National Insurance Fund Account 1997–98*, HC 130, Session 1998–99 (London: The Stationery Office, 1999).

NACAB, *The Cost of Living* (London: NACAB, 1992).

NACAB, *Failing the Test: CAB clients' experience of the habitual residence test in social security* (London: NACAB, 1996).

National Committee of Inquiry into Higher Education, *Report of the National Committee* (London: DfEE, 1997).

National Council for One Parent Families, *The Insecurity System* (London: National Council for One Parent Families, 1985).

National Consumer Council, *Of Benefit to All. A Consumer Review of Social Security* (National Consumer Council, 1984).

National Insurance Advisory Committee, *The Availability Question*, Cmd 8894 (London: HMSO, 1953).

National Insurance Advisory Committee, *Social Security (Non-Contributory Invalidity Pension) Amendment Regulations 1977*, Cmnd 6900 (London: HMSO, 1977).

National Insurance Advisory Committee, *Report on Unemployment Benefit for Students*, Cmnd 7613 (London: HMSO, 1979).

National Federation of Housing Associations, *Inquiry into British Housing* (National Federation of Housing Associations, 1985).

Nicholls, Sir G., *A History of the English Poor Law Vol. 1. A.D. 924–1714* (Westminster: P. S. King and Son, 1904).

Nicholson, F., and Twomey, P. (eds), *Current Issues of Asylum Law and Policy* (Aldershot: Ashgate, 1998).

Nielsen, R., and Szyszczak, E., *The Social Dimension of the European Union* (Copenhagen: Handelshojskolens Forlag, 1997).

Novak, T., *Poverty and the State* (Milton Keynes: Open University Press, 1988).

Nove, A., and Smith, N., *The Employment Service National Customer Satisfaction Survey 1994*, ES Research and Evaluation Report No. 103 (London: HMSO, 1995).

N.U.S., *Response of the National Union of Students to the Green Paper 'Reform of Social Security'* (London: N.U.S., 1985).

N.U.S., *Value for Money Survey* (London: NUS, 1995).

N.U.S., *Student Hardship—the facts* (London, NUS, 1996).

N.U.S., Press Release, 'Student hardship hits record high', 12 July 1997.

O'Connor, J., 'US Social Welfare Policy: The Reagan Record and Legacy' (1998) 27(1) *J. of Social Policy,* 37–61.

O'Donovan, K., 'Gender Blindness or Justice Engendered', in Blackburn, R. (ed.), *Rights of Citizenship* (Oxford: Mansell, 1993), 12–30.

O'Higgins, M., 'Welfare, redistribution and inequality', in Bean, P., Ferris, J., and Whynes, D., *In Defence of Welfare* (London: Tavistock, 1985), 162–79.

O'Kelly, R., 'The Principle of Aggregation', in Silburn, R. (ed.), *The Future of Social Security. A Response to the Social Security Green Paper* (London: Fabian Society, 1985), 73–85.

Office for National Statistics, *Informal Carers* (London: The Stationery Office, 1998).

Ogus, A. I., 'Great Britain', in Kholer, P. A., Zacker, H. F., and Partington, M., *The Evolution of Social Insurance 1881–1981* (London: Frances Pinter, 1982), 150–264.

Ogus, A. I., 'SSAC as an independent advisory body: its role and influence in policymaking' (1998) 5 *J.S.S.L.* 156–74.

Ogus, A. I., and Barendt, E. M., *The Law of Social Security*, 3rd edn. (London: Butterworths, 1988).

Ogus, A. I., Barendt, E. M., and Wikeley, N., *The Law of Social Security*, 4th edn. (London: Butterworths, 1995).

O'Keeffe, D., 'The Uneasy Progress of European Social Policy' (1996) 2 *Columbia Journal of European Law*, 241–63.

Oldfield, N., and Yu, A., *The Cost of a Child: Living Standards for the 1990s* (London: Child Poverty Action Group, 1993).

Oliver, D., 'Active Citizenship in the 1990s' (1991) 44(2) *Journal of Parliamentary Affairs*, 157–71.

Oliver, D., *Government in the United Kingdom: The Search for Accountability, Effectiveness and Citizenship* (Milton Keynes: Open University Press, 1991).

Oliver, M., *The Politics of Disablement* (Basingstoke: Macmillan, 1990).

Oliver, M., *Understanding Disability* (Basingstoke: Macmillan, 1996).

Oppenheim, C., and Lister, R., 'Ten years after the 1986 Social Security Act' (1996) *Social Policy Review*, 8 84–105.

Oppenheim, C., 'The growth of poverty and inequality', in Walker, A., and Walker, C. (eds), *Britain Divided* (London: Child Poverty Action Group, 1997), 17–31.

Oppenheim, C. (ed.), *An Inclusive Society: Strategies for Tackling Poverty* (London: Institute for Public Policy Research, 1998).

Oppenheim, C., 'Poverty and Social Exclusion: An Overview', in ibid.

Oppenheim, C., and Harker, L., *Poverty: The Facts*, 3rd edn. (London: Child Poverty Action Group, 1996).

Oxley, D., *Poor Relief in England and Wales 1601–1834* (Newton Abbot: David and Charles, 1974).

Page, R., 'New Labour's New "Welfarism": Time to Re-write the Script' (1998) *Benefits* (April/May) 10–11.

Pahl, J., *Money and Marriage* (Houndmills: Macmillan, 1989).

Parker, H. (ed.), *Low Cost but Acceptable: A minimum income standard for the UK, families with young children, January 1998 prices* (London: Polity Press and Zachaeus 2000 Trust, 1998).

Parker, J., *Social Policy and Citizenship* (Oxford: Clarendon Press, 1975).

Partington, M., 'Supplementary Benefits: Interpretation and Judgment' (1981) 131 *N.L.J.* 547–8.

Partington, M., 'Adjudication and the Social Fund: Some preliminary observations' (1986) *Legal Action*, 10–11.

Partington, M., *Secretary of State's Powers of Adjudication in Social Security Law* (Bristol: School for Advanced Urban Studies, 1991).

Partington, M., *Claim in Time: Time Limits in Social Security Law*, 3rd edn. (Legal Action Group, 1994).

Partington, M., 'Judicial Review and Housing Benefit', in Buck, T., *Judicial Review and Social Welfare* (London: Pinter, 1998), 182–201.

Partington, M., and Bolderson, H., *Housing Benefit Review Procedures: A Preliminary Analysis* (Uxbridge: Brunel University, 1984).

Partington, M., Bolderson, H., and Smith, K., *Housing Benefit Review Procedures* (Brunel: Brunel University, Department of Law, 1984).

Pascall, G., *Social Policy: A New Feminist Analysis* (London: Routledge, 1997).

Payne, J., and Range, M., *Lone Parents' Lives,* DSS Research Report No. 78 (London: The Stationery Office, 1998).

Pearce, N., and Hillman, J., *Wasted Youth* (London: Institute for Public Policy Research, 1998).

Pearson Commission, *Report of the Royal Commission on Civil Liability and Compensation for Personal Injury*, Cmnd 7054 (London: HMSO, 1978).

Pelican, J., *Studying on the Dole* (London: Youthaid, 1983).

Philimore, P., Beattie, A., and Townsend, P., 'Widening inequality of health in northern England' (1994), 308 *British Medical Journal*, 1125–8.

Phillips, A., *Democracy and Difference* (London: Polity, 1993).

Piachaud, D., *The Cost of a Child* (London: Child Poverty Action Group, 1979).

Piachaud, D., 'Poverty', in *The Guardian* 'Society', Beveridge Report 50th Anniversary Special, 4 March 1992.

Piachaud, D., 'Means Testing and the Conservatives' (1996) *Benefits*, No. 15, 5–7.

Piachaud, D., 'The Growth of Means-Testing', in Walker, A., and Walker, C. (eds), *Britain Divided* (London: CPAG, 1997), 75–83.

Piven, F., and Cloward, R., *Regulating the Poor* (London: Tavistock, 1972).

Plant, R., 'The very idea of a welfare state', in Bean, P., Ferris, J., and Whynes, D., *In Defence of Welfare* (London: Tavistock, 1985), 3–30.

Plant, R., 'The fairness of workfare', *The Times,* 16 November 1988.

Plant, R., 'Supply Side Citizenship' (1999) 6 *J.S.S.L.* 124–36.

Plant, R., Lesser, H., and Taylor-Gooby, P., *Political Philosophy and Social Welfare* (London: Routledge and Kegan Paul, 1980).

Pollard, D., 'Attention in connection with bodily functions' (1998) 5 *J.S.S.L.* 175–94.

Policy Studies Institute Press Release, 12 January 1998 and DfEE, *DfEE Departmental Report* (London: Stationery Office, 1998), Cm 3910, Annex Bii.

Policy Studies Institute Press Release, 21 March 1988, 'Government social security reforms "ignore independent research" ' (London PSI, 1988).

Powell, M., and Hewitt, M., 'The End of the Welfare State' (1998) 32(1) *Social Policy and Administration,* 1–13.

Priest, J., 'Departure Directions in the Child Support Scheme' (1998) *J.S.S.L.* 118–38.

Prime Minister, The, *The Citizen's Charter: raising the standard,* Cmnd 1599 (London: HMSO, 1991).

Prosser, T., 'Poverty, Ideology and Legality: Supplementary Benefit Appeal Tribunals and their Predecessors' (1977) 4(1) *British Journal of Law and Society,* 39–60.

Prosser, T., 'Politics and Judicial Review: The Atkinson case and its aftermath' [1979] *P.L.* 59–83.

Prosser, T., 'The Politics of Discretion: Aspects of Discretionary Power in the Supplementary Benefits Scheme', in Adler, M., and Asquith, S., *Discretion and Welfare* (London: Heinemann, 1981), 148–70.

Prosser, T., *Test Cases for the Poor* (London: Child Poverty Action Group, 1983).

Rahilly, S., 'Housing Benefit: the Impact of Subsidies on Decision-making' (1995) 2 *J.S.S.L.* 196–207.

Rahilly, S., 'Housing for the Homeless and Immigration Control: the Provisions of the Housing Act 1996 and the Asylum and Immigration Act 1996' (1998) 20 *J.S.W.F.L.* 237–50.

Randolph, B., 'The Re-privatisation of Housing Associations', in Malpass, P., and Means, R. (eds), *Implementing Housing Policy* (Open University Press, 1993), 39–58.

Ranson, S., 'From 1944 to 1988: Education, Citizenship and Democracy', in Flude, M., and Hammer, M. (eds), *The Education Reform Act 1988: Its Origins and Implications* (London: Falmer, 1989), 1–20.

Rathbone, E., *The Disinherited Family* (London: Allen and Unwin, 1924).

Rawls, J., *A Theory of Justice* (Oxford: Oxford University Press, 1972).

Rees, G., and Rees, T. L., 'Juvenile Unemployment and the State between the Wars', in Rees, T. L., and Atkinson, P., *Youth Unemployment and State Intervention* (London: Routledge, 1982), 18.

Reich, C., 'The New Property' (1964) 73/5 *Yale Law Journal,* 733–87.

Reid, K., 'Combating school absenteeism: main conclusions', in Reid, K. (ed.), *Combating School Absenteeism* (London: Hodder and Stoughton, 1988), 208–12.

Reid, K., 'The Education Welfare Service—some issues and suggestions', in Reid, K. (ed.), *Combating School Absenteeism* (London: Hodder and Stoughton, 1988), 160–2.

Report of the Committee on the Procedure and Evidence for the Determination of Claims of Unemployment Insurance Benefit, Cmnd 3415 (London: HMSO, 1929).

Review Team, Department of Health and Social Security, *Social Assistance* (London: DHSS, 1978).

Rhodes, L., 'Living Below Benefit Level' (1991) *Poverty,* No. 79, 15–17.

Rhodes, M., and Mény, Y., 'Europe's Social Contract under Stress', in Rhodes, M., and Mény, Y. (eds), *The Future of European Welfare: A new social contract* (Basingstoke: Macmillan, 1998), 1–19.

Ritchie, J., *GPs and IVB: A Qualitative Study of the Role of General Practitioners in the Award of Invalidity Benefit*, DSS Research Report No. 18 (London: HMSO, 1993).

Roberts, K., *Youth Labour Markets: The Class of '83*, Department of Employment Research Paper No. 59 (London: Department of Employment, 1985).

Robson, W. A., *Welfare State and Welfare Society: Illusion and Reality* (London: Allen and Unwin, 1976).

Rogers, B., *The Battle Against Poverty. Vol. 2. Towards a Welfare State* (London: Routledge and Kegan Paul, 1969).

Room, G., Lawson, R., and Lackzko, F., '"New Poverty" in the European Community' (1989) 17(2) *Policy and Politics*, 165–76.

Ross, G., *Jacques Delors* (Cambridge: Polity, 1995).

Rowe, P., 'Case Analysis' (1994) 1 *J.S.S.L.* 133–8.

Rowell, M. S., 'The Social Fund—Transitional Measures and Possible Alternatives' [1987] *J.S.W.L.* 137–49.

Rowell, M. S., and Wilton, A. M., 'Supplementary Benefit and the Green Paper' [1986] *J.S.W.L.* 14–31.

Rowland, M., *Medical and Disability Appeal Tribunals: The Legislation* (London: Sweet & Maxwell, 1998).

Rowlingson, K., and Berthoud, R., *Evaluating the Disability Working Allowance* (London: PSI, 1994).

Rowlingson, K., and Berthoud, R., *Disability, Benefits and Employment*, DSS Research Report No. 54 (London: HMSO, 1996).

Rowlingson, K., and Whyley, C., 'The Right Amount to the Right People? Reducing Fraud, Error and Non Take-Up of Benefit', *Benefits*, January 1998, 7–10.

Rowntree, B. S., *Poverty: A Study of Town Life* (London: Macmillan, 1901) and (1918) and (1937) editions.

Rowntree, B. S., and Lavers, G. R., *Poverty and the Welfare State* (London: Longman, 1951).

Royal Commission on Unemployment Insurance, *Final Report*, Cmd 4185 (London: HMSO, 1932).

Royal Commission on Long Term Care, *With Respect to Old Age: Long Term Care—Rights and Responsibilities*, Cm 4192–I (London: Stationery Office, 1999).

Sadler, B., 'Unemployment and Unemployment Benefits in Twentieth Century Britain: A Lesson of the Thirties', in Cowling, K., et al., *Out of Work. Perspectives of Mass Unemployment* (Coventry: University of Warwick, 1983).

Sainsbury, R., *Survey and Report into the Working of the Medical Appeal Tribunals* (London: HMSO, 1992).

Sainsbury, R., 'Internal Reviews and the Weakening of Social Security Claimants' Rights of Appeal', in Richardson, G., and Genn, H. (eds), *Administrative Law and Government Action: the courts and alternative mechanisms of review* (Oxford: Clarendon Press, 1994), 287–307.

Sainsbury, R., *Consultation on Improving Decision Making and Appeals in Social Security: Analysis of responses* (London: Department of Social Security, 1997).

Sainsbury, R., 'A Critique of the Case for Change', in Adler, M., and Sainsbury, R. (eds), *Adjudication Matters: Reforming Decision Making and Appeals in Social Security*, New Waverley Papers SP14 (Edinburgh: University of Edinburgh, Department of Social Policy, 1998), 23–9.

Sainsbury, R., and Eardley, T., *Housing Benefit Reviews. An evaluation of the effectiveness of the review system in responding to claimants dissatisfied with housing benefit decisions*, DSS Research Report No. 3 (London: HMSO, 1991).

Sainsbury, R., and Eardley, T., 'Housing Benefit Review Boards: a Case for Slum Clearance?' [1992] *P.L.* 551–9.

Sainsbury, R., Hirst, M., and Lawton, D., *Evaluation of Disability Living Allowance and Attendance Allowance*, DSS Research Report No. 41 (London: HMSO, 1995).

Sainsbury, R., Hutton, S., and Ditch, J., *Changing Lives and the Role of Income Support*, DSS Research Report No. 45 (London: HMSO, 1996).

Saunders, P., 'Selectivity and Targeting in Income Support: The Australian Experience' (1991) 20 *J. of Social Policy*, 299–326.

Save the Children Fund, *Unemployment and the Child* (London: Longmans, 1933).

Sayers, S., 'The need to work: a perspective from philosophy', in Pahl, R. E. (ed.), *On Work* (Oxford: Basil Blackwell Ltd, 1988).

Schechter, E., 'Work While Receiving Disability Insurance benefits: Additional Findings From the New Beneficiary Follow-up Survey' (1997) 60 *Social Security Bulletin*, 3–17.

Schnieder, C. E., 'Discretion and Rules: A Lawyer's View', in Hawkins, K. (ed.), *The Uses of Discretion* (Oxford: Oxford University Press, 1992), 47–88.

Scott, J., *Development Dilemmas in the European Community: Rethinking Regional Development Policy* (London: Open University Press, 1995).

Secretary of State for Social Security, *Annual Report of the Secretary of State for Social Security on the Social Fund 1997/98*, Cm 4003 (London: Stationery Office, 1998).

Secretary of State for Social Security, *Annual Report of the Secretary of State for Social Security on the Social Fund 1998/99* Cm 4351 (London: The Stationery Office, 1999).

Secretary of State for Social Security and Chief Secretary to the Treasury, *Social Security Departmental Report, The Government's Expenditure Plans 1996–97 to 1998–99*, Cm 3213 (London: HMSO, 1996).

Secretary of State for Social Services, Annex to SSAC, *The Supplementary Benefit (Requirements and resources) Amendment Regulations 1982 (Etc)*, Cmnd 8598 (London: HMSO, 1982).

Secretary of State for Social Services, *Reform of Social Security* (Green Paper) Vols 1–3, Cmnds 9517–9519 (London: HMSO, 1985).

Secretary of State for Social Services, *The Reform of Social Security: A Programme for Action* (White Paper) Cmnd 9691 (London: HMSO, 1985).

Sen, A., 'Poor, Relatively Speaking' (1983) 35(1) *Oxford Economic Papers*, 153–69.

Shaw, A., Walker, R., Ashworth, K., Jenkins, S., and Middleton, S., *Moving Off Income Support: Barriers and Bridges*, DSS Research Report No. 53 (London: HMSO, 1996).

Simkins, J., and Tickner, V., *Whose Benefit?* (London: Economist Intelligence Unit, 1978).

Smedmark, G., 'The Swedish social insurance system: A model in transition' (1994) 47(2) *I.S.S.R.* 71–7.

Social Exclusion Unit, *Truancy and School Exclusion: Report by the Social Exclusion Unit*, Cm 3957 (London: The Stationery Office, May 1998).

Social Security Advisory Committee, *First Report* (London: HMSO, 1982).

Social Security Advisory Committee, *Second Report* (London: HMSO, 1983).

Social Security Advisory Committee, *Third Report* (London: HMSO, 1985).

Social Security Advisory Committee, *Fourth Report* (London: HMSO, 1985).

Social Security Advisory Committee, *The Supplementary Benefit (Conditions of Entitlement) Amendment Regulations 1986, report by the SSAC*, Cmnd 9813 (London: HMSO, 1986).

Social Security Advisory Committee, *The Supplementary Benefit (Miscellaneous Amendments) Regulations (Etc),* Cmnd 9813 (London: HMSO, 1986).

Social Security Advisory Committee, *The Draft Social Fund Manual. Report by the SSAC* (London: SSAC, 1987).

Social Security Advisory Committee, *Fifth Report* (London: HMSO, 1987).

Social Security Advisory Committee, *Proposals for Regulations Regarding Benefits for Children and Young People,* Cm 106 (London: HMSO, 1987).

Social Security Advisory Committee, *Sixth Report* (London: HMSO, 1988).

Social Security Advisory Committee, *The Benefits for Disabled People: A Strategy for Change* (London: HMSO, 1988).

Social Security Advisory Committee, *Report of the SSAC on the Social Security Benefits (Student Loan) Amendment Regulations 1990,* Cm 1141 (London: HMSO, 1990).

Social Security Advisory Committee, *Seventh Report* (London: HMSO, 1990).

Social Security Advisory Committee, *The Social Fund—A New Structure* (London: HMSO, 1992).

Social Security Advisory Committee, *State Benefits and Private Provision: The Review of Social Security Paper 2* (Leeds: BA Publishing Services Ltd, 1994).

Social Security Advisory Committee, *Housing Benefit. The Review of Social Security,* Paper 3 (BA Publishing Services Ltd, 1995).

Social Security Advisory Committee, *Social Security Provision for Disability: A Case for Change?* (London: The Stationery Office, 1997).

Social Security Research Consortium, *Cash Limited, Limited Cash* (London: AMA, 1992).

Sohrab, J., *Sexing the Benefit: Women, Social Security and Financial Independence in EC Sex Equality Law* (Aldershot: Dartmouth, 1996).

Spicker, P., *Poverty and Social Security: Concepts and Principles* (London: Routledge, 1993).

Stafford, B., et al., *Moving into Work: Bridging Housing Costs,* DSS Research Report No. 79, (London: The Stationery Office, 1998).

Stagg, P., *Overpayments and Recovery of Social Security Benefits* (London: LAG, 1996).

Stagg, P., 'The Social Security (Overpayments) Act 1996', (1997) 4 *J.S.S.L.* 155–77.

Steiner, J., 'The principle of equal treatment for men and women in social security', in Hervey, T., and O'Keefe, D. (eds), *Sex Equality Law in the European Union* (Chichester: Wiley, 1996).

Stewart, G., Lee, R., and Stewart, J., 'The Right Approach to Social Security: The Case of the Board and Lodgings Regulations' (1986) 13 *J.L.S.* 371–99.

Stone, D., *The Disabled State* (London: Macmillan, 1985).

Storey, H., 'United Kingdom Social Security Law: European and International Dimensions— Part 1' (1994) 1 *J.S.S.L.* 110–32.

Stapleton, J., *Disease and the Compensation Debate* (Oxford: Clarendon Press, 1986).

Streeck, W., 'Neo-Voluntarism: A New European Social Policy Regime' (1995) 1(1) *European Law Journal,* 31–59.

Sullivan, M., 'From personal tragedy to social oppression: the medical model and social theories of disability' (1991) 16 *N.Z. Journal of Industrial Relations,* 255–72.

Supplementary Benefits Commission, *Annual Report 1975* (London: HMSO, 1976).

Supplementary Benefits Commission, *Annual Report 1976* (London: HMSO, 1977).

Supplementary Benefits Commission, *Annual Report 1977* (London: HMSO, 1978).

Supplementary Benefits Commission, *Response of the Supplementary Benefits Commission to 'Social Assistance'* (London: HMSO, 1979).

Supplementary Benefits Commission, *Annual Report 1979* (London: HMSO, 1980).

Swain, H., 'Benefit changes could hit poorest students' (1999) *Times Higher Education Supplement*, 29 October, 56.

Swales, K., *A Study of Disability Living Allowance and Attendance Allowance Awards*, DSS In-house report 41 (London: DSS Social Research Branch, 1998).

Swanton, O., 'Higher Education: Burden of debt' (1997) *The Guardian*, 3 June.

Taylor, D., 'Citizenship and Social Power' (1989) 9(2) *Critical Social Policy*, 19–31.

Taylor, M., *The Modernisation of Britain's Tax and Benefits System—2. Work Incentives* (London: HM Treasury, 1998).

Taylor-Gooby, P., 'Two cheers for the Welfare State: Public Opinion and Private Welfare' (1982) 2(4) *Journal of Public Policy*, 319–46.

Taylor-Gooby, P., 'Paying for Welfare: The View from Europe' (1996) 67 *Pol.Q.* 116–26.

Taylor-Gooby, P., 'The Response of Government: Fragile Convergence?', in George, V., and Taylor-Gooby, P. (eds), *European Welfare Policy: Squaring the Welfare Circle* (Basingstoke: Macmillan, 1996), 199–218.

Taylor-Gooby, P., and Lawson, R., 'Where do we go from here?: the new order in welfare', in Taylor-Gooby, P., and Lawson, R. (eds), *Markets and Managers: New Issues in the Delivery of Welfare* (Milton Keynes: Open University Press, 1993), 132–49.

Taylor-Gooby, P., and Lakeman, S., 'Back to the Future: Statutory Sick Pay, Citizenship and Social Class' (1988) 17 *J. of Social Policy*, 23–39.

Thane, P., 'Childhood in History', in King, M. (ed.), *Childhood, Welfare, Justice* (London: B. T. Batsford, 1981), 17.

Thomson, D., *England in the Nineteenth Century* (Harmondsworth: Penguin, 1975).

Thornton, P., Sainsbury, R., and Barnes, H., *Helping Disabled People to Work: A Cross-National Study of Social Security and Employment Provisions,* SSAC Research Paper 8 (London: The Stationery Office, 1997).

Timmins, N., *The Five Giants. A Biography of the Welfare State* (London: Harper Collins, 1995).

Titmuss, R., M., 'The social division of welfare' in *Essays on the Welfare State*, 2nd edn. (London: George Allen and Unwin, 1955).

Titmuss, R. M., 'Welfare "Rights", Law and Discretion' (1971) 42 *Pol.Q.* 113–32.

Titmuss, R. M., *Commitment to Welfare* (London: Allen and Unwin, 1968).

Titmuss, R. M., *Social Policy: An Introduction* (London: Allen and Unwin, 1974).

Townsend, P., *Poverty in the United Kingdom* (Harmondsworth: Penguin, 1979).

Townsend, P., *A Poor Future* (London: Lemos and Crane, 1996).

Townsend, P., and Gordon, D., 'What is Enough? New Evidence on Poverty Allowing the Definition of a Minimum Benefit', in Adler, M., Bell, C., Clasen, J., and Sinfield, A., *The Sociology of Social Security* (Edinburgh: Edinburgh University Press, 1991), 35–69.

Travis, A., 'Straw moves to quell asylum bill rebellion' (1999) *The Guardian*, 9 June.

Trevelyan, G. M., *English Social History* (London: Reprint Society/Longmans, Green & Co, 1948).

Trickey, H., Kellard, K., Walker, R., Ashworth, K., and Smith, A.,*Unemployment and Jobseeking: Two years on,* DSS Research Report No. 87 (London: The Stationery Office, 1998).

Tweedy, J., and Hunt, A., 'The Future of the Welfare State and Social Rights: Reflections on Habermas' (1994) 21(3) *J.L.S.* 288–316.

Twigg, J., and Atkin, K., *Carers Perceived: Policy and Practice in Informal Care* (Buckingham: Open University Press, 1994).

Twomey, P., 'Case Analysis' (1995) 2 *J.S.S.L.* 208–14.

Unemployment Assistance Board, *Report for 1938* (London: HMSO, 1939).

University of Liverpool, *Report on Co-operation between The Unemployment Assistance Board, the Local Authority and Voluntary Associations in Liverpool* (Liverpool and London: University Press of Liverpool and Hodder and Stoughton, 1938).

Van der Mei, A. P., 'Cross-border access to Medical Care within the EU' (1998) 5 *Maastricht Journal of European and Comparative Law*, 277–97.

Veit-Wilson, J., 'Condemned to Deprivation: Beveridge's Responsibility for the Invisibility of Poverty', in Hills, J., Ditch, J., and Glennester, H., *Beveridge and Social Security: An International Retrospective* (Oxford: Clarendon Press, 1994), 97–117.

Veit-Wilson, J., *Dignity not Poverty—A Minimum Income Standard for the UK* (London: Commission on Social Justice, 1994).

Vincent, A., and Plant, R., *Philosophy, Politics and Citizenship* (Oxford: Basil Blackwell, 1984).

Vincent, D., *Poor Citizens* (London: Longman, 1991).

Wadham, J. and Mountfield, H., *Blackstone's Guide to the Human Rights Act 1998* (London: Blackstone, 1999)

Walker, A., and Walker, L., 'Disability and Financial Need—The Failure of the Social Security System', in Dalley, G. (ed.), *Disability and Social Policy* (London: PSI, 1991), 20–56.

Walker, A., and Walker, C., *Britain Divided* (London: Child Poverty Action Group, 1997).

Walker, C., *Managing Poverty. The Limits of Social Assistance* (London: Routledge, 1993).

Walker, R., *Housing Benefit: the experience of implementation* (London: Housing Centre Trust, 1985).

Walker, R., 'Springing the Poverty Trap' (1994) 1(3) *New Economy*, 163–7.

Walker, R., 'Social Security Reform—Ten Years On' (1996) *Benefits*, No. 15, 1.

Walker, R., Dix, G., and Huby, M., *Working the Fund*, (London: HMSO, 1992).

Walker, R. and Lawton, D., 'The Social Fund as an exercise in resource allocation' (1989) 67 *Public Administration*, 295–317.

Wallace, C., *For Richer, For Poorer. Growing Up In and Out of Work* (London: Tavistock, 1987).

Walley, J., 'Children's Allowances: an economic and social necessity', in Bull, D. (ed.), *Family Poverty*, 2nd edn. (London: Duckworth, 1972).

Ward, S., 'Pensions', in Silburn, R. (ed.), *The Future of Social Security* (London: Fabian Society, 1985) 22–41.

Ward, S., *An Unfit Test: CAB clients'experience of the medical test for incapacity benefit* (London: National Association of Citizens Advice Bureaux, 1997).

Watson, M., 'Citizenship and Welfare' in Lavalette, M. and Pratt, A. (eds.), *Social Policy—A Conceptual and Theoretical Introduction* (London: Sage, 1997), 182–95.

Watson, P., *Social Security Law of the European Communities* (Oxford: Mansell, 1980).

Weatherill, S., 'Beyond Preemption? Shared Competence and Constitutional Change in the EC', in O'Keeffe, D. and Twomey, P. (eds), *Legal Issues of the Maastricht Treaty* (London: Wiley Chancery, 1994), 13–33.

Weatherill, S., *Law and Integration in the European Union* (Oxford: Clarendon Press, 1995).

Webb, S., 'Social insurance and poverty alleviation: An empirical analsyis', in S. Baldwin and J. Falkingham (eds), *Social security and social change: New challenges to the Beveridge model* (Hemel Hempstead: Harvester Wheatsheaf, 1994), 11–28.

Weir, T., *C.L.J.* [1998] 204–6.

Wellens, N., and Borchardt, D., 'Soft Law in European Community Law' (1989) 14 *ELRev* 267–321.

White, R., 'Editorial' (1999) 24 *ELRev* 119–20.

Whiteford, E., 'Occupational Pensions and European Law: Clarity at Last?' in Hervey, T. and O'Keeffe, D. (eds), *Sex Equality Law in the European Union* (Chichester: Wiley, 1996), 21–34.

Whiteford, E., *Adapting to Change: Occupational Pension Schemes, Women and Migrant Workers* (The Hague: Klewer Law International, 1997).

Whiteford, P., and Kennedy, S., *Income and Living Standards of Older People*, DSS Research Report No. 34 (London: HMSO, 1995).

Wikeley, N. J., 'Housing Benefit Review Boards; the New Slum?' (1986) 5 *C.J.Q.* 18–25.

Wikeley, N. J., 'The Future of Social Security Appeal Tribunals' (1987) 17 *Family Law*, 133–5.

Wikeley, N. J., 'Migrant Workers and Unemployment Benefit in the European Community' (1988) *J.S.W.L.* 300–5.

Wikeley, N. J., 'Social Security Adjudication and Occupational Lung Diseases' (1988) 17(2) *I.L.J.* 92–104.

Wikeley, N. J., 'Targeting, Training and Tightening Up: the Social Security Act 1988' [1989] *J.S.W.L.* 277–292.

Wikeley, N. J., 'Unemployment Benefit, the State and the Labour Market' (1989) 16 *J.L.S.* 291–309.

Wikeley, N. J., 'Tort and the Clawback of Social Security Benefits' (1991) 10 *C.J.Q.* 10–15.

Wikeley, N. J., *Compensation for Industrial Disease* (Dartmouth Publishing Co, 1993).

Wikeley, N. J., 'The New Prescribed Disease: coalminers' chronic bronchitis and emphysema' (1994) 1 *J.S.S.L.* 23–36.

Wikeley, N. J., 'Income support and mortgage interest: the new rules' (1995) 2 *J.S.S.L.* 168–78.

Wikeley, N. J., 'The Jobseeker's Act 1995: What the unemployed need is a good haircut . . .' (1995) 25 *I.L.J.* 71–6.

Wikeley, N. J., 'The Social Security (Incapacity for Work) Act 1994' (1995) 58 *M.L.R.* 523–33.

Wikeley, N. J., 'Decision making and appeals under the Social Security Act 1998' (1998) 5 *J.S.S.L.* 104–17.

Wikeley, N. J., 'Severe mental impairment and the higher rate mobility component of DLA' (1999) 6 *J.S.S.L.* 10–32.

Wilcox, S., 'More Tough Choices' (1998) *ROOF*, Sept/Oct, 12.

Wilcox, S., *Unfinished Business: Housing Costs and the Reform of Welfare Benefits* (Chartered Institute of Housing, 1998).

Williams, D. W., *Social Security Taxation* (London: Sweet and Maxwell, 1982).

Williams, D. W. W., 'Poverty and Unemployment Traps and Trappings' [1986] *J.S.W.L.* 96–107.

Wilson, E., *Women in the Welfare State* (London: Tavistock, 1977).

Wilson, M., 'The German Welfare State: A Conservative regime in crisis', in Cochrane, A., and Clarke, J. (eds), *Comparing Welfare States* (London: Sage, 1993), 141–71.

Witherspoon, S., Whyley, C., and Kempston, E., *Paying for Rented Housing*, DSS Research Report No. 43 (London: HMSO, 1996).

Wood, P., *International Classification of Impairments, Disabilities and Handicaps* (Geneva: World Health Organisation, 1980).

Woodfield, K., and Finch, H., *Unemployed Couples: attitudes towards proposals affecting partners of job-seekers*, DSS Research Report 47 (London: The Stationery Office, 1997).

Woodward, K., 'Feminist Critiques of Social Policy', in Lavalette, M., and Pratt, A. (eds), *Social Policy—A Conceptual and Theoretical Introduction* (London: Sage, 1997), 98–100.

Wraith, R. E., and Hutchesson, P. G., *Administrative Tribunals* (London: Allen & Unwin, 1973).

Wynn, M., *Family Policy: A study of the economic costs of rearing children* (Harmondsworth: Penguin, 1972).

Young, I., 'Polity and group difference: a critique of the ideal of universal citizenship' (1989) 99(2) *Ethics* 250–74.

Zarb, G., *Social Security and Mental Health; Report on the SSAC Workshop*, SSAC Research Paper 7 (London: HMSO, 1996).

Zarb, G., 'Social Security and Mental Health: Defining the Issues', in ibid., 3–10.

Zebedee, J., and Ward, M., *Guide to Housing Benefit and Council Tax Benefit* (Shelter and Chartered Institute of Housing, 1999).

Zollner, D., 'Germany', in Kholer, P. A., Zacker, H. F., and Partington, M., op. cit., 1–92.

Index

Note: numbers in **bold** refer to tables.

National Health Service (NHS) 254, 282, 426
national insurance 98
  benefits 42, 112, 146, 211
  contributions 146, 165–76, 261, 375
  see also contributory and non-contributory
     benefits; insurance
national insurance local tribunals (NILT) 211,
  212, 213
National Union of Students (NUS) 331, 333–4
NCIP (non-contributory invalidity pension) 100,
  376
neo-liberal market model 232–3
Netherlands 4, 106, 250, 251, 455
*New Ambitions for Our Country: A New Contract for
  Welfare, see* Green Paper (1998)
New Contract for Welfare: Support for Disabled People
  Green Paper (1998) 363, 387, 493
  see also Green Paper (1998)
New Deal 27, 30, 305–7, 321–5
  contractarian approach 34, 38, 194, 296
  for the disabled 55
  lone parents 53–4, 286–7
  and young people 52–3, 342, 357
New Insurance Contract 168
New Labour 9–10, 12–14, 38, 259
  see also Labour Government 1997–
New Poor Law 291
  see also Poor Law
New Right 9–11, 20, 106, 119, 146, 265–6, 283
  see also Conservative Governments 1979–1997
new welfare contract (New Labour vision) 9–10
Next Steps Agencies 147
NHS (National Health Service) 254, 282, 426
night care 381, 383–4, 388–9, 395, 396
NILT (national insurance local tribunal) 211, 212,
  213
non-advanced education 335–45
non-contributory invalidity pension (NCIP) 100,
  376
non-dependant deduction 141–2, 417
  see also housing benefit
non-means-tested benefits 158–61, **159**
  see also means-tested benefits; means-testing
notional capital and notional income 186, 187
  see also incomes
nursing homes, *see* residential care and nursing
  homes
NUS (National Union of Students) 331, 333–4

occupational diseases, *see* diseases, occupational
occupational injury, *see* industrial injury
Occupational Pensions Regulatory Authority 183
OECD (Organisation for Economic Co-
  operation and Development) 8–9, 467
Office of Population and Census Surveys (OPCS)
  148, 365, 385, 386, 390, 395

oil crisis 1973, 116
Old Age Pensions Act 1908, 73–4
Old Age Pensions Act 1919, 74
ombudsmen, local government 418, 425
one parent benefit 105, 190, 265
  see also parents, lone
one parent families, *see* parents, lone
ONE programme (single gateway) 357, 373–4
OPCS, *see* Office of Population and Census
  Surveys
oral and paper reviews and hearings 226–8, **227**,
  425, 455–7
Organisation for Economic Co–operation and
  Development (OECD) 8–9, 467
orphans 79
out of work donation 77–8
own occupation test 369
owner occupation 193, 404, 427, 428

PACs (public assistance committees) 82, 83, 84
paper and oral reviews and hearings 226–8, **227**,
  425, 455–7
parents 260–280
  absent 54–5, 267, 271, 274–80, 284–6
  contributions to student finances 330, 333, 335
  lone 19, 53–5, 262–80; and child benefits
     105, 265–6, 275–80; and employment
     49–50, 149, 281, 286–9, 397; and family
     benefits 105, 124, 190, 285; and income
     support 60, 127–8, 267–70, 273, 275,
     276–7; housing 403–4; mothers 60,
     263–5, 276–7; and New Deal 305–7; and
     poverty 47, 106, 168; responsibilities of
     96, 260; and social fund 447–8, 449–50,
     450; as partners of prisoners 197; as
     students 343; and take-up of benefits 63
  see also children; maternity benefits; mothers;
     widows
parishes and poor relief 70–2
part-time work 61, 168, 205, 263, 285,
  and incentives 315–16, 318–20
partners, *see* couples; parents
passported benefits 163
pay, *see* incomes
PAYE (pay-as-you-earn) 15, 172
payments, *see* grants, loans and awards
Pearson Committee (1978) 469, 472
Pension Schemes Act 1993, 183
pensioner premium 182, 190–1
pensioners:
  and benefits 63, 65, 150
  cold weather and winter fuel payments 443,
     458
  and income support 128, 149, 404
  and poverty 47, 106
  and social fund 449–50, **450**
  and take-up of benefits 63, 65, 166